Łódź Ghetto

Łódź Ghetto

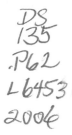

A HISTORY

Isaiah Trunk

Translated and edited by Robert Moses Shapiro

Introduction by Israel Gutman

*Published in association with the
United States Holocaust Memorial Museum*

INDIANA UNIVERSITY PRESS
BLOOMINGTON AND INDIANAPOLIS

This book is a publication of
Indiana University Press
601 North Morton Street
Bloomington, IN 47404-3797 USA

http://iupress.indiana.edu

Telephone orders	800-842-6796
Fax orders	812-855-7931
Orders by e-mail	iuporder@indiana.edu

A principally Yiddish edition of Isaiah Trunk's *Łódź Ghetto* was published as *Lodzher geto* by YIVO Institute for Jewish Research and by Yad Vashem, copyright 1962 by Yad Vashem Martyrs' and Heroes' Memorial Authority, Jerusalem, and YIVO Institute for Jewish Research, New York, as part of their Joint Documentary Projects, Monograph Series No. 1. The preparation and publication of that edition were made possible by a generous grant from the Conference on Jewish Material Claims Against Germany. The United States Holocaust Memorial Museum, Indiana University Press, Gabriel Trunk, and Robert Moses Shapiro express their deep appreciation to the aforementioned organizations, as well as to the authors and proprietors of supplementary material included in this translated, annotated, and augmented edition, for their gracious cooperation and valuable contributions.

The paper used in this publication meets the minimum requirements of American National Standard for Information Sciences—Permanence of Paper for Printed Library Materials, ANSI Z39.48-1984.

Manufactured in the United States of America

Cataloguing information is available from the Library of Congress.

ISBN 0-253-34755-6 (cl. : alk. paper)

CONTENTS

Major Tables, Charts, and Maps

BfG	*Bleter far geshikhte* (Warsaw)
B.G.K.B.Z.N. (H.)	*Biuletyn Głównej Komisji Badania Zbrodni Niemieckich (Hitlerowskich) w Polsce,* Warsaw
BZIH	*Biuletyn Żydowskiego Instytutu Historycznego* (Warsaw)
Doc.	Document
G.V.	Gettoverwaltung
H.T.O.	Haupttreuhandstelle Ost
JHI	Jewish Historical Institute, Warsaw (ZIH)
Mk	mark
n.d.	no date
n.n.	no number
O.D.	Ordnungsdienst
O.S.	Order Service
RM	Reichsmark
TA	Trunk annotation: Notes for corrections and emendations written by Isaiah Trunk on the pages of his personal copy of *Lodzher geto.* Most consist of references to specific documents in the Zonabend Collection.
YIVO	YIVO Institute for Jewish Research, New York City
ZIH	Żydowski Instytut Historyczny (Jewish Historical Institute, Warsaw)

Isaiah Trunk's study of the Łódź Ghetto, originally published in 1962 by the YIVO Institute for Jewish Research in New York and Yad Vashem in Jerusalem, was written in Yiddish, the principal language of Eastern European Jewry. Trunk sought to describe and explain the remarkable tragedy that befell the Jews imprisoned in the first major ghetto imposed by the Germans after they invaded Poland in 1939. Łódź had been home to a community of nearly a quarter million Jews, more than a third of the population of the city that was the center of Poland's textile industry. When the Soviet military arrived in Łódź in January 1945, they found 877 living Jews and the remains of a vast industrial enterprise that had employed masses of enslaved Jewish laborers.

Amid the detritus of the former ghetto and in abandoned German offices, researchers of the Central Jewish Historical Commission found and retrieved a vast array of the most varied documents that would enable scholars to reconstruct the travails of the more than 200,000 Jews who passed through the Łódź Ghetto during its more than four and a half years of existence. The sheer bulk of this documentation is daunting, far exceeding the equivalent sources for the Warsaw Ghetto by a factor of ten or more. To discover and describe the course of events in the Łódź Ghetto demanded a unique set of historiographic and linguistic skills. It was Isaiah Trunk who undertook to describe the creation and development of the Łódź Ghetto on the basis of the most primary of sources available. It is a testament to the significance of Trunk's achievement that his book remains the fundamental study of the Łódź Ghetto. This underscores the importance of making *Łódź Ghetto* accessible to the majority of researchers and students who do not have access to Yiddish.

Isaiah Trunk, Polish Jewish Historian

Isaiah Trunk was born in 1905, a son of Rabbi Isaac Trunk, the distinguished rabbinic leader of Kutno (hometown of the Yiddish author Sholem Asch), located north of Łódź and west of Warsaw. Rabbi Trunk, a founder of the religious Zionist movement Mizrachi, saw that his son received a thoroughly traditional Jewish education in Torah and Talmud. At age fourteen or fifteen, Isaiah Trunk went to Łódź for two years to attend the bilingual Polish-Hebrew secondary school established by the distinguished Rabbi Dr. Markus (Mordechai Zev) Braude. He went on to the University of Warsaw, graduating in 1929 with an M.A. in history, having written his thesis under Prof. Majer Bałaban on the early history of the Jews in the region around Warsaw.[1]

Warsaw was arguably the intellectual center of the Jewish Diaspora, with its plethora of Jewish daily newspapers and periodicals in Yiddish and Polish and broad spectrum of Jewish cultural, political, social, and religious organizations. Trunk was attracted to intellectual circles associated with the Bund, the Jewish socialist party that emphasized the role of Yiddish as the language of the Jewish working masses. He also joined the group of Jewish university students and graduates who gathered around Dr. Emanuel Ringelblum to study the problems of Jewish history. The circle published several Yiddish collections of studies by its members, including works by Isaiah Trunk. The Young Historian group eventually affiliated with the YIVO Institute for Jewish Research, founded in 1925 and based in Vilna. YIVO was committed to objective, rigorous, but engaged scholarship about all facets of the Jewish past and present. Trunk was actively involved in the major effort to collect primary sources from Jewish communities all over Poland and beyond.

During the economically depressed 1930s, as anti-Jewish violence and discrimination increased on Polish university campuses and prospects for academic employment for Jews were negligible, Trunk taught for a year or two in a Yiddish elementary school. He went on to become a history teacher in several Jewish secondary schools, generally teaching in Polish, but also in Yiddish and Hebrew. These Jewish schools contended with constant financial difficulties and frequent harassment by the Polish authorities.

Amid the chaos of the German invasion in September 1939, Trunk was among the flood of able-bodied males directed to go east to join in continuing the Polish resistance. Like tens of thousands of others who fled Warsaw, Trunk soon found himself in the Soviet-occupied zone of Eastern Poland. For a time, he resumed his teaching career in the state Yiddish schools funded by the Soviets in Białystok.

For having declined to accept Soviet citizenship, in June 1940 Trunk was exiled to the Soviet Far East, to the Komi Autonomous Soviet Socialist Republic, where he became a woodcutter, living in conditions of severe privation. He knew little of the course of the war or the specific fate of the Jews caught under German occupation. As late as 1943, the Soviet press rarely carried details regarding Jews, but wrote only of "murdered Soviet citizens." In the wake of the Soviet victory at Stalingrad, Trunk was sent to the Ukrainian city of Kherson, but it was not until late in 1944 that he read the detailed Soviet reports about Majdanek, with the first references to gas chambers, ovens, and crematoria.

Repatriated to Poland in 1946, Trunk saw Warsaw in ruins. Łódź was relatively intact and there he found two cousins who had survived the Warsaw Ghetto, unlike his mother and two sisters who had been sent to Treblinka. Trunk joined in the work of the Central Jewish Historical Commission, founded by Philip Friedman to document the recent catastrophe. For several years, Trunk collaborated in the collection and initial analysis of the evidence about the fate of Poland's millions of Jews during the German occupation. The Historical Commission, which was succeeded by the Jewish Historical Institute in Warsaw, published a number of important collections of documents and the first monographs on aspects of the Holocaust. Trunk's first published postwar works examined the fate of Jews in the Wartheland region that included Łódź. As part of his research, he assiduously examined the accumulated documents left by the German authorities and the Rumkowski ghetto administration in Łódź.

In 1948, Trunk married the former Celia (Cyla) Baar, a survivor of five concentration camps; their son, Gabriel, was born the following year. Sensing a change in the methods and policies of the Jewish Historical Commission, as Poland became ever more clearly a Soviet satellite, Trunk initially applied for a visa to France, only to find his departure blocked by Communist authorities. When Poland agreed in 1949 to allow Jews to emigrate to the new state of Israel, Trunk decided to go there, arriving with his family in January 1951. For two years, he worked at Kibbutz Lohamei Ha-getaot, the Ghetto Fighters' Kibbutz north of Haifa, collaborating in the development of an important research institution and museum devoted to the memory of the Warsaw Ghetto fighters and other ghettos and camps. A huge collection of documents was assembled, including many eyewitness testimonies, as well as originals and copies of many documents, paving the way for Yad Vashem, which was founded only in 1953.

Israel was in the midst of severe austerity, including food rationing and a shortage of housing. Trunk decided to leave, as both his wife and young son were ill. They went to Canada, where Trunk was engaged to be the principal of a Yiddish school in Calgary. An invitation from YIVO led to another move, to New York City in 1954.

Trunk brought with him from Poland and Israel a library of books and extensive research notes accumulated during the immediate postwar years. These were the foundation for his major research projects and writing on the Nazi-imposed ghettos. At YIVO he became a senior research associate and chief archivist. Trunk's most significant works during his American period were his monographs on the Łódź Ghetto and the hundreds of Judenrats or Jewish councils. His book *Judenrat* (Macmillan, 1972) was distinguished with the National Book Award, bringing renown to a man dedicated to diligent research and writing. In 1969, Trunk earned a doctorate of Jewish literature from the Jewish Teachers' Seminary of New York, having written his Yiddish dissertation on the inner life of Jews during the Holocaust. While emphasizing the value of contemporaneously produced primary sources, Trunk recognized the worth of postwar memoirs and testimonies that could corroborate and illuminate other documents. YIVO itself carefully collected and transcribed over 3,000 original testimonies. Trunk published a collection of sixty-two such testimonies, translated from Yiddish by his son, Gabriel.[2]

Dr. Isaiah Trunk continued to write and teach, both as a guest at various American and Israeli universities and in his seminars in the Max Weinreich Institute for Advanced Jewish Studies at YIVO. I had the privilege of studying with him in the 1970s. He died suddenly on March 28, 1981, leaving behind an important body of research and a model for diligence that subsequent historians would do well to emulate.

The Range of Sources Used (and Not Used) by Trunk

Trunk's *Łódź Ghetto* appeared in print only seventeen years after the Nazi German defeat. The peculiar circumstances of the city of Łódź during the Second World War contributed to the survival of a vast quantity of diverse documentary sources, created by both Germans and Jews. The sheer quantity dwarfs by far the documentation on the fate of any other ghetto. Nevertheless, Trunk did not have easy access to all the materials he wanted to examine. The authorities of Communist Poland refused to extend him a visa in the 1960s.

Nevertheless, Trunk had several advantages in approaching the study of the Łódź Ghetto. A former resident of Łódź, and fluent in Yiddish, Hebrew, Polish, German, and Russian, Trunk was well positioned to understand the documents denotatively and connotatively in context. From 1946 to 1950, he diligently studied the records, took notes, and copied the most useful items in Warsaw and Łódź. During his two years in Israel, he helped assemble the Lohamei Ha-getaot (Ghetto Fighters House) archival collection of original documents and testimonies, including a wealth of material related to Łódź. At YIVO, he had access to the Nachman Zonabend Collection from the archive established within Rumkowski's administration.

To accompany his portrayal and analysis of the Łódź Ghetto, Trunk included a selection of about 140 original documents in Yiddish, Polish, and German that are also translated into English here. The array of sources is quite broad. The daily *Chronicle* produced within the ghetto archive by a staff of about fifteen co-workers provides a record that is nearly complete from 1941 to the end of July 1944. Trunk made use of the *Chronicle* very frequently, although he apparently did not have access to a full set of the *Chronicle,* the first two volumes of which were published only in 1965–1966. At times, Trunk had to make do with selections of the *Chronicle* quoted by A. Wolf Jasny, a former Yiddish journalist from Łódź. There are numerous instances when there are divergences between Trunk's quoted text from the *Chronicle* and the versions published in English, Polish, and Hebrew.

Trunk makes extensive use of selected official German documents that survived in the collections of the *Gettoverwaltung* and other divisions of the German regime in Łódź. The most convenient source of such documents was the collection published by the Jewish Historical Commission and edited by Artur Eisenbach already in 1946. Then there are the trial records of Hans Biebow and Artur Greiser, as well as of Adolf Eichmann.

Included among the Zonabend Collection are copies of most of Rumkowski's hundreds of poster announcements to the ghetto population. There are also impressive commemorative albums prepared by the divisions of the ghetto industry and administration, as well as the Yiddish *Getto-tsaytung* fortnightly published by Rumkowski.

Trunk makes extensive use of a number of diaries written in the ghetto, especially those by Hiler, Hurwitz, Poznański, and Frank. Yisroel Tabaksblat's volume is also one of a number of detailed memoirs by survivors who held responsible positions within the ghetto administration or the remnants of the clandestine organizations.[3]

Trunk's Yiddish edition makes little use of the thousands of surviving photographic images from the Łódź Ghetto. It was presumably too costly to include photographs in the volume. Moreover, the several hundred color images made by the German official Walther Genewein were unknown until the mid-1980s, while other color slides made by him were discovered even more recently.[4] Trunk did include copies of some of the complex charts and maps prepared by the ghetto's statistical office.

Vast quantities of primary sources remain to be examined for data to add to the mosaic of the history of the Łódź Ghetto. Polish and German scholars have been handicapped by being unable to access the Yiddish sources, although an effort has been made in recent years to publish translations of sources. Some, like the work *Łódź Ghetto* (1989), compiled and edited by Alan Adelson and Robert Lapides, and the edition of *The Diary of Dawid Sierakowiak* (1996), edited by Adelson, in my opinion supply significantly less than the full potential value of the translated documents through the quality of their editing, sometimes combined with an apparent lack of full knowledge. Hanno Loewy's German edition of the anonymous diary written in the margins of a French novel, *Les Vrais Riches*,[5] in English, Polish, Yiddish, and Hebrew, is a valuable and moving document. Also an important recent addition to the literature on the Łódź Ghetto is the publication of the notebooks of Oskar Rosenfeld, a Viennese Jewish writer and co-worker in the ghetto archive.[6] In 1990, a major exhibition on the Łódź Ghetto was mounted at the Jewish Museum in Frankfurt, inspiring an accompanying book rich in photographs and documents in German and German translation, with particular emphasis on the writing of Oskar Rosenfeld and Oskar Singer, as well as many German passages from the daily *Chronicle*.[7] Jakub Poznański's diary, originally published in 1960, was a very important source for Trunk; a new, reportedly fuller version of the diary was published in 2002.[8]

Israeli scholar Michal Unger edited another very valuable museum catalogue in association with Yad Vashem's exhibition on the Łódź Ghetto. A revised edition of Unger's Hebrew University doctoral dissertation on the inner life of the Łódź Ghetto is in preparation, soon to be published in both Hebrew and English.[9]

Especially valuable has been the publication since the 1960s of various editions of the Łódź Ghetto *Chronicle* in Polish, English, and Hebrew. The Polish edition was left incomplete in the wake of the notorious "anti-Zionist" campaign of the 1960s,[10] while the American English-language edition is a one-volume selection that includes only about a fourth of the entire *Chronicle,* although it is enriched with an extensive introduction and annotations by Lucjan Dobroszycki.[11] The "complete and unabridged" Israeli Hebrew-language edition[12] is extensively annotated and includes introductions by both Dobroszycki and Israel Gutman.[13] A complete edition of the *Chronicle* in both of its original languages is now in prepration by a team coordinated by German scholar Dr. Sascha Feuchert.

Memoirs by Jewish survivors of Łódź continue to appear. Among the most important is the volume by Arnold Mostowicz, a medical doctor in the ghetto.[14] Lucille Eichengreen, a German Jewish woman who was deported to the Łódź Ghetto, has provided unique eyewitness testimony to Rumkowski's abusive behavior.[15] An unusual source unavailable to Trunk is the nearly seven hours of recorded audio interviews with former ghetto police official David

Gertler, conducted in Munich in 1974 by Isaiah Kuperstein and only recently made available for scholars at YIVO.

The State of Research Today

In August 2002, a two-week research workshop was organized and chaired by Robert Moses Shapiro at the Center for Advanced Holocaust Studies at the United States Holocaust Memorial Museum. The effort to find those actively involved in research about the Łódź Ghetto revealed few senior scholars, but a small cadre of more junior researchers. Dr. Michael Thaler of San Francisco has undertaken important research into the German administrative and insurance records related to the Łódź Ghetto, while Peter Klein is a doctoral student in Berlin writing on aspects of the German administration's Jewish policies in Łódź. Dr. Sascha Feuchert of the University of Giessen is a literary historian focusing on the Holocaust; he has edited and published works by ghetto author Oskar Singer,[16] and is coordinating publication of the full original texts of the Łódź Ghetto *Chronicle* in German and Polish. Helene Sinnreich has written her doctoral dissertation at Brandeis University on questions of food supply in the Łódź Ghetto;[17] for three years she resided in Łódź, doing research and teaching at the University of Łódź. Joanna Podolska is a journalist with *Gazeta Wyborcza,* who writes frequently on issues of Jewish and Holocaust history in Łódź, and is actively involved in the preservation and marking of the sites remaining from the ghetto period. Prof. Carol Zemel of York University in Toronto is a specialist in the history of visual art, currently writing on photography in the ghetto, with emphasis on the work of Mendel Grossman and Henryk Ross. Irena Kohn is a doctoral student at the Ontario Institute for Studies in Education of the University of Toronto, working on questions of testimony and historical memory, and is looking at how the events of the Łódź Ghetto have been remembered. Also participating in the Washington workshop was Dr. Marian Turski, a survivor of the Łódź Ghetto who is historical editor of the Polish weekly *Polityka* as well as chairman of the board of the Jewish Historical Institute of Poland.

The deliberations of the workshop were especially valuable because of the varied themes, but also because of the array of languages that the group as a whole commanded. Significantly, only a minority of the participants were able to use sources in all the relevant languages (German, Polish, Yiddish, Hebrew, and English). This reinforces the need to promote language study, especially of Yiddish, and to promote translation of primary sources into English as the most widely accessible language.

The largest repository of original documents related to the Łódź Ghetto is the State Archive in Łódź. Julian Baranowski, that archive's principal specialist on records connected with the Łódź Ghetto, has compiled a valuable and compact guide to the history of the ghetto and to the relevant documentation available in Łódź.[18] The small book has parallel Polish and German texts, outlining in concise chapters the history of the Jews of Łódź and establishment of the ghetto. The German and Jewish administrations are described, as well as the effects of starvation and diseases in the ghetto, and the terror and extermination actions. Throughout the book are many illustrations: photographs taken in the ghetto, of official posters, of ghetto money, of other documents, of objects produced in the ghetto workshops, and much more. There are maps of the ghetto, as well as alphabetical lists of German street names with Polish equivalents and vice-versa (112–115); a list of the addresses of all the ghetto factories, workshops, and offices (102–109); and a list of surviving ghetto buildings (111). All in all, Baranowski's book clearly suggests the treasure trove of resources available for reconstructing the history of the doomed world of the Łódź Ghetto. The bibliography lists thirty-four published items, mainly in Polish, some in German, and a few in English. Significantly, no Yiddish or Hebrew works are cited, including Trunk's fundamental book on the Łódź Ghetto. It is important that Trunk's views and data are made accessible to Polish and other scholars.

Criticism of Trunk

At present, there is no reliable, comprehensive history of the Łódź Ghetto that exceeds Trunk's work with its admitted limitations. However, special reference must be made to Icchak Henryk Rubin's massive Polish study of the Jews in Łódź under German occupation,[19] particularly because he forcefully raises a number of criticisms of Trunk's work. Rubin was born in Łódź in 1913 and survived the Second World War, although he lost numerous family members, including his mother sent to Chełmno in 1942. Research on Rubin's book commenced as a doctoral dissertation proposal in 1959 at Copernicus University in Poland. Ultimately, Rubin received his doctorate from the College of Education (Wyższa Szkoła Pedagogiczna) in Gdańsk, where he was sheltered for two years during the anti-Jewish campaign that flared in 1968. He then immigrated to Denmark, where he cultivated and edited his book for almost twenty years, until its publication in Polish in London.[20] Rubin had access to all the principal archival collections in Warsaw and Łódź, as well as to all the published sources in Polish, German, Yiddish, and Hebrew. His scholarship is thorough, but some may see it as energized by a not fully controlled rage against German crimes and perceived failures of other scholars.[21]

Trunk's book appeared while Rubin was researching his dissertation. Rubin was very familiar with most of the sources cited by Trunk and addresses a number of very sharp criticisms against him. First and foremost, Rubin accuses Trunk of being negatively prejudiced and biased against Rumkowski and his policies. Rubin holds that Rumkowski is, in fact, a heroic figure acting to save what he could and almost succeeding in bringing out 70,000 Jews, if not for the failure of the Soviet Army to move the last sixty-five miles to Łódź in summer 1944. Rubin expands his position into one of sympathetic defense of the Jewish councils who acted energetically and daringly within the limits of what was possible to save some Jews. In fact, Rubin's allegation of bias is excessive, for Trunk clearly distinguished between collaboration and coerced cooperation.[22]

Rubin does catch Trunk in an error in regard to the identity of the author of the diary by Engineer Leon Hurwitz (Hurwicz), whom Trunk misidentifies as a pseudonym for Dr. Józef Klementynowski, first director of the ghetto archive.[23] This error was also pointed out by Lucjan Dobroszycki.[24] Rubin holds that Trunk's book is based on too narrow and meager a set of sources that led Trunk to put too much trust in YIVO's Zonabend Collection and not enough in the documents of the *Gettoverwaltung* and in the daily *Chronicle*. Rubin also objects to the structure of Trunk's book, with too many statistical tables and not enough description of the texture of day-to-day life and relationships in the ghetto. For Rubin, Trunk's book lacks a sense of the ghetto atmosphere. Nor does Trunk sufficiently present the evolution of German policy toward Jews and the dependence of that policy on the international military-political situation.[25]

Rubin sees Trunk's analysis as a fundamental misrepresentation of reality. Trunk portrays Rumkowski as having had total control, suppressing all competitors in economic and political affairs. Rubin counters that there was a free (or black) market in personal goods and foods. Moreover, Rumkowski went out of his way to save party activists and even negotiated with them; yet they betrayed him in 1943 when the Germans transferred power to Jewish police official Marek Kligier.[26] Rubin declares that Trunk either ignores or is ignorant of the April 1943 *Chronicle* report of how Rumkowski chose to punish a potato thief not with death, but with a sentence of three years in prison.[27] Rubin argues that Trunk is wrong to blame Rumkowski for the relatively high proportion of Western Jews deported in the first half of 1942, for it was Biebow who ordered it.[28]

According to Rubin, Trunk falsely accuses Rumkowski of making a deal with the Germans during the September 1942 roundups, substituting 200 other people for favored individuals who had escaped from the hospitals. Rubin challenges the value of a passage that Trunk cites from Zelkowicz's extraordinary account of the September 1942 *Aktion*. Rumkowski did not intervene even to save the father of his own new wife.[29]

The overall value of Rubin's book is not enhanced by what I perceive as manifestations of injudicious rage which surface at intervals in the book's text and notes. It is unfortunate that the book was not more skillfully edited, for it is not taken as seriously as it deserves to be, even if one may disagree with some of Rubin's conclusions.

Among other criticisms that might be raised regarding Trunk's book is the lack of consistent clarity in references to documents cited from the YIVO Zonabend Collection. The documents are referred to both by their number in the inventory of the Zonabend Collection and by their number in the series of documents appended to the chapters of the book. It is important to note that the Zonabend Collection was reorganized in the 1980s, so that to find a given document cited by Trunk requires recourse to a conversion table kept at YIVO. Generally, references to documents by number in the main text refer to texts appended to the book's chapters. Another annoyance is that at times Trunk presents data drawn from a given document, but he cites only the folder or document number without describing the document itself.

Trunk left behind annotations and some corrections in his own handwriting in his copy of the Yiddish *Łódź Ghetto*. These have been incorporated in the present translation as notes: TA: Doc. ##. Annotations by the translator-editor have been included as footnotes. Annotations include updated source references, as well as some corrections and supplemental information to elucidate the text.

Whatever the limitations and gaps in Trunk's work, his book is a serious attempt at comprehensively addressing the question of what happened to the Jews in Łódź during more than five years of German occupation and oppression. By conscientious recourse to sources in Yiddish and other languages, Trunk has been able to discern and describe many threads of the tapestry of what happened to the Jews. By examining and publishing documents intimately created by those Jews and by others around them, Trunk allows us to approach an understanding of how they perceived and responded to their disastrous circumstances. Much more work is needed to advance down the path that Trunk has pioneered. I hope that publication of his book in English will enable others to make progress in paving the road to memory and understanding.

Isaiah Trunk

JOSEPH KERMISH[1]

With the sudden death of Isaiah Trunk, one of the most important researchers of Holocaust history and a prolific historian of Polish Jewry has departed. He was a younger contemporary of Emanuel Ringelblum, who, like him, principally dealt with the history of Jews in Poland. Trunk sought to interpret every matter on the basis of archival sources and occupied himself with historical problems in an innovative fashion.

The young Trunk participated in the Seminar for Jewish History that Ringelblum founded at the Jewish Academic Home in Warsaw. A few years later, with the establishment of YIVO, the seminar became the Historical Circle of the YIVO Society in Warsaw. The circle consisted of young historians who already had completed their studies at university. It published four Yiddish anthologies of Jewish history, initially entitled *Yunger Historiker* (Young Historian; 1926, 1929), and edited by Emanuel Ringelblum and Rafael Mahler. In the course of time, as the "youngsters" matured, the publication was renamed *Bleter far geshikhte* (Folios for History; 1934, 1938).

In volume one of *Bleter far geshikhte*, Trunk published a monograph on the Jewish community in Kutno at the end of the eighteenth century; that work expressed the author's special connection with his hometown. In the second volume, published in 1938, there appeared "The Legal Status of the Jews in Płock in the 16th Century," a chapter of his major work on the Jews in Płock. These works were produced, as were other studies about Jewish communities authored by young historians, under the stimulating influence of Emanuel Ringelblum. Each of these younger researchers laid out a lifetime of projects for himself. The topics touched upon in these works published in *Yunger Historiker* and *Bleter far geshikhte* were linked to the contemporary reality of the Jews in Poland and attempted to respond to the problems and questions of Jewish life. As Ringelblum expressed it in 1938, "For them, Jewish history is an important public duty."

Trunk was also very active in the Historical Commission set up at the Warsaw section of YIVO, of which Ringelblum was one of the founders and builders. Under Ringelblum's leadership, in 1937 this commission sought to register the minute books of Jewish communities and associations in Poland. Questionnaires were distributed to almost all the Jewish communities in Poland. Detailed responses came in concerning 293 minute books and associations in over 200 communities, dating from 1628 to 1916. The survey material was analyzed by Trunk and published in the Yiddish bulletin, *Yedies fun yivo* (News from YIVO), no. 83–84.

It is worth recalling that this group of young historians led by Rafael Mahler and Ringelblum (the outstanding student of Dr. Yitshak Schiper) appeared at a time when Yiddish literature, schools, publishing houses, the Yiddish press, the theater, and so forth were blossoming, in the period when the social-cultural development of East European Jewry reached its zenith.

This group of young historians advanced research into the history of the Jews in Poland and shifted to new methodological and conceptual questions. Ringelblum, flag-bearer of the younger generation of Jewish historians in Poland, together with other historians with a sociological orientation, held that history as a social science must bring out the societal conflicts that are the motive force of historical development.

In his research, Ringelblum missed no opportunity to uncover the social stratification of Jewish society in previous generations and the social injustice that the exploitive communal oligarchy inflicted on the masses of the people. Ringelblum also underscored the duty of the historian to include in his research and description all fields of life in their full form.

Trunk's Yiddish study, *History of Jews in Płock 1237–1657,* published by YIVO in 1939, before the outbreak of the Second World War, was his first broad-scale work, based on rich archival material and on his great expertise in the historical literature. Even though it has the character of a local monograph, the book illuminates the history of the Jews in Poland and spreads out before the reader a multi-faceted picture of Jewish life in all the turmoil of national and social interests. Like Ringelblum, Trunk thought in categories of historical issues and was not satisfied with mere recitation of facts. Here originated his tendency toward synthesis and finding the common denominator and pattern in the colorful fabric of historical events.

These achievements before the outbreak of the Second World War had already earned Trunk a reputation as one of the most outstanding young historians of the Jews in Poland.

After the war broke out, Trunk left Warsaw on 7 September 1939 together with the refugee masses streaming toward the East.

I happened to meet him in Kałuszyn on 8 September and saw no more of him until he returned from the Soviet Union in summer 1946. He immediately joined the little group of researchers then concentrated around the Jewish Historical Commission in liberated Poland. The commission's temporary seat was in Łódź.

At the time, research on the Holocaust was still in its first stage, that of collecting and concentrating the documentation. Everybody was involved in assembling the facts, one detail after another. This means that the writing of the Jewish history of the Holocaust was also still in its infancy.

Among the archives collected at the time, the most important were those from the German organs of government in Łódź. First and foremost was the archive of the German Ghetto administration (including the files of the Gestapo, the Kripo, the city government, and so on), which had exercised unlimited dominion over hundreds of thousands of Jews in Łódź and in the other localities in the Warthegau. The Germans did not manage to destroy those records before they fled the city. There also remained the ghetto archive of the *Ältestenrat* in Łódź with all its institutions, the largest surviving archive for the history of a Jewish community in Eastern Europe during the Second World War. The various documents written in the ghetto have great value for research about the ghetto's history and especially of the history of the forms of resistance. In those immediate postwar days, the Jewish Historical Commission saw its principal tasks as collecting the largest possible quantity of different historical sources and the publication of a selection of instructive historical documents on the history of destruction and resistance. All this was in preparation for subsequent historical works. Trunk directly applied himself to making use of this colossal collection of documentary material, with the goal of undertaking research on the history of the Jews in the Warthegau, and publishing it in the form of a historical monograph that should serve as a basis for a comprehensive history of the Holocaust and its causes.

Three years passed and Trunk published his first two monographs in the field of Holocaust research, doing so in the renewed *Bleter far Geshikhte,* organ of the new Jewish Historical Institute in Warsaw (itself a continuation of the Jewish Historical Commission): "Jewish Labor Camps in Wartheland"[2] and "Study of the History of Jews in Wartheland in the Period of Destruction (1939–1944)."[3] In these studies, Trunk paved his own road in Holocaust research, intending to uncover the truth about the inner life of the Jews in the ghettos and camps.

For a time, working together with Nahman Blumental, Tsvi Shner, and the present author, in the years 1951–1952, Isaiah Trunk was among the founders of the Israeli archive at Bet Lohamei Hagetaot (Ghetto Fighters' House), named after the martyred poet

Yitshak Katzenelson. Trunk also helped establish the scholarly publications of Bet Lohamei Ha-getaot (*Dapim le-heker ha-shoa ve-ha-mered*). However, lack of suitable housing at that time compelled him and his family to leave Israel and depart initially for Canada and then America.

The years Trunk spent at YIVO in New York beginning in 1954 were the most fruitful period of his life. An extraordinarily diligent scholar with great talents, he was entirely engaged in research. His interests were extensive and therefore the range of his studies was broad. He occupied himself with the problems of social and cultural history no less than with the economic problems of Polish Jewry. But he devoted his primary interest to Holocaust research. He chose the path of a series of separate research articles, in effect laying down bricks for a larger structure. A portion of these studies are scattered among various periodicals and anthologies.

It is worth singling out a few of his most important works. For example, he published "The War against the Jews through Spreading Diseases" in the Yiddish *YIVO-bleter* in 1954 (58–100). Or consider his study, "The Bund and Its Activities from Its Genesis until the Poland Period," in the Hebrew *Diaspora Encyclopedia: Warsaw* (Tel Aviv, 1959, vol. 2, cols. 59–92), and others. His major book in Yiddish about the Łódź Ghetto (*Łódź Ghetto: A Historical and Sociological Study,* New York, 1962) is a clear indication of the fundamental and manifold nature that characterized Trunk's research. This is a model of deep research that analyzes every document of whatever provenance, primarily from Jewish sources, that can aid him in getting to know his subject as closely as possible, a research study that punctiliously documents everything and accompanies it with a mass of analytic notes. This monograph gives full expression to the attempt at fundamental analysis, coupled with rich documentation; therefore, this volume is somewhat differently constructed than other books by Trunk. The book is rich in themes and problems and is provided with an abundance of documents appended to each chapter. Indeed, its uniqueness consists in this. The author succeeded in giving a profound analysis of the socio-ideological dynamic of this major Jewish community and of the metamorphosis that took place in its structure. Trunk's emphasis is not only on the torments and the annihilation, but rather on the life of Jews in circumstances that threatened destruction and especially on the phenomena of resistance.

Following the 7 February 1960 death of Philip Friedman, Trunk took over the study of the Nazi-imposed Jewish councils, a project on which Friedman had labored for years. Friedman had been founder and first chairman of the Jewish Historical Commission in Poland and the first historian to assemble a mass of substantive sources about the *Judenrat,* about which he wrote a series of research articles that dealt with very important aspects of the topic. Nevertheless, Friedman did not manage to write a comprehensive monograph on this controversial and emotionally distressing theme.

Trunk did not satisfy himself with the large collection of material that Friedman left him. He possessed his own collection: notes and documents that he gathered during his work in Poland and in Israel between 1946 and 1951. In addition, at Trunk's initiative, Yad Vashem and YIVO conducted a survey about the social background and behavior of the members of the Jewish councils and of the Jewish police in the ghettos in occupied Poland, as well as in the Baltic States, Belorussia, eastern Poland, and Ukraine. This was a complementary preparatory project for his research and his own contribution was great in the gathering of a wealth of photographic material. Trunk immediately published the results of the survey.[4] Before he published the entire research study, he dealt with various aspects of the topic in a series of research articles, including "The Organizational Structure of the Jewish Councils in Eastern Europe"[5] and "The Relationship of the Jewish Councils to the Problems of Armed Revolt against the Nazis."[6] The latter work presented many instances of active resistance in the years of the German occupation, in which participation by members and staff of the Jewish councils was not lacking.

Trunk's *Judenrat: The Jewish Councils in Eastern Europe Under Nazi Occupation* occupies a special place as the result of his years of gathering sources and preparatory work.[7] It embraces 405 Jewish communities in which Jewish councils functioned. This work comprises an important link in the research about one of the central topics in inner Jewish life during the Holocaust, a question about which there remains on-going historiographic controversy. This is the first detailed analysis of the phenomena of the "self-government" that was imposed upon the Jews by the German regime.

Together with this central theme, *Judenrat* also clarifies other aspects of internal Jewish life. Trunk set himself the task of giving a balanced picture of the activity of the Jewish councils. When he evaluates the qualities and deeds of the members of the Jewish councils in the given circumstances, he avoids simplifications or generalizations. Concentrated in the book is a wealth of detailed material about the Jewish councils' conduct in the areas of life that were under their partial or full control. The book also sketches out the relations between the Jewish councils and the Germans on the one hand, and with the underground—where it existed—on the other hand.

Trunk sees the Jewish councils as one of the central arenas in which the struggle for rescue and for Jewish survival was conducted. He presents the attempts that the Jewish councils made to defend the interests of the Jewish public.

It is impossible not to emphasize the sheer breadth of Trunk's grasp of the problems of the Jewish council, as he does not overlook any aspect linked with them. How profoundly sensitive he is to the various and contradictory elements in the work of the Jewish council, elements which he attempts to classify. He categorizes the types of Jewish councils according to moral-national criteria and he is the first to differentiate between cooperation and collaboration in carrying out the orders of the Germans.

Trunk's massive book had broad repercussions and contributed to a renewed interest in the activity of the Jewish councils. He continued with his research, as demonstrated by his essay "National Polyarchy in the Situation of the Jews in the Occupied Territories."[8] At the International Conference on Holocaust Research held in Jerusalem at Yad Vashem in April 1977, Trunk delivered a lecture, "Typology of the Jewish Councils in Eastern Europe."[9] There he expressed the wish that subsequent research about the Jewish councils should go in the direction of searching out sources that would facilitate making a classification according to already indicated and new criteria, because "such an analysis will make it possible to penetrate more deeply into the inner conditions in the ghettos and will also facilitate development of methodological concepts for the typology of the Jewish councils."

Beyond this, every year Trunk wrote historical essays and articles on a whole series of topics, mainly related to interwar Polish Jewry, that had blossomed not only in the partisan sense, but became the center of Jewish culture and of Jewish national life in the Diaspora. His essays and articles particularly excel from the thematic point of view. Trunk invested massive amounts of time and effort into essays that deal with a whole series of aspects of Jewish social and cultural life in Poland and in various eras.

So that the interested reader could have easy access to a systematically organized selection of his instructive essays and articles, Trunk assembled them in a Yiddish collection that appeared in 1962 in Buenos Aires.[10] Among the included articles are, for example, "Simon Dubnov and Eastern European Historiography" and an essay about the eminent Jewish folklorist Samuel Lehman, who collected whole treasure troves of folksongs and folk sayings all his life—but managed to publish little of this material.

Trunk himself prepared and delivered to the publisher another collection[11] of his own historical essays and articles that were originally published in various places in the 1960s and 1970s. This collection includes, for example, "Economic Antisemitism in Poland between Both World Wars,"[12] a work that admittedly does not greatly surprise but does present the data in a concentrated and organized form. Moreover, it includes an analysis of the economic structure of Polish Jewry. Also included in Trunk's new Yiddish collection is his essay "YIVO and Jewish Historical Science."

In another essay, "Emanuel Ringelblum: Historian and Social Activist," included in the new collection, Trunk focuses particularly on Ringelblum's social and historical work in the Warsaw Ghetto, on the problem of documenting the unprecedented catastrophe of the Jewish people under Nazi rule. Trunk rightly holds that Ringelblum's greatest scholarly and organizational accomplishment during the war was *Oyneg Shabes,* the cryptonym for the unique underground ghetto archive that was planned and assembled in conditions of strict conspiracy. In truth, this archive came into being mainly in order to serve as a documentation center of the time, in order to secure the nation's tragic epoch historically. Therefore, the *Oyneg Shabes* archive, which comprises a wonderful national cultural treasure for the Jewish people, safeguards more than any other archive from that time the spiritual inheritance left by those generations that departed on the most gruesome road of destruction.

After Trunk discusses in a brief overview the most significant materials from the *Oyneg Shabes* archive, whose largest part consists of monographs about annihilated communities, he comes to the conclusion that, unfortunately, very little is known among us about the wealth of materials in the Ringelblum archive, that "what has been published until now . . . is a small fraction of the existing material." Therefore, "a multi-volume edition of the Ringelblum archive is really a debt owed by the Jewish people to someone who enriched the knowledge of its past with his creative life and who, while constantly facing the danger of death, wrote for future generations the chronicle of our greatest national catastrophe until his last breath."

Among the numerous occasions that I had the pleasure to spend with Isaiah Trunk, who was a dear person, a good friend, and one who excelled in modesty in all his actions, I could often appreciate his mode of working; it was a model of meticulous intellectual integrity. Nothing emerged from beneath his pen that he had not carefully checked several times. And more than once I was utterly amazed by his diligence, by his broad knowledge, by his deep proficiency in all branches of Holocaust research, as well as by the broad scope of his bibliographic knowledge.

As a member of the scientific staff of YIVO and as the one who for many years directed the institute's archive, he devoted much time to training young researchers. Many of his students were educated on his writings and research studies, and among those individuals were not a few educators who are teaching their pupils Jewish history.

Over the course of more than forty years, since his first historical treatise appeared, until his last day, Trunk untiringly did fruitful work in the field of historical research. Thanks to his industry and his devotion, he left behind a very important lifetime's work, rich in quantity and quality—substantive and interesting books, essays and articles.

The passing into eternity of this creative historian, Isaiah Trunk, is a painful loss for historiography of the Holocaust, an irreplaceable loss.

Introduction:
The Distinctiveness
of the Łódź Ghetto
Israel Gutman[1]

Łódź and its Jewish community were well known for their rapid development, which, over a few generations, transformed a remote village into one of the largest centers of economic activity in Europe. In 1808, Łódź had a population of 434, including 58 Jews; by the eve of the Second World War and the Nazi occupation—in the span of about 130 years—its total population had soared to 672,000 and its Jewish population to 233,000. The Jews contributed greatly to the city's development, both as founders of businesses and of industrial enterprises (of the 156 factories built in the city between 1881 and 1900, 105 were under Jewish ownership) and as workers and craftsmen in the textile industry, which fueled the city's rapid growth and gave it the sobriquet, "the Manchester of Poland."[2]

After the Nazis occupied Łódź in September 1939, the city was included in the Warthegau area in the northwest of Poland, which was annexed to the Reich. The Third Reich authorities originally considered leaving Łódź in the ethnic-Polish enclave of the occupied area, the Generalgouvernement, but Hitler honored a request from the governor of the Warthegau, Arthur Karl Greiser, and the many Germans who lived in Łódź, and proclaimed the annexation of Łódź to the Reich in November 1939. The importance of this decision transcended its political and administrative aspects; it meant that Łódź was to be transformed into a German city. The Jews were to be eliminated from Łódź as from the rest of the Warthegau, and the Polish population was to be thinned out and subjected to a regime of political and sociocultural repression. Greiser was adamant about the transfer of Jews from Łódź; in a meeting of representatives of the central Reich authorities in Berlin on 1 April 1940, where a moratorium on the transfer of Jews from the annexed territories to the Generalgouvernement was bruited, Greiser argued that Łódź should be exempted from the moratorium.[3] An initial order on 10 December 1939, which mentioned the establishment of a ghetto in Łódź, clearly had in mind only a temporary concentration of Jews in the ghetto, for "the immediate evacuation of the Jews is not possible."[4] Another document by the mayor of Łódź, dated July 1941, states that, according to the "promise made at the time, the Łódź Ghetto was to have existed only as a provisional measure (*Übergangsmassnahme*) until October 1, 1940."[5]

Consequently, the Łódź Ghetto (Litzmannstadt-Getto), sealed on 1 May 1940, was meant to serve as a short-term transit point until Jews could be altogether deported from the city. Throughout the years 1939–1943, various ghettos were established in the Generalgouvernement and the annexed territories, and various explanations and excuses were given for the need to imprison the Jews in them. In other words, no general one-time order was given to create ghettos, and the decision on when to form them evidently was made by local authorities for reasons of their own.[6] Additionally, the internal regimes and the quarantining of the ghettos were neither uniform nor identical in all places. In some ghettos, such as that of Warsaw, Jews were cut off from the rest of the city by walls, while elsewhere they were allowed to leave for short periods in order to obtain basic provisions.

The Łódź Ghetto was one of the first set up in occupied Poland and, as stated, was meant to be temporary. Paradoxically, it outlasted all the other ghettos in occupied Eastern Europe. It became institutionalized, and its organizational structure became a model for emulation. Jewish and Gentile officials and representatives from various localities were sent to Łódź in order to study the ghetto system there and to fashion their own after it.[7]

Several aspects that distinguished the Łódź Ghetto from ghettos in other cities affected the conditions in this ghetto and did much to determine its fate. This review emphasizes these distinctive features that may help us understand what happened in Łódź and comprehend the history of its ghetto.

* * *

The Łódź Ghetto, the second-largest in German-occupied Eastern Europe after that of Warsaw, was also the most isolated from the outside world. Although some 233,000 Jews lived in Łódź at the outbreak of the war, only about 164,000 of them were confined in the ghetto in May 1940. This drastic decrease, more than one-third of the Jewish population of the city within several months, may be attributed to several factors. From the very beginning of the occupation, the Nazis invoked a system of terror and persecution that, while also directed at the Poles, targeted Jews above all. In addition to suffering assaults in the city streets, Jews were immediately subjected to a set of orders and prohibitions. One such order forced each Jew to wear a yellow armband, which was swiftly replaced by a yellow star on the chest and the back. Jews were enjoined from leaving their homes in the afternoon hours and were barred from traveling on the main thoroughfare and from using public transportation. A separate set of economic decrees dispossessed the Jews of their property and deprived them of any possibility of earning a livelihood. Jews lost their jobs, factories, and businesses, and were forbidden to trade in textile goods. Their bank accounts were frozen, and they were not allowed to possess cash in excess of the small sum of 2,000 zlotys. In December 1939, the Nuremberg Laws were applied to Łódź as to all of the Wartheland.

From the very first days of September, Jews began to flee Łódź and join the flow of refugees eastward. After the Reich annexed the city, the German authorities began evacuating Jews and Poles from dwellings that were reserved for Germans, and a methodical deportation from the city was set in motion. Deportations to the Generalgouvernement, characterized by violence and plunder, took place in December 1939 and January 1940. By the end of the latter month, Jews had been evicted from dwellings in the downtown area to specific parts of the Old City and Bałuty quarters, where the ghetto subsequently was set up. On 8 February, the chief of police in Łódź, *SS* Brigadeführer Johannes Schäfer, issued an order that included a list of streets where Jews might dwell and a precise schedule for the evictions.[8] On 1 March, evidently dissatisfied with the alacrity of the transfer, the Germans perpetrated a pogrom in which many were murdered, and thousands more were forced into the ghetto with no possessions whatsoever. This frenzy of violence delivered all the Jews to the ghetto except for several dozen individuals who were allowed to remain outside temporarily for work reasons. Between February and April, Jews continued to leave Łódź for the Generalgouvernement, chiefly Warsaw. Those who joined the successive waves of escapees and deportees until the sealing of the ghetto included many of the affluent local Jews and much of the intelligentsia.

The ghetto was surrounded by a wooden and barbed wire fence in March-April 1940 and was officially sealed off in late April. On 10 May, Schäfer gave orders concerning the guarding of the ghetto fences and gates, and announced that "any attempt by a ghetto resident to leave the ghetto without permission, in any way whatsoever, shall be [prevented] at once with the use of firearms."[9] This grave punishment was introduced at no other ghetto, except at a later stage of the ghettoization process.[10] The Łódź Ghetto was soon hermetically sealed, impenetrable and isolated. Two units of German police were entrusted with guarding its outer perimeter, and Jewish police were in charge of the ghetto interior. Unlike in other ghettos, the two types of police were not allowed to interrelate in Łódź. At first, small quantities of food were smuggled into the ghetto, and business relations between Jews and Gentiles continued sporadically. However, both these activities soon came to an end. The chief of police warned of an absolute ban on "any form of commerce with

Jews; transport of goods into the ghetto is deemed to be smuggling and is punishable."[11] The Łódź Ghetto was evidently the only ghetto where smuggling was absolutely impossible. Consequently, food was not brought in clandestinely, and the ghetto inhabitants could not produce goods illegally to sell on the outside. Because groups of laborers did not leave the ghetto for work elsewhere, this avenue of smuggling and liaison was precluded. Unable to smuggle and manufacture clandestinely, the Jews depended completely on such food supplies as the authorities provided, and all goods manufactured in the ghetto were for German use only.

The ghetto scrip, called the "chaimke" or "rumki" in the ghetto argot (after the name of the Judenrat chairman, Mordechai Chaim Rumkowski), also frustrated smuggling. This scrip, bearing the signature of the chairman of the Judenrat, was valid in the ghetto but utterly worthless outside it. The introduction of specious currency was also an effective device in the plunder of Jewish property. In their state of pervasive hunger, the Jews were forced to sell their property, including valuables, foreign currency, and Reichsmarks, for ghetto scrip, for only with it could they buy even the smallest quantities of food. Some allege that it was Rumkowski who had proposed to the Germans the introduction of alternative currency; others, however, conclude that this was a German measure consistent with their methods. Be that as it may, the ghetto scrip was introduced shortly after the quarantining of the ghetto, and was enforced as the only legal tender.

* * *

In February 1941, the ghetto administration employed 5,500 people, 6 percent of the adult population. By late 1941, the number of administration employees rose to 10,000, and to 12,000 in early August 1942.

The ghettos were established at various times and under various orders and were sealed in different ways. In contrast, the institution of the Judenrat (Jewish council) was introduced in Jewish localities at the beginning of the occupation, under ordinances that pertained to all the Nazi-occupied areas and outlined the council's major functions and responsibilities.[12] However, the Judenrat of the Łódź Ghetto and, in particular, its dominant and authoritarian chairman, Mordechai Chaim Rumkowski—"President" or Chairman of the Council of Elders (Judenälteste),[13] or simply "the Chairman" or "King Chaim," to mention just a few of the appellations applied to him—were considered exceptional among Judenräte and Judenrat leaders in all of occupied Poland.

The chairman of the Łódź Kehilla (Jewish Community) Board, Leib Mincberg of Agudath Israel, like most communal, political, and social activists, fled Łódź before the Germans arrived.[14] During a brief transition period, the remaining council members who had stayed behind, including Rumkowski, functioned as the heads of the community. A month after the Kehilla Council reorganized as the first Beirat, the thirty-one members of this new board were ordered to report to the authorities. Most never saw their homes again. Rumkowski, one of three members to be released, was instructed to form a new Beirat to which he appointed many of his cronies.

The eradication of the first Beirat under hazy circumstances left a deep impression. Rumkowski's most adamant critics among the survivors blame him for the physical liquidation of the previous council. Philip Friedman articulated this accusation, asserting that Rumkowski had borne a grudge against those first Beirat members who "did not accede to his every demand and [who] objected to his internal policies." Therefore, alleges Friedman, he had "handed them to the executioner."[15] This serious indictment seems to have no solid basis; rather, it belongs to a relentless predisposition to hold Rumkowski responsible for any adverse or tragic event that befell the Jews of Łódź. There is no proof of his involvement; on the contrary, the available documentation indicates that Rumkowski had tried to save his colleagues on the council.[16]

Rumkowski was born in 1877 in Ilino, Russia.[17] The exact date of his arrival in Łódź is unknown, but it is fairly certain that he reached the town as an adult. The future head of the Łódź Ghetto had no higher education; some claim that his formal education ended after the first few primary grades. He earned his living in trade and industry, sometimes amassing considerable wealth, experiencing ups and downs. In the years preceding World War II, he worked as an insurance agent and earned a regular income. Rumkowski was attracted to public service, in which he invested much time and energy. He belonged to the General Zionist Party and represented its interests on the Jewish community council, but his relations with colleagues in the faction soured after he, unlike the others, refused to resign his seat in response to a confrontation with Agudath Israel. Rumkowski was among the founders of an orphanage in Helenówek, an institution that became renowned, and was considered its indefatigable custodian. Although Rumkowski's political activities and devotion to the orphanage were apparently not totally altruistic,[18] even his many adversaries admitted that this man, who was childless and for many years a widower, harbored sincere and deeply felt fatherly feelings and concern for his charges. In the years preceding the war, the traits that intensified to unbridled proportions in the ghetto period were already visible in Rumkowski: pursuit of honor and power, authoritarianism and persistence, powers of persuasion, organizational skills, and wanton exploitation of those around him for the goals he set himself.

Rumkowski, who acquired absolute control of the second largest ghetto in Europe, has piqued the curiosity of historians, authors, and memoirists alike.[19] Many writers have attempted to understand the force that drove the Łódź Ghetto Judenälteste to behave and believe as he did, and to discover the secret of the power and durability of the man who ruled the Jews of Łódź and the ghetto highhandedly from the beginning of the occupation until the liquidation of the ghetto in the summer of 1944.

A primary source of his power was evidently the authority that the German authorities vested in him, a degree of power unmatched in any other ghetto. On 13 October 1939, German city commissioner of Łódź Leister ruled that, for the discharge of his duties, the Judenälteste was free to travel through the city day and night, to meet with the governing authorities, and to choose the members of his "Council of Elders" at his own discretion.[20] One day later, the German commissioner augmented and expanded Rumkowski's powers by stating that all existing Jewish public agencies and institutions would be dissolved and reconstituted under the Judenälteste's jurisdiction. This document also stipulated that community members who evaded their lawful obligations would be reported and that Leister would "see to their immediate detention." Rumkowski was empowered to levy taxes to cover the expenses resulting from the discharge of his functions.[21] In April 1940, with the establishment of the ghetto, Rumkowski was given vast prerogatives that effectively placed him in control of all vital aspects of the Jews' internal affairs. The relevant document stated, inter alia: "You must particularly ensure order in economic life, food provisions, use of manpower, public health, and public welfare. You are authorized to take all necessary measures and issue all necessary instructions to attain this goal, and to enforce them by means of the Jewish police force that is under your command."[22]

Rumkowski's loyalty to the German authorities became well known and has been cited on several occasions in testimonies of former ghetto inhabitants and in the records of persons who came into contact with him. In his Warsaw Ghetto chronicle, Emanuel Ringelblum wrote the following entry in September 1940: "Today, September 6, Rumkowski of Łódź, where he is known as 'King Chaim,' came for a visit. He is an old man of seventy or so, with uncommon ambition and of somewhat confused intellect. He described the ghetto in miraculous terms. There is a Jewish state with four hundred policemen and three prisons. He has a foreign minister and all other ministers, too."[23]

Adam Czerniaków, head of the Warsaw Ghetto Judenrat, wrote in his diary on 17 May 1941: "He is replete with self-praise, a conceited and witless man, and a dangerous man, too, since he keeps telling the authorities that all is well in his preserve."[24]

Nathan Eck was a teacher in Łódź who had fled the city, first to Warsaw and, during the large deportations in the summer of 1942, from Warsaw to Sosnowiec. In his memoirs he related that

Moshe Merin, chairman of the Judenrat in the Zagłębie area who, like Rumkowski, was considered a compliant Judenrat chairman who ruled the Jews despotically, had told him: "Heaven knows what punishment this Rumkowski deserves . . . because he showed the Germans the way."[25] J. Poznański, who kept a diary in the Łódź Ghetto, wrote in his entry for 15 September 1943 that Rumkowski had visited his workplace (*ressort*) and delivered a lengthy speech: "He said that we must devote ourselves to work and, God forbid, not deal in politics."[26]

Several historians subject Rumkowski to assessments even more critical than those of the aforementioned diarists and authors of memoirs. Isaiah Trunk portrays him as having "carried out Nazi policy in the ghetto. . . . As forceful and domineering as he was with those who depended on him in the ghetto, so was he submissive and disciplined vis-à-vis the authorities."[27] Philip Friedman was yet more vehement. In "Pseudo-Saviors in the Polish Ghettos," Friedman draws a bizarre parallel between the false messiahs throughout Jewish history and specific Judenrat chairmen in the Polish ghettos (Rumkowski in Łódź, Merin in Zagłębie, and Gens in Vilna). Friedman does admit: "The inmost urgings of the people, their hopes and their dreams, found expression in the messages of the false messiahs. Thus the term 'false messiah' does not really suit those Jews who arose in the ghettos of Nazi-occupied Poland and took upon themselves the task of saving Israel. They were false saviors, not false messiahs."[28] Subsequently, however, Friedman notes:

> By twisted and strange paths, "messianic" notions had become central to fascism, especially Nazism. In distorted fashion, the false messiahs of the fascist states promised salvation to their masses, spoke about their mission and their election, announced that their regime would endure for a thousand years, and sacrificed to their nation's glowing future tens of thousands of human lives. . . . The pseudo-messiahs of the ghettos were, consciously or unconsciously, influenced by the great "messianic" craze of the fascists, and aspired to be saviors of their people in ways that were devoid of Jewish spirit. They were ruthless men who ruled, like their Nazi masters, by coercion. They believed that they would manage to save at least a portion of their people by autocratic deeds in the spirit of the German Führer.[29]

Friedman thus accuses Rumkowski of hallowing the malevolent, non-Jewish spirit of fascism and adopting Nazi methods. Even if he does not allege explicitly that Rumkowski accepted fascist principles as his ideological credo, he certainly does not stop far short of this assertion.[30]

Researchers who have dealt with the issue of collaboration have differentiated carefully between willful collaboration (e.g., Quisling), the result of conceptual identification with and adoption of Nazi political tactics, and submission and collaboration under duress, in which leaders in the occupied countries participated against their will, regarding this as the only way to remain alive. Trunk seeks to express this distinction in terminology, by calling collaboration under duress by Judenräte "cooperation," as opposed to willing cooperation, which he terms "collaboration."[31]

Friedman's harsh assessment seems to reflect the bitterness toward the Judenräte, and the abjectly negative characterization of the institution, that lurked in the shadow of the tragedy and trauma in the early post-war years. This unequivocally accusative stance is based, to some extent, on the criticism and flagellation that the chroniclers and survivors heaped on the Judenräte in their memoirs. Only research that also takes account of the writings of Judenräte chairmen and material from the Judenrat archives, and that attempts to compare the Judenräte with non-Jewish players in the occupied countries (especially in the concentration camps), where collaboration was a basic prerequisite for survival, can reach more balanced assessments.

It is clear that the Nazis deliberately set up the Judenräte for a direct confrontation with the population of the ghetto. The Nazi authorities forced Judenräte to carry out their orders and decrees, and the Jews of the ghetto dealt with the Judenrat chairman and authorities rather than with the Nazis, who remained offstage as it were, directing and masterminding events from afar. The commissioner of the Warsaw Ghetto, Heinz Auerswald, regarded the Judenrat, which stood in the front line and bore the brunt of Jewish criticism, as an important asset to the regime.[32] The commissioner of the Łódź Ghetto, Hans Biebow, behaved similarly, sometimes preferring to improve the lot of the ghetto inhabitants in order to sow even greater confusion, intensify the resentment of the *Ältestenrat*, and exacerbate internal conflicts among the Jews.

Rumkowski was no coward. He had been beaten several times by the Germans, including Biebow. The latter, the German official in charge of the Łódź Ghetto, applied his tactics efficiently; instead of merely criticizing things from afar, he delved into the details of the council's appointments and modus operandi. The German administration drew up an indictment against Rumkowski in June 1942,[33] and their purpose in doing so is clear. It was their way of informing Rumkowski that they were watching his every move, and that his tenure would not last long if he deviated from their instructions in the slightest or attempted to act independently. The claim that Rumkowski behaved during the ghetto years as a "despotic autocrat," to use Trunk's term, misrepresents the stage-by-stage development of the ghetto leadership. He was evidently uncertain and reluctant as he assumed the office of Judenälteste.[34] At first he solicited advice and support from authoritative public figures, including political functionaries in the ghetto. Janni [Jacob] Szulman, a close acquaintance of Rumkowski's and a former journalist who belonged to the left flank of the Zionist movement, wrote the following in early March 1941: "In the early days of Rumkowski's public duties, he attempted to gain the cooperation of many former friends and colleagues in the party."[35]

Israel Tabaksblat, in his book *Khurbn lodzh* (Destruction of Łódź), argues that Rumkowski could not convert the community from a tradition of democracy to absolute rule all at once. Therefore, he says, Rumkowski's Beirat still had room for "influential, respectable, intelligent people. It seems that he was not yet willing or able to display his autocratic tendencies at the start, and had no choice but to take account of the community, a factor that he later suppressed and totally uprooted."[36]

Some of Rumkowski's senior appointments in his administration went to individuals with strong political identities, such as the Zionist Baruch Praszkier and J. Jachimek of the Bund. In the spring and summer of 1940, when unemployment, poverty, and hunger provoked riots in the ghetto, Rumkowski convened public and political forces for a consultation. Trunk writes that the relocation of the collective kibbutz extensions of youth movements and political organizations to Marysin (an area of small farms and small houses that was annexed to the ghetto in May 1940) was the result of "Rumkowski's public initiative and administration." The public and political groupings also controlled centers of power and organization such as house committees, soup kitchens, and labor cooperatives. When forced to make decisions on the selection of Jews for dispatch to labor camps or for deportation, Rumkowski initially included public figures in his considerations and in the leadership of the ghetto.

However, the sporadic contacts with public figures, the participation of small numbers of politicians, and the existence of structures and institutions in which public and political representatives had a say were all eliminated in the course of 1941. The question is what induced Rumkowski to reject the public agencies in favor of almost unlimited autocracy and reliance on obsequious, ambitious, and efficient sycophants, who introduced a quasi-Byzantine servility toward the Judenälteste, corruption and intrigue in ghetto life, and a ghetto atmosphere without any traditional public guidance. Rumkowski may have feared excessive intervention on the part of traditional public forces, which might have made him look suspicious in German eyes. It is also possible that Rumkowski's self-confidence grew as the system of ghetto services became institutionalized, thus fueling his narcissism and lust for power. In early 1941, the Łódź Ghetto turned into a massive workplace, and all essentials of life such as food, shelter, and welfare were centered in the Judenrat administration. The dynamism that gave the Łódź Ghetto its "autonomous" image made Rumkowski more popular with the inhabitants. He strolled the ghetto streets confidently, delivered speeches to groups of people who gathered around him, and enveloped himself in a blanket of endless admiration. According to Tabaksblat, in those days Rumkowski "was driven by one obsession: to acquire power, as much power as possible, power for the sake of power!" This explains his reliance on boot-lickers and intriguers, who exploited his weakness. He deteriorated to the point at which he could not bear to have around him people who did not acknowledge his qualities as an infallible leader, and he showed no quarter in banishing anyone who took public exception to his methods, by including them in the transports that hauled workers and deportees out of the ghetto. He deliberately adopted proprietary affectations, speaking frequently of "my Jews, my houses, my factories . . . my bread."[37]

Some conjecture that not only did Rumkowski become a megalomaniac within the walls of the Łódź Ghetto, but he even entertained ideas about becoming a Jewish leader under German patronage in Nazi-dominated Europe. However, there seems to be no real evidence of such ambitions. According to Szulman, Rumkowski often declared that he had "packed his [political leanings] in a little box that [he] put aside for the time being." He adds, however: "The *Älteste* had set his heart on going to Palestine immediately after the war. . . . He was dominated by the idea that his name would be recorded in history. Before he moved into the sealed ghetto, he already believed in the great mission that was awaiting him. . . . But he never lost sight of the main goal: the welfare of the Jewish people."[38]

In a speech on 3 January 1942, Rumkowski delivered the following remarks: "I hope that, with your help, I shall be able to fulfill my mission and create the conditions that will make it possible to survive this period, stay alive, and sustain the health of large segments of the ghetto population and the young generations within it."[39]

These sound like irreconcilable contradictions. There is no denying the contradictions that nestled in Rumkowski's complex personality. However, Rumkowski seems to have been fully aware of his limitations. His dynamism, ambition, and other traits equipped him to be a powerful local ruler and caused him to imagine that the ghetto was an autonomous mini-state under his heel. His strength, however, did not lie in grand politics or the world of ideas. The cult that he deliberately fostered leaves a repugnant, sickening impression. In Warsaw, too, attempts were made to exalt and praise Czerniaków in song and acclaim, but, as the diary of the Warsaw Judenrat chairman shows, Czerniaków was well aware of the meaning of these hollow acts of sycophancy and spoke of them with an irony tempered by sadness. Not so Rumkowski; he exuded the arrogance of yesterday's slave newly empowered. The conditions that excised standard norms and destroyed a sound social structure reduced this uncultured man, with his inflated historical perspective, to grotesque behavior. He would walk around the ghetto, visiting workplaces and apportioning extra rations to those he favored, appointed himself supreme judge, officiated at young couples' weddings, and so on. The strange thing was that Rumkowski took his position and importance with the utmost seriousness and gravely acknowledged the pomp, praise, and poems that were written in his honor in the ghetto calendars and official newspaper. He was not alone in believing in the historical mission that had come his way; Gens in Vilna and even Barasz in Białystok entertained similar beliefs. They, however, were more aware of the dangers; they also understood that they were on thin ice and did not take the external manifestations of praise too seriously. Even if they were not entirely indifferent to the praise that was heaped on them, they were nevertheless endowed with a sense of reality.

This, it would seem, is what set Rumkowski apart from other Judenrat chairmen who adopted the attitude of "salvation through labor." Barasz and Gens also sought to make work a guiding principle in the Jews' lives. They aspired to raise productivity; they took pride in their achievements and efficiencies. They took credit for the Jews' accomplishments, efficacy, and abilities on the job, and regarded work as an "antidote" to annihilation. In so doing, however, they understood the clear demarcation of turf, the outer turf occupied by the dangerous enemy lying in ambush, and the inner domain of the ghetto and its Jews, whose fate they shared. Therefore, they addressed the Jews and the ghetto in one register, uninhibited and free, and the authorities in another register, adapted to the requisites of the situation. Their loyalty was purely tactical: to carry out any order that had to be carried out, and to refrain from carrying out orders, and to aid and abet illegalities, as long as these could be concealed from the Germans. At some point, probably in the course of 1942, Rumkowski disassociated himself from this covert partnership with the Jewish community and its interests, a partnership guided by this two-edged tactical policy. At this point, the Judenälteste appeared to be working hand in hand with the German authorities, "always ready to carry out their orders without protest, even if this required very serious measures."[40] True or not, this is how many Jews in the ghetto perceived the situation. In a discussion on the Judenräte at the Residence of the Presidents of Israel, Zalman Shazar remarked that he considered Rumkowski's case different from the tragic dilemma in which other Judenrat leaders found themselves: "I was not amazed by this despot, the head of the Łódź Judenrat, who displayed all kinds of strong-arm, power-satiated affectations. He gave me the impression of being a degenerate who drank up power as a drunkard drinks his wine."[41]

Rumkowski's self-confidence and unchallenged status were seriously undermined by the murderous deportation in September 1942, which will be discussed below. From then on, he made few public appearances and his status was gravely diminished. The signs of weakness that Rumkowski began to show—in reflection of either his own doubts or distrust of the community, which had ceased to view him as a savior and protector—opened the door for schemers who aspired to step into the Judenälteste's shoes or, at least, to get a piece of the action. Biebow deprived Rumkowski of two crucial aspects of ghetto management and handed them to two of the toughest members of the newly evolved ghetto elite. The supply division was transferred to David Gertler, head of the *Sonderabteilung* (special unit) and a trusted agent of the Gestapo. Responsibility for the *ressorts*[42] (the ghetto labor apparatus) was handed to Aaron Jakubowicz, who had previously administered the network of factories and showed no inclination to terminate his subordinate relationship with Rumkowski. Despite his diminished status, Rumkowski remained at the top of the pyramid until 30 August 1944, when he expressed his desire to join a transport to Auschwitz unless his brother and family, who had been included in the transport, were freed. Rumkowski's reception at Auschwitz and his subsequent death are the subjects of many stories of unproven veracity.[43]

Rumkowski's personality and role have elicited much controversy among the ghetto inhabitants and the survivors. One of the latter wrote: "It is strange that Rumkowski's personality remains controversial among the surviving inmates of the Łódź Ghetto. His defenders have many arguments to fall back on, including that his policies and his attitude toward the Germans kept the Łódź Ghetto intact until the summer of 1944. These [survivors] insist that the positive aspects and results of his actions should not be disregarded. This positive side was particularly evident, they say, at the time when the ghetto was being organized."[44]

Isaiah Trunk, who spares Rumkowski no measure of criticism and condemnation, concludes the discussion of the latter's personality by stating that the Judenälteste of the Łódź Ghetto imagined that he would go down in history as the hero who had succeeded in saving thousands of Jews from death in the Łódź Ghetto. Trunk adds: "And who knows whether he would not have succeeded, if the Soviet army had not halted its offensive on the Polish front from August 1944 until January 1945? There were still 68,500 Jews living in the ghetto on 1 August 1944."[45]

Other historians and authors concur with Trunk and have taken up this theory. This hypothesis is unacceptable, not only because historians tread on dangerous ground when they indulge in hyperbole along the lines of "what if." It has been proven on more than one occasion that the Nazis managed to massacre tens of thousands within a matter of days, as in the camps around Lublin in November 1943, and to evacuate tens of thousands of inmates on death marches, as in Auschwitz and the complex of camps adjacent to it in January 1945.

* * *

The Łódź Ghetto excelled in the organization of its labor and its achievements in production. The production system in the ghetto, set in motion immediately after the ghetto was established, quickly expanded until the enclosure became, in Trunk's words, "a milder version of a labor camp." The first sewing workshop went into operation in May 1940, and by September 1940 there were seventeen *ressorts* including seven sewing factories. By 1943, there were 117 operational factories, workshops, sorting houses, and merchandise warehouses in the ghetto. By July 1940, 40,000 of the 146,000 Jews in the ghetto were employed in the *ressorts* and offices, and by March 1942, the number of production workers alone had risen to 53,000.[46] Tabaksblat claims that, in early 1941, the upper-limit goal was to achieve 25 percent employment; in 1942–1943, 95 percent of the adult population in the ghetto was working.[47] The output of the Łódź Ghetto was of enormous value, and Greiser declared in his trial after the war (Poznań, 1946) that the Łódź Ghetto was one of the largest industrial centers in the Reich.[48]

The ghetto was not endowed with large factories. Jews were dispossessed of their enterprises, and the confiscated property included essential production equipment. The Ältestenrat made an effort to prevent the plunder of equipment owned by small Jewish enterprises and requested the return of confiscated machinery and equipment, but was only partially successful. The "productivization" process—the effort to turn a diverse population into an army of brute laborers using primitive manual methods—was difficult to carry out. Work conditions in the ghetto factories are described in the Łódź volume of Yad Vashem's *Pinkas ha-kehilot*:

> Labor in the ressorts was exhausting and poorly paid. Deadlines were hard to meet; wages were low and arbitrarily set. When urgent orders came in, a twelve-hour workday was compulsory. Working conditions at the ressorts were harsh: small, poorly lit and inadequately ventilated rooms, wholly unsuited to the various types of production. Many operations ordinarily done by machine had to be done manually for lack of equipment. The work quotas for Jews were very high when one considers that the workers were starving. Biebow himself wrote in a report to his superiors in April 1943 that Jews were, for example, assigned a quota of 300–320 wooden shoe soles per day, while the daily quota for Polish workers in Łódź factories was only 180–200 soles.[49]

The ghetto turned out a broad selection of products. The list of *ressorts* included sewing, undergarments, furs, leather goods, carpentry, metalwork, paper, brushes, shoes, and electrical goods. One of the compilers of these lists, who was intimately familiar with the ghetto economy, wrote:

> Every type of work was performed there. There was no kind of manufacturing that lacked its craftsmen. Work was done for military and civilian purposes. Usually there was little civilian work, because only orders from the military provided Biebow with appropriate cover. The ghetto was never bombarded, so companies in the Reich willingly sent their orders there. At times, output from a certain company in the Łódź Ghetto was all that remained of a German company's assets after the rest of its domestic assets were destroyed in the bombings. A lot of manufacturing was done free of charge for Germans with influence. Officials from the city administration and the [German] ghetto administration, from the Gestapo and the Kripo, dressed like kings from the results of Jewish toil.[50]

The German ghetto administration was housed in several locations. Officially, it was a department of sorts attached to City Hall (*der Oberbürgermeister Gettoverwaltung in Litzmannstadt*). At its head was Hans Biebow, a businessman from Bremen whom the Germans entrusted with control of the ghetto. Biebow maintained ramified and favorable connections with various economic institutions throughout the Reich, but his power derived mainly from the support that Greiser gave him. In other cities, control of the ghetto was segmented among civilian authorities, the SS, and, at times, other players, and tensions between these authorities were clearly reflected in the circumstances and events that took place in the ghetto. Conditions in the Łódź Ghetto were different. The principal authority was wielded by Biebow, who ruled with the backing of the Civil Administration. Biebow had an interest in ghetto production for two reasons: its contribution to the labor effort in the Reich, and the personal advantage and profit that he derived from it. According to some accounts, relations between Biebow and Rumkowski were marked by tension and clashes, but both officials were interested in the continued survival of the ghetto.

The administration office at Bałuty Square was a "headquarters" for the *ressorts*—a place that dealt with orders, accounts, and deliveries. The workers were starving. Although they were sometimes rewarded with rations in addition to the meager standard portion of bread and watery soup, their diet did not meet minimum nutritional needs, and fainting from hunger was a frequent occurrence at work. Nevertheless, as one of the survivors points out, the ghetto inhabitants still preferred to go to work, because those who did so found their hunger pangs to be weaker, and the extra food received at the *ressort* was an appreciable incentive. "If somebody was absent from work without a note from the doctor, he was arrested by the Jewish police and forced to return to the ressort."[51] Most of the Jewish foremen and supervisors, few of whom were experienced professionals, took a tough attitude toward rank-and-file workers. In several cases, however, supervisors treated their subordinates considerately and tried to help and protect them as much as possible.

The Łódź Ghetto, unlike the ghettos in Warsaw and many other localities, excelled in eliminating social disparities and instituting a brand of egalitarianism. Very few inhabitants were exempted from food shortages and allowed to dip into the public stores without limit. Any individual who possessed an extra portion of food was usually considered the beneficiary of good fortune. However, even the egalitarian distribution, which Rumkowski implemented stringently, did not prevent mass starvation.

Artur Eisenbach provides comparative mortality statistics in the Warsaw and Łódź Ghettos:

| | Warsaw | | Łódź | |
Year	General Mortality	Deaths per Thousand	General Mortality	Deaths per Thousand
1940	8,981	23.5	6,197	39.2
1941	43,238	90.0	11,378	75.7
1942	39,719	140.0	18,134	159.8

In the pre-war years, the death rate was 9.6 per thousand.[52] Mortality in Łódź approximated that in Warsaw and even exceeded it slightly in relative terms. In both ghettos, death from hunger and disease caused the ghetto population to diminish significantly even before the "Final Solution."

* * *

According to conventional wisdom, the maximum mobilization of Jews in Łódź for work was a means of defending them against the threat of deportation and murder. It is true that the purpose of labor mobilization in the ghettos of eastern Poland, such as those of Białystok and Vilna, was to make the Jews effective partners in the German work effort and thereby to prevent their murder. Vast areas of eastern Poland, occupied immediately after the beginning of Operation Barbarossa in June 1941, were swept by waves of massacres by the Einsatzgruppen in the second half of 1941, and the communities and ghettos there turned to labor as a means of survival.

This was not the case in Łódź at first. The purpose of developing the labor system and operating the *ressorts*, at least in the early stages of the ghetto period, was to alleviate the economic hardships of the

Jewish inhabitants. The Jews of Łódź had been totally dispossessed in the first few months of the occupation, and the plunder continued throughout the ghetto years. Similarly, most of the affluent Jews of Łódź had fled the city, and Rumkowski, the Ältestenrat, and the Jews themselves had to face the seemingly insurmountable problem of how to feed the masses of Jews quarantined in the impoverished suburb of Bałuty. In one of his speeches in the ghetto in 1941, Rumkowski boasted that before moving to the ghetto, he had informed the mayor of Łódź that their ghetto was a "gold mine." Noticing the mayor's amazement, the Judenälteste explained: "I have a labor force of 40,000 people, and this is my gold mine."[53] On 1 February 1941, Rumkowski informed senior ghetto officials, "Most members of the property-owning classes left before the ghetto was sealed. Left behind were the middle classes, the lower classes, and the working classes—the workers who account for most of the element of Bałuty. . . . I have assumed the task of seeing that life continues normally at any cost. This shall be achieved above all by general employment. Therefore, my main goal is *to provide jobs for as many people as possible.*"[54]

Memoirs reinforce our understanding that the most urgent issue facing the nascent ghetto was subsistence. Thus, the first impetus to enlist craftsmen and exploit the ghetto's productive potential was the need for employment and sources of nourishment. Only later were work and productivity in the ghetto considered not only a means of subsistence for the inhabitants but also an anchor that might keep the ghetto in existence and spare those whose labor was essential.

As we have seen, in 1940 the local officials and the Wartheland authorities wanted to expel all the Jews and were willing to accept the establishment of the ghetto only as a temporary evil. It was the central Reich authorities who halted the deportations of Jews from the Wartheland to the Generalgouvernement. Subsequently, these roles were seemingly reversed: local elements benefited from the ghetto and regarded it as a source of income that they did not want to lose; whereas the central authorities in the Reich (not the economic branches but the chief office of the SS [the RSHA] and its economic bureau, *SS-Wirtschaftsverwaltungshauptamt* [WVHA]) sought to liquidate the ghetto and appropriate its economic resources. Biebow and his superiors agreed to pare down the ghetto and deport some of its population to the death camp at Chełmno, but for reasons of profit they wished to preserve the working, productive ghetto core.

In July 1941, Hoeppner, a police officer at SS headquarters in Poznań, wrote to Eichmann: "I believe that Uebelhoer, president of the Łódź district, does not favor the liquidation of the Łódź Ghetto because it gives him an opportunity to earn a great deal of money."[55]

A Jewish source points out: "At that time, with black clouds hovering over the ghetto, Biebow gave instructions to show a flood of orders that would prove the ghetto's importance to Germany. In this fashion, the survival of the ghetto was prolonged from time to time."[56]

A letter written on 4 July 1941, apparently by Dr. Marder, mayor of Łódź, asserts that the Germans had originally considered liquidating the ghetto by October 1940. Therefore, until then the ghetto administration dealt primarily with

> extracting something valuable from the ghetto inhabitants in order to cover the expense of keeping them alive. When it transpired that the ghetto would not be liquidated by the time stipulated, they began to organize an extensive labor enterprise there. In view of the resulting structure, the ghetto is no longer regarded as a labor or concentration camp of sorts, but rather as a significant element in the economic system [Gesamtwirtschaft], a kind of vast factory. To date, 40,000 of the 160,000 ghetto inmates are employed; this corresponds to the general employment [rate] in the Reich. In the near future, [the number of workers in the ghetto] is due to rise. I believe the conditions that apply to any other economic enterprise in the Reich should apply to an enterprise of this kind.[57]

Local German officials in the Łódź Ghetto and in other ghettos exploited the ghetto for power and profit. Middle-ranking bureaucrats exerted absolute control over tens of thousands, if not hundreds of thousands of people. Their positions protected them from being posted to the Eastern Front and afforded them a comfortable life and a quick path to wealth. Therefore, these people—guided not by humanitarian principles or motives, but primarily by broad and narrow self-interest—sought to keep the ghetto going.

Himmler strove to eliminate the ghettos and other Jewish civilian concentrations, and in July 1942 issued an order to "evacuate the entire Jewish population from the Generalgouvernement" by the end of 1942, except for a small number of locations that would serve as temporary concentration and selection centers. Starting in early 1943, Himmler focused on a campaign of mass liquidation and murder of Jews outside the Generalgouvernement. In early 1943, about 11,000 Jews were interned in approximately 100 small labor camps in the Poznań (Posen) area. In the summer of that year, these camps were liquidated by order of Himmler, and most of the laborers were killed. At this time, Himmler instructed Globocnik, chief of the SS and police in the Lublin district, to liquidate the Łódź Ghetto and transfer its productive labor force to the network of ghettos in the Lublin area, which was under SS supervision. Globocnik had orchestrated the mass murder of Jews in the Generalgouvernement (Operation Reinhard) and was in charge of the economic section (the Eastern Economic Authority—Ostindustrie [Osti]).[58] This order was never carried out because Albert Speer, Hitler's minister of armaments, was empowered to curb the economic expansion of the SS, and because Greiser resisted the order. Events in the Lublin area also helped thwart Himmler's stratagem. The uprising of Jewish inmates of the Sobibór extermination camp in October 1943 alarmed the Nazi authorities, and the swift advance of the Soviet forces added to the sense of unease. As a result of all these factors, the Jewish inmates of the camps in the Lublin area were murdered in November 1943. Hence the plan to transfer the productive core of the Łódź Ghetto was cancelled.

In December, Himmler ordered the transformation of the Łódź Ghetto into a concentration camp. Officials from the Economic Office (the WVHA) and SS headquarters, including Max Horn, were sent to Łódź to consider how to carry out this order and turn over the ghetto to Osti. The outcome of their discussions was a decision to conduct a selection among the ghetto inhabitants and have a core group of workers, provided that the regime and security arrangements corresponded to those of concentration camps. Another issue was who would claim the property of the ghetto inhabitants: the civilian district authorities or the SS. Albert Speer intervened at this point, and a military delegation from the Wehrmacht and armaments control staff in Poznań and Łódź arrived in December 1943. Concurrently, Biebow left for Berlin in order to interdict the SS and protect the status quo and his control over the ghetto. According to Eisenbach, the decision to leave the Łódź Ghetto in place was made by Hitler's general staff in a January 1944 meeting, at which the staff agreed that the resolutions taken would apply to the Łódź Ghetto as well as other localities.[59]

Interestingly, Osti director Max Horn expressed a dim view of the management of the ghetto enterprise and argued that its output was very low. Eisenbach construes this as evidence that the slogan of the underground forces in the Łódź Ghetto, "Go slow" (PP—*Pracuj powoli*), was effective. It is also possible, however, that Horn's negative assessments of the profitability of the Łódź Ghetto factories were meant to back the SS in its demand for transfer of the ghetto to its control. As the bargaining continued, the issue of property and ownership came up again; the civilian authorities demanded 18–20 million Reichsmarks for the factory machinery and equipment. In February 1944, Himmler and Greiser held a decisive meeting in Poznań and made a final ruling on the Łódź Ghetto. Instead of making the ghetto a concentration camp, they decided to turn it into a central ghetto for the district, reserved only for such Jews as were needed for production.[60] Pursuant to this decision, a "division of spoils" was concluded among the authorities involved.

Summing up, it may be stated with certainty that the primary reason for the longevity of the Łódź Ghetto was its labor and production system and the local authorities' vested interest in its continuation. Approximately 205,000 Jews passed through the ghetto, but only 70,000 were left when it was liquidated in June 1944. This shows clearly that the Łódź Ghetto, like all other localities, was the victim of barbaric living conditions and deportations to death camps. At this point in time, however, Łódź was the only ghetto and the location with the largest Jewish population in Nazi-occupied Eastern Europe.

* * *

There are various estimates of the extent to which the Jews in the Łódź Ghetto knew about and understood the meaning and purpose of the deportations and the Nazis' ongoing extermination of Jews.

It is clear that information did not reach the Łódź Ghetto in the way and at the time it reached most of the other ghettos. Furthermore, the gradual implementation of the deportations in the Łódź Ghetto, along with the relentless influx of refugees and deportees from other countries and surrounding localities, made it hard for the Jews of Łódź to understand and gauge the full significance of the events that ensued.

Reports on mass murder in the territories occupied by the Germans from June 1941 reached most of the ghettos directly from Vilna and the locations of these atrocities, or from Warsaw, to which and from which youth-movement emissaries spread the horrifying news throughout the occupied areas. These reports, printed in clandestine publications and in the press run by underground organizations in the Warsaw Ghetto, found their way to other ghettos. Łódź, however, was hermetically sealed; outside envoys could not reach it, and it had no ties with underground centers throughout Poland. On 1 January 1942, in a secret meeting of pioneering youth movements in the Vilna Ghetto, a statement prepared by Abba Kovner was read out; it not only mentioned the murder of deportees from Vilna, but asserted that Vilna and Lithuania were merely the first victims in an overall design culminating in the annihilation of the entire Jewish population of Europe.[61] This sweeping assertion, based on mere intuition and conjecture at the time it was made, was received with rejection and much vacillation. Among underground youth-movement circles and their leadership, however, it was generally accepted as a sober, truthful, and accurate view of reality and was gradually adopted by the underground leadership and some of the Jewish population in the ghettos. This assessment, like the others, never reached Łódź as far as we know, and we have no evidence of any controversy concerning the broader significance of the deportations within the Łódź Ghetto.

The death camp in Chełmno was about sixty kilometers from Łódź and belonged to the Wartheland. First activated in December

1941, it was actually the first death camp and murder site outside the jurisdiction of the Einsatzgruppen in occupied Soviet territory. Beginning in December 1941, terrifying rumors of impending evacuation spread through the Łódź Ghetto. The stated reason for the evacuation was the large size of the ghetto population, because in October 1941 the ghetto had received from the Reich and the Czech Protectorate another 20,000 refugees, whom it found difficult to support. On 20 December 1941, Rumkowski officially announced the forthcoming evacuation and spoke of three categories of undesirables whom he had designated for removal: criminal elements, welfare recipients who shirked labor, and speculators who snapped up the personal belongings of refugees as they reached the ghetto. In all, 20,000 Jews were earmarked for evacuation, offsetting the population growth caused by the refugees. An "evacuation committee" was set up, composed of the chief of the ghetto police, the registration officer, and others. According to Tabaksblat, the question of whom to deport was raised in a consultation with Rumkowski. Some argued that children and the elderly should be dispatched in order to leave the able-bodied in the ghetto for work. Others believed it best to select young adults, because the Germans' promises to resettle the deportees in nearby villages were untrustworthy; if the deportees had to set out on a lengthy march, young adults would survive the ordeal while children and the elderly would not. Tabaksblat adds parenthetically that nobody ever imagined that the deportees might be transported to a place set aside for their summary extermination. "Nobody dreamed of it," he writes.[62] Doctors examined the deportation candidates to determine whether their health was bad enough to exempt them, and rabbis arranged divorces overnight. Each deportee was allowed to take specified quantities of personal belongings and money. In the space of fourteen days, 16–29 January 1942, fourteen transports left the ghetto, bearing 10,103 people to the death camp in Chełmno. A moratorium followed—"the ghetto breathed a sigh of relief"—but the deportations to the death camp resumed on 22 February. The numbers of Jews transported to Chełmno from Łódź were 7,000 in February; 24,700 in March; 2,350 in April; and 11,000 in May. By 15 May, 55,000 people had been deported in sixty-six transports.[63]

Tabaksblat states: "After the first few weeks passed and the number of deportees had passed 20,000 with no end in sight, people began wondering: How long? They had been willfully duped. . . . Rumors spread that the ghetto was about to be liquidated and that everyone would be deported. Whither? For what purpose? There was no answer. This went on for about four months until the long-awaited signal was given: Stop! Satan had had his fill for the moment."[64]

Party activists took part in the debate about which population groups should be included in the transports. Party circles in the underground made sure to excuse their people from the evil decree. Although a member of the Bund states in his memoirs that his colleagues refused to take part in these consultations, Bundists were also known to attempt to secure the release of Bund members.[65]

A close associate of organized religious circles in the ghetto testified, "During the first deportation, no one knew why the Germans needed these people"; and, convening a consultation, Rumkowski expressed his preference: deport the elderly and the children. When the Judenälteste asked the rabbis who they believed should be deported, they said: "They can only declare who may not be handed over: young children and the sick, who do not even come into consideration. As to who should be handed over, the person conducting the negotiations must decide."[66]

In the course of 1941, thousands of Jews (more than a thousand per month in some months) were sent from the ghetto to various labor camps. Their families in the ghetto received reports on them and even a paltry salary. One gets the impression that the ghetto inhabitants were unable to differentiate, or at least differentiate clearly, between these transports and the deportations to Chełmno that began in January 1942. Abraham Wolf Jasny presumes that Rumkowski knew the significance of these deportations, because in the past he had been apprised of the deportees' destination, whereas this time he was not.[67] Furthermore, according to the Łódź daily Chronicle (10–14 April 1942), the Gestapo had mentioned off the record that the deportees were to be transferred to a camp near Koło, where 100,000 Jews had already been taken. From these two facts, to which persons other than Rumkowski were privy, it is hard to reach a firm conclusion as to whether the fate of the deportees was known.

The historian Shaul Esh, relying on a German source, described a visit by a German to the Łódź Ghetto, the purpose of which was to make contact with a German-Jewish family who had been deported there. In his article, Esh states that the visitor met with Leon Rozenblat, chief of police in the Łódź Ghetto, who had told him that he could guess the deportees' fate and that they were being gassed to death. According to Esh, the German was a reliable person, an author named Friedrich Hilscher, a radical conservative who, disgusted with the Nazis, "began to deal in underground activities." However, the story itself contains many puzzling details; the fact that the Jewish chief of police revealed his deepest secrets to a casual German visitor to the ghetto is only one of them. The most puzzling detail of all, perhaps, is the date of the visit: September 1941, a time when there were as yet no German Jewish refugees in the Łódź Ghetto, no transports to death camps from Łódź, and no extermination by gas in the camps.[68]

While the Łódź Ghetto was immersed in uncertainty and ignorance as to the destination and fate of the deportees, the Jews in Warsaw knew fairly early about Chełmno and the atrocities perpetrated there. In January 1942, Jacob Grojanowski, a Jew from the town of Izbica, escaped from the Chełmno camp, where he and a detachment of Jews from the transports had been forced to bury their murdered compatriots. In late January or early February 1942, Grojanowski reached Warsaw and gave detailed testimony about Chełmno, the transports that reached the camp, and the methods of mass murder invoked there. The testimony, collected by the staff of the Warsaw Ghetto underground archives, was forwarded to London through Polish underground channels.[69] The February-March 1942 edition of the underground newspaper of the Gordonia movement in Warsaw, *Słowo Młodych,* carried an article with the following information:

> Apart from the Jews of Koło and Dąbie, others have been slaughtered in Chełmno: Gypsies from the Łódź Ghetto on January 2–9, Jews from Kłodawa on January 10–12; Jews from Bugaj on January 14; Jews from Izbica Kujawska on January 14–15; and Jews from the Łódź Ghetto from January 15 on. There is no doubt whatsoever that this Aktion was deliberately planned. The local headquarters of the gendarmerie had detailed knowledge of the fate that awaited the deportees. Nevertheless, not only did they fail to inform the victims, they went so far as to lie to them with cruel hypocrisy, asserting that they knew nothing of any malevolent plan to displace them. The Gestapo, which perpetrated the massacre in the castle, followed an elaborately contrived plan. The main principle of the whole operation was complete secrecy. Apart from the specific transport of victims, no outsider was ever found within the boundaries of the farm, and never, ever, were two groups of deportees allowed to meet anywhere. The foregoing details originate in the testimonies by the surrounding population, to whom, despite all precautions, ripples of the terrible tragedy taking place in the Chełmno redoubt filtered through; and also, and above all, from written accounts that the unfortunate gravediggers threw out of the windows of their buildings. There is no doubt whatsoever as to the reliability of these accounts.[70]

Chaika Klinger, of the town Będzin in Zagłębie, wrote in her diary that Mordechai Anielewicz, who had reached the town in May 1942 while on a mission to Zagłębie, "corroborated the rumors about Chełmno and stated that there were accurate records of the layout of the place and the murder process."[71] Ringelblum wrote in his diary in June 1942, "In the past few weeks, English radio has broadcast frequent news items on atrocities against Polish Jews: Chełmno, Vilna, Bełżec, etc."[72]

Was the Łódź Ghetto truly impervious to reports of what was happening in Chełmno, even as the details were known in Warsaw, in other ghettos, and even abroad?

Trunk argues that "there is absolutely no doubt that Rumkowski already knew of the tragic fate of the deportees in the early spring of 1942." From the accounts of Jews who had survived the liquidation of ghettos in nearby towns and had been transported to Łódź in May 1942, the deportees' destination was known. An evacuee from Brzeziny brought a postcard sent by a rabbi from Grabów (near Łęczyca) dated 19 January 1942, which explicitly mentions the death camp at Chełmno. "When Rumkowski was informed of this, he replied that he was already aware of the fact." The source cited by Trunk to verify the information available to Rumkowski does not seem absolutely certain, and other sources do not confirm Trunk's assumption.[73]

However, the postcard sent by the rabbi from Grabów is mentioned by other witnesses and is apparently real. The contents of the missive, penned by Rabbi J. Silman of Grabów, have been published in several places, although we have not managed to obtain the original. The rabbi says that he was hesitant to mention the fate of the deportees as long as nothing was known for certain. "But today there arrived a witness who had been there, inside that hell. It is the village of Chełmno near Dąbie, and they are all buried in a forest known by the name of Łochów. The same happened with Koło, Dąbie, Kłodawa, and Izbica Kujawska. They also brought thousands of Gypsies there from Łódź, and the same was done to them. Since last week, thousands of Jews from Łódź have also arrived. All of them are gassed or shot to death."[74]

Even if we lack documented information on the Grabów rabbi's postcard and its circulation among the Jews of Łódź, it is clear that the September 1942 deportations left no doubt about the fate of future deportees.

The deportation of 5–12 September 1942 had a severe and traumatic impact on everyone who witnessed and wrote of it. Even the *Chronicle,* which was generally restrained in style, printed the following report on 14 September: "The week of September 5–12, 1942, will leave an indelible imprint among those in the ghetto who will be lucky enough to survive the war. One week, eight days, as long as eternity. Today it is still hardly imaginable. A maelstrom passed through the ghetto, sweeping 15,000 people away (the exact number is as yet unknown), and life only seems to have returned to its former path."[75]

The significance of the deportation is most tangibly expressed in a speech by the Judenälteste on September 4, 1942: "The ghetto has taken a grievous blow. They have asked us for the ghetto's most precious people: the children and the elderly. Unfortunately, I never had the merit of bearing a child of my own, and therefore I devoted my best years to children. I lived and breathed with them. I never imagined that my hands would be forced to bring the sacrifice to the altar. In my old age, I am forced to stretch out my hands and plead: 'My brothers and sisters—give them to me! Fathers and mothers—give me your children!' . . . (Anguished wailing wracks the assembled audience.)"[76]

Tabaksblat describes the *Sperre* (shperre), as the September deportation was known:

> At dawn, street after street and house after house were blockaded and the entire population, large and small, old and young, was forced to assemble in the yard or on the sidewalk near their homes, as the murderers, armed with pistols or machine guns, selected some for life and some for death. Anybody who looked withered or sickly to them was made to stand aside. Those who remained, the fortunate ones—those not selected—were allowed to go home. Home they went, some without a mother, some without children, heads bowed, but nevertheless breathing more easily. Their lives had been spared. Waiting in the street were the transport trucks, to which those selected were herded after being counted. The fortunate ones returned home, mute and despondent like mourners. There were no shattered hearts; there was no boiling blood.[77]

Could there have been any vestige of doubt about the fate of the children, the elderly, and the ill who had been separated so savagely from their mothers and loved ones? Many years later, one of the women survivors remarked: "It is hard to say, 'They knew.' There were conjectures, and we believed that it was so. In late 1942, one of the proofs we had was the *Sperre*. Why would they take the ill and the children? What would they do with them? To kill them, to exterminate them—but we did not know for sure until nearly the end."[78] An important Communist activist, Barbara (Hinda) Beatus, testified after the war: "Even we had disagreements about the evacuations. We were not sufficiently oriented; we did not believe that all the evacuees were being murdered. After a while, by 1943 or so, we were almost fully convinced that elderly and ill people and children had been murdered."[79]

Paradoxically, the September 1942 deportation, which proved that the deportees were being taken to their deaths, did not make the Jews of Łódź more aware and cognizant of the "Final Solution." In other words, it did not help them understand that the Germans were not targeting specific categories of Jews but were orchestrating the extirpation of the entire Jewish people. The very selection of persons who could not or did not work led them to conclude that the Nazis—while not averse to killing Jews who brought them no benefit—would protect their workers, who therefore had a chance to survive. From the September 1942 deportation to June 1944, relative calm prevailed in the Łódź Ghetto.

The rumors and reports of deportations from provincial towns, information about Chełmno that filtered into the large ghetto, and, particularly, the traumatic deportation of September 1942 made some of the ghetto inhabitants suspect, and made others certain, that murder was being committed and that at least some of the deportees were the victims. However, the Jews of the Łódź Ghetto—both the masses and the underground groups—never deduced that total and methodical murder was being perpetrated against the Jews. The Jews in Łódź neither knew nor understood the significance of the "Final Solution" until the ghetto had been liquidated.

* * *

Below we attempt to review underground activities and manifestations of resistance in the Łódź Ghetto.

In chapter 8 of his book on the Łódź Ghetto, regarding the "problem of resistance in the Łódź Ghetto," Trunk asks: "Why in the Łódź Ghetto, with its large Jewish population and a proletariat with a tradition of struggle, was armed resistance not mounted, at least in the final phase of liquidation, as happened in Warsaw, Częstochowa, Białystok, and several smaller ghettos in the eastern sector?"[80]

It should be emphasized that the absence of physical resistance and armed revolt in the Łódź Ghetto does not imply disorganization or apathy in the underground channels of the ghetto. Although the Łódź Ghetto did not give rise to a fighting organization, political and public organizations worked in the underground, focusing their energy on specific areas. As early as May 1940, starving Jews held their first spontaneous demonstrations in Łódź. The agitation grew in August; the number of demonstrators rose to 2,000 demanding food and work. The ghetto police hesitated to use force against the masses. Rumkowski asked the Germans to intervene, and the German police dispersed the demonstrators by firing into the air. On several occasions, desperate, starving mobs raided warehouses and wagons stocked with furniture, which they used for fuel. According to reports, these riots were instigated by famished Jews whose gnawing hunger drove them to acts of despair, by political activists, and by opportunists who sought to inflame the hungry masses and derive some benefit from the ensuing chaos.[81]

Rumkowski responded to the riots with crackdowns but was not impervious to the cries of the destitute. Political party representatives were convened and proposals meant to improve the situation were bruited. Corrective measures that brought slight relief to the most afflicted were introduced, and initial opportunities for public activism were created. Various political parties established soup kitchens and cooperative relief organizations came into being. These centers also hosted cultural and political gatherings. Rumkowski won over several party activists and installed them in positions in which they could influence important decisions in ghetto life. The Bund activists chose to abstain from the consultations with Rumkowski as representatives of their party, but they saw to it that their people were delegated to meetings as representatives of the workplaces.[82] In the early phase of the ghetto, the period of the mass protests, Rumkowski sought the advice and backing of the functionaries who directed the political party cells, immersed themselves in ghetto affairs, and had high status in the *ressorts*. These relations with political and public figures facilitated initiatives such as soup kitchens and consumer cooperatives; moreover, the "kibbutzim" and collective farms at Marysin, as well as the cultivation of vegetable gardens, were evidently the results of the intervention of these persons. According to various activists, Rumkowski's contacts with party activists were accompanied from the start by vacillation and distaste. Even this complex relationship, typified by maneuvering among groups and individuals amid exploitation of their contradictory interests, came to an end in 1941. Loyal public figures were dismissed from their posts, the house committees were abolished, the soup kitchens that doubled as rendezvous points for secret political cells were shut down, and the verdant collectives of Marysin were abandoned.

The political groups, however, did not cease to exist. They merely became more insular, withdrew from the general arena, and transferred most of their activities to the *ressorts*, where they orchestrated the organizing efforts and the protests. Starting in 1941 strikes and protest demonstrations erupted in the *ressorts*, one after another, engulfing the sewing factories, the carpentry workshops, and others. The spontaneous nature of these outbreaks indicates that the general hardship and pressure caused by starvation, piecework, and the especially heavy workload assigned to certain groups had driven the labor force to the breaking point. Even if the political activists were not the sponsors of these eruptions, as the events unfolded they positioned themselves at the head of the struggle and provided the workers with guidance. Several of the protests alleviated the worst aspects of food distribution and the work regimen, but there were also cases where the Germans intervened, leading to arrests.

The underground cells that helped the workers in the *ressorts* organize were under the influence of Bund activists headed by Moshe Lederman; the Poalei Zion Left under Emanuel Walinski; and the Communists (or the "Organized Left," as they called themselves in the ghetto) under Ziula Pacanowska, a figure respected throughout the ghetto. Additional Zionist factions and organized groups of observant Jews were also active. They were not large-scale organizations but rather small cells that continued to preserve their movements' political traditions. Their unity was most evident on the personal and social levels, and their aim was to provide their immediate circle of comrades with material support.

The targets of the fury and protest that manifested themselves in the street demonstrations of 1940 and the strikes at the *ressorts* in and after 1941 were the ghetto administration, Rumkowski, and the work managers—but not the German authorities who oversaw these policies and persecutions. The structure of the Łódź Ghetto, more than that of other ghettos, reserved a prominent place for the Jewish officials who ran the internal administration, and it was they who served as the focal points and targets of the bitterness and outbursts of despair.[83]

One of the most notable political initiatives was the Polish slogan PP ("*Pracuj powoli*" [Work slowly]), which the leftist activists disseminated among the *ressort* workers.[84] We cannot assess the true impact of this watchword, but it evidently led to the sabotaging of production toward the end of the ghetto period. We know that such acts of sabotage infuriated Rumkowski, and any significant damage to the production process obviously threatened the ghetto's very existence, as everyone knew.

In 1940–1942, the parties' efforts focused on provided information and mutual assistance in the underground. The domains of activity and public work at this stage are reminiscent of organizational work and action plans in Warsaw and other ghettos. Parties held meetings and assemblies to mark anniversaries and special events, and debated the tactics to use in response to issues on the agenda. Through mutual assistance they tried to obtain small quantities of food, help the ill and the distressed, arrange less arduous jobs, and protect people from deportation.

The youth movements persevered in their activism and dynamism. They organized clandestine study, issued internal bulletins, and set up meetings at which they freely and enthusiastically discussed forbidden opinions and ideas. They read forbidden literature and observed the anniversaries of the deaths of Jewish and non-Jewish leaders and intellectuals. The youngsters encouraged a spirit of mutual assistance: "Young boys and girls, aged twelve to sixteen, undernourished for years, denied themselves morsels of food in order to place them in the community chest: 20 grams of flour, 20 grams of bread, a portion of soup and two potatoes. . . . In this fashion they managed to save comrades who had refused to report for deportation, had gone into hiding, and no longer received food rations."[85]

"I doubt," wrote a member of a Communist organization in her memoirs, "that so many handwritten copies of articles and works by Marx, Engels, and Lenin were made in any other place whatsoever."[86] A young Bund activist describes how his party observed May Day in 1941, bedecking the ghetto streets with posters: "In all [in a demonstration that took the form of a kind of festive parade in the ghetto streets], 1,087 people took part, including 514 party members, 390 members of Tsukunft, and 180 children of SkiF."[87]

An article on the activities of the Zionist pioneer movements states that in 1941 Gordonia sponsored a seminar on Jewish history, Palestine geography and history, the history of socialism, and literature.[88] Members of Ha-shomer Ha-tsair published their own paper in the early occupation and ghetto period.[89] Another group of religious youth as well as young Zionists coalesced in the ghetto: *Hazit Dor Bnei Midbar* (Sons of the Desert Generation Front), who aspired to imbue their movement with an overarching, pan-Zionist spirit.

These activities, however, are reminiscent of those of the early period in the Warsaw Ghetto, before news of the Final Solution filtered through. Once their fate became known, the activists in Warsaw pledged most of their efforts to resistance and the establishment of a general, all-embracing fighting organization. In other ghettos, members and leaders of youth movements rejected adult patronage, organized themselves in radical cells, and plotted rescue missions, uprisings, and armed resistance. In Warsaw, they even formed an effective public leadership in the last months of the ghetto period and during the uprising. The Łódź Ghetto did not follow this pattern.

In Łódź, several radio sets were secretly preserved and assembled using underground methods, and news of developments on the front and the general political scene spread by word of mouth. These radios were in the possession of organized political groups (one was owned by Bund members) or of groups and individuals, the best known of whom were the Zionist Chaim Widawski and Moshe Taffel, cantor at the Ohel Yaakov Synagogue. The listeners were able to carry on for quite some time without betrayal. Groups of radio listeners and news disseminators worked undisturbed for five years of the war, day after day. They learned of events such as the Warsaw Ghetto uprising in this way, and the ghetto even observed the anniversary of the uprising. Many inhabitants of the ghetto knew the individuals who took part in this illegal endeavor (radio sets had been confiscated at the start of the war, and their possession was completely prohibited). Not until June 1944 did an informer emerge, at which point the culprits were arrested and executed. Chaim Widawski managed to escape from prison but took his own life for fear that he would not have the strength to withstand torture upon capture.[90] It seems, however, that the June downfall did not unearth all the radio receivers in the ghetto, because there are reports of ghetto inhabitants listening to the radio and circulating news in July 1944.

Several individuals in the Łódź Ghetto excelled in preserving and saving documents and other clandestine documentary material. In this context, the name of Nachman Zonabend is noteworthy.[91] Many photos of the ghetto survive, some attesting to intentions of resistance and risk-taking. The most outstanding ghetto photographer was Mendel Grossman.[92] Vague reports suggest that during the last few weeks of the ghetto, in the midst of the final evacuation, organized resistance was proposed but never reached the organizational stage, let alone that of practical action.[93] The only resistance effort carried out was the hiding of dozens of people, perhaps a hundred or even more, in bunkers within the ghetto. At this time, the Germans left nearly 800 people behind to gather the victims' remaining property and the factory equipment.[94] When one of the bunkers was discovered, one of its occupants, Dr. Daniel Wajskopf, assaulted Hans Biebow. Even the concealment operation, however, was neither organized nor led; it was the spontaneous action of individuals and families who made up their minds to go into hiding as the final deportation loomed.

We now return to the key question: Why was protest activity in Łódź restricted to social agitation directed against the ghetto strongman and his lackeys, not against the true source of their privation, persecution, and death? Why did the youth movements and young adults fail to coalesce in the cause of resistance and revolt? Why was there no organized action in this direction? Why were there no rescue operations? Why were there no attempts made to flee the ghetto, link up with underground forces, and slip through the frontiers?

Survivors' memoirs and scholarly analysis attribute the absence of certain manifestations of resistance to several major factors:

a. The hermetic quarantining of the Łódź Ghetto and the ensuing lack of contact with other Jewish centers.

b. The strong German presence in the city of Łódź. The Polish underground was hardly active here, and there were no liaison cells such as those in other ghettos.

c. The large-scale evacuations and mass deportations from the Łódź Ghetto. These deprived the Jewish community of many of its public activists, youth movement leaders, and political party functionaries—the human potential of which underground and resistance movements are made. Such people did not return to Łódź at a later stage, as they did to other ghettos.

d. Rumkowski's policy, power, and influence, and the infiltration of the German administration into the internal affairs of the ghetto.

e. Total or partial ignorance of the "Final Solution" and its true significance.

All of these factors created a reality in Łódź different from that in the other ghettos. By describing and analyzing the features that made the Łódź Ghetto unique, we gain a better understanding of the Jews' situation there.

Łódź Ghetto

YAD WASHEM MARTYRS' AND HEROES' MEMORIAL AUTHORITY
Jerusalem

YIVO INSTITUTE FOR JEWISH RESEARCH
New York

JOINT DOCUMENTARY PROJECTS
Monograph Series No. 1

ISAIAH TRUNK

GHETTO LODZ

A Historical and Sociological Study, Including Documents,
Maps, and Tables

NEW YORK
1962

Street Map of the Łódź Ghetto

Łagiewnicka

Stefana

Kowalska

Franciszkańska

Żabia

Krzyżowa

Rymarska

Tokarszewskiego

Gęsia

Zgierska

Goplańska

Dolna

Mickiewicza

Wawelska

Spacerowa

Mlynarska

Pasterska

św. Wincentego

Szeroka

Pucka

Flisacka

Lekarska

Niecała

Urzędnicza

Wrocławska

Drukarska

Ciesielska

Lotnicza

Masarska

Ceglana

Dworska

Limanowskiego

Bałucki
Rynek

Zawiszy Czarnego

Wrześnieńska

Modra

Gnieźnieńska

Ciemna

Wróbla

Mroczna

Podwórzowa

Krótka

Berka Joselwicza

Pieprzowa

Old
Jewish
Cemetery

Miodowa

Rybna

Pawia

Piwna

Wrocławska

Bazarowa

Wesoła

Lutomierska

Kościelna

Żydowska

Majowa

Piwna

Rawicka

Żytnia

Ślusarska

Stodolniana

Stary Rynek

św. Jakuba

Drewnowska

Podrzeczna

Nad Łódką

Wolborska

Jerozolimska

Piłsudskiego

Północna

0   100 200   400   600   800   1 KM

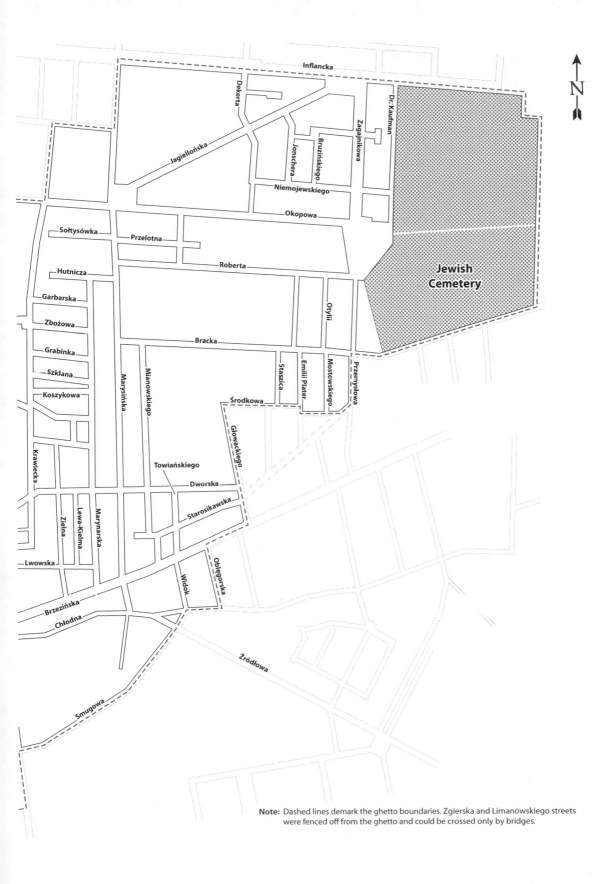

N

Inflancka

Dekerta

Jagiellońska

Jonschera

Bruzińskiego

Zagajnikowa

Dr. Kaufman

Niemojewskiego

Okopowa

Sołtysówka

Przelotna

Roberta

Hutnicza

Garbarska

Otylii

Jewish Cemetery

Zbożowa

Grabinka

Bracka

Szklana

Marysińska

Mianowskiego

Staszica

Emilii Plater

Mostowskiego

Przemysłowa

Koszykowa

Środkowa

Głowackiego

Krawiecka

Towiańskiego

Dworska

Starosikawska

Zielna

Lewa-Kielma

Marynarska

Lwowska

Widok

Oblęgorska

Brzezińska

Chłodna

Źródłowa

Smugowa

Note: Dashed lines demark the ghetto boundaries. Zgierska and Limanowskiego streets were fenced off from the ghetto and could be crossed only by bridges.

Poland Under German Rule
1939-1944

LATVIA

BALTIC
SEA

LITHUANIA

Vilna

Danzig

GERMANY
(EAST PRUSSIA)

Nowogródek

GERMANY

DANZIG-
WEST PRUSSIA

Toruń

Białystok

BEZIRK
ZICHENAU

Poznań

Treblinka

Chełmno

Brześć

Warsaw

WARTHELAND

Sobibór

Łódź

Other Polish territories
occupied by Germany
after June 22, 1941

Lublin

Kielce

Majdanek

Łuck

GENERAL
GOUVERNEMENT

Bełżec

UPPER
SILESIA

Kraków

U.S.S.R.

Lwów

Auschwitz

Tarnopol

Stanisławów

N

CZECHOSLOVAKIA

ROMANIA

0   50   100 MILES

Foreword
JACOB ROBINSON[1]

Is there a need for another book on the Ghetto of Łódź? This is a natural and legitimate question when addressed to the Documentary Projects, a group that is supposed to know the present state of research on the Jewish Catastrophe, particularly the research on the Łódź Ghetto.

A few elementary facts should serve as an answer.

First, our research activities extend over a catastrophe of global, continental, regional, and local dimensions; it is one that affected millions of human lives.

Second, not fewer than 100,000 men had a direct hand in the process of Jewish destruction, including 60,000 murderers decorated with the Iron Cross 2nd Class, which was legally reserved for frontline fighters only.

Third, the nature of the events created a situation in which days seemed to be years. In brief, we deal with a tragedy that will challenge researchers not for years, but for centuries.

What is true of the Catastrophe as a whole is also true—*mutatis mutandis*—of the specific subject of Łódź. Therefore, all literary "genres" that deal with the Łódź Ghetto are justifiable and welcome.

What is the state of the special Łódź research? We find the following: "objective" documentation in Eisenbach's collection;[2] personal experiences in the diaries of Dawid Sierakowiak,[3] Jakub Poznański,[4] Shlomo Frank,[5] and J. L. Girsht;[6] and a combination of personal experiences and post-mortem reflections in Israel Tabaksblat's book on the destruction of Łódź,[7] and Wolf Yasny's *History,*[8] of which the second volume has not yet been published. Although the genre of the latter volume is nearer than the others to that of Trunk's, Yasny has stated in the preface that his book "does not claim to be of strict scientific nature." These are important materials for the historian, and Isaiah Trunk utilized them well for his work.[9]

The Trunk volume, however, does claim to be of a "strict-scientific nature." Among the sources Trunk presents are at least a few dozen generally unknown and formerly unused collections of documents such as the reports by Josef Zelkowicz, a considerable number of documents from the Rumkowski Archives, and the files of the *Gettoverwaltung*. Needless to say, the approach to these and other sources is both critical and analytical. Finally, after almost all the analytical chapters the reader will find in their original language the documents referred to therein.

This work is not the definitive history of the tremendous complex simplistically called the Łódź Ghetto. Not all the sources have been detected and not all the detected sources are easily accessible. But within the limits of the sources mentioned in the preface, Trunk's study is an attempt at a definitive analysis.

This is the first substantive research published by the New York group of the Joint Documentary Projects of Yad Vashem in Jerusalem and the YIVO Institute for Jewish Research in New York. We hope it will provide useful information on one of the most important local sectors of the Jewish tragedy.

The book hereby presented to the reader is an attempt at a historical and sociological study of one ghetto—that of Łódź. It is a study of a large Jewish community (the second largest in Poland) that struggled under the extreme conditions of a Nazi work ghetto for well nigh five years and lived during that period in the constant shadow of ineluctable extermination.

Prior to the Hitler period, history had not known of such a social organism as was constituted by the Jews in the Nazi ghettos. A study of the life of such a "compulsory community," to make use of H. G. Adler's deft expression, under conditions of existence that have no parallel in the history of civilized mankind, has in addition to its Jewish and human significance also great interest for the social sciences. As will be indicated in the following chapters, the Łódź Ghetto had certain characteristics that make it deserving of a special study. It was a ghetto with a pronounced character and of a special type. There, too, the enormity of the Nazi horror and the perfection of Nazi perfidy were unique. Elements of this uniqueness were also discernible in other communities, but nowhere did they appear in such sharpness and persistence as in Łódź.

Although a monograph, a number of problems of the Catastrophe of a general nature may be illuminated by it. It may help us to a better understanding of certain aspects of the Catastrophe in general.

A few remarks about the sources of this book:

The Łódź Ghetto has left behind possibly the largest collection of documents on its existence. In contrast to the large ghettos, such as Warsaw, Białystok, and Kaunas, the Łódź Ghetto, like the city of Łódź, was left intact by the Germans in their panic flight. The documents concealed in the last few months of the Ghetto's existence were not destroyed in the interval between its liquidation and the liberation in January 1945. They were later unearthed or found concealed in walls and other accessible hiding places. To be sure, after the liberation the remaining local Polish population in its search for hidden treasure did considerable damage to the ghetto and incidentally destroyed portions of the concealed archives. Nor had the German authorities succeeded in destroying their own archives. In sum, for the history of the Łódź Ghetto there is to our disposition a comparatively abundant collection of source materials.

The main source of documents is the Zonabend Collection in the YIVO Archives, consisting of 1,700 documents and photographs clandestinely gathered and concealed in the Łódź Ghetto by Nachman Zonabend and later donated to the YIVO. These documents were part of the Rumkowski Archives, and most of them are originals or copies of originals. In addition, we have utilized for this book other collections of documents, such as the photograph albums of the ghetto, retrieved by Abraham Sutskever, the late Shmerke Kaczerginski, Abraham Feferkorn, and Leyzer Ran, numbering 300 documents and photographs. Moreover, good use was made of copies and notes on documents of a large part of the Rumkowski Archives, found after the war in the ruins of the ghetto and now in the Archives of the Jewish Historical Institute in Warsaw. Of special note are the *Ghetto Chronicle,* in German and in Polish (*Tages-Chronik, Biuletyn Kroniki Codziennej*), which appeared periodically from January 1941 to July 1944 as a semi-official internal publication of the Rumkowski Archives; the numerous reports of Western European Jews who were brought to the Łódź Ghetto in October and November of 1941; and the reportages of that sensitive Łódź writer, Joseph Zelkovitsh (Józef Zelkowicz), penetrating all corners of the ghetto. The archives also contain highly valuable statistical materials.

These documents have furnished the most important material about the inner life of the Łódź Ghetto. The *Tages-Chronik* is an inexhaustible treasure of facts and descriptions, on the basis of which the inner history of the Łódź Ghetto could be written in the form of a daily chronicle. Patently, its attitudes and interpretations, as a semi-official publication of the Rumkowski administration, must be taken with great reservations.

The second source of our present work is the large archive of the Łódź *Gettoverwaltung;* the Germans had not succeeded in destroying these documents in their evacuation of the city in January 1945. These archives are now in the Jewish Historical Institute in Warsaw.[2] They have furnished the materials on the role of the Gettoverwaltung and other German bodies in the spoliation, starvation, enslavement, and ultimate extermination of the ghetto population. They also shed light on Rumkowski's position in the ghetto, on the attitudes of the prisoners of the ghetto toward him, as well as on certain aspects of the ghetto's inner life, such as industry, sickness, and mortality. Without these archives, the discussion of forced labor outside the ghetto in chapter 4 could not have been written.[3]

A few words about the credibility of Nazi documents. In the light of Nazi duplicity and deception—fields in which they have attained unchallenged supremacy—these documents, frequently written in the specific Nazi jargon and for the purpose of deliberate deception and alibi, must be taken with a grain of salt. Nevertheless, they can be used as more or less reliable sources in two instances: when the statements contained in them were made without awareness of their significance (which occurred surprisingly often among the arrogant but dull Nazi bureaucrats) and when they present their subjects in a frankly unfavorable light.

A third group of documents consists of diaries written in the ghetto, memoirs, and testimonies of eyewitnesses. These diaries are generally in manuscript in various archives. In recent years three diaries have appeared in print (by Shlomo Frank, Dawid Sierakowiak, and Jakób Poznański).

The value of the diaries, memoirs, and eyewitness testimonies as reliable historical sources varies considerably. It depends upon a number of objective and subjective conditions under which these documents were written or recorded and upon the author or witness. Ostensibly, the moment of inevitable subjectivism is bound to reduce the source value of this group of documents. This qualification holds particularly for memoirs and testimonies written or recorded a number of years after the events. I collated this group of documents, wherever possible with at least one independent source dealing with the same fact or opinion, and indicated variations, divergencies, and nuances.

One thing must be stated here. There is a surprising unanimity among the authors of the diaries, the later memoirists, and eyewitnesses concerning several basic phenomena in the Łódź Ghetto, namely the Rumkowski regime and its negative influence on life in the ghetto, the role of certain offices and the persons heading them, and the unmistakable social differentiation in the ghetto. The fact that these data derive from persons of diverse social background and diverse communal position in the ghetto—an engineer, a writer, a laborer, a trained business employee, a ghetto policeman—makes this unanimity even more striking. It also adds solidity to our conclusions.

A few words about the statistical value of the sources. Ostensibly—and I shall expatiate on this point in the book—the bizarre ghetto conditions render the statistical materials not fully reliable. The special figures on illness, for example, do not coincide with the factual figures. Because of the brutal methods adopted by the Germans to combat epidemics and the fear of deportation, to which in the first place the ill were subject, cases of infectious diseases such as typhus, typhoid fever, tuberculosis, and the like were not reported, if possible. In all likelihood, Rumkowski, who was anxious to impress the authorities with the inhabitants' great vigor and capacity for work, deliberately exaggerated the numbers of the workers in the ghetto shops and their overall production, and, on the other hand, minimized the number of ill due to starvation, exhaustion, and the like. In the reports of Rumkowski's Division of Health, the sanitary conditions in the ghetto, for which he was responsible, were presented in colors presumably more favorable than in reality. Similarly, the production in the fields, in which the authorities were especially interested, was slightly exaggerated in the reports of the managers in the ghetto shops, in accord with the tendency of "joyful creativity."

All these elements have a negative effect upon the statistical value of our sources. However, if the absolute figures are not fully correct, the relative quantities are nearly correct, since the coefficient of error in our calculations applies equally to all official figures. The underlying factor of possible errors with respect to absolute numbers holds, for example, for official figures on infectious diseases and on mortality alike. Hence the statistical picture of demographic conditions, ghetto production, morbidity, and mortality, which I present later, may be relatively correct, although it may show slight deviation in absolute numbers.

A final source of materials included in the present volume is the documents that the Israeli police collected for the Eichmann trial.

The historical literature on the Łódź Ghetto published in the postwar era has, of course, been taken into consideration.

For presentation, the materials have been divided into eight main topics. Combined, these furnish an all-encompassing picture of ghetto life, and tell the story of the Łódź Ghetto in its chronological development from establishment to final destruction. The various aspects of ghetto life dealt with in the eight chapters were, of course, not isolated phenomena. Rather, they were intricately intertwined: a change occurring in one area invariably brought about changes in the others. While the thematic arrangement of the material is a necessary means of presentation, it should not convey the impression that the individual aspects dealt with were discrete from one another. On the contrary, they were closely connected links in a chain, which during a period of nearly five years fettered the people of the Łódź Ghetto.

Finally, a few remarks of a technical character. Each chapter consists of two parts: an extensive account and analysis, and several significant documents illustrative of the subject or the problem. The documents at the end of each chapter have their own current numeration, to which the text refers. The documents in the notes at the foot of the text are given the numbers or the code letters they bear in the catalogues of the respective archives.

The chapter titled "Diseases and Mortality" is based almost

exclusively on documents of the Rumkowski Archives and of the Archives of the German Ghetto Administration *not* in the Zonabend Collection. It therefore contains no separate documentary section but extensive excerpts in the text.

Unless otherwise indicated, every quoted document is from the Zonabend Collection. The signature YI before the number of a document indicates the YIVO Institute for Jewish Research.

I wish to express my thanks to the YIVO Institute for Jewish Research; Mrs. Rebecca Tcherikower and E. Lifschitz of the YIVO Archives; the Jewish Historical Institute in Warsaw and its director B. Mark; Bet Lohamei Ha-getaot and its secretary, Zvi Shner; and the Archives of the Jewish Labor Movement in the name of Franz Kursky and its director, David Meyer, for making their collections accessible to me.

I also am indebted to Mr. S. Dawidowicz for his help in preparing the manuscript for the printer; Mr. Chaim Finkelstein, administrator of the Documentary Projects at YIVO, for his painstaking supervision of the production of this book; the staff of the Projects; Dr. Shlomo Noble for translating into English parts of the manuscript; and Mr. Israel London, president of Marstin Press, Inc., who spared no effort to give this book an attractive appearance.

Special thanks go to Dr. Jacob Robinson, who read the manuscript in its first and final version, for his valuable suggestions and emendations. However, responsibility for the views expressed is mine.

I

Establishment of the Ghetto

The ghettos were one of the most effective instruments to facilitate and expedite the Nazi extermination process against the Jewish population in the occupied territories. Except for the name, the Nazi-German imposed ghetto had nothing in common with the so-called medieval ghetto. The Jewish ghetto in the early Middle Ages was in fact a neighborhood or a street where, in most cases, Jews concentrated out of their own free will, in order to live together, to isolate and close themselves off from alien influences, and more easily defend themselves against attacks by their Christian neighbors. In the Middle Ages Jews felt more secure and free within their ghetto, behind the protection of the guarded ghetto gates. (It is worth noting that Jews in Verona, Italy, annually celebrated the day when they were locked into the Jewish residential quarter.) The pre-modern ghetto was a sort of Jewish "refuge" in a hostile Christian environment. Moreover, during the day, Jews were allowed to move about freely in the Christian parts of town.

Although Nazi propaganda attempted to portray the imposed ghettos and Jewish councils (*Judenräte*) to the outside world as a return to the former Jewish autonomy in medieval Europe, the Nazi ghetto was planned with entirely different goals. By imprisoning the Jewish population in ghettos the Nazis achieved two aims. First, concentration of Jews into a limited and heavily guarded area facilitated control over the ghetto and eased the process of economic ruination and physical prostration for the German authorities, both through severe restrictions on food deliveries into the ghettos and blockage of all sources of livelihood. Second, the isolation and separation from the outside world deprived the ghettos of every opportunity to obtain aid from outside.

Already in the secret *Schnellbrief* (express letter) of 21 September 1939 from Heydrich, chief of the *Reichssicherheitshauptamt* (Reich Security Main Office, RSHA), the concentration of the Jewish population is considered a prerequisite for realizing the final objective (*Endziel*), that is, the extermination of the Jewish population (par. 1).[1]

The first attempt to create a ghetto in a major Jewish center in Poland was in Łódź.[2] Even before the establishment of the ghetto, a series of ordinances was issued in November 1939, whose purpose was to identify and single out the Jewish populace. Jews were ordered to wear the Jewish identification badge (doc. no. 1: First Ordinance, 14 November 1939, by the Kalisz *Regierungspräsident,* in whose district Łódź was located);[3] to identify Jewish businesses through a special yellow sign with the inscription *"Jude"* (doc. no. 2: Ordinance published in *Lodzer Zeitung,* 30 November 1939);[4] and to be bound to remain in their town and place of residence (doc. no. 3: Ordinance of the Higher SS and Police Leader in Wartheland, Wilhelm Koppe, 13 November 1939).[5]

On 10 December 1939, Kalisz *Regierungspräsident* (district administration chief) Übelhör distributed a "secret, strictly confidential" memorandum about creating a ghetto in Łódź. The addressees were the Nazi party organs, city administration, regular and security police, and other concerned administrative offices. In this memorandum, Übelhör revealed the real intention of the higher German authorities. He concludes with the following characteristic sentences: "The formation of the ghetto is, of course, only a transitional measure. When and with what means the ghetto and thereby the city of Łódź will be cleansed of Jews—I reserve for myself to determine. In any case, the final objective must be that we shall completely burn out this pestilence" (doc. no. 4).[6]

Übelhör's plan, inter alia, foresaw the division of the Jewish population into two groups: one group—the overwhelming majority—who must be enclosed in an isolated and guarded area, designated principally for the Jews incapable of working; and a second group remaining outside the ghetto area, but who must be housed in special barrack blocks under strict guard. Any Jews in the second group who fell ill or became incapable of working were to be transferred into the ghetto. The entire northern part of the city, that is, Old Town and the Bałuty neighborhoods principally inhabited by Jews, was initially to be enclosed within the boundaries of the projected ghetto. Übelhör cites an exaggerated Jewish population figure of 320,000 souls.

Regardless of whether Übelhör himself modified his plan or received the decisive approval of Wartheland[7] *Statthalter* (Governor) Greiser, it is a fact that the 8 February 1940 police ordinance on the creation of the ghetto (see below) makes no distinction at all between Jews capable of work and those incapable of work. It applied to all Łódź Jews without exception. Nonetheless, a small group of waste-sorters and highly trained experts received the right to work outside the ghetto, although only for a short time.

Übelhör also erred both in regard to the length of the ghetto's existence and the competence of the government body that was supposed to decide on the ultimate fate of the ghetto. A "transitional measure" (*Übergangsmassnahme*), the Łódź Ghetto nevertheless led a lonely existence for almost five full years, until the end of August 1944, very near the collapse of the Third Reich. Whether the time had come "for burning out the plague" was decided not by the Łódź district Regierungspräsident, but by *Reichsführer SS und Chef der deutschen Polizei* Heinrich Himmler. In December 1939, the "solution of the Jewish question" in Łódź seemed much simpler to Übelhör than it later turned out to be in reality.

For a couple of months, various government agencies and offices conducted a discussion about the essential question of whether to leave Jews in Łódź or deport them into the *Generalgouvernement* (the central provinces of former Poland, administered under Hans Frank). Wartheland Reichsstatthalter Greiser, a member of the Nazi ruling hierarchy, in fact wanted to purge Łódź of Jews. On 8 November 1939, it was agreed between Greiser and the authorities of the Generalgouvernement that in the first phase of the general evacuation of non-Germans from Wartheland, from 15 November 1939 until the end of February 1940, 200,000 Poles and 100,000 Jews, including 30,000 from Łódź, would be expelled.[8]

From a later 4 July 1941 memorandum by the mayor of Litzmannstadt (as Łódź was renamed in November 1939),[9] we learn that at the founding of the ghetto it was understood that this was to be only a temporary matter and that by 1 October 1940 all Jews were to be completely eliminated from the city.[10]

At the beginning of December 1939 the official Łódź Jewish Community (*kehile* or *gmina żydowska*) received written instructions about the planned evacuation, although there was no public announcement about it. Registration of candidates for evacuation commenced on 13 December. When the required quota for evacuation was steadily increased (1,700 on the thirteenth, 2,100 on the fourteenth, etc.), panic broke out among the Jewish population and the registration nearly came to a halt. On the seventeenth, the German authorities themselves ordered a stop to further registration due to transportation difficulties and crowding in the collection points. In all, about 6,000 people were expelled from Łódź on the basis of this registration. Simultaneously,

Jews of Łódź are forced to move into the ghetto, in the Bałuty section of the city, 1940. Photographer unknown. USHMM, courtesy of Frank Morgens (Mieczysław Morgenstern).

during the period 11–16 December, the authorities deported from Łódź numerous Jewish doctors, attorneys, teachers, and the residents of two streets of the subsequent ghetto area (total number unknown).[11] However, Greiser's plan was cancelled by Goering's 23 March 1940 circular, which ordered a standstill of any "resettlement" action, pending a new decree. On this basis, Koppe, the Higher SS and Police Leader in Poznań, in turn ordered a halt to the evacuation of Jews from Wartheland, including from Łódź.[12]

Even before the matter of crowding the Łódź Jews into a ghetto took on organizational forms, these Jews were forbidden to show themselves on the two most important streets, the chief arteries of the city. Jews also began to be driven from their apartments, and with such brutality that they did not manage to take with them the most necessary personal items. When Rumkowski, whom the authorities had designated on 13 October 1939 as the head of the Jews, intervened so that these people should not be left in the midst of winter naked and deprived of everything, he received a cynical reply. On 2 February 1940, the Łódź branch office of the "Office for Implantation of Balts at the Higher SS and Police Leader, Warthe[land]"[13] wrote that the Jews certainly could have taken with them the "most necessary things," in particular children's clothing and personal documents (doc. no. 10).[14] On 13 February, Rumkowski received from the aforementioned office a permit to

View of the wooden and barbed wire fence that separated the Łódź Ghetto from the rest of the city. Signs forbidding entrance to Poles and Germans were posted at all entrances to the ghetto, 1940. Photographer unknown. USHMM, courtesy of Frank Morgens (Mieczysław Morgenstern).

contact the new residents of the former Jewish apartments, to retrieve the "unneeded children's things," or linens and clothing, documents, and other objects (doc. no. 11).[15]

Like almost everywhere in Eastern Europe, in order to "justify" among the non-Jewish population the creation of the ghetto, the Jewish residential area had previously been portrayed as a "nest of infection" (*Infektions-Herd*) and the population was warned against coming into contact with Jews (doc. no. 5: Announcement by the Łódź police-president, 9 January 1940).[16] At the borders of the Jewish residential area, whose largest part later became the ghetto area, warning signs were erected with the inscription "Residential Area of Jews, Entry Forbidden." After the soil was psychologically prepared for the isolation of the Jewish population, an ordinance was issued on 8 February 1940 by Łódź Police-President Johannes Schäfer concerning "residential rights of Jews," that is, about creation of a closed Jewish residential area (doc. no. 6).[17] Under the same date were published "executive instructions" for the latter ordinance (doc. no. 7).[18] According to this ordinance and the related instructions, Jews were forbidden to dwell outside the precisely defined area, and they had to move into the ghetto within designated deadlines, according to an established plan and order. But the tempo of moving such a large mass (after the sealing of the ghetto in June 1940, the number of Jews was 160,423) into a cramped, isolated neighborhood did not, it appears, satisfy the chief of police. On 1 March he announced that, as a penalty for the lively traffic that Jews continued to maintain with the rest of the city, a raid had occurred on 29 February, a result of which was that "a large number of Jews were arrested" (doc. no. 8).[19] On 2 March, Rumkowski received a directive from the police-president to see that the relatives of those arrested pay a fine of 150 RM for each and provide them with food (doc. no. 9).[20]

At the same time, the authorities carried out two "actions": on the night of 1–2 March, 500 Jewish and Polish families were "evacuated"; and before dawn all Poles who still resided in the area that bordered the ghetto were arrested. After interrogation by the Kripo and Gestapo, some of them were turned over to the military court (*Standgericht*), although their transgressions are not indicated in the document. Some Poles were transported into the Polish residential quarter, while the rest were designated for evacuation on 4 March. On the same day, the Jews from the center of town were to be deported in place of the Poles transferred into the Polish residential quarter. The document does not state to where the arrested Jewish and Polish families were evacuated, although they were probably sent into the Generalgouvernement.[21]

On the same day, probably at the order of the police-president, Rumkowski issued a public warning not to leave the Jewish residential area, this under threat of police penalty.[22] In the above-cited announcement of 1 March 1940, the police-president communicated that in the future he would deal ruthlessly with such transgressions, and he kept his word. On the evening of 6 March and the night of 7–8 March (the day that entered the history of the Łódź Ghetto as "Bloody Thursday"),[23] German police and SS—both uniformed and in civilian clothing—shot several hundred Jews on the streets and in residences (chiefly on Piotrkowska, the main street of Łódź). All Jews were ordered to leave their apartments within five minutes. Whoever did not manage to do so was shot on the spot. Simultaneously, Jews were hauled into transfer points, where they were abused and robbed. Nearly 500 Jews were deported into the Generalgouvernement and about 160 were sent into the Zgierz woods, where they were killed.[24] On the same day (7 March), a police ordinance cancelled all temporary passes (*Passierscheinen*) that had allowed certain categories of Jews (among others: doctors, pharmacists, midwives, and rag dealers) to move about in certain hours outside the ghetto (doc. no. 12).[25]

The police-president had his way: After 7 March people no longer walked, but ran in panic into the ghetto.

An eyewitness, Y. Tabaksblat, thus describes the march of the Łódź Jews into the ghetto: "The long, tragic procession of pedestrians with parcels and bundles on their backs, with small children in their arms and larger ones at their sides with little handcarts, laden with old baggage, pushed and shoved by various scoundrels, accompanied with wanton, cynical catcalls. . . ."[26]

According to the second and third "executive instructions" of 15 March and 3 April 1940, Jews were forbidden to stay in the farther western and southern quarters of the city, and the local inhabitants were required to report to the relevant police precinct (docs. nos. 13–14).[27]

On 8 April, the police-president issued a new ordinance that modi-

Jewish men and women entering the Łódź Ghetto, March 1940. Photographer unknown. USHMM, courtesy of Raphael Aronson.

fied the former plan, and as a result the residential area designated for Jews was enlarged over that described in the police ordinance of 8 February. However, the expanded areas were mainly in the north and east, with the area around the Jewish cemetery and the undeveloped portion in Marysin (doc. no. 15).[28]

The Jewish residential area encompassed two Łódź neighborhoods: Bałuty, which only in 1916 had been annexed to the city; and the so-called Old Town, the oldest neighborhood of Łódź, which had been the Jewish district (*rewir żydowski*) until 1861. Both neighborhoods were among the most impoverished, dirty, and neglected parts of the city. A couple of statistics speak clearly about the housing conditions in this part of Łódź, where the ghetto was created. During the second half of 1940, of 3,361 buildings, 1,402 were wood and 1,959 masonry and mixed. Fully 1,300 buildings were one-story structures and 969 were two-story. Of 31,962 dwelling units, 19,721 consisted of a single room and 8,710 of two rooms, altogether about 89 percent of all the ghetto dwellings. About 95 percent—30,624 dwellings—had no hygienic facilities, water piping, or sewerage. Only 49 dwellings possessed all the comforts, even a bathroom. As for population density, when the ghetto was sealed there were about 164,000 souls crowded into 4.13 square ki-

Łódź Ghetto Jews behind a wooden and barbed-wire fence that separated the Łódź Ghetto from the rest of the city, 1940–1941. Photographer unknown. USHMM, courtesy of Frank Morgens (Mieczysław Morgenstern).

lometers. If we deduct from this 0.22 square kilometers designated for police needs and construction work, as well as 1.5 square kilometers of undeveloped and uninhabited land, then no more than 2.41 square kilometers remained for the actual residential area. Thus, more than 68,000 people lived on one square kilometer. (It is worth noting that in 1931 the density in Łódź averaged 10,248 people per square kilometer, only about one-seventh that in the ghetto in May 1940.) As for the number of people per room, it was almost 3.5 persons per room—about 164,000 souls in 48,102 residential rooms. Naturally, this is the average. During the panicked flight into the ghetto it happened not infrequently that 15–20 people were crammed together in one room.[29]

Regardless of all projected schedules and instructions about *"Ordnung,"* the move into the ghetto took place in an unorganized, almost chaotic fashion. It was physically impossible to provide each family with a roof over their heads. For those who did not have anywhere to turn, a collective-camp was created, where an epidemic of spotted typhus broke out in April (doc. no. 16). Adding to the chaos was the fact that the non-Jewish residents of the designated ghetto area, particularly those who lived in their own and better housing, did not want to abandon their apartments and admit those expelled. If they had to, then they wanted to earn something in the deal. They would lock the apartments and take the keys with them (doc. no. 17, about Rumkowski's intervention to open such apartments). Private initiative, money, and strength began to decide who would get an apartment or remain without a roof over his head. People began to seize apartments on their own.

So as to gain some control over the situation, on 8 April Rumkowski issued an admonition that no one might take over without his permission any apartments located within the area assigned to the ghetto according to the police ordinance of 8 April. Transgressors would be evicted from the apartments and severely punished (doc. no. 18). This apparently had little effect, for Rumkowski reiterated his warning on 25 April.[30] However, it appears that Rumkowski could no longer master the situation. The landlords, building administrators, and superintendents took to demanding "key money" for admission into the apartments, or rent in advance (Rumkowski's appeal to them on 28 April).[31] On 3 May, he was compelled to allow homeless families to move on their own into available single rooms, with the exception of those he had confiscated for communal needs. He directed that occupied rooms must be immediately reported to the Housing Office of the Jewish Community (doc. no. 19). In occupying apartments, people often had physical encounters with Poles and so-called *Volksdeutsche* (ethnic Germans), who would— out of anger at having to leave their apartments—break the Jews' furniture and beat up the new tenants. But the situation gradually stabilized. On 19 April the police-president announced that the formation of the ghetto had progressed so far that its "complete isolation" was already possible (doc. no. 21). Two days earlier, on 17 April, he ordered Rumkowski to have the Jewish Order Service (see chapter 2, "Organization of the Ghetto") immediately take over the guarding of the ghetto enclosure (doc. no. 20).[32] On 7 May 1940 came the fifth and final "executive ordinance" to both of the police ordinances of 8 February and 8 April 1940; these finally sealed the ghetto from the outside world. All communication was cut off, including trade traffic between the Christian population and Jews; a penalty (fine or imprisonment) was announced for transgressing this prohibition (doc. no. 22).[33]

Thus, the Łódź Ghetto became a fact. But it appears that there were in certain circles of the occupation regime those who did not want to accept the idea and still viewed the ghetto as a "temporary measure." That the Łódź Ghetto "must continue to remain" was finally determined only around the middle of October 1940. On 18 October 1940, a meeting was held under the chairmanship of Übelhör with the participation of the heads of the administrative and police organs. At this gathering, the unpleasant fact of ghetto continuity was noted and on the agenda. As the heading on the surviving protocol shows, the question was "administering and supporting the ghetto in Litzmannstadt" in such manner that it should be able to maintain itself. Principles of ghetto autarchy were declared: the immediate "realization" of confiscated gold objects and precious stones, completion of the ghetto industry, and Jewish labor.[34]

Documents 1–23

No. 1. YIVO 39/3[35]

Decree of Kalisz Regierungspräsident Übelhör of 14 November 1939, concerning the obligation of all Jews regardless of gender or age to wear a yellow armband under threat of the death penalty. [in German]

The very deplorable state of affairs caused by the Jews in the public life of the administrative area of the Regierungspräsident at Kalisz cause me to order for the administrative area of the Regierungspräsident at Kalisz:

1.

As a special distinguishing mark, Jews regardless of age or gender wear a ten-centimeter wide armband in Jewish-yellow color on the right upper arm directly beneath the armpit.[36]

2.

In the administrative area of the Regierungspräsident at Kalisz, Jews may not leave their residence without a special permit from 5 P.M. until 8 A.M. . . .[37]

3.

Offenses against this decree will be punished with death. . . . In the presence of extenuating circumstances, a fine of unlimited amount or imprisonment alone or in combination can be imposed. . . .

4.

Except for the order in par. 1, this decree immediately comes into force, while par. 1 comes into force from 18 November 1939.

(Lodzer Zeitung, *16 November 1939*)

No. 2. YIVO 39/6

Decree by the Łódź City Commissioner concerning identifying Jewish businesses through a yellow sign with the inscription "JUDE." [in German]

3. Jewish businesses are to be marked with signs in Jewish-yellow with the imprint "JUDE." The signs of Jewish businesses until now are insufficient. These signs must have a minimum size of 20 by 35 cm. . . . They are to be placed in clearly visible positions at eye level, namely both a sign on the show-window and also a sign on the business' entrance door. . . .

(Lodscher[38] Zeitung, *30 November 1939*)

No. 3. YIVO 39/2

From the Higher SS and Police Leader in Wartheland, Wilhelm Koppe, 13 November 1939, who forbids Poles and Jews to leave their place of residence. [in German]

re: Prohibition on migration and movement for Poles and Jews
1. For the purpose of a final personal status registration, I forbid with immediate effect Poles and Jews to make any change of residence and

any migration within the Wartheland Reichsgau. Likewise, every move from outside into the Wartheland Reichsgau is prohibited.

2. In justified cases, the local police authorities can issue permits.

3. Anyone who changes his place of residence or his residence without police permit will be arrested and severely penalized.

4. With this regulation, all migration and movement permits not issued by the competent local police authorities are no longer in force.

(Lodscher Zeitung, 15 November 1939)

No. 4.

Secret memorandum by Übelhör, 10 December 1939, concerning creation of a ghetto for Jews in Łódź. [in German][39]

Regierungspräsident at Kalisz

Łódź, December 10, 1939
Secret!
Strictly confidential!

Formation of a Ghetto in the City of Łódź

There are in my estimate ca. 320,000 Jews living today in greater Łódź. Their immediate evacuation is not possible. Thorough examinations by all the relevant offices proved that bringing all Jews together into a closed ghetto *is not possible.*[40] The Jewish question in the city of Łódź must be solved *temporarily* in the following way:

1. Jews residing north of the line Listopada (Novemberstrasse, Freiheitsplatz, Pomorska) Pommerschestrasse are to be put into a closed ghetto, so that on the one hand the space needed around Freiheitsplatz[41] for the formation of a German center of power will be cleared of Jews, and on the other hand the northern part of the city that is almost exclusively inhabited by Jews will be included into this ghetto.

2. Jews capable of work residing in the remaining part of the city of Łódź are to be combined into labor units and put into blocks of barracks and kept under guard.

The preparations for and implementation of this plan are to be carried out by a project staff into which the following authorities or departments are to delegate representatives:

1. N.S.D.A.P.
2. Łódź Office of the Kalisz Regierungspräsident
3. City administration of Łódź (Housing, Construction, Health, Food Departments, etc.)
4. Order Police
5. Security Police
6. Death's Head Unit
7. Chamber of Industry and Commerce
8. Finance Office

. . .

Moreover, the following preparations are to be made:

1. Defining the facilities for cordoning off (installation of road-blocks, barricading of building fronts and exits, etc.).
2. Plotting of measures for guarding the perimeter of the ghetto.
3. Obtaining the required materials for sealing off of the ghetto by the Łódź city administration.
4. Taking of measures to see that the health care of Jews within the ghetto is guaranteed through transfer of medicaments and medical instruments (from Jewish stocks), especially from the standpoint of the fight against epidemics (Health Department).
5. Preparations for the later arrangement for the removal of feces from the ghetto and arrangement for the transportation of corpses to the Jewish cemetery, or establishment of a cemetery within the ghetto (city administration).
6. Securing the quantities of heating materials needed in the ghetto (city administration).

After completion of these preparations and after provision of sufficient guard forces, the establishment of the ghetto will suddenly take place on a day designated by me; that is, at a given hour the designated perimeter of the ghetto will be occupied by the hereby planned guard units and the streets closed by barbed wire barricades [*spanische Reiter*] and other cordoning devices. At the same time, walling up of building fronts will be commenced by Jewish laborers to be taken from the ghetto. In the ghetto itself a Jewish self-government will immediately be installed, consisting of the Eldest of the Jews and a greatly expanded community board.

. . . [42]

The Food Office of the City of Łódź will deliver the required foodstuffs and fuel to specified points in the ghetto and transfer them to the representative of the Jewish self-government for distribution. The basic principle must thereby be that foodstuffs, fuel, and the like must be paid for only through barter goods, like textiles and so forth. In this manner we will succeed in completely extracting the most concealed material assets hidden by Jews.

. . .

When combing the remaining quarters of the city for Jews incapable of work, which is simultaneously to be postponed in the ghetto until shortly after the ghetto's establishment, Jews capable of work who reside there [outside the ghetto] are also to be secured. They are to be combined into labor units and to be accommodated and guarded in blocks of barracks prepared in advance by the city administration and the security police. These Jews are designated for a closed work gang.

. . .

From the foregoing, it follows that first of all the Jews who have their place of residence outside the ghetto will be taken for work deployment. Those Jews in the labor barracks who are incapable of working or become ill are to be transferred into the ghetto. Those Jews still capable of work who reside in the ghetto are to fulfill jobs that arise in the ghetto. I will later decide whether Jews capable of work will be extracted from the ghetto and brought into the labor barracks.

The establishment of the ghetto is of course only a transitional measure. I reserve to myself the decision at what point in time and with which means the ghetto and thereby the city of Łódź will be cleansed of Jews. In any event, the final goal must be that we completely burn out this pestilential boil.

signed Übelhör
(Eisenbach, Dokumenty, *vol. 3,* Getto Łódzkie, *26–31)*

No. 5. YI-39/11

Announcement on 9 January 1940 by Łódź Police-President SS-Brigaden-führer Johannes Schäfer, concerning avoiding coming into contact with the Jewish residential quarter as a source of epidemic. [in German]

Due to the nasty conditions in regard to hygiene, the north of the city of Łódź, particularly the part inhabited virtually exclusively by Jews, is a constant focus of infection, above all for typhoid fever, dysentery, and typhus, so that the danger of these diseases spreading exists.
Every unnecessary contact with this part of the city must therefore immediately cease.

The urgent order is hereby issued to all Germans, both Reich Germans and ethnic Germans, who do not reside in the north of the city and are not involved in the health service, as for example physicians, nurses, health attendants, disinfectors, and so forth, to avoid this part of the city in all circumstances. Moreover, I expect that the Polish population will restrict visits to relatives or acquaintances that reside in the designated city quarter to absolutely necessary visits. The region of the city in question is bounded by the rail line running northward, beginning as follows: "Goplańska, Żórawia, Żabia, Tokarzewskiego, Marysinska, Brzezinska, Franciszkańska, Północna, Piłsudskiego, Łódka, Nowomiejska, Podrzeczna, Stodolniana, Drewnowska, Rymarska, Lutomierska, Rybna, Limanowskiego, Lotnicza, Zgierska until the intersection of Goplańksa."

(Lodscher Zeitung, 10 January 1940)

No. 6. YI-39/16–17

Ordinance of 8 February 1940 by Łódź Police-President SS-Brigadenführer Johannes Schäfer, concerning formation of a ghetto. [in German]

POLICE ORDINANCE
concerning the residential rights of Jews on the basis of the Police Administration Law of 1 June 1931/G.S.S.-J.J.u.F., the following police ordinance is being issued:

Par. 1
A residential area is being established for the closed accommodation

of all Jews resident in the city of Łódź, in the section of the city north of Deutschlandplatz, bordered by the following streets: Wirkerstrasse /Stefana/, extension of Drechlerstrasse /Sadowa/ until Froschweg /Żabia/, Froschweg Goldschmiedegasse /Tokarzewskiego/ until Siegfriedstrasse /Marysińska/, Siegfriedstrasse until Kuehlen Gasse /Chłodna/, extension of Siegfriedstrasse until Veit Stoss Strasse, Buschlinie /Kilinskiego/ Nordstrasse /Połnocna/ until Lodkabach, then Lodkabach until Oststrasse /Piłsudskiego/, then Tizianstrasse /Nadłódka/, then extension of Tizianstrasse until the Poznański Factory, property boundaries of the Poznański Factory until Holzstrasse /Drewnowska/, then Holzstrasse itself until Bierstrasse /Piwna/, Bierstrasse, then Reiterstrasse /Urzędnicza/ property boundaries until Spulergasse /Adwokacka/, then Spulergasse itself.

The precise drawing of the boundary follows the delineation by the municipal administration of Łódź.

For through traffic with vehicles of all sorts, Neustadtstrasse /Nowomiejska/, Hohensteinerstrasse /Zgierska/ and Alexanderhofstrasse /Limanowski (!)/ will be kept free until further regulation. All pedestrian traffic on these open through-streets will be forbidden from a soon-to-be-fixed point in time.

Par. 2

All the ethnic Germans and Poles who still reside in this part of the city must vacate by 29 February 1940 at the latest, with their families, their household furnishings, their professional and other movable property.

The affected ethnic Germans will be assigned suitable residences, insofar as they do not themselves obtain residences with the agreement of the municipal Housing and Resettlement Office, on application to the Housing and Resettlement Office within the city of Łódź. Lodging will be assigned to Poles by the same office in another part of the city enclosed as follows: in the north by the Kalisch-Łódź railline until Wendischstrasse, Wendischstrasse, /extension of Kątnastrasse/, Warenstrasse /Towarowa/, Otternstrasse /Łaska/, Eichhoernchengasse /Wołowa/, Ludendorffstrasse /Żeromski/, Albert Breyer Strasse / Księdza-Skorupki/ Glockengasse /św. Stanisława/, Adolf-Hitler Strasse /Piotrkowska/, Boehmische Linie /Napiórkowskiego/, Wuppertalerstrasse /Milionowa/, in the East, South and West by the city limits.

Par. 3

Implementation of the total resettlement takes place in accord with the applicable executive ordinances that designate for each affected residential block which day and to which new housing area the inhabitants of the affected block must move. All building owners or Polish or Jewish building maintenance boards are obligated to admit persons assigned by the police or the city into their residences.

These executive ordinances will also name the items, which the individual groups should take with them during the resettlement.

Those affected by the outsettlement must have ready for their move on the designated day a compilation of the number of rooms occupied until now and the nature and extent of any industrial facilities, professional plants, or warehouses existing in that area.

Par. 5

The landlords or managers of all of the apartments affected by the resettlement, with the exception of the residential area of the Jews designated in par. 1, will be made responsible to see that all the ethnic Germans and Poles moving in with them report to the relevant police precinct about their change of residence.

Par. 6

Jews employed in vitally important branches of industry and whose replacement by other persons is not possible can, at the application of the employer, continue to be employed, if [the employer] commits himself for the food supply and secure housing of these Jews in closed accommodation, without their families, on the property of the employer [who is] really prepared to care for them in every manner. Further security police measures remain reserved.

Par. 7

Violations against these police ordinances will be punished with fines of up to 150 RM or with corresponding imprisonment.

Par. 8

This police ordinance comes into force immediately. It goes out of force on 31 December 1940.

(Lodscher Zeitung, *9 February 1940)*

No. 7. YI-39/18–22

Executive regulations to the ordinance of Police-President Schäfer of 8 February 1940. [in German]

In the execution of my ordinance of 8.2.1940, I hereby ordain the following:

Par. 1

(Area of Resettlement)

Each week, a schedule will be made public, which is hereby made a component of the abovementioned police ordinance. This plan identifies the blocks affected by implementation of the required resettlement during the following week under the above ordinance, in each case on publication.

Par. 2

(Residential Curfew on Moving Days)

To assure the carrying out of an orderly resettlement, the prohibition is hereby issued that all persons, who are affected by the resettlement on the given day according to the schedule below for each residential block, must not leave their apartments except for carrying out the resettlement. All persons affected have to provide themselves in advance with the necessary supplies for the day of their resettlement.

Par. 3
(Taking Along Objects)

All persons who will be affected by the resettlement may take along basically one suitcase with their linens, personal clothing, and family keepsakes (family pictures and the like), but in a quantity such that each individual can carry it with him without special means of transport.

The timetable regulates which additional objects may be taken along.

Par. 4
(Moves)

The movement of Poles out of the area designated according to par. 1 of the police ordinance as residential districts of Jews and the settlement of Jews into this area take place in principle only in organized groups under the direction of the designated transport manager, who also carries out the assignment of new apartments to the Jews and Poles. Every other movement of Jews and Poles, as well as of all ethnic Germans who are not directly included by this resettlement measure, is forbidden until further notice.

Par. 5
(Housing Cards)

Everyone affected by the resettlement must, on the day before the resettlement, very legibly fill out a blank housing card that he himself has to obtain and that is available in the stationery of the nearest precinct. The housing card includes the following questions:

a) First and last names of the person being resettled;
b) Number of rooms of the apartment occupied by him until now;
c) Stocks of goods by any chance present in the apartment, by type and quantity;
d) Professional equipment that may be present;
e) Name and address of the person entrusted with his apartment key (see par. 7).

On arrival at the assembly point, the duly filled out cards are to be neatly turned in to the transport manager without being asked.

. . .

Par. 10
(Sick Persons)

Medically certified sick persons affected by the resettlement, who are capable of being transported, will be provided with transport by the resettlement manager in conjunction with the municipal Health Office.

No later than on the day prior to the resettlement, the Housing Office is to be notified in writing of the number of persons and apartments with attachment of the requisite medical certificates.

Par. 11
(Abandonment of the Transport Group)

The entire resettlement of Poles and Jews and assignment into new apartments takes place exclusively in organized transport groups. None of those concerned may abandon his transport group until the local assignment into the new apartment takes place and the required housing certificate has been handed to him by the transport manager of his group. Violations will be considered as an attempt to escape, resulting in immediate use of weapons.

. . .

Par. 15
(Move of Jews)

Under the management of the transport leader, Jews move daily into their new residential area in 6 groups of at most 300 heads:

> Group 1 at 8 A.M.
> Group 2 at 10 A.M.
> Group 3 at 12 noon
> Group 4 at 2 P.M.
> Group 5 at 4 P.M.
> Group 6 at 6 P.M.

and namely from the assembly point designated in the timetable.

The Jews are responsible to see that the required number from the designated residential area are standing by for departure at each time with filled out housing cards.

Should this privilege not lead to success, it will be ordered that the entire housing block of the relevant day will have to stand ready in the morning, reporting together in closed ranks. Every act of resistance or attempt at flight will result in immediate use of weapons.

Par. 16
(Admission of Jews)

Within the new residential area of the Jews, the Eldest of the Jews regulates admission into individual buildings and apartments according to the orders of the transport manager. The Eldest of the Jews can employ officials provided by himself, identified with white-yellow armbands, whose orders are then to be obeyed in the same fashion as his own orders.

When the transport manager transfers a transport group designated for a residential block to the Eldest of the Jews or his officials, all the members of this group are to be accommodated in the designated housing block.

Any relaxation of this rule can only be decided in the further course of the resettlement. In the meantime, it must remain that the transport manager successively admits groups into designated residential blocks of the new residential area of the Jews.

Par. 17

(Housing Ban for Jews)

With the proclamation of this ordinance, all Jews who already reside within the residential area of Jews, [defined] according to par. 1 of the police ordinance, will henceforward be forbidden to live outside this assigned area. The same applies for all Jews who in the course of the resettlement are admitted into this area. Occupation of apartments vacated by Germans and Poles in the new residential area of the Jews in the course of the resettlement is regulated by the timetable and the individual orders of the transport manager.

Unauthorized use of unassigned rooms or equipment will be treated as theft and punished. Resistance to the transport manager's orders results in use of weapons.

(Lodzher Zeitung, *9 February 1940*)

No. 8. YI-39/36

Police-president's announcement of 1 March 1940 about the arrest of a large number of Jews for maintaining a brisk traffic with the city. [in German]

In spite of the police ordinance issued on 8.2.1940 and the repeatedly expressed warnings, a brisk traffic of JEWS out of the GHETTO into the city and back is still taking place. In order to put a final stop to this impudent activity of the Jews, that over and over works against the authorities' efforts for order and cleanliness, I yesterday ordered a POLICE RAID to be carried out, with the result that a large number of Jews, who until now paid no heed to the issued police ordinance, were arrested. In the future, I will also unrelentingly proceed against this sort of violations and am not inclined to allow any exceptions.

In this connection, I once more state that all Reich Germans and ethnic Germans must also support me in my efforts to bring the conditions in Łódź into order, and above all to refrain immediately from entering without authorization into the ghetto area, that is sufficiently marked out.

(Lodscher Zeitung, *1 March 1940*)

No. 9. YI-621/49

Directive from the police-president to Rumkowski, 2 March 1940, concerning payment of the fine for those arrested and provision of food for them. [in German]

The Jews entered on the attached list were arrested on 29.2.1940, as they violated par. 7 of the executive instructions for the police ordinance of 8.2.1940.

I have directed their punishment with fines of 150 RM each. The ability of those concerned to pay has been determined. You are requested immediately to see that the relatives of the Jews appearing on the list pay at the Łódź Police Headquarters, Hermann Goering St. 52, Dept. V. (par. 7, Police Ordinance 8.2.1940 [!]), with reference to my demand in the amount of 150 RM.

Prisoner release takes place only after payment of the sum of money. The relatives must likewise see to feeding the detainee, while food and drink, provided with a name label, are to be delivered to the head of the guard unit, Luisen St. 25.

No. 10. YI-621/6

Letter from the Łódź branch of the Office for Settlement of Balts [Amt fuer Balteneinsatz] at the Higher SS and Police Leader, Warthe[land], to Rumkowski, dated 2 February 1940, concerning things that the expelled Jews left behind in their apartments. [in German]

In reply to your letter of 26.1.40, I inform you that it was entirely in the Jews' possibility to take along from the apartments the now requested objects, particularly since the officials charged with enforcement constantly informed the Jews that the most necessary items, especially children's linen as well as personal documents, should be taken along.

I leave [it to your] discretion in urgent cases to submit to my office, *Amt fuer Wohnungseinsatz* [Office for Housing Assignment], a petition for transfer of children's things as well as personal documents.

No. 11. YI-621/11

Letter from the same office to Rumkowski of 13 February 1940, concerning coming into contact with the new inhabitants of the Jewish apartments. [in German]

In regard to your letter of 6.2.40, I leave it to your discretion to make contact with the present residents of the cited apartments for the purpose of delivery of the mentioned objects.

The apartment residents are requested to turn over the expendable children's things, documents, souvenirs, passes, as well as a set of underwear and items of clothing.

No. 12. YI-39/38

Police ordinance of 7 March 1940, that invalidates all temporary permits to move about outside the boundaries of the ghetto. [in German]

All passes issued to Jews, in particular

- a) For walking on Adolf Hitler Street between 8 A.M. and 5 P.M. or from 8 A.M. to 8 P.M.;
- b) For unhindered passage on the streets of Łódź City from 8 A.M. to 5 P.M. or 8 A.M. to 8 P.M.;
- c) For Jewish physicians, pharmacists, and midwives to walk the streets in Łódź City at night;
- d) Special passes issued to Jewish rag dealers and scrap iron collec-

tors for the District of Kalisch and for the Government for the time from 8 A.M. to 8 P.M.;

are hereby declared immediately invalid regardless of their term of validity. There is to be no future use of this pass. Whoever will be found in unauthorized use of passes in spite of this [order], exposes himself to arrest and a severe fine.

(Lodsher Zeitung, *9 March 1940*)

Nos. 13, 14: YI-39/40, 42

Second and third executive instructions of 15 March and 3 April 1940 that prohibit the lodging of Jews in designated western and southern quarters of the city. [in German]

In the execution of my ordinance of 8.2.1940, I direct the following: I hereby forbid all Jews to stay in the area west from the Łódź Central Train Station railline until the city limit (area of police precincts 23 and 27), as well as in the southern part of the city, which on the north is bounded by the following streets:

. . .

I hereby demand that all Jews still residing in the designated areas that are now closed for Jews immediately report to the nearest police precinct for the purpose of resettlement.

Excluded are those Jews designated in par. 6 of the Police Ordinance of 8.2.1940, provided that on publication of this executive regulation they are already QUARTERED IN BARRACKS.

. . .

Effective immediately, I forbid all Jews to remain in the southern part of the city that is bounded on the north by the following streets:

. . .

All the Jews still residing in the designated restricted area must report to the nearest police precinct for the purpose of resettlement. Excepted are those Jews named in par. 6 of the Police Ordinance of 8.2.1940, provided that at the publication of this executive regulation they are already quartered in barracks.

(Lodscher Zeitung, *19 March and 4 April 1940*)

No. 15. YI-39/43

Police-president's Ordinance of 8 April (4th executive regulation to the ordinance of 8 February 1940), that modifies and somewhat enlarges the area of the ghetto. [in German]

On the basis of par. 37 of the Police Administration Law of 1.6.1931, pars. 1 & 2 of the police ordinance of 8 February 1940 are amended as follows:

par. 1.

For the closed housing of all the resident Jews in the city of Łódź, a residential area (GHETTO) is established in the part of the city north of Deutschlandplatz that is bounded by the following streets:

> Buchbinderstrasse (Goplańska), Kranichweg in the northern direction over Wirkerstrasse until Winzerweg, Winzerweg to Hanseatenstrasse, Gaertnerstrasse, Jewish Cemetery inclusive, both sides of Wolfgangstrasse, Ewaldstrasse, Gewervestrasse until Krimhildstrasse, Krimhildstrasse until Winfriedstrasse, Konradstrasse, Kuehle Gasse, Veit-Stoss Strasse until Nordstrasse until Lodka stream, along the Lodka until Tizianstrasse, further along the Lodka over Am Bach, in the northern direction until Holzstrasse, boths sides of Maienstrasse, both sides of Luetzowstrasse, both sides of Hamburgerstrasse, both sides of Blaue Gasse, Koenigsbergerstrasse, Bierstrasse, Reiterstrasse until Balutkabach along Balutkabach until Hohensteinerstrasse. All the streets that are not designated as both sides belonging to the ghetto fall with the street side that borders on the ghetto area into the ghetto area.

Pars. 2 and 3 remain in the old formulation.

Par. 2

All Germans and Poles still residing in this part of the city must clear out of it by 30 April 1940 with their families, their household goods, their commercial and other movable possessions, and report to their nearest police precinct.

Suitable apartments etc. within the city of Łódź will be assigned to the affected Germans and Poles, insofar as they do not themselves obtain apartments with the agreement of the municipal Resettlement and Housing Office [Umsiedlungs- und Quartieramt].

All JEWS still residing in the city area have to move into an apartment in the ghetto area by the 19th of April 1940.

Pars. 3 through 8 remain in their old text.

(Litzmannstaedter Zeitung, 9 April 1940)[43]

No. 16. YI-621/86

Letter from the municipal Health Department to Rumkowski, 11 April 1940, concerning outbreak of typhus in the assembly camp. [in German]

Lately, cases of typhus illnesses contracted in the Rembrandtstrasse 10 collective camp are constantly mounting.

You are immediately to report in what scope the camp still exists, what the spatial and hygienic conditions of the camp are, and whether all has been done for prevention of spread of the infection.

In any case, you will carefully remove vermin from the entire camp through your own arrangements or through a private firm and immediately delouse the inmates.

A report about the measures taken is to be turned in to the Health Department's Hygiene Section.

No. 17. YI-621/68

Letter from Rumkowski to the Resettlement and Quartering Office, 30 March 1940, concerning issuing to him the keys to a locked building in the ghetto. [in German]

Since according to the police ordinance of 8.2.40 a residential area for Jews is ordered and all the empty premises in this Jewish residential area are at my disposal, I hereby respectfully request release of the vacant building at Schneidergasse no. 3 and delivery of the key.

Hoping that you will grant my request, I sign, thanking you very much in advance, . . .

No. 18. YI-92

Rumkowski's Announcement no. 13 of 8 April 1940 that prohibits unauthorized occupation of apartments in the ghetto.[44] [in German]

I hereby announce that the apartments that lie within the expanded ghetto, according to the police ordinance of 8.4.1940, may be moved into only with my authorization.
Anyone who moves into an apartment in this area without my authorization will be forcibly removed from the same and most severely penalized.

No. 19. YI-106

Rumkowski's Announcement of 3 May 1940, permitting occupation of individual rooms in the expanded ghetto area. [in German]

I hereby permit all homeless families to move into individual rooms in the expanded Jewish residential area /new ghetto/, with the exception of those that are in those buildings that have been confiscated by me for public uses.

Immediately after moving into the room, this must be reported at the Community's Housing Assignment Office, Hamburgerstrasse no. 13 /Lutomierska/ and be certified by it.

Anyone who neglects to report will be evicted from the apartment.

No landlord, building manager, or janitor is to demand key money or rent.

Those who pay key money or rent will, after discovery, be evicted from the apartment.

Larger apartments can be sought out, but they can be moved into only when certified in advance by the Housing Assignment Office.

No. 20. YI-762

Letter from the police-president to Rumkowski, 17 April 1940, stating that the Jewish Order Service should immediately take over guarding the ghetto enclosure. [in German]

Since the formation of the ghetto has progressed so far that the sealing off can take place on 30.4.[1940], the Jewish Order Service must immediately take over the surveillance of the ghetto's enclosure. The Jewish Community will be responsible for all damages arising in future. Should the occasion arise, I will also punish the responsible leader of the Jewish Order Service pursuant to the Police Ordinance of 20 February 1940 on the formation of a Jewish Order Service.

No. 21. YI-39/46

Police-president's Announcement of 19 April 1940, concerning the possibility of totally sealing off the ghetto. [in German]

FORMATION OF THE GHETTO in the north of Litzmannstadt is already so advanced that the total sealing off can take place. From 15 April, the ghetto area was to be entered by ethnic Germans only for the purpose of resettlement. In this regard, I reiterate that all German and ethnic German officials, as well as all Army personnel, must support me in my efforts to arrange the conditions in Litzmannstadt.

I request that this document be announced to all authorities and Army personnel and in this sense to influence them.

(*Litzmannstädter Zeitung, 20 April 1940*)

No. 22. YI-39/47

5th and final executive ordinance by the police-president of 7 May 1940 to both police ordinances of 8 February and 8 April 1940, concerning the final sealing off of the ghetto. [in German]

Since the final sealing of the ghetto was carried out on 1.5.1940 on the basis of the above ordinances of 8.2.1940 and 8.4.1940, I ordain the following immediately:

Every contact with Jews, also including commercial traffic of the civilian population, is forbidden as of now. Contravention against these executive regulations will be punished according to par. 7 of the police ordinance of 8.2.1940 with a fine of up to 150 mk or with corresponding arrest.

(*Litzmannstädter Zeitung, 9 May 1940*)

No. 23. YI-1301

Map of the Łódź Ghetto [in German, see pages lx–lxi][45]

II

Organization of the Ghetto

Before we move to describing the organization of the Łódź Ghetto, it is worthwhile to discuss briefly the real nature of the Jewish "self-government" in the ghettos and the role that the authorities allotted to it in relation to the policy of extermination toward the Jewish population in the occupied countries. This is necessary in order to see in proper historical perspective the "ghetto autonomy" with its broadly constructed administrative apparatus, behind which in fact was the hypocritical intent to harness the victims themselves into the executioner's machinery of destruction.[1]

It is clear that the entire ghetto structure had to serve the realization of the Nazi plans for the isolated ghetto population. The ghetto's ramified organization was created first of all in order precisely and effectively to carry out all decrees and commands of the supervising regime. Its role is thus sketched in the ordinance of 28 November 1939 concerning introduction of the *Judenrat* (council of Jews) in the Generalgouvernement and in all other official and unofficial Nazi pronouncements.[2]

The Nazis did not consider the Jewish council (*Judenrat* in the Generalgouvernement, *Ältestenrat* in the annexed territories) to be a body to organize life in the ghettos so as to strengthen the ghetto socially and make it capable of resistance, but just the opposite. The *Judenrat* was to be an entity that would help realize Nazi Germany's extermination plans. (At most, the Jewish councils should maintain "calm and order" in the ghettos, as the Nazis understood it.) It is far from a coincidence that in Heydrich's famous *Schnellbrief* of 21 September 1939, where he already hints at the "final objective" (*Endziel*) of solving the Jewish question in the occupied territories, there is in the introduction a special segment (2) devoted to the Jewish councils and their help in concentrating the Jewish population in designated city quarters.

A Jewish council striving to achieve positive tasks for the benefit of the Jewish population would not have been tolerated by the German authorities for even one day. We know of enough cases of removal or even murder of members of the councils, whom the regime considered disruptive in the realization of the Nazi Germans' plans.

Therefore, if the Jewish councils wanted to exist, and considered their existence to be the sole possibility at least to soothe the pain and suffering of the ghetto population, they had to maneuver between two contradictory fronts—the internal Jewish and the external Nazi. Naturally, such maneuvering was often a sort of tightrope walk that could not long endure. The Nazi front was the stronger, decisive one, and it dictated the councils' policies.

Thus, the councils' field of activity was restricted in advance to a single task—to help realize the Nazi plans in regard to the Jewish population. Everything else that the councils did, with the agreement of the supervising regime in the field of internal ghetto life (social welfare, economic and cultural activities), was of a temporary character and was intended to camouflage the Nazi strategy in order to conceal from the Jews the final objective (*Endziel*) as long as necessary. The representatives of the councils were reassured, "You can live calmly in the ghetto, nothing threatens you," or "This is the final action, there will be no more actions."

With the councils' help, the Nazis were often able to spread rescue illusions among the Jewish population and to dull its alertness to the impending danger.

In the Łódź Ghetto, this maneuvering between the two fronts and the role that the authorities assigned to the *Ältestenrat* (more precisely, to Rumkowski) were very clearly evident.

One person placed the deepest imprint on the internal organization of the Łódź Ghetto: Mordechai Chaim Rumkowski, a member of the prewar Jewish Community Board.[3] According to the confirmation (*Ausweis*) by the Łódź city-commissioner on 13 October 1939, as "the eldest of the Jews in the city of Łódź [he was] given the mandate to carry out all measures of the German civil administration in regard to all persons belonging to the Jewish race." They were unconditionally obligated to obey his orders or be punished by the German authorities. Rumkowski also received permission to assemble a circle of coworkers (*Ältestenrat*) to consult with him (doc. no. 26).[4]

Mordechai Chaim Rumkowski rides through the Łódź Ghetto in a horse-drawn carriage, 1940–1944. Photograph by Walter Genewein. USHMM, courtesy of Robert Abrams.

A day later, on 14 October, the city-commissioner directed Rumkowski to dissolve all existing institutions and administrative organs of the Jewish community and reorganize them from scratch. Any persons declining to carry out the duties placed on them would be arrested. The order also gave Rumkowski the right to levy taxes. As a result of this directive, all Jewish philanthropic and social institutions of a public character were liquidated (doc. no. 27).[5]

To carry out the aforementioned instructions, Rumkowski convened a conference. He invited thirty-one representative persons from among the Jewish population in Łódź, and thus the so-called *Beirat* (advisory council) was constituted, consisting of thirty people.[6] This first Beirat did not last long. On 7 November, the entire council was required to report to the building of the Gestapo. With the exception of Rumkowski and two others, all were sent to prison and from there into a nearby penal camp in Radogoszcz (Radegast), where some were murdered by shooting and torture and five members were deported to Kraków in December.[7]

Mordechai Chaim Rumkowski is driven in a horse-drawn carriage through a street of the Łódź Ghetto, 1940–1944. Photograph by Walter Genewein. USHMM, courtesy of Robert Abrams.

This was the tragic end of the first Beirat. Only on 5 February 1940 did Rumkowski notify the *Sicherheitsdienst* (SD, Security Service of the SS) about formation of a second council of twenty-one members (doc. no. 28).[8] The second Beirat consisted of persons characterized by someone very knowledgeable about the history of the Łódź Ghetto as "persons of the third rank, with little public sense and still less sense of responsibility for the great tasks that stood before them."[9] Symptomatic for the evolution of the *Ältestenrat* (Elders' Council) or Beirat is the fact that in the graphic schematic chart of the ghetto's internal organization of September 1941, it is degraded to a "Consultative Commission with the Eldest of the Jews" (*Beratungscommission beim Ältesten der Juden*); it does not appear at all in the ghetto's organizational chart of August 1943.

In fact, until after the September deportation of 1942, a system of autocratic rule by the *Judenältester* (Eldest of the Jews) M. Ch. Rumkowski was installed in the Łódź Ghetto. In the authorization of 30 April 1940, sent by the mayor of Łódź to Rumkowski, the latter was made exclusively and personally responsible to "carry out all measures which are and will be necessary to maintain an orderly public life in the Jewish residential area" and carry them out with the help of the Jewish Police (*Ordnungsdienst,* Order Service) placed under him. Not a single word refers to the existing Beirat. There is only talk of an eventual deputy of Rumkowski (doc. no. 29).[10] Only on 17 January 1941 did Rumkowski, in agreement with the German authorities, nominate as his deputy Dr. Leon Szykier, the medical director of the Health Department, and this only during his absence (doc. no. 30).[11] But because this physician evinced too much independence, Rumkowski removed Szyk-

Four members of the Łódź Ghetto administration (left to right): Mordechai Lajzerowicz, head of the ghetto bakeries; Max Szczęśliwy, head of food supply; Leon Rozenblat, chief of the ghetto police; and Dr. Leon Szykier, head of the health department, 1940–1942. Photographer unknown. USHMM, courtesy of Gila Flam.

ier from his position on 12 June 1941 (doc. no. 31).[12] Only in September 1941 did Rumkowski nominate the commandant of the Jewish Police and the director of the Central Bureau of the Labor Departments as his deputies (see below and doc. no. 32).[13] But these were only pawns, who mixed little in the general affairs of the ghetto administration. In reality, the system of one-man rule took hold in the ghetto. In those fields of ghetto life where the German authorities left the Jews free hands, Rumkowski was the sole and final arbiter.

In accord with the above-mentioned decree about dissolving all Jewish institutions and absorbing them into Rumkowski's administration, on 5 March 1940 he forwarded to the German security authorities a list of institutions and facilities that he had taken over: three hospitals, two clinics, one first aid station, one kitchen for the poor, four orphanages, one home for infants, thirty-two former state elementary schools for Jewish children,[14] one kindergarten, and one Talmud Torah.[15] In addition, he extended subsidies to one home for the aged, three shelters for the homeless, one home for the disabled, a kitchen for the poor, a school for deaf-mutes, six private schools, and a Talmud Torah.[16] This was the social patrimony that Rumkowski inherited from the former Jewish community, for whose maintenance he had now to worry in the catastrophically changed circumstances of Nazi rule. New and urgent tasks arose.

The first urgent task in regard to the German authorities that confronted Rumkowski was organization of forced labor by the Jewish population, due to seizures of people on the streets and even from homes. The brutal abuse during the work became a horrible plague for the Jewish population. On 15 October 1939 arrived the demand from the chief of the civil administration at the German Army Field Command (*Armeeoberkommando*) to the rabbinate to supply 600 laborers daily (doc. no. 33).[17] On the same day, the *Arbeitseinsatz I* (Labor Conscription Office) was formed, whose function was to deliver Jewish laborers to various assembly points for employment by German offices and agencies. Before the end of the month, the *Arbeitseinsatz* registered males ages eighteen to sixty and women ages twenty-two to fifty-five. In December 1939, the number of Jewish forced laborers delivered rose to 2,000–3,000 daily. The prosperous could buy exemptions through substitutes for a specified sum. The Jewish community paid men 1.75 RM per day and women 1.25 RM. After the municipal welfare bureau decreed that requests for Jewish workers must go through it, there arose in December the *Arbeitseinsatz II,* headed by Rumkowski, whose task was to supply the required number of laborers. Until May 1940, the *Arbeitseinsatz* expended 285,000 RM for wages and had a deficit of 175,000 RM. This bureau existed until 1 September 1940 (according to another source, until 1 July), while until that date Jewish workers still labored in the city beyond the ghetto limits (doc. no. 34).[18] The *Arbeitseinsatz* later became the Department for Public Works in the ghetto itself (see chapter 4 on this matter).

The second urgent task was aid for the poor, for segments of the population impoverished due to the war and for those left without means of support due to the confiscatory policies of the occupation authorities. On 1 November 1939, the city administration terminated public assistance for Jews. The Jewish communal treasury was empty, since the communal funds in the banks, like all other Jewish bank accounts, were blocked. On 15 October 1939, the Department for Social Aid was created, existing until 27 September 1940. In that month, Rumkowski shifted to another form of public assistance (about the activity of the Department for Social Aid, see below).

Rumkowski also had to take over support of, or at least subsidize, the Jewish hospitals and provide for the Jewish patients after the municipality refused to treat them in the city hospitals. The health situation of the Jewish population was generally difficult because many physicians had left the city since the war's outbreak or had been deported. In October 1939, the nucleus of the Health Department was formed, which later strongly developed in the ghetto.

The third serious task was to organize the resettlement of the Jewish population into the ghetto. According to the executive instructions to the police ordinances of 8 February 1940 (see chapter 1 and doc. no. 7), Rumkowski was empowered to regulate the quartering of those expelled in the ghetto's buildings. The Housing Office was formed on 23 January 1940. But as already noted (in chapter 1), the move into the ghetto took place largely in panic and chaos, so that the operation of the Housing

Office was disorganized in great measure not due to Rumkowski's fault. Though the housing situation in the ghetto later stabilized somewhat, the Housing Office continued to exist.

The administrative apparatus grew mightily in the ghetto, while under Rumkowski's personal authority the broadly expanded bureaucracy regulated life in the ghetto down to the smallest details. In fact, all the ghetto inhabitants were Rumkowski's employees. He would refer to all the ghetto institutions and economic enterprises as "my."

In February 1941 the ghetto administration's departments employed 5,500 workers,[19] which amounted to about 6 percent of the total ghetto population old enough to work. The number of employees (office workers and physical laborers) subsequently increased even more, and in July 1941 totaled 7,316 employees (aside from temporary workers). By 1 December 1941, there were 9,221 and on 1 August 1942 fully 12,880 employees on the payroll.[20]

A surviving Department List (*Abteilungs-Verzeichnis*), apparently from the second half of 1940, reckons seven administrative groups with seventy-three departments and workshops (doc. no. 35).[21] In time, new departments were added and desks (*referatn*) in departments turned into independent departments themselves. Thus, for example, on 3 December 1941, after 3,082 Jews from Włocławek and its vicinity (September-October) and 19,953 Jews from Germany, Vienna, Prague, and Luxemburg (October-November) were deported into the Łódź Ghetto, the Department for the Resettled was created, which in large scope existed until 30 November 1942.[22] By that date, the overwhelming majority of these deportees had departed with the "outsettlement" (*Aussiedlung*) of May 1942, or had already died (over one-fifth of their initial number). This department, starting from mid-May 1942, also dealt with the matters of those expelled to Łódź from the liquidated provincial ghettos.

After introduction of the food rationing system on 15 December 1940, a Ration Card Department was created on 1 January 1941. When feeding (soups) was introduced in the workshops on the basis of coupons and the system of distributing food coupons was extensively expanded, a Coupons Department was formed on 29 January 1941. In April 1940 the Agricultural Desk at the Economic (*Virtshaft*) Department was established to deal with leasing out vacant land parcels in the ghetto for planting. In January 1941, the Work Desk at the Welfare Department turned into an independent Office for Public Works.

A euphemistically named Department for Special Affairs was formed on 1 June 1942, after huge transports of clothing, shoes, bedding, and household goods arrived from the liquidated ghettos in Wartheland and after the German ghetto administration (*Gettoverwaltung*) directed that the sorting of the bloody inheritance from the victims take place in the ghetto. A Resettlement Commission (founded 5 January 1942) functioned during the resettlement actions in the ghetto during 1942, and there was an Inter-Factory (*Tsvishn-Resort*) Commission during the final deportation in June-August 1944.

Particularly strongly developed was the network of industrial enterprises in the ghetto. From a single tailor shop with about 300 workers in May 1940, it grew to 101 factories, workshops, and other workplaces that at the end of 1943 employed 73,782 persons. That amounted to about 85 percent of the entire ghetto population at the time.

We now briefly describe the organization and functions of the departments of the ghetto administration listed in doc. no. 35.

Group One: General Administration

1. **The Secretariat at Kościelna 4,** also called the Secretariat of the Presidial Department, was the most important center in the ghetto. From there emerged all significant decisions within the framework of the ghetto's "autonomy." Initially, the work of all the departments and offices was concentrated there. Also from there was conducted the correspondence with the German organs of power (mainly with the *Gettoverwaltung*). Contacts with the German authorities were conducted through the Secretariat at the Bałuty Marketplace (*Baluter Mark, Bałucki Rynek*), where the *Gettoverwaltung* had its administrative offices that also employed Jewish workers (during the years 1942–1944, almost exclusively Jews). In February 1944, the Secretariat at the Bałuty Marketplace had to vacate the buildings (barracks) to make way for the *Gettoverwaltung*'s bureaus, which moved from the city to Bałuty Marketplace. Only the Central Bureau of the Labor Office remained at this "neutral territory."

2. **The General Secretariat at Dworska 1** dealt with correspondence (letters, circulars) with the various departments and work divisions (*arbet-resortn*) in the ghetto. Proposals and applications from individuals were also accepted there.[23]

3. **The Personnel Department** (established on 10 June 1940) kept the records of all employees and workers in all offices and workplaces. Rumkowski alone decided all personnel matters of hiring, firing, or penalizing offending employees. He controlled the entire population in the ghetto through this office.

4. **The Central Treasury** *(hoyptkase)* played a very important role in the ghetto administration. It regulated all monetary circulation in the ghetto and thereby influenced salaries and prices, as well as consumption suited to the low standard of living in the ghetto. On 28 June 1940, the so-called "mark-receipts" (*mark-kvitungen*) were introduced in place of the Polish and German currencies that were withdrawn from circulation (doc. no. 36).[24] Ghetto money was printed in denominations from 50 pfennig up to 50 marks, a total of 8.5 million ghetto marks. Only 1.8 million ghetto marks were released into circulation, while the balance of ghetto banknotes was secured in a special vault. Thus, there was an average of between 11 and 12 marks in such scrip per ghetto resident. In spring 1942, due to the feverish trade on the black market during the "resettlement" action, the money turnover in the ghetto rose

to 5.5 million scrip-marks. The daily cash desk volume in June 1941 amounted to about 300,000 marks, while the monthly turnover for the first half-year of 1941 was about 3.5 million.[25] On 1 January 1941, Central Bookkeeping was separated from the Central Cash Desk as an independent department that kept the books of all existing ghetto institutions and compiled monthly and annual financial reports.

5. **The Supreme Control Office** (abbreviated in Yiddish as H.K.A. or in Polish as N.I.K. [*Najwyższa Izba Kontroli*]) was introduced on 6 November 1940 (doc. no. 37),[26] replacing the former Central Control Office (*tsentrale kontrol-shtele*). It primarily had the task of combating the widespread plague of corruption and embezzlement in the ghetto. The office consisted of 9 members and 13 controllers. Formally, the H.K.A. had broad competencies, but when it attempted to look into matters of supply, where Rumkowski admitted no one, he dissolved the old administration on 4 July 1941 and on the same day named a new leadership of four persons, with himself as temporary chairman. As reasons for this decision, Rumkowski declared that the office had internal wrangling over competence and had "not properly understood my wish."[27]

But the new administration of the H.K.A. did not last long either. On 16 August 1942, Rumkowski named an administration of five new members with his brother Joseph as chairman (doc. no. 38).[28] He dissolved this administration, too, only four months later (doc. no. 39).[29]

The H.K.A. not only audited the activities of the departments and had the right to remove those guilty of misdeeds from their posts and even have them arrested, but it also regulated questions of the innermost administration in the labor sites, such as wages, rations for the sick, child laborers, and so forth. Naturally, all sorts of complaints would come in to the H.K.A.[30]

6. **The Order Service** (O.S.; German, *Ordnungsdienst* or O.D.) played an extraordinarily important role in the ghetto administration. It was founded on 1 March 1940 on the basis of the Łódź Police Chief's order of 20 February 1940.[31] The ghetto populace was officially informed about this only on 1 May 1940 (doc. no. 40).[32] The O.S. was not armed (the Germans presumably feared giving Jews weapons). It did make use of rubber truncheons in its "work" and had its own uniform and badges (a round blue cap with a red stripe and on the sleeve a two-colored ribbon, mostly white-yellow, with little stars and badges for various ranks). The O.S. grew into a large, hierarchically developed organization with commissioners, deputy commissioners, investigators (*aspirantn*), captains (*eybervakhmaysters*), sergeants (*vakhmaysters*), and ordinary O.S. men. Even in April 1943, when the entire Jewish population in the ghetto numbered no more than 86,000 souls, the O.S. had 530 men, including 5 commissioners, 18 investigators, 10 captains, 50 sergeants, and 10 specialists (*referentn*). In addition, 52 O.S. men (loosely linked with the actual O.S.) were at the disposition of Rumkowski and the various departments.[33]

(Opposite top) Leon Rozenblat, chief of the ghetto police at a roll call, 1940–1944. Photographer unknown. USHMM, courtesy of Gila Flam.

(Opposite bottom) Group portrait of Jewish policemen in the Łódź Ghetto, 1940–1944. Photographer unknown. USHMM, courtesy of Żydowski Instytut Historyczny Instytut Naukowo-Badawczy.

Leon Rozenblat, chief of the ghetto police, poses with a newlywed couple in the Łódź Ghetto, 1940–1944. Photographer unknown. USHMM, courtesy of Gila Flam

The O.S. was initially divided into four precincts and later into five (the fifth in Marysin). One section of the O.S., called by the German term *Ueberfallkommando,* had the task of swiftly suppressing any disturbance among the ghetto inhabitants; it was dissolved on 25 September 1941. There were also two offices for price control and sanitary facilities (*sanitar-vezn*), as well as an examination department or juridical department, which was the sole judicial entity in the ghetto until the creation of a court.

Initially, there was also an auxiliary O.S. that was, however, dissolved on 3 November 1940. The women's department of the O.S. was established in October 1942. Its duty was to supervise children in the streets, fight against prohibited street trade, maintain order at ration distribution shops, and so forth. The women's department did not exist long. While most were later assigned to the work sites, a certain number were transferred to the so-called Special Unit (*Sonderkommando*).[34] The O.S. was subject to Rumkowski, with a commandant at its head as the chairman's deputy. How the leadership of the O.S. understood its duties in the ghetto is clearly evoked by the "Order of the Day" of 1 March 1943, celebrating the third anniversary of its founding (doc. no. 41).[35]

7. **The Special Unit** (*Sonderkommando*) occupied a position unusually independent from the O.S. in the ghetto. Its initial task consisted principally in confiscation, both independently, according to Rumkowski's instructions, and in cooperation with the German Criminal

Mordechai Chaim Rumkowski, chairman of the Jewish council in the Łódź Ghetto, in conversation with Hans Biebow, head of the Gettoverwaltung, the German ghetto administration, 1940– 1944. Photographer unknown. USHMM, courtesy of Al Moss.

Police (*Kripo*). The Special Unit also conducted political espionage ("political secret service") in the ghetto against opposition elements and had secret agents at its disposal (doc. no. 42).[36] Due to its constant contacts with the German police of all sorts, beginning in October 1942 it developed into a major power in the ghetto independent of Rumkowski. On 9 October 1942, through Biebow (the German custodian over the ghetto), the Special Unit was designated the highest control authority over the economy and food supply in the ghetto. Thus, for example, the ghetto bakeries came under its authority at the end of October 1942, and in 1944 it decided about such important matters as exemption from deportation, postal shipments, and so on.[37]

8. **The Brigade of Firefighters and Chimneysweeps** was subjected to the command of the O.S. from September 1941. In addition, there was a firefighters reserve of 230 men. During the various "actions" in the ghetto, the Firefighters and Chimneysweeps Brigade played the role of auxiliary police.[38]

9. **Ghetto Courts:** As mentioned above, until the formation of a court, the juridical department of the O.S. was the only judicial organ in the ghetto. Due to serious abuses that were uncovered, the department was reorganized by transferring its judicial competence to the newly formed court headed by a prominent attorney.[39] In June 1940, Rumkowski created the Ghetto Court and named ten judges. This court consisted (in July 1941) of three divisions: penal, civil, and prosecution.[40] On 16 March 1941, Rumkowski announced introduction of a summary judgment court (*shnelgerikht*), consisting of two judicial panels, each staffed by one judge and two associates (*bayzitsers*), named by Rumkowski. The summary courts judged without a prior investigation and without the participation of the accused or defenders (doc. no. 43).[41] These courts did operate swiftly and arrived at a substantial number of verdicts daily. Thus, for example, during the course of a couple of days (around 20 June 1941) summary courts sentenced seventeen persons to one to three months of hard labor, mainly for stealing in the workplace or falsifying ration coupons.[42]

Apparently this was too little for Rumkowski to halt the plague of "crimes" in the ghetto. For stealing four boards from the Paper Department, a carpenter received two months of severe imprisonment; for stealing a bottle of oil, one month, and so forth. Therefore, on 30 May 1941 he entrusted to one of his closest co-workers, the lawyer Henryk Neftalin (director of the Records Department), very broad competence as a sort of supreme investigative judge over employees and workers in the ghetto offices and factories. Rumkowski himself claimed the right to punish transgressors administratively on the basis of Neftalin's reports (doc. no. 44).[43]

On 1 July 1941, Rumkowksi dissolved the summary judgment court and himself took over its functions.[44] On 22 July, he directed the aforementioned special investigator to form a court for minors with a separate jailhouse in the prison (outside the general Central Prison). Such a court already functioned in August. In the same month, a sixteen-member board of guardians (*kuratorn-krayz*) was formed at this juvenile court.[45]

In the general court, in the first instance a single judge heard the case, while in the second instance (only in cases when the penalty exceeded 50 RM or two weeks arrest) there was a panel of three judges. In important cases, the court chairman could rule that three judges should hear the case in the first instance. Rumkowski had the power to grant amnesty for all penalties (doc. no. 45).[46] He carried out a partial amnesty in honor of Rosh Hashana and Hanuka in 1941,[47] as well as for Passover in 1943.

The penalties imposed by the summary judgment courts or by Rumkowski himself consisted primarily of being sentenced to forced labor. Those sentenced would not be put into prison but would have to perform unpaid labor for the ghetto nine hours daily for one to six months, receiving the food designated for arrestees. In the event of failure to report for work punctually or to perform it properly, the penalty was lengthened and the convict incarcerated in prison. Rumkowski, at the demand of the German authorities, required the judges to issue death sentences on serious criminals. When a number of judges and prosecutors refused to obey the order, they were dismissed and Rumkowski forbade giving them any employment. Thanks to their courageous stand, the issue of a death penalty was removed from the ghetto court's agenda.[48] It must be taken into account that lengthier prison sentences ultimately actually meant a death penalty, for the convicts were the first candidates to be sent to death during the deportations from the ghetto.

10. **The Ghetto Post Office** was established on 15 March 1940. In February, the municipal post office had halted regular delivery of correspondence and other postal items for Jews. Instead, the mail for Jews was delivered to the Jewish Communal Building, where it was sorted by street and building and the addressees themselves would pick it up. Later (May 1940), the delivery of mail to the ghetto was regulated by an agreement between Rumkowski and a representative of the German Post Office.[49]

In December 1940, the Ghetto Post Office employed a staff of 139, including 62 office workers, 50 letter carriers, and 27 messengers.

The postal communication between the ghetto and the outside world was continually disrupted by the German restrictions, which led in certain periods to a total postal embargo.

On 3 June 1940, receipt of food parcels from the city was halted and instead it was permitted to pay a certain sum into the bank account of the *Ernährung-und Wirtschaftsstelle—Getto* (Food Supply and Management Office—Ghetto) for which the addressee was to receive the equivalent in foodstuffs. Simultaneously, it was forbidden to export from the ghetto any objects whatever, aside from old clothing.[50]

On 12 July, Rumkowski announced that censorship had been introduced at the Ghetto Post Office, which would destroy correspondence and parcels that were in contradiction to regulations (doc. no. 46).[51]

Between 17 July and 16 September 1940, communication between the ghetto and the outside world was absolutely halted, with the exception of registered letters and telegrams. Postal communication was eventually renewed, although with a whole series of severe restrictions.[52]

Confiscation of food parcels that arrived by mail for the ghetto was a regular practice during the ghetto's entire existence. Rumkowski's motive was that there was an on-going speculative trade in products from the received parcels (doc. no. 47).[53] Postal service in the ghetto was also interrupted between 8 January and 8 March 1942, with the exception of money remittances, apparently in connection with the first deportation actions (16 January to 15 May 1942). When service was resumed, ghetto inhabitants were allowed to send only postcards with an established printed text.[54] Under such conditions, postal communication between the ghetto and the outside world continued until the end. Starting from 9 May 1944, the restrictions regarding letters were abolished and a couple of hundred surviving Jewish families from Prague were also permitted to pick up their parcels through the mediation of the Jewish Special Unit (*Sonderkommando*).

11. **The Records Department** (registration department, registry bureau, statistical division, records office) was created on 9 May 1940 in connection with the conclusion of the expulsion into the ghetto. There had already been a registration of men and women of working age due to the imposition of forced labor. Now, the entire population had to report to the Registry Bureau (*meldbyuro;* doc. no. 48). The registration of inhabitants was assigned to 100 designated building superintendents. To expedite the work, the house committees formed on the basis of Rumkowski's announcement of 26 March 1940 were also involved.

According to the ghetto census on 16 June 1940, there were 160,423 residents. The German authorities also required that the population be categorized by occupations. The final tabulation of the ghetto population according to age, gender, and occupation was ready on 15 July 1940. It was prepared at the Registry Bureau's **Statistical Office** (established on 4 June). Recording of the subsequent vital statistics records of the ghetto residents according to these rubrics was delegated to a specially designated **Statistical Department** in September 1940.

In time, the Statistical Department's activity came to embrace almost all the fields of the ghetto administration. The work was shared among a large number of specialists: for demography, employment, health, social work, food, judiciary, security, and so forth. The department also possessed a graphic and photographic laboratory. All the departments of the ghetto administration and work sites were obligated to submit reports and statistical data to it. The department's staff reached forty-four persons in May 1944. After the "resettlement" of Western European Jews into the ghetto, a certain number of intellectuals from Germany and Prague worked in the statistical department.[55]

The **Vital Statistics Office** (*tsivilamt*) was organized at the start of June 1940[56] and divided into four sections: births, marriages, deaths, and personal documents (the Germans initially gave their assent only for a section for deaths). Within the office, there was a panel of fifteen officially recognized rabbis. After the September 1942 deportation, the rabbinical panel was abolished and Rumkowski himself took over the function of performing marriage ceremonies. The German authorities systematically received monthly reports on deaths and births, which would be entered into the books of the municipal office of vital statistics.[57] In April 1941, the ghetto's Vital Statistics Department employed eighty persons.[58]

Jews in the Łódź Ghetto reading and posting announcements on the side of a building. Among those pictured is Nachman Zonabend, holding a briefcase, and Pinchas Szwarc (later Shaar) at the far right, 1941–1942. Photograph by Mendel Grosman. USHMM, courtesy of Instytut Pamięci Narodowej.

12. The **Archive** was created on 17 September 1940 to receive and preserve copies of all the outgoing correspondence (letters, circulars, notices, and so on) from all departments and in general to collect all materials related to the ghetto. The Archive's co-workers, among whom were also several deported intellectuals from Vienna and Prague, composed monographs and reportages on ghetto life. At the beginning of 1944, the co-workers of the Archive compiled an encyclopedia about the Łódź Ghetto, which was intended to provide exhaustive information about affairs and people there.

From 12 January 1941, the Archive issued, as mentioned, an internal information bulletin (daily, weekly and monthly) in Polish and German, which continued until July 1944 inclusive, under the titles *Biuletyn Kroniki Codziennej* (Bulletin of the Daily Chronicle) and *Tageschronik* (Daily Chronicle). These bulletins for the years 1941–1944 are among the most important sources for the history of the Łódź Ghetto.[59]

Group Two: Supply Branches

13. **The Provisioning Department** created in October 1939 expanded greatly in the ghetto. It employed 657 persons in July 1940; but in March 1941, it had grown to over 2,500 clerical and physical workers[60] and had been decentralized. Around the end of January 1941, the department was divided into four sub-departments: for bread and groceries, for vegetables, for milk and dairy products, and for meat. The central and most important sub-department was the first named, which was divided into a number of offices, such as shipping, distribution points, bakeries, and so forth.

After the reorganization of the distribution points on 18 May 1941, there was a network covering the entire area of the ghetto: forty-five bread and grocery shops, forty-five greengroceries, sixteen points for dairy products, and sixteen meat shops[61] (previously, there had been fifty-seven distribution points).[62] In addition, over the course of time four special dietetic food stores were opened for the sick and other privileged individuals, the so-called R/1, R/2, R/3, and R/4 (the first was opened 30 January 1941.)

The Provisioning Department also established a series of enterprises, like the sausage factory, the factory for wood (methyl) alcohol, for sugar products, and so forth.

14. **The Coal Department** (established 8 May 1940) was separated from the Provisioning Department on 1 January 1941 and dealt with the supply of coal and charcoal briquets, with the dismantling of derelict wooden buildings and other structures for fuel, and its distribution among the populace. When first established, this department employed 10 workers; in May 1942 it had 570, and in May 1943 there were 702 employees. By March 1944, the department had distributed 51 million kilograms of coal, 28 million kilograms of briquets, and 13.5 million kilograms of wood from dismantled wooden structures. (More details about the activity of separate branches of the provisioning organization in various periods of the ghetto are presented in chapter 3.)

Group Three: Economic-Financial Branch

15. **The Financial-Administrative Department** occupied a central and leading position. It was established in November 1940 from existing separate departments for finance and administration (the latter founded 1 May 1940).

The Finance Department had to see to raising the financial means for the ever-growing expenditures of the ghetto administration, as the Jewish Communal Treasury had already been emptied during the first month of the occupation. Rumkowski levied a new communal tax that the still well-to-do willingly paid, living under the constant fear of confiscation of money and goods by the German occupation authorities.

Private loans were also taken out, mainly from wholesale merchants and from bakers as advances against the expense of flour and other foodstuffs purchased.

Rent was also supposed to be a source of revenue. On 24 April 1940, the City Commissioner transferred to Rumkowski guardianship over all the real estate in the ghetto (starting from 1 April), with the right to collect rent, and he had to pay the appropriate taxes (doc. no. 49).[63] Revenue from rent was projected as 323,000 marks monthly. "But the result was negligible; a total of 220,844 marks [in rent] came in over 5 months, averaging out to 44,000 marks a month."[64] The clear reason was the great impoverishment of the ghetto population, incapable of paying any rent.

Another source of communal revenue could also have been the sums that Rumkowski was authorized by the Main Trusteeship Office East, Łódź Branch (*Hauptreuhandstelle-Ost, Nebenstelle Litzmannstadt*), to withdraw weekly from the blocked Jewish accounts in five Łódź banks.[65] But the banks raised major obstacles, as they did not want to recognize Rumkowski's general authorization and required in each individual case a direct instruction from the Trusteeship Office (*Treuhandstelle*) in Łódź, or from the appointed administrators of the relevant confiscated enterprises.[66] Moreover, the Trusteeship Office soon entirely withdrew the authorization from Rumkowski.[67] It held in March 1940 that "the Łódź Jews have abundant financial means at their disposal."[68]

As a result, the financial situation of the ghetto became catastrophic. Rumkowski's access to short-term credit was halted. He had used it to purchase foodstuffs obtained from German and Polish firms in the city through the intermediation of the Chamber of Commerce. Outright starvation threatened the ghetto. The difficult situation was in a certain measure eased thanks to the loan of two million RM that Rumkowski received from the German supervisory authority on 19 September 1940.[69]

The ghetto's financial situation began to improve with the expansion of the ghetto industry in 1941. In the autumn months of 1941, the item "work pay" for the goods produced in the ghetto amounted to over two million RM.[70]

A report about the activity of the Jewish Community in Łódź for the period from 1 January until 27 July 1940 shows a sum of 8,384,181.70 RM in expenditures and 8,361,307.93 RM in revenues (doc. no. 50).[71] It is worth noting that the prewar Jewish Communal budget in 1939 was projected at 1,566,491.76 złoty.[72] Even taking into account the rise in prices, the expenditures in the budget had sharply increased. The following statistics also testify about the growth of the Jewish communal finances: the total spending of the Łódź Jewish community for the month of November 1939 amounted to 181,500 RM, but reached 2,442,000 RM (in round numbers) in October 1940.[73]

The Finance Department also collected taxes and rent. Later, a separate **Department for Rent and Taxes** was established. Although the ghetto population was exempted from payment of municipal taxes on 1 August 1940,[74] there remained internal ghetto taxes, like the wage tax, income tax, and head tax. When wages were paid out, deductions were made not only for taxes, but for rent and fees for ration coupons. Rent was set on 6 January at 4 percent of salary, aside from the so-called luxury apartments (flats with gas or toilets), for which rent was reckoned at 150 percent of the prewar rate.

The wage tax was reckoned against salaries starting from 104 ghetto marks a month. The lowest wage tax was 1.30 marks a month, while the highest (on wages from 494 marks and higher) was 46.80 marks and more. The wage scale in January 1942 ranged between 84.50 and about 500 marks a month.[75]

The most important task of the **Management Department** (*Virtshaft-opteyl*) consisted of directing the management of buildings in the ghetto. Tenants' house committees themselves raised money for maintaining the buildings until November 1940. From then on, that task was transferred to the building administrators under the department's supervision. The building watchmen, who were mainly volunteers and until then received their meager salary from money collections among the tenants, also went onto Rumkowski's budget from November 1940.[76]

In the period from the establishment of the ghetto, the Management Department was also occupied with transferring communal property into the ghetto (the equipment of soup kitchens, orphanages, schools, shelters, and so forth).[77] On the other hand, the department delivered to German offices various factory equipment and tools, as well as goods from the factories and stores within the ghetto,[78] and exercised technical supervision over the industrial enterprises in the ghetto.[79]

Subsequently, the Management Department's functions expanded mightily. It saw both to the removal of waste from the ghetto, which was a difficult and responsible matter in view of the strict German guard and police harassment, and to arranging the leasing of vacant or cleared lots for cultivation (from April 1940).

16. **The Department for Animal Husbandry** was established on 1 January 1941 (from the former Department for Cattle Breeding) and took over supervision not only of the live communal inventory but also of privately owned animals. Beginning in July 1941, this department took over all the means of transport in the ghetto, which previously lay primarily in private hands. The department's name was changed to **Animal Husbandry and Transport Department.** All means of transport in the ghetto went into its possession. Its inventory steadily increased (383 peasant wagons and 37 oxen came into the ghetto in September 1941; on 1 January 1944, the department had at its disposal 143 horses). From the end of 1941 onward, it was officially called the **Transport Department.**[80] When limited passenger trolley service was permitted in the ghetto from May 1942, it operated this service.

17. **The Labor Office** (*Arbeitseinsatz*) regulated work in the ghetto (aside from the ghetto industry, which was assigned to a separate labor office; see below) and consisted of the following five desks (*referatn*): data (*evidents*), work outside the ghetto, public works, permanent employees, and employment service.[81]

18. **The Construction Department** (established 10 June 1940) performed construction and demolition work, including dismantling at official order certain buildings in the ghetto or at the border of the ghetto and clearing ruins, whose lumber was used for heating fuel and for construction purposes;[82] building of three bridges over the two "Aryan" streets that cut through the ghetto;[83] and construction of barracks for infectious patients[84] and for Jews deported from provincial towns and from Western Europe, at the transport station in Radogoszcz,[85] and so forth. On 12 June 1942, Construction Department II was established, whose task was executing rush construction projects at the demand of the authorities.

19. and 20. **Electricity and Gas Departments** regulated the consumption of electricity and gas in the ghetto. According to an agreement, concluded on 28 February 1940 between the German enterprise Electrizitätwerk, Łódź A.G. and a representative of Rumkowski, a branch of the electricity company was set up in the ghetto under its jurisdiction, but financed by the ghetto administration.[86]

View of Łódź Ghetto residents crossing the pedestrian bridge over Zgierska Street at Kościelny Square, circa 1941. Photographer unknown. USHMM, courtesy of Instytut Pamięci Narodowej.

The consumption of gas and electricity in the ghetto was very restricted. Use of electric cooking equipment was banned on 3 March 1941, along with light bulbs stronger than 15 watts per room.[87] Use of gas kitchens required a special permit. Initially, there were only a couple of gas kitchens in the ghetto, where one could cook for a fee of 30–50 pfennig an hour. They were constantly crowded.[88] On 15 June 1941, the administration took over operation of the gas kitchens at its expense, increased their number, and introduced a fixed tariff (40 pfennig to cook a liter of food). The Electricity Department, which was under the jurisdiction of the municipal electrical works, was to a large extent independent of Rumkowski's administration. This fact found expression during various deportation actions in the ghetto, when the department's workers were exempted as municipal employees.

Group Four: Purchasing (Confiscation)

Jewish property was initially de facto and later de jure[89]declared to be state property, and right from the start of the occupation there took place a systematic and often frenzied seizure of Jewish property. All sorts were after Jewish wealth: the Treuhandstelle in Łódź, the *Gettoverwaltung*, the Criminal Police, and every German official and soldier. The Łódź Treuhandstelle and the *Gettoverwaltung* subsequently came to an understanding about the matter in March 1942.[90]

Łódź Jews did what people do in such cases: they concealed whatever they could, however they could. Nevertheless, the German regime did not give up on its goal of extracting wealth from the Łódź Jews. Rumkowski also had to pay for the ghetto's food with valuable objects and goods, as well as with hard currency, which was extracted from the ghetto inhabitants in a variety of ways.

21. On 13 August 1940, Rumkowski announced the opening of a Purchasing Point (*aynkoyf-shtele*) for gold, silver, precious stones, furs, stocks, garments, and so forth, which would be appraised by reliable evaluators (doc. no. 51).[91] Even earlier, he announced the establishment on 4 August of a purchase point for old goods; on 29 August, for purchasing kitchenware.[92] There was also a special purchase point for down and feathers. On 17 December 1940, Rumkowski notified the ghetto population about the obligation to sell all sorts of furs and hides at his "bank" by 1 January 1941 (doc. no. 52).[93] On 6 January 1942, he announced the compulsory sale of mountain shoes and ski boots (doc. no. 53).[94]

When the deportations from the ghetto began, the purchase points bought up the home furnishings of the candidates for deportation, paying with worthless ghetto money (doc. no. 54).[95] An exception was the final deportation of June-August 1944, discussed in chapter 6 below.

Since the public was suspicious of the purchase points and refrained from selling to them, the Special Unit came to the purchase points' assistance by unvarnished confiscation of valuable items, raw materials, and goods. Appeals to the population to "sell" to the Special Unit valuable items and goods that were concealed both within and outside the ghetto were frequently repeated.[96]

Group Five: Ghetto Industry

On 5 April 1940, even before the sealing of the ghetto, Rumkowski turned to the city's mayor with a plan to create workshops in the ghetto, which would operate with raw materials provided by the German regime for German needs (doc. no. 55).[97] On 13 May, Rumkowski notified the mayor that he had registered 14,850 tailors and seamstresses and he requested an order as quickly as possible.[98] The following statistics demonstrate the huge growth of the tailoring industry and of the ghetto industry in general.

The first tailoring workshop in the ghetto opened on 20 April 1940 with approximately 300 tailors. At the end of 1940, there were nine tailoring shops operating in the ghetto, led by a tailoring center (*shnayder-tsentrale*). In December 1940, they employed over 5,600 tailors, and in January 1943 about 8,000 workers (in spite of the great deportations of 1942).[99]

The growth of the ghetto industry was a result both of Rumkowski's ideology of "rescue through labor" and the labor shortage that became ever more apparent in Germany and in the occupied territories. As already mentioned, there were 101 factories, workshops, and other work sites in operation in the Łódź Ghetto in the second half of 1942. At the end of 1943, the 117 factories, workshops, sorting sites, and warehouses employed 73,782 men and women, which then amounted to over 85 percent of the population (about 83,400 people).

22. **The Central Bureau of Labor Sites** (*Arbet-resortn*),[100] founded on 1 October 1940, managed the entire ghetto industry. The Central Bureau's most important desk (*referat*) was the **Trades and Control Desk.**

At the head of each workshop or factory stood a manager (*resort-layter*), who kept the records of the workers and his workshop. It was his obligation to provide periodic reports to the General Secretariat about the number of workers, salary disbursements, production figures, and so on.

The workshop and factory managers were mostly recruited from people who had initially served in the ghetto police and were assigned to the workshops as commissioners (*komisarn*) to maintain order and introduce strict work discipline. Instructors and so-called group leaders also belonged to the administration in the workshops and factories. The factory managers in the ghetto were a specially privileged caste, who externally differentiated themselves by wearing uniform caps inscribed with the letter W for *Wirtschaft* (management). (More precise information about the organization and production of the ghetto industry is provided in chapter 4.)

Group Six: School and Health Institutions

23. **School Department.** On 25 October 1939, the Łódź city-commissioner empowered Rumkowski to take over the Jewish elementary schools and support them by levying a tax on the Jewish population (doc. no. 56).[101] Even earlier, on 18 October, the city-commissioner had directed him to dismiss all Polish teachers, but to pay them their salary with an appropriate severance;[102] simultaneously, all Jewish teachers were eliminated from the general schools without any severance pay.

At the start of the 1939–1940 school year, Łódź had thirty-one elementary schools for Jewish children with 17,902 pupils, twelve *khedorim* (private religious primary schools) with 1,452 students, ten Jewish secondary schools with 1,861 pupils, and ten elementary schools affiliated with the secondary schools with 1,112 pupils. Of the thirty-one elementary schools, only eight had buildings located within the area of the future ghetto, while all the other school buildings were outside the ghetto.

In May 1940, the ghetto had thirty-five elementary schools with 6,263 pupils, two religious schools (283 pupils), one secondary school (728), and one vocational school (92)—with 7,336 pupils altogether (in comparison with 22,327 in September 1939). Over three-fourths (5,542) of the pupils were fed in the ghetto schools.

The school year began on 11 September 1939, but the Jewish school network was entirely disorganized and the number of pupils fell drastically as eight major school buildings (mainly the high schools) were requisitioned and teachers left the city, were arrested, or were seized for labor due to the insecure, often dangerous situation for Jews who appeared on the streets. In the 1939–1940 school year, Jewish children numbering 10,462 studied in the elementary schools, 633 in secondary schools, and 56 in the artisans school.[103] Attendance in the schools increased thanks to the additional food for school children, introduced on 30 November 1939. But the schools could not stabilize due to the constant changes in the situation of the Jewish population. Classes concluded in the schools on 15 December, and were only resumed after the end of the expulsion into the ghetto (early March). Classes met in two or even three shifts and were overcrowded (in the gymnasium 90 pupils in a class). Due to the major interruption in studies, the first school year was extended until September, and the vacation holidays fell during the Jewish holy days (doc. no. 57).[104]

In October 1939, a School Commission (later changed to a School Council), consisting of six members nominated by Rumkowski, began to function. The council's membership changed often as members left the city. In September 1941, the leadership of the School Department consisted of a chairman and two inspectors. Two school visitors would inspect the schools.

In August 1940, a "convalescence home" for children of school and pre-school age opened in Marysin. In the same month, day camps for children ages four to seven were also opened in Marysin; campers attended from 8:30 A.M. until 7 P.M.[105] Children numbering 6,178 attended the convalescence home in Marysin during the summer and autumn of 1940, while the day camps hosted 7,611 children.

The second and final ghetto school year began on 29 October 1941 with forty-five schools: forty elementary schools (including four religious schools and two for retarded and deaf-mute children), two pre-schools, two secondary schools (gymnasium and lycée), and one vocational school. Average total school attendance in January 1941 amounted to 14,944 pupils; the monthly average was 10,300 children.[106] On 19 January 1941, in connection with the reduction in the ghetto's area set for the start of February 1941, several schools were closed in order to provide housing for about 7,000 people from the two eliminated streets.[107] At Rumkowski's order, the two secondary schools and the vocational school were closed. The gymnasiums remained closed until May, while the lycée was closed during February and the vocational school until June 1941. They were transferred to Marysin and there continued with their work. The number of teachers in all types of schools in July 1941 was 482, including 295 women and 187 men.[108]

After a lengthy interruption, school meals were reinstituted in August 1941.

Under pressure from the German authorities, the second school year 1940–1941 broke with the former curriculum modeled on the program and spirit of the former Polish schools. At Rumkowski's initiative, a rich program of Jewish studies (Yiddish, Hebrew, Bible, Jewish history) was introduced, with Yiddish as the language of instruction. (In the first school year, the teachers still taught in the language to which they were accustomed.) The teaching staff, consisting mostly of former teachers in the Polish state elementary schools for Jewish children (319 out of 482), was not ready to teach in Yiddish (some knew no Yiddish at all) and it was necessary to set up teacher courses for Yiddish. On 15 May, the "Seminar for Yiddish Proficiency" opened in four groups and continued until 21 September 1941.[109]

School courses were also introduced into the institutions in Marysin (children's camp, orphanage, religious school). On 31 May 1941, there were 1,512 children there, including 1,261 of school age. From January until August 1941, the number of students in the schools rose from 452 to 1,250. As mentioned, two gymnasiums (together with the lycée classes) and the vocational school were transferred to Marysin and the students who resided in the ghetto had to travel two kilometers to get to school each day.

The children in Marysin were under systematic medical supervision. Generally, the children sent out to Marysin were weak and sickly.

The entire school system came to an end in October 1941, when the school buildings were turned into shelters for the nearly 20,000 Jews from Western Europe who began to arrive in the ghetto on 17 October. Even earlier, hundreds of children were taken away from the school bench for a variety of reasons and mobilized into the ghetto industry. Already in March 1941, a restructuring commission was established at the School Department to integrate youths ages fourteen to twenty-one into economic life. The vocational school and the one-year program of "Supplementary Courses for Young Artisans" served that purpose. This process particularly intensified in winter and spring 1942, during the ghetto's first period of "resettlement." In August 1942, almost all the ghetto workshops employed nearly 13,861 adolescents and even children, who composed about 20 percent of all those employed at the time.[110] At the end of July 1942, at the decree of the German authorities, Rumkowski ordered a stop to all sorts of lessons and discussions with children, which until then were still being carried on in the children's home in Marysin.[111]

In some sites, for example in the tailoring and hat factories, and in the electro-technical factory, the employed children and adolescents were in special courses studying some general subjects (Yiddish, arithmetic) in addition to vocational skills.[112] Other workshops (for example, underwear and clothing) founded their own day shelters for the small children of parents employed there. There were also elementary school studies for the children.[113] In general, children were taught clandestinely in many factories, even in an unorganized manner. This was done mainly by former teachers who had gone to work in the ghetto factories after the schools were closed.

24. **Health Department.** During the establishment of the ghetto, two Jewish hospitals, the Poznański Hospital (250–270 beds) and the maternity clinic,[114] found themselves outside its borders. Within the ghetto remained only the hospital for the insane.[115] The hospital buildings had to be abandoned and the equipment moved into the ghetto, to the extent that the German authorities had in the meantime not confiscated certain expensive medical devices. The Poznański Hospital finally moved on 25 April 1940.

In the same month, Rumkowski was given use of two non-Jewish hospitals located within the area of the ghetto: the North Hospital (Nord-Krankenhaus) and Saint Joseph Hospital. But the Jewish communal treasury had to cover the costs of remodeling[116] and pay for the supplies that were left behind there.[117] Rumkowski also made efforts to retrieve confiscated clinics (for example, the physiotherapy clinic)[118] and medicines from the confiscated and closed Jewish pharmacies, for which the German Apothecary Society (that had taken over the Jewish pharmacies) demanded to be paid a substantial sum (77,005 RM).[119]

The Health Department, whose leadership lay in the hands of two managers, one medical and one administrative, developed broad-branched preventive care and treatment programs. Initially, there were three hospitals: one each for infectious diseases, respiratory patients, and internal diseases. Due to the catastrophic growth of illness in the ghetto, both from the frequent epidemics and due to hunger, it was constantly necessary to expand the number of hospitals, outpatient clinics, and so forth. In March 1942, the ghetto had five hospitals, one maternity clinic, and a children's hospital in Marysin. In addition, there were five outpatient clinics, two preventive care clinics (*preventoryes*) for children, two first aid stations, one dental clinic, seven pharmacies, a disinfection facility, a milk point for preparing milk for small children, an institution to combat tuberculosis, an electro-medical facility, and a station for insulin treatment.[120] During the outbreak of the typhus epidemic, a quarantine center for 100 persons was set up in Marysin.

On 3 December 1940, all physicians, medics,[121] nurses, and midwives were mobilized to work. They were responsible to the representative of the Health Department, whose orders they had to carry out under penalty of losing the right to practice and up to three months imprisonment (doc. no. 58).[122] Rumkowski firmly suppressed a strike by hospital personnel that broke out on 1 December 1940 due to the extension of the workday to more than eight hours.[123]

All children born in 1939 were vaccinated against small pox in August 1940, while children born in 1940 were vaccinated in 1941 and 1942.[124]

Doctors were authorized to issue food coupons for patients, initially at their own discretion and from 6 July 1940 with a certification from the Health Department. For the coupons one received special food in the aforementioned dietetic stores. Until April 1941, nearly 2,000 food coupons were issued, while during all of 1941 there was a total of 2,585 coupons for children sick with tuberculosis.[125]

The following statistics testify to the activity of the hospitals, clinics, preventive care centers, first aid stations, and other branches of the Health Department in the ghetto. In May 1940, the ghetto hospitals had 227 beds at their disposal, while in March 1942, they had 2,100; during the months August–December 1940, the five ghetto hospitals admitted 4,297 new patients, while during the entire year of 1941 they admitted 11,981 patients. In 1942, the hospital for infectious diseases alone admitted 7,301 patients, while in 1943 only 3,746. In the outpatient clinics, from June–December 1940, there were 122,841 visits by patients to the clinics and 48,568 housecalls; in 1941, these statistics were 242,249 and 65,390; while in the months January–June 1942, they were 125,028 and 26,692, respectively. In the children's clinic in Marysin, during the course of 1941 there were 29,143 patient visits and 3,555 housecalls to sick children. The first aid station handled 10,505 cases during June–December 1940, rising to 21,040 cases in 1941; while in the first half of 1942, the first aid station handled 7,272 cases.[126]

There were about 170 doctors working in the ghetto hospitals and clinics. In May 1941, Rumkowski brought a group of twelve doctors from Warsaw, while a larger number of physicians, including the famous cancer researcher Wilhelm Caspari, arrived with the transports of Western European Jews in October–November 1941. The community employed all the doctors, who received a monthly salary. A minimal fee for housecalls to the sick was set, although many doctors did not observe it.

Through an intensive campaign of disinfection and quarantine, the Health Department did all that was in its limited abilities to combat in an effective and decent way the spread of the spotted fever and typhus epidemics in the years 1941 and 1942.[127]

The department's budget totaled 575,157.94 marks during the first seven months of 1941. Y. Tabaksblat writes about the work of the Health Department:

> The number alone actually says nothing, but if one takes into account that the patients were much better nourished than everybody else in the ghetto, even better than some of the higher officials in the ghetto, then it will give an idea of what the budget meant. In the first two years, when the "autonomy" blossomed, the hospitals were provided with all possible medical means that the city had, and the patients lacked nothing. In the later years it became much worse.[128]

The hospital system was wrecked in the first two days of the September Action (1–2 September 1942). All patients capable of being transported were loaded onto trucks and taken to destruction. Seriously ill patients, who could not be removed from their beds, were shot on the spot. Three hospital buildings were turned into workshops. The children's hospital in Marysin was also liquidated and the children were shipped out of the ghetto to their tragic fate. There remained only two hospitals for internal and respiratory diseases and two clinics. The activity of the Health Department shrank sharply. After September 1942, only healthy and young people capable of working were in principle allowed to be in the ghetto. A graphic outline of the ghetto's organizational structure in August 1943 does not note any hospitals at all, only a hygiene department for the factories and three bath and disinfection facilities.

Group Seven: Social Welfare

This group embraced ten departments of various branches of public welfare, such as the monetary dole (untershtitsung), homes for infants, orphan care, daycare, homes for the elderly, shelters for the homeless, for refugees, for solitary and forlorn people and for the disabled, summer camps and day camps, and so forth.

25. **The Department for Social Aid** existed from 15 October 1939 until 27 September 1940. It was the Jewish Community's first department to resume operation and the most urgently needed. In November 1939, the department was reorganized and took over two existing public soup kitchens, which issued an average of 500 dinners daily over the

course of the month. The number of those benefiting from the public kitchens grew constantly and in September 1940 reached its zenith, an average of 18,060 daily. For the entire period from November 1939 until September 1940, the daily average was 7,825 dinners daily; that is, about 5 percent of the population had to resort to the soup kitchen dinners. This department also provided aid in cash and in raw products. The money grants for various categories of the needy ranged between five and six złoty. During the entire period of its existence, the department disbursed grants in cash (also for rent) and in kind totaling 343,682.52 marks to 52,058 persons.

This department's activity evoked sharp criticism against it at the time. The soups were so bad that people would spill them out on the spot and only take the 200 grams of bread. The arrangements in the kitchens were unpleasant. "Moreover, there was no system of rational support in the cash grants, but there were privileged individuals to whom 30 zł and more is given, and common people for whom the average amounted to five and six zł" (doc. no. 59).[129]

On 22 July 1940, the just-established Central Control Office (*tsentrale kontrol-shtele*) commenced its supervision over the operation of the Department for Social Aid. As a result, on 4 September searches were carried out among all the employees and officials and several were arrested. The department was put under direct management by the Control Commission and formally ceased to exist on 27 September.[130]

26. **The Welfare Department** (*untershtitsung-opteyl*) was formed on 21 September 1940, after a severe food and financial crisis in the ghetto that caused stormy hunger demonstrations.[131] On the basis of a two-million-mark loan that Rumkowski obtained from the German authorities, the Welfare Department began to distribute financial grants for indigent families according to the following pattern: adults received 9 marks monthly, children up to fourteen years of age 7 marks, and the elderly over sixty years of age 10 marks, while those eighty and older received 20 marks. Recipients were required to undertake any paying job to which they would be assigned (doc. no. 60).[132]

A relief commission (*untershtitsung-komisye*) was formed, consisting of eight members. To it were co-opted another four persons as representatives of social groupings. The ghetto was divided into twenty-seven regions and each relief applicant had to submit a form with the regional manager.[133]

The first relief campaign from September until 20 October 1940 embraced 124,773 persons (79 percent of the population) with a total sum of 1,077,176 marks. The twelfth relief campaign, in September 1941, included only 58,000 recipients (48 percent of the ghetto population) with a total of 535,165 marks (doc. no. 61).[134] On 17 January 1941, the relief amount was increased: for adults to 10 marks and for the elderly from 12 to 16 marks according to three levels of seniority: over sixty, over seventy, and eighty and older.

In July 1941, the relief amounts were again increased. Children up to fourteen years old received 12 marks monthly (instead of 7); adults ages fifteen to sixty-five collected 15 marks (instead of 10); those ages sixty-one to seventy received 17 marks (instead of 12); and those seventy-one and older, 20 marks (instead of 16).

But from 1 September 1941, Rumkowski reintroduced the former lower norms with the motive that the recipients were evading the obligation of fourteen days unpaid work per month. During the winter months of 1941–42, the relief sum for both adults and children was equalized at 12 marks a month.[135]

The decline in the number of those entitled to relief is explained by the fact that with time certain categories of the gainfully employed were deprived of the right to benefit from relief. At first, the relief sum for each self-supporting wage earner was reduced 15 marks, and from 1 April by 10 and 5 marks from the sum of each employed family member. Whoever earned only up to 15 marks (family members up to 5 marks) a month received the full relief sum. From 1 July 1941, the families of untenured (*nisht-etatirte*) employees in the ghetto administration, as well as workers in the ghetto factories, lost the right to relief. From that date, the tenured (*etatirte*) employees and workers received the so-called "family supplements" according to the number of family members. From 1 September, independent craftsmen were also excluded from relief.[136] In addition, the obligation of unpaid heavy physical labor (although the announcement about the relief system mentioned payment) scared off a lot of people who waived the benefit. By September 1941, the relief department paid out a total of about 10.4 million marks.

27. **Orphans' Care:** Until the war's outbreak, the Łódź Jewish community had possessed six institutions for orphans (among them a large orphanage in Helenówek outside Łódź, and a home for infants founded and managed by TOZ).[137] On 12 March 1940, two orphanages were transferred into a single building within the ghetto. Another orphanage was also transferred subsequently. Due to the war, the number of children in the orphanages grew substantially.

An orphanage was set up in Marysin in July 1940 with 366 children, increasing to 391. A separate small building was devoted to sixty religious boys. At the start of February 1941, by order of the German authorities, it was necessary to evacuate the Marysin orphanage and transfer the home into another building near the ghetto's center. (The secondary school, vocational school, and the home for infants were also transferred there from Marysin.) In time, two small buildings were added. The food supply in the orphanages was always much better than the average nourishment of the ghetto population. Thus, the children would get meat, a rare article in the ghetto, three times a week. Also, the factories would supply the orphanage with all needed goods, like underwear, clothing, and shoes. Without doubt, Rumkowski's prewar social work in this field and his sentiment for children in general and orphans in particular were decisive here.[138]

28. **The Home for the Aged** maintained by the Jewish community also had to move into the ghetto on 19 April 1940. In December 1941, after the deportation of nearly 23,000 Jews into the Łódź Ghetto, a second home for the elderly was founded, in order to admit the older folk among the new arrivals. People ages sixty-five and older comprised 14 percent of all the deportees.[139] The institution consisted of four buildings with about 100 rooms. Until July 1942, there passed through this home for the elderly 1,178 men and women. During the May 1942 "outsettlement," 395 of them were deported, while 340 had died in the meantime. In all, in July there remained 277 old folk in the home.[140]

Establishment of a **summer camp** for children ages four to seven, as well as children of school age, was announced on 21 June 1940. The summer camp was located in Marysin, and in September 1940 numbered about 1,050 children. In May 1941, there were 1,213 children who enjoyed the Marysin camp, rising by the end of July to 1,573, of whom 62.4 percent had lost one or both parents.

On 31 July 1941, the camp employed thirty-three instructors (*lerers*), forty-three educators (*dertsiyers*), including nineteen prewar teachers and educators, and fifty-five technical personnel. Medical staff for the clinic and children's hospital included three doctors, ten nurses and hygienists, and thirteen trainee nurses (*praktikantkes*). Altogether, the summer camp employed 217 persons. The number of beds in the children's hospital ranged between eighteen (in February) and thirty-six (in May 1941). During the year from September 1940 until September 1941, operation of the Marysin camp with all its facilities cost 562,269 marks.[141]

The decline of the Marysin camp began during the first phase of the deportations in winter 1942, when some of the children left with their parents, and older children were gradually incorporated into the ghetto industry as protection against "outsettlement." The final liquidation of the summer camp took place in September 1942 during the action against the elderly, the sick, and children. Workshops were set up in the deserted buildings.

30. Aside from the **convalescent home** (*erholungs-heym*), during the summers of 1940 and 1941 there also existed so-called **daycamps** (or half-camps) for children ages four to seven. The first was announced on 21 June 1940, and others on 30 July (doc. no. 62).[142]

31. Also under the supervision of this branch of the ghetto administration was a **home for solitary** (*elnte*) **people and for cripples.**

32. Separated in a certain measure from the general ghetto administration was the so-called Marysin Board (*Forshtand Maryshin*), that autonomously managed a certain number of economic enterprises and institutions in that ghetto quarter and was formed as an independent unit on 15 June 1941. Initially, its director was the commandant of the ghetto prison. After he was deported in March 1942, a collective management of six persons was formed. In October 1942, the autonomy of Marysin was liquidated and the institutions were subjected to the general administration.[143]

33. Noteworthy was the so-called **Scientific Department,** which actually had no relation to the ghetto and fulfilled (earlier in the city, later within the ghetto) a typically Nazi order (*bashtelung*) for "cultural" and propaganda purposes. When a treasure trove of sacred works, ritual objects, and artworks was assembled from among the confiscated Jewish property, the *Gettoverwaltung* set to establishing a permanent museum. Placed at the head of this undertaking was a teacher and modern rabbi (*rabbiner*) from Danzig, who moved to Łódź and resided in the city even after the establishment of the ghetto. In May 1942, Rumkowski received an order to found a "scientific department," at whose head the aforementioned rabbi was placed.[144]

The department, which employed twenty-two persons (among them two painters, two graphic artists, and eighteen skilled women, the majority from Germany), constructed figures of Eastern Jewish types and scenes of Jewish customary ways, such as "Hasidic Wedding in Poland," "Sabbath Eve in a Shtetl in Volhynia," "Candle Lighting in a Jewish Home," among others. Also displayed were works with Jewish motifs by Łódź Jewish painters. This all occupied five rooms in a building at the Bałuty Marketplace. The figures and scenes, in accord with the goal for which they were created, were actually grotesque caricatures of Jewish life.

Due to lack of material, the work in subsequent years was extremely limited and the number of workers reduced to six (including the director). The work still continued in January 1944 and this "artistic" production still filled the "halls" of the scientific department.[145]

Documents 26–64

No. 26.[146] YI-1201

The Łódź City Commissioner on 13 October 1939 names Mordechai Chaim Rumkowski the "Eldest of the Jews in Łódź." [in German]

IDENTIFICATION CARD
The Eldest of the Jews in the City of Łódź

RUMKOWSKI has been given the commission to enforce measures of the German civil administration of the City of Łódź that apply to all members of the Jewish race.

He is personally responsible to me for this.

For the execution of these tasks, he has permission

1. to move about on the street freely at all times of day and night;
2. to access the offices of the German administration;
3. to enlist a circle of coworkers /Aeltestenrat/ and to hold meetings with it;
4. to announce by wall posters the measures he has taken;
5. to supervise the Jewish deployment of labor.

Each member of the Jewish race is unconditionally obligated to follow all directives of the Eldest RUMKOWSKI. Resistance offered against him will be punished by me.

[signed] Leister
City Commissioner

No. 27. YI-1202

City Commissioner's Ordinance of 14 October 1939 addressed to Rumkowski to dissolve all institutions and administrative organs of the Jewish Community. [in German]

For the carrying out of the written commission granted to you on the 13th of this month, according to which you are personally responsible to me for all measures to be carried out, I order that:

All existing institutions of the Israelite Religious Community of Łódź are placed under you or officials named by you.

Heretofore existing boards, councils, councilors, or similar so-called administrative offices are to be dissolved, their offices to be dissolved and to be reconstituted by you in sole responsibility.

Persons of your community who evade such tasks are to be reported to me. I will immediately place them in custody.

You have the right to levy a fee to cover all costs arising in the execution of the measures imposed on you.

[signed] Leister
City Commissioner

No. 28.

Rumkowski's letter to the Sicherheitsdienst in Łódź, 5 February 1940, concerning the second Beirat.[147] [in German]

For the members of the new Jewish Council of Elders [*Aeltestenrat*] in the city of Łódź appearing on the enclosed list, I hereby respectfully request that "Passes be issued so that they can walk the streets of Łódź City (including Adolf Hitler Street), even after the curfew hour and so that they will not be conscripted into any other work." These passes are essential in order to be able to comply punctually with the tasks demanded by the authorities, whereby I would like to note expressly that these gentlemen must work for the community during the day and the meetings can take place only in the evenings. These conferences must take place in order to allocate the jobs in the Jewish community in an orderly fashion and to supervise the work of the staff.

I would also not want to leave unmentioned that meetings can only occur in the evening for the reason that the members of the Aeltestenrat will then not be pestered by the many petitioners.

No. 29. YI-1204

The Łódź Mayor's authorization of 30 April 1940 for Rumkowski to organize life in the ghetto. [in German]

On the basis of the police-president's ordinance of 8.4.1940, leaving the ghetto is forbidden to all residents from 30 April 1940. I hold you responsible for the strict enforcement of this prohibition.

Furthermore, on the basis of the authorization granted to me by the *Regierungspräsident* on 27 April 1940, I task you with carrying out all measures that are necessary and will be necessary for the maintenance of an orderly social life in the Jews' residential area. In particular, you have to secure the order of economic life, nutrition, labor deployment, public health, and welfare. You are thereby entitled to undertake all necessary measures and directives and to enforce these with help of the Order Service placed under you.

I authorize you immediately to set up registry offices in which all of the inhabitants of the ghetto are to be compiled in lists. Religious and ethnic affiliation must also be shown in this list. Carbon copies of this list are to be submitted to me weekly in five sets—starting from 13 May 1940.

All dealings with the German authorities take place only and solely through you, or a deputy yet to be nominated to me by you, in the administration office that is going to be set up on Bałuty Marketplace. The admission of further representatives is to be proposed in advance from case to case.

To secure the nourishment of the ghetto's population, you are authorized to confiscate all the collected stockpiles and to see to distribution.

Since all Jewish property is considered confiscated according to the Reich's legal regulation, you are to list and secure all the Jews' assets insofar as they do not belong to direct vital necessity (e.g., for clothing, nourishment, and housing).

You are further authorized to engage all Jews for unpaid labor duty.

All measures of a fundamental nature require my prior written consent. If measures that cannot be postponed are concerned and must be undertaken to avert an immediately impending threat, my consent is to be sought immediately by telephone or in writing according to the regulation.

The powers of the police-president of Litzmannstadt remain uninfringed by this regulation.

No. 30. YI-54A

On 17 January 1941, Rumkowski nominates as his deputy Dr. Leon Szykier, the medical director of the Health Department. [in German]

Circular to all departments.

I hereby announce that I have named the chairman of my Health Department, *Dr. Leon Szykier, Hohensteinstr. 11*, as my deputy.

No. 31. YI-18

Rumkowski dismisses Dr. Leon Szykier from his office on 12 June 1941.[148]
[in Yiddish]

DR. LEON SZYKIER REMOVED FROM OFFICE AS THE CHAIRMAN'S DEPUTY.

On the basis of a special written notice by Chairman Rumkowski of 12 June 1941, Dr. Leon Szykier was removed from his office as the Chairman's deputy.

No. 32. YI-18

Rumkowski nominates his two deputies, September 1941. [in Yiddish]

THE CHAIRMAN'S DEPUTIES.

Chairman Rumkowski has named these gentlemen as his deputies: Leon Rozenblat, head of the Order Service, and Aaron Jakubowicz, director of the Labor Divisions [*arbets-resortn*].

(Geto-tsaytung, *no. 17, 14 September 1941*)

No. 33.

Letter from the Chief of the Civil Administration at the German Army Field Command [Armeeoberkommando] to the Łódź Rabbinate, 13 October 1939, concerning delivery of 600 Jews daily for forced labor. [in German]

From 15 October 1939, you have to make available to the Labor Deployment [*Arbeitseinsatz*] 600 workmen daily, for the time being, at 7:30 A.M., namely 150 men each to the following indicated four assembly points. The work time is set as follows:

>from 7:30 A.M. to 12 noon and
>from 2 P.M. to 5 P.M.
>List of Assembly Points:
>1. Suwalskastrasse no. 6
>2. Południowastrasse no. 10
>3. Lipowastrasse no. 31
>4. Zgierskastrasse no. 17

(*Eisenbach,* Dokumenty, *vol. 3,* Getto Łódzkie, *19*)

No. 34: YI-630

Internal memorandum concerning forced labor in 1939/1940 [no date]. [in Polish]

[p. 6 of original]

While initially several hundred persons sufficed, not speaking of those who were regardless of this seized on the streets for labor etc., in a short time the demand for laborers constantly rose and soon reached 3,000 persons daily. Not many of those summoned reported for work, and it was therefore necessary to keep ca. 1,000–12,000 [*sic*] persons constantly in readiness, in order not to come into collision with the Authorities. It was simultaneously necessary to reorganize the method of call-ups.

A new office was formed at Cegielnana 17, named *Arbeitseinsatz* II, in contrast with the first, whose task was supplying the required quantity of laborers. At the head of this bureau stood Mr. Zygmunt Reingold, who set to the matter with his characteristic scrupulousness.

Immediately after taking office, he sent out summonses to landlords and building administrators, this time demanding compilation of lists of Jews of both genders ages eighteen to sixty, according to individual precincts. On the basis of these lists, in the first half of December 1939 a card index was compiled of all Jews residing on the territory of Łódź.
[p. 7]

It was apparent that not all those summoned were reporting to work, some fearing to leave home, others due to incapacity; and consequently it was difficult to foresee in advance what quantity of laborers the bureau of summonses would have at its disposal the next day. Nevertheless, not to supply the required quantity of workers was impermissible. It was thus necessary to sanction the institution of official substitutes, who would be paid from the revenues for the non-appearance of those summoned. In the middle of December 1939, the community registered about 1,000 such substitutes who received one-day and seven-day labor coupons, and later the so-called labor card [*Arbeitskarte*]. On these coupons, the "employer" entered a notation about the work done. For substitute labor, the community paid men 1.70 marks each, while paying women 1.25 marks each daily.

However, even though the internal operation of the labor deployment offices [*Arbeitseinsatzów*] became normalized and consolidated in a certain measure, the demand for laborers on the part of the authorities continued to arrive in a chaotic fashion, not even to mention that seizures on the streets and extraction from homes did not stop in the least. Independent of this, soldiers and representatives of other formations turned up at the community. Not caring that the workers in the community's courtyard had already been designated for a particular job, the soldiers and officials assembled them and took them to work for them. By this they introduced chaos and disorganization. This matter had to be regulated and here Atty. Henryk Neftalin deserves mention. From December 1939, he occupied a higher position in the Department of Labor Conscription [*w Wydziale Powołań do pracy*].
[p. 8]

As a result of Atty. Neftalin's intervention, a regulation also appeared from the Commissioner of the City of Łódź on 27 December 1939, with the following content:

Announcement [in German]

To channel the demand for Jewish laborers in regular paths, the following is ordered:

> Jewish laborers are in future to be claimed only at the municipal Welfare Office, Zawadska Street 11. The Welfare Office forwards the notice to the Eldest of the Jews, who is responsible for the provision of workers.
>
> *The Commissioner of Łódź City.*

And thanks to this, daily at 5 P.M., the community received a list of sites to which workers were to be directed the next day.

There were about 100 sites (see the Welfare Office's requisition) to which groups of laborers were directed. The biggest customer for laborers was the Gestapo, at ul. Anstadta 7, which daily submitted a requisition for 1,000 persons for hard labor.

[p. 9]

As is apparent from the statistical data preserved in the Archive, a small percentage of those summoned reported to work. Now it arises from the daily reports of Mr. Reingold, then director of the Department of Summonses [*Arbeitseinsatz*][149] no. 2, that in the period from 15 December 1939 to 5 January 1940 combined: "Of 30,068 persons summoned for work, ca. 35 percent or 10,590 persons paid a substitute to work; ca. 15 percent or 4,492 persons were directed to work; ca. 15 percent or 4,584 persons lodged an appeal; ca. 35 percent or 10,402 persons did not report."

Consecutive reports for the subsequent period are lacking, although from the eighty-six daily reports for the period from 22 January–10 May 1940, which are in the Archive, it arises that during eighty-six of the reported days:

[p. 9a]

184,686 persons were summoned to work, for a daily average of 2,148 persons—100 percent

71,496 persons did not report, for a daily average of 831 persons—38.9 percent

16,995 persons paid for a work substitute, for a daily average of 198 persons—9.2 percent

31,529 persons were directed to work, for a daily average of 367 persons—16.9 percent

64,666 persons submitted an appeal, were exempted and left Łódź, for a daily average of 752 persons—35 percent

and the average revenue from the nonappearance of those summoned amounted to 684 marks.

. . .

[p. 12]

In fact, the authorities continued to seize Jews for labor at the end of April and even after the ghetto's closure, but in such cases Chairman Rumkowski effectively intervened, pointing to how this behavior by the authorities was in contradiction with their guideline. In this manner, the matter of sending [laborers] to work in the city was liquidated; the *Arbeitseinsatz* was wound up and in its place arose the Department of Labor, which was directed from 1 July 1940 by Engineer Waldman.

. . .

No. 35. YI-1207

List of departments and workshops of the ghetto administration.[150] [in German]

LIST OF DEPARTMENTS

Group I
1. Secretariat and Information Dept.
2. Secretariat, Dworska 1
3. Secretariat, Bałuty Marketplace
4. Personnel Dept.
5. Central Cashier
6. H.K.K. [Supreme Control Chamber]
7. Central Bookkeeping
8. Order Service
9. Special Unit [*Sonder-Abt.*]
10. Firefighting
11. Court
12. Postal Dept.
13. Registry Bureau [*Meldebüro*]
14. Statistical Office
15. Registry Office [*Standesamt*]
16. Archive
17. Rabbinate
18. Burial Dept.
19. Control Commission

Group II
1. Vegetable Dept.
2. Grocery Dept. [*Kolonialabt.*]
3. Dairy Products Dept.
4. Bread Dept.
5. Meat Dept.
6. Sausage Dept.
7. Coal Dept.
8. Kitchens Dept.
9. Smoked Goods Dept.
10. Bakeries

Group III
1. Finance and Management Dept.
2. Labor Deployment [*Arbeitseinsatz*]
3. Construction Dept.
4. Metal Dept.
5. Gas Dept.
6. Electricity Plant
7. Bank, Marynarska 71
8. Cattle Husbandry

Group IV
1. Central Purchasing Office
2. Purchase of Old Goods
3. Purchase of Kitchen Utensils
4. Down and Feathers
5. Bank of Purchase [*Bank-Einkauf*]

Group V
1. Tailoring Dept.
2. Quilts Dept.
3. Felt Slippers Dept.
4. Shoe Dept.
5. Rag Slippers I
6. Rag Slippers II
7. Furrier Dept.
8. Upholstery Dept. [*Tapezier-Abt.*]
9. Tricot Dept.
10. Linens Dept. [*Wäsche-Abt.*]
11. Knitting Factory
12. Hat Dept.
13. Rubber Coat Dept.
14. Gloves and Stockings
15. Furniture Dept.
16. Tannery Dept.
17. Rubber Factory
18. Textile Factory
19. Central Office of the Labor Divisions, Bałuty Marketplace

Group VI
1. Health Dept.
2. School Dept.

Group VII
1. Welfare Dept. [*Unterstützungs-Abteilung*]
2. Individual Aid Grants
3. Orphanage
4. Infants Home
5. Children's Home
6. Rest Home
7. Summer Camp
8. Home for the Elderly
9. Home for Cripples [*Krüppelheim*]
10. Collection Point

No. 36. YI-130

Announcement no. 71 of 24 June 1940, concerning introduction of the ghetto money (Mark-Quittungen). [in German]

In execution of my Announcement no. 70 regarding means of payment within the ghetto, I hereby announce that my Provisions Department, food shops, meat shops, pharmacies, clinics, hospitals, tax and rent payment offices, as well as all other departments subject to me *will from Friday, 28 June 1940, not accept any German Reichsmarks, but only the mark receipts [Mark-Quittungen] issued by me.*

Consequently, it is necessary that the population in the ghetto promptly and as of now provide themselves with my mark receipts, so as to be in a position to be able to supply themselves with the needed foodstuffs, medicines, and so forth.

I therefore ask the population in the ghetto in its own interest immediately to commence the exchange of Reichsmark notes, Reichsmark coins, as well as 1 złoty coins *in my bank at Kelmstrasse 71, as well as in the bank branch at Alexanderhofsstrasse 56.*

No. 37. YI-208

Announcement no. 158 of 6 November 1940, concerning the formation of a Supreme Control Office. [in Yiddish]

Since I have determined that abuses are being committed, concern for the welfare of all residents in the ghetto has moved me to create a *Supreme Control Office [hekhster kontrol-amt]* with the duty to fundamentally annihilate all abuses and to prevent such from occurring in the future. I have entrusted the broadest powers to the Supreme Control Office:

a) supervision over the activity of all departments;
b) supervision over all manifestations of collective life of the population in the ghetto.

In order to fulfill these tasks, the S.C.O. has the right to penetrate into the administrative and financial activity of the community at large and of each individual resident.

Where it will be necessary, the S.C.O. has the right:

a) to remove officials immediately from their posts, regardless of which posts they occupy;
b) to conduct searches in offices and in private homes; to carry out personal searches and make provisional arrests until my decision or the decision of the court.

The Supreme Control Office will operate in accord with the court in the ghetto.

The successful and positive activity of the S.C.O. depends to a certain measure on the cooperation of all the residents of the ghetto.

Therefore, I call upon the entire population *to assist the S.C.O.* as the highest jurisdiction that has been named by me *to root out all abuses* and to uproot all harmful elements from public life.

All accusations must be turned in personally at the bureau of the Supreme Control Office, Plac Kościelny 4, from 9 to 12 noon daily.

No. 38. YI-609

Rumkowski's circular of 16 August 1942, concerning naming new members to the Supreme Control Office.[151] [in German]

I hereby announce that I have undertaken a recasting of the members of the Supreme Control Office with immediate effect.

All heretofore members are hereby removed from the Supreme Control Office and the following persons are named to be members of the Supreme Control Office: Eng. B. Kopel, L. Neumann, M. Rosenblat, Dir. Josef Rumkowski, secretary: Szaja Pachter.

As chairman of the Supreme Control Office, I have named Dir. Josef Rumkowski.

As you know, the Supreme Control Office has among others the task of checking whether all issued instructions were followed and is independently entitled, upon confirmation of any abuses, to institute dismissals and to arrange for arrests when needed.

No. 39. YI-615

Rumkowski's circular of 1 November 1942, concerning dissolution of the Supreme Control Office. [in German]

Circular
To All Departments, Workshops, and Factories.
Re: Dissolution of the Supreme Control Office.
I hereby announce that the Supreme Control Office is *dissolved* with immediate effect.

No. 40. YI-150a

Announcement no. 30 of 1 May 1940, concerning the Order Service. [in German]

On the basis of the authority entrusted to me, I have established an Order Service Guard for the protection of the Jewish population and for the maintenance of calm and order.

I call on all Jews in the Jewish residential area /Ghetto/ to be strictly obedient to the men of the Order Service and to obey their commands unconditionally. Acts of resistance and contravention will be punished.

Simultaneously, I hereby call on all Order Servicemen for strict discipline and expect that each Order Serviceman will behave calmly and politely toward the public.

No. 41. YI-788

Order of the day of the commandant of the Order Service, 1 March 1943. [in German]

ORDER OF THE DAY NO. 8

For the third time comes the anniversary of the day on which, at the direction of the Eldest of the Jews, I summoned the Order Service into being.

My thoughts extend back over the past three years. In the course of three years of existence the O.S. has developed from its initial form, conditioned by specific circumstances, into an organization suitably perfected for its tasks and duties.

I recall the initial foundation stage, when on 25 February 1940 I was appointed by the Eldest of the Jews to organize the Order Service. In the course of two days, the framework of the Order Service came into being and began its activity from 1 March 1940.

Out of the gravity of the time grew the enormous tasks with which the O.S. had to cope. Its development shows that our range of functions extends far beyond the framework of a normal police force. The ghetto's erection and development brought with them problems of immense significance. When the Order Service manages to overcome these problems, it demonstrates the colossal, selfless effort of each individual, the really determined conduct and the sympathetic mutual effort of my co-workers.

Right from the start of the ghetto, there was only one slogan: totally dedicated devotion to service. Thus, it was possible for us, through our public spirit and through our helpfulness, to alleviate the harsh fate of our brothers and sisters, who had become homeless in the city. Often for up to forty-eight hours without a break, the Order Service aided in the accommodation of those evacuated from the city.

[p. 2]

Here it was valuable to lend a hand in order to transfer the sick and frail, as well as small children with their luggage. The Order Serviceman jumped in everywhere, giving his utmost for the people in need of assistance.

In proper realization of the organizational structure of the O.S. necessary to maintain calm and order in the ghetto, in 1940 I established five precincts, whose seats I designated appropriate to the territorial needs. Moreover, an investigation department was created, which comprised the sole legal tribunal until the establishment of the court. Specialized functions came into the Order Service with subsequently instituted departments like *Hiod* [?], O.S. Board [*O.D.-Vorstand*], Price Surveillance, and Sanitation Office, as well as the Flying Squad [*Ueberfallkommando*].

To the first year's range of activity also belonged, among others, the fight against smuggling, escorting wagons of provisions, maintenance of calm in general and in particular in the lines in front of the cooperatives and kitchens.

The practical police deployment of the O.S. men who had been torn from their civilian occupations demanded of them total discipline and appreciation of a necessary subordination and domination for disciplined exercise of duty. With the help of my co-workers, I could also see that proper discipline was accepted in the ranks of the O.S., by which the necessary authority and due respect were externally won among the ghetto population.

In the second service year, 1941–42, we had to reinforce our efforts. The care and accommodation of 23,000 new arrivals brought the Order Service an abundance of tasks, which could be mastered thanks to the entire concentration of our forces.
[p. 3]
In spite of the most difficult circumstances, we still managed to secure lodgings for our sisters and brothers. Without any personal consideration, the Order Serviceman applied himself rain or shine, by day and night, and thereby earned universal recognition. If the settlement of new arrivals [*Einsiedlung*] demanded the full effort of each individual, then the outsettlements [*Aussiedlungen*] of many thousands of people that took place in this year required further increase of the performance standards placed on us. I therefore had to direct my attention to seeing that the normal service did not undergo any variations.

In combating infectious diseases, the Order Service achieved excellent pioneering work that contributed much to the far-reaching reduction of the danger of the epidemic's spread. For this purpose the O.S. Isolation Service was formed, which took the necessary measures for prevention of epidemics, working jointly with the Hygiene Section [*Sanitäts-Sektion*] of the Health Department.

Nor did the third year, 1942–1943, lag behind in regard to events falling directly within the sphere of activity of the Order Service. There were again settlements of newcomers [*Einsiedlungen*], this time from the nearby surroundings, which kept the O.S. man on the alert day and night. A highpoint in the demands on the O.S. were the further outsettlements [*Aussiedlungen*] that again became a touchstone of our sense of duty. The founding of the O.S. Women's Department, entrusted with special functions, occurred in the O.S.'s 3rd service year.

In view of territorial changes that occurred, I dissolved the 5th Precinct on 1.2.1942.

No. 42. YI-808B

Letter from the 2nd Precinct of the Order Service to Rumkowski, 14 August 1940, concerning hiring 5 agents for the political secret service at the Sonderkommando's recommendation. [in Polish][152]

We hereby make known to the Chairman that in accord with the recommendation of the Sonderkommando, the following were admitted to service in the II Precinct of the O.S. from 9.8.1940:

Symcha Kutas, Plac Kościelny 4; Leon Margulies, Młynarska 8; Samuel Frenkiel, Zawiszy 36; Szlama Feld, Bałucki Rynek 3; Menachem Tenenbaum, Rybna 12.

Those named are assigned to the political secret service and over the last several days have yielded us much benefit. Through them we caught a majority of the agitators. On Monday, they also delivered at Bałuty Marketplace a whole group from Berka Joselewicza Street, who had put up proclamations.

No. 43. YI-279

Announcement no. 233 of 15 March 1941, concerning formation of a summary court. [in Yiddish]

I hereby announce that, from the 16th of March, the entirely independent *Summary Court* called into existence by me, commences operation in its office at Franciszkańska 27[. *Its] task is to persecute every sort of crime that is directly against the essential interests of the community at large.*

The Summary Court is fully independent from the general court already existing at Gnieźnieńska 20.

The verdicts of the Summary Court will be issued through two tribunals, each consisting of one judge and two associates [*bayzitsers*], who were named by me from among the ghetto residents.

The court deliberations do not foresee any prior investigation and also exclude the participation of prosecutor and defender.

The court panel issues the verdict on the basis of free conviction [*ibertsaygung*].

No. 44. YI-18 (322)

Announcement no. 275 of 30 May 1941, concerning reporting all sorts of thefts, abuses, and swindles. [in Yiddish]

In recent days, I have been heavily burdened by unceasing reports about various thefts, abuses, and frauds that are being committed by a portion of my officials employed in various offices, departments, divisions, distribution points, bakeries, etc. This takes away a lot of my time from my more productive work, which ought to serve the benefit of the ghetto public.

In order to remove from myself in large measure the work of receiving the mentioned reports, hearing out the guilty, summoning witnesses, and so forth, I have decided to turn over this part of the work to the attorney, Mr. Henryk Neftalin.

Everyone who uncovers whatever theft or abuse to the detriment of the ghetto, or knows about any sort of activity harmful to the ghetto, must unconditionally report this immediately to Atty. Henryk Neftalin, who will investigate the matter and later present me with an exact report. On the basis of these reports, I will measure out the level of administrative punishment. In urgent cases, the verdict will be issued even more swiftly than in the Summary Court.

In order to carry out this task, I entrust to Atty. Henryk Neftalin the broadest powers in connection with the relevant matters, like ordering arrests, conducting searches, etc.

All community offices, including the court and the prosecutor, must give him the necessary help. The Order Servicemen must absolutely carry out his orders and commands even when they are not on duty.

In more serious matters, Atty. Henryk Neftalin is authorized to consult with the chairman of my court, Atty. S. Jakubson.

Atty. Henryk Neftalin will officiate daily at Bałuty Marketplace from 9 to 11 o'clock in the morning. In the event that his intervention will be necessary in the remaining hours of the day, it is possible to learn where he is through the intermediation of the telephone station.

This ordinance goes into force from today. From now on, no one may take up any of my time with any notifications and accusations; all must be put into the hands of Atty. Henryk Neftalin.

(Geto-tsaytung, *no. 11–12, 18 May 1941*)

No. 45. YI-862A

Criminal law procedure in the ghetto [1940]. [in Polish]

Criminal Law.

Principle: Punishable is each action that infringes upon generally accepted principles of criminal law, as well as regulations of the German authorities and the Eldest of the Jews, that are binding in the ghetto.

Administration of punishment: retribution for the act committed, repair of the damage, deterrence, admonition-reprimand, fine, arrest, prison, delivery to the German authorities. Besides that, a fine is an additional penalty. The limit of the extent of punishment is not fixed, being left to the judge's discretion.

Arrest from 1 day to 4 weeks. Imprisonment from 2 weeks (degrading punishment, intensification in rigor).

Costs of the proceedings can be assessed.[153]

Territorial jurisdiction: All offenses committed on the ghetto's terrain are prosecuted; additionally, crimes committed during the war on the terrain of the city of Łódź, only according to the finding of the Chairman of the Court.

Generally accepted principles of criminal law are binding.

Private prosecutions: —defamation, insult, battery, light bodily injury, breach of domestic peace and infringement of ownership of agricultural and garden produce. Payment 5 RM (duplication [*dwutorowość*]).

[Added in pencil:] (in breaking into agric. prop. 2—)

Proceedings: 1 judge rules in the I instance
3 judges rule in the II instance

In the event that the assessed penalty does not exceed 50 RM fine or jailing for up to two weeks, 1 judge rules in the II instance.

In more significant cases, the Chairman of the Court can assign 3 judges to the matter in the first instance. The same happens at the motion of the ruling judge or the Public Prosecutor.

Principle of orality and directness.

The official language is German. All written motions and arguments can occur in 3 languages: German, Polish, and Yiddish.

Judicial independence in the matter of adjudication.

The Court's Chairman has insight into each case.

An appeal must be announced within 3 days and submitted in writing within 14 days from the date of adjudication. Motives are drawn up in writing within 4 days (Possibility of restoring the deadline for submission of an appeal, in the event of a delay in drawing up of the motives). *Appeal only from:* fine over 20 RM and arrest of 7 days. Possibility of entering an ex officio appeal in each case by ruling of the Public Prosecutor or the Chairman of the Court.

Dependence of the Public Prosecutor on the Chairman of the Court; the same applies to the marshals in this segment of their activity.

Accusers: public prosecutor's office and the marshals delegated by it.

Denunciations: The precincts of the marshals of [public] order accept reports about the commission of crime only in cases involving the need for immediate intervention. In a given incident, they carry out the most essential actions and direct the matter to the public prosecutor.

2. The Office of Investigations accepts all reports that do not flow into the precincts, conducts investigation, applies security measures, and also directs the case to the public prosecutor.

Variation of the means of inquiry is exclusively up to the Prosecutor. Moreover, the Office of Investigation carries out all actions ordered by the Prosecutor, in its own sphere or also transfers them to the precincts.

Arrest and search must be confirmed by the Public Prosecutor within 24 hours.

3. The Public Prosecutor accepts reports only in writing and in the German language. In matters transferred to the Public Prosecutor by the police precincts or also by the Office of Investigation, the public prosecutor conducts its own investigation, or also assigns the matter in total or partially to the Office of Investigation.

The Marshals of Public Order themselves identify misdemeanors and apply a penalty up to 10 RM or 3 days arrest.

The prosecutor is the executor of all penal judgments.

The Chairman of the Eldest of the Jews enjoys the right of pardon in all criminal cases. Appeals for pardon must be submitted to the Chairman in writing.

No. 46. YI-139

Announcement no. 81 of 12 July 1940, concerning introduction of censorship of outgoing correspondence. [in German]

By order, I have introduced in my Postal Department inspection of all letters, postcards, and other outgoing written items from the ghetto. All letters, postcards, as well as other written items that contain orders to firms or private persons, or in which the recipient is requested to send foodstuffs or other items into the ghetto against payment or gratis (as gifts), will be destroyed.

There is only one way of support and that is for all acquaintances or relatives who live outside the ghetto and who want to help anyone to transmit the intended contribution to him in cash.

The outgoing request for aid must contain this addendum:

"The payment is to be made to account no. 700 Ghetto Food and Management Office at the Municipal Savings Bank in Litzmannstadt." I refer in this connection to my Announcement no. 53 of 3 June 1940.

It should also be noted here:

The sender of the money must give his exact address in making the deposit and clearly note who the recipient is on the deposit slip.

The credit voucher comes into my hands and I will then pay out to the addressee the arrived sum in cash ghetto money or have foodstuffs issued in the value of the paid in deposit irrespective of the allocation of foodstuffs.

No. 47. YI-267

Announcement no. 221 of 26 February 1941, concerning confiscation of all parcels with foodstuffs that arrive for the ghetto. [in Yiddish][154]

I hereby make known that by order of the authorities, all *parcels with foodstuffs* that have arrived by train, as well as the parcels that will yet arrive by train, *must be confiscated by me* for the benefit of the population of the ghetto.

No. 48. YI-110

Ordinance no. 35 of 9 May 1940, concerning the obligation to register in the newly formed registration bureau. [in German]

On the basis of the powers entrusted to me, I order the following:

All inhabitants of the ghetto in Litzmannstadt are obligated to register at the registration bureau established by me.

Whoever evades the duty to register will be severely penalized.

I hereby task the building managers with enrollment of inhabitants of the ghetto[. They] can carry this out with the possible help of the house committees.

For registration, forms will be filled out in duplicate. These are available only from the building managers of the Eldest of the Jews in Litzmannstadt for the price of 0.05 RM apiece.

The registrations will be undertaken so that each of the designated houses will in turn be registered.

After the registration has taken place in a given house, every person who then moves into the house, as well as whoever leaves it to move into another house, must register or cancel registration within 24 hours.

Whoever omits this will be severely penalized.

This ordinance comes into force on 10.5.40.

No. 49. YI-621/161

Letter from the mayor to Rumkowski of 24 April 1940, where he transfers to him the administration of the real estate in the ghetto. [in German][155]

I hereby transfer to you immediately the trustee management of all the real estate located in the residential area of the Jews. You are obligated to keep the properties in orderly condition and for the regular payment to the city of taxes that apply to the properties, insofar as this tax flowed into the Finance Office until now. The payment obligation and the authorization for collection of rents come into effect from 1.4.1940.

I hereby empower you to make this statement known to all property managers who were employed by the city or the Trustee Office East.

The mandate of these managers expires with the assumption of real estate management by you.

No. 50. YI-40

Financial report of the activity of the Jewish Religious Community for the period from 1 January until 27 July 1940. [in German][156]

SPENDING

1. *Tax and Finance Department*

Community Tax Refund	853.	
House Expenditures	43,391.91	
Deposits	675.	
Overhead	5701.97	
Various for confiscated goods	400.	
Fund for Finance Dept.	4,050.	55,071.88

2. *Cemetery Department*

Expenditures		33,798.67

3. *School Department*

School Salaries	122,941.31	
Pensions, Subventions and Other Expenditures	17,589.03	140,530.34

4. Social Welfare

Money Grants and Products	244,980.14	
Feeding Facilities (Kitchens)	128,560.73	
Home for the Aged, Children's		
Home, and Orphanages	116,036.58	
Summer Camps	30,762.11	
Exempted from Rent Payment	64,407.45	
Hachshara*	8,857.03	
Various Overhead	2,450.37	596,054.41

5. Labor Deployment

Payments	220,963.85	220,963.85

6. Feeding Department

Payments		1,626,626.89

7. Resettlement Department

Various Overhead		15,175.27
Carry Over		**2,668,221.31**

INCOME

1. Tax and Finance Department

Communal Tax Receipts	378,213.29	
Registration Card Fees Receipts	31,051.11	
Rental Receipts	243,975.97	
Rental Receipts through Bailiff	3,809.41	
Various Taxes	23,977.49	
Contributions	7,077.39	
Deposits	874.82	
Wage Tax	6,725.15	
Various Fees	2,850.50	
Rent for Miscalculations	1,185.08	
Overhead Refund	4.32	700,243.53

2. Cemetery Department

Receipts		38,068.20

3. School Department

School Fees	7,263.13	
School Salaries Refund	433.80	7,696.99

4. Social Welfare

Chancellory Fees Receipts	4,044.22	
Kitchens	308.24	
Home for the Aged, Children's		
Home, Orphanages	5,872.60	10,225.06

5. Labor Deployment

Receipts		56,755.70

6. Feeding Department

Receipts		1,396,859.29

7. Resettlement Department

Receipts		20,058.35
Carry Over		**2,229,907.12**

---

*Editor's note: Hebrew—Agricultural training.

SPENDING

Carry Over		**2,668,221.31**

8. *Health Department*
Clinics	46,854.25	
Hospitals	111,739.54	
Infectious Disease Hospital	122,286.74	
Rescue Preparedness	6,163.21	
Pharmacies	10,719.07	
Diverse Expenditures of the Health Office	277,389.13	575,151.94

9. *Management Department*
Heating Overhead	21,075.45	
Fecal and Rubbish Removal	14,447.88	
Building Manager Salaries	9,438.10	
Various Expenses	82,495.20	
Chimneysweep	62.95	127,519.58

10. a) *Order Service*
Various Expenditures		105,954.84

   b) *Auxiliary Order Service*
Various Expenditures	712.61	
Building Guards	37,888.38	
Special Unit [*Sonderkommando*]	4,631.65	43,232.64

11. a) *Postal Department*
Various Expenditures		43,579.30
b) *Postal Remittances*		
Paid Out Postal Moneyorders		164,536.80
c) *C.O.D. and Customs*		
Advanced for C.O.D. and Customs		5,478.99
d) *Postal Department Separate Account*		
Expended in RM for Printed Postal Items		82,503.59

12. *Registration Bureau*
Various Expenditures		2,390.15

CARRY OVER		**3,818,569.14**

INCOME

Carry Over		**2,229,907.12**

8. *Health Department*
Clinics	29,273.04	
Hospitals	1,868.50	
Infectious Disease Hospital	21.25	
Rescue Preparedness	1,407.07	
Pharmacies	41,632.	
Chemical Laboratory	349.	
Various Receipts of the Health Office	50,237.02	124,787.88

9. *Management Department*
Receipts for Heating	402.30	
Fecal and Rubbish Removal	24,409.45	
Various Receipts	5,886.70	
Chimneysweep	3,336.70	34,033.70

10. a) *Order Service*
      Various Receipts   6,469.49
    b) *Auxiliary Order Service*
      Building Guards   380.59

11. a) *Postal Department*
      Various Receipts   155,861.05
    b) *Postal Remittances*
      Receipts through the Ghetto Food
          and Management Office   126,391.66
    c) *Postal Dept. Separate Account*
      Behobene [Withdrawals??]**   104,713.48

12. Registry Bureau
      Various Receipts   21,877.15

CARRY OVER   **2,804,422.12**

INCOME***
13. *Agricultural Department*
      Various Receipts   1,757.15
14. *Labor Division*
      Various Received Payments   43.91
15. *Management Department* Đ
For Accounting Clearing [Zur Verrechnung]   92,571.90
16. *Control Commission*   —
17. *Division for Public Works*   —
18. *Health Office* Đ
For Accounting Clearing [Zur Verrechnung]   194,322.95
19. *Firebrigade Department*   —
20. *Personnel Account*
      Repayments   1,042.98
21. *Deposits and Securities*   1,751.10
22. *Loans*   8,994.02
23. *Accounting Clearing [Verrechnung]*
Account   5,870.59
24. *Various Expenses [Refunds]*   76.60
25. *Reichsvereinigung der Juden in Deutschland*
      Behobene [?Withdrawals?]****   50,000.
26. *Kassa Account*
      [Out] Payments   3,247,803.23
27. *Złoty Currency Account*
      [Out] Payments   7,788.
28. *Transitory Sums [Durchlaufende Summen]* 17,855.36
29. *German Pharmacists Association*
      For seized pharmacies   37,617.35
30. *Various Expenses (Rent)*   —
31. *Issuing Bank (Emissions-Bank)*
      For *behobene* (?Withdrawals?) in RM   1,412,588.50

    **Editor's note: *Behobene* is an odd term that seems to imply withdrawals. Perhaps this item refers to money seized from outside remittances sent for people in the ghetto.
    ***Editor's note: Although Trunk labels this "SPENDING," it is clearly a listing of revenue items. This was confirmed by checking the original document at YIVO.
    ****Editor's note: This may refer to funds transmitted from the official organization of German Jewry and then seized by the Rumkowski administration.

32. *Dresdner Bank*
  Deposited   224,594.19
33. *Emissions-Bank Scrip Account*
  Refunds   45,500.
34. *Tax and Social Contributions*
  Various Tax   4,702.64
35. *Moveables [Mobilien] Account*   1,276.

            8,361,301.93

EXPENSES
CARRY OVER   **2,804,422.12**
13. *Agricultural Department*
  Various Expenditures   38,836.99
14. *Labor Division*
  Various Expenditures   60,103.55
15. *Management Department – For Accounting* 95,047.96
Clearing Account [Zur Verrechnung]
16. *Control Commission*
  Various Expenses   195.85
17. *Public Works Division*
  Various Expenditures   26,103.48
18. *Health Office –*   180,175.29
For Accounting Clearing Account
[Zur Verrechnung]
19. *Fire Brigade Department*
  Salaries   7,555.40
20. *Personnel Account*
  Salaries of All Departments   305,115.68
21. *Deposits and Securities*   9,640.
22. *Loans*   4,410.
23. *Accounting Clearing Account*   6,598.66
[Verrechnung Conto]
24. *Various Expenses*   38,731.43
26. *[sic] Kassa Account*
25. ————————
Receipts   3,449,367.87
27. *Złoty Currency Account*
  Receipts   285.
28. *Transitory Sums [Durchlaufende Summen]* 40,366.74
29. *German Pharmacists Association*
————————
30. *Various Expenses (Rent)*   4,013.06
31. *Bank of Issue (Emissions-Bank)*
  Expenses   113.
32. *Dresdner Bank*
  Behobene [?]   299,296.17
33. *Bank of Issue (Emissions Bank)*
   Scrip Account
  Behobene in ghetto currency (*Quitt.*) 177,500.
34. *Tax and Social Contributions*
————————
35. *Moveables Account*   ————

            8,361,301.93

    Cash on Hand as of 27 July 1940 218,176.77
    Debit Balance of the Feeding Dept. 241,056.54

No. 51. YI-159

Announcement no. 105 of 13 August 1940, concerning the opening of a purchase office. [in German]

I know that many people who have no way to make a living are selling their personal things in order not to be compelled to turn to the Welfare Department.

In the sale of these things, they are frequently exploited in that too low prices are bid.

In order to help out, I am opening on Friday, 16 August 1940, at Kelmstrasse 71

a Purchase Office.

Reliable people will be employed by me there, who will appraise the value and pay for the purchase of offered objects like jewelry, gold and silver, precious stones, furs, securities, pieces of clothing, linens and so forth, to prevent exploitation of the plight of these people.

No. 52. YI-228

Announcement no. 179 of 17 December 1940, concerning compulsory sale of furs and fur items. [in German]

By order of the Authorities, I hereby make known that all women's and men's fur coats, foxes, collars, and hides of all sorts

by no later than 1 January 1941

must be offered for purchase in my bank, Bleicherweg 7. *Buying commences on Sunday, 22 December 1940, 9 A.M.* After 1 January 1941, fur pieces that are still found in private possession will be confiscated.

No. 53. YI-394

Announcement no. 350 of 6 January 1942, concerning compulsory sale of men's ski- and mountain-shoes. [in Yiddish]

By order of the authorities, I make known that *all men's ski- and mountain-shoes from size 40 on must be surrendered.* The mentioned shoes are being purchased through *my bank, Ciesielska no. 7.* The surrender of the aforementioned shoes will last *until the 15th of January 1942.*

After this deadline, men's ski- and men's mountain-shoes that are found will be requisitioned and the owner will not receive any compensation and will also be punished.

No. 54. YI-411

Announcement no. 368 of 2 March 1942, concerning sale of furniture and houseware by those designated for deportation. [in Yiddish][157]

Concerning the pieces of furniture and housewares of the families designated for departure, *as well concerning taking along money.* In connection with my announcement no. 353 of 9 January 1942, I point out that

in addition to the carpentry shop at Drukarska 12, *all sorts of furniture pieces, house- and kitchen-items can also be sold at Franciszkańska 35.*
The Central Purchasing Office, *Plac Kościelny 4,* buys all sorts of goods and various house- and kitchen-items.

Concerning taking along money. In order to prevent abuses, I have set up *a place for the acceptance of money* at the following locations: 1. Jonshera Street no. 25 and 2. Jagiellońska no. 16, Marysin.

Families designated for departure, who have ghetto money in their possession, can leave [money] before departure and indicate to whom the money left should be paid out.

An account will be opened there for each depositor.

I have appointed reliable persons to the operation of the aforementioned point.

No. 55. YI-1212

Rumkowski's letter to the mayor of 5 April 1940, concerning creating workshops in the ghetto that would work for the German authorities. [in German]

I hereby permit myself to submit to you the following proposal about my plan regarding the question of life in the ghetto:

There are in the ghetto ca. 8–10,000 experts of various branches: shoe- and bootmakers (manual and mechan[ized]), saddlers, leather galanterie-makers, tailors (made-to-order and mass production), sewers of linen (made-to-order and mass production), hat and cap makers, tinsmiths, locksmiths, cabinetmakers, masons, painters, bookbinders, upholsterers.

I could arrange for these [skilled artisans] to work for the authorities, with the authorities supplying the raw material and fixing the pay rate. The jobs will be performed in the ghetto and I would allocate the work among the experts through a department named by me. These [experts] must then deliver the completed items back to the department concerned, and delivery to the authorities ensues from me against cash payment of the fixed labor payment or equivalent delivery of food products that I receive allocated for the entire Jewish population. Payment of wages to the experts then follows through me.

Moreover, there are in the ghetto many dealers in old products that are also very necessary for the authorities.

After the trustees and appointed managers of the houses in the ghetto are withdrawn, I politely request that I be authorized to collect the rents; whereby I must note that a large part of the population in the ghetto consists of the poor, who must be freed from payment of rent. I obligate myself to pay off all taxes of the houses and to have the necessary repairs undertaken. The remaining surplus will go into the Community treasury.

Further, I respectfully request the right to house [*einzuräumen*], to issue business certificates, whereby I would also have a benefit. Moreover, I would levy an assessment, to which I am already authorized.

In order to be able to carry all of this out now in an orderly fashion and without difficulty, the authorities must free me from the assignment of compulsory workers to the authorities and duty stations, so that the Jews will not have to leave the ghetto. I would request that, if necessary, an ordinance be issued that no one is authorized to come into the ghetto and take people away from the street to work, for that would signify an exceptional disruption.

[p. 2]

I hope that I and my co-workers in all this will succeed in obtaining a suitable subvention from the authorities in order to carry out the budget in the ghetto: to properly support the Order Service, to keep the poor and needy viable, and to protect the population against diseases, as well as to do justice to all the other needs of the Jewish population in the ghetto.

No. 56. YI-931

25 October 1939 authorization from the City Commissioner for Rumkowski, concerning taking over operation of the Jewish elementary schools. [in German]

The Eldest of the Jews in Łódź, Mr. Ch. Rumkowski, is obligated and empowered to take all measures for the Jewish elementary school system and to apportion all the related expenses on the totality of the Jews and to collect the sums from those affected.

No. 57. YI-959

Anonymous report concerning the school system in the Łódź Ghetto in the years 1939–1941. [in Polish]

[p. 8]

Deprivation of School Sites

Adding to the various difficulties with which Jewish education wrestled, which we partially mentioned above, there came in October and in November [1939] partial seizure of the sites of Jewish schools for various military purposes, hospitals, and offices. In the first rank, the best buildings and accommodations were subject to that fate. And thus [were lost] Cegielniana 63, Wierzbowa 17, Sieńkiewicza 11, Zawadzka 42, Kilinskiego 63, Gdańska 90, Składowa 15, Magistracka 18. In view of the lack of other sites, the displaced schools were relocated at still functioning schools, as a second shift (afternoon).

By order of the Chairman, private schools (at that time barely vegetating or completely non-functioning) were also requisitioned for this purpose. But in time these too were subject to eviction. Some schools repeatedly wandered from site to site. Of course, in those conditions there could be no talk of normal attendance. Aside from moves, too many factors operated negatively: seizures for labor, fear of strange faces, and so many others.

But regardless of this, how many times were pupils and teachers seized along the way by those empowered and not empowered, to [do] the most varied tasks without any connection to their profession, which was traded for sweeping and cleaning apartments and offices, moving out requisitioned furniture, even delivering parcels which it did not suit the members of the Master Race to carry.

But in many cases, this was possibly the easiest to bear. In some locations, the crew gave full play to their sadistic or plain marauding tendencies.

In these conditions, whoever could refrained from going out. However, it did not help much, when victims began to be sought in their apartments.

It would happen that, for fun or from a desire to annoy, a teenaged lad found pleasure in seizing Jews in order to free them after holding and threatening them for a few hours. At times the epilogue was much sadder.

All these incidents very depressingly affected Jews not accustomed to such demeaning treatment. Whoever could, whoever was not compelled by any sort of reasons to remain, left for the Gen.-Government or abroad. Teachers, being younger and spiritually otherwise inclined, particularly set out for Russia.

So a lack of teachers began to be perceptible, which was dealt with by trying to engage new people.

[p. 15]

. . .

But in spite of everything, the Jews' vitality was extraordinary in these hard times, and despite these hard times. The scramble to study was elemental; the number of pupils applying is ever larger. In a short time, it reached seven hundred. Instruction takes place in eighteen classes and in two shifts.[158]

[p. 20]

. . .

The fundamental task of the school in this period is possibly not only instruction, but rather supplemental feeding of the children and supervision over their health. In accord with the Chairman's instructions, the teachers operate kitchens at the schools as part of their duties, pay attention to the quality of the portions served, and extend health supervision, in common with physicians and school hygienists, over the children entrusted to them.

Instruction

Instruction is taking place on the basis of the old (Polish) school curricula. The language of instruction continues to remain Polish.

Attempts to introduce Hebrew as a subject of instruction encounter many difficulties and only from June 1940 are they becoming realized.

Irregular instruction in the first months of this school year was most often entirely fruitless. For completion of the course, the term of instruction was extended to September, so that in this way the summer holiday had to fall in the period of the autumn Jewish holidays.

State of the Pupils

It is to be seen from the report for the month of April [1940] that in that period 6,265 [pupils] attended the communal elementary schools; 728 were in the gymnasium; 220 in the united boys religious schools; 63 in the united Bajs-Jakow [Bet-Yaakov] girls religious schools; 92 in the schools of the Assoc. of United Yiddish Schools; altogether 7,366.

[p. 21]

To the extent that life in the ghetto began to normalize, the number of children attending schools simultaneously grew: in September 1940 it reached the respectable height of 9,915, of whom 5,542 are being supplementally fed.

[p. 23]

. . .

School Year 1940/1941

The 1940/1941 school year started under two slogans: involvement of all children in schooling, even if in compulsory form, and redoubled consideration of Yiddish language and Judaic subjects in the broadest extent.

As to the first point, in spite of the worst living conditions (the relief grants introduced at that time were given to 80 percent of the inhabitants), the ghetto's populace splendidly recognized the value and significance of education for their children.

The number of registrations grew constantly, so by the nature of things instruction became universal. To promote the enrollment of the few children still remaining outside school, a card file of all the children of school age was compiled.

[p. 24]

. . .

Under pressure of external factors, there occurred a break with the previously introduced spirit and tendency of the Polish schools. There were no dictates, but the Chairman took advantage of the situation to introduce the idea long cherished by him that in a Jewish state, like the ghetto indubitably was, education [should be] conducted in a Jewish national and religious spirit, to relate to the ancient Jewish tradition and so bring up a youth aware of their nationality and human origin.

He ordered introduction of Yiddish as the language of instruction, along with a simultaneous deepening of Judaic learning.

Since then, the schools have had to devote at least half an hour to religious study and to the Yiddish and Hebrew languages.

But this reform brought with it the necessity of creating suitably prepared teaching cadres, since, despite the fact that a previously conducted survey among the teachers [showed] a significant percentage fluent in the Yiddish language, this was rather mere home learning, entirely inadequate for teaching in schools.

So the School Department confronted the task of training a sufficient quantity of teachers who would be able to teach in Yiddish.

Four courses of 50–60 students each were organized. They lasted from May to September 1941 and produced satisfactory results.

The School Department also created a programmatic commission, which elaborated curricula for each class of each subject.

No. 58. YI-221

Ordinance no. 171 of 3 December 1940, concerning placing all medical personnel in the ghetto under the authority of the director of the Health Department. [in German]

All physicians, medics, nurses, and midwives, who reside within the area of the ghetto, are from today joined together and subordinated to the director of the Health Department, whose orders for the practice of all medical and health functions are to be obeyed unconditionally.

Every contravention against the above ordinance will be punished with loss of position, lasting deprivation of the right to practice in a profession caring for the sick, and up to three months of severe imprisonment.

Moreover, in especially serious cases, I reserve for myself application of the most far-reaching and harshest measures.

No. 59. YI-1002

Monograph about the organization and activity of the Department for Social Aid by [Józef Zelkowicz].[159] [in Yiddish]

[p. 7]

At the conference that took place while still in the former Jewish community building at number 18 Pomorska, Ch. Rumkowski called on the employees present to stay at their posts and to do their work thoroughly, while also pointing out the need to reorganize the Department for Social Aid.

Nominated at that meeting as director of the Department for Social Aid, or *Opieka Społeczna*,[160] as the institution later became popular among the public, was the honest and energetic Mr. Samuel Faust; Mgr. S. Bunin as the office manager; as the treasurer, Y. M. Birenshtok [*sic*] and controller, Mr. Buchwejc [Bukhveyts].

At the time, there existed two so-called cheap kitchens in the city: at the philanthropic society *Tomkhey Orkhim* at number 26 Zachodnia Street and the kitchen of the competing organization *Noysen Lekhem* on Solna Street.[161] The Chairman took over these kitchens together with their personnel and let them operate under the supervision of the Jewish Community's Department of Social Aid.

The aforementioned kitchens had to provide the dinners [*mitogn*], or the products in kind used to prepare the dinners, first and foremost, as already noted, to those poor folk who until now had been supported by the city administration.

[p. 42]

Table 14
Number of Dinners Issued through the Jewish Community
from November 1939 until September 1940

Year	Month	Operating Days	Dinners for Adults	Others
1939	November	18	19,130	00,000 [sic]
1939	December	31	88,063	16,219
1940	January	31	133,088	18,407
1940	February	28	119,621	18,045
1940	March	31	97,607	1,249
1940	April	26	75,201	—
1940	May	31	161,369	86,024
1940	June	30	135,328	112,905
1940	July	31	186,626	118,906
1940	August	31	351,596	157,774
1940	September	25	451,640	100,537
	Total	313	1,819,269	630,066

If we divide the number of dinners for adults by the number of days of operation (1,819,269 divided by 313), we obtain a daily average of 5,812 dinners. If we do the same with the dinners that figure in the table in the rubric "Others" (630,066 divided by 313), we have a daily average of 2,013 dinners. Both averages together give a total daily average of 7,825 dinners, that amount to 5 percent in relation to the number of people who lived in the ghetto at that time (around 155–156 thousand). In other words: Almost two thousand families who lived in the ghetto had to turn to the dinners that the kitchen issued.
[p. 66]

. . .

And when the leadership of the DSA (Department for Social Aid) realized that its accomplishment did not help, and the situation in the ghetto was becoming ever worse and an even greater congestion was expected, only then did it consent to the path of control.

True. The control system was archaic, introduced by the prewar Jewish community, and was also employed in the beginning by the new community. In the first declarations that were submitted by the poor, still in the city [before the ghetto], for the months of November and December 1939, one finds notices of the checking made, and often even special control protocols, signed by Controller Buchwejc, who was presumably specially hired in the community for this purpose. Only later do the controls vanish, and a submitted declaration [of need], particularly when it was furnished with a recommendation, was enough to become a "client" of the "*Opieka*" and to receive a grant. Of course, such a system could only give rise to abuses and corruption, for there was no checking whether the applicant was really a pauper; nor was the accuracy checked of the number of souls that he claimed as dependents in his declaration (because in the end this circumstance was a certain criterion in setting the amount of the aid grant); nor was it checked

whether any of the souls dependent on the applicant was employed privately or in community institutions.
[p. 69]

. . .

On the 27th of September, the Department of Social Aid as such ceased to exist. Together with the closure of the DSA, the system by which it had operated the whole time was also brought down. The institution that arose on the ruins of the DSA, the Relief Department [*untershtitsungs opteyl*] will efface the concepts of "proper" and "respectable" ["*sheyn*," "*bekoved*"] and will operate according to entirely different methods and systems, about which we will have occasion to speak further.
[p. 81]

. . .

If we take the prewar conditions and compare them with the current ones, we get this picture:

Before the war, Łódź reckoned the Jewish population at about 260 thousand souls. At that time, the Jewish community estimated 182 thousand marks (364 thousand złoty) for relief needs in its budget, which amounted to an average of 70 pfennig per capita, or 1.40 złoty. But now, in the period that we are dealing with, the ghetto population consisted of about 155 thousand souls, for whose relief was expended, as we see, over 272 thousand marks, amounting to an average of over 1.70 marks per capita, and thus more than two and a half times as much.

Even if we compared the relief sums to the bread prices, calculated in marks, according to the ratio of the former złoty (formerly, a two kilogram bread cost 55 *groszy* and now 55 *pfennig*), the average relief will also be larger than before the war.

Table 26[1]
Direct and Indirect Relief Grants from the Department of Social Aid during its Existence: [no year, in Yiddish]

Month	Direct Relief Grants				Together		Indirect Grants	
	In Cash		In Products					
	Applicants	Amount	Applicants	Amount	Applicants	Amount	Applicants	Amount
November	2,448	22,132.52	—	—	2,448	22,132.52	—	—
December	1,409	11,137.45	—	—	1,409	11,137.45	—	—
January	2,072	14,313.70	—	—	2,072	14,313.70	—	—
February	451	3,109.50	—	—	451	3,109.50	—	—
March	37	266.45	1,803	10,442.00	1,840	10,708.45	—	—
April	868	6,656.	87	880.00	955	7,536.	—	—
May	137	1,496.30	3,438	19,212.50	3,575	20,708.80	—	—
June	314	3,481.75	4,120	23,023.50	4,434	26,505.25	2,116	25,461.97
July	2,364	14,038.	5,690	31,657.—	8,054	45,695.	2,340	21,191.11
August	10,793	62,493.45	555	3,077.—	11,348	65,570.45	1,800	16,196.48
September	4,792	27,075.50	3,418	17,793.—	8,210	44,868.50	1,006	8,547.34
TOTAL	25,685	166,200.62	19,111	106,085.—	44,796	272,285.62	7,262	71,396.90

1. Ed. Note: *Lodhzer geto*, 94, no source cited, although it likely was part of the previous Zelkowicz report, doc. No. 59.

No. 60. YI-1470

Announcement no. 123 of 20 September 1940, concerning introduction of the relief system. [in Yiddish][162]

Residents of the Ghetto

In order to introduce calm and order in the ghetto and not have any hungry people here, I have decided to reconstruct the social aid on new foundations, until I receive sufficient work for my Labor Department[163] and there will be work.

According to my information and registrations, there are around a hundred thousand people who have been left without work in the ghetto.

I must have around one million marks a month in order to satisfy the hungry and to be able to conduct a just and fair relief campaign.

My plan is that the grants will be issued only in cash money according to the following arrangement:

Money relief grants will be received by

About 60,000 adults at 9 marks a month	540,000 marks
" *15,000 children up to age 14 at 7 m.*	105,000
" *7,000 persons over age 60 at 10 m.*	70,000
" *15,000 children are being supported in the camps, orphanages, homes for infants and the elderly in the home for the aged*	230,000
Special relief fund	50,000
	995,000 marks

Workers with families, who earn less than 9 marks a month, are reckoned as unemployed and receive the full sum of the aid grant.

The aid grant will be sent through the mail after registration and confirmation.

All grants are reckoned from today. Those who receive aid grants are free from paying rent.

In the entire ghetto, kitchens exist and will further be organized by me and the house committees, that will issue dinners for 15, 20, and 25 *fenig* each. Breakfasts will be issued at low prices.

Workers with families who earn more than 9 marks a month receive a supplement if the aid that is due them according to their family situation amounts to more than their monthly earnings. Everyone who receives relief is obligated to carry out the work to which he is assigned by me and for which he will also get paid. If he will not do the required work honestly and conscientiously, he will be removed from the job site and loses the right to relief aid.

I note that I also have the following expenses monthly:

Health Department	250,000 m.
Administration	360,000 m.

Public Works	40,000 m.
Building Repairs and Construction of Kitchens	20,000 m.
Unforeseen	10,000 m.

665,000 m.

Altogether, monthly expenses of 1,650,000 marks.

According to the plan, all Jews in the ghetto are considered working people. Until today, I have managed by my own efforts without aid from outside to cover my budget, which until now amounted to about 700,000 marks. Now, when the ghetto is uniformly sealed and dependent on self-government, the expenses of which amount to 1,650,000 marks, and the revenues to only 600–700 thousand marks, I have had recourse to a loan that was approved for me. In this way, I can cover my current budget and carry out my plan.

I now appeal to you to support me in my work for the public good and not to hinder me in it.

I also want to care for the entire ghetto public through a broad winter relief campaign, i.e., for clothing, shoes, and heating.

I ask of you good will and loyal fulfillment of your obligations. I warn anyone making malevolent attempts to disturb the calm and the enforcement of my plan, who spreads false rumors and incites the population.

The penalties and repressions that I will now apply against them will be immeasurably greater and sharper than those until now.

No. 61. YI-1001

Anonymous report concerning the activity of the Relief Department from September 1940 until September 1941. [in Polish]

. . .

[p. 9]

XV.

The first applications were received in the Medical Points on the 21st of September.

On the very same day, they were forwarded to the Management Department [*Wydziału Gospodarczego*].

From that moment commenced work that went on for 24 hours a day for a long time.

By day, administrators conducted interviews, while at night applications were sorted according to districts, entered into indices, checked as to whether the applicant had submitted an application twice, and [after being] checked as to whether he had died, were [then] issued to the administrators.

They were returned with an opinion to the Management Department, which further forwarded them to the CUK [Central Control Office, *Centralny Urząd Kontroli*] for a second check.

Thanks to the enthusiastic collaboration of the officials of the Manag. Dept. and the CUK, as well as to the operating procedure that was well designed by Atty. Neftalin and Mr. Rozenblum, the tempo was extraordinary. Consequently, after three days 544 applications flowed in to the Relief Grants Department [*Wydział Zasiłkowy*].

XVI.

Instantly created, in an alien site (an empty office of the Finance Department was opened on 24 September in the afternoon, which had to be ready to deal with the work that was to commence that evening), with personnel assembled from the most varied offices, without set patterns, without forms and diagrams, the Relief Grants Department confronted an unprecedented, difficult task, even more difficult, since all knew that every delay means hunger for those affected.

The work, still not systematized at the start, was already regulated after the first day by division of function between both principal heads: while decisions were made jointly, Mr. Zażujer dealt with external matters, hiring of officials, while Mr. Neftalin dealt with technical issues and the internal apparat.

The simplification of procedure and the file system, etc., introduced by them, streamlined the Department's activity to a significant degree,

[p. 10]

as proven by the constant increase of cases dealt with daily.

And so:

25.9[164] handled	544 cases	30.9 handled	3,165 cases
26.9 "	1,076 "	1.10 "	2,945 "
27.9 "	2,027 "	2.10 "	2,537 "
28.9 "	2,175 "	6.10 "	7,918 "
29.9 "	2,664 "		

XVII.

How did the work take place in the Relief Grants Department?

The first activity was sorting the submitted applications by opinion and affixing of attachments (this took place if they were negative but required explanations). This group is assigned to jurists.

The following matters are distinguished [by coded letters]:

"P"[165]—certain . . . . both opinions positive
"O"—rejected . . . . both opinions negative
"S"—case . . . . insufficiently clarified matters
"R"—various . . . . divergent opinions, undecided
"L"—wage lists . . . . one or more members of the family have sources of income from work, but inadequate.

All went to the desk of the Commission (which exclusively had the right to award grants), some directly, some after additional transfer to a third examination by special trusted controllers ("S" and "R" matters).

Without exception, each application was reviewed by the Commission and each decision was signed by its chairman, Mr. Zażujer, or by another member in the event of his absence.

Accepted applications are immediately directed to bookkeeping, where a detailed registration card for the given family is filled out in the card file, calculating on it the amount of the grant, to which the chairman subscribed, [then] postal orders are filled out and by the very next morning letter-carriers paid out the allotted grants.

A maximum of 24 hours elapsed from the moment of the application's arrival until the payment. A couple of thousand cases are now handled daily.

. . .

[p. 14]

XXVI.

On 1 July commenced the realization of the second part of the basic concept underlying the formation of the relief campaign: the obligation to work.

Relief recipients had to be called to auxiliary work, odd jobs, or jobs not requiring skilled knowledge, like cleaning offices and workshops, sweeping and hosing down streets, peeling vegetables in public kitchens, at vegetable and coal sites, at field and road works, in excavation of pits according to the orders of OPL,[166] or as a reserve for the Firefighters.

The money saved in this way amounted to around 340 thousand marks, which previously was expended to employ day-laborers at the aforementioned jobs. Not wanting to profit from the unemployed, the Chairman totally allocated [these savings] to increasing the relief grants.

The rate increase introduced simultaneously (for the X period) was very significant, because it amounted, for example, to 50 percent in the principal group aged 15 to 60 years old.

To bring this plan into effect, a Labor Desk [*Referat Pracy*] was formed at the Department, under the direction of Miss Fuchs, director of the Labor Office [*Arbeitseinsatz*].

[p. 15]

. . .

Those reporting to registration of people conscripted for labor included 13,354 men aged 17 to 47 and 11,434 women aged 17 to 40 (so long as they do not have children under 14 years old to look after).

XXVIII.

During July and August, relief recipients put in about 220,000 working days.

It turned out, however, that the work, to which great hope was tied, was wholly disappointing due to the relief recipients' careless attitude toward it.

Consequently, with the 1st day of September 1941 (XII aid grants) there was a reversion to the former situation: lower rates (7 marks to age 14 and 10 marks above) without working it off.

The Labor Desk was changed into the Labor Brokerage Desk [*Ref. Pośrednictwa Pracy*].

Only one innovation was introduced: if someone is employed with independent paid labor of whatever character, steady or occasional, regardless of the amount of income attained, he loses the right to a relief grant, together with his immediate family.

On one hand, this was to induce elements capable of working to undertake productive labor, on the other hand—to clarify the situation on the free market of labor.

[p. 20]

. . .

Statistical Table No. 2

Registration of Persons Eligible for Free Dinners
Conducted by CUK at the end of August 1940

Needy . . . . 16,177 people   On 1 September 1940, the Ghetto
Very Needy . . . . 25,535 "   numbered 158,042 residents.
Most Needy . . . . 41,100 "   52.4% of residents needed aid.

[p. 22]

Statistical Table No. 9

Relief Grants	As of the date	Ghetto Population	% of Pop. Receiving Relief Grants	Number of Cases	New Cases
I	1 Oct. 1940	157,079	79.5%	39,191	—
II	1 Dec. 1940	155,743	78.9%	38,473	561
III	1 Jan. 1941	153,588	73.3%	35,810	334
Chanuka	"	"	78.0%	38,448	169
IV	1 Feb. 1941	151,969	67.5%	33,187	204
V	1 Mar. 1941	150,959	66.7%	32,658	279
VI-VII	1 Apr. 1941	149,569	67.3%	35,245	96
VIII	1 June 1941	146,547	55.5%	27,424	98
IX	1 July 1941	145,625	49.8%	25,372	121
X	1 Aug. 1941	144,959	44.0%	23,729	51
XI	1 Sept. 1941	144,401	39.4%	22,692	—
XII	"	—	—	22,918	—

Statistical Table No. 10

Relief Grants	Sum Allotted in Marks	Deductions in Marks	Overhead[1] in Marks	Overhead Per Person in *Fenig*
I	1,078,906	50,577	—	—
II	1,426,727	72,404	68,185	55
III	979,052	58,097	61,811	55
Chanuka	310,670	—	—	—
IV	980,298	50,206	57,267	55
V	963,866	69,599	55,876	55
VI-VII	1,922,288	?	107,117	53
VIII	776,073	43,191	46,242	56
IX	702,215	30,167	41,5261/2	58
X	969,726	35,952	37,9791/2	59
XI	928,666	31,851	36,3741/2	58
XII	584,074	48,909	33,8591/2	—

––––––––––
1. *Wydatki domowe.*

No. 62. YI-938

Announcement (no number) of 30 July 1940 concerning establishing day camps for children ages 4 to 7. [in Polish]

ANNOUNCEMENT

I hereby make known that *at 85 Franciszkańska Street* and *at 22 Zawisza Street* I am starting another day camp for the most impoverished children ages *4–7 years,* who reside in the neighborhood of these locations.

Registrations will take place in the schools at *76 Franciszkańska Street and 25 Młynarska Street on the days of July 30, 31, and August 1, 1940, during the hours 9–3* P.M.

No. 63. YI-58

Statistical Table: The Ghetto Population on 12 July 1940, by Occupation, Gender, and Age (between Lodhzer geto, *pp. 93 and 94). [in German, see pages 96–97]*

No. 64.

Graphic Representation of the Labor Divisions and Internal Administration of the Litzmannstadt Ghetto, August 1943 (pull out in Lodhzer geto*). [in German, see pages 98–103]*

The Ghetto Population on 12 July 1940
by Occupation, Gender, and Age
(according to registrations)

Occupations[1]	MEN								
	Age to 8 years	Age 9—14	Age 15—19	Age 20—25	Age 26—35	Age 36—45	Age 46—60	Age over 60	All Men
Physician	—	—	—	—	22	15	16	13	66
Pharmacist	—	—	—	2	17	17	16	8	60
Worker (untrained)	—	23	801	1,008	1,595	1,319	1,196	593	6,535
Baker	—	2	51	80	242	257	252	78	962
Construction worker	—	—	4	6	16	25	14	11	76
Bookbinder	—	1	18	22	41	48	63	24	217
Office and Business Employee	—	16	426	792	1,369	1,317	1,181	446	5,548
Printer	—	—	22	44	71	54	68	16	275
Electrician	—	—	43	68	97	73	41	7	329
Dyer	—	—	8	11	35	59	37	17	167
Barber or Hairdresser	—	1	32	68	147	143	81	23	495
Wagoners	—	1	57	83	199	192	180	87	799
Fancy Goods Worker[2]	—	2	23	45	48	33	19	7	177
Tanner	—	—	4	10	13	16	16	12	71
Health Personnel	—	1	6	21	41	38	26	12	145
Business Agents	—	—	1	19	86	131	205	137	579
Artisan Apprentices	—	9	77	17	2	1	—	—	106
Building Manager	—	—	1	5	36	54	73	48	217
Hat maker	—	1	36	72	112	75	64	25	385
Engineers and Technicians	—	—	5	12	32	32	37	6	124
Jurists	—	—	—	1	4	3	1	1	10
Merchants	—	3	150	353	1,288	1,686	2,531	1,876	7,887
Plumber[3]	—	—	24	34	61	69	63	39	290
Furrier	—	—	25	52	93	66	43	5	289
Agric. Workers and Gardeners	—	—	6	7	11	17	14	12	67
Teachers	—	—	19	65	125	141	218	159	727
Rag Sorters	—	—	1	3	6	7	5	2	24
Painters	—	2	52	81	161	137	152	49	634
Manipulators[4]	—	—	—	5	6	8	17	13	49
Metal Workers, Locksmiths and Mechanics	—	3	131	108	218	146	121	26	753
Corset makers	—	—	2	1	8	2	2	—	16
Packers	—	—	5	17	36	84	109	37	288
Saddler	—	—	6	6	13	24	12	6	67
Box maker	—	—	26	48	45	33	19	10	181
Tailors and Underclothing Sewers	—	22	675	883	2,109	1,187	997	429	6,302
Shoemakers[5]	—	6	128	229	705	629	548	211	2,456
Knitter	—	—	9	23	41	29	24	15	141
Upholsterer[6]	—	1	10	23	64	59	35	4	196
Cabinetmaker	—	6	127	144	253	185	314	96	1,125
Watchmaker and Engraver	—	—	5	26	37	47	42	36	193
Weaver	—	2	330	486	668	714	1,192	679	4,068
Stocking Maker[7]	—	13	286	567	876	553	310	74	2,679
Dentist	—	—	—	1	1	8	9	2	21
Dental Technician	—	—	5	6	9	14	5	—	39
Other Occupations	—	—	47	97	23	286	336	196	1,215
Without Occupation	10,711	9,487	3,600	159	80	47	38	55	24,177
TOTAL	10,711	9,602	7,284	5,812	11,392	10,077	10,747	5,602	71,227

---

1. Ed. Note: In the German original, the occupations are listed alphabetically in German. The sequence of entries has been retained here without attempting to alphabetize them in English.]

2. *Galanteriearbeiter*

3. Or sheetmetal worker (*Klempner*).

WOMEN									All Men and Women
Age to 8 years	Age 9—14	Age 15—19	Age 20—25	Age 26—35	Age 36—45	Age 46—60	Age over 60	All Women	
—	—	—	—	9	4	12	0	26	92
—	—	—	9	30	18	11	—	68	128
—	13	536	1,022	1,696	886	505	134	4,792	11,327
—	—	1	5	8	4	4	3	25	987
—	—	—	—	—	—	—	—	—	76
—	—	3	9	17	6	8	4	47	264
—	5	262	738	925	414	59	41	2,541	8,092
—	—	3	2	2	—	1	—	8	283
—	—	—	—	—	—	—	—	—	329
—	—	—	—	1	3	1	—	5	172
—	—	15	52	93	82	33	6	281	776
—	—	—	—	—	—	—	—	—	799
—	—	13	35	34	16	1	—	99	276
—	—	3	—	1	—	—	—	4	75
—	2	19	14	103	73	39	19	319	464
—	—	1	1	2	5	20	3	32	611
—	—	5	—	—	—	—	—	5	111
—	—	2	—	2	4	6	6	20	237
—	—	40	8	141	92	42	9	405	790
—	—	—	2	3	1	—	—	6	130
—	—	—	—	—	—	—	—	—	10
—	—	32	132	371	397	459	287	1,678	9,565
—	—	—	—	—	—	—	—	—	290
—	—	1	2	3	2	1	—	9	298
—	—	—	1	2	2	4	—	9	76
—	—	9	70	164	151	123	26	543	1,270
—	—	2	5	9	11	2	—	29	53
—	—	—	1	—	3	1	—	5	639
—	—	—	—	2	1	2	—	5	54
—	1	—	2	1	1	1	—	6	759
—	—	41	84	59	38	10	—	232	248
—	—	—	—	—	—	—	—	—	288
—	—	2	2	2	—	1	—	7	74
—	—	9	8	15	4	2	—	38	219
—	33	1,345	2,170	2,879	1,411	707	137	8,682	14,984
—	—	—	1	2	—	1	—	4	2,460
—	1	38	70	148	55	22	5	339	480
—	—	—	—	—	—	—	—	—	196
—	—	—	—	—	—	—	—	—	1,125
—	—	—	—	—	—	—	—	—	193
—	4	180	367	584	390	268	56	1,849	5,917
—	8	259	569	766	329	126	21	2,078	4,757
—	—	—	3	5	23	9	—	40	61
—	—	2	4	1	—	2	—	9	48
—	—	3	10	26	18	7	4	68	1,283
10,115	9,064	5,252	2,919	7,274	8,885	10,805	6,545	60,859	85,036
10,115	9,131	8,078	8,440	15,380	13,329	13,395	7,307	85,175	156,402

4. *Manipulanten.*
5. *Schuster u. Scheftemach.*
6. *Tapezierer*
7. *Wirker*

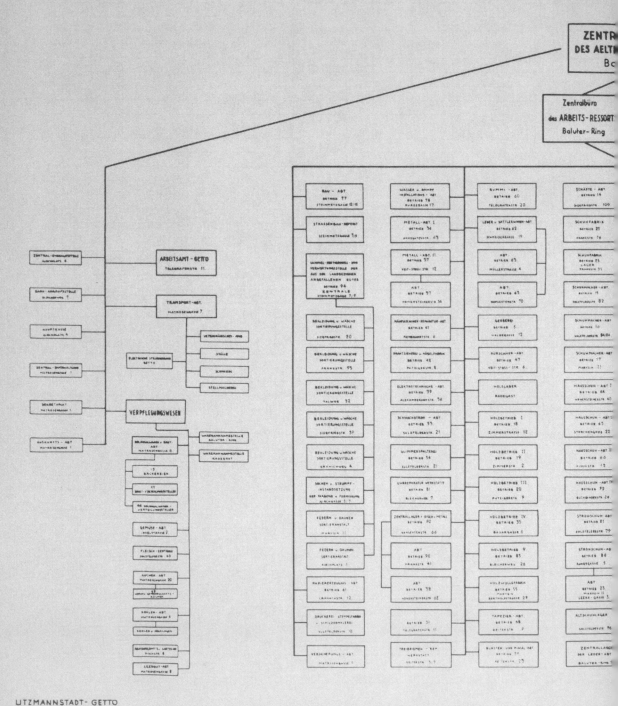

UTZMANNSTADT- GETTO
AUGUST – 1943

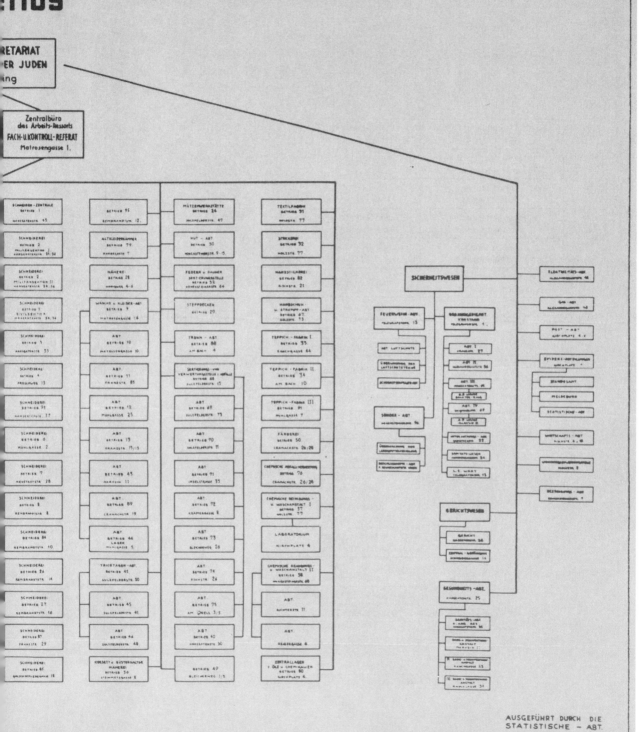

AUSGEFÜHRT DURCH DIE
STATISTISCHE - ABT.

Central Purchasing Office Kirchplatz 4	Ghetto Labor Office Telegrafenstr. 11		Construction Dept. Plant 77 Steinmetzgasse 12-15
Purchasing Office Bank Bleicheweg 7			
Main Cashier Kirchplatz 4	Transport Dept. Matrosengasse 7		Road Building Bureau Steinmetzgasse 7/9
Central Bookkeeping Matrosengasse 1	Electric Streetcar Service Ghetto	Veterinary Dept.	Collection-Sorting-Utilization Dept. for the Resulting Goods from Country Districts Plant 94 Chief Office Steinmetzgasse 7/9
Secretariat Matrosengasse 1		Stalls	
Information Dept. Matrosengasse 1	Food Supply System	Smithy	Clothing and Undergarments Sorting Dept. Siefriedstr. 20
	Groceries and Bread Dept. Matrosengasse 6	Wheelwright	Clothing and Undergarments Sorting Dept. Franzstr. 93
	15 Bakeries		
	11 Bread Food Supply Stations	Goods Receiving Station Baluter-Ring	Clothing and Undergarments Sorting Dept. Talweg 32
	44 Groceries Distribution Stations	Goods Receiving Station Radegast	Clothing and Undergarments Sorting Dept. Siegfriedstr. 39
	Vegetables Dept. Inselstrasse 2		Clothing and Undergarments Sorting Dept. Kranichweg 4
	Central Meat Office Sulzfelderstr. 40		Socks and Stockings – Repair Bureau of Dye-works and Formation Kirchgasse 5/7
	Kitchens Dept. Matrosengasse 20		
	48 Welfare [?] and Community Kitchens		
	Coal Dept. Matrosengasse 4		
	Coal and Wood Storehouse		
	Food Supply Ration Cards Dept. Fischstr. 8		
	Empties Dept. Matrosengasse 8		

cont'd A

GRAPHIC REPRESENTATION OF THE LABOR DIVISIONS AND INTERNAL ADMINISTRATION OF THE GHETTO
Litzmannstadt Ghetto, August 1943
Prepared by the Statistical Department

Central Secretariat of the Eldest of the Jews
Baluter Ring

Central Bureau of the Labor Divisions Baluter Ring	Central Bureau of the Labor Divisions Craft and Control Bureau Matrosengasse 1

Water and Steam Installation Dept. Plant 78 Kurzegasse 17	Rubber Dept. Plant 60 Telegrafenstr. 20	Handle-shaft Dept. Plant 14 Siegfriedstr. 100	Tailoring Central Office Plant 1 Hanseatenstr. 45	Plant 95 Rembrandtstr. 12	Capmaking Workshops Plant 24 Sulzfelderstr. 47	Textile Factory Plant 31 Holzstr. 77
Metal Dept. I Plant 36 Hanseatenstr. 63	Leather and Saddle Goods Dept. Plant 62 Schneidergasse 19	Shoe Factory Plant 25 Franzstr. 76	Tailoring Plant 2 Military Sector I Hanseatenstr. 34/36	Old Clothing Depot Plant 79 Rungegasse 7	Hat Dept. Plant 30 Hohensteinerstr. 9-15	Knitting Plant 32 Holzstr. 77
Metal Dept. II Plant 37 Voit-Stoss-str. 12	Dept. Plant 63 Müllerstrasse 4	Shoe Factory Plant 23 Storehouse Franzstr. 31	Tailoring Plant 2 Military Sector II Hanseatenstr. 34/36	Sewing Shop Plant 28 Honigweg 4-6	Feather and Down Sorting Shop Plant 52 Hohensteinerstr. 64	Handknitting Plant 82 Fischstr. 21
Dept. Plant 37 Hohensteinerstr. 56	Dept. Plant 63 Hanseatenstr. 70	Shoemaker Dept. Plant 15 Sulzfelderstr. 82	Tailoring Plant 2 Civilian Sector Hanseatenstr. 34/36	Underwear and Clothing Dept. Plant 9 Matrosengasse 14	Quilts Plant 29	Glove and Stocking Dept. Plant 67 Holzstr. 75
Sewing Machine Repair Dept. Plant 41 Rembrandtstr. 6	Tannery Plant 5 Halbegasse 12	Shoemaker Dept. Plant 16 Sulzfelderstr. 84/86	Tailoring Plant 3 Hanseatenstr. 53	Dept. Plant 10 Matrosengasse 10	Detaching [Seams] Dept. Plant 88 Am Bach 4	Carpet Factory I Plant 33 Rauchgasse 44
Wire and Nail Factory Plant 42 Putzigerstr. 8	Furrier Dept. Plant 47 Veit-Stoss-Str. 6	Shoemaker Dept. Plant 17 Marysin II	Tailoring Plant 4 Froschweg 13	Dept. Plant 11 Franzstr. 85	Sorting and Utilization Shop for Scraps Plant 68 Sulzfelderstr. 15	Carpet Factory II Plant 34 Am Bach 10
Electro-technical Dept. Plant 39 Alexanderhofstr. 36	Lumberyard Radegast	Slipper Dept. I Plant 64 Hohensteinerstr. 40	Tailoring Plant 93 Hanseatenstr. 37	Dept. Plant 12 Mühlgasse 25	Dept. Plant 69 Sulzfelderstr. 73	Carpet Factory III Plant 91 Mühlgasse 7
Low Voltage Dept. Plant 53 Sulzfelderstr. 21	Wood Dept. I Plant 18 Zimmerstrasse 12	Slipper Dept. II Plant 65 Storchengasse 22	Tailoring Plant 6 Mühlgasse 2	Dept. Plant 13 Franzstr. 13/15	Dept. Plant 70 Sulzfelderstr. 11	Dye-works Plant 50 Cranachstr. 26/28
Mica-slate Splitting Shop Plant 54 Sulzfelderstr. 21	Wood Dept. II Plant 19 Zimmerstr. 2	Slipper Dept. III Plant 66 Fischstr. 15	Tailoring Plant 7 Neustadtstr. 28	Dept. Plant 43 Marysin II	Dept. Plant 71 Inselstrasse 33	Chemical Waste Utilization Plant 76 Cranachstr. 26/28
cont'd B	cont'd C	cont'd D	cont'd E	cont'd F	cont'd G	cont'd H

GRAPHIC REPRESENTATION OF THE LABOR DIVISIONS AND INTERNAL ADMINISTRATION OF THE GHETTO
Litzmannstadt Ghetto, August 1943
Prepared by the Statistical Department

Central Secretariat of the Eldest of the Jews
Baluter Ring

Central Bureau of the Labor Divisions Baluter Ring				Central Bureau of the Labor Division Craft and Control Bureau Matrosengasse 1		
cont'd A	cont'd B	cont'd C	cont'd D	cont'd E	cont'd F	cont'd G
Feathers and Down Sorting Facility Marysin 11	Watch Repair Workshop Plant 81 Bleicherweg 7	Wood Dept. III Plant 20 Putzigerstr. 9	Slipper Dept. IV Plant 92 Buchbinderstr. 26	Tailoring Plant 8 Rembrandtstr. 8	Dept. Plant 89 Cranachstr. 19	Dept. Plant 72 Krämergasse 8
Feathers and Down Sorting Facility Kirchplatz 1	Central Storehouse: Iron-Metal Plant 90 Hanseatenstr. 66	Wood Dept. IV Plant 35 Basargasse 6	Strawshoe Dept. Plant 21 Sulzfelderstr. 79	Tailoring Plant 84 Rembrandtstr. 10	Dept. Plant 44 Storehouse Mühlgasse 5	Dept. Plant 73 Bleicherweg 26
Paper Production Dept. Plant 61 Cranachstr. 12	Dept. Plant 90 Franzstr. 41	Wood Dept. V Plant 83 Bleicherweg 26	Strawshoe Dept. Plant 86 Rungegasse 5	Tailoring Plant 26 Rembrandtstr. 14	Tricotware Dept. Plant 45 Sulzfelderstr. 50	Dept. Plant 74 Fischstr. 26
Printshop, Rubber-stamp Factory and Sign-painting Sulzfelderstr. 10	Dept. Plant 38 Hohensteinerstr. 62	Wood Shavings Factory Plant 55 Marysin Bertholdstrasse 29	Dept. Plant 23 Marysin II Leere-Gasse 3	Tailoring Plant 27 Rembrandtstr. 16	Dept. Plant 45 Sulzfelderstr. 41	Dept. Plant 75 Am Quell 3/5
Insurance Dept. Matrosengasse 1	Plant 51 Telegrafenstr. 11	Upholstery Dept. Plant 48 Reiterstr. 9	Old Shoe Store-house Sulzfelderstr. 96	Tailoring Plant 87 Franzstr. 29	Dept. Plant 46 Sulzfelderstr. 48	Dept. Plant 40 Hanseatenstr. 50
	Drive Belt Repair Workshop Reiterstr. 5/7	Brush Dept. Plant 59 Reiterstr. 23	Central Storehouse of the Leather Dept. Baluter-Ring 5	Tailoring Plant 85 Goldschmiede-gasse 18	Corset and Brassiere Sewing Plant 56 Steinmetz-gasse 8	Plant 49 Bleicherweg 1/3

cont'd H

Chemical Cleaning and Laundry Facility I
Plant 57
Holzstr. 77

Laboratory
Kirchplatz 4

Chemical Cleaning and Laundry Facility II
Plant 58
Hohensteinerstr. 68

Dept.
Richterstr. 11

Dept.
Reigergasse 4

Central Storehouse for Oils and Chemicals
Plant 80
Kirchplatz 4

Security System		Electricity Dept. Alexanderhofstr. 46
Fire Brigade Dept. Telegrafenstr. 13	Order Service Directorate Telegrafenstr. 1	Gas Dept. Alexanderhofstr. 40
Air Defense Dept.	Dept. I Franzstrasse 27	Postal Dept. Kirchplatz 4-4
Supervision of Air Defense Practices	Dept. II Alexanderhofstr. 54	
[illegible] Dept.	Dept. III Hanseatenstrasse 61	Records Departments Kirchplatz 4
Special Dept. Hanseatenstr. 96	Order Service Guard Post Baluter-Ring	Registry Office
Supervision of [illegible]	Dept. IV Siegfriedstrasse 69	Registration Office
Confiscation Dept. Of [illegible] Goods	Order Service Guard Post [illegible] II	Statistical Dept.
	Investigation Dept. Hohensteinerstr. [?] 24	
	Air Defense Warden Telegrafenstr. 13	Management Dept. Fischstr. 4-6
		[illegible] Fischstr. [illegible]
	Judicial System	Burial Dept. [illegible]str. 9
	Court [illegible]str. 24	
	Central Prison Schneidergasse 14	

Health Dept.
Hanseatenstr. 25

Health Dept. for Labor Divisions
Hanseatenstr. 25

Bath and Disinfection Facility
Marysin I

II Bath and Disinfection Facility
Rauchgasse 13

III Bath and Disinfection Facility
Rauchgasse 39

III

Provisioning

The German army's penetration into Polish territory immediately washed away the economic basis of Polish Jewry, especially in the regions that were annexed into the German Reich. Organized and unorganized plundering of Jewish possessions proceeded parallel with the great devastation and impoverishment directly resulting from combat.

The Main Trusteeship Office-East (*Haupttreuhandstelle-Ost,* HTO) was created at Goering's order on 1 November 1939. In time it became the chief organ of the occupation regime in Poland for matters of confiscation of Jewish and Polish property. Another Goering decree of 28 November 1939 created the "legal" basis for confiscation of all raw materials and unfinished goods in the occupied territories for the German war economy. In practice, systematic looting of the Jewish population commenced immediately after the German military marched in, and the subsequent decrees only sanctioned the factual situation.[1]

In Łódź, for example, already in September 1939 the authorities confiscated Jewish wholesalers' stocks of fabrics and groceries. Trustees (*Treuhändler*) were placed in control of factories and stores. Food shops were liquidated under the pretext of their unsanitary conditions, while cash, jewelry, garments, household objects, and so forth were stolen.

Overnight, the majority of Jews who had no businesses and no capital and had always lived from hand to mouth were left without the means to live. Food could only be purchased at Christian shops where one had to contend with "the hell of standing in the lines, into which Jews were not admitted."[2]

On 16 October 1939, Rumkowski established a Provisioning Department whose initial task was to supply provisions to the Jewish charitable institutions, like hospitals, schools, soup kitchens, and homes for the evacuees, refugees, and so forth.[3]

According to the City Commissioner's decree of 14 November 1939, the Jewish community was supposed to receive 25 percent of the foodstuffs consigned for the city, but food allocation by the city administration took place in an irregular, chaotic manner and food shipments were minimal in comparison with the needs of the Jewish population.[4] It would also happen that already allotted products were confiscated. The Jewish food merchants were cut off from their former suppliers and only Rumkowski and his authorized agents had any access to the Christian wholesalers and to German institutions and firms.[5]

The Provisioning Department thus had to deal with the overall supply of food for the Jewish population. Due to lack of money, Rumkowski turned to the Jewish wholesalers, who would lay out the necessary funds for the community and bring food products from the countryside, often risking their health and, indeed, their lives in the process. Security deposits for repayment were also taken from bakers and concessionaires of food shops. Since they subsequently exploited their monopoly for purposes of speculation, this system was abolished. The same happened with a partnership of former vegetable dealers to whom Rumkowski had entrusted the sale of vegetables.

At the start of March 1940, Rumkowski opened communal food shops (doc. no. 65) and gave concessions to private food dealers to receive food allocations for the population.[6] The Provisioning Department also opened a milk store that not only distributed milk products brought in from the city, but later also produced dairy products for children and the elderly. Thirty-two shops for the sale of bread and milk were opened.[7]

To raise the funds needed to buy food products, on 25 May 1940 Rumkowski ordered that each tenant should pay three marks per family member to the house committees that were to forward the money to the Provisioning Department.[8] The allocation of rationed foods (aside from bread, which was not yet rationed) began on 2 June 1940 through the house committees.[9] Until 12 December, when Rumkowski announced the rationing of bread and the introduction of new bread and food ration cards, eighteen announcements about food allocation were issued, more or less every ten to fourteen days.

The need among the impoverished Jewish population was so great that almost half the Jews often did not possess the necessary couple of marks to buy up their allotted food. During the ninth distribution, on 29 August 1940, those who did not buy up their allotted items amounted to 47.1 percent of the population. Once cash relief payments were introduced on 20 September 1940 (see above) and with the enlistment of large parts of the population into the newly formed ghetto workshops, the percentage buying their rations rose, reaching 96.7 percent by October 1940.[10]

The introduction of full-scale rationing of food on 15 December 1940 (doc. no. 66) was a breakthrough moment in the provisioning situation of the ghetto because this eliminated the possibility of free consumption of meals in public kitchens and private restaurants. Whoever wanted to eat in a given soup kitchen or restaurant had to be registered and turn in his ration cards so that the given kitchen could collect his food portion from the Provisioning Department.

Provisioning of the ghetto was put entirely under the Provisioning Department when Rumkowski announced, on 24 and 27 December 1940, that he had taken over sixty-four building kitchens, five factory kitchens, thirteen private restaurants and other feeding points, and that from 30 December foodstuffs would be distributed not through the house committees, but through the stores of the Provisioning Department.[11]

In this connection, the Provisioning Department expanded mightily. In July 1940, its thirteen sub-departments employed 651 persons (the major-

(Above) A soup coupon issued by the Łódź Ghetto's Jewish Council, 1940–1944. Photographer unknown. USHMM, courtesy of Jack J. Silverstein.

(Below) Crowd gathers in front of a soup kitchen in the Łódź Ghetto, 1940–1942. Photographer unknown. USHMM, courtesy of Żydowski Instytut Historyczny Instytut Naukowo-Badawczy.

ity—327—in the *referat* for distribution points).[12] Even after the department was decentralized in January 1941, when the departments for meat, vegetables, and milk were separated from it, the remaining units, including baking and distribution of bread and groceries, employed 834 persons in December 1941.[13]

The huge increase in the Provisioning Department's scope of activity is also vividly reflected in the sums of its business volume: in February 1940 it amounted to 42,904 marks, in May (in the first month after the sealing of the ghetto) 932,899 marks, and in November 1940 2,770,786 marks. The overall total financial gross of the department for eleven months of 1940 amounted to 16,611,302 marks and for the whole of 1941 totaled 20,502,765 marks.[14]

These statistics reflect only the relative growth of the activity of the Provisioning Department in the ghetto itself, but not the actual value of the foodstuffs that the Germans granted for the ghetto. The ghetto paid for them not with its worthless ghetto money, but with its confiscated property and with the slave labor of its inhabitants. This was in accord with the principle imposed by the German regime that the costs of supplying the ghetto must be covered by the Jewish workforce's salary, that is, according to the value of the ghetto production and of the "sale" of Jewish property through the Judenälteste's bank. According to the *Gettoverwaltung's* calculations, provisioning the ghetto cost more than the ghetto brought in. In its letter to the Łódź *Regierungspräsident,* dated 21 September 1941, the *Gettoverwaltung* complained that supplying the ghetto with foodstuffs amounted to an average of 1.3 to 1.7 million RM a month, while the revenue (*Lohn*) from the four most important employment divisions, namely tailoring readymade clothing, furniture carpentry, shoemaking, and manual weaving, was no more than 105,000 RM and the sale of valuables not more than 100,000 RM monthly.[15]

The sealed off ghetto, robbed of the possibility of feeding itself, became completely dependent on the mercy of the German provisioning system. And here, with complete blatancy, appeared the war of extermination against the Jewish population. In the Łódź Ghetto, the nourishment norm for a Jew was set at 30 pfennig a day, lower even than the prison norm (40–50 pfennig) that was supposed to be the projected nourishment level of the Łódź Ghetto.[16]

Even Biebow, the head of the *Gettoverwaltung,* who was personally interested in maintaining the production of the ghetto industry, complained in a 4 March 1942 memorandum to the Łódź Gestapo that the

A supplementary ration coupon issued to workers on the night shift in the Łódź Ghetto by the Jewish Council, 1940–1944. Photographer unknown. USHMM, courtesy of Jack J. Silverstein.

Hans Biebow, head of the Germans' Łódź Ghetto administration or Gettoverwaltung, at his desk, 1940–1944. Photograph by Walter Genewein. USHMM, courtesy of Robert Abrams.

nutritional norm in the ghetto had been beneath the prison norm for a year; that the health condition of the Jewish workers put into doubt their productivity and ability to work.[17]

According to an agreement of 14 June 1941, between the *Landesbauernschaft* (Farmers' Organization) of Poznań and the *Gettoverwaltung,* the following food norms were set for the Łódź Ghetto:

1. Bread (starting from 3 July): 2,250 grams a week for workers; 1,143 grams of flour a week for nonworkers.
2. Meat: 200 grams for workers; 160 grams a week for nonworkers. However, since meat was inaccessible at the time for the ghetto, two eggs a week should be issued instead.
3. Fats: 100 grams a week per person.
4. Potatoes: 5.25 kilograms a week.
5. Sugar: 600 grams a month (until then only 300 grams was foreseen).
6. Other nutritional items: 100 grams a week.[18]

In reality, even these starvation norms remained only on paper. In 1941, when the entire provisioning in the ghetto was already firmly regulated and all were dependent upon the ration portions, the Department for Bread and Groceries provided 12.85 million kilograms of flour to the bakeries and distributed among the population 5.8 million kilograms of other foodstuffs (aside from vegetables, meat, and dairy products). The result is a daily average per person during 1941 of 235 grams of flour and 105 grams of other foodstuffs (the 303,000 kilograms of additional foodstuffs that were distributed during the year for the hospitals and other philanthropic institutions do not essentially change this tragic picture of food supply). One must also take into account the large variations in the quantities of the delivered food transports. Thus, for example, during the month of January 1941, the bakeries received only 345,000 kilograms of flour, while in March 1941, a sum of 380,000 kilograms of foodstuffs was distributed in the ghetto, which works out to ludicrously small quantities per day of not more than about 100 grams of flour and 40 grams of other foodstuffs (doc. no. 67). At the end of October 1940, there was no bread at all in the ghetto for three days.[19] During long periods, a product as important as potatoes would be lacking, for example during two weeks in September 1940 and from January to April 1942, and so forth. A major part of even the already authorized shipments would not arrive in the ghetto. In his aforementioned letter to the Gestapo of 4 March 1942, Biebow states that for the year 1941 the ghetto received 107 tons less than authorized of various food products, 289 tons less of meat, 323 tons less of marmalade, 10,865 tons less of potatoes, 503 tons less of vegetables, and 151 tons less of ersatz-coffee. From these colossal deficits in the feeding of the ghetto, one can form a concept of what indeed arrived.[20]

The worsening of the provisioning situation in the ghetto would sometimes lead to hunger disturbances. In July 1940, when the situation in the ghetto markedly declined due to the ban on receiving parcels and due to the introduction of the ghetto money, which halted trade and smuggling with the outside, a crowd of hungry social assistance clients, who had not been paid their cash relief grants, entered the community's building and began to demolish the office. Rumkowski had then ordered the issuance of coupons for free dinners to each who asked for it.[21] But this could not substantially ease the hunger in the ghetto, particularly when the distribution of products for the needy fell sharply due to shortage of food.

On 10 and 11 August 1940, hunger drove masses of people into the street twice on two consecutive days. On the first day, the demonstration was not large and not very numerous; the police easily dispersed it. But on the second day, thousands flooded the streets, with cries of "We want bread, we're dying from hunger." The Jewish police, seeing the large crowds of demonstrators, refused to intervene and withdrew. At Rumkowski's notification to the German authorities, the German police shot into the air, dispersing the crowd, and then they assaulted the workers fleeing into the houses. The result was only a few lightly wounded. On 12 August, Rumkowski issued an appeal for calm to the population, promising to increase the food supply in the soup kitchens. A number of teahouses were opened and several thousand workers each received 5 kilograms of potatoes to take home.[22]

But this was like a drop in the ocean. The majority continued to go hungry and at the start of October 1940 a large crowd attacked a potato store and looted the entire stock of potatoes there. German and Jewish police drove the crowd away, with two killed and four injured.[23] Hunger disturbances with attempts to loot food wagons and a lumberyard also took place on 11 and 12 January 1941; only strong patrols by the ghetto police restored order (doc. no. 68).

The severe supply situation was eased a little by increasing the food supplied in the public kitchens. In August 1941, the number of dinners issued was twice as large as in July, averaging 11,340 meals a day, rising to 16,505 dinners in September. Additionally, introduction of the cash relief payment system at the end of September 1940 gave the poor and impoverished segments of the ghetto population the opportunity to purchase at least a portion of their food ration at the distribution points. The ability to buy the food rations in full also improved thanks to the fact that the factories in the ghetto industry were employing an ever larger number of workers, whose monthly earnings averaged about 20 ghetto marks.

Nevertheless, with a very small exception of a thin segment of the ghetto elite, the Jewish population suffered from an unceasing state of hunger throughout the ghetto's existence, that is, for over four years.

A series of factors influenced the provisioning situation in the ghetto: first, food delivery by the German supervisory authorities in a given period; second, the supply policies of Rumkowski and his provisioning bureaucracy; and third, objective economic factors in the ghetto itself in connection with the various circumstances and shakeups that the

Men, women, and children carrying various containers in line for food at a soup kitchen in the Łódź Ghetto, 1940–1942. Photographer unknown. USHMM, courtesy of Gila Flam.

ghetto endured during its existence. We have already described the first factor above. We will now discuss the latter two factors in more detail.

In general, although there were deviations for reasons of patronage or favoritism, Rumkowski applied the German provisioning policy of differentiating between workers and nonworkers in the ghetto's population in regard to food. This was also in accord with Rumkowski's own ideology of "rescue through work."

In time, a provisioning pyramid formed in the ghetto, and the size of one's portion of the meager ghetto supplies was dependent upon the position an individual occupied on the steps of the pyramid. At the pinnacle of the supply pyramid stood all those who had the right to benefit from the so-called "*Beirat*" allocations (ration cards with the letter B). To this category belonged members of the *Beirat,* high officials of the Jewish ghetto administration, like the directors of departments and factories, master craftsmen, and technical instructors, and the members of the physicians' and pharmacists' cooperatives. Beyond the normal rations, they would also receive a supplement of various articles, mainly meat, flour, and sugar, at the four special shops or in the so-called cooperatives. This most privileged group was not large. In the first half of May 1942 these privileged people numbered nearly 1,500 persons.[24]

In 1942, *Beirat* supplements in various lower gradations—BI, BII, BIII C.P. (Polish: *ciężko pracujący,* hardworkers)—also included certain other categories of workers. These included, for example, those working in hazardous sanitary conditions: excrement transporters (*fekalistn*), pressers, tanners, and highly qualified skilled workers, as well as so-called hardworkers and overtime laborers who, after a normal day's work, would still perform urgent jobs at night, like unloading arriving shipments and so forth.[25]

At the start of November 1943, when the *Gettoverwaltung* was preparing to take over provisioning matters in the ghetto, the B-rations were "temporarily" halted.[26] These coupons were reintroduced at the start of May 1944.[27]

On the second rung of the provisioning ladder stood the general officials, workers in the ghetto factories, building watchmen, those employed in public works, Jewish police personnel, firefighters, and chimneysweeps. Aside from the normal allocations for all, they would also get supplements, among others including foods that were rarely distributed in the ghetto, like meat, sausage, and potatoes (doc. no. 68). These supplements would be issued on so-called "extra-coupons" from time to time, or (from March 1942) on systematically introduced supplemental ration cards, number 1 for laborers (with a better ration) and number 2 for office workers (with a weaker ration)[28] (doc. no. 69).

Workers in the factories would each also get one or two soups daily (not on their ration cards) for a price of 25 to 30 pfennig at the workplace. From 1 June 1942, the meal for workers in the factories was replaced with 15 dekagrams of bread, four dekagrams of sausage, or possibly butter, and coffee. Six weeks later, on 14 July, the former soup system was resumed at the workplaces.[29]

At the end of May 1943, Rumkowski shifted over to a system of preferentially supplying better food to certain categories of workers, presumably those employed in the most important branches of the ghetto industry and to overtime- and hard-laborers. Kitchens were opened for them to provide so-called "strengthening dinners" (*krefti-kungs-mitogn*). The first kitchen of this sort opened on 31 May for 1,500 workers. And by 26 October, three more such kitchens were in operation for 5,600 persons, thus altogether over 7,000 people. At the start of November 1943, Rumkowski halted the issuance of additional soups (*tsuzatz-zupn*) for the workers in the factories (only one soup daily). But from 15 November 1943, Biebow took over direct supervision of provisioning issues in the ghetto and cancelled Rumkowski's order; he even promised an improvement of the food supply situation for those working (doc. no. 70).[30]

In fact, the additional soups were temporarily reinstituted only for the "deserving" (*fardinstfule*) 10 percent of workers and employees. This meant essentially for those doing heavy labor for long hours.[31] On 16 November, a special kitchen was opened for this category of about 3,000 workers.

The sick, the weakened, and mothers of newborns (*kimpetorins*) were also in a sort of privileged position in regard to nourishment, for they would receive special products in the dietetic shops, on prescription coupons filled out by doctors and certified by the Coupon Department.[32] The Health Department was very vigilant that the doctors not be too liberal in such cases. Only a couple of thousand benefited from this privilege, while the number of sick in the ghetto was in the tens of thousands. But even these very limited food allocations for the sick lasted only until winter 1942. On 14 February 1942, when the hunger in the ghetto had intensified, a circular from the Health Department abolished the special food rations for the sick. The circular was repeated on 26 May.

The worker or employee received his supplemental nourishment so long as he worked. If he fell ill and the sickness lasted longer than seven days, he lost his job and simultaneously the right to supplemental food. Moreover, a worker's eligibility for supplemental feeding on the basis of his work card was dependent on whether he worked on a designated key date (*shtikhtog*). If for some reason he was not at work on that day, he lost his right to benefit from his work card.[33]

As mentioned, during the first years of the ghetto the feeding of the sick in the hospitals was satisfactory. Until the end of June 1942, the hospital personnel did not have any ration cards, but would be fed at the hospital during their work. From 30 June, the hospital workers received their own cards and also the supplemental food for workers, primarily "B.W.K." (German abbreviation for bread, sausage, and cof-

A family eating their daily
ration of soup in their
apartment in the Łódź
Ghetto. Note that all are
wearing coats due to the cold,
1940–1943. Photographer
unknown. USHMM,
courtesy of Żydowski
Instytut Historyczny Instytut
Naukowo-Badawczy.

fee).[34] Younger children were for a time in a better condition in regard
to food supply; until the closure of the schools, the children would receive dinner there.

From the first day of Rosh Hashana 1941, Rumkowski also introduced hot evening meals for children ages two to seven on special nourishment cards for the price of 15 or 5 pfennig (5 pfennig for those who
received relief; on the days of Rosh Hashana the suppers were given out
to the children free of charge).

On the bottom rung of the provisioning pyramid were those not
working, which was most of the population in the years 1940–1942.

There were two categories of food allocations: a larger one for the
so-called homecookers, who did not benefit from the public kitchens,
and a smaller one for those who registered in the kitchens and received
their dinners there (docs. nos. 71, 72).

Before the introduction of the ration card system, the Kitchen Department, founded on 12 December 1940, had under its supervision 130
public kitchens and restaurants (November 1940): five central kitchens,
the former building kitchens it had taken over, and other public and private kitchens with 145,000 consumers (about 95 percent of the ghetto
population) and 2,500 employees. The kitchens issued up to a half million servings of soup daily. There were, as mentioned, special factory

kitchens for tailors, shoemakers, carpenters, and others. Police and firemen had their 10 canteens. The public kitchens operated by Zionists and Bundists had great success. The nine Zionist and two Bundist kitchens (with about 4,000 consumers) were, in the ghetto conditions, a surrogate for public life (doc. no. 73).

After introduction of total food rationing, the number of public kitchen consumers fell to about 15,000. A series of kitchens therefore had to be closed. In general, the number of kitchens was fluid due to various conditions, as the following shows.

Due to the major disorder and corruption that reigned in the majority of kitchens, they were closed in May 1942, with the exception of the kitchens for intelligentsia and the strictly Orthodox, and a few minor ones. The number of consumers fell to 6,000. After the conclusion of the "May outsettlement" in 1942, the number of kitchens increased and rose to fifty, yet by 1 June only five were left. One reason was that the food allocations for the homecookers were much better in quantity and quality than for those who ate in the public kitchens. On 1 July there remained only two kitchens (the kitchen for the intelligentsia and the kitchen for the devout) with no more than about 560 consumers.[35] Also continuing were the factory kitchens that endured the various transformations mentioned above.

We shall now see what the ghetto population received for their ration cards.

As for bread, the portion grew continually smaller (with a brief exception). At first, people were given 300 grams per head daily. For factory workers, there was a supplement of another 300 grams and later even 500 grams daily. On 21 January 1941, an equal bread ration of 400 grams for all without exception was introduced. Each person would receive two kilograms for five days in advance. But even this small bread ration could not be maintained and it was in fact reduced to 330 grams, as instead of five days the two kilograms of bread had to last for six days. From 4 November 1941, after the resettlement of Jews from Włocławek and Western Europe into the Łódź Ghetto, the bread ration was reduced to 280 grams per person. From 31 July 1942, it was further reduced to 250 grams.[36] At first, there were still sporadic bread distributions. Thus, for example, in January and February 1941 the population was allotted one-time bread supplements of 500 and 600 grams, respectively.[37] The elimination of the bread supplements for workers in January 1941 evoked a stormy strike among the carpenters (see chapter 7). Briefly, from 1 June to 15 July 1942, the workers received 150 grams of bread on the job instead of the factory soups. Bakery workers had the privilege of an extra portion of bread (in the amount of half a kilo), but only during their work. (In 1943, physically weakened workers were assigned to the bakeries so that they could build up their strength there.)

The pitiful bread portions (two kilograms for seven days, later for eight days) were consumed in the hungry ghetto within the first couple of days after they were received. Few still had any bread left by the last couple of days before the distribution of a new ration, and people had to rely solely on the meager soup.

Bread, therefore, belonged to the most expensive articles in the ghetto and played the role of a universally recognized measure of value and item of trade. In February 1944, a kilogram of bread reached the fantastic price of 1,100 marks.

As for milk, until May 1942, the ghetto would receive city deliveries of 1,000 liters of whole milk and 3,000 liters of skim milk. From June, only about 4,000 to 6,000 liters of skim milk was received. If the milk was in good condition, it was used in the hospitals. If it was already half-spoiled, which happened frequently, the Department for Dairy Products would produce cottage cheese from it, distributed to the population at the bread and milk points, more or less once a week.

As for the allocation of other food items (such as vegetables and groceries), it was on a starvation level during the ghetto's entire existence. Meat and fats were very seldom distributed. As a rule, food was issued for a period of ten to fourteen days, but there would occur longer breaks between one distribution and the next. As an example, we present the range of products and their caloric values from the food rations in different periods.

Thus, for example, the following was allocated per capita for the last third of May 1942:

Product	Quantity (grams)	Approximate Caloric Value (calories)
1. Potatoes	1,000	550
2. Beets (canned)	350	47
3. Rye flour (*kornmel*)	300	996
4. Peas	60	178
5. Rye flakes (*kornflokn*)	100	322
6. Sugar (white and brown)	150	570
7. Marmalade	200	498
8. Margarine	150	1,152
9. Sausage (lean)	200	400
10. Rye bread (*kornbroyt*)	2,500	6,175
TOTAL	5,360 grams	10,888 calories

Thus the number of calories per day amounted to an average of not quite 1,100. The official price of the ration was 3.50 ghetto marks.

For the middle third of January 1943, the ration and its caloric value were as follows:

Product	Quantity (grams)	Approximate Caloric Value (calories)
1. Potatoes	4,000	2,200
2. Rye flour	450	1,594
3. Sugar	320	1,216
4. Margarine	300	2,304
5. Oil	100	899
6. Beets	4,000	52
7. Bread	2,500	1,175
8. Other (salt, vinegar)	200	———
TOTAL	11,870 grams	14,440 calories

Therefore, the number of calories per day was 1,444. The ration's price was 7.20 marks.

For the fourteen days from 24 April until 7 May 1944, the allotted ration was as follows:

Product	Quantity (grams)	Approximate Caloric Value (calories)
1. Rye flour	660	1,992
2. Rye cereal (*korene kashe*)	200	664
3. Sugar	400	1,520
4. Oil	50	450
5. Marmalade	350	872
6. Soup extract in cubes	150	389
7. Canned beets	500	90
8. Beet juice	100	[?]
9. Rye bread (*kornbroyt*)	4,000	9,880
TOTAL	6,410 grams	15,857 calories

This ration for 14 days had a value of about 15,857 calories, or 1,132.6 calories a day.

Excluded from these calculations are the ersatz coffee and a series of minor products, like "*saga*," vinegar, whose quantity and caloric value were minimal and could not substantively change the results of our calculations.

We see that the nutritional value of the product allocations on the cards varied in different periods between about 1,000 and 1,400 calories daily. To these numbers ought to be added the caloric value of the soups in the factory kitchens (only for workers and other employees), which was—with few exceptions—minimal. Thus, for example, the average value of the factory soups in 1941, according to the data of the Statistical

Department, amounted to 388 calories. However, in June until mid-July, bread, sausage, and coffee were distributed in the worksites instead of soup; this portion had an average value of 552 calories. Together, then, the nutritional value of the food supplied to a working person for one day is maximally calculated at about 2,000 calories. Our calculations are more or less in agreement with the data from the Statistical Department, according to which the average value of the nutrition of a worker or an employee in 1941 amounted to 2,040 calories (including 43.55 grams of egg whites, 19.26 grams fats, and 411 grams carbohydrates); for a nonworker, the value was 1,620 calories (including 34.1 grams egg whites, 16 grams fats, and 326.6 grams carbohydrates). In the subsequent years (with the exception of 1943), the situation was, if not worse, certainly not improved.

As we see, the products from the official food allocation for the non-working population in the Łódź Ghetto covered only between 46 and 58 percent of the minimal caloric need that is necessary to keep the organism alive (2,400 calories), while for a working person it was about 66 percent of the minimum required (3,000 calories). In such a nutritional situation, combined with difficult physical labor, the organism could not survive longer than six to eight months.[38]

The food supply situation in the Łódź Ghetto was actually even worse, for the population was exclusively dependent upon the official provisioning. In other ghettos in the *Generalgouvernement* and in *Ostland*,[39] smuggling initially gave the segments of the population who were still well-to-do and earning well the possibility to turn to the black market to cover their enormous food deficit.

In the hermetically sealed Łódź Ghetto, both the German authorities and Rumkowski conducted a ruthless struggle against food smuggling. Right from the start, the Order Service systematically confiscated smuggled products and strictly banned street trade in bread, sweets, and the like.[40] A group of smugglers based in Marysin, supposedly as a kibbutz, was liquidated in autumn 1940.[41] The German ghetto guards fired without warning at anyone who approached the ghetto fence. On 9 July 1940, in accord with a German decree, Rumkowski issued a strict prohibition against even talking across the wire fence.[42]

In one document we read: "Many smugglers' families and still more innocent people, who were shot on the roads from the [beginning] until the end of July 1940, have the aforementioned laconic, but strict prohibition to lament." Between 2 and 28 July, twenty-four Jews were killed.[43] Introduction of the ghetto marks, worthless outside the ghetto, also cut off the possibility of food smuggling. The ban on receiving food parcels made it impossible to bring additional food into the ghetto in a legal way. The ghetto had to be satisfied with what officially arrived. But very little came into the ghetto.

The food products on the black market came from people compelled by various, often tragic reasons to sell a portion of their food rations to buyers and speculators. The prices were relatively high and continually tended to increase. They were effectively inaccessible for the overwhelming majority of the ghetto population. Here is a sample of the most important articles in various periods as they were noted in the daily entries of the ghetto *Chronicle*:

Items	10 Sept. 1942 Black Market Price	27 Dec. 1942 Black Market Price	27 Feb. 1944 Black Market Price
Rye bread (kilogram)	90 mk	360 mk	1,050–1,100 mk
Rye flour (kg)	——	280 mk	700 mk
Potatoes (kg)	9 mk	60 mk	200 mk
Butter (kg)	400 mk	1,300 mk	2,000 mk
Sugar (white)	110 mk	420 mk	1,000 mk
Oil, margarine	ca. 150 mk	1,300 mk	1,800 mk
Factory soup	——	12–14 mk	42 mk

When we take into account that a highly qualified worker in the Łódź Ghetto initially earned on average about 20 marks, and later, in 1943, when the wage was increased, to 50 marks a month, it is clear why a Jew in the Łódź Ghetto was entirely dependent on the official food supply. Rumkowski applied the German policy of "freezing" the prewar wages and salaries, so that a ghetto worker ought not to earn more than enough to purchase food rations for himself and his family. The result could only be a slow death from starvation. The nonworking population that lived from the money relief grants was often not in a position to buy up even the meager official allotments whose price oscillated between 2 and 7 marks and would sometimes reach up to 10 to 12 marks.

It should also be noted that food arriving in the ghetto was generally of low quality, frequently even in an unusable condition. These were no accidents, but a result of a conscious provisioning policy toward the ghetto, which was adopted at a conference on 25 October 1940, attended by representatives of the local authorities under the chairmanship of *Regierungsvicepräsident* Dr. Moser.[44] Thus, for example, on 1 July 1942, a transport of 800 kilograms of meat for the sausage factory in the ghetto arrived in a putrid state with green, yellow, and white chunks. The Meat Headquarters refused to accept the shipment. After an intervention at the *Gettoverwaltung,* it was decided that the meat should be set aside until an inspection by the official veterinarian, who later directed that it be withdrawn from use. A short time earlier, a transport of 10,000 kilograms of rancid (*fareyletste*) butter, already black in color, was shipped to the ghetto. There was no other solution than to remove the bitterness by rinsing the spoiled product a couple of times, and in that condition it was distributed among the ghetto residents, "whose stomachs were used to everything" (doc. no. 74). In wintertime, potatoes and other vegetables arrived half-frozen or rotten. From the rotten frozen vegetables the Milk Department would produce a special ghetto delicacy, the so-called "*salatke,*" that was distributed to the ghetto population. Highly sought after in the ghetto were the potato peel flakes (*shubekhts*) (doc. no. 75).

Add to this a corrupt, incompetent provisioning system that was wasteful, subject to thievery, and in which shameless favoritism reigned.

The oft-cited Y. Tabaksblat characterizes the provisioning system with the following words:

> Provisioning! I must lay down my pen. It is really difficult to write. Does there exist an expression, a description for what has taken place in that muck, which was at first called the Provisioning, later Grocery and Bread Department? Laziness, clumsiness, mixed with meanness, predatory management, arbitrariness—this altogether still does not give the least concept about what went on in that department. When all were starving, not plain "hungry," but simply flooding the cemetery with corpses, swollen from hunger, they buried millions of kilos of potatoes and vegetables in the fields on account of laziness. They conducted a predatory management, sharing out right and left products in the thousands of kilos for their own kin and acquaintances, for high dignitaries because . . . one hand washes the other. . . . Such a condition lasted the whole time—even after the Gettoverwaltung itself [from 15 November 1943] took over the provisioning and supposedly designated a commission of three persons to manage it. . . . No screams or protests helped. Not even strikes. And all because the bigshots wanted it that way. No control was allowed. And when one by chance grabbed the chairman's arm and made him aware, he played as if he did not know, or glossed it over. . . . When the Supreme Control Chamber was formed . . . everything was supposed to be checked by it—except the provisioning. There was a case when a controller began to probe in the books and to raise questions. Right away, within the same quarter-hour, a telephone call came from the chairman personally in a rage—the controller must immediately break off the inspection and leave the Provisioning Department. . . . When people were arrested and beaten bloody, when people were dispatched to forced labor for the sin of grabbing a potato or a chunk of coal from a wagon, the whole Provisioning Department gang had honor and [ration] coupons bestowed upon them and were allowed to party. . . . When the population was starving and the patients in the hospitals were fasting, the Special Unit, on taking over the remainder on 30 June 1944, found huge quantities of products, like rice, cereal [kashe], cocoa, chocolate, and big barrels of wine, liquors, and still many more products in the Provisioning Department's warehouses.[45]

We find criticism of the provisioning system in a number of documents from that time. The *Daily Bulletin of the Ghetto Chronicle* sometimes also permitted itself a careful criticism of the ghetto circumstances. Writing under the date of 26 July 1942, about the abolition of sale of vegetables in the bread and grocery shops (in June 1942) and transfer of this task to the vegetable places, it states that "experience has proven that customers are best and most swiftly handled by the grocery points, that differentiate themselves for praise in contrast with the eliminated and missed-by-nobody vegetable points, which will long remain in the consumers' memory as an example of clumsy and irrational service."[46] The huge disorders and swindles during distribution of vegetables are also described in a reportage from the same period (doc. no. 76).

Disorder and embezzlements also plagued the general soup kitchens, where a significant percentage of the population ate, until the moment of their reduction. Even the factory kitchens, under the supervision of the workers themselves, suffered from abuses (doc. no. 77). In his speech of 1 June 1942, Rumkowski declared that the introduction of dry food in the factory kitchens, instead of soup, took place because of theft and corruption that reigned in the kitchens.[47]

A certain easing in the ghetto's catastrophic food supply situation was supposed to come from the cultivation of land to bring forth some vegetables from the hard ghetto soil. Aside from the parcels of land in Marysin, formerly inhabited mostly by Polish state and factory workers, where almost every cottage had a garden around it, arable land was artificially created in the ghetto by removing the cobblestone pavement and rocks from the earth. People even planted vegetables in window boxes. As mentioned, these matters were managed by the agricultural desk at the Economic Management Department.

The origins of farming in the ghetto are linked with the *Hakhshara kibbutsim* established in Marysin in the spring months of 1940. There were 360 young people of both genders located there in March 1941. (For more about the *kibbutsim* in the ghetto, see chapter 7.)

The Economic Management Department also set aside for itself in May 1940 a series of fields and gardens in Marysin, some of which were later designated for leasing out to private persons (doc. no. 78).

By the end of September 1940, a public auction of crops from the communal fields was held.[48] But the shrinking of the ghetto at the beginning of February 1941 cut off from it the fields that were its chief source of vegetables in that period.[49]

Plots of land were also leased out for cultivation in subsequent years (1942–1944). In 1941, the norm was 200 square meters for a family. Families of more than five persons could lease 400 square meters. At the start of April 1941, about 44,000 square meters had been leased. The children and adolescents in the camps in Marysin were also employed in cultivating land. They sowed vegetables on 11,492 square meters of land in 1941.

In May 1942, an advisory office for those leasing plots of land was opened,[50] and in the first half of June three issues were published of *Informator far kleyngertner* (Guide for Small Gardeners).[51] Public lectures were also held to guide the new ghetto "agriculturalists," few of whom had anything to do with gardening before the war.[52]

Starting in June 1942, the agriculturalist desk also leased out fruit trees and bushes, whose price was determined by three appraisal commissions.

The bacillus of favoritism and corruption also penetrated here. In spring 1942, large areas (nearly two-thirds of the land) were leased to tough guys ("kulaks, big gardeners, and deal-makers") who employed the "ghetto pariahs." These were people designated for deportation but who hoped to save themselves from expulsion through this work for influential people. These pariahs were exploited disgracefully.

Average people, facing the prospect of starvation, jumped at the opportunity to lease plots of soil, but had to act forcefully to extract a plot of ground for themselves (doc. no. 79).

At the end of May 1942, Rumkowski ordered that the vegetables harvested by those leasing major plots (there were twenty such leasing groups) would have to be sold in the so-called R-shops; naturally, with a certain profit for the lessee and a surcharge of 10 percent for the ghetto administration.[53]

Private lessees had a right to sell their vegetables in private trade at prices set by the department.[54] A change in favor of small lessees occurred in spring 1943, when the big "commercial areas" (!) were broken up into parcels, improving an individual's chances of getting a bit of land to sow.[55]

Frequent theft of often half-ripe vegetables from the sown areas was a big plague for those leasing plots of land in the hungry ghetto. Rumkowski's stern admonitions (the first was on 11 May 1941) did not help.[56] The seeds that arrived for the ghetto were of poor quality and would only partially germinate. This was also in great measure due to the inexperience of the majority of ghetto Jews in this new field. The big drought in August 1942 also had a fatal effect on agriculture in the ghetto.[57]

In sum, the ghetto agriculture was incapable of stilling the hunger, particularly due to the meagerness of the cultivated areas. Nevertheless, individuals laboring intensively, often after a long and hard workday, were in a position to raise some vegetables for their poor meals.

A third factor that, as mentioned, influenced the food supply of the ghetto population in general and of individual groups in particular was the economic conditions in the ghetto itself and the various shocks that took place there.

The first strong economic shock that fatally affected the food situation was experienced by the ghetto with the "resettlement" of nearly 20,000 Western European Jews in October-November 1941. The arrival in the ghetto of such a large number of people who brought along with them a rich baggage of clothing and valuable objects distorted the food market in the ghetto. The westerners included a large proportion of older people unaccustomed to physical labor. Hunger and great unemployment among these "settlers" compelled them to sell off their valuable baggage.

The demand for food products rose tremendously along with the inflation on the free market. Objectively, the most favorable conditions

A woman wrapped in a blanket sells socks in the market in the Łódź Ghetto, circa 1941. Photographer unknown. USHMM, courtesy of Instytut Pamięci Narodowej.

for trade between the exiles and the residents were created. The local population felt a major shortage of underwear, clothing, shoes, and other items of personal use, while the new arrivals were first of all interested in food products. This commerce between both population groups blossomed in a feverish bull market while both parties constantly increased the prices of their goods. The result was that the ghetto money became devalued, which most impacted the working people who had only ghetto marks at their disposal (doc. no. 80).

Rumkowski attempted to combat food speculation with stern measures, as well as to fight the inflation in the ghetto that disrupted his plan to transform the ghetto into a labor barrack, where need would compel everyone to work. The ghetto police made confiscations and carried out arrests among the trading partners.[58] But all this could not halt the trade that grew out of objective ghetto conditions.

The food supply situation in the ghetto endured a second, still stronger shock during the deportations from the ghetto in the months from January to May 1942. All those who received summonses to report at the assembly points naturally exerted themselves for any price to be rid of the ghetto marks that were worthless outside the ghetto. The demand on the free market for foodstuffs again grew tremendously as each deportee attempted to supply himself for the journey "in the unknown direction" (no baggage, except small hand parcels, was allowed to be brought along). Once again the prices shot up to a dizzying height.

Prices rose particularly during the final stage of the deportation in the first half of May 1942, when the Western European Jews were banished. The price of a kilogram of bread, for example, rose to 600 marks (from 360 marks in April) and of margarine to 1,000 marks, while potatoes rose to 50 marks (doc. no. 81). There was a parallel barter trade in goods whose prices testify plainly about the devaluation of things in comparison with food. Thus, for example, a man's suit was exchanged for a half kilo of bread, a pair of shoes for two kilo of potatoes or half a kilo of flour, and so forth.[59]

The value of the Reichsmark also rose in relation to the ghetto mark, from 1:1.60 to 1:10; that is, ten ghetto marks bought one RM.[60] After the conclusion of the deportations, prices for food fell sharply. Thus, for example, in early June the price of bread fell to 130 marks, of margarine to 100 (instead of 1,000), potatoes to 24, and so forth. The rate of the Reichsmark settled at the end of May to three ghetto marks for 1 RM.[61]

During the deportation roundups between 5 and 12 September 1942, distribution of food to the population was entirely halted until the ninth, and only on that day did limited sale of bread and food resume in that part of the ghetto where the bloody *Aktion* had already ended. The rule was that no food could be sold where police raids were continuing.[62] In those dreadful days of the *Shpere* or "September Blockade," both murderous shootings and hunger felled victims.

When the liquidation actions commenced in the ghetto in February 1944, the ghetto administration applied the sharp weapon of starvation against the recalcitrants who hid from the registration and refused to report to the departing transports. Rumkowski threatened to confiscate the food ration cards from them and their families and to halt the issuance of food at the workplaces.[63] Moreover, such fugitives did not dare to use their ration cards or come in to their workplaces for fear of being arrested by the ghetto police.[64] Later, their food cards were invalidated ("blocked") and their names in the food shop rolls were stamped with the letter E (perhaps for *Einziehen,* "confiscated").[65] Those concealing and feeding persons who did not report for deportation were themselves threatened with invalidation of their own ration cards.[66]

Rumkowski exploited this tragic situation of those who were in effect condemned to die from hunger, when on 16 June he announced that people who registered "for work outside the ghetto" (a euphemism for deportation) could immediately collect their food rations without standing in line.[67]

In August 1944, in the days of the final liquidation of the ghetto, food distribution was halted in whole neighborhoods whose residents had to "evacuate."[68] Thus, hunger was applied as a whip to drive the victims to the deportation trains.

This was one of the functions that hunger fulfilled in the ghetto.

However, in accord with the German plans, its permanent task in the ghetto was to exterminate the ghetto population. The unceasing hunger in the ghetto not only caused a large number of direct victims of diseases of malnutrition (edema, scurvy, exhaustion, weakening of the bones), but in great measure intensified and increased the incidence of other diseases, particularly tuberculosis (see chapter 5).

Cold was the ghetto's other great plague. During its entire existence, in contrast with its needs (especially for the ghetto workshops, various departments, and hospitals), the ghetto received minimal quantities of coal, as well as the so-called briquets and coal dust. No wood at all was supplied to the ghetto, which had to provide its own wood, mostly by dismantling old ruined buildings at the ghetto's periphery or in the ghetto itself, as well as by taking apart sheds, fences, and so forth.

In summer 1940, ghetto residents still received some coal and wood from time to time.[69] But the situation became tragic when the first autumn and winter crept in. The catastrophic shortage of fuel in winter 1940–1941 caused the closure of the 45 *tsholnt* bakeries and five newly opened bread bakeries.[70] For 2½ months, from November until the middle of January 1941, no fuel at all was distributed and only on 17 January 1941 was a special ration of four kilograms of coal dust and two kilograms of firewood per person given out.[71] The desperate ghetto people burned their own furniture, floorboards, doors, and walls, while the more energetic dismantled ruined wooden buildings, booths, fences, and even the wooden steps and outhouses in order to heat their cold dwellings.

During the first, very frosty winter in the ghetto, the dismantling of fences took on such a mass character that the wooden partitions between the houses vanished and the rows of courtyards became passable for long stretches. The cold drove people out into the street. On 11 and 12 January 1941, as already mentioned, there occurred street demonstrations, whose participants demanded heating fuel. At this occasion, a lumber store was looted; one person was killed and a couple of people injured when the roof collapsed.[72]

We find a portrayal of the severe heating problem in the ghetto in one of the included documents (no. 82).

Among the 1,218 deaths in January 1941, the most frequent cause was hunger and cold.[73] Children and adults were found frozen to death in their homes.[74]

Rumkowski continually threatened punishment for those obtaining wood illegally, both for those who tore boards from wooden buildings or ruined structures or fences and for those who purchased this wood.[75] Among those convicted by the summary courts from March to July 1941 were a substantial number of people punished with heavy prison terms for stealing wood.[76]

After introduction of the ration-card system, on rare occasion a certain quantity of coal, briquets, coal dust, and firewood was given out for the so-called "home-cookers." Thus, for example, the Coal Department issued fifteen kilograms of coal per person for the period from 13 February until 24 March 1941.[77] Twelve kilograms of briquettes were given out at the end of December 1941 for a period of one and a half months (16 January–28 February 1942).[78] During the entire period from 15 October 1942 until 5 November 1943 (over eleven months), fuel was given out to the population only four times (in February, March, and twice at the end of June) for a total of one hundred kilograms of coal, twenty-three kilograms of briquets, and nine kilograms of wood per person.[79]

Due to the shortage of wood and coal, so-called "coal miners" appeared. These were mostly young people as well as older men and women. Armed with spades, cleavers, shovels, and other primitive digging tools, they would set out to the undeveloped areas at the northern limits of the ghetto, to which trash was taken at one time. They dug into the piles of trash in order to find small bits of coal or unburned chunks of wood. It appears that people would also dig in the built-up areas, closer to the central ghetto (doc. no. 83).

The Rumkowski administration struggled against the "coal miners," with the accusation that "at the same time . . . [that] they destroy the cultivated land, chop down the fresh little trees and plants . . . [they] also undermine masonry foundations of houses, not taking into the least account the great danger that threatens the residents and themselves." Building watchmen were directed not to allow the digging up of the areas under their supervision, while the ghetto policemen were ordered to arrest those doing damage and bring them in for trial.[80]

In addition to the "coal miners," another category of miners appeared in the ghetto in April 1944: "garbage miners." Whole groups of young people would dig in frozen garbage pits for the rotten and contaminated remnants of potato peels and other vegetables thrown out from the neighboring kitchens.[81] This was a vivid token of the catastrophic level the hunger reached. There were also cases of a family member's death not reported for a long time, in order to make use of his food ration card in the interval.[82] Three cases of murder took place in the ghetto due to hunger (two in 1942, one in 1943; see chapter 7).

Documents 65–83

No. 65: YI-621/51

On 2 March 1940, the police-president permits opening three grocery shops in the ghetto for the Jewish population. [in German]

It is permitted to the Board of the Jewish Community, for Regina Plywaka,[83] representing the City of Lodsch, to open the shops of Itze Hochnitz, Kościelna 6, of Pinches Zynger in Fa. Wiener Fyjge, Zgierska 8, and of Gurke, St[ary] Rynek 15, that are located in the Jewish district and to make use of the shops for distribution of foodstuffs to the Jewish population.

No. 66: YI-234

Announcement no. 186 of 27 December 1940, concerning obtaining the food allotment on the newly introduced food cards. [in German]

I hereby make known that from Monday, 30 December 1940, the population obtains all foods on the [basis of] food ration cards. Distribution of food through the house committees ceases from that date. It is always noted on the ration cards where the products are to be purchased. My shops, in which foods on the ration cards are to be picked up, maintain customer lists. I hereby ask every ghetto resident, immediately, on Sunday, the 29th and Monday, the 30th.12.1940, to check in the stores near them, as well in the bread shops near them, whether he is included in the list of customers.

The cards of the entire family are to be brought along for the purpose of stamping. From Monday, 30th.12.1940, the following products per person on Coupon No. 81 of the foodstuffs card will be issued for the total fee of 1.34 Mk.

> 3 kilograms potatoes
> 150 grams salt
> 250 grams sugar
> 50 grams oil
> 1 box matches

and on Coupon No. 82
per person for the total fee of 1.30 mk

> 100 grams coffee mixture
> 100 grams honey
> 150 grams rye flour
> 50 grams margarine
> ¼ kilograms soda
> $\frac{1}{10}$ liter vinegar
> ½ piece soap
> 1 box matches
> 10 grams bicarbonate of soda

One person from each family can pick up the foods for the entire family. Due to shortage of paper, everyone must bring along a paper or cloth bag or an appropriate receptacle in clean condition when collecting the products. It is not compulsory to buy both allotments. Each person can take either one of the two or both allotments. Whoever purchases only one allotment does not lose the right to collect the other allotment, but can also purchase that one later.

The foodstuffs are paid for directly in the store during collection. I expressly draw attention to the fact that when picking up the products, the entire food ration card is to be brought along. The coupons are cut off in the store at payment for the foodstuffs. Loose, cutoff coupons have no validity. The distribution of bread on the bread cards begins on Wednesday, the 1st of January 1941 in the bread shops.

No. 67: YI-1021

Report concerning the organization and activity of the Department for Groceries and Bread [1942]. [in Polish]

[p. 24]

. . . .

The Provisioning Department possesses 45 distribution points right in the Ghetto and 1 independent distribution point in Marysin and distribution of foods takes place in total peace and quiet. If formerly it was necessary to arm oneself not only with patience but also with strong fists in order to persevere many hours at one's post in front of the cooperative, today it suffices to have money, to conform to the distribution plan, which appears in front of every cooperative and is comprehensible for everybody; and it is possible to contend with a minimal loss of time.

The causes of this efficiency must be sought in a certain reduction of the sphere of work of the Provisioning Department (from which, as we have seen, some locations were eliminated), and in an increase of personnel of some desks [*referatów*], which were previously overburdened with work.

Thus the employment in individual cells of the Department of Groceries and Bread in 1941 appeared as follows:

1941

	July	December
Central Bureau	54	61
Bałuty Marketsquare	7	6
Radogoszcz	4	6
Warehouses	20	23
Bakeries Desk	135	163
Distribution Points Desk	560	575
TOTAL	**780**	**834**

The average number of consumers going to one distribution point amounted in 1940 to

May [2nd half] 4,970
September 4,776
December 4,580

The year 1941 also commences with an average number of 4,520 consumers in January and 4,420 in the first half of May, but from the second half of May 1941, after the increase in the quantity of shops from 32 to 45, this figure fell to 3,130 and amounts to 3,016 in September and in December 3,120.

Lack of some record books made it impossible to produce statistics of products distributed in 1940, but in 1941 there was given out monthly in thousands of kilograms:

1941	In Allotments[84]	To Bakeries	To Hospitals and Other Institutions
Jan.	710	345	19
Feb.	571	701	13
Mar.	380	1,649	20
Apr.	458	1,327	14
May	361	1,420	19
June	253	1,200	22
July	646	1,302	28
Aug.	482	920	40
Sept.	354	1,223	42
Oct.	538	680	28
Nov.	502	932	33
Dec.	545	1,151	25
TOTAL	**5,800**	**12,850**	**303**

and the financial gross of the Department of Goods and Bread[85] in 1941 amounted to:

Jan.	1,538,893.26 mk.
Feb.	1,447,823.31 mk.
Mar.	1,674,073.50 mk.
Apr.	2,787,098.74 mk.
May	2,092,686.69 mk.
June	1,776,304.81 mk.
July	1,761,288.45 mk.
Aug.	1,678,067.60 mk.
Sept.	1,626,455.82 mk.
Oct.	1,380,385.37 mk.
Nov.	1,250,340.65 mk.
Dec.	1,489,346.76 mk.
TOTAL	**20,502,764.96 mk.**

[p. 26]

And thus, in spite of the separation of various Departments from Provisioning (the turnover of the Vegetable Department also reached nearly 18 million marks), the volume for 1941 was nearly 20 percent higher than in the previous year. The percentages of people buying up their rations was higher and reached:

1941

January	93 %	July	98.9 %
February	93 %	August	92.5 %
March	90.7 %	September	98 %
April	70.4 %	October	89.4 %
May	71.5 %	November	99.4 %
June	95.3 %	December	92 %

. . . .

No. 68: YI-43

Notice in the ghetto Chronicle of 12 January 1941, concerning street demonstrations in the ghetto. [in Polish][86]

STREET DEMONSTRATIONS

Demonstrations by crowds demanding an increase in the food and fuel rations that started yesterday also took place today in the morning hours.

It is worth recording that since the time of the September events the peace in the ghetto was not disturbed even once. It was irrefutably ascertained that this action was organized by irresponsible individuals, striving to disrupt the harmony and public order organized by the consistent effort of the ghetto's authorities, who watch over the calm, safety, and provisioning of its residents. Characteristic is the fact that the individuals inciting the crowd were recruited from among those employed who benefit from supplemental food allowances, but who sold at black market prices the very rations they had obtained for themselves. The demonstrations occurred in front of the building of the hospital at Łagiewnicka Street as well as in several places on Brzezińska Street. The crowd repeatedly attempted to loot foods being transported in wagons. Thanks to the energetic posture of the Order Service these attempts were frustrated. Heavy police patrols supervised the ghetto's streets throughout the entire day. Calm was fully restored in the afternoon hours.

No. 68a: YI-251

Rumkowski's Announcement no. 203 of 28 January 1941, concerning supplemental food coupons for workers, building watchmen, police, firefighters, and chimneysweeps. [in Yiddish]

I hereby make known that all workers in my workshops and factories (but only those which are now actually operating), building watchmen, those employed at public works, police, firefighters and chimneysweeps will, from Friday, the 31st of January 1941, receive the second ration for the current week on special coupons: 58 deka of meat and 2 kilo of potatoes. The directors of each department will distribute these coupons for their subordinates.

No. 69: YI-1089

Announcement of 3 April 1942, concerning food distribution for the general population and those possessing the supplemental nutrition cards. [in German]

I hereby make known that from tomorrow, 4 April 1942, the following ration per person will be issued for all on the basis of the vegetable identification papers in the vegetable distribution points pertaining to them:

2 kg potatoes
1 kg vegetables (turnips, carrots, or beetroots)
and 5 dkg parsley, radish, or horseradish.

This ration costs 1 Mk.

Moreover, from tomorrow, 4 April 1942, for all [consumers] in their respective milk shops on coupon no. 76 of the food ration card

10 dkg margarine per person

will be given out.

For possessors of supplemental food ration card 1, in their respective groceries and bread distribution points, from tomorrow, 4 April 1942, on coupon no. 103 of that card

20 dkg soup spices
10 dkg coffee mix
2 packets fruit soups

will be given out.

This ration comes to 1 Mk.

For the possessors of supplemental food ration card 2, likewise from tomorrow, 4 April 1942, on coupon no. 108 of that card in their respective groceries and bread distribution points

20 dkg soup spices
10 dkg coffee mix
2 packets fruit soups

for the amount of 1 Mk

will be given out.

Furthermore, from tomorrow, 4 April 1942, for all [consumers] in their respective meat shops on coupon no. 75 of the food ration card

10 dkg meat per person

will be given out.

No. 70: YI-1399

A notice from the German ghetto administration [no date, early November 1943] that it is taking over supervision of supplying food in the ghetto. [in German]

Regarding: *Nourishment of the Worker!*

With Announcement no. 401 of the Eldest of the Jews of 3.XI.1943, the ghetto's working population was informed that a reduction of food allocations would be necessary due to smaller food deliveries, in particular that the rations of the factory kitchens were reduced.

With immediate effect, I order the reinstitution of the food rations that existed before the above action, whereby the nourishment of the worker is guaranteed. In order to eliminate acts of favoritism, the issuing of coupons, strengthening dinners, and so forth is immediately halted by me.

For the time being, a plan is being worked out concerning the nourishment of those who work. It will be fundamentally more advantageous than the one that existed before the above action.

All food questions will be fundamentally *regulated by the [German] ghetto administration* from 15 November 1943, since various abuses have been confirmed. I have therefore from today put the food warehouses and distribution points under me, and they must operate only according to my instructions.

No. 71: YI-1087

Announcement of 11 February 1942, concerning product allocation for those who benefit from the dinners in the kitchens. [in Yiddish]

I hereby make known that from Thursday, the 12th of February 1942, on coupon no. 53 of the food ration card, for the period from 16 February until 28 February 1942 inclusive, the following food allotment will be given out in my groceries and bread points for each person who registered for cooking dinners at home:

500 grams rye meal,
200   "   noodles [*farfl*],
40   "   barley pellets [*groypn*],
400   "   white sugar,
100   "   margarine,
50   "   coffee,
50   "   synthetic honey or marmalade,
250   "   salt,
100   "   spice-soup [*gevirts-zup*],
10   "   citric acid,
10   "   tea soda [*tey-zode*],
5   "   paprika,
1½ kilograms canned beets.

This ration costs 3.80 marks.

I simultaneously make known that the old kitchen ration from 26 January on coupon no. 46 is valid until 16 February 1942 inclusive.

No. 72: YI-1091

Announcement concerning the product allotment of 26 July 1942 for home cookers and kitchen eaters. [in German]

I hereby make known that from Sunday, the 28th of June 1942, on coupon no. 33 and coupon no. 34 of the food ration card, [but] only for those persons who have registered for cooking dinner at home, the following ration will be given out in their respective groceries and bread distribution points per person for the period from 1 July 1942 until 10 July 1942 inclusive:

2 ½ kilograms potatoes,
200 grams rye flour,
100 grams rye flakes,
120 grams sugar,
120 grams margarine,
100 grams synthetic honey,
90 grams coffee mix,
250 grams salt,
10 grams soda [*Natron*],
10 grams paprika,
10 grams citric acid,
250 grams wash soda,
1 box matches,
¹/₁₀ liter vinegar

This ration costs 4 marks.

Simultaneously, also from Sunday, the 28th of June 1942 on coupon no. 34 of the food ration card, those persons who have registered for eating dinner in the kitchens receive in their respective groceries and bread points the following ration per person:

120 grams sugar,
100 grams synthetic honey,
90 grams coffee mix,
100 grams salt,
5 grams soda [*Natron*],
10 grams paprika,
250 grams wash soda,
¹/₁₀ liter vinegar,
1 box matches.

This ration costs 1.50 marks.

On Saturday, the 27th of June 1942, all persons who were employed on the key-date [*Stichtag*] of 26 June 1942 must bring along their food ration cards to their workplaces.

There they receive certificates, on the basis of which from Saturday, the 28th of June 1942, in their respective groceries and bread distribution points for the period from 1 July 1942 until the 10th of July 1942 inclusive:

1 kilogram potatoes
100 grams tomato pulp
100 grams pearl barley [*Graupen*]
200 grams sugar
50 grams cooking butter [*Kochbutter*]
10 grams paprika
1 packet of fruit soups

for the sum of 2.00 marks

will be given out. The food ration cards must be brought along when collecting the foods.

No. 73: YI-43

Report about the activity of the Kitchens Department in the ghetto Chronicle of 29 January 1941.[87] [in German]

Kitchens Department: supervises the activity of ca. 100 public kitchens and eating-places. There are the following categories: 1) central kitchens of the Community (five); 2) kitchens formerly operated by the house committees and recently taken over by the community; 3) cooperative kitchens and eating places; 4) private restaurants. Until the introduction of coupon presentation for the kitchens, the latter issued up to 145,000 meals daily. Now, one can eat only after presentation of coupons from the food ration card, aside from the exception of those entitled to rations for "cooking at home." After that introduction, the number sank to 15,000. This is explained through the fact that formerly a series of people profited from the food in different feeding places, which would now however be impossible. Moreover, practice has shown that the population prefers to collect the products in kind and because at this time it was no longer possible to draw from both sources, the population itself is thus deciding whether they want to be fed in the kitchens or at home. Thus the existence of the kitchens is being decided automatically. Therefore, a series of kitchens must be liquidated. Consequently, a natural selection is taking place: those that are well run and also provide good food continue to have success.

There are eighteen private restaurants, seventy-seven kitchens of the former house committees, and five community kitchens.[88] There are three under construction. Then there are special factory kitchens: shoemakers, tailors, rubber coat, carpenters, and so forth. The police and the fire department also operate a total of ten canteens.

The so-called "social kitchens" have had great success: there are 12 (political partisan) [including] Zionists with 2,500 dinners daily, Bundists (two) under joint management with 1,500 dinners daily. Of the community kitchens, the intelligentsia kitchen[89] was the most patronized with 1,100 dinners daily. The mentioned kitchens credit their success to the fact that they really put into the pot what they received. They were also well managed in the most difficult periods, when meat and vegetables were lacking.

In the existing circumstances, the demand to cook at home instead can be explained by the fact that the population sells one part of their food and that the cooking warms the house. If all the kitchens served good food, the volume [of dinners] would not have fallen so sharply. With the arrival of the warm weather, the proportion will likely change again. The Kitchens Department has the following functions: organization of kitchens, allocation of kitchens to suitable locations, liquidation of the superfluous ones, supervision of the food served, issuance of products to the kitchens. It is still young, established only on 12 XII 1940.

No. 74: YI-30

Notice in the ghetto Chronicle *of 2 July 1942, concerning spoiled food that was being delivered to the ghetto.*[90] *[in Polish]*

[p. 4]

WHAT'S BEING DELIVERED TO US.

1. Yesterday, a shipment of 800 kilograms of meat in a state of advanced decay arrived in the ghetto. There were green, yellow, white pieces. Upon receipt, communal officials, after communicating with the Meat Headquarters, questioned the shipment, declaring that they could not use the meat, designated for sausage for workers, in view of the catastrophic effects that could be wreaked on their health. The ghetto administration delegated two officials to the Meat Headquarters to check, but the spoilage was so obvious that they acknowledged themselves incompetent and ordered a halt in the processing and that the meat be kept cool until Thursday morning, until the arrival of the official veterinary from the city.

2. Not long ago, we wrote about the arrival of 10,000 kilograms of butter. It was completely rancid and black. Experts state that it had been lying around for at least six months. After repeated washing, the Milk Department managed to remove the bitterness and derive a product that was relatively clean and digestible for the ghetto's residents' stomachs that are used to everything.

3. Recently, one of the bakers of Litzmannstadt with his own horses and his own wagon sent to Bałuty Marketsquare a significant quantity of flour that had begun to spoil in his storehouse. He did this apparently in fear of punishment that he might encounter for allowing the flour to spoil. It was not usable in the city, but it was more than good enough for the ghetto.

No. 75: YI-28

Notice in the ghetto Chronicle *of 16 May 1942, concerning the large demand for potato peels. [in Polish]*[91]

Peels. An eloquent symptom of the hunger situation that reigns in the Ghetto is the pursuit after potato peels. The starving population is racing for this delicacy with admirable persistence. Obtaining peels is not among the easy things. On the basis of medical certificates, the Department of Kitchens issues instructions to individual kitchens for allotments of peels in the amount of 3 kilograms daily. Such long lines of applicants form in front of the kitchens that there is no way to share out a full portion to everyone. How sought after this article (completely worthless in prewar times) is now can testify the fact that during the general boom for peels 15 marks were paid for 1 kilogram. People not only prepare themselves dishes [*potrawki*] from these peels, but cook plain soups.[92]

No. 76: YI-46–A

Fragment from reportage by Joseph Zelkowicz of 8 July 1943, concerning the disorder and abuses during the distribution of vegetables. [in Yiddish]

[pp. 2–3]

And this is the chief defect of the system, that rarely did the Vegetable Department send enough goods of one type for all the consumers of the given point: For example, Distribution Point 1 that has 1,500 consumers received 600 kilograms of carrots with the order to give out a half kilogram per head. If nothing would be missing from this shipment on the way, if it even turned out on the hair, the shipment could suffice for only 1,200 consumers and the remaining 300 had fruitlessly pushed into the line and wasted time for nothing. The result of such a delivery: No sooner was it heard that a certain product had arrived at the point—and it was heard several hours yet before its arrival—the entire "clientele" as big and strong as it was, with kit and caboodle, with kith and kin, was clustered in the narrow distribution shop. Everyone pushed; everyone shoved; everyone wanted to be as early as possible, no one wanted to remain among those for whom there would not be enough, but this would not yet have been the worst. The pushing and shoving could have been easily prevented if the consumer would have the certainty: "I didn't get [any] today, so I'll get [some] tomorrow." . . . But the story is that in most cases, the consumer cannot have this certainty because—and this is the rub—the issuance of vegetables occurs only on the basis of the vegetable identification card that is again a quite broad field for different abuses and machinations:

A. The Card Department never made any problems for anybody in issuing duplicates of vegetable identification cards, particularly in winter, in the no-vegetables season, when they did not play any practical and actual role. It was enough just to report to the Card Department that identification card so-and-so, number this-and-that had been lost and to pay the relevant fee of several pennies in order to obtain a second identification card. This circumstance was widely exploited, particularly by those who had, so to say, "wide acquaintance" with the personnel of the distribution points. This sort of fellow is equipped with two, or even several, identifications that he hands in "around back," so that the cashier won't have to specify his name . . . He also leaves the necessary money with his acquaintance from among the personnel and he thereby gets one and the same products several times, even in one and the same day . . . (Bread and other products are issued only on the basis of cards that must be recorded each time into the roster when picking up [rations] and the relevant coupons are cut out of them, thus precluding this sort of tricks).

B. If the entire "clientele," or even only a significant part of it, had at one time clustered in one place in the store (and why they had gathered is understandable, as we have already pointed out)—if each of those assembled said not more than even one word, and presumably the personnel were interested in handling them as quickly as possible, to free themselves as soon as possible from that Gehenna . . . and, under such conditions one cannot demand from anyone, that he work with the exactness and precision of a Swiss watch, no one can demand of him that he keep relevant notations in the roster, or even only on the identification card. This situation, that vegetables are being given out and it's not noted even on the identification card, is again strongly and widely exploited by shrewd, strong-elbowed and broad-shouldered consumers; that sort of fellow collects goods once on his identification card, turns it in a second time (he gets up to the window a lot faster and swifter than another . . .), and if God helps and he manages it—a second and a third time, too. . . . Not to speak of those who don't need to push at all—those that have a "side in the bowl"—an acquaintance or a relative among the "cooperative's" personnel, who get their goods "around back" and are always the first: These certainly have time, to bring in their identification another time. . . . And those who cannot push and don't have a "side in the bowl," as long as one has some brains, he can easily cope: Simply stand in the line two together—in front the father, at the end of the line—the daughter. When the father has already paid and received back the booklet, he then turns it over to the daughter and she pays another time. . . .

C. If the "cooperative's" personnel know that the arrived products are not sufficient for distribution for all the consumers, they reserve products—each for his own acquaintances and friends: They simply and plainly write out order forms under the numbers of the identification cards that their friends and acquaintances have, pay for them, select from the best-looking [items] and send it off to their home; and the next day, or even on that very same day, the same friends and acquaintances come in, totally innocent, and they pay on their booklets, as if nothing had ever happened . . .

With this sort of trickery and machinations that are regrettably too frequent phenomena, the consumer can never have the certainty that he will get his products tomorrow if he does not manage to shove his way up today. Tomorrow, there are more preferred people who receive, tomorrow there's a tough guy, a friend, a soup-server, a peeler-woman from the kitchen, who will receive a second or yet a third time. For the weak, simple, and naive consumer, [goods] will always be lacking, for him it would never suffice . . . and, when that sort of fellow comes with a justified complaint: "Why has that other guy already received two times, both yesterday and today, and for me there wasn't any?" you will always hear the stereotypical and innocent excuse: "We didn't eat up the products: As much as arrived to us we have distributed. Moreover, why are you yelling? It's coming to you? What, was it a 'ration,' that you must receive it?[93] It was a few carrots. Whoever was there and pushed himself forward, he received. You couldn't push yourself up? What kind of gripe do you have against us? Go and complain to Rumkowski, about why he sends so little and it doesn't suffice for everyone! . . .

No. 77: YI-28

Notices in the ghetto Chronicle *of 6 and 14 May 1942,[94] concerning the disorders and embezzlements in the ghetto kitchens. [in Polish]*

[p. 5]

TRIALOG[95] IN THE MATTER OF THE KITCHEN DINNERS
The attitude toward the matter of kitchen dinners varies among people of different camps in the ghetto. The consumer sees it differently, the kitchen manager sees it differently, and totally different is the view of the agent, who is assigned to check on both the preparation and the distribution of the dinner and who, in his own well-comprehended self-interest, manages at the appropriate moment to screw his eye shut and not see what he ought to see. The consumer says, "I'm not surprised that the dinners are so watery and lacking substance, for the personnel are the first in line to get thick portions (until 5 May of this year, staff each received 4 soups daily), then come the favorites, then the favorites of the favorites, and finally what's left . . . the gray mass." From here also comes the general dissatisfaction among consumers and the universal flight from public kitchens.

In these conditions it would be much more rational to distribute products to people in place of factory soups, for the same quantity of food cooked at home will be very tasty and rich. Cooking at home does not cause anyone special difficulties, for a huge majority today already cook at home.

The KITCHEN MANAGER thinks instead that the cause of such thin dinners recently is principally the very small allocation of products and to this adds allocation of a poor class of potatoes, of which the lion's share is peeled off. During extended cooking, these potatoes are boiled to a pulp and little remains of them in the soup. Not a small sore point, he says, are the various dignitaries or also pseudo-dignitaries who could not be denied better soups, whether with regard to the positions they hold, whether also at a threat with which they shake us down. And how to behave here, when these persons show up personally at the kitchen with a pot?

And finally, clients' complaints about the poor soups are not always justified. Sometimes at fault is only the server, who is in the end only a human being and can make mistakes. Sometimes she can give a better portion to one but a worse portion to another.

[p. 4]⁹⁶

CONTROLLER: Everything is in the best order in the kitchens! The soups are rich and tasty, equitable service for everyone; I didn't find any injustices or any shortcomings.

CLOSURE OF KITCHENS

According to information from the Department of Kitchens at no. 20 Dworska Street, on the 9th of this month the following communal kitchens will be closed: Nos. 302, 322, 348, 363, 415, 434, and 451. The aforementioned seven kitchens include kitchen no. 363, the so-called ritual kitchen at no. 26 Zgierska, and no. 302, the oldest kitchen in the ghetto at Żytnia Street. As the cause of closure, the Department of Kitchens cites the huge fall in the number of consumers. In the kitchen at no. 26 Zgierska Street, it fell from ca. 1,800 in the holiday period to 120. This phenomenon can be explained on the one hand by various copious allotments for those cooking at home, while on the other was the constant worsening of the dinners in the kitchens. The controllers assigned, subject to the Supreme Control Chamber, were even transferred repeatedly, but the result was rather the opposite. During these movements, they entered into ever closer contact and in result they acquire for themselves and their families only larger quantities of soups, while closing their eyes to what was happening in the kitchens. It did not matter that [not only] were the kitchen personnel dining on potatoes in various forms before the eyes of consumers, but that families of kitchen personnel and various casual guests were enjoying this benefit, completely ignoring those looking on around them.[97]

[p. 14]⁹⁸

Nowhere more than in the ghetto was the thesis confirmed that those sitting at the bowl eat the best. The judicial chronicle and the administrative punishments often imposed by Mr. Chairman himself gave us the most varied proofs of this. It is sad that all these measures have until now not produced a positive result, but rather that only the actors were changed. The old ones are not stealing; it's new ones who are stealing.

In order to prevent unjust division of dinners in the factory kitchens, Mr. Chairman ordained delegation to the kitchens of worker representatives, to whose obligations belong scrupulous supervision of both the preparation and the distribution of dinners. It would seem that there could be no more ideal invention, for the interested parties themselves are acting in their own cause and that of their closest comrades. But nevertheless, here and there is heard that for a few extra-curricular soups the delegates themselves are closing their eyes to what is happening around them and their comrades continue to be robbed. They realize that tomorrow their colleagues can do the same thing and they in turn will fall into this handicapped position, but it does not offend them—they are living for today. And thus, before their eyes, as is heard from the most varied factories, the kitchen staff, administration, friends, and even acquaintances of members of the administration are stealing from the factory soups in the heretofore manner to the detriment of all those employed at the given site.

Mr. Chairman at one time established several independent controllers of kitchens; we say independent, for they did not bear any obligation to prove themselves before the Department of Kitchens, but, as we already reported, on this fire they only baked roasts for themselves. This position turned out to be very seductive, for through frequent transfers they established acquaintance in nearly all of the kitchens and took excellent advantage of this for their own ends. Such depletion of the food of comrades in adversity is a very sad symptom of moral decay, but a completely worse and sadder phenomenon is the reprehensible manipulation of sausage rations.

Those handling distribution leave the packed sausage (as is reported from several factories) overnight in water. The sausage swells, increasing in weight, and the next day colleagues get a full 5 dkg of waterlogged sausage. The increase in weight is significant enough that those distributing take off the supposed excess weight in advance.

This manipulation with sausage is absolutely detrimental, for workers complain that they are getting moldy sausage. But what this means—we dare say does not need to be explained.

Controllers over controllers, delegated controllers from the workers' own circle, the most severe punishments for the least transgression! It would seem that Mr. Chairman is doing everything in order to prevent the corruption rampant in the ghetto, but nevertheless he cannot prevent it and is not up to bringing the situation in this area under control!

The hunger situation in the ghetto cannot be any excuse and especially for those to whom was entrusted the honorable mission of fair distribution of food. Rather they ought to understand best for barely yesterday they were in the same situation . . .

And yet they continue to act, in spite of the admonitions of Mr. Chairman, who really shows himself utterly at a loss regarding recent events. Where could proper controllers finally be recruited? Certainly not from outside?

No. 78: YI-275

Rumkowski's announcement of 7 March 1941, concerning leasing garden allotments for the year 1941. [in Polish]

Desiring to enable the general population to acquire land for cultivation and its rational utilization, as well as to prevent exploitation, I have decided to parcel out a large part of the ghetto's cultivable land for allotments of 200 square meters, i.e., enough to suffice for feeding a family. Every family, with the exception of families having steady income, can lease an allotment of 200 square meters.

Families comprised of more than five persons can compete for a double allotment, i.e., 400 square meters.

Part of the grounds as well as some of the gardens will be leased out in total. The lease fee for an allotment of 200 square meters is 20 marks, together with the tax, payable 50 percent at signing of the contract, 50 percent by 30 April 1941. The lease fee for fertile gardens is by agreement.

Building tenants can lease grounds located on the same real estate parcel at the administrator's application for permission from the Farming Office. The aforementioned grounds are exempt from lease fees in so far as:

a. they will be utilized exclusively by the tenants of that house,
b. the size of the plot does not exceed 100 square meters.

In return for this, tenant-lessees of the above allotments are obligated to care for the aesthetic appearance around the trash pile and the privy, in so far as they are located at the allotment. The Farming Office without refund of payments and costs will confiscate allotments that are leased but not cultivated by the lessees. Abandonment of allotments in whole or part is not to be tolerated without the Farming Office's acceptance.

Lessees are entitled to benefit from free expert consultations with communal gardening instructors.

The Farming Office provides seeds to lessees for a fee.

Applications should be directed to my Farming Office at the Financial-Management Dept., 11 Lutomierska Street, starting from Sunday, 9 March 1941.

No. 79: YI-28

Notice in the ghetto Chronicle *of 27 May 1942, concerning the situation in the cultivation of land.*[99] *[in Polish]*

[p. 34]

The run on allotments this year was exceedingly large, but admittedly it was necessary to apply the greatest efforts in order to obtain parcels in the Farming Department. The one who conducted this policy of selection and patronage, Mr. Pomeranc of disreputable memory, was punished by Mr. Chairman and removed from the affairs of this Department. Unfortunately, this occurred a little late. If his removal had taken place earlier, more than one of the Ghetto's residents could still have received this or that tiny allotment, which, thanks to Mr. Pomeranc's policy, was absorbed by large commercial tracts leased out to speculators or else to "ghetto dignitaries." Thanks to the fact that Mr. Pomeranc rammed through the keeping in the ghetto of a whole army of those who were initially predestined for outsettlement, but were kept for agricultural work, the privileged had the possibility to make use of the labor of the hands of hundreds of people, on whom this labor was imposed. There arose a new type of slave, who had to work off his tribute for the fact that he was not deported and the least dissent by him was met with Mr. Pomeranc's threats. The threats were more than persuasive enough so that nobody would dare not to take them seriously.

And thus, big tracts of land were plowed, excavated and sown by strange hands, most often even without the knowledge of the owners of the parcel. The community paid the workers, most often the workers received dinners (soups), and if the need for plowing had arisen, the Transport Department's bill was sent to the interested party. Bills varied, depending on the field and the time . . . but this already enters the field of mathematics, over which it is not worth thinking about in this place.

Curious is another phenomenon, which in recent times has become quite common in the ghetto. Following after the example of "great dignitaries" went lesser ones, "administrators" who were apparently completely insignificant in the ghetto.

To each of these administrators is awarded the right to cultivate a certain allotment with an area of 150–200 square meters and it appeared that they themselves were working manually, or with the aid of their closest family. We have seen more than one gray citizen, who, after a whole day's work in a factory, hungry and haggard, went out into the field with his immediate family, so as to work with their last strength the allotment assigned to him with such toil.

Administrators, on the other hand, appeared to be in a completely different situation. At their request, the Community sent out people to clear the site and this in such quantity that in normal times could clean whole streets. For particularly large properties, the community sent out 20–30 persons each with carts and tools, while 6, 8, or 10 persons labored on smaller ones. It seemed peculiar that this administrator, who gazed with such an indifferent eye at mountains of garbage and filth through the whole winter and spring, was suddenly energetically urging people on to work. The cleared allotments were placed under cultivation; on the other hand, he did not see to it that the toilet pits would be emptied and on several properties they are inoperative until today (in a heat of 35 degrees C)!

Sometimes twenty and more properties belong to the administrator's region, but of course he was allowed to lease only one parcel. So he enters into an understanding with one of the tenants, plays out the role of one not interested and then as guardian of cleanliness submits a requisition at the community for a group of workers, brings the property to the proper condition and to the tenant who is in on the secret he issues a certificate that it was he who cleaned the courtyard and deserves the grant of a parcel. Of course, the brazenness of some of these administrators carried things so far that not only did they at communal cost clear the site on which they intend to cultivate vegetables jointly with the former tenant, but they outright submit a requisition for laborers and employ them in cultivation of their own parcel and an ally's parcel in which they had an interest.

Workers questioned by me bluntly declared that they were subject to the administrator's orders and although they know that they were working in this case for a private person, they are too small to make a stand against it.

Of course, they receive money from the community and they know that this is an abuse on the administrator's part, but they do not lodge any complaints because it is ultimately all the same to them what they do, so long as they somehow survive the day.

And what of the Management Department in this? Does it not maintain a whole throng of controllers? And is it happening right in the closest vicinity to the Department, close by 7 Lutomierska Street, 34 Zgierska, 38 Zgierska, not to speak of more distant properties?

In other places, the administrator divides such a group into ones who clear the properties and others who cultivate his allotments, but nevertheless they are always abusing the community's trust. When we reflect on how many worthy people concealed themselves with agricultural jobs in fear of deportation, we will understand not only the unlimited daring and effrontery of the administrator, but also the profound physical and moral pain of this new type of hired laborers.

No. 80: YI-25

Notice in the ghetto Chronicle *for the month of November 1941, concerning the food speculation and inflation in the ghetto in connection with the arrival of the West-European Jews. [in Polish]*[100]

[p. 10]

REVIVAL IN THE RESTAURANTS. From the moment of the arrival of transports from Germany, all the restaurants and pastry shops existing on the terrain of the ghetto, until now blessed with practically complete vacancy, were really besieged by the strangers. As a characteristic phenomenon it must also be underscored that from the first moment the strangers began selling their personal possessions, and for the cash received simultaneously commenced to buy up literally everything, whatever was available on the private food market. In the course of time, this phenomenon caused both a shortage in the supply of food articles and what comes of that, a horrendous boom in prices, whose tempo was simply difficult to grasp. On the other hand, the offering of the most varied objects that for a long time were completely unavailable in the Ghetto caused a revival in trade and the shelves of the few shops in the ghetto filled up with goods long unseen in the ghetto. During the month of November, the doors of the shops were never closed before the newcomers, popularly called *yekes*[101] here. They sold clothing, shoes, linens, cosmetics, travel accessories, etc., etc. For a short time, this phenomenon caused a reduction in prices of the most varied objects; however, the extent of the boom in prices on the food market led the new arrivals to begin to increase in the same degree the prices of the things they were selling. On account of the above, from the point of view of collective interests of the veteran population of the ghetto, introduction of private commerce on a relatively broad scale caused rather undesirable commotion and difficulty, and, what is worse, thanks to the newcomers there began in a short time a devaluation of the [ghetto] money in circulation.

This phenomenon was especially a hardship for the working throngs, the most important segment of ghetto society, having at their command only the money received from the treasury of the Eldest of the Jews.

No. 81: YI-28

Notice in the ghetto Chronicle *of 9, 10, and 11 May 1942, concerning the commercial boom and the inflation in the ghetto in relation with the outsettlement of the West European Jews. [in Polish]*

[p. 9]

THE FOOD MARKET.[102]

In connection with the further continuing business frenzy that pervaded the entire ghetto at the outsettlement of Western Jews, such complete chaos reigns on the food market that setting of prices even within broad ranges is impossible.

The only fact remains that all the prices, both of food and of everything, are mushrooming. Depreciation of money is in full swing. It's said that the price of bread reached 600 marks, margarine 1,000 marks, potatoes 50 marks, a box of matches 2 marks, etc. etc. It is worth emphasizing that during the outsettlement action, by order of superior authorities, the price control organs of the Order Service are looking through their fingers at the existence of the food market, tolerating it, so as not to prevent those departing from making a purchase of food for the money made from sale of things. There continues to be a great rush in furtive transactions for the German mark. Its exchange rate was set in the reported days at 10. Particularly sought after are small banknotes, which are practically completely unavailable. In barter transactions, the permanent population of the ghetto earned for itself the worst report card.[103] Fortunately, the ever present head of the ghetto paid attention to this atrocious phenomenon and commanded ruthless combat. On the first day of this order, twenty-four individuals were already put in jail.

Reportage by Joseph Zelkowicz (no date), concerning the distribution of wood, winter 1941. [in Yiddish]

A LITTLE ORGANIZATION

When prices for wood in the ghetto reached 4 marks for a kilogram, the Chairman in his grandiosity wrote out for January a heating fuel allocation of six kilograms of coal and fifteen kilograms of wood per head.

No wood is arriving in the ghetto from outside. The ghetto must be autarchic in lumber goods. With this allotment of fifteen kilograms of wood per head, the ghetto had to deliver nearly four and a half million [kilograms] only for the population, aside from the offices and factories.

This wood, as already mentioned, on account of the fact that none is arriving from outside the ghetto, had to be provided from the ghetto itself. All the wooden buildings had to be dismantled, both in the portion that was cut off from the ghetto in [the streets] Brzezińska, Franciszkańska, etc., and uninhabitable wooden buildings in other streets.

Because this wood allocation was supposedly already foreseen a few weeks ago, a large site was reserved at no. 27 Ceglana Street on which the wood that originated from the dismantled buildings was stacked.

Immense chaos and disorganization prevailed even while there was still an opportunity to pick up the wood allocation. It truly hurt one's heart to see how the coal site that was considered one of the best organized facilities in the ghetto, how the coal site where the applicant was dealt with in the fastest possible way, without lines and without hue and cry—how this very site's organization begins to falter and go off its rails.

Unusual things happened at this place: A whole staff of employees worked at it. They were constantly sawing there and splitting into smaller pieces the construction lumber that arrived whole from the dismantled buildings and yet . . .

Except for the policemen, firemen and other similarly uniformed persons, or the well connected, no one could get a piece of the sawn and reduced lumber. If someone wanted to collect his wood, it was not given to him—he had to go get it himself; he himself had to seek out from the great stacks a piece of wood and because the piece of wood is much too large and much too heavy, several men had to cooperate and with combined efforts had to make it small. At that, one had to bring along a saw and a hatchet from home. It was impossible to obtain such a tool on the site.

Such a situation was the reason that there were always hundreds of people at the place, arguing, actually fighting, over a little board or a piece of wood, like a dog around a bone. But—

The place also had the quality that if one wanted to waste a day, one could get from it the several kilograms of wood.

It became much worse when wood began to run out at the place and the applicants were sent to the locations where houses were being dismantled every day at a different location and another address.

Dantesque scenes are played out at these locations: Like locusts, the freezing crowd attacks the building that must be dismantled. The Jewish community laborer does not work here, but the consumer himself. And here the law of the jungle applies: The stronger wins. Whoever has a crowbar, an axe, a saw and whoever also has healthy arms and still healthier shoulders and also has several people to help—that one can attain a piece of wood.

The freezing crowd threw themselves on a building, like crows on carrion, like jackals on a found carcass, ripping, chopping, sawing, as walls collapse, beams fly, chunks of plaster cover people alive, but no one yields the position he occupies:

Each wants something with which to cook up his little pot of warm food. Each has a child at home or a sick person who is freezing, but—

Not everyone can bring along a crowbar from home. Not everyone has an axe at home, or a saw, and not everyone is strong enough to carry from the place the beam that he has already sawed up or chopped up. Women and children get away with thin little boards, with thicker chunks, that they gather among the pile of grass, clay and lime, but while they collect their 15 kilograms and race for this board or that chunk, what they have collected until now is meanwhile stolen away right from under their noses. And—it's no surprise that every minute there's another outbreak of violence and other fights occur:

Here the bit of wood was stolen, together with the sack. There someone stole another's sled. A ten-pound beam simply fell on the leg of a third one and broke it and a fourth was buried by the plaster from a beam. . . . Most beautiful of all is, however, that at such a location where a wooden building is being dismantled by thousands of people, there is a single scale in use and because not everyone could chop up or saw up a suitable quantity of wood, the line in front of this scale stands for hours and it does not move at all, until . . .

The crowd does not lose its patience and it drags off its sawed up or chopped up heap, not weighed and probably without turning in any coupons, in order the next day to come to another location and in such manner again supply themselves with wood. . . .

It is understandable that it would be easier to collect the wood each time at the location where it is produced. It is understandable that in such a manner the community wants to economize on labor and transportation costs, but with the organization that reigns at these locations, amid the terrible chaos and confusion, the fact is that the community not only does not save anything, but just the opposite—50 percent of the wood is mislaid and stolen and moreover people are turned into beasts and vandals. Would it not be worthwhile on account of this . . . to introduce a bit of order into this chaos and a bit of organization, at least on account of this alone,—to enable the weak, the gray, honest person, who cannot fight, who cannot steal and cannot tear down any buildings, to get his several kilograms of wood, to enable him not to freeze, to give him a chance to cook up his bit of turnips?

No. 83: YI-Diary

Fragment of diary of Engineer Leon Hurwitz,[104] August 1941, about the coal miners in the ghetto. [in Yiddish]

[pp. 28–29]

Coal Miners in the Ghetto.[105]

As everybody knows, there is no coal or coalmines in the ghetto, but there are "coalminers." This is not a paradox, not a joke, and not said for no reason, but is true. On the eastern side, the ghetto ends with desolate places that once served as dump sites for trash brought out from the city. And these trash sites border sites that had belonged to a brick factory that is in a state of total ruin. But in the north the borders of the ghetto lie much further and these desolate fields link the center of the ghetto on one side with the oasis that is called Marysin, and on the other side with the cemetery. A few chosen individuals indeed know the naked fields only from a distance, riding by in the droshkies that bear the sign of the ghetto boss to the royal summer residence, i.e. in R's Tsarskoye Selo,[106] to Marysin. I personally, just like all the other plain, unprivileged Jews, have become more closely acquainted with the unfruitful fields, while striding both through the hills of trash, that have collected there for years, and through the moist muddy places in order to shorten the way to the cemetery.

And the unfriendly fields, which for years only the trash haulers and sand and clay diggers saw, are now suddenly revived. Hundreds of adults and still more children sit from morning until the sun sets and tunnel down like moles to two meters and sometimes still deeper into the earth, or more accurately into the rubbish. With bent iron hatchets, with small shovels and still other primitive instruments, they dig and scratch into the rubbish trenches, quite crowded, quite densely close to one another. Barely two meters separate one group of workers from the next, so that from a distance one sees only hunched and bent backs.

And what are they digging for in the rubbish, what are the hundreds of people searching for here? They are digging up coal and creating still another "industrial branch" in the ghetto, which has almost the same relation, the same similarity to the real coal industry as many other official industries that were created in the ghetto and are only a parody, a distorted mirror of real enterprises. But these people who are digging coal in the rubbish fields do their work seriously, without clamor. They perform their work so as to earn enough for a watery soup, to be able to purchase a ration. However, the big shots who daily create new industrial branches in the ghetto, even though they know right well that these are the same "coalmines and rubbish bins," make a fuss and a clamor about it, form commissions with chairmen and secretaries with handsomely furnished offices, with waiting rooms, with surveys and with soap-bubble statistics!

And where, however, do the coals come from that the coal or rubbish miners dig out? There were, of course, normal times before the war, when every more or less prosperous house stocked up on coal for the winter, and each time there remained small bits which the servant girls did not want to use, neither in the heating ovens nor in the kitchen. And even though the "madame" wanted to run her household economically and made a point of wanting to use the coal dust and the tiny bits of coal, the serving-girls unceremoniously tossed the bits into the rubbish bin. From there, they were taken outside of town, where they collected for years and heaped up until two genial inventions were made: the closed ghetto and the coalminers on the rubbish fields in the ghetto.

IV

Forced Labor

Within the Ghetto

According to Rumkowski's program, labor was one of the chief pillars on which the ghetto had to base its existence. At various occasions, in his numerous public appearances, Rumkowski never tired of underscoring this labor principle as the main foundation of his entire ghetto philosophy (see chapter 7).

As mentioned, two weeks after the sealing of the ghetto, Rumkowski on 13 May 1940 sent the mayor a letter where he states that he has registered 14,850 skilled workers (9,550 tailoring workers, 2,500 knitwear workers, and 3,200 sewers of underwear), as well as a list of over 70 articles that the ghetto can produce, and for which he requested that orders be placed (chapter 2). In another letter dated 21 May 1940, he presents to the German mayor a new list of 3,345 skilled workers (carpenters, leatherworkers, locksmiths, sheet-metal workers, and hatters) and again mentions orders for the ghetto.

After the registration was carried out, a commission comprised of experts for all the registered branches set to organizing the workshops in the ghetto.

The Central Bureau of Factories (*Tsentral-byuro fun arbet-resortn*)[1] was created on 1 October 1940, at first managing the work in all the

A sign in German and Yiddish bearing Mordechai Chaim Rumkowski's slogan, "Our only path is work!" 1940–1944. Photograph by Walter Genewein. USHMM, courtesy of Robert Abrams.

workshops formed. Later, when the ghetto industry had significantly expanded, a certain decentralization occurred. For the technical management of the large number of tailoring workshops, a special Tailor Headquarters (*Shnayder-tsentrale*) was created. On 6 April 1941, the administrative and technical management of the ghetto industry was taken over by the separate Central Trades (*fakh*) Commission (also called the Trade and Control Commission). The Central Bureau of Factories represented the ghetto industry to the German authorities in the daily contacts with the *Gettoverwaltung*, and would receive from the latter various tasks and orders for goods.

The area of the city where the ghetto was located possessed few major factories; those factories that were there mostly belonged to the category of light manufacturing or small industry. Rumkowski exerted himself to save from German confiscation at least the small number of machines that were left within that region.

On 15 April 1940, in a letter to the Łódź branch of the HTO, Rumkowski requested permission to leave in the ghetto the machinery that was there, or that the HTO come to an understanding with him in each case of removing machines from the ghetto.[2] This request had only a partial effect. Confiscations, particularly of valuable equipment, occurred constantly. It was only on 18 October 1940, at a conference attended by the vice-president of the District Administration (*Viceregierungspräsident*), police-president, the mayor's deputy, and others, that the *Viceregierungspräsident,* speaking on behalf of the HTO, expressed his agreement to open for production all factories located in the ghetto, as well as to request a permit to apply all raw materials subject to confiscation to this purpose. Rumkowski was requested to look after the condition of all machinery located in the ghetto.[3] However, as we learn from a subsequent letter (26 March 1942) from Biebow to the Łódź branch of the HTO in the Warthegau (Poznań), the *Treuhandstelle* had already sold a portion of the ghetto machinery while the remainder was loaned to the "Jewish community." He adds that the stock of equipment in the ghetto had been substantially increased in some branches, like shoemaking, locksmithing, furs, and tailoring, partly thanks to the purchase of new machinery by the German ghetto administration.[4]

Machinery also came in from the liquidated provincial Jewish communities and ghettos. In an instruction dated 31 March 1942, from the Finance Ministry to all chief financial administrators (*Oberfinanzpraesidenten*, except in Prague) about how to utilize Jewish property left behind by those deported, it is pointed out inter alia that sewing machines should be sold to the Łódź *Gettoverwaltung* for use by the tailoring industry in the ghetto.[5]

As we shall further see, a large portion of the machinery was assembled in the ghetto itself from dismantled parts or entirely new ones. According to a report from the end of December 1942, over 7,000 machines were in operation in the ghetto.[6]

Equipment for the ghetto industry was also obtained through compulsory means. On 26 October 1940, Rumkowski issued an announcement (no. 148) about the obligation "voluntarily" to lend sewing machines under the threat of confiscation.[7] A month later, on 20 November, an announcement (no. 168) was again issued about the obligation "to lend" carpentry equipment for the newly established carpentry shops; if not, then it would be confiscated.[8] In August 1942, shoemakers working privately were searched out and any equipment, tools, and so forth found was taken away from them.[9] There were also instances when, at the founding of the relevant worksite (underwear sewing shop, paper production), the craftsmen voluntarily contributed their own workshop equipment.

The history of the rise and development of the ghetto industry indicates, on the one hand, a high degree of Jewish adaptability, endurance in the most difficult of circumstances and inventiveness, and on the other hand demonstrates Nazi exploitation of Jewish slave labor. Industry began to be created in the ghetto *ex nihilo*, "from nothing," as a contemporary document expresses it,[10] without the necessary machinery and without a suitable supply of raw materials. The Metal Department, the Electrotechnical Department, and the Department for Repair of Transmission Belts, with virtually nothing but their own meager capabilities, mechanized the entire ghetto industry. In the Metal Division (*resort*) were concentrated so many sub-branches of the metal industry (repairs, foundry, smithy, production of tools, and all sorts of instruments, including galvanizing), that a document observes: "Never have so many branches been coupled together in a metal factory as here out of necessity."[11] The same could be said about the textile mill that had to specialize in all sorts of yarn and produced both wool and cotton, both

Teenagers work in Łódź Ghetto metal workshop no. 16, 1940–1944. Photograph by Walter Genewein. USHMM, courtesy of Robert Abrams.

vicuna and wadding, "which is a sort of operation people were not capable of in prewar Łódź."[12]

The Electrotechnical Division conducted a highly ramified, multi-branched operation in the ghetto factories that had to be electrified due to the shortage of fuel in the ghetto. The same held true for the Transmission Belts Repair Department that had to see to maintaining the condition of the old belts and find surrogates for them, since no new transmission belts were provided to the ghetto at all (doc. no. 84).

As for raw materials, the most important sources for the ghetto industry were old things and junk. The *Gettoverwaltung* not only did not, as a rule, supply the ghetto with any raw materials, but it also took away for the German market the stock of old clothes and refuse that was in the ghetto, and which was, out of need and Jewish inventiveness, turned into various goods. All the private warehouses of rags and old clothes were, according to Rumkowski's order of 2 November 1940 (no. 154), placed at the disposition of the ghetto industry. It was strictly forbidden, under penalty of confiscation, to produce any articles whatsoever from them for private purposes. In July 1942, after the arrival of huge quantities of clothing, underwear, and so forth from the liquidated ghettos in the provinces, the Łódź ghetto warehouses had three-quarters of a million kilograms of rags at their disposal.[13] Only the orders for the military by the *Heeresbekleidungamt* (Army Clothing Office) and from

A Jewish policeman accompanies a supervisor inspecting Jews sewing on machines in the saddle-making workshop in the Łódź Ghetto, 1940–1944. Photograph by Walter Genewein. USHMM, courtesy of Robert Abrams.

a couple of German firms (see below) were covered with their own fabrics and accessories.

Typical in this respect was the construction of the textile factory established in the ghetto at the end of October 1940. The question of raw materials arose sharply after installation of a spinnery, a dye plant, and a carbonation plant (*karbonizatsye*), pulled together with great effort and exertions, using parts from half-ruined factories. A large quantity of old rags (345,462 kg) and yarn (25,000 kg) was acquired from the Purchase Point of Old Materials. In addition, after Rumkowski's request to the population to sell yarn to the textile department had negligible effect,[14] the Special Command of the Jewish police requisitioned 6,000 kilos of yarn from private persons. At the end of October 1940, this improvised textile mill employed ninety-three workers in production and fifteen workers in assembly (*montazh*). In November, the factory possessed fourteen cord workshops (*kordvarshtatn*) and twenty-five manual workshops. In June 1941, the textile factory produced 9,144 kilos of spinning material with 123 employees and had a stockpile of 111,306 kilos of rags.[15] Similar difficulties also had to be overcome in the building of the paper factory (doc. no. 85).

The ghetto industry was and had to be mainly for export. In one of the documents, we read: "The ghetto did not need anything for itself,

Four Jewish men haul a heavily laden wagon through the streets of the Łódź Ghetto, 1942. Photograph by Mendel Grosman. USHMM, courtesy of Nachman Zonabend.

the ghetto was not permitted to need. If people in the ghetto wanted to work and live, then this work had to be calculated for "export," to outside the ghetto, whence food could come in as an equivalent for this labor."[16]

In producing for its own consumption, the ghetto had to make do with a minimum, like a sausage factory, two factories for sweets, marmalade, rapeseed oil (*ribneyl*), production of wooden clogs and rag shoes, and repair of old garments and footwear.

Beginning with a tailoring shop in May 1940, the number of factories, workshops, and workplaces grew constantly, until August 1943, when there were 117 factories, workshops, sorting places, and goods warehouses, of which over 90 were factories and workshops.

The ghetto industry of Łódź grew, especially after the liquidation during May through August 1942 of the ghettos in the Łódź province (Pabianice, Brzeziny, Ozorków, Bełchatów, Sieradz, Zduńska-Wola, and others), which until their destruction were also involved in the slave labor for German firms. German orders were transferred from these destroyed ghettos to the Łódź ghetto for fulfillment.

Table 1
The Łódź Ghetto Industry, 1940-1943

Resort	First Report Period*				Subsequent or Maximal State			
	Founded	Workers	Machines	Production	Date	Workers	Machines	Production
Tailoring	V 40	3,500	800	25,000 pieces	IV 42	4,956	2100	370,553 pieces
Carpentry and Woodworking	15 V 40	407	20	181 pieces	II 42	936	450 Work-shops	1,586 large pieces; 100,000 small pieces
Metal	V 40	22	11	—	II 42	852	141	—
Shoeworks; Shoeworks Branch in Marysin	7 VII 40 12 XII 40	303	—	— —	Until mid-42	900	—	320,000 wooden shoes; repaired 20,000 pairs**
Shoe factory	—	—	—	—	XI 42	—	—	18,958 pairs
Quilting	—	286	83	21,247 pairs	II 42	742	121	35,094 pieces
Underwear and Clothing	20 VII 40	225	110	11,000 pieces and 442 dozens of kerchiefs	II 41	1,356	755	86,796 pieces
Upholstery	1 VIII 40	ca. 100	4	370 mattresses and 5,284 kg sea weed (*yam-groz*)	II 42	61 (adolescents)	15	2,205 pieces
Felt shoes	26 VIII 40	70	18	4,035 pairs	II 42	298	18	23,118 pairs
Corsets, etc.	IX 1940	258	231	1,772 doz.	VII 42	1,250	450	—
Knitting	10 X 40	25	26	2,500 sweaters	1941-1942	500 (150 home-workers)	120	160,000 sweaters; 2,960,000 earmuffs
Manual Knitting	1 XI 42	—	—	—	IV 43	—	—	11,411 pieces
Textile	X 40	106	48 and 300 spindles	14,950 kg and 8,883 meters	II 42	262	937 (with spindles)	35,335 kg, 12,745 meters
Knitted goods (*trikotazh*)	XI 1940	68	38	11,064 pieces	II 42	nearly 750	395	51,767 large pieces; 73,200 small pieces
Furrier	8 X 40	22	10	191 pieces	II 42	367	113	3,856 pieces
Brushes	—	20	—	2,617 pieces	II 42	55 (adolescents)	3	10,408 pieces
Rubber coats	15 XI 40	70	6	85 pieces	Until VIII 41	250	—	35,039 pieces
Hats	13 XI 40	72	14	6,000 pieces	II 42	622	45	5,046 pieces, 11,693 meters of straw mat (*shtroy-geflekht*)

First Report Period*					Subsequent or Maximal State			
Resort	Founded	Workers	Machines	Production	Date	Workers	Machines	Production
Gloves and socks	I 41	105	—	580 doz. gloves, 1,907 doz. stockings, etc.	II 42	600 (200 home-work-ers)	120	7,338 doz., 17,389 pieces
Saddlers and belts	I 41	124	18	28,708 pieces	II 42	1,706	445	140,000 pieces, 3,500 kg
Paper	27 II 41	67	—	—	End of VI 42	450	58	4,050 pieces, 19,150 pairs
Caps	7 III 40	67	35	1,430 pieces	II 42	127	80	11,398 pieces
Chemical laundry	III 41	—	—	—	1st half 43	595	—	683,026 pieces
Rugs	28 VI 41	156	—	500 pieces	VII-VIII 42	1,620	—	ca. 1,500 sq. meters weekly
Low Voltage Dept. (tele-phones)	2 VIII 42	—	—	For 6 months: Repaired 1,000 table units and 1,200 wall units		868	—	—
Tannery	10 VIII 40	26	7	566 differ-ent hides	II 42	47	7	3,190 hides
Printshop and Stamp factory	Summer 1940	—	—	—	Until IV 43	—	—	25,000,000 printed things
Wood shavings	—	19	3	600 pieces + 61 kg	II 42	20	4	8,385 pieces

---

* Includes mostly the months Oct.-Nov. 1940.
** Also an unknown number of slippers from rags.

Aside from those listed in the table, other workshops and warehouses were also active in the ghetto, producing straw shoes, rubber goods, arts and crafts goods (employing 220 workers, mostly women, and 17 machines in May 1941), repair workshops for transmission belts, sewing machines, and watches and clocks, warehouses of leather, metal and chemical goods, as well as warehouses for collection, sorting and utilizing the Jewish possessions sent in from the liquidated provincial ghettos (in July 1942 this employed over 2,000 workers; in August 1942 they worked in 8 branches of this department), and a department for collection and utilization of scraps (*opfal*; in August 1943, ten branches were in operation).

With all reservations regarding the statistical value of the materials, on the basis of which we have compiled the above table (reports by factory division managers, reports by the *Gettoverwaltung* and Joseph Zelkowicz's reportages about the separate divisions, these figures indicate the huge growth of the ghetto industry from its genesis in May 1940 until its peak development in summer 1943.

The greatest growth was recorded by the clothing branches that were the backbone of the entire ghetto industry; the German buyers were most interested in them. Thus, for example, the number of machines in the tailoring shops increased from May 1940 until April 1942 by a factor of more than 2.5 (from 800 to 2,100) and the production by a factor of nearly 15 (from 25,000 to 370,553 pieces); in the knitting works, between Oct. 1940 and Dec. 1942, increased by nearly 5 times (from 26 to 120); in the furrier workshops, from Oct. 1940 until Feb. 1942, by 11 times as much (from 10 to 113), etc. The growth was also vivid in certain segments of the leather industry. Thus, in the saddler and belt workshops the number of machines increased from May 1941 until Feb. 1942 by 445, and so forth. In accord with this, the number of those employed grew everywhere.

Workers roll up coils of straw in the straw shoe factory of the Łódź Ghetto, 1940–1944. Photograph by Walter Genewein. USHMM, courtesy of Robert Abrams.

Table 1 shows the growth of the most important branches of the ghetto industry during the years 1940–1943. The growth of the number of people employed in the ghetto is shown in the following statistics:

1 Sept. 1941—	40,288 employed
29 June 1942—	68,896 "
29 Sept. 1942—	74,568 "

During the course of a single year, the number of those employed rose by 86 percent.[17] In three summer months of July–September 1942, another 5,672 new employees had been drawn into the labor process. Grouped by chief branches, the distribution of workers employed in the Łódź Ghetto's manufacturing at the end of August 1943 was:

Textile and clothing	30,631	56.8 %
Leather	12,354	22.9 %
Metal	5,251	9.8 %
Wood	4,569	8.5 %
Paper	1,089	2.0 %
TOTAL	53,894	100.0 %

The remaining 20 percent of ghetto workers were employed in subsidiary trades and in the administration.[18]

In comparison with the prewar structure of the Jewish population in Łódź, the development of the ghetto industry caused fundamental changes in the occupational structure of the ghetto population, as shown by Table 2.

Table 2
The Occupational Structure of the
Jewish Population in 1931 and 1944

Branch	1931*		January 1944**	
	Number	% Total Work-ing Population	Number	% Total Working Population
1. Industry Total	48,035	56.8	60,200	81.2
Metal	681	0.8	5,317	7.1
Wood	1,381	1.6	4,463	6.1
Leather (Shoe-making)	3,069	3.5	11,570	15.7
Clothing	15,246	18.3	28,754	38.9
Other industry	27,658	32.6	10,096	13.4
2. Employed in public and social service	1,028	1.2	13,943	18.8
Total number of workers	84,605		74,143	
% total Jewish population	41.8		92.6	
3. Commerce, insurance	23,691	27.5***	—	—

---

* According to Y. Leshtsinski, "Yidn in varshe un Łódźh," in *Yidishe ekonomik*, 1938, no. 1-2, Table VIII; and A. Melezin, op.cit., p. 24.
** According to a report that Maks Horn, a leading official in the *Wirtschaftsstab* of the S.S., forwarded to his chief (Poln). Doc. NO. 519 in the National Archives in Wash., DC, microfilm in YIVO Archive.
*** In relation to the entire economically active Jewish population.

As we see from this table, a radical change occurred in the occupational structure of the Jewish population during the existence of the ghetto, a change that was achieved essentially through coercive means. In 1931, the working portion of the Jewish population in Łódź (physical and intellectual workers) amounted to 41.8 percent of the total Jewish population, while in January 1944 this category was 92.6 percent!

The commercial class, which in 1931 was 27.5 percent of the economically active Jewish population in Łódź, had completely vanished by 1944. In connection with this, it is worth observing that according to the results of the first ghetto census (16 June 1940) the rubric "without occupation" included 85,036 souls, that is, 54 percent of the total number of 156,402 people in the ghetto.[19] Most of this category doubtless consisted of former merchants, shopkeepers, business employees, and agents, who for understandable reasons did not want to state their profession, which in the ghetto lost any economic basis and could only attract repression by the German confiscation officials.

This commercial element largely disappeared earlier, in the first weeks of the war, during the panicky mass flights from the city, during the forced expulsion in December 1939, and later, in the ghetto, during the great mass deportations. A certain portion, as far as was possible, changed occupations and became involved in the ghetto industry.

Table 2 also indicates major changes in the occupational structure of Jewish artisans and workers. For example, the number of Jews employed in the metal branch increased from 0.8 percent in 1931 to 7.1 percent in 1944, almost nine times as many. The same can be seen in the wood branch: from 1.6 to 6.1 percent, nearly a four-fold increase; and in the leather branch, which rose from 3.5 to 15.7 percent, a more than four-fold increase.

The relative number of those employed in public service also grew sharply, from 1.2 percent in 1931 to 18.8 percent in January 1944, almost sixteen times greater. These statistics reflect the huge growth in those employed in the internal ghetto administration (officials, judges, medical personnel, ghetto police, and so forth) to manage all the branches of the "autonomous" Jewish life in the ghetto.

A major change also took place in the organization of work. Before the war, the organizational structure of Jewish industry was dominated by the small workshop that rarely exceeded 100 workers, but on average had fewer than ten. In the big ghetto workshops hundreds of Jewish workers were concentrated in one place. Thus, for example, there were 1,200 workers employed in the big tailoring shop on Jakuba Street. "The Jewish tailor had . . . never worked in such large groups," notes a contemporaneous document.[20] There was no equivalent in prewar Łódź of the large ghetto factory for furniture and other wood products, which in the summer of 1941 concentrated nearly 800 workers in its three divisions. At the end of July 1942, the four divisions of the house-slipper factory employed 4,500 skilled and unskilled workers.[21]

In connection with this, in a series of industrial branches, like tailoring, shoemaking, and so on, the labor process changed in the direction of the assembly line (*band-system*), which enabled the employment of a larger number of unskilled workers (doc. no. 86).

A whole series of workplaces, like the workshops for rugs, house-slippers, mica splitting, and so forth, employed armies of unskilled laborers, former shopkeepers, women, old people, adolescents, and children, who first learned their skill only in these very workshops.

Parallel with this, a retraining process took place in the ranks of the ghetto's labor force itself. For example, highly skilled tailors, who had previously worked on individual orders, now had to adapt to the so-called "cheap work" (*tandeyt-arbet*). When there were no orders for garments, they had to sew military shirts and furs.[22]

This "productivization" process filled Rumkowski and the managers of the ghetto industry with pride. At the end of December 1942, at the opening of the exhibition of five work divisions' production, a factory manager emphatically underscored the "activation into the labor process of a community of nearly 50 thousand souls, whose majority was transformed overnight from a nonworking into a working element . . . by the great restructuring process that was reflected in the ranks of the workforce itself."[23]

Jewish youth cut blocks of wood in a furniture workshop in the Łódź Ghetto, 1940–1943. Photograph by Walter Genewein. USHMM, courtesy of Robert Abrams.

Rumkowski, in his speech at the aforementioned exhibition opening, emotionally cried out that "the reward [for those being honored] will not be the bit of paper or the trinket that they will receive; it will be the most proud heritage that they will leave to their coming generations. Our children and grandchildren will recall with pride the names of all those who assisted in the creation of the most important positions of Jewry in the ghetto—by their work opportunities that gave them entitlement to life and existence."[24]

This feeling of joyous creation was, however, possessed only by the members of the leadership, most of whom only became important in the ghetto thanks to the roles they played. The directors of the factories were almost entirely randomly chosen people who previously had not had any contact with the given industrial branch.[25]

Most ghetto workers had an entirely different attitude on this toil for the German war machine. They considered it a necessity and a condition for the ghetto's existence and for their own passive vegetation and survival without exertion of the mind. "The worker who went to his job at that time [in the first period of the ghetto] did it more in order to fulfill his social obligation than for his own benefit. . . . Only thanks to that social consciousness were we enabled to work and thereby to exist," said one of the chief managers of the factories at the exhibition.[26]

However, due to Rumkowski's heavy hand, this social motive quickly evaporated among the mass of workers, and they lost any interest in the work. "It had ceased for [the majority of workers] to be a question of existence, because with it or without it [the worker] could not exist anyway. . . . He could not buy anything [for his wage]."[27]

As a rule, the ghetto worker labored only enough so as to be able to afford to buy the ration allotment. The total wage did not matter to him, for with what was left over from his earnings he could not do anything anyway, as it was negligible compared to the swollen prices in the illegal food trade.

The average wage of a skilled worker in the summer of 1941 ranged between 15 and 30 marks a week; an unskilled worker received between 12 and 20 marks (depending on the factory). In 1942, the minimum weekly wage of a worker (unskilled?) was a little higher, amounting to 19.90 marks.[28] In the same time period, a master craftsman earned up to 60 marks weekly (in the shoe workshops).

The wage scale was very broad and highly differentiated. The above-mentioned document (see note 28) outlined twenty-five wage categories, the highest being 108 marks a week. Among employees in the administration, the lowest monthly salary was 84.50 marks (21.12 marks weekly), while the highest was over 500 marks.

The inflation that broke out in the ghetto during the "outsettlement" in April–May 1942 sharply reduced the real value of wages, particularly since to combat the inflation the official prices for food articles in the rations were increased by 50 to 100 percent. Fees for electricity and gas also became more expensive,[29] but wages, as we shall further see, were not increased. Rumkowski in this regard apparently had to abide by the German general economic policy of "freezing" prices and wages at the prewar level. From an economic standpoint, this was a fiction: While prices rose in multiples in comparison with the prewar period, wages were increased only a little.

In May 1943, weekly and daily wages were abolished and an hourly wage was introduced according to the following categories:

A. Unskilled Workers
  Category I: Men 0.39 marks per hour, Women 0.33 marks per hour.
  Category II: Men 0.33 marks per hour, Women 0.28 marks per hour.
B. Skilled Workers (so-called half specialists)
  Category I: Men 0.45 marks per hour, Women 0.42 marks per hour.
  Category II: Men 0.42 marks per hour, Women 0.39 marks per hour.

Since the workday was nine hours (plus one hour designated for the lunch break), the workweek was fifty-four hours. Thus, the wages of unskilled workers ranged between 17.82 and 21.06 marks weekly for men and between 15.12 and 17.82 marks weekly for women. For the semi-skilled workers, wages ranged between 22.68 and 24.30 marks a week for men and between 21.06 and 22.68 marks weekly for women.[30] The wage for highly skilled workers is not listed in this document. The 18 May 1943 circular also abolished the higher tariff for working overtime and Sundays and banned adding supplements to contractual wage rates, such as paying the workers during interruptions in production if they had worked at least four hours a day.

Thus, we see that the wages of the overwhelming majority of the mass of workers in the ghetto factories (categories A and B) remained at the same level in comparison with summer 1941, while the official prices of the rations sharply rose during the course of two years, from 1941 to 1943.

If, for example, the price of a food ration in 1941 ranged from about 2.50 to 6 marks (depending on how "plentiful" the supply), the price during the years 1942–1944 ranged between 3.50 (5.20 for those employed with a supplemental coupon) to about 20 marks. The allocations were given out on average three times a month, so that the earnings of an average, less skilled worker barely sufficed for buying his food rations, particularly when one takes into account that the above-mentioned wages were gross wages. In reality the worker received much less when paid. Each pay packet was debited for the supplemental coupons (for soup, or bread with sausage), for rent (4 percent), and a wage tax ranging from 1.25 to 9.45 percent, and so forth.[31]

These wretched wages and the hard labor regime (see further) engendered among the mass of workers a deep reluctance toward this slave labor for the hated enemy and for justifying the existence of all sorts of factory managers, big and small. This deep reluctance would even evoke a covert sabotage in the form of defective production, reduced productivity, and so on. A slogan was widespread in the ghetto, consisting of the Polish abbreviation "p.p." (*Pracuj powoli!* Work slowly!). Whether the fires that broke out so frequently in the workshops at the end of 1942 were due to intentional sabotage cannot be determined on the basis of the meager documentation. At a special gathering of the factory managers convened on 6 January 1943, the danger that these conflagrations could cause for the ghetto was drastically described.[32]

The ghetto production would indeed drop sharply in certain periods. Thus, for example, under the headline, "The Fall in Production," the ghetto *Chronicle* of May 1942 reports the following reasons for this phenomenon:

1. Due to the worsening of the provisioning, the workers were weak, incapable of the least effort. Hunger caused the 25 percent fall of production.
2. The deportations had brought an influx of people incapable of working who could not fit into the group work and hampered the production in the workshops. The old workers adapted to the weak pace of the new ones.
3. The workers were not interested in the wage. If a worker sold his portion of soup or bread with sausage distributed in the factory, he was paid just as much as a skilled worker for a whole week's labor (doc. no. 87).

The chronicler also mentions "reasons of principle" that he does not explain, but it is clear that he has in mind the reluctance of the population to work for the hated foe.

In order to maintain production at the proper level a strict labor regime was introduced into the workshops. Special "commissioners," mostly former ghetto policemen, were assigned to maintain discipline. In the course of time they became the bosses of the workshops. For example, a report about the tailoring division states, "If not for the heavy hands of the commissioners, the situation would have resulted in unpleasant occurrences [in the large tailor workshops]. . . . The workers jeer."[33]

Y. Tabaksblat tells us about the conduct of the factory managers in the workshops and their relation to the workers:[34]

> They kept the workers in a disciplined barracks regime, where for the least transgression (so-called) they imposed the most serious, severe penalty, which they had available: taking away the worker's soup. The taking away of a worker's single bowl of factory soup was a daily occurrence. How many tears did workers shed, women as well as men, silently and aloud, biting their lips . . . and they had to be silent. Protesting and yelling were not allowed. At first, people attempted not to allow it and stood up. There was a case when a foreman with a human heart and conscience asked for better feeding on behalf of the pressers in the tailoring shop. . . . For this impudence, the foreman was removed and when the workers went on strike, they were dealt with short and sharp: seventeen delegates were summoned to the Gestapo and under threats of hanging they had to commit themselves to be diligent and obedient. Such foremen were very few in number. The rest were no more than satraps, who slapped and kicked the workers for the least failure to obey.

Rumkowski's administration ignored the brutal treatment by the workshop bosses. In the rich documentation about the Łódź Ghetto we have encountered only one instance of removal of a factory manager from his office for maltreatment of his workers. The case involves the textile division manager who, in August 1942, was dismissed from his post for the sin "of abusing the workers."[35] Symptomatic of the attitude of the workers toward their "leaders" in certain factories is the fact stated by the diarist Y. Hiler[36] that the workers rejoiced in January 1944 when a German commissioner was assigned to manage Metal Factory no. 2.

The work regimen in the ghetto workshops was very intense and from the beginning of 1943 became even more severe due to a shortage of workers for the German war production.

In the beginning, work was six days a week for eight hours daily. The day of rest was initially Saturday, but later was in fact Sunday. From 29 April 1941, a ten-hour workday was introduced in all ghetto offices, with a one and a half hour lunch break. In the central ration cards offices and distribution points, staff worked eleven and twelve hours a day with a one hour lunch break. But from 20 July 1941 the lunch break was abolished in the offices with the admonition that exceptions could be made for the bureaus of the Labor Office and of the distribution points.[37] In the workshops and factories where work was in several shifts, this announcement (see note 37) gave the managers free hands. When there were urgent orders for the German authorities, and this occurred often, people worked longer and also on Sundays. Only on 29 January 1943 was the ten-hour workday (from 7 A.M. to 5 P.M.) officially instituted with Sunday as a rest day that, however, did not apply to contract workers. In spring of that year, due to the shortage of skilled staff, a twelve-hour, two-shift workday was introduced in a series of factories and workshops.[38]

The system of control over the workers was applied with a sharp precision. All departments and workshops kept record books, attendance lists, and daily control lists (the latter served as a basis for distributing the factory dinners and product coupons).[39] Workers in all the workshops and sorting places were individually searched at the exit at the end of their workday. During work hours, no one employed in the departments and workshops was allowed to appear outside his worksite without a special permit, and the ghetto police patrols kept a sharp lookout for this.

The German supervisory authority naturally also kept an alert eye on the course of the ghetto production and intervened in its fashion. Thus, for example, the manager of the nails department in the metal division was summoned to the Criminal Police where he was shown in a "beating manner" [wordplay in Polish: *dobitnie przedstawiono*] how unsuitable his behavior was in carrying out an order from the German regime.[40]

The workers labored mostly in small, cramped, unsuited quarters and in unsanitary conditions.

A report about the rug division states that "the weaver workshops are very primitive, banged together in the ghetto . . . in small rooms, three looms each [in each room], with a woman who rolls up the thread on paper spindles." The capmaker division was located "in small rooms, in a former private apartment, densely packed with workers," while the knitwear division occupied the "structure" of a burned-out dyeing plant, where only the first floor could be used. Bitter cold reigned there in fall and winter. The arts and crafts division (*Kunstgewerbe ressort*) was located adjacent to the Jewish cemetery and occupied a couple of small cottages that lacked doors and window frames.[41] In the rubber division's building, where the air was contaminated with sulfur, lead, and chlorine, there were cases of poisoning and fainting during the work.[42]

Only a couple of divisions, like for example the clothing factory on Dworska Street, were located in "large and bright work halls."[43]

In the Mayor's 24 September 1941 memorandum to the Łódź District *Regierungspräsident,* it is reported that, in order to make space for the ghetto workshops, it was necessary to renovate somewhat a whole series of wrecked factory buildings that were supposed to have been torn down, and that the families who resided in those ruins were evicted from there without consideration.[44] After the September Action of 1942, when the hospitals were cleared of patients, workshops were set up in the large hospital buildings (see chapter 6).

The backbreaking labor in the ghetto workshops exhausted the workers' last strength. It was claimed that labor was saving the ghetto's existence, that labor was its right to survival. Yet the slave labor did not save the ghetto, but instead achieved the final wrecking of the factory workers' health even before their extermination in the death camps.

Writing in his 4 March 1942 memorandum to the Gestapo, Biebow refers to the fact that workers were collapsing in the ghetto workshops.[45] A year later, he raises the same argument for the necessity to improve the provisioning of the ghetto's working population in his letter to Mayor Ventzki, dated 19 April 1943.[46]

A Health Department report to Rumkowski, dated 18 June 1941, states that during four days, from 3 to 6 January, there were 172 recorded cases of fainting while working. On a single day, 5 January, there were 113 such instances.[47]

In certain factories, where the work conditions were especially harmful to health and the nourishment was miserable, mortality took on catastrophic proportions. Thus, for example, at the ghetto printing shop during the course of one year, from August 1941 until July 1942, twenty-eight printers died from a total of over forty.[48] In June 1943, among workers in some of the divisions, there was found a high rate of scurvy, as well as fever, linked with white tongue boils.[49] If a worker fell ill and did not come to work for seven days, he was dropped from the workshop and another took his place. So-called sick commissions or committees were formed in autumn 1943 in the departments and workshops. Their task was to help those who were ill and enfeebled with a bit of food, subsequently also with money collected mainly among their workshop colleagues. Occasionally, management would be able to obtain a food allocation from the Provisioning Office for this purpose. In spring 1944, several commissions arranged performances and lotteries in order to increase their funds.[50] Nevertheless, all this could not put a sick worker on his feet and his fate was sealed. A Jewish journalist expelled from Prague into the Łódź Ghetto melancholically concludes his reportage on the situation of the sick workers in the ghetto: "The ghetto has only one place for the sick—in Marysin [at the cemetery]" (doc. no. 88).

The hard labor in the factories played no small role in the sickness and death of thousands of ghetto workers. The German supervisory authority allowed such a catastrophic health situation among the workers in the ghetto industry, disregarding the fact that it highly valued the productivity of the Jewish worker. In his above-cited letter of 19 April 1943 to the mayor, Biebow writes that "the productivity of the Jewish worker stands much higher than that of the Polish worker. . . . Only one example: A Polish worker completes 180–200 wooden soles a day, while in the Jewish factories production amounts to 300–320 daily. Ignoring this, a Polish worker gets . . . 321 grams of bread and the Jewish one . . . 271 grams a day."[51]

The Jewish worker in the ghetto carried out the most difficult work in the most difficult conditions. If he were not suffused with a sense of responsibility for the community at large, it would have been nearly impossible to achieve what he did.[52]

In arguing for improvement of the food supply situation of those laboring in the ghetto, Biebow was naturally not out for the good of the Jewish worker. He was, like a number of the Nazi ghetto rulers who benefited materially from bribes, gifts, and a chance to evade the despised Eastern Front, personally interested in maintaining the ghetto's existence and therefore the ghetto's production capabilities. But the Nazi policy of extermination toward the Jewish population also encompassed in its plan the exhausting, hard physical labor in a permanent state of hunger as a means of annihilation, while squeezing from the Jews their strength for the maximum labor at the lowest cost.

The German ghetto administration also drew substantial profits from the Jewish labor for its own budget. In his file memo (*Aktenvermerk*) of 20 April 1940, Alfred Hall, empowered (on the part of the German city administration?) to organize and exploit the Jewish craftsmen in the ghetto, made a calculation that with 50,000 Jewish artisans employed the city could have a surplus daily income of 50,000–70,000 RM (doc. no. 89).

In 1942, the income of the German ghetto administration from various Jewish sources (appropriated remittances from the Generalgouvernement and abroad, confiscation and labor) amounted to 9,827,343.71 RM. In passing, the finance report observes that, since during the coming financial year (1943) a series of Jewish income sources will fall away, the productivity of the ghetto industry must be increased, that is, to squeeze out even more labor from the ghetto factories.[53]

Jewish workers in the Nazi period can be divided into four groups:

1. Those who worked individually for private entrepreneurs in or outside the ghetto, a form customary only in the first period of the occupation;
2. Those who worked collectively ("in columns") on public works, or for private construction firms (outside the ghetto);
3. Those who worked collectively in the ghetto for private firms and others, chiefly military clients. This group can be further divided into
   a. Those working for German firms with their own raw materials and goods; and
   b. Those who received their raw materials from outside (mainly with military orders); and finally,

4. Those who worked throughout for the internal needs of the ghetto.[54]

The German military provided the largest number of orders through the *Reichsarbeitsdienst* (Reich Labor Service, R.A.D.) or *Heeresbekleidungsamt* (Army Clothing Office, H.B.A.), directly through the Quartermaster's Office (*Intendantur*) or through contracted private firms. According to a report by the ghetto administration of 22 September 1941, during the eleven months from 1 October 1940 until 1 September 1941, there were produced 2,505,704 units of clothing, underwear, and other garments for the army. The Navy (*Marine-Behoerde, Kiel*) would also send in military orders. The tailoring workshops had eighteen different military clients, designated with the Roman numerals I to XLI.

On 24 September 1941, the Mayor sent to the District Governor (*Regierungspräsident*) a memorandum opposing "resettling" 20,000 Jews from Germany and the Czech Protectorate and 5,000 Gypsies into the Łódź Ghetto. He states, among other things, the total of orders from the *Wehrmacht,* namely:

In the saddler- and leather division	2,669,000 items
In the shoemaking workshops	721,000 items
Metal	1,717,000 items
Textiles	2,474,000 items
Furrier	9,000 items
TOTAL	7,590,000 items
From Private Firms	382,505 items

This means that 95 percent of the orders were from the *Wehrmacht.* The value of the raw materials of the military orders together with the labor charges is estimated in this memorandum at 50–60 million RM.[55]

In certain periods, when large military orders arrived, the whole operation in the majority of ghetto workshops was applied to military production. Thus, for example, all the tailor workshops in December 1941 rushed to finish an order for 56,000 pairs of so-called "camouflage suits" of white fabric for the Eastern Front. A similar order for 140,000 pairs arrived in August 1942.[56]

In 1941, the embroidery division completed 1,053,000 earmuffs for the military, while in August 1942, the specially designated division for military hats was employed in the production of 15,000 padded winter caps for armored troops.[57] The Łódź Ghetto also mass-produced wooden shoes and rag shoes for the labor camps and prisoner of war camps.[58]

Various military items were produced in the ghetto, from epaulets and badges to uniforms, boots, winter fur coats (*vinterpeltsn*), and helmets. In November 1942, ghetto production amounted to 68,165 kilos; 3,009,763 items; 515,468 pairs; 8,995,600 meters; 1,516 square meters; 11,358 dozens; and other minor quantities of the most varied textile, leather, metal, and wood products and so forth.

According to a calculation by the German ghetto administration, in 1941 it received 12,881,300 RM for the wages for the ghetto workshops and 3,312,500 RM from sale of ghetto products, altogether 16,193,800 RM. For the year 1942, the respective figures were 8,667,400 and 19,014,800, totaling 27,862,200 RM.[59]

At his 1946 trial in Poznań, former Wartheland *Statthalter* Greiser characterized the Łódź Ghetto as one of the largest war enterprises in the Reich.[60] In a document from the *Gettovervaltung*, there is a statement to the effect that the Łódź Ghetto's production was first and foremost creating opportunities for business in Wartheland.[61]

Various German commissions, from the military, the civil administration, and police organs, frequently visited the ghetto. The commissions were interested above all in the ghetto workshops and their production. Even Himmler personally visited the Łódź Ghetto on the fifth or seventh of June 1941 and had a conversation with Rumkowski.[62]

On 4 June 1942, *Statthalter* Greiser with his large retinue visited several ghetto workshops.[63] Visitations by various commissions became especially frequent during January–June 1944, when the fate of the ghetto was being decided.[64]

Private German firms were also anxious to send orders to the Łódź Ghetto and benefit from the almost free Jewish labor. Also interested in

Mordechai Chaim Rumkowski greets Heinrich Himmler as he visits the Łódź Ghetto, 5 June 1941. Photograph by Walter Gerewein. USHMM, courtesy of Robert Abrams.

exploiting Jewish slave labor were civilian Germans in Łódź, including officials of the *Gettoverwaltung,* the city administration, and the like. Nevertheless, the German ghetto administration, through whose mediation passed the bulk of orders for the *Wehrmacht,* strove to monopolize the entire Jewish labor force for these purposes.

In his letter of 28 October 1940 to Rumkowski, Biebow warned him "for the last time" to halt any work for private persons; only orders that had Biebow's signature or his contracts were to be carried out. This letter was to serve Rumkowski as an indication that he could not work for private clients.[65]

However, greedy German officials were not scared off by this. On 9 November 1942, Biebow had to issue a new stern warning that "all those employed by the *Gettoverwaltung* are strictly forbidden to export goods or products from the ghetto" without his permission, and he threatened to arrest every workshop manager who transgressed his prohibition (doc. no. 90).

The German ghetto administration also urged the District Governor (*Regierungspräsident*) to forbid private entrepreneurs to employ Jewish workers because they must be employed only for military needs (letter of 3 December 1940). In his reply of 18 December 1940, however, the *Regierungspräsident* refused to issue such a ban, explaining that it would make the employment of Jewish workers impossible in the entire Warthegau, and that there was no legal basis for such a ban.[66]

Indeed, various German firms both in Łódź and in the Reich broadly exploited this favorable set of circumstances and placed large orders. They supplied the ghetto not only with raw materials and accessories, but sometimes even their own machinery. Thus, for example, the largest client for underwear and clothing in the ghetto was the Berlin firm of Josef Neckermann Underwear and Clothing Factory.[67] The German Łódź shoe company Heine ordered 10,000 pairs of so-called "*ganduvkes*" (sandals of linen and cardboard) between 25 June and 8 July 1941 from the felt shoe factory. The demand for them in the city was very large, because "no clothing ration cards are needed for them, [they] are produced from Jewish materials and are inexpensive."[68]

For its orders for corsets, the firm Spieshauer und Braun in Haubach in July 1941 delivered to the ghetto, aside from materials, seven machines which were previously unknown in Łódź, and in November another five machines together with a large order. The firm required that only its orders be processed on the machines it sent in and asked for a separate building for itself. The corset department created at the time worked for a long time only for that firm. Like a monopolist, the German company dictated its conditions and paid very low wages (5–12 marks a week). In time, the division made itself independent of this firm and the weekly wages were increased from 12 to 30 marks.[69]

The arts and crafts (*Kunstgewerbe*) division that worked entirely on old clothes and rags would fulfill orders from the Berlin firm, Oldenburg;[70] while the small appliances department (*shvakhshtrom-optayl*, "low voltage department") was principally employed with repair of outdated model telephones that a German firm shipped into the ghetto by the wagonload from the conquered eastern regions,[71] and so on.

The work in the ghetto factories often had to be partially halted or reduced due to irregular delivery of materials and accessories. Almost all reports about the ghetto production underscore the point that, due to the sporadic and irregular delivery of raw materials and accessories by the German clients (even for the military), urgent orders from the government could not be filled and this also caused lengthy interruptions and partial reductions of labor personnel.[72]

Thus, for example, the ghetto *Chronicle* of 25 March 1941 reports that due to the reduced deliveries of material, the number of workdays in the tailoring shops was reduced to two to three days a week, while only two shops for military uniforms and civilian garments were working a full week.[73] The *Chronicle* of 16 December 1941 reports similar information about the situation in the factories for rugs, belts and saddles, shoes, brushes, and leather.[74]

There were also public construction and paving projects carried out in the ghetto by order of the supervisory authority. They were executed initially by the Construction Department (One and Two), and then, from the beginning of July 1942, by the Office for Special Tasks. On 21 July 1942, there were 530 workers employed on public works in the ghetto (construction work and the like).[75] In the second half of 1943 and in February–March 1944, when many employees were dismissed from the administrative departments, they were assigned to the workshops and to build barracks at Radogoszcz. The latter project was part of the preparations for the final liquidation of the ghetto.[76] As already mentioned, all who benefited from relief were obligated to work gratis fourteen days in a month. They were chiefly employed in public works.

In time of need, the ghetto's entire adult population was mobilized for urgent work. In March 1941 and in April 1942, Rumkowski required all men and women (in 1941, from eighteen to forty years old; in 1942, from fifteen to fifty years old) to report for work in clearing the ghetto of snow and ice. Also mobilized for this job in 1942 were even workers in the factories and workshops, which were closed on the given day, 6 April.[77]

It would happen that the Order Service simply seized people for work off the streets and from houses. Thus the *Chronicle* of 6 December 1941 reports that, in connection with the necessity to unload a large transport of foodstuffs for the ghetto, the police on the evening of the fifth forcibly pulled people they encountered at random (adolescents, elderly, even workers on their way to their jobs) into the police precincts. Late that night, due to the deep resentment evoked by the "great impetuousness of the police" (namely beatings), an order arrived to release the detainees and to send to work only volunteers and for a suitable wage.[78]

Workers at the saddle-making workshop stand next to their work tables in the Łódź Ghetto, 1940–1944. Photograph by Walter Genewein. USHMM, courtesy of Robert Abrams.

As mentioned, the ghetto also produced a number of food articles for its own consumption, like sausage, vegetable oil, and candies. A typical example of this "food industry" in the ghetto was the manufacture of the so-called "*salatke*" and cottage cheese. "Vegetable salad" was manufactured from vegetable scraps (leaves, the good bits from rotten potatoes, and the like) and old bread that had begun to mold. The production of these so-called "ghetto preserves" rose from 380 kilos in January 1941 to 29,000 kilos in May 1942. The other item, cottage cheese, was produced from the skim or spoiled milk that the city delivered to the ghetto. Just as the delivery was very irregular, the production of this item varied greatly; from 13,050 kilos in September 1941, to 50 kilos in December 1941 and 62 kilos in January 1942, but 41,500 kilos in July 1942. Workers would each get 15 deka of cottage cheese twice a week, as well as "*salatke*" from time to time.[79]

The clothing and shoe workshops also operated partially for the ghetto population's needs. On 28 October 1941, when the nakedness and barefootedness of the ghetto population was already most vividly apparent and it was literally "the waters have reached my neck,"[80] the Clothing Department was formed that sought to ease the catastrophic clothing situation in the ghetto.

In spring 1942, this department's card file of clients numbered 28,000 family cards that included nearly 120,000 souls, which was nearly the entire ghetto population at the time. The shoe workshops took to manufacturing wooden shoes, the so-called *"trepes"* (30,000 pairs for all those employed in the factories); 23,700 pairs of various sorts of repaired shoes and slippers were also distributed. In September 1942, the Clothing Department spun off a separate Department for Ready-Made Clothing and Haberdashery Goods (*konfektsye un galanterye-khfeytsim*) to sell old, used, or repaired garments and underwear at its four warehouses for cheap prices (free to the needy). The number of the beneficiaries until a certain period (not given) amounted to 30,082, who purchased 73,846 items of clothing in the value of 270,614 ghetto marks.[81]

To complete the image of work in the ghetto it is worthwhile to discuss at least briefly the problem of adolescent and child labor. After the closing of the schools in October 1941, the ghetto was confronted with the question of what to do with the huge multitude of children and adolescents. The Restructuring Commission at the School Department, formed on 1 March 1941, had set itself the task of teaching the youth various trades and integrating them into the production process. It carried out a survey and registration, and by 20 July 1942 nearly 13,000 adolescents and children ages ten to seventeen were sent into the ghetto workshops. This was nearly 19 percent of the entire working population in that period.[82]

Especially numerous was the influx of children during the first deportation actions in the winter and spring months of 1942. "Whole families enlisted in the work, from ten-year-old children to gray old men."[83] Work was considered a remedy against being deported from the ghetto. In some workshops, the September Action of 1942 led to real devastation in regard to children. In the slipper factory, for example, that employed a large number of older women and children, of 2,200 employees only 600 (including 150 adolescents and children) remained after the action. A fresh wave of children, as young as seven to nine years old, who had been saved with blood and sweat, poured into the workshops after the "Children and Elderly Action" of September 1942, and found there a legal justification for their endangered existence.

There were workshops where adolescents and children comprised a very significant percentage, in some workshops almost half of the entire workforce. Thus, for example, on 19 July 1943 the Small Appliances Department ("Low Voltage Department") employed 93 men, 363 women, and 412 children. The children made up almost half of all those doing physical labor in this department[84] (doc. no. 91). In the metal division, there were 184 apprentices and 384 adult workers in June–July 1941. In May 1942, the number of young people employed in the division reached a record of 1,500 and it was planned to increase to 2,000.[85] Due to a shortage of trained workers, the adolescents who learned the trade in the factory played a decisive role there. Certain departments, like for example the nail mill, employed almost only adolescents.

In the large tailoring factory on Łagiewnicka Street, which employed 300 adolescents, there were two halls occupied wholly by children, who were graduates of the tailoring school on Franciszkańska Street (sixty-seven children). These two halls were called showrooms (*pokazowe*). "The German visitors marveled at the 2 halls, [where] they make a pair of trousers within 8–9 minutes, produce as much as adults—60 pairs a day."[86]

Certain divisions, like metal, electrotechnical, and tailoring, conducted vocational courses for their young workers, in time training groups of skilled workers (doc. no. 92).

As for wages, they initially received only soup, or bread with sausage. After a certain degree of experience or training, they were paid. A circular from the Trade and Control Commission of 12 October 1942 set their minimum wage at 8 marks weekly. If the wage was smaller, they had to be paid the difference. In an incomplete workweek, each adolescent was to be paid up to 1.15 marks for each day worked. For the meals that they received at work, 2.50 marks were to be deducted weekly, as well as the wage tax. Adolescents who were under the supervision of the Department for Child Protection received no adjustment of their salaries (that is, up to the minimum of 8 marks weekly).[87] At the end of June 1943, when the principle was introduced that adolescents must also be paid in general according to contract work, the following tariff was established: untrained 1.35 marks a day, partially trained 1.70 marks, fully trained 2 marks. Adolescents who were attending vocational courses or were included in vocational training groups also received a free additional soup.[88]

With a tragic pride, children and adolescents bore on their weak shoulders part of the difficult slave labor in the ghetto, which gave them, these "superfluous creatures," a right to live and an illusory chance to survive.

Forced Labor Outside the Ghetto

The ghetto also delivered its slaves for work outside the ghetto, mainly in the work camps in Wartheland, where they were employed in draining swamps, regulating rivers, building roads, laying train rails, and so on. The *Reichsautobahn* (R.A.B.) employed the largest number of Jewish slave laborers in constructing the Frankfurt-Oder-Poznań, Kutno-Poznań, Lissa-Ostrowa, and other highways. For the period between 10 December 1940 and 29 August 1941, 4,045 persons were dispatched from Łódź into the R.A.B. camps.[89] The *Deutsche Reichsbahn* (German Rail System) also had a large number of camps with Jewish laborers. Jews from the camps in Inowrocław worked on various train lines, including the Krotosin-Lissa line, on various rail stations, and in the train workshops in Zbąszyń. The *Reichswasserwirtschaftsamt* (Reich Water Management Office) in Poznań also had a large number of Jewish laborers in its camps. The Jewish camp laborers carried out regulation projects on many rivers and streams and improvement projects in various regions in Wartheland. The *Hauptbauamt* (Central Construction Office) in Poznań, the *Kreisbauämter* (District Construction Offices in the rural districts), and *Stadtbauämter* (Town Building Offices) in this province also employed many Jewish workers from the ghettos, including from Łódź. The organs and officials of the civil administration (*Landraten* and *Amtkommissaren*) also employed Jewish laborers from the ghettos. We find Jewish workers on various private and government estates engaged in forest and fieldwork. Camps were to be found at almost every major construction site, at all points of the road and improvement projects, at almost all factories, large workshops, and agricultural estates. They were thickly scattered across the entire territory of the province. According to surviving sources in the archive of the Łódź *Gettoverwaltung*, the number of camps in their most numerous period (second half of 1942–first half of 1943) totaled at least 160.[90]

In September 1940, a proposal circulated among German government organs to dispatch Jews from the Łódź Ghetto to labor on various public works, firstly for the *Reichsautobahn* construction of the Frankfurt-Poznań highway. On 10 December of the same year, the first party of 638 persons was sent out and it continued that way constantly, with shorter or longer breaks, until the liquidation of the ghetto.

According to the data of Rumkowski's Statistical Office, 1941 saw 5,179 persons sent out (in April and May 2,981) and in the first half-year of 1942 (until 30 June) another 1,383 people. Thus, from 10 December 1940 until the end of June 1942 a total of 7,200 persons were dispatched.[91]

Nineteen forty-one was the year of intensive dispatching to the labor camps. However, the number of those sent out steadily declined during the second half of 1942, with the strong development of the ghetto industry and its large capacity to absorb workers. Thus only 240 persons were sent to work outside the ghetto during the second half of 1942, and in 1943, when the ghetto industry's development reached its zenith, a total of 1,512 persons were sent out, for an average of 126 people a month.[92]

Already in 1942, it happened that skilled workers and specialists, who found themselves on the lists of candidates for outside labor, were detained by their workplaces. Thus, the ghetto *Chronicle* of 6 and 7 June 1942 states that of 300 candidates there were only 130 left, because the majority consisted of specialists that the ghetto workshops did not want to release from their work.[93] There was even noted a case when the German supervisory authority itself demanded that the holders of labor cards, that is those employed in the ghetto workshops, be removed from the list of an already prepared worker transport.[94]

In the final year of the ghetto's existence, only two transports were sent out, on 9 and 10 March 1944, with 1,600 persons, who were sent to the ammunition factory in Skarżysko and to Częstochowa in the

Generalgouvernement.[95] All other transports, ostensibly also "for work outside the ghetto," were sent to Auschwitz. An exception was the final transport in which there were a number of officials of the Jewish ghetto administration, managers of workshops and specialists (precise number unknown); it was sent on 21 October 1944 to Königswusterhausen (near Berlin) for work.[96] All in all, according to available data, about 11,000 persons were sent for work outside the ghetto during its entire existence.

Recruitment of candidates to leave, particularly in the beginning, was in principle "voluntary." Through wall posters, Rumkowski would from time to time call for registration for work outside the ghetto (doc. no. 93). The masses of poor, who were anyway menaced by death from hunger, at first voluntarily registered to leave with the illusory hope of finding a possibility to exist outside the ghetto. But when the truth about the murderous conditions in the work camps began to penetrate back into the ghetto with returned workers, Rumkowski had to apply coercive means. People were dragged from their beds at night and taken to the Central Prison.[97]

Even earlier, Rumkowski had used being sent out for work as a means to be rid of a turbulent and rebellious element, or of those who had committed some transgression against him. From the end of March until the start of April 1941, he sent out for work about 800 wagoners, butchers, and fishmongers[98] who had shown too great a measure of independence and too little subordination toward his totalitarian ghetto regime.[99]

Those arrested and held in the ghetto prison and the remnants of the provincial Jews were ready-made candidates for being sent out for labor, sent into Łódź when the liquidation of the local ghettos commenced (an exception was made only for the skilled specialists). These physically and emotionally broken people, violently torn away from their families and brought to a strange place, were already incapable of resisting. The immeasurably worse food supply situation in the Łódź Ghetto, in comparison with the ghettos from which they came, also moved some of them to report "voluntarily" for departure.

Recruitment of candidates for external labor would also encounter difficulties due to the disastrous health situation. The ghetto *Chronicle* for November 1941 reports that the Jewish physicians' commission approved barely 25 percent of the candidates for work outside the ghetto and that the German examination in the city rejected another portion of those certified.[100]

Wartheland governor Artur Greiser regulated the working and living conditions in the labor camps. A decree of 12 August 1941 (there was also a prior decree of 9 April, but it has not been preserved), consisting of eight paragraphs, set the wage scale for a working hour at 30 pfennig (par. 1). It deprived the Jewish workers of the right to insurance in case of illness, disability, or unemployment. It introduced the rule that

Jewish laborers could benefit from medical treatment only by a Jewish doctor or medic, thereby excluding any hospital treatment. Sick workers whose recovery was in doubt were to be delivered for "removal" (par. 2). The decree further established that the costs for feeding a Jewish worker must in no case exceed the sum of 1.50 RM daily (par. 4). Paragraph 5 regulated the wage allocation in such a fashion that, of what was left after the deductions for subsistence and taxes,[101] the worker was to receive 20 percent as "pocket money." The balance was to be forwarded each week to the administration of the ghetto, or community, from which the worker originated for "supporting the families" (par. 6). The same decree also set the weekly feeding norms at 2,250 grams of bread, 250 grams of horsemeat, and 100 grams of fats. It was emphasized that Jewish laborers did not get any of the additional rations for which those employed in heavy physical labor were eligible (par. 7). The eighth paragraph discussed the guarding of the camps, which had to be organized so as to make escape impossible.

In reality, the situation in the camps was much worse than would appear from this decree. The designated wage rate of 30 pfennig an hour was, of course, terribly low. This wage was by no means enough to support the families left in the ghettos. The German ghetto administration itself even admitted this. In its memorandum to the Łódź *Regierungspräsident* of 1 September 1941, it writes that "the new wage of 30 pfennig an hour is far from adequate to nourish the remaining relatives, because the bulk of the earnings is retained by the construction firms or the camps [in order to cover the expenses] for feeding and upkeep [of the workers themselves]."[102]

In reality, at this wage rate, the earnings of a camp worker, for an eight-hour workday, could total at most 10.40 RM weekly. After deducting the so-called social tax (15 percent) and 1.50 RM daily for subsistence (together 12.66 RM), there remained 1.74 for the family for an entire week! (And this only in the event that the worker refused the 20 percent in "pocket money.")

The families left behind in the ghetto indeed could little count on the earnings from the husbands and sons sent out to the labor camps, and Rumkowski paid out to them relief grants in the amount of 12 marks weekly. As Biebow writes in the memorandum to the *Regierungspräsident,* support through 30 August 1941 for the families of those sent out of the ghetto had cost Rumkowski 961,921 RM, while the total wages transferred from the camps for families in the ghetto amounted to at most 100,000 RM.[103]

With arrival of the year 1942, there began the mass extermination of the Jewish population in Wartheland, with the Łódź Ghetto in the lead. From 16 January until 15 May 1942, there were deported to destruction 54,990 Łódź Jews, over 40 percent of their average total population during that period. The deportation waves swept away the overwhelming majority of families of those sent out for work. Since the

Jewish labor camp worker had lost his family, there was no longer any "humanitarian" consideration for paying the Jewish worker a wage so that he could supposedly support his family in the ghetto. And indeed, Greiser's secret decree of 25 June 1942 arrived, introducing the principle of unpaid Jewish labor ("*Jüdische Arbeitskräfte erhalten keinen Lohn*" [Jewish workers receive no salary]). Only in exceptional cases was it permitted to reward Jewish workers for significantly exceeding the work norm and that only up to 1.50 RM weekly (par. 3, subpar. 2). The fourth paragraph of the decree introduced the principle that, in order "to maintain the Jews incapable of work," the entrepreneurs who employ Jewish workers were obligated to pay the Łódź ghetto administration (regardless of the place of origin of the camp worker) a daily 70 pfennig "Jew-rental fee" (*Judenleihgebühr*) per Jew, both for when he worked and for when he was not engaged in a task for certain reasons. The costs of upkeep of a camp worker were set at a maximum of 1 RM a day (par. 3, subpar. 1). As for camp clothing and medical aid, whose only aim was to prevent epidemics, the principle was set that the allocation of garments and footwear in the labor camps was the responsibility of the ghetto administration (par. 5), but provision of medical care was the responsibility of the entrepreneur (par. 6). Finally, a ten-hour workday was instituted (par. 7; doc. no. 94).

Greiser's decree illustrates vividly the final stage of the Nazi policy toward the "Jewish work force" located behind the camp fences. The goal of the decree is clear, to accelerate the physical destruction of the Jewish labor camp worker, to break him both physically and morally. The paragraph about *Judenleihgebühr* in the amount of 70 pfennig a day had to result in such an intensification of the work regime that under this burden weak and sick workers must quickly collapse. The German entrepreneurs were now interested in being rid as soon as possible of this unproductive labor force. Not enough that they had to feed the worker, but they also had to pay an additional 70 pfennig daily for him. If previously the camp worker could still have had the illusory comfort that with his labor he was supporting, at least in a minimal measure, his family left behind in the ghetto, the elimination of the wage could not leave him in any doubt regarding the family's fate. Greiser's decree of 25 June 1942 was in force in the Jewish labor camps in Wartheland until the moment of their final liquidation.[104]

But the real situation in the camps was much worse even than the draconian regulations of Greiser's latter decree, in large measure because of the unscrupulous greed of the German entrepreneurs. Regardless of the established norm of an eight-hour and later (from 2 July 1942) a ten-hour workday, they compelled workers to toil even longer, particularly in the summer months. Touching on the question of overtime, Biebow writes in the aforementioned memorandum of 1 September 1940, "This caused debilitation and sicknesses in a terrible measure. The result is that of every 1,000 Jews, 200–300 remain sitting in camp, because they are no longer able to do the work." He relates that of 4,045 workers sent out, 921 returned to the ghetto, filling up the hospitals, and that the promise was broken that "Łódź will no longer see any Jew incapable of work."[105]

Food in the camps reached a condition of outright starvation. On the basis of Greiser's decree of 12 August 1941, the daily feeding norm amounted to 420 grams of bread, 14 grams fats, and 35–36 grams of meat, which was the norm of the Jewish nonworking population (*Normalverbraucher*). But in fact not even these hunger norms were adhered to. In the Poznań city camps the nutritional value of the daily norm amounted on average to 800 calories, while the minimal caloric requirement of a physical worker is 2,500–3,000 calories. Moreover, the systematic theft of the pitiful starvation rations by the corrupt camp administration reduced the nutrition to an unheard of minimum.

In order to silence their hunger somewhat, people ate all that came to hand: raw potatoes (it was strictly forbidden to cook in the camps), kernels of grain, and so on. They would eat roots and grasses on the way to work. After work, they rummaged about in the kitchen garbage in order to pull out the half-rotten bits of vegetables. For leaving the work site in order to look for a bit of food in a nearby village, the penalty was hanging.[106] Such nourishment naturally resulted in epidemic sicknesses of the digestive organs and caused an increase in mortality.

Sicknesses and mortality were also caused by the fact that the workers went about in rags and tatters. The decree of 12 August 1941 did not regulate the question of who had the obligation to supply clothing and shoes in the labor camps. Only the decree of 25 June 1942 placed this obligation on the German ghetto administration (par. 5). Thus until this date, that is, for a year and a half, none of the interested parties even formally had any duty to see to the clothing of the camp slaves. They were dependent in this respect on aid from the families left behind. Until 1 September 1941, according to a report by Biebow, 1,500 parcels worth 22,500 RM had been sent from the ghetto to the camps.[107]

After Greiser's decree of 25 June 1942 appeared, the *Gettoverwaltung* took on the duty of clothing. Moreover, it was easy to accede to the requests from the entrepreneurs in regard to camp clothing: The ghetto administration's warehouses were then, in summer 1942, laden with huge quantities of garments, underwear, and shoes that it had "inherited" from the tens of thousands of murdered Jews of Wartheland. According to Greiser's two secret decrees of 18 March and 1 May 1942, the Łódź ghetto administration was designated the chief heir of the looted property. But it employed the camp clothing as a means of putting pressure on the entrepreneurs in regard to paying for the Jewish camp laborers. The sending of clothing for the Jewish labor camps was made dependent on regular payment of the *Judenleihgebühr*. Therefore, the clothing situation was especially unfortunate at the firms that were, in the opinion of the ghetto administration, in arrears with their payments. The firms themselves write about this clothing condition of their slave laborers. The Otto Trebitsch firm, for example, had already asked the ghetto administration a couple of times without success to send out "Jew-clothing" (*Judenbekleidung*). It substantiated its renewed, this time menacing request, of 12 November 1942 with the argument that "it cannot be imagined that I should send the Jews barefoot (in November!) to the construction site, because this is not permissible, since the naked body is partially visible and it allows the danger of provoking public distress."[108]

The condition of the camp clothing is described in the Fritz Hilgenstock firm's letter of 14 August to the *Gettoverwaltung*: "The Jews find themselves in regard to clothing in such a down-at-heels state that, in order to avoid public offense at the construction site, it is unconditionally necessary to replace the ragged garments with others."[109] In a letter of 20 March 1943 to the ghetto administration, the M. Hamann firm complains that the Jews who are in its camp have not received any clothing for a year and a half.

On the job, there was in fact a pattern of sadistically tormenting the Jewish laborers, supposedly for negligent work or for too slow tempo. The workers would frequently return to the camp from the work site with serious bodily injuries. In the city work camps in Poznań, stretchers were taken along to work since almost every day it was necessary to carry back from work laborers who were seriously injured or even beaten to death.[110]

The sanitary facilities in the camps were simply a mockery of the most elementary rules of hygiene. In the Obra firm's camp there were a total of twenty bowls for eating by forty-five camp workers, so two people had to eat from one dish. The Gruen und Vielfinger firm that employed several hundred Jews from the *Gemeinschaftslager* Gutenbrun explained to the ghetto administration (in a letter of 28 July 1942) that it did not deduct for the Jew-leasing fee (*Judenleihgebühr*) with the excuse that the camp was closed for weeks due to lice infestation.[111]

It is no wonder, then, that various diseases rapidly decimated the camps. As an illustration we bring statistics from the Poznań camp Kreising that constructed the Poznań airport and employed a large number of Łódź Jews. In this camp, which on 30 November 1942 numbered 900 men, there were 180 deaths during that month, about 20 percent. During seven days (from 22 to 28 November) 61 men died, an average of 9 daily; on one day, the thirteenth, 19 men died, and on the nineteenth, 11 died. After the Gestapo shipped the hopelessly ill in "an unknown direction" (363 men on 31 December), mortality naturally declined and in January 1943 amounted to only 4 percent.

It was no better in other camps. In the R.A.B. camp in Necklo, there were on average 263 men in July 1942; in the course of that month 37 workers died (14 percent). On one day, 17 July, 16 workers died according to the official status report.[112]

Also high was the incidence of disease. At the Kreising construction site (a branch of the camp), the proportion of those sick during the first half of September 1942 ranged between 36.8 and 61.7 percent. There were periods of time when an overwhelming majority—even 100 percent of the laborers—were unable to go to work due to illness. Such days were 29–30 November and 5–6 December in 1942. In the week between 27 December 1942 and 3 January 1943, out of 319 worker days, there were 250 days of sickness (64 percent).

We also see a similar picture in other camps. In the monthly report for May 1942 from the barracks camp in Konin, which belonged to the Otto Trebitsch firm, we find that on 3 May, of 302 workers, 186 were sick; on 10 May, of 266 workers, 214 sick; on 12 May, 224 workers and 149 sick; on 17 May, 242 workers and 225 sick.[113] But in many camps, illness did not spare one from work, and seriously ill workers were compelled to go to work, or went out of fear.[114] According to a secret decree, the Gestapo had to be notified about all workers who were ill or incapable of work. These workers were taken from the camp, killed in the nearest vicinity, or they were sent to an extermination camp. This was called *Rücktransporten* (return transports). Only in very rare cases, in the beginning, would the sick workers be returned to their ghetto of origin. According to Biebow's letter of 30 August 1941, the first transports of the sick began to be assembled in July 1941, and some did indeed return to the Łódź Ghetto (143 men, by the mentioned date). The rest vanished without a trace. Biebow himself states that during two or three weeks no word arrived about them and that the correspondence arriving for them in the camps is returned to Łódź.[115]

For example, on 7 July 1942, 308 sick workers were taken from the camp in Necklo (Schroda district), more than half of the entire company (599 men). On 1 December 1942, 363 men (40.3 percent) were taken away from the Kreising camp. Although the reason is not stated, knowing the health situation in this camp, it is not difficult to presume why.[116]

What sorts of diseases decimated the camp prisoners? During almost three months (from 25 August until 21 November 1942), the aforementioned Kreising camp exceptionally sent to the Łódź ghetto administration systematic notifications about deaths, stating the cause (in general the notices do not state the cause of death, an exception being executions). Thus of 285 reported instances of death, heart disease was the cause in 168 cases (58.9 percent), catarrh or tuberculosis of the digestive organs in 32 cases (11.2 percent), gangrene of the legs and other limbs or general poisoning (*allgemeine Fargiftung*) in 22 (7.7 percent), general debilitation in 19 cases (6.6 percent), tuberculosis in 13 (4.5 percent), and weak blood circulation in 10 cases (3.4 percent). The balance of deaths came from other diseases, like avitaminosis, limb damage, and inflammation of the lungs.[117]

These statistics speak clearly and should be accepted as not only characteristic for this camp, but rather typical for all labor camps in Wartheland. The overwhelming majority of deaths had as their cause diseases that arose due to hunger, exhaustion due to hard labor, and unsanitary conditions. This fact is underscored even more vividly by the ages of those who died, as Table 3 shows.

One deduces from this table that 189 (68 percent) of those who died were born in the years 1900–1920, that is, that they left this world in their best years (from twenty-two to forty-two years of age). To these must be added a large number of those born in the years 1920–24, that is, those seventeen to eighteen years of age (as we see from the table, children as young as fourteen were enslaved in this camp). In total, we see a terrible picture: almost 75–80 percent of those who died were ages eighteen to forty-two, their premature deaths caused only by the murderous camp regime.

The sick had almost no medical care at all. As already noted, the Jewish labor camps, according to Greiser's decree of 12 August 1941, could benefit only from medical care by a Jewish physician, or in a case

Table 3
Ages of Those Who Died in Kreising Camp

Born in the years	Number	%
1882-1900	38	13.4
1900-1910	91	31.9
1910-1920	98	34.4
1920-1928	58	20.3
TOTAL	285	100.0

when there was no doctor, a Jewish medic. Transporting a patient to a hospital outside the camp was forbidden. The designated primitive sickrooms in the camps naturally could not substitute for a hospital.

Greiser's decree of 25 June 1942, as mentioned, placed the responsibility to support and treat sick laborers on the chief entrepreneurs, or on the firms that leased the Jewish workers from the chief entrepreneur. It is easy to imagine what the medical care looked like in the camps in a situation when the firms themselves had to cover the costs for treatment. The sick camp worker was a double burden for them. Financially it was better for the contractor to hasten the death of the sick workers and thus be rid of useless expenses, rather than treating them for various diseases which was almost impossible under camp conditions. In any case, this would have to take a very long time. A letter from the Poznań contractor Hochtief to the Łódź ghetto administration reveals the sort of difficulties encountered in treating a sick Jewish worker. The firm complains about the Poznań pharmacies that refuse to provide medicaments whose value exceeds the sum of 100 RM and only rarely deliver smaller quantities.[118] Some firms, like Heino Hecht in Poznań, compelled their Jewish workers to treat their sick comrades.[119]

It was none other than Heusler, councilor (*Regierungsrat*) to the Poznań governor (*Statthalter*), who wrote about the German contractors in his letter of 3 November 1943 to the factory manager of the *Ost-Deutsche Chemische Werke* (East German Chemical Works):

> Dieser generellen Regelung . . . den Pauschalbetrag zu erheben liegt im uebrigen der Gedanke zugrunde, dass die Auftraggeber—mehr als es bedauerlicherweise der Fall gewesen ist—wenigstens das Notwendigste tun, um diese Arbeitskräfte einsatzfähig zu erhalten.

> The general rule . . . to levy the lump sum moreover is based upon the idea that the contractor—more than regrettably has been the case—at least takes the most necessary measures to keep this manpower capable of working.

The result was just the opposite. A female Jewish doctor who was employed in the Poznań city women's camps describes the "treatment conditions" in one of them:

> The sleeping places of the rest of the sick were exactly as primitive [as the earlier mentioned]; here also the sick lay on bunks in three layers. . . . In this poisoned air where there were dozens of seriously ill people, I had to admit still other patients and conduct operations. A wooden bunk served me as an operating table. I always had to do the operations without anesthesia, because there were no anesthetics for Jews. There was also no possibility to sterilize the instruments. Only after a time did I find a possibility to obtain an electric cooker and to sterilize the instruments. . . . While the district doctor [*Gauarzt*] allowed use of the necessary salves, the pharmacist only deigned to grant half of them, observing that one had not come here to treat "Jewesses.". . . All those who were sent over to the so-called 'hospital' were lost people and rarely did anyone return to her camp. The patients, therefore, did not want to leave their camp and preferred to die in their daily environment. . . . Each day the number of sick in the individual barracks had to be reported. The diagnosis of "hunger-edema," "weakness," etc. was forbidden. The number of those sick could not exceed 5 percent. Camp doctors who stated a larger percentage were considered saboteurs and were deported to the East.[120]

The unbearable camp conditions, the permanent hunger, the physical and moral torments, all these brought the people to despair. They attempted to save themselves from unavoidable death. Yet over the most minor transgression of the draconian camp code there hovered the threat of the severe penalty of the lash and in most cases the death penalty. People tried to save themselves in various ways: by "organizing" (stealing) food and clothing, by "doing business" within or outside the camp, with concealed money and valuables, and finally through escaping. The camp authorities responded harshly to all these transgressions: with dungeon, lash, and executions. The first two sorts of punishments are rarely noted in the documents. They were apparently considered less significant. In contrast, we find in the documents frequent reports about executions as a penalty for unsuccessful attempts to escape or for leaving the camp in order to get food. We bring here several cases of the large number of executions in the camps:

On 7 February 1942, the ghetto administration notified Rumkowski that, according to a report from the Labor Office in Lissa, on 22 January 1942 five Łódź Jews were hanged for an attempt to escape (the names are listed and their dates of birth) in Altgule (Golina Wielka, Rawicz district) (doc. no. 95). Two weeks later, on 25 February, a report from the Łódź Labor Office again announced that 14 Łódź Jews were hanged for escaping in the Friedrichsweiler camp (Rawicz district). Among those hanged were seven nineteen-year-old young men. In the period from 19–30 August 1942, six Łódź Jews were hanged in the Kreising camp,[121] and so forth.

Even a minor was not spared. Thus, for example, on 9 June 1942 five Jews were hanged (four from Pabianice) in Zbąszyń camp; among them was a boy of thirteen.[122]

In some instances, those captured were brought back not to the camp but into the Łódź Ghetto and were there publicly hanged, or executed inside the central prison. On 22 July 1942, two escapees from a labor camp outside Poznań were publicly hanged on Bazarna Street; one was a sixteen-year-old boy (Grynbaum) from Pabianice. On 3 December of the same year, three young women from Łódź were hanged in the ghetto prison for the same sin; one of them, Gitl Aronowicz, was seventeen years old at the time of execution.[123]

Generally, the camp inmates themselves had to carry out the death sentences on their comrades. In the Poznań city camps the executions took place in the presence of prisoners from other camps, including delegates from the women's camps who were forced to dance around those hanged.[124]

The liquidation process of the labor camps took place in waves, just like the general extermination process. Actually, the liquidation process was constant, for diseases and high mortality on the spot killed the camp prisoners. Moreover, the sick were liquidated in the so-called "*Rücktransporten*," which become a very frequent occurrence in the second half of 1942 and the first half of 1943. In the first half of 1943, the number of people in the camps was sharply reduced. There remained isolated remnants of creatures, who had once been people. The final phase approached, the period of their final annihilation. After two or three years of slave labor and hunger had exhausted the camp workers' last strength and turned them into human shadows, the plan became ripe for the German regime finally to liquidate them, particularly since the political goal, the total physical annihilation of the Jewish population, no longer had to be restrained on account of economic considerations. It must also be noted that the labor camps in Wartheland belonged to the German regime's tertiary category of economic significance.[125] As camps that carried out capital investment projects, land improvement, and construction, they had become unnecessary for war purposes.

The first annihilation wave known to us was still small in its scope, encompassing four camps in the Łódź province in August–September 1942.[126] According to existing reports, at least sixteen camps were liquidated before August 1943. The intensive extermination process took place in the month of August 1943, when at least 107 labor camps were liquidated, while from September until the end of the year a further fifteen camps were cleared. Thus, during that year nearly 80 percent of all the camps that had existed in Wartheland were destroyed. Of the nearly 10,000 Jews who were sent out from the Łódź Ghetto to the various labor camps in and outside Wartheland during the years 1940–1943, a negligible number were saved. All the rest died either a "natural" death, tormented or killed in the nearby woods and cemeteries, or were transferred to the extermination camps at Chełmno and Auschwitz.[127]

Documents 84–95

No. 84: YI-41F

From J. Zelkowicz's reportage, "In the Transmission Belt Repair Shop," dated 10 August 1943. [in Yiddish]

[p. 3]

. . . . [128]

Someone else in Mr. Rozenmuter's place would have been satisfied with the status quo. He would maintain the records of the transmission belts warehouse, he would issue a suitable belt for use on an order, if it just fit and it would not be necessary to make any changes, and he would have accepted the old, worn out, and no longer usable belts from a factory. But Mr. Rozenmuter understood that such a position cannot long endure: the bit of belts he has in stock will quickly run out and one bright day he would be left with empty shelves, aside from a mountain of old, unusable material that he would not be in a position even to repair, and the factories will be left without motive power.

He therefore entered on the difficult, although already well known path in the ghetto of creation *ex nihilo*. There are no transmission straps, the old ones cannot be repaired, and no fresh ones from outside the ghetto will arrive—so substitute straps must be procured. . . .

The logic of this way of thinking is clear: there are already in the ghetto so many things made from nothing, so why should straps be an exception? It was only necessary to find the suitable material that can be used as the substitute.

Indeed, all Mr. Rozenmuter's effort went in that direction and, after he searched well and willingly, he found: in the ripping department [*tren-opteyl*], at no. 4 Podrzeczna Street, there had just arrived a large shipment of old military backpacks and belt straps [*gurt-rimen*]. In the ripping department, these bags and straps were ripped apart and they were supposed to serve the ghetto for the same purpose that all old tatters and rags do. However, Mr. Rozenmuter discovered that drive belts could be made from certain parts of these backpacks and almost all the belt straps, if they were only properly treated and processed, and during a shortage one could make do with them as transmission belts. And when the first attempt succeeded, he established near his warehouse the first operating branch of his subsequent factory producing drive straps from old belts [*gurt-pasn*] and linen backpacks.

Nevertheless, due to lack of space, this work could not be conducted on a broad scale either, as already mentioned. It was therefore done primitively, by only four artisans, and with them he could barely manage to cover the ghetto's needs.

Ultimately, the authoritative factors had to realize and recognize the usefulness and necessity of the freshly created institution, whose fate will be to become the breath of life of the entire ghetto and it had to be given the possibility to develop and grow.

On January 1 of 1943, Mr. Rozenmuter was assigned the site at no. 5 Rayter Street for his factory, neighboring the ghetto's tannery, and here it had an opportunity to spread its wings.

Here he had an opportunity to set up the already long yearned for equipment: the sharp machine and the heavy strap machine. Thanks to them, he can go on with the work, repairing not only the damaged cloth transmission belts, but also the torn leather ones. Now it is possible to cut, to piece together. And not only this—

[p. 4]

Now the factory is even capable of constructing its own leather transmission belts from start to finish, if only it will have the raw material for them—suitable leather.

The vicinity of the tannery factory was indeed very broadly exploited for this purpose: by instruction, the tannery produced leather for the straps, and from these leathers were produced transmission belts.

This was the second stage in the activity of our factory: Production of new leather drive belts and repair of old, damaged leather drive belts sent to the factory.

. . . .

[p. 5]

Thanks to the establishment of the three mentioned areas of operation of the transmission belt factory, in the course of a very short time not only were all the ghetto's needs met, but partially also [orders] from outside the ghetto. Drive belts from this factory were even taken to Dąbrówka,[129] for motors there. Aside from the ghetto factories, transmission belts were provided to the wells, kitchens, laundries, hospitals, coal and vegetables sites, etc.

It would, however, be an error to assume that everything is being driven with the power of the leather belt. Leather is still consistently too expensive an article and, although the factory produces new leather belts from scratch, it is not possible to go everywhere with the luxury of leather. By the way, the management of the factory never forgot its original duty to conduct a rational operation and to do without expensive leather anywhere that the least opportunity exists; the leather is replaced with an ersatz belt made from cloth, from scratch-straps [krats-rimen], from old, so-called gum [balate] straps, from camelhair, even from old harnesses, and the like.

. . . .

[p. 7]

Today, our factory employs sixty-two workers, including eighteen youths, who earn an average of 5 marks a day.

If we recall that the factory began operation with 4 craftsmen in all and that its tasks were initially only to manage the ghetto's supply of drive belts, we also need to know that

a. Aside from the fact that the factory produces drive belts, it also has control and supervision over everything in the ghetto that is operated with the power of electricity or steam, and it also produces parts not actually entirely belonging to its tasks, like for example couplings [kiplinges?] for wells, that had always been made from rubber, different leather parts for the textile industry, like shlag-shikh [?], spool-leathers [shpiln-leders, so-called "harmonicas"] from parchment leather, buffers (that are composed of various leather scraps), shaft-belts [shaft-rimen], etc.

b. Aside from the fact that the factory covered the ongoing needs of all the divisions, factories, workshops, and the like, it still always has in stock and is ready at a moment's notice to serve with several thousand meters of cables [rund-shnurn] for manual and mechanized sewing machines; with several thousand meters of cloth and leather transmission belts of different sizes and widths; and also always has a large reserve of raw chromium leather [khrom-leder] from which an appropriate number of transmission belts can be produced at any time.

c. Each order and request is immediately and precisely fulfilled, without disappointment, not at all in the ghetto style.

No. 85: YI-742

From J. Zelkowicz's reportage, "In the Paper Factory," dated the 26 and 28 June 1943.[130] [in Yiddish]

[1st Part, p. 4]

. . . .

One needs to hear what one of the workers who participated in collection design tells about that time:

> It was easy to say: "put together a collection," but we actually did not know what we were supposed "to put together." Should one make an album, fancy stationery, a paper basket—[all] useful things, or should

we impress with trinkets, truly beautiful things that are, however, not so very useful, particularly in wartime? . . . Maybe it was only an accident that we did not go with trinkets; maybe we were too hungry and frozen to have baubles on our minds. We decided to put together a collection of useful things and here starts the real history:

[p. 5]

Decided is indeed decided, but how does one carry out the decision?

If one of us still had a złoty, he didn't want to spend it on buying the materials. Nobody felt like tossing good money after bad. Each thought it would be better for that złoty to buy several dekagrams of barley cereal for the children . . .

But he was right after all, Bajgelman.[131] One could really have thought that we couldn't do more than bind a little prayerbook! So now our ambition was involved and we took up collections among ourselves, of fifty, twenty, or even ten pennies apiece, as much as each could and wanted [to contribute] and we went into the shops and bought materials that we needed to put together a collection.

And how many of us, do you think, literally worked on their knees? How many of our folk in their new ghetto apartments actually did not have even a little table on which to work? And how many of us, do you think, literally chopped up the last chair in order to heat up the glue that was freezing in our hands?

In short, with need, with sweat, we put the collection together. A collection of the most useful things: envelopes, blotters, letter files, paper baskets, and so forth, and we turned it over to Bajgelman as if to say: "Here's your little prayerbook and now off you go to *kheyder*."[132] . . . We've done our part and your thing is to see to it that the collection gets into the right hands.

When Bajgelman turned the collection over to Bałuty Marketsquare,[133] just then there was taking place an exhibition of things that were and could be produced in the ghetto. His exhibit items were included in the exhibition and the result was that after several days the Chairman turned over to him the keys of the sealed building at no. 8 Żydowska Street, where there had been a small bindery before the war; and together with the keys, he received the commission to establish a factory for paper production.

This occurred on the 27th of February of the year one thousand nine hundred forty-one and since then dates the true rise of the paper division.

[2nd Part, p. 1]

. . . .

However, the factory still did not have an established pattern. It still did not have a trodden road to follow and advance along. For several months, nothing was heard of the collection it had delivered to the city. No orders arrived. When the management of the factory began to search for the reason for this, it came to the sad conclusion that with its primitive ghetto facility it was simply not able to be competitive with other factories that make more attractive and cheaper goods. The management, desiring nevertheless to exist, decided to go over to manual work, with the calculation of being able to compete with larger and technically better-equipped factories on the basis of cheap skilled labor costs.

And again it was necessary to put together a collection. This time not of goods produced on machines that until now had not amazed anyone and were nothing new for anybody, but of goods—fresh articles— brain products, that are produced by hand. . . .

And remarkably: This collection was a hit. Masses of orders arrived for this sort of articles and the factory thereby got a defined line. Now it knew at least which sort of goods are wanted from it and which sort of goods it could market.

In connection with the large orders for its products, the factory had to increase the number of workers and, together with them, also expand the site.

Today, the factory employs 450 workers and almost all of its departments are operating in two shifts of 7 hours each. While the first payroll of the factory as salary amounted to about 100 marks, the
[p. 2]
payroll last week exceeded the sum of 4,000 marks.

If one looks closely at the work, we must here, just like elsewhere in every labor division in the ghetto, marvel at the Jewish inventiveness that borders almost on genius! All of these trinkets, all of the truly beautiful albums, all of the various little crates and boxes that are produced here, the ashtrays that look like marble, the inkwells that look as if made from some unfamiliar stone, the paper baskets that can occupy the place of honor in the most elegantly furnished office—all of these things are
[p. 3]
made from the most common, most ordinary paper, from bits and pieces, from old boxes in which margarine was packed, from old paper sacks that had held baking soda or flour, from pieces of waste paper that at one time a good housekeeper tossed out as worthless and here, in the paper factory, an entire industry is built thereupon, an industry that competes with technically well-equipped factories.

. . . .

[p. 4]
In a fourth room are produced special children's playthings like paper buckets, purses, and various other toys. Here, in this room, the work is much more interesting: The work is playful, easy, colorful; but less interesting [is the fact that] the workers do not earn much. But it's the same story: indeed, thanks to the small wage cost, the ghetto is still
[p. 5]
competitive. . . . Thanks to the small wages of the workers, the ghetto

receives big orders from outside and can thereby maintain factories, employ workers, and still maintain itself with a livelihood, even if difficult and stressful. . . .

. . . .

No. 86: YI-738

From a speech at the production exhibition of five labor divisions on 26 December 1942. [in Yiddish]

[p. 4]

. . . .

As already mentioned, due to the scarcity in orders, a crisis has entered the tailoring industry and many tailors have become saddlers and the like. Suddenly, there arrived an order for 200,000 so-called camouflage suits[134] that had to be finished immediately.
[p. 5]

. . . .

Even if we would have had the entire complement of our old workers, even if we had twice as many craftsmen, in the present labor system we did not have any prospects at all to be able to disentangle ourselves from our commitments on which the existence of the ghetto actually depends.

. . . .

No. 87: YI-28

Notice in the Ghetto Chronicle of 13 and 14 May 1942, concerning the causes of the decline of productivity in the labor divisions.[135] [in Polish]

[p. 16]
FALL IN LABOR PRODUCTIVITY
The fall in labor productivity is too significant a question for the security and even the existence of the ghetto altogether to be able to skip over it to the daily agenda. In addition to fundamental causes, more secondary factors are broached that are very characteristic for the current situation, and worth reflecting upon. The workers unanimously declare that the decline in labor productivity is directly connected with the worsening of the food. People are exhausted to such a degree that they are incapable of making the least exertion. Perhaps the replacement of manual with mechanical power initiated recently where possible will resolve this issue in a certain measure, since it will contribute to a reduction of physical exertion. Moreover, a very important element should not be forgotten. In many factories, the system of group work existed until now. Brigades were composed of specialists and auxiliary workers, who received a certain task to do and divided earnings according to a fixed key. Lately, in connection with the deportations, very many persons have been hired who are not only untrained, but simply unsuited for the given work. These were often individuals with pull, lacking

comprehension for the work, and inclusion of these individuals in work groups reduced productivity, not only due to the fact that these individuals did not manage to adapt to the work tempo, but simply held up the work of others, discouraged them and as a result the rest of the people adapted to the weak work tempo. Managers affirm from their side that underfeeding of the worker negatively affects the intensity of production and significantly causes its decline, which in several factories reaches 25 percent. On the other hand again, the complete lack of interest in wages influences the decline of production, since a worker cannot buy anything for the money earned, aside from the scanty ration, and therefore seeks only to earn the sum that he needs "for the ration."

An indisputably demoralizing influence on the workers is the presence of a hired element, "workers" who in reality produce nothing, but hang around the workshop, getting soup and sausage. This drawing of rations is most seductive, since its price rose lately to 32 marks. Without working and without effort, they are thus earning
[p. 17]
daily as much as a skilled worker makes—weekly!

. . . .

No. 88: YI-1031

Reportage by O[skar] S[inger] about the situation of sick workers in the ghetto, 14 July 1942. [in German]

The principle of feeding the working person in the ghetto better than the unemployed is correct. The idea is certainly not new. Not an invention of the ghetto. The supplemental food coupons correspond to the hard-worker card in the Reich. Of course, with a grain of salt, for the worker is by far not the best fed man in the ghetto through the additional food coupon. After all, the idea reigns: He who works should eat!

The results of this great theory are in practice very small. The additional foodstuffs are truly decisive for the maintenance of life, but they do not suffice for the supply of the energy that the physically working person expended. In other words: the decline in strength is only slowed, but it is not stopped. There can also be no talk at all of the storage of only a minimal reserve of strength. Lacking above all is the most necessary item—fat. But, one could ask, what then of thinking of reserves! One wants only to make it through to the next day, more accurately from one ten-day ration period to the next.[136] If this were the only worry of the day, it would be as simple as a slap in the face. But things are just not so uncomplicated.

Let's take the most favorable case: that the worker does not have to share his additional ration with unemployed family members, so he himself can consume all of it. He enjoys this benefit only as long as he works. This is a nasty thought and as unsocial as possible. But thus was the idea of work created in the ghetto. This has its good grounds, hidden reasons. The worker must deliver up the last of his strength. If that happened, he can perish. The only place the ghetto has for sick people is—in Marysin.[137] A nasty idea, but—an idea born in the war and in the special war.

But how is it when the worker, wanting to prevent a serious sickness, uses a day in order to seek out the doctor or to stretch out for a day? He'll be sorry if he has bad luck! The day can be fateful. For the worker ration is linked to a qualifying date [*Stichtag*] on which the worker or employee must be present. The qualifying date is unknown. Only at the announcement of the ration does one find out just which day was the fateful one. The loss of that ration is a fateful blow.

The ghetto is not organized for eternity; it has its social laws only for today, at most for tomorrow. If the worker falls ill so that he misses a qualifying day, then the stone starts rolling—and it rolls unstoppably all the way . . . to Marysin!

No. 89

From Dr. Philip Friedman's collection.[138] File memorandum by Alfred Hall, authorized by the city administration [?] to organize the exploitation of Jewish craftsmen for the economy [no date, 1940]. [in German]

[p. 1]

. . . .

3. The specially authorized official[139] mediates payment orders only for firms that pay the unit price to the city and a supplementary fee, for the time being of 20 percent, to the specially authorized official, out of which all of his expenses must be covered. The surplus is, just the same as the total unit price, at the disposition of the city.

4. The city administration promises all useful support without thereby taking on an obligation.

5. The city administration and the specially authorized official are in agreement that revenues for the city administration will only exist when paying orders come in. In the clothing sector orders are without doubt certain; in the rest, the efforts of the specially authorized official will be aimed at attaining, as quickly as possible, employment of from 30,000 to 50,000 men, whereby of course there should not be any disadvantage to Aryan workers.

6. With the employment of 15,000 men, the city administration can receive daily revenue of 75,000 RM; with 30,000 people, it would be 150,000 RM and with a possible maximum figure of around 250,000 RM.

7. All revenue means a reduction of the city's expenditures, since food must be procured until the Jews have been transported away. [p. 2] With employment of 50,000 men, the city can have a surplus of 50–75,000 RM per day.

8. The city administration protects the specially authorized official

against any allegations regarding friendliness to Jews; his task has nothing to do with that; it is rather only a question of practicality for the public.

No. 90: YI-1190

Letter from Biebow to Rumkowski of 9 November 1942, concerning prohibition on giving out goods to, or accepting orders from, officials of the ghetto administration without his agreement. [in German]

Regarding: Private Manufacturing in the Ghetto

I request that you immediately instruct your factory managers, the Jakubowitsch[140] Office, the Central Office at Bałuty Marketsquare, etc., that it is most strictly forbidden to every employee of the ghetto administration to take out of the ghetto any goods or articles, for which an application is not authorized by the undersigned. All major deliveries from your inventory are not hereby affected, but pass over as usual to the Goods Exploitation Department [*Warenverwertung Abt.*]. As soon as one of my co-workers utters any private wishes, he is to be directed to me immediately. If one of your enterprises still deals against this order, I will have the relevant manager arrested by involving the Secret State Police or the Criminal Police. In connection herewith let me tell you that improvements in the branch offices, like for example at the Radegast Train Station, Bałuty Marketsquare, disinfection facility, etc., are also not allowed to be carried out unless an approval by the undersigned was submitted for it.

A copy of this order is to be passed on to all the ghetto's workshops, purchasing offices, etc, and you will have it confirmed in writing by all the responsible people in the ghetto that they have taken note of this order. The copy of this directive is to be carefully preserved, for it serves as proof should the occasion arise that this or that job cannot be done because the office director's confirmation is lacking.

No. 91: YI-41–B

From J. Zelkowicz's reportage, "Impressions from a Visit in the Low Voltage Department," dated 19 July 1943. [in Yiddish]

[p. 3]

Finally, we are in the so-called "*glimmer*"[141] or mica splitting shop. Around long tables are seated for the most part "former" people—old men, old women, and ordinary "obituaried"[142] faces. A little heap of the mica mineral that must be split lies before each of them. From the little pieces must be made the very thinnest bits. No matter that the piece may be so small and unsuited to the old, weakened eyes, that it can slip out from the tremulous hands—it must be split. Three pennies are paid for a split gram. A gram is a whole pile and the little heap is still so small and the day is already almost through. . . . The hands tremble and they want to urge on the pointy and sharp knife to separate thereby layer from layer, but the knife infrequently and barely penetrates into bread, so how should it strike into the hair-thin sliver? . . . When the knife is urged on, when it's harnessed it crawls along . . . into the hand, into a finger and there is a first aid station, a woman medic, too; she will bandage the injured finger, the injured hand, admittedly, not with iodine, but with some sort of stinking and burning fluid. But the hand will be bandaged, and it will tremblingly continue to push the knife, because what else should he do, the old Jew, what else should she do, the sick Jewish woman, or that "obituaried" face? Push a wheelbarrow? Haul boards? Wash floors or windows? So it's still fortunate that there is the little bit of mica. No strength needs to be applied, only a little patience and some nerves. And patience isn't lacking in the ghetto. . . . The main thing is, of course, the soup . . . and sometimes a supplemental ration and to go on. Only to go on, only without sinning, so as to keep up the little bit of life, as long as one can. . . .

And the actual work, the mica splitting, is a special matter for the ghetto. In all the countries everywhere that had prisons for serious criminals, this is work done by those criminals. It is a job that never paid, it is a job that no healthy and sane person, who has two arms, ever wanted to take up, because the dust from the mica damages and consumes the lungs—a job, an ideal one for the ghetto, where all that live must work, where all that have a hand and a mouth must be employed. So really, this is work done by people who cannot do anything else, [p. 4]
—by impaired eyes, by trembling hands and by ghetto lungs already corroded and punctured anyway and . . . by children, who have a prospect to survive the war and to "repair" their lungs later. . . . But among the children, the job is completely different. Their eyes still see; they discern the tiniest little heap. Their small young hands do not tremble. Confidently and proficiently, they insert the knife into the thick of the ore, to make it thinner, still thinner, still finer than a hair, to split it as thin as it lets itself be split. They don't let themselves be satisfied with only the soup and three times a week the "fiftieth supplement." They have greater aspirations; they also want to be breadwinners. . . . During their five-hour workday, they must finish as much as their grandpa or granny. Their little bodies, their hands, their eyes are much, much more mobile, and as for the dust—they still understand little of the dust and just as they don't understand it, so may it also not do them harm. . . .

. . . .

We believe you, little fourteen-year-old Goldberg, even if you would have sung fifty percent less heartily, or if you would not have sung at all. We also believe that your soul is pure, just as we see the purity of the souls of your friends, boys and girls, who sit at their prisoner-work with fleet hands and open mouths, who are paying attention to your really emotion-laden and heartfelt singing.

But the truthfulness of these very children often stands beneath a big question mark

[p. 5]

for if little Zilbershtrom with the green, emaciated, lemony face [*esrig-peniml*] wants to convince me that he is already eleven years old not only in the factory but at home; if little Beyle Palka wants to convince me that she has long been thirteen years old, that she had already turned thirteen a long time ago, even at home . . . I know that they are deceiving me. They are intentionally deceiving me. . . .

Only once again the same story: They are not the ones deceiving. They were the ones who were tricked! They were talked into believing that they are already old and must already work! . . .

No. 92: YI-747

From a reportage by an anonymous author, concerning adolescents in the Electrotechnical Department, dated 8 April 1943. [in Polish]

[p. 1]

One of the most indispensable and popular factories is the Electrotechnical Department, whose task is to electrify the entire ghetto. In connection with the above goal, entailing the necessity of a careful division of the work, the department broke off from itself two large segments. The workshops division is occupied with preparation and repair of electrical equipment, while the installation division took over area electrification.

The factory gives youth broad working opportunities in the chosen direction. Mathematics and physics enthusiasts applied en masse to study electrical skills, providing a practical basis beneath their former theoretical studies, while their younger colleagues, graduates of elementary schools or the first or second secondary school grades, arrived here to learn a trade suited to their masculine preferences. Among around 500 workers, Electrotechnical employs as many as 211 boys, with over a hundred of them assigned to each division.

[p. 2]

. . . .

Of the total number of youths, 151 boys are working by the job [*pracuje na akord*]. The pay amounts to from 15 to 55 pfennig per hour. According to a balance sheet, 69 boys earn from 8 to 12 marks weekly, 68 from 13 to 20, while the rest are receiving more. Mastery of the profession, requiring on average over a year of training, is based both in the workshops and in installation on a practical basis. The facts are that the pupils mechanically carry out operations entrusted to them without understanding the totality of the matter. This applies chiefly to the youngest pupils, to whom school did not manage to provide elementary knowledge. For prevention of a similar state of affairs, to support training in theory, the Regrouping Commission [*Komisja Przewarstwowie-*

nia] organized Professional Continuing Education Courses. On the 1st and 15th of February, two groups were started, numbering 30 students each. A condition of admission was completion of a minimum of the 6th grade of elementary school, as well as demonstrating progress in jobs in the factory. Instruction takes place daily, except Sunday, in the hours from 9 A.M. to 11:30, as well as from 12 to 2:30 P.M. and includes three forty-five-minute class periods

[p. 3]

with five-minute breaks. Each course therefore includes eighteen lessons weekly, of which six fall to secular subjects, namely Yiddish and bookkeeping. Of the vocational subjects, electronics occupies first place with four hours allotted weekly, and there are also collateral two-hour courses on commercial materials, surveying, construction of machines, as well as professional drawing. The lecturers are engineers and masters who are chiefly employed in the department. The courses' meet in a large and bright room on the third floor in the vicinity of the factory offices.

· · · · · · · · · · ·

[p. 4]

Instruction in Yiddish, the other secular subject, commenced in both groups from the basics. The extent of preparation was discussion and designation of the parts of speech together with analogy to known languages. Currently, the boys have started to decline nouns and

[p. 5]

verbs, at the same time getting to know the most important principles of orthography. One class in the week is devoted to reading popular and accessible Yiddish authors.

The courses are a real blessing for the youth. In a period of four months, the reckoned program of instruction is supposed to give a future electrician basic vocational education. Classes of a more chatty nature narrowed theory to the limits of practical application. Visible everywhere is scrupulously integrated knowledge from the fields of mathematics, physics, chemistry, and even arithmetic. The lecturers accurately reword the material, often making use of previously prepared notes. The children's effort and eagerness for work are also apparent. Initially unruly classes, deprived for nearly two years of the guiding hand of a teacher, returned to the bounds of school discipline. Calm and concentration pervade the classroom. Pupils' advances are apparent in their utterances. In each group, a handful of more capable students excel above the average level, as also do those for whom better home conditions make possible deeper comprehension of the subject. Of course, dull boys are not lacking here, too, employed in this factory by chance and sitting uselessly on the school bench. But attendance at the courses and being in the surroundings of peers exert a beneficial influence even on them. For the young people at large, the class hours are the brightest point of the working day in the ghetto, to which they look forward.

No. 93: YI-297

Rumkowski's Announcement no. 250 of 16 April 1941, concerning registration of men and women for work outside the ghetto. [in German]

Regarding: *Registration of men and women for work outside the ghetto.*
The registration of men in the ages from 18 to 43 years, as
well as of women in the ages from 20 to 30 years, for
work outside the ghetto continues to take place in the
        Work Deployment Department, 13 Telegraph Street.
Those men and women, who have already registered previously, do not
need to register again. Identity card with photograph is to be brought
along to the registration.

No. 94: Archive of the Jewish Historical Institute

Ordinance of Reichsstatthalter Greiser of 25 June 1942, about employment of Jewish workers. [in German]

No. 112

Reichsstatthalter in Warthegau
Labor Department
Field
"Reich Trustee of Labor"   Poznań, 25 June 1942
                             Directive
                  on the employment of Jewish workers
                     in the Reichsgau Wartheland.
                             Par. 1
        The employment of Jewish workers is permissible only with the consent of the Reichsstatthalter's Labor Department.
        The application for assignment of Jewish laborers is to be directed to the Labor Office appropriate for the place of employment.
                             Par. 2
        Jewish workers may be employed only for the purpose for which they were assigned.
                             Par. 3
        The Jewish workers receive free room and board, whose costs are not to amount to more than 1 RM daily.
        Jewish workers receive no wages; however, release of rewards for exceptionally exceeding a normal production quota or the enforcement of piecework for the attainment of increased production is permissible. The rewards for the Jewish worker may not amount to more than 1.50 RM each workweek.
                             Par. 4
        A charge of 70 pfennig each calendar day is to be paid for each assigned Jewish worker, for support of Jews not fit for employment. The sums are always to be transferred on the 1st and 15th of the month to ac-

count no. 12300 at the Litzmannstadt City Savings Bank for the Mayor of Litzmannstadt.

The transfer has to be paid in principle exclusively by the responsible party for whose purpose the Jewish workers are assigned. If the assignment is not for the responsible party of a given measure, then the transfer is to be paid by the entrepreneur who is employing the Jewish workers.

The Mayor of Litzmannstadt, ghetto administration, can make regulations divergent from the aforementioned provisions on the transfer or crediting of the fees.

Par. 5

In case of need, the Mayor of Litzmannstadt, ghetto administration will provide clothing for the Jewish workers, including footware.

Procurement of items of clothing through third parties, in particular offsetting the costs arising for it against the transferred sums, is permissible only in agreement with the Mayor of Litzmannstadt, ghetto administration.

Par. 6

For the absolutely necessary maintenance of the Jewish work force's ability to work, the guidelines of the Reichsstattshalter's Department II (particularly enactment of 20.2.1942—II B 226/1–2)[143] are to be followed.

The contractor employing Jews is liable to pay for the costs of carrying out necessary medical care and the required measures for the prevention of epidemics, in so far as someone else responsible for the measure is not available.

Par. 7.

The working time of the Jewish workforce should in principle amount to 10 hours daily.

Par. 8

This directive comes into force on 1 July 1942. From the same day, directives and rules issued until now go out of force, in so far as this directive stands in contradiction to them.

No. 95: YI-18T

Letter from Łódź Mayor to Rumkowski of 7 February 1942, concerning hanging of five Jews in the Altguhle labor camp as a punishment for running away. [in German]

The Lissa Labor Office notifies me that on 22.1.42 in Altguhle, Rawitsch District, the following named Jews were hanged on account of flight from work:

Lipski Moses	born	4.12.22
Rettmann Viktor	"	26.9.11
Malinowski Josef	"	18.12.97
Horowitz Jakob	"	21.3.19
Lisek Josef	"	20.5.23

In addition to this, there died:

Rosenberg Max	born	6.9.97	died	21.1.42
Jacubowicz Pesach	"	14.4.01	"	21.1.42
Perla Abraham	"	5.10.98	"	14.1.42
Gutter Chaim	"	19.5.13	"	17.1.42

V

Diseases and Mortality

Today there is no doubt that the creation of conditions in the ghettos that would cause Jews to expire in masses "naturally," that is, without gas chambers and executions, occupied a significant place in the Nazi plan to annihilate the Jewish population.[1]

The same applied in the Łódź Ghetto. Here, too, the sealing of the Jewish population in the ghetto caused a growth of epidemics, diseases, and mortality. Thus, for example, the number of cases of spotted typhus rose from 16 in February 1940 to 75 in March and to 102 cases in April 1940. Likewise, typhoid fever rose from 51 in May to 217 in August. Most widespread in the years 1940–1941 was the dysentery epidemic that broke out in spring 1940. The following figures give us an impression of the spread of this epidemic in the second half of 1940:

May	73	cases
June	2,538	"
July	3,413	"
August	1,929	"
September	815	"
October	490	"
November	186	"
December	91	"

Pallbearers carry a corpse on a stretcher to the Jewish cemetery in the Łódź Ghetto, 1940–1944. Photograph by Walter Genewein. USHMM, courtesy of Robert Abrams.

As we see, the dysentery epidemic had a stormy, explosive course. From 73 cases in May, it rose at a dizzying tempo to 2,538 in June and 3,413 in July. This is expressed even more vividly when we compare the number of cases of dysentery with the total number of infectious illness cases in the individual months of 1940 and 1941.

As we see from Table 4, the epidemic was most intensive in the months June–July 1940 and August 1941, when the dysentery cases amounted to 84.3, 92.5, and 77.0 percent of all infectious illnesses in the given months. Starting from August 1940, it becomes weaker in absolute numbers and from November also relatively weaker. At the end of 1940, the number of dysentery cases amounted to not even a third of the total number of infectious diseases. In the subsequent winter and spring months in 1941, the epidemic continues to decline (in the months of May–June only 12.5 percent of all infectious illnesses). But suddenly in July of that year it starts to rise again, peaking in August (45.4 percent of all cases of dysentery during the whole year and 77 percent of all infectious diseases during August). It falls quickly in the autumn months, but a fresh rise of short duration can be noted in December. Nevertheless, the disease no longer has an epidemic character. Overall, 12,088 cases of dysentery were officially registered during the entire ghetto period, including 11,570 cases in the years 1940 and 1941.

These official statistics are not exhaustive. Due to the reasons touched on above in the foreword, a quite substantial percentage of the sick probably was not reported to the Health Department.

How many deaths did this epidemic cause? The sources are very contradictory. At a conference with representatives of the German

Table 4
Dysentery Epidemic and Other Infectious Diseases
in the Łódź Ghetto, May 1940–December 1941

Month in 1940	Dysentery Cases	Total of Infectious Diseases Cases	% Dysentery Cases	Month in 1941	Dysentery Cases	Total of Infectious Diseases Cases	% Dysentery Cases
				Jan.	82	225	36.4
				Feb.	92	263	34.9
				Mar.	94	334	28.2
				Apr.	50	317	15.7
May	73	389	18.7	May	40	317	12.6
June	2,538	3,009	84.3	June	45	360	12.5
July	3,413	3,688	92.5	July	188	493	38.2
Aug.	1,929	2,288	83.7	Aug.	924	1,200	77.0
Sept.	815	1,045	74.4	Sept.	333	541	61.5
Oct.	490	767	63.8	Oct.	54	359	15.0
Nov.	186	345	54.1	Nov.	81	260	11.9
Dec.	91	290	31.4	Dec.	92	313	29.3
Total	9,535	11,821	80.6	**Total**	2,035	4,982	40.7

sanitary authorities, held on 16 July 1940, the chairman of the ghetto's Health Department, Dr. Szykier, reported that 20–25 percent of dysentery cases resulted in death. Thus, the number of deaths would have totaled 2,000–2,500.[2] But a printed table from the Statistical Department of the Rumkowski administration states 1,191 deaths among an overall number of 10,042 cases of dysentery in the months May–December 1940. The mortality amounts here to no more than 11.8 percent.[3]

A third source states a mortality figure that is very near the latter. There it is stated that from 1 May until 30 June 1940, 236 people died of dysentery, a bit more than 9 percent. According to this source, the relatively largest number of victims was among children up to 8 years old, and among the elderly from 61 years of age up.[4] As the epidemic spread, mortality rose. While in May the weekly number of deaths was a bit more than 100 on average, in the third week of June (16–22) it was 210.[5]

How the German regime related to the outbreak of the dysentery epidemic in the ghetto shows a characteristic aspect. One of the factors that tremendously impeded the fight against the spread of dysentery was the danger that was linked with emptying the latrines and transferring the waste out of the ghetto. Since the work had to be done at night, after the curfew, it happened that the guards shot at the Jewish workers employed in this labor.[6] The German guards had no instructions about allowing the night work of these workers.[7]

The Łódź police-president did not want to give permission to open the wire fences of the ghetto for a short time, disregarding the fact that, as *Obermedizinalrat* Dr. Melkert himself asserted, this made impossible the emptying of the latrine pits in a large number of buildings.[8] In addition, the number of waste wagons that the German authorities made available for the ghetto was insufficient. They were outdated and not hermetically sealed.

Concerned over the epidemic and fearful that it could spread to the "Aryan" city quarters, particularly to German officials and police who came in contact with the ghetto, the German authorities called one conference after another. In the course of ten days, three conferences took place (on 16, 21, and 25 June), with the participation of Jewish representatives. At the first conference, Doctors Szykier and Kwiat reported about the extent and course of the epidemic, that from 1 May until mid-June there were 4,200 cases and nearly 600 of them were treated in a hospital.[9] At the second session, Dr. Falk, the specialist for epidemic diseases at the Health Department who was responsible to the German authorities, spoke about infectious diseases in the ghetto, particularly about the awful epidemic of diarrhea. Falk also formulated the measures that were necessary to combat the epidemic:

1. Opening the wirefencing around nearly 180 especially endangered buildings on Hohenstein and Aleksander streets, in order to conduct disinfection there.
2. Supplying medications of good quality and in sufficient quantity to the ghetto.
3. Supplying an adequate quantity of milk for the children.

At this conference, it also became clear that no products containing soap could be provided to the ghetto as disinfectants. As for medications, particularly if it involved such items as bismuth preparations, glycerin, quinine, and codeine, the ghetto must apply directly to the Chamber of Pharmacists in Poznań, and this procedure was taking, as noted in the protocol, a long time.

Regarding milk (until now, the ghetto would receive milk that was already sour), it was determined at the second session that it was "impossible to furnish" for the ghetto the daily quantity of 4,000 liters (for 7,800 children under three years of age, for a few older children and pregnant women). There was talk about a substitute in the form of goat milk (the ghetto had a total of five cows) and the meeting ended with the wish that perhaps the ghetto could get about 2,000 liters of milk daily, which would have barely sufficed for a third of the number of children up to age three.[10]

The German authorities were well informed about the sanitary situation in the ghetto. In a memorandum of 24 September 1941, from

Mayor Ventzki to the Łódź *Regierungspräsident,* the hygienic condition in the ghetto is characterized in the following fashion:

> The hygienic facilities in the ghetto are as pitiful as one can only imagine. The hospitals that were included within the ghetto are overcrowded. And those that were established by the head of the Jews are equipped in a primitive fashion. . . . What sort of danger threatens only from the insufficient number of outhouses, due to the lack of sewerage and the shortage of waste wagons. . . . The buildings are in an unbelievable state. Very many wooden buildings are neglected, because they have not been repaired for decades and they could be considered only as carriers of infectious diseases. . . . So if due to the density of the population an epidemic breaks out, it will be a danger not only for the ghetto population [with which the Nazi dignitary probably concerned himself little], but also for the city.[11]

This characterization of the situation in the ghetto needs no commentary. And even though the mayor had a motive to present the capacity of the ghetto to take in new human material in dark shades (he opposed the plans to send into the Łódź Ghetto fresh transports of Jews from the province and from the Reich), nevertheless one should not suspect him of having painted the situation in too bleak colors.

Just as in other ghettos, the authorities here, too, refused to see the true reasons for the epidemic: overcrowding, filth, and hunger. In the fight against the epidemic the Germans satisfied themselves only with the means of disinfection. But even in this limited aspect the security system (the hermetic sealing of the ghetto) overwhelmed the health considerations (for example, by impeding the removal of waste from the latrines), because the German regime was very little interested in really combating the epidemics in the ghettos; they only strove to localize them.

Typhus and Typhoid Fever
Epidemics in the Łódź Ghetto

Typhus (*flektifus*) was also an attendant phenomenon of ghetto conditions, like hunger, filth, and infestation with lice, that naturally did not spare the Łódź Ghetto.

We have already indicated above that when over 160,000 Jews were pressed into Bałuty, the number of cases of typhus rose sharply: from 16 cases in February to 102 cases in March. In the subsequent months of 1940, the number of cases of this disease substantially declined (in December only five). During all of 1940, there were 416 officially noted cases. The number of cases was also relatively low in 1941; during the entire year 124 were registered, an average of ten a month.[12] Only in the first half of 1942 did the curve of the epidemic rise strongly: from 15 cases in December 1941 to 237 cases in April 1942. For the entire year of 1942, there were 981 registered cases, an average of nearly 82 cases a month.

Fecalists dispose of sewage in the Łódź Ghetto, 1940–1944. Photograph by Walter Genewein. USHMM, courtesy of Robert Abrams.

Table 5 illustrates the growth of the typhus epidemic during the years 1940–1944 in comparison with other infectious diseases.

The epidemic's greatest intensity falls during 1942, when the number of cases of typhus reached 13.4 percent of all infectious illnesses in that year. The typhus epidemic was most widespread in the months of March–April 1942, when the number of cases totaled almost half of all infectious diseases (471 of 981 cases). On 1 March, there were 281 typhus patients among a total of 326 patients in the hospital for infectious diseases.[13] The epidemic was also intensive in the ghetto's first months, March–May 1940. In May almost a fourth of all infectious disease patients had typhus.

A certain growth of the typhus epidemic can be seen in June 1942 (160 cases). This occurred in connection with the "resettlement" in the Łódź Ghetto of parties of Jews deported from the neighboring ghettos, for example from Brzeziny, among whom there were some infected with typhus.[14]

Thus, for example, the number of typhus patients in the infectious diseases hospital among the deportees from Warthegau in the period May–July 1942 totaled 88 percent of all cases of infectious diseases among this group.[15] Thanks to careful preventive measures by the Health Department, the epidemic did not spread into the ghetto. Pa-

Table 5
Epidemics of Typhus in the Łódź Ghetto, 1940–1944

Year	Months	Typhus Cases	All Infectious Diseases	% of Typhus Cases Among All Infectious Diseases
1940	May–Dec.	205	11,821	1.7
1941	Jan.–Dec.	124	4,982	2.4
1942	Jan.–Dec.	981	7, 301	13.4
1943	Jan.–Dec.	37	3,476	1.1
1944	Jan.–July	8	1,471	0.5
TOTAL		1,355	29,051	4.6

tients suspected of having typhus were sent to the hospital; a quarantine unit was set up in Marysin for 100 people.[16]

Typhus was imported into the ghetto in December 1943, when an epidemic broke out in the camp for Polish youths located near the ghetto. The German authorities at the time ordered the emptying of the infection hospital on Matrosen Street to make space for the sick from the Polish camp. The Jewish patients, some with active tuberculosis, were evacuated from the hospital to home or to relatives on 22 December, a cold winter day. In January 1944 there were 170 Polish adolescent patients in the hospital, but the course of the epidemic was very mild. The patients would recover quickly, so that in February there were a total of 28 patients in the hospital and on 1 March there were no more typhus patients and the hospital returned to the ghetto's control.[17] This time, too, thanks to the Health Department's energetic sanitary measures, like quarantine, disinfection of factory workers, and so forth, spread of the epidemic into the ghetto was prevented.

In 1944 there were only individual cases of typhus. Thus, for example, during January–July only eight cases were officially registered, that is, just over one case a month.

In all, 1,355 cases of typhus were officially registered for the whole period, amounting to 4.6 percent of all registered infectious diseases during the ghetto's existence.

Regarding the coefficient of mortality of this disease, it was quite variable. In the first period of the epidemic, in the second half of 1940, mortality was quite high. Among 205 patients there were 47 deaths, i.e., almost 23 percent of all cases ended in death. In 1941 mortality fell more than half: of 124 patients, 13 deaths (10.4 percent). In the first half of 1943, it was an average of 14.6 percent: of 887 patients, 130 died. In the most intense period of the epidemic, in the months of March and April of 1943, mortality was a little higher: 90 deaths among 471 patients, i.e., 19.1 percent. In general, mortality from typhus in the Łódź

Ghetto was higher than in the Warsaw Ghetto, where in 1942 it reached no more than 8–9 percent of the cases. Compared with the course and extent of typhus in the Warsaw Ghetto, this epidemic in Łódź was much weaker. While 1941, the most intensive year of the epidemic in the Warsaw Ghetto, saw 15,449 patients with typhus official registered, amounting to about 3 percent of the total population, during 1942, the most intensive year of the epidemic in the Łódź Ghetto, only 981 patients were registered, comprising only 0.86 percent of the average number of ghetto inhabitants in that year. The number of cases in the Warsaw Ghetto was almost four times higher than in the Łódź Ghetto.

This phenomenon can be explained by the fact that an intensive disinfection and quarantine campaign was effective against the spread of the typhus epidemic—in contrast to the dysentery epidemic that broke out in the first months of the Łódź Ghetto, when the Health Department was still in an organizational stage and the situation in the ghetto was still very fluid. In contrast with Warsaw, we do not here have a phenomenon like the corrupted disinfection columns, the notorious "*paruvkes*" (steam-baths), which the German and Polish sanitation authorities turned into a "modern Inquisition" for the ghetto population and contributed to the growth of the epidemic. It must also be noted that in the Łódź Ghetto the problem of refugees and expellees did not constitute such a serious danger of epidemic as in the Warsaw Ghetto, where the "[refugees-] points became nests for the spread of typhus."[18]

As for typhoid fever (*boykhtifus*), its scope and intensity were stronger than those of typhus (*flektifus*). Typhoid fever was a regular resident in the ghetto during the entire period. The permanent hunger and the anti-sanitary condition created excellent soil for the spread of this disease. During the years 1940 until August 1944, there were 4,403 officially noted cases of typhoid fever. Its course and relation to other infectious diseases in the aforementioned period is shown by Table 6.

The largest number of typhoid fever cases occurred during 1942, over 50 percent of all the cases in the entire period. Relatively, the number of typhoid fever cases fell during 1943, comprising more than a third of all infectious diseases in that year.

The epidemic broke out during the ghetto's first summer months. The most intensive diffusion of the epidemic, both absolutely and relatively, occurred during the months of September–December 1942. In those months, the number of typhoid fever cases was from 82.8 percent to 84.0 percent of all infectious diseases and 88 percent of all cases of typhoid fever during the entire year.

From December 1942, the curve of the epidemic falls until in the months of April–May 1943 it reaches absolutely and relatively its minimal points (5.5 and 5.4 percent of all infectious diseases). In the summer months of 1943 it rose again, reaching in August 64.4 percent of all infectious diseases in that month. In October the epidemic was on the downswing (as opposed to in 1942) until it vanishes almost completely in the winter months of 1944.

Table 6
Typhoid Fever in the Łódź Ghetto, 1940–1944

Year	Months	Cases of Typhoid Fever	As % of All Infectious Diseases
1940	May-Dec.	709	6.0
1941		226	4.9
1942		2,251	30.8
1943		1,194	34.3
1944	Jan.-July	23	1.5
TOTAL		4,403	15.1

For the entire period, 4,403 cases of typhoid fever were officially noted, which works out to 15.1 percent of all cases of infectious diseases in the ghetto.

However, these official statistics do not exhaust the real number of instances of disease. Dr. Miller, chairman of the Health Department of the *Ältestenrat,* estimated the number of those ill with typhoid fever in the thousands at the beginning of November 1942. In many cases, the illness remained concealed from the sanitary authorities because there was no obligation to report the illness.[19]

Generally, according to the statistics of the Health Department, during 1942 nearly 3 percent (exactly 2,923) and in 1943 1.2 percent of the average ghetto population in the given years was sick with typhoid fever. Thus, according to official data 4.12 percent of the ghetto population contracted this disease, almost five times more than the number that contracted typhus.

The intensity of the epidemic in the mentioned months of 1942 becomes even more vivid when we take into account that during the first half of September almost all of the patients of the hospitals were "outsettled" and after this action the population was reduced by about 20,000 souls.

In the *Chronicle* of the Łódź Ghetto we find the following description of the cause of the spread of typhoid fever in the mentioned months of 1942:

> The hospitals were liquidated . . . but there are many people. Among the infectious patients typhoid fever predominates. . . . Due to the crowding, there can be no talk of isolation. The sanitary aid service was abolished and neither the family members nor the apartments [of the sick] are isolated. With a [relatively] large quantity of vegetables and warm weather, typhus has a broad field, but the deciding factor in these conditions is the filth. . . . The vegetables are not properly cleaned. There is no warm water to boil them, there is no time to prepare the food properly after

a whole day of work. . . . Out of hunger, people consume half-raw foods and that in most cases is the cause of the illness.[20]

To these causes must only be added the anti-sanitary situation in the ghetto, which impeded the fight against the epidemic. The latrine pits and the outhouses contaminated the well water; there was also a lack of transport to empty the pits. The situation was still more tragic, in that there was a lack of whole series of elementary medicines like *tonalbina,* opium, and so on.

As for mortality due to typhoid fever, in the most intensive period of the epidemic (October–December 1942), it amounted to 10.5 percent of all patients (196 deaths among 1,857 sick). In the winter months of 1943, mortality from typhoid fever rose and exceeded 17 percent of the number of sick. However, it fell during the second period of the epidemic's intensification, in July–October 1943, and in August reached 2 percent (5 deaths among 250 patients); yet, in September we find a further growth to 10 percent (23 deaths among 233 cases). The mortality figure among the patients in the infection hospital varied in different periods of the epidemic. Thus, for example, in the months July–December 1940, it was 19 percent (82 deaths among 420 patients), against only 8.9 percent in 1941 (17 deaths among 192 cases).

We can assume that the mortality due to typhoid fever averaged 10–12 percent, and the number of deaths from this disease for the whole period can be estimated at about 500–600 according to the officially registered cases. The actual number was, of course, larger.

Diseases of Hunger and Tuberculosis

Neither the dysentery epidemic in 1940, nor typhus and typhoid fever in the subsequent years, caused the high mortality in the ghetto. The angel of death of the Łódź Ghetto was hunger. The results of the enduring, unceasing hunger became simply catastrophic for the health condition of the ghetto population and produced, both absolutely and relatively, the largest number of victims. The starvation caused not only a large number of direct victims of the hunger diseases (swelling, scurvy, debilitation, decalcification of the bones, and so forth), but in a huge measure aggravated and increased the number of cases of other diseases, like tuberculosis and heart disease.

Table 7 presents causes of deaths among Łódź Jews from the first half of 1940 until the second half of 1942.

From this table we see that during the second half of 1940 until the second half of 1942, the number of deaths due to tuberculosis and hunger expanded immensely. Tuberculosis rose from 9.1 to 19.1 percent (in 1941 it was even more, 24.2 percent), while hunger increased from 1.8 to 25.9 percent. If during eight months of 1940 there were 623 deaths from tuberculosis and 121 deaths from hunger, that works out to an average of 78 cases of tuberculosis and 15 hunger deaths a month. During six months of 1942 there were 2,189 deaths from tuberculosis and 2,811

Table 7
Causes of Deaths in the Łódź Ghetto, May 1940–June 1942

Period	May–Dec. 1940		Jan.–Dec. 1941		Jan.–June 1942	
Cause of Death	Number of Deaths	%	Number of Deaths	%	Number of Deaths	%
1. Dysentery	1,191	17.4	244	2.1	168	1.4
2. Typhoid Fever	83	1.2	22	0.2	13	0.2
3. Typhus	47	0.7	13	0.1	130	1.2
4. Pulmonary Tuberculosis	589	8.6	2,552	22.3	1,995	17.5
5. Tuberculosis of other organs	34	0.5	213	1.9	194	1.6
6. Lung diseases	544	7.9	606	5.3	460	4.0
7. Heart diseases	2,061	30.1	3,221	28.2	3,066	27.1
8. Diseases of the digestive organs	663	9.7	740	6.5	498	4.4
9. Nervous system diseases	244	3.6	380	3.3	353	3.1
10. Cancer and other diseases	142	2.1	139	1.2	80	7.0
11. Aging weakness	373	5.4	505	4.4	819	7.1
12. Whooping cough	—	—	—	—	37	0.3
13. Hunger	121	1.8	2,134	18.6	2,811	25.9
14. Others	759	11.0	668	5.9	649	5.5
TOTAL	6,851	100.0	11,437	100.0	11,273	100.0

from hunger, thus a monthly average of 365 deaths from tuberculosis and 468.5 from hunger: The monthly average of tuberculosis deaths rose by a factor of almost 4.6 times, while hunger deaths skyrocketed by a factor of more than 30.

Mortality was very high among the tuberculosis patients. For example, with 298 new cases during the second half of 1940 in the hospital for tuberculosis patients, 92 patients died (30.8 percent); and in 1941, 38.7 percent of tuberculosis cases among those admitted to the hospital ended with death (727 deaths for 1,876 patients). Tuberculosis was especially destructive among patients of certain ages. Thus, for example, in the second half of 1940, of 165 patients ages 15–35, over half (86, or 52.1 percent) died in the hospital; and in 1941, of 846 patients in the same age range, 413 (48.8 percent) died. That is, almost every second case of tuberculosis during the years 1940–1941 concluded with death. In the subsequent years, it certainly did not look any better, if not worse. Those sick with tuberculosis in the ghetto were condemned to an inexorable death.

The destructive effect of tuberculosis and hunger in the ghetto becomes even more apparent when we take into account that during the mentioned period the average ghetto population declined by 24 percent, from 158,116 in the latter half of 1940 to 130,023 in the first half of 1942. But the absolute number of deaths from tuberculosis grew to nearly four times as many, while deaths from hunger diseases grew by more than 23 times.

The absolute number of deaths from heart diseases also grew, from 2,061 in the eight months of 1940 to 3,066 in the first six months of 1942, doubling from an average of 257 deaths a month in the former period to 511 cases in the latter period. Deaths attributed to old age also rose, both absolutely, from 46.6 cases to 136.5 cases a month, nearly triple as many, and relatively, from 5.4 percent of all deaths in 1940 to 7.0 percent during the second half of 1942. The ghetto did not provide the conditions for longevity.

As for other causes of deaths due to diseases, there were either no great changes (aside from the large number of deaths from dysentery during the epidemic in 1940), or we observe even a reduction (pulmonary diseases, diseases of the digestive organs, cancer, and others).

Among the causes of death in 1940, cardiovascular diseases hold first place, with diseases of the digestive organs in second, tuberculosis third, and hunger in one of the last places. In 1941 and the first half of 1942, the order in the table "Causes of Death" would be heart diseases, tuberculosis, and hunger in 1941 and heart disease, hunger, and tuberculosis in the first half of 1942. Of course, there is a close connection between the growth in the number of deaths from hunger and heart diseases. Hunger without doubt caused the spread and intensification of these diseases.

To compare Table 7 with the prewar mortality of the Jewish population in Łódź is more difficult than to make such a comparison regarding the Jews in Warsaw,[21] because for Łódź we do not possess suitable statistical material regarding the prewar period. But taking into account the similarity of the socioeconomic and general environmental conditions, we can with a certain measure of confidence assume that among the Łódź Jews the ranking of causes of death was approximately the same place as among Warsaw Jews.

Thus, if we take data from Warsaw as a basis for comparison, we see that in heart diseases, which had been the leading cause of death in the years 1931–1936 (23.9 percent), the change is relatively negligible, a growth of 6.2 percent in the second half of 1940 and of 3.3 percent in the first half of 1942. In contrast, we can note a huge relative growth of tuberculosis as a cause of death in comparison with the prewar years, from 8.2 percent to 24.2 percent in 1941 and to 18.9 percent in the first half of 1942.[22] Diseases of the digestive organs (except diarrhea among children) also rose as a cause of death, from 2.3 percent in the prewar period to 9.7 percent in the latter half of 1940 and 4.4 percent in the first half of 1942. In contrast, diseases of the pulmonary organs (lung diseases except tuberculosis) fell from an average of 17 percent in the prewar period to 7.9 percent in 1940 and 3.9 percent in the first half of 1942.

Table 8 illustrates this process.

Table 8
Comparison Among the Causes of Death
among Łódź Jews in 1931–1936 and 1940–1942

Cause of Death	1931–1936 %	May–Dec. 1940 %	%-/+	Jan.–June 1942 %	%-/+
1. Heart diseases	23.9	30.1	+6.2	27.1	+3.2
2. Tuberculosis	8.2	9.1	+0.9	19.1	+10.9
3. Diseases of the Digestive Organs	2.3	9.7	+7.4	4.4	+2.1
4. Lung Diseases	17.0	7.9	−9.1	4.1	−12.9

The victims of hunger diseases were quite rarely admitted to hospital, where the infectiously ill had primary consideration. As a result, only a small portion of those ill from starvation passed through the hospital records. Only those found to have, aside from the hunger diagnosis (*inanitio*), other infectious diseases of the digestive organs (e.g., dysentery, gastritis, typhoid fever) would be hospitalized. For example, during the period from 1 January to 10 August 1942, the infection hospital admitted 2,787 patients, among whom only 162 (5.8 percent) had the diagnosis *inanitio* in connection with other diseases; among 128 of them (79.1 percent) dysentery with fever was also diagnosed.[23] This category of hunger-sick, of course, is far from exhausting the actual number. The sources testify that a significant part of the ghetto population suffered from edema or swelling due to hunger in 1942.

The following statistics testify to the tragic growth of the hunger diseases in the ghetto during the period from January to August 1942. While in January the number of patients diagnosed with *inanitio* as the principal illness was 1.4 percent of all those hospitalized in the Łódź Ghetto, it amounted to 5.8 percent in April, 8.2 percent in June, 19.5 percent in July, and during the first ten days of August 23.3 percent of all newly admitted patients in the hospital.[24]

The mortality among the hunger-sick was very high. From 1 January until 10 August 1942, of 162 patients, 144 (88.8 percent) died, after an average hospital stay of no more than four to five days.[25] Mortality figures among all other patients admitted into the infection hospital in the same period show that of 2,787 patients, 739 (26.5 percent) died after an average stay in the hospital of 11.6 days. When we compare these statistics it becomes apparent that mortality among the hunger-sick was more than three times higher than among all other infectious patients combined. In certain periods, the mortality among the hunger-sick was still higher. In June and July 1942, over 90 percent (precisely 92.5 percent and 95.8 percent, respectively) of all patients diagnosed with starvation died in the infection hospital.

A characteristic letter from Biebow to Rumkowski, dated 5 March 1942, directly testifies about the high mortality from hunger. The letter notes that the Łódź *Standesamt* (Civil Registry Office) is complaining that lately the cause of death given in the death certificates is "hunger" or "hunger-swelling." Biebow instructs Rumkowski that such "diagnoses are prohibited. In such cases, the cause must be given as *Unterernährung*,"[26] undernourishment.

Characteristic of the German hypocrisy is the fact that after 7 March 1943 even this careful diagnosis vanishes from Rumkowski's daily reports for the German ghetto administration. At the time when hunger took thousands of victims, there was no trace of it in the official documents.

The ghetto entered 1943 with a heavy legacy from the previous two years of hunger. Although the nutritional situation in 1943 was relatively better than in the prior two years, the rations were nevertheless still far too meager, and they were received too irregularly to save the people who were already worn out from the two previous years of hunger.

In that year, hunger disease only took on other forms. In the ghetto *Chronicle* for 3 February 1943, we read: "In the past year, many cases of hunger swelling have appeared among the ghetto population. . . . In contrast to this phenomenon we now often find decalcification of the bones and also loss of muscle . . . results from deficiency in vitamin D and fats." The *Chronicle* of 16 April recounted: "People drag themselves through the streets, everyone complains of horrible weakness in the legs. . . . The principal reason is the lack of potatoes for the bones. . . . In contrast to the previous year, fewer people swollen from hunger are seen, conversely conspicuous are the number of gaunt faces, like the typical tubercular faces, but not the full ruddy ones seen in previous years."[27]

In 1943, tuberculosis became the terrible angel of death of the Łódź Ghetto. This disease now took the lead position in the mortality table. Table 9 illustrates the horrible growth of this destructive illness.

The percentage of tubercular sick among the ghetto population officially rose from 0.73 percent in the second half of 1940 to 2.56 percent in 1943, that is, more than three and a half times as many. In 1944, according to official statistics, the percentage of tuberculosis fell. This can be explained by the frequent "outsettlements" in 1944 when the Jewish police would fill the missing quota through night raids on the sick, particularly tuberculosis patients. This artificially reduced the percentage of tuberculosis patients among the population.[28]

In 1944, tuberculosis had become an *endemic* disease in the Łódź Ghetto. People sick with tuberculosis worked everywhere, in the departments, kitchens, and factories. In such conditions the disease could spread undisturbed by any obstacle.[29]

The expansion and scope of tuberculosis can be seen even more clearly when we compare the numbers of cases of the disease with the

Table 9
Tuberculosis in the Łódź Ghetto

Year	Number of Cases of Tuberculosis (Official)	% of All Infectious Diseases	Average Population	% Relative to the Population
1940, May–Dec.	1,165	9.8	158,116	0.73
1941	2,221	45.8	150,516	1.47
1942	2,934	40.2	113,509	2.49
1943	2,181	62.4	85,054	2.56
1944, Jan.–July	1,226	83.3	75,258	1.62
Average 1940–1944	1,945.4	33.5	116,490	1.67

number of cases of registered infectious diseases in general. As we see from Table 9, the percentage of tuberculosis patients rose swiftly, from 9.8 percent in the second half of 1940 to 83.3 percent in the first half of 1944. On average during this period, every third illness in the ghetto was tuberculosis. If we exclude 1940, with the large number of dysentery cases during the summer epidemic that would reduce the scope of tuberculosis in the ghetto, the average percentage of tuberculosis patients for the years 1941–1944 amounts to more than half (54.5 percent) of all infectious diseases in this period.

Parallel with the rise in incidence, mortality from tuberculosis also increased. From January to July 1943, the percentage of deaths from tuberculosis rose from 30.6 percent to 67.3 percent of all deaths in those months.

It must also be taken into account that the previous figures include only the officially registered cases of tuberculosis, which passed through the records of the Health Department. In fact, the number of those sick with consumption was much larger, because a significant number of the sick remained at home and avoided registration. They feared "outsettlement," especially after September 1942, when the patients in the hospitals fell victim to the roundup during the first days of the month. In April 1943, the doctors estimated the number of those sick with tuberculosis at 10,000 and the total of those predisposed at about the same number.[30]

That a negligible percentage of tubercular patients received hospital treatment can be inferred from the fact that in both ghetto hospitals for infectious diseases in early March 1943 there were a total of 168 patients, of whom 60–70 were sick with tuberculosis, at a time when the number of officially registered new cases of consumption in the prior two months (January and February) was 433. When in July 1942 the epidemic of typhoid fever intensified (165 cases) and there was a shortage of beds for the sick in the infectious diseases hospital, even the minimal number of tuberculosis patients were removed in order to make space for the typhoid patients. The small hospital on Richter Street with its nearly twenty beds was not in a position to admit even the most urgent cases of pulmonary inflammation.[31]

Pulmonary tuberculosis took on such a mass character in winter 1943 that Rumkowski's Health Department saw itself compelled to send out a circular to all physicians (dated 22 February 1943), asking them to restrict sending patients with lung illnesses for X-rays to urgent cases only, "since the *wholesale* [emphasis added] dispatch for X-raying impedes the work and creates a situation in which the sick must wait weeks for their turn."[32]

We now proceed to the final year of the ghetto's existence, 1944. As we have already shown, in the first half of 1944 the number of officially registered cases of consumption amounted to 83.3 percent of all the reported cases of infectious diseases (Table 9). Tuberculosis was also the cause of 63.9 percent to 65.7 percent of all the deaths in the months April–June 1944.

Although the material for the next-to-last month of the ghetto's existence (July) is fragmentary, it indicates the ever-growing mortality from tuberculosis in comparison to other diseases. For the two days, 17–18 July, of 39 deaths, 34 were from tuberculosis (87.1 percent) (mainly pulmonary tuberculosis, 32 cases) and on 19 June, 12 of 18 deaths were from pulmonary tuberculosis and two cases of tuberculosis of other organs. That is, 77.7 percent of all deaths were due to tuberculosis.

When we recall that in the prewar period tuberculosis occupied the fifth place in the table of causes of death among the Jewish population in Warsaw (and likely about the same also in Łódź) and in the years 1931–1936 accounted for only 8.3 percent of all causes of death, we comprehend the horrible scope of the bloody harvest that tuberculosis made in the Łódź Ghetto.

Diseases and Mortality among Those "Resettled"

We read about this in a document:

Contraction of infectious diseases by Jews who arrived from outside into this sealed Jewish community, in the initial period, or after the closure of the ghetto, earns special consideration for the following reasons: 1) On the basis of existing material, as well as from the number of "settlers" [ayngezidlte], one can calculate the intensity of infectious diseases among this group. Observing these phenomena from time to time, we would get a guide in the search for answers to the following questions:

a) Were certain infectious diseases brought into the ghetto from outside and to what extent?

b) Have already extinguished epidemics of certain infectious diseases broken out anew due to the arrival of a new human-element, or also among the residents?

The intensity of the infectious diseases among the deportees, after a certain time of being in the ghetto, in comparison with the mortality from the same diseases among the resident population in the same period, gives us an indication of how far the new arrivals surrendered to the influence of the new living conditions that are not in all aspects similar to their living conditions until now.

If we here also add the statistics that relate to the sick among the deportees in the hospital for infectious diseases, among whom the diagnosis inanitio was made (as an independent disease, or in connection with other diseases), we will obtain another aspect of the destructive effect that the new, worse living conditions had on these people uprooted from the soil where they grew up.[33]

In considering the question of morbidity and mortality among the deportees, this population group must first of all be divided into two categories: those deported from the province and those deported from Central and Western Europe (Germany, Austria, Luxembourg, and Czechoslovakia). Major differences between these two groups will become apparent in the degree of adaptability to the new environment and in their capacity to resist in the struggle with the changed living conditions.

Table 10 illustrates the extent of the spread of infectious diseases and hunger diseases among the "resettled" in comparison with the [veteran] residents.

As we see from the table, the percentage of diffusion of infectious diseases among the ghetto's local residents and among the deportees from Kujawy is very close, 4.3 percent among the residents and 6.2 percent among the deportees from Włocławek and environs. In contrast, it is a third smaller among the Western European Jews (2.89 percent) in comparison with the residents, and half in comparison with the deportees from Kujawy. In regard to tubercular diseases, we see a remarkable difference between the resident population and these two categories of deportees. While among the ghetto residents 2.17 percent suffered from this illness, it amounts to 0.40 percent to 0.35 percent among the deportees. Again, in regard to hunger diseases, among the ghetto residents they are less than among the deportees from Western Europe (among the former 0.26 percent and among the latter 0.43 percent) and they are not found at all among the deportees from Kujawy. Among the latter element from the provincial ghettos, which were mostly open ghettos where the food supply situation was immeasurably better than in Łódź, the starvation conditions in the new ghetto had not [yet] managed to evoke visible symptoms of illness at the time.

As for the relative significance of the various infectious diseases among the designated three categories of the population in the period under consideration, we find that among the local population tuberculosis was the most prevalent (51 percent of all infectious diseases), 2,880 out of 5,634 cases in all. Next was typhus with 1,007 cases (17.9 percent), dysentery with 634 cases (11.2 percent), whooping cough with 499 cases (8.7 percent), and typhoid fever with 370 cases (6.4 percent).

Among the deportees from Kujawy, whooping cough's 78 cases (50 percent) was most prevalent among all infectious diseases. This can be

Table 10

Diseases among the Deportees from the Province and from Central and Western Europe in Comparison with the Resident Population in the Łódź Ghetto, September 1941–August 1942

Group:	Veteran Residents*		Deported from Kujawy		Deported from Central and Western Europe	
Period:	27 Sept. 1941–August 1942*		27 Sept. 1941–August 1942*		28 Oct. 1941–August 1942	
Average Number	ca. 132,450		ca. 2,500		ca. 15,100	
Diseases	Number of Cases	% of the Group	Number of Cases	% of the Group	Number of Cases	% of the Group
All Infectious Diseases	5,634	4.30	156	6.20	437	2.89
Typhus	1,007	0.76	52	2.08	131	0.87
Whooping Cough	499	0.37	78	3.12	10	0.07
Typhoid Fever	370	0.27	2	0.08	38	0.25
Dysentery	634	0.47	2	0.08	80	0.53
Tuberculosis	2,880	2.17	10	0.4	54	0.35
Hunger Diseases Linked with Other Diseases	350**	0.26	—	—	65	0.43
Others	294	0.22	12	0.44	124	0.82

* For the days 27–30 September 1941, we have the number of cases of diseases [among veteran residents] calculated approximately according to the average daily number of cases.
** From 1 January to 10 August 1942.

explained as due to the comparatively large number of children, ages 1–15, among this group, composing 37.6 percent of all deportees.[34] The next most common was typhus, with a third of all infectious illnesses among this group, followed by tuberculosis, dysentery, and typhoid fever. The latter two were a minimal percentage (0.06 percent).

Among the Western European Jews, typhus was the most common, with 131 cases (30 percent), followed by dysentery (80 cases, 18.3 percent), tuberculosis (54 cases, 12.3 percent), typhoid fever (38 cases, 8.6 percent), and whooping cough (10 cases, 2.2 percent).

The higher percentage of typhus among the deportees of both categories in comparison with the local population apparently is explained by the worse housing and sanitary conditions in which these groups lived, in the "asylums," so-called "collectives" where the opportunity for infection was much greater. Moreover, in some of the "collectives," for example of the 4th Prague transport, the typhus infection was spread by a doctor who had served in the Gypsy camp where a severe typhus epidemic raged in December 1941.[35]

Table 11 illustrates the mortality among the deportees from Central and Western Europe in comparison with the local population. (We

Table 11

Mortality among the Local Population and among
Western European* Jews in the Łódź Ghetto, 1941–1942

Group	Period	Average Number in the Group	Number of Deaths	Per 1,000 per Month
Local (including Kujawy group)	Oct.–Dec. 1941	155,264	2,589	5.5
	April 1942	112,954	1,888	16.7
Central and Western European	Oct.–Dec. 1941	19,820	400	6.7
	April 1942	17,628	670	37.5

*Under this designation, we also include those deported from Central Europe.

do not possess separate statistical material about deaths among the deportees from Kujawy. They were reckoned together with the resident population.)

From this table can be clearly inferred the huge jump in the mortality rate among the Western European Jews during the period from autumn 1941 until spring 1942. In general, mortality among them was higher than among the resident ghetto population. While among the latter mortality rose in the mentioned period from 5.5 to 16.7 per thousand (more than three times more), among the Western European Jews it rose from 6.7 per thousand to 37.5 per thousand (more than five times as much). In autumn 1941, mortality among both population groups was still very similar (5.5 versus 6.7 per thousand), but in spring 1942 mortality among Western European Jews was more than twice as high (37.5 versus 16.7 per thousand).

There were periods when mortality among the Westerners was still higher in comparison with the local residents. On 3 May 1942, for example, 72 persons died in the ghetto, of whom 34 (47.2 percent) were Western Europeans; and on 5 May, 57 people died, including 22 (38.6 percent) Western Europeans. The Western European Jews at the time comprised about 7 percent of the ghetto population, but produced a mortality figure that was on average six times higher than it should have been according to their number. The large number of deaths among the deportees from Western Europe in the first half of May 1942 is also explained by the suicides committed by desperate victims of the May "outsettlement."

There is also a difference between the mortality among men and women in the two population groups. While the mortality rate among the locals, calculated for the first eight months of 1942, was on average

18.86 per thousand among men and 10.59 per thousand among women, among the Western Europeans during approximately the same period (nine months) it was 47.60 per thousand among men and 20.30 per thousand among women, that is, about 3.5 times more among men and almost two times more among women.[36]

From these statistics one could also infer that, in comparison with men, women in both categories of the ghetto population demonstrated a greater sturdiness in the radically changed conditions. This phenomenon, the unnaturally higher mortality among men in comparison with women, can also be explained with the difficult, physically exhausting labor by the men, that the women were, as far as possible, spared.

Overall, during the period from October 1941 until June 1943, there were 4,476 deaths among the Western European Jews, amounting to 22.4 percent of their initial number (19,953). Their average monthly mortality during these twenty-one months was 10.6 per thousand.

If one could evaluate these figures in the sense of endurance and adaptability to the Łódź Ghetto conditions on the part of the three mentioned population groups, we see that the least able to adapt were the deportees from Western Europe: in almost all age groups they produced the largest mortality figure, except among women ages 15–45. The provincial deportees, particularly their women, demonstrated the greatest hardiness. Among them, the respective mortality rates were 17.83 per thousand (men) and 2.73 per thousand (women). However, this data relates to a period of only three months.

Let us now see how their cities of origin affected mortality among the deportees from Western Europe.

As we see from Table 12, the highest mortality rate was among the Berliners, as almost a third of their initial number died during twenty-one months.[37] Then came the Jews from Frankfurt (30.1 percent), Emden (24.6 percent), Vienna (22.9 percent), Hamburg (20.1 percent), Luxembourg (19.3 percent), and Cologne and Duesseldorf (over 16 percent). A more precise social-medical analysis could possibly determine the causes of the difference in the mortality among the different hometown groups of Central and Western European Jews in the Łódź Ghetto. But that is already a purely medical matter.

Summary of Mortality among Łódź Jews, 1940–1944

In the previous chapters, we have often spoken about the mortality rates in the Łódź Ghetto as a result of various diseases and epidemics in different periods. In this section, we give a summary of mortality in the ghetto. Table 13 illustrates the mortality curve among the ghetto population during the ghetto's five years in comparison with 1938.

The table reveals that mortality in the Łódź Ghetto reached its maximum in 1942, with an annual average of 159.6 per thousand. This was almost sixteen times greater than in 1938 for the Jewish community of Łódź.

Table 12
Mortality Rate Among Deported Western European Jews by City of Origin, October 1941–July 1943, in the Łódź Ghetto

Deported from:	Number	Deaths	Deaths per Thousand
1. Berlin	4,054	1,257	31.0
2. Frankfurt	1,186	357	30.1
3. Emden	122	30	24.6
4. Vienna	5,000	1,140	22.9
5. Hamburg	1,063	214	20.1
6. Luxembourg	512	99	19.3
7. Prague	5,000	871	17.4
8. Cologne	2,012	337	16.7
9. Duesseldorf	1,004	164	16.3
TOTAL	19,953	4,476	22.4

Starting from 1940, we have a continually rising mortality curve until 1943, when it fell to 53.9 per thousand on average. This phenomenon can be explained first by the elimination of the sick from the hospitals during the September Action of 1942, that in a mechanical fashion reduced the mortality rate within the resident ghetto population; and second, by the far-reaching winnowing of human material during the previous two years, during which the older and more physically weak died or were deported from the ghetto. Additionally, control of the epidemics of typhus and typhoid fever in 1943 caused a reduction in the number of deaths. The period from January to August 1942 was critical, for then the average number of deaths reached 1,876 a month.

Mortality peaked in absolute numbers in March 1942, with 2,249 deaths (the month's mortality rate was 17.4 per thousand),[38] and relatively in July 1942, with 2,025 deaths producing a mortality rate of 19.7 per thousand. The lowest mortality occurs in the autumn months of 1943. For the months September–December, the average monthly number of deaths was 216 (2.6 per thousand), that is, eight times less than in July 1942.

However, in winter 1944 the mortality curve rose slowly but steadily and attained another relative zenith in July, with 505 deaths (7.1 per thousand).The increase in mortality in 1944 resulted from the wholesale spread of pulmonary tuberculosis. This increase also shows that even the healthiest human material that was left after all the selections (both natural and German) could not withstand the conditions of the Łódź Ghetto.

Table 13
Mortality in the Łódź Ghetto, 1940–1944

Year	Average Population	Number of Deaths	Average Number of Deaths per Thousand
1938	ca. 225,000	2,340	10.8
1940 (from May)	158,116	6,851	43.3
1941	150,516	11,437	75.9
1942	113,509	18,117	159.6
1943	85,054	4,589	53.9
1944 (until Aug.)	76,677	2,749	35.8
Average 1940–1944	110,798	(Total) 43,743	394.8
Maximum (July 1942)	101,402	2,025	19.7
Minimum (Nov. 1943)	83,293	178	2.6

Data about age and gender of the dead is instructive. Sadly, it is not complete and includes only the period from May 1940 to July 1942. But it permits certain conclusions of a general character. We present the statistics in the following table.[39]

From Table 14, we see first of all that during the eight months of 1940 (May–December), there was a high mortality among children up to one year old (12.7 percent of all deaths) and among the elderly over age 60 (44.8 percent of all deaths). As observed above, this phenomenon was a result of the dysentery epidemic whose victims in large measure were children up to one year old (due to lack of milk) and the elderly over 60. In the most intensive months of the epidemic (June–July 1940), of a total of 2,254 deaths, 584 (25.9 percent) were among children up to age one and 897 (39.8 percent) among the elderly over age 60. In the subsequent years, the mortality among children up to age one fell relatively sharply: in 1941 it was only 1.3 percent of all deaths, in the first half of 1942 even less, 1.1 percent. This was due to a simple reason: the birthrate had fallen sharply. For the entire year 1941, there were 586 live children born, that is nearly four live births for each 1,000 residents, while in the prewar years, 1936–1938, the average birthrate among Polish Jews was 19.3 per thousand. Thus, in 1941 it fell to almost five times less. We see the same phenomenon in 1942 also. During that year, there were in all 497 live births in the ghetto, or 4.4 per thousand.

The relative decline of the mortality rate among the elderly over age 60 in 1941–1942 in comparison with 1940 can also be explained by the larger number of deaths from dysentery among the elderly in 1940, and not that the ghetto promoted longevity.

Table 14
Deaths in Łódź Ghetto According to
Gender and Age, May 1940–July 1942

A. May–December 1940

Ages	Male	%	Female	%	Together	%
To 1 year	484	55.5	338	44.5	872	12.7
1–8	190	56.2	148	43.8	338	4.9
9–14	39	48.7	41	51.3	80	1.2
15–19	107	60.1	71	39.9	178	2.6
20–25	84	50.3	83	49.7	167	2.4
26–45	401	46.9	454	53.1	855	12.6
46–60	673	52.0	619	48.0	1,292	18.8
61–	1,470	47.8	1,599	52.2	3,069	44.8
Totals	3,448	50.3	3,403	49.7	6,851	100.0

B. 1941

Ages	Male	%	Female	%	Together	%
To 1 year	83	53.9	71	46.1	154	1.3
1–8	148	48.8	155	51.2	303	2.6
9–14	105	51.9	97	48.1	202	1.8
15–19	470	68.8	213	31.2	683	6.0
20–25	411	67.7	196	32.3	607	5.3
26–45	1,487	60.8	956	39.2	2,443	21.4
46–60	2,084	64.9	1,130	35.1	3,214	28.1
61–	2,168	56.5	1,663	43.5	3,831	33.5
Totals	6,956	60.8	4,481	39.2	11,437	100.0

C. January–July 1942

Ages	Male	%	Female	%	Together	%
To 1 year	72	58.0	52	42.0	124	1.1
1–8	156	49.6	157	50.4	313	2.8
9–14	78	51.3	74	48.7	152	1.3
15–19	310	62.6	185	37.7	495	4.4
20–25	341	68.1	160	31.9	501	4.5
26–45	1,402	62.2	851	37.8	2,253	20.0
46–60	2,223	64.9	1,202	35.1	3,425	30.3
61–	2,191	54.6	1,819	45.4	4,010	35.6
Totals	6,773	60.0	4,500	40.0	11,273	100.0

We further see a sharp increase in deaths among adolescents ages 15–19 and among adults ages 20–45. In comparison with 1940 (May–December), the absolute number of deaths among adolescents in 1941 almost quadrupled and relatively more than doubled: 683 cases (6.0 percent) in 1941 in contrast with 178 cases (2.6 percent) between May and December 1940. In the first half of 1942, the number of deaths among adolescents fell somewhat (4.4 percent). But it was still more than 1.5 times as great as in the eight months of 1940. The number of deaths among boys during the entire period amounted to two-thirds or even more (in 1941, 68.8 percent) of all deaths in this age category.

We encounter the same phenomenon among adults ages 20–25 and 26–45: in 1941 the number of deaths among adults ages 20–25 almost quadrupled absolutely and more than doubled relatively, and in the first half of 1942 tripled absolutely and almost doubled in comparison with 1940. At that, the situation strongly changed in percentages regarding both sexes. If during the eight months in 1940 the number of deaths among both sexes was almost equal (50.3 and 49.7 percent), it changes in 1941 and in the first half of 1942 strongly shifts to the disfavor of the male gender that produced more than two-thirds of all deaths in this age category (67.7 and 68.1 percent).

Among adults ages 26–45 and 46–60, mortality in 1941 and in the first half of 1942 rose from 12.6 percent and 18.8 percent of all deaths in the eight months of 1940 to 21.4 percent in 1941 and to 20 percent in the first half of 1942 in the age category 26–45, and to 28.1 percent and 30.3 percent in the age category 46–60. As with the previous age categories, the proportion between the genders worsened strongly for the male sex: if in 1940 (May–December) the number of deaths among men ages 26–45 did not make up even half of all deaths in that age category (46.9 percent), in 1941 and in the first half of 1942 it amounted to almost two-thirds of all deaths (62.2 percent and 60.8 percent). The proportion changed similarly for the age group 46–60: from 52 percent in 1940 to not quite two-thirds (64.9 percent) in 1941 and in the first half of 1942.

The absolute and relative growth of the number of deaths among adolescents from 15–19 years old, and among adults ages 20–46, resulted from the fact that forced labor affected these age groups primarily; it was from these groups that those sent "to work outside the ghetto" in the various labor camps were recruited, as well as the workers in the ghetto factories, where the toil itself caused sicknesses and death. Also, apparently tuberculosis, the angel of death in the Łódź Ghetto, had a richer harvest among these age groups than among others.

The age curve of the dead appears in the Łódź Ghetto quite different than in normal times. Normally, we have the first mortality maximum in the first year of life, while the first minimum occurs in the range of 10–15 years old. From that year on the curve rises slowly until age 50 and reaches the second peak in the years of advanced age. In the ghetto, the first minimum actually did occur in the first year of life, with the exception of 1940, due to the on-going effect of the prewar birthrate on the one hand and the large toll from dysentery among infants under age one on the other hand. This demographic phenomenon is not explained by the fact that relatively few children died (from May 1940 until December 1941, 38 percent of all children died in their first year of life),[40] but rather due to the catastrophic fall in the birthrate.

Starting from age 20–45, the mortality curve rises strongly: in the eight months of 1940 it rose among this age group on average from 2.4 percent to 12.6 percent (more than five-fold) and in 1941 from 5.3 percent to 21.4 percent, a four-fold increase. Thus, in this age group, whose mortality index normally is near to the minimal points of the death curve in general, we have mortality rate indices that are near to its maximal points.

Premature death among these age categories, which normally are the most vital, underscores even more vividly the destructive results of the German ghetto regime.

The largest number of victims came from the masses of Jewish poor, which right from the first day of the war felt the ruthless whip on their backs. We can confirm this indirectly when we compare the number of free funerals in the ghetto with those that were paid (Table 15).

During May–December 1940 nearly 70 percent and during 1941 over 70 percent of funerals were gratis. The conclusion is clear. Nearly 70 percent of the dead in this period belonged to the ghetto's impoverished and degraded masses.

In the Łódź Ghetto, whole families died within short periods of time. In the six-member Tusk family, consisting of parents 45 and 47 years old, two sons ages 21 and 22, and two daughters ages 15 and 17, during barely eighteen days (10–28 July 1942) the parents, the older son, and the older daughter died. Remaining alive were the two younger siblings.[41]

Finally, it is also worthwhile to compare the mortality in the two former largest Jewish centers in Poland, which in the conditions of a ghetto regime turned into death centers for large Jewish masses.

The average maximum monthly mortality rate in the Łódź Ghetto in 1942 was 13.3 per thousand. In the Warsaw Ghetto, the maximum monthly mortality rate was 11.1 to 12.0 per thousand a month (in April–May 1942). Thus we see that the maximum mortality rate in both ghettos was almost the same, and in both occurred in 1942. The minimum mortality rate in the Warsaw Ghetto occurred in December 1940 and amounted to 1.47 per thousand,[42] while in the Łódź Ghetto the minimum monthly mortality rate was never less on average than almost 5 per thousand. Thus, it emerges that mortality in the Łódź Ghetto was relatively higher than in Warsaw. The reasons are understandable. The ghetto regime with all its results was harsher than in Warsaw, so the number of its victims was relatively greater.

Table 15
Paid and Free Funerals in the Łódź Ghetto,
May 1940–December 1941

Period	Total Funerals	Free Funerals	% of Free Funerals
May–Dec. 1940	6,802*	4,714	69.3
1941	11,567	8,139	70.4
Total	18,369	12,853	69.8

* The number of funerals is smaller than the number of deaths in the same period (6,851—minimal number). This arises from the fact that not all the dead in the given time period were buried immediately. In contrast, in 1941 the number of funerals exceeds the number of those who died by 130. A certain number of those who actually died at the end of 1940 were only buried at the start of 1941. Corpses would lie and wait several days for their turn because the cemetery staff could not manage to carry out the funerals in time due to the great mortality (*Chronicle* of March 1941).

How many victims of a "natural" death did this ghetto regime cause? From May 1940 until August 1944 nearly 43,800 Jews died in the Łódź Ghetto. The prewar mortality among the Łódź Jews in 1938 amounted to 10.8 per thousand a year. The number of deaths in the Łódź Ghetto for the given period (51 months), assuming that the average number of the ghetto population during the ghetto period was about 110,800, should have been about 5,100 souls. Thus, an excess of about 38,700 Jews died not during "actions" and "resettlements" but in a "natural" manner through hunger and disease. This amounts to about 16.6 percent of the Jewish population in Łódź at the beginning of the war (about 233,000) and nearly 35 percent of the average number of Jews in the ghetto from May 1940 until August 1944.

For comparison, it is worthwhile to point out that a similar calculation for the Warsaw ghetto brought out that 19 percent of the average number of Jews who resided in Warsaw during September 1939–July 1942 expired due to hunger, diseases, and epidemics (76,000 out of about 400,000).[43]

VI

Persecutions, Murder, and Deportations

With the arrival of the German military in Łódź on 8 September 1939, a week after the war's outbreak, there commenced for the Łódź Jews a bloody period of constant persecutions and outrages that continued throughout the entire nearly five-year existence of the ghetto. In the first days of September, a large number of victims fell to German bullets on the roads to Warsaw, during the panicked flight from Łódź. Those who made their way back had to endure persecution and torment by the German military units they encountered.[1]

From the first day on, over the course of several weeks, there was a brutal hooligan rampage on the streets of Łódź, mainly conducted by the local ethnic Germans (so-called *Volksdeutsche*), who in the blink of an eye became the loyal helpers of the occupation authorities, and by the Polish anti-Semitic rabble. They would haul Jews from their beds in the middle of the night and drive them from their homes just as they were. Mostly ethnic Germans moved into the deserted apartments. Robbery and beating of Jews on the streets became regular daily occurrences. Thus, for example, the so-called *Volinyakes* (ethnic Germans from Volhynia who, on the basis of the transfer agreement between Germany and Soviet Russia, were transported to Łódź into a transit camp housed in the building of a home for the elderly) would every day wait for Jews in the building entries and drag the better dressed ones into their camp, supposedly to work, but in fact to extort payoffs from them of 1 to 10 RM. Whoever did not pay would emerge from the camp beaten up (doc. no. 96).[2]

> On the afternoon of 18 October 1939, a group of SS-men drove up to the Jewish popular café Astoria with revolvers in their hands and arrested everyone there, about 100–150 people, and took them away on trucks to their quarters. There the real bacchanalia began. Like enraged wild beasts, dozens of them threw themselves on their victims with iron bars, rods, and rubber clubs and beat them continuously. This was only a prelude. Later, the individual action began. Each one was interrogated separately in a sophisticated way. By breaking arms and fingers, they squeezed out whatever anyone may still have possessed, and commanded ransom payments of several hundred marks each. Whoever did not have it with him had to identify his family who were told by special messengers to bring the designated ransom. In result . . . forty-six people were shot to death on the spot, fifty were freed for larger sums, and the rest were led off to the temporary jail-camp in Radogoszcz.[3]

Those seized during the large police raid on 29 February 1940 (see chapter 1) experienced brutal torments during the five days of their arrest (those who could pay 150 RM each were released earlier). The intent was to extort ransom money. Some were killed on the spot and fifty persons were removed from the group and shot to death in a neighboring forest. On the fifth day, the majority of those seized were freed, after their relatives had brought ransom money.[4]

Soldiers and members of Nazi formations sponsored these actions and themselves participated in these nocturnal ambushes. Already discussed in chapter 1 were the continual "legal" prohibitions for Jews to move about or reside on certain principal streets and parts of the city (before introduction of the ghetto) and other anti-Jewish decrees, like wearing the Jewish badge, the ban on using the municipal tramway, and so forth.

A particular scourge was seizure for forced labor, whose purpose was mainly to torment those who were seized, both physically and morally. They were compelled to fill in the air-defense trenches, unload coal, move rocks and bricks, and do other unskilled labor. They were not given any work tools, but were forced to fill in the trenches with their hands or with tin cans. They had to clean toilets with their hands, to scrape and clean the floors with their nails. Women were forced to wash the floors with their own underwear.[5] Groups of Jews were locked up in several large factories that belonged to Jews (Poznański, Rosenblatt, Eitingon); they were forced to clean the factory halls and were beaten terribly while laboring.[6]

There were also cases of humane treatment: workers were given food and even cigarettes.[7] Jewish technical specialists, if they were needed, could even exploit their privileged position and help their brothers in distress with food or release from heavy, humiliating work.[8] It was all, of course, dependent on the measure of humanity that remained in this or that soldier, officer, or policeman.

Jews also had big problems in supplying themselves with food in the public shops. It was enough if a Pole pointed out Jews standing in line for the German policeman to drive them away and beat them as well.[9] Jews were eliminated from the normal food supply system and had to buy food at horribly high prices.

The Jew's property was also free for the taking. In practice, from the first moment there began a brutal expropriation of Jewish property, and the subsequent decrees only sanctioned the factual situation and divided the loot among the various interested takers.

Regardless of the highest authorities' explicit decrees that regulated the competence of the relevant organs in the question of confiscation of Jewish and Polish property,[10] each German soldier, policeman, and official felt entitled to participate in the open theft of Jewish possessions. Here was acted out the whole greed of the arrogant and overbearing Nazi military. Even officers would barge into Jewish residences, order the Jews to pack up the clothing, jewelry, and furs, and hurriedly ship it back into the Reich "out of fear that a higher officer might take it away for himself."[11] Very active in the matter of taking over Jewish factories, warehouses, and businesses were the ethnic Germans who immediately put themselves at the service of the occupant.

Symptomatic in this respect are the Kalisz *Regierungspräsident*'s message of 10 January 1940 to the Lodz *Polizeipräsident,* and the latter's declaration in the Łódź German press of 17 January 1940, notifying their subordinate offices about the frequent cases of unauthorized confiscations (*wilde Beschlagnahmen*) by military, civilian, and party organs that were not entitled to do so and were endangering economic life in the occupied territories.

This had negligible effect. When it involved seizing Jewish property, Germans would lose their exaggerated sense of subordination, and on 4 December 1940 the *Regierungspräsident* once again sent to all his offices a circular about halting the "wild confiscations."[12]

In the end, the H.T.O. became the chief organ for seizing and managing Jewish requisitioned property in the annexed territories. The large scope of the confiscation campaign is attested to by the fact that by February 1941 there were under the H.T.O.'s management in the entire Wartheland province 264 large, 9,000 medium, and 76,000 small industrial enterprises, and 9,120 large and 112,000 small commercial enterprises.[13] A major part of these confiscations occurred, of course, in Łódź, as the largest industrial and commercial center of the province.

The wanton requisitions together with the devastation and impoverishment as a result of the invasion immediately washed away the economic base of the Łódź Jews. They arrived in the ghetto in a state of economic ruin, with very limited possibilities of material existence.

In the first months, the people driven into the ghetto comforted themselves with an illusory feeling of security. They hoped to be free of the persecutions and insults that they had to endure in the city in the pre-ghetto period. But this hope quickly evaporated. Disregarding the fact that Rumkowski had delivered thousands of laborers at each demand of the German organs, the seizure for forced labor did not halt even in the ghetto (only from 1 July 1940 did Jewish laborers cease to work outside the ghetto).[14]

A new terrible plague commenced in July 1940, particularly for those who lived on the streets adjacent to the wire fences. The German guards would capriciously shoot across the ghetto fence. For some, this was a sort of entertainment, for others an act of hatred or revenge. Between 2 and 26 July, thirty-five Jews fell at the hands of these uncontrolled guard personnel.[15] One of them, the notorious *"Geler Yanek"* (Blond Jack), himself shot twenty-four Jews. He was a Polish gentile youth who had previously been a porter among the Jewish merchants at the "Green Market." After the arrival of the Germans, he became a *Volksdeutsche* and was appointed a ghetto guard.[16] An incomplete report by the Order Service to Rumkowski, dated 21 July 1940, lists seven Jews (five men and two women) shot before curfew "in the last week; it is also pointed out that two of the victims were eighty meters from the fence."[17]

In April 1941, the bloody bacchanalia at the ghetto fences resumed, and in December of that year it took on such a character that people fled in panic from the houses neighboring the ghetto borders, abandoning their last possessions. It was dangerous to move about anywhere near more than ten guardposts.

During the month of December, the ghetto *Chronicle* noted ten cases of shooting deaths (including one case on 30 November; this number is certainly not complete, because we do not possess the entire set of the *Chronicle* for December).[18] In order to calm the ghetto public, which was moreover shocked due to the announced *Aussiedlung* ("outsettlement") from the ghetto, Rumkowski issued an appeal to the ghetto population on 25 December, in which he announces that after an intervention with the authorities he obtained from them an assurance that these events would not be repeated any more. But as for smugglers and those who leave the ghetto illegally, the guards would behave ruthlessly (doc. no. 97).[19] Yet regardless of this official assurance, on the evening of 29 December a deportee from Kassel was shot by the ghetto watch.[20] This fresh murder naturally was not going to calm the strained emotions in the ghetto, so Rumkowski issued another appeal (no. 348) on 1 January 1942, in which he reiterated his previous assurance and declared that the Jew was shot because the guard assumed he was a smuggler. (He supposedly was carrying two heavy valises.)[21]

Sporadic cases of shooting by the guards at the ghetto fences happened during almost the entire existence of the ghetto.[22] The ghetto sentries shot relentlessly at all who attempted to get out of the ghetto,[23] at those who left their homes after curfew,[24] or who wanted to put an end to their sad lives in the ghetto and, not having the strength themselves, would approach the wires and ask the sentries to shoot them.[25]

The Nazis would employ provocations to instigate a mood of terror in the ghetto. Thus, for example, on 4 June 1941 Rumkowski issued a poster announcement (no. 278), stating that on the night of 27 May someone had fired from two places within the ghetto and one bullet fell near the German sentry post. The authorities wanted to punish the entire ghetto population severely, but thanks to his intervention they settled on a total curfew in which Jews were not to go out on the street for a night and a day: from 9 P.M., Friday, 6 June, until 8 P.M., Saturday, 7 June. The only exceptions were to be the Jewish police, firefighters, and chimneysweeps, as well as physicians, first aid personnel, and those with a special permit (doc. no. 98).[26]

According to the testimony of a surviving printer from the Łódź Ghetto, the Jewish printers and their manager, Sh. Rozenshteyn, were roused by Gestapo men in the middle of the night and were ordered to print up a prepared text of the aforementioned announcement. They knew that the story about the shooting from inside the ghetto was invented from start to finish, and the only purpose of this provocation was to throw a scare into the ghetto.[27]

Public executions also served as a means to terrorize the ghetto population: even before the sealing of the ghetto (exact date unknown, probably on 9 November 1939), the Nazis hanged three Jews at the Bałuty Market square, supposedly as a penalty for denouncing Łódź Germans to Polish government organs during the first days of the war. The three Jews were left hanging for forty-eight hours and only then were they permitted to be buried.[28]

On 19 January 1942 an announcement was posted on the ghetto walls in which Rumkowski made known that Dr. Ulrich Georg "Israel" Schulz, a deportee from Prague (born in 1897) was shot for "resisting German police officials."[29] The ghetto *Chronicle* for the second half of January 1942 presents this information with the following explanation: the man shot was placed in prison immediately after his arrival in the ghetto. On the way from Prague to Łódź, he had a fit of insanity and insulted the police officials who were in the railcar as escorts.[30] The date of this report, 19 January, when the "resettlement action" was in full swing and over two months after Mr. Schulz was arrested, is surely no accident. It was supposed to show what awaited anyone resisting the German police.

Less than a month later, on 21 February, one day before the start of the second stage of the "resettlement," a deportee from Cologne, Max Hertz, was publicly hanged. He had been arrested at the city train station while purchasing a ticket. About 8,000 Western European Jews, among whom were also the wife and the young daughter of the condemned, had to attend the public execution.[31]

The public execution on 22 July 1942 of two escapees from a labor camp near Poznań was discussed in chapter 4.

The German authorities employed every means to humiliate the Jews in the ghetto. To this category belonged the decree to greet each

German official, both civilian and military, with a military salute (Jewish police and firefighters) or through removing their hats (men) and bowing their heads (women).[32]

The First Deportation Phase (16 January–15 May 1942)

Preparations for the annihilation campaign against the Jewish population in Wartheland began in summer 1941. From a 16 July 1941 letter by Heppner, later the director of the Population Department (*Bevölkerungswesen*) in the provincial governor's administration (*Statthalterei*) in Poznań, to Adolf Eichmann, the official designated for Jewish affairs in the Reich Security Main Office (*Reichssicherheitshauptamt*), it can be clearly inferred that officials in the governor's administration were at the time considering various means to "resolve the Jewish question" in Wartheland. Heppner writes:

> There is a danger that in the coming winter it will not be possible among other things to supply all Jews with food. It must be seriously considered whether a liquidation of all Jews not capable of working, with the aid of a fast working means, would not be more humane; in any case it would be more pleasant [!] than to let them die out from hunger. . . . The governor has not yet expressed himself on this question. It is likely that the Łódź Regierungspräsident Uebelhoer would prefer that the Łódź Ghetto not be destroyed because he is presumably earning not too badly from it.[33]

The decision for physical mass extermination was made no later than October 1941, because the preparations were already under way in the months of October and November for the extermination camp in Chełmno, which began to function on 8 December.[34]

The Germans began the extermination action with the mentally ill. In March 1941, more than forty patients were taken from the Jewish hospital for the insane on Wesoła Street. On 28 July 1941 this hospital was emptied of its last sixty patients and simultaneously, as Y. Tabaksblat relates, the cripples were taken from their asylum. By order, the mental patients were injected in advance with anesthetizing scopolamine. They were taken to death in a half-unconscious state, while at the same time only five of the sixty nearly cured patients were sent home.[35]

On 2 January 1942, Greiser issued his decree about "dejewification" (*Entjudung*) of the Warthegau.[36] However, even earlier, at the end of September or the beginning of October 1941, the Germans began to experiment with methods of mass killing. The first "experiment" took place in Konin district. The entire Jewish population of the district, numbering nearly 3,000 souls, was concentrated at the end of September or the start of October 1941 in Zagórowa (German: Hinterbergen, a small town near Konin). Earlier, each had to undergo a medical examination and pay 4 RM "head money." Included were males from ages 14 to 60 and females from 14 to 50 years old, supposedly to determine their ability to work. Then the "outsettlement" (*Aussiedlung*) commenced. The story was that they were going by truck to the neighboring town of Koło and from there by train to Łódź. In groups of sixty in a truck, they were driven into the nearby Kazimierzów forest, where they were killed. A witness, a former Polish arrestee whom the Germans took with two other prisoners into the woods in order to bury the dead and sort their garments, recounts that the Jews were thrown alive into trenches filled with quick lime on which water was poured. Simultaneously, trucks were brought from the forest with gassed Jews who were also buried there.[37] Here we have the extermination action still in the testing stage.

After the Chełmno extermination camp was set in operation, the liquidation of the Jewish population in Wartheland proceeded at full speed: From 7 December 1941 to 14 January 1942, the Jews of five small communities were killed there (Koło, Dąbie, Kłodowa, Iżbica, and Bugaj), about 6,400 people. On 16 January 1942, the first party of those being "outsettled" from the Łódź Ghetto arrived at Chełmno.[38]

Around mid-December 1941, alarming reports began to spread in the ghetto that the German authorities were asking Rumkowski to deliver people for deportation. The official motive for this was that it was impossible for the German regime to feed such a numerous population. On 1 December 1941, according to the official statistics, there were 163,623 people living in the Łódź Ghetto, including the deportees from Western Europe and the provincial towns. Therefore, the ghetto must be reduced by at least half.[39]

Rumkowski gave the first official notice about a deportation in his speech of 20 December 1941, delivered in the Culture House after a concert especially organized for the ghetto elite. He announced that candidates to be sent out of the ghetto were in the first place the criminal element, after them relief recipients who evaded compulsory labor, as well as speculators occupied with buying up personal possessions from the newly arrived. In this speech, Rumkowski stated a figure of 10,000 people and boasted that it had been possible to reduce by half the number the authorities had initially demanded from him.[40]

On 5 January 1942, the Outsettlement Commission (*Oyszidlungskomisye*) began operation, named by Rumkowski and composed of five persons. Belonging to it were the chief of the Vital Statistics (*Evidents*) Department, the ghetto police commandant, the chairman of the ghetto court, the commandant of the ghetto prison, and the director of the criminal division of the ghetto police.

According to the commission's plan, operating on the basis of Rumkowski's instructions, the 10,000 candidates for deportation were to be recruited in the following fashion: 2,000 from the provincial refugees, then the families whose husbands or sons had been dispatched for work outside the ghetto and had received relief of 12 marks a month, and finally all those who came into conflict with Rumkowski's harsh penal code.[41] These were, with few exceptions, the very poorest and socially weakest part of the ghetto population.

As Y. Tabaksblat reports:

> At a conference in the Chairman's office the question [was] raised whom
> to send out. Some thought that old folk and children should be sent, in
> order that the young and healthy and those able to work and support the
> ghetto should remain in the ghetto. Others construed the matter differ-
> ently. Not one hundred percent believing the assurances about the ar-
> rangement for those sent out into countryside (too big a favor for Jews),
> but sooner believing that there would be a migration to distant places
> . . . and the old and sick will not survive. Therefore, it is more reasonable
> to send younger people, who can more readily take care of themselves
> (no one dreamed that those sent out were going to annihilation. . .). It
> was left that no distinction would be made between young and old, but
> to send entire families, to keep them together and so that they should
> help one another on the way.[42]

A transport of about 1,000 people was supposed to depart each day.

As soon as the first summonses were received (in the ghetto they
were called "wedding invitations"), turmoil broke out in the ghetto.
Work in the factories and offices was virtually paralyzed. Rumors, one
more terrible than the next, spread through the ghetto. The candidates
to be sent out would hide with relatives or friends. Foreseeing these desperate escape attempts, Rumkowski already on 30 December 1941, before the Outsettlement Commission officially began to operate, issued a
severe warning to the ghetto population against giving shelter or a place
for the night to strangers or relatives who were not registered in the relevant buildings; those transgressing this prohibition would be forcibly
deported from the ghetto.[43] Rumkowski repeated this admonition in his
announcement of 14 January, adding that the doorkeepers (*vekhter*) of
buildings where people designated for deportation were hidden would
themselves be sent out of the ghetto.[44]

The desperation that caught up the ghetto inhabitants was beyond
measure. There were intense frosts at the time and the ghetto found itself in one of its frequent periods of hunger. The delivery of supplies was
minimal. In a diary written in those tragic days, we read the following
lines under the date of 17 January [1942]:

> Early today [should be yesterday] the first transport of evacuees was sent
> out. Altogether, the transport numbered 780 men, 853 women, and 154
> children. Most of them—poor, broken, naked, and starved. Their depar-
> ture was extraordinarily tragic. All of them cried mournfully. Mothers
> embraced their little children . . . and screamed aloud: If we will die,
> you at least stay alive in order to be able to get revenge on those who are
> banishing us. . . . Terror, rage, deadly turmoil combined to annihilate a
> community of Jews. With our own eyes we saw how Jews were going to
> destruction.[45]

Y. Tabaksblat writes:

> Each day in the afternoon hours whole families shuffled out . . . load-
> ed up with large and small bundles of bedding, pots, bowls, and other

household things, surrounded with children, barely dragging themselves to the place, so that quite early in the morning they would make their way to the train [in Radogoszcz]. The same each day during the course of long weeks . . . severely ill people, taken from their beds, did not survive even the short way from prison to the train and died in the middle, so they were . . . transported in wagons . . . and they were also counted for the total.[46]

According to the deportation procedure, probably so that it would look like they were really being "sent to work," each deportee could take along 12.5 kg of baggage. The exiles could sell their furniture and household goods in the carpentry workshops at prices set by appraisers. Furniture could also be left in storage, to be collected "when they return." Each could also exchange the ghetto scrip and receive an equivalent of 10 RM, and as for the rest of the money, designate to whom to give it. An account was opened for each deportee.[47]

The rabbinical council issued conditional divorces according to a simplified and speedy procedure. Health Department doctors examined those who submitted appeals that they could not go due to illness.[48] Matters continued in this way until 29 January, when a short interruption took place in the deportation. During these fourteen days, fourteen transports left with 10,103 people,[49] an average of over 700 in each transport. This and subsequent deportations were carried out through the Jewish Outsettlement Commission and the Order Service. Only at the train station did the victims go over to the jurisdiction of the German police.

On 30 January, the ghetto breathed more freely. It was claimed that the deportation was completely halted, that life was going back to "normal." But not for long. A further series of deportations began on 22 February, continuing without interruption until 2 April 1942.[50] The forty transports dispatched from the ghetto during those forty days swallowed up 34,073 victims (12,847 men and 12,226 women).[51]

In order to make people desperate and compel them to appear "voluntarily" at the assembly points to be sent out, the authorities applied the tactic of starvation during the winter months of 1942 (and also during subsequent "actions"). The delivery of supplies for the ghetto shrank from day to day. Thus, for example, in January 1,336,050 kilos of rye flour and 19,000 kilos of wheat flour came in, but in February only 923,980 kilos of rye flour and 3,328 kilos of wheat flour. Vegetables were not delivered at all. The public kitchens did not have anything to cook in the soups.[52] The hunger often forced people to emerge from their hiding places and report to the assembly point in the central prison, where the victims received soup, meat, and bread. Those who hid themselves could not even collect their meager food allotments because their names were reported to the stores and distribution points. The renewal of the deportation in February, during the coldest frosts, evoked a mood of deep despair in the ghetto. The image of groups of men, women, and children, wrapped in tatters, shivering from cold, marching through the ghetto in the direction of Marysin shocked people, particularly because the interruption in the action from the end of January until 22 February was considered a sign that the deportation was halted, at least for the winter months. People now sensed that they were confronting a total liquidation of the ghetto.

When rumors spread that the action was halted, Rumkowski twice, on 22 and 25 March, came out with admonitions, denying the rumors and threatening that those who did not show up would be sent out without baggage (doc. no. 99).[53]

On 2 April, the first day of Passover, the deportation was interrupted for a short time. Pious Jews saw in this a Passover miracle and a "beginning of redemption."[54] But this breathing spell for the ghetto, which was like a seriously ill person living on his last strength, did not long endure. On 18 April came Rumkowski's announcement (no. 374) calling on all unemployed ghetto inhabitants from ten years of age and older to appear for a medical examination. Exempted from this obligation were all those actually employed, all possessing a job assignment from the Labor Office (*Arbeitseinsatz*) or from the Personnel Department, as well as the newly arrived.[55] During the week from 21 to 28 April, Rumkowski issued another four announcements categorically calling for people to report to the medical commission that consisted of German physicians (on the twenty-eighth the deadline was extended another day).[56]

Suddenly, a new announcement (no. 380) posted on 29 April radically changed the situation in the ghetto. This notice spoke not about appearing before the German commission, but informed the ghetto population that on 4 May deportation would begin of the newly arrived people from the *Altreich,* Luxembourg, Vienna, and Prague (with the exception of those with jobs and recipients of the Iron Cross and medals for those wounded in the First World War). Until now, and according to the announcement of 18 April, they had been exempt from appearing for the medical examination.[57]

The next day, on 30 April, Rumkowski issued another summons to all those who had not yet reported to the commission of doctors, that they must do this on 1 May. Like the announcement of 18 April, the deportees from the Reich, Vienna, Prague, and Luxembourg were again excluded.[58]

How can one make sense of the contradictory announcements of 18, 29, and 30 April? It is clear that between 18 and 29 April a radical change took place in the "outsettlement" plan. According to the first plan, those to be deported were supposed to be unemployed and ghetto residents incapable of work, while the Western European Jews, who had been in the ghetto only six months, were supposed to be spared from the action. But in the meantime, between the eighteenth and twenty-ninth, there matured a second plan to deport the newly arrived Jews from the West instead of residents.

Why had the May deportation struck only the deportees from Western Europe (with very minor exceptions; see below)? The question was raised at the time in a number of documents. Various theories were heard about this in the ghetto, reflecting both the character of Rumkowski's regime and the position of the Western European exiles in the ghetto. An anonymous author (Dr. Oskar Singer?), himself one of the Western European Jews, writes:

> An opportunity to kill two birds with one stone has come to hand for the chairman in the new outsettlement in May: to measure out equal justice to both sides and get rid of an unproductive human element. Although in principle no distinction is made, the psychologist must understand: the resident is a real brother, the new fellow—a step-brother. He does not even understand the language of the ghetto. Moreover, there coincided here the high percentage of older people and such whose possibilities of adapting were hopeless. . . . If it came to an outsettlement of only residents, then the chairman would have to target his productive elements. . . . Who can be offended at a good father, when he spares with all his strength his favorite child?[59]

Thus did a representative of the deportees themselves, who by the way belonged to the category of those spared, attempt to justify the sentence on his countrymen.

The same author is not certain whether the outsettlement of the newly arrived took place on the basis of an explicit decree from the German authorities or was a result of negotiations: Rumkowski received an order to resettle residents, but he later negotiated and got a free hand to replace the residents with the new people.

This tragic change is also similarly commented upon in other documents. For example, the ghetto *Chronicle* from the end of April or beginning of May writes: "The opinion generally reigned [among the new arrivals] that in order to save the hometown population it was consigned to the factories and offices, and the Western European Jews were shipped out."[60] Another document comments similarly on this question: Since the majority of residents who reported to the medical examination commission were old people, women and children whom the commission rejected, the foreigners here became the scapegoat for the local population.[61]

Whatever motives may have been decisive, there is no doubt that Rumkowski bears in larger measure the responsibility for such a selection of human material for the May deportation. It is enough to become familiar with the threats that he made in speeches addressed to the deportees from Western Europe[62] to be convinced that Rumkowski, who reckoned quite little with human lives, willingly exploited the opportunity in a radical fashion to be quit of the "intruders" from the West, with whom he could not cope and who impeded the carrying out of his plans.[63]

According to the announcement of 29 April, as already mentioned, holders of the Iron Cross, First Class and Second Class, and those wounded in the First World War and their families, were exempt from deportation. Also, a group of scholars who were assigned as translators of various languages was exempted from the obligation to report to the transports. In the first category of those eligible to benefit from this privilege were 289 persons, constituting a relatively large percentage, when one takes into account that this figure does not include some of the transports—for example, the transports from Berlin—from which the exiles "could not" take any personal documents along with them.[64]

The other category (translators of Hebrew, English, French, Serbian, modern Greek, Spanish, and Latin) included a group of seventeen persons with their families. There had been twenty, but three died in the meantime.

As for those employed, specialists and tenured employees (*etatizirte ongeshtelte*)[65] were taken into account, but the condition was that they had to be employed starting from 31 March.[66] Only those physicians and nurses who were employed at the Health Department (the majority) were exempted.

Characteristic of the mood of despair that reigned among the Western European exiles is the fact that many of the privileged decided not to make use of the right to remain in the ghetto and did not declare their military decorations. "The five months in the ghetto, on the floor, in hunger and cold . . . could not motivate them to struggle for their lives. They say that wherever they may be, it will not be any worse for them. Therefore, they willingly want to leave their present place."[67] This mood of apathy was widespread among the broadest circles of the exiles, and they passively and obediently went to the assembly points. Among some the calculation was thus: "Since sooner or later everybody will be sent out, why be sent away with *Ostjuden* when one can travel with his own."[68]

Therefore, relatively many volunteers reported for deportation (for example, the former transport leaders). A reason for this phenomenon was also the fact that the appeals commission had taken into account only immediate family members when making exemptions. Brothers and sisters of privileged people did not enjoy this right. People did not want to part from relatives and therefore they traveled together.[69]

Characteristic of the cruel methods that prevailed during the deportations is the fact that even privileged people also received summonses to report to the central prison and only there, after a check, were they exempted. On returning to their homes, they encountered havoc there, for everything had been dragged out and stolen.

Similar things happened with the disbursement of the sums of money sent from abroad. Only when nothing could be done with the money (paid out in ghetto currency) did the post office start to pay out without difficulties "as if in a sort of malicious spite."[70]

The sequence of the deportation was as follows:

> In the morning hours, those designated for the outsettlement gather in the central prison, or in the cottages surrounded with barbed wire. . . . They spend the night here and in the morning they are conducted under guard [of the Order Service] into the assembly camp in Marysin. . . . At 4 A.M. they are conveyed by the Jewish Order Service to the Radogoszcz train station. Departure takes place each day at 7 A.M. Seating in the railcars takes place under the control of the [German] police and then comes the order to cast away the baggage. . . . As a rule, the smallest parcels are taken away from them. They are left with only bread and sometimes a few food articles. Larger parcels are confiscated by the O[rder] S[ervice] in the assembly points and are sent off to the Department for the Newly Arrived. Sick people and the elderly are carried into the railcars by porters. A first aid station is on duty at the rail station. The train consists of 7 third-class cars and everyone has a guaranteed seat.[71]

Although the decree of 29 April explicitly permitted baggage of 12.5 kilos per person, people were convinced by the events at the departure of the first transport that they were not being permitted to take anything along (aside from bread and sometimes a small quantity of other food). Those designated for deportation started to sell off their garments and personal items en masse. In this, they were exploited in an ugly fashion by unconscionable buyers even from their own ranks. "The handsomest suit for three kilo of potatoes . . . a women's suit for a ¼ kilo of margarine." In addition to this, buyers lied about the quality and falsified the food products.[72] The prices for foodstuffs in the ghetto rose with dizzying speed. On 4 May, the first day of the deportation, people paid 360 marks for bread (it later reached to 600 marks) and 750 marks for a kilo of margarine (later reaching 1,000 marks). The extent of embitterment that prevailed among the exiles on account of this harmful exploitation is attested to by the fact that the second Cologne transport, which lived in a "collective," burned their goods left over after selling off. The *Chronicle* adds "that the fact alone that such a report could arise and spread [apparently people doubted its accuracy] characterizes sufficiently the mentality of the foreign Jews, their attitudes to us and vice-versa our attitudes to them."[73]

The first transport, numbering 1,000 souls, departed on 4 May; the twelfth and final one left on 15 May. Altogether, 10,914 people were sent out in the third stage of the deportation. Among them were also 753 veteran residents of Łódź, people who had in some way sinned against Rumkowski, or volunteers. In the earlier transports (January–April), 340 newcomers had been deported, so that in the first phase of deportation a total of 10,501 Western European Jews (3,408 men and 7,093 women) were sent away. They comprised about 61 percent of all the Western Europeans who were in the ghetto on the eve of the deportations.[74] Ninety-four candidates for exile died, while 25 persons were deported from the hospitals. Among the dead were a relatively large number of suicides. According to information in the ghetto *Chronicle*,

Table 16
The May 1942 Deportation of Western European Exiles*

Place of Origin	Initial Number	Died**		Deported		Remained in Ghetto	
		Number	%	Number	%	Number	%
Berlin	4,054	992	24.4	2,267	55.9	745	18.1
Vienna	4,999	733	14.7	3,085	61.7	1,100	22.0
Prague	4,999	355	7.1	1,945	38.9	2,470	49.8
Frankfurt am Main	1,186	213	17.9	538	45.3	325	27.4
Hamburg	1,063	130	12.2	534	50.2	340	31.9
Cologne	2,014	143	7.1	1,057	52.4	730	36.2
Düsseldorf	1,004	68	6.7	487	48.6	400	39.7
Luxembourg	512	45	8.7	248	48.4	200	39.0
TOTAL	19,831	2,679	13.5	10,161	52.2	6,310	31.7

* Not included in these figures are the Emden transport (122 people), as well as those who had been sent to the Poznań labor camps (nearly 700 people). The figures come from *Chronicle* of 29 May 1942.[1]
** The number of those who died is not complete because reliable figures are available only until the end of April 1942, a couple of days before the deportation started. According to a source cited by Melezin (op.cit., p. 12), there were supposedly a total of 5,672 Western European Jews in the Łódź Ghetto on 30 June 1942.

1. Ed. Note: *Chronicle* (1984), 188, entry dated 27 May 1942, states that there were 6,310 Western European Jews left in the ghetto and gives the totals for each city as in this table. But no such data is in the entry dated May 28–29.

suicide was committed out of fear of deportation by 23 Western European Jews out of 29 cases in all. Among them were two joint suicides of couples.[75] One of the suicides was carried into the railcar, with the veins cut in his arms. The sixth transport, which departed on 9 May, carried away 260 Jews of the Christian faith.[76]

Table 16 provides more precise details regarding the changes in the number of Western European newcomers:

During the first phase of deportations from 16 January until 15 May 1942, a total of 54,990 souls (20,767 men and 34,223 women) were sent out of the Łódź Ghetto, that is, over a third of the number of Jews in the ghetto on 1 January 1942 (162,681). On 1 June 1942, there remained 104,470 people in the ghetto, among them over 6,300 of the Western European newcomers.

As we see from the table, at the end of May 1942, there remained less than a fifth of the Berliners, somewhat more than a fifth of the Viennese, almost half of those from Prague, a bit more than a fourth of the Frankfurters, and of the rest more or less a third of their initial number. The Berliners, Frankfurters, and Viennese also produced the largest number of dead. From mid-October 1941 until May 1942, almost 25 percent of the Berliners died, among the Frankfurters almost 18 percent, and among the Viennese almost 15 percent. The Viennese gave the largest number of deportees, almost two-thirds of their earlier number, followed by the Berliners (almost 56 percent), those from Cologne, and the Hamburgers (over 50 percent of their earlier number). The "least" victims were among those from Prague (nearly 40 percent).

These differences in the percentage of deportees can be explained by the demographic structure of the respective city groups. This structure also determined the extant of employment. Since in this respect those from Prague were in the best situation, the largest number of those remaining was among them. Moreover, the Viennese and Berliners, the Düsseldorfers and those from Cologne, found themselves in a worse state due to the fact that most of them still resided in the "collectives" that were more intensely afflicted by the deportations. Prague possessed only one large "collective." This was the fifth arrival transport that was almost entirely deported, delivering to the deportations 558 souls, i.e., almost a fourth of all the "outsettled" Praguers.

In all, on 29 May 1942 less than a third (31.7 percent) of the Western European Jews remained. Of the other two-thirds, during the course of six months 17 percent died or were sent out to a slow death at the Poznań labor camps and over 50 percent were sent directly to death at Chełmno.

The Deportation in the First Half of September 1942

A month passed after the last stage of the deportations in May 1942, and again the ghetto was seized by disturbing rumors about a new deportation, this time of children up to ten years old. The *Chronicle* of 23 and 24 June 1942 noted these rumors, characterizing them as unfounded and adding that some of the higher officials of the ghetto administration categorically deny these "*plyotkes*" (rumors). According to the *Chronicle*, 24 June, the rumors grew from the fact that Rumkowski had ordered the compilation of a list of persons over age ten, who had at one time been stamped by the German medical commission, in order to have statistical material prepared in case the authorities would demand it.[77] This "innocent" explanation about the necessity to have statistical material ready about the ages of the ghetto inhabitants has a tragic sense in light of the subsequent developments.

Rumkowski already knew as early as the beginning of June 1942 that a fresh threat of deportation was approaching the ghetto. To this testifies his speech delivered on 6 June, during a revue performance at Culture House, where he expressly stated "that the ghetto will in the near future be confronted by severe experiences, yet he hopes that he will manage to temper the eventual danger."[78]

One of the means to blunt the approaching danger was the broad campaign to integrate children ages ten and older into the ghetto production, particularly children and adolescents who were registered in April 1942. On 20 June 1942, nearly 13,000 children and adolescents were employed in the ghetto workshops (together with those who had been recruited into the ghetto production during the winter and spring deportations).[79]

Simultaneously, the registration continued of all those who had been "stamped," supposedly in order to find whether or not any of them had in the meantime obtained work and yet still benefited from communal relief.[80]

However, all these official explanations could not calm the mood of the sorely tried ghetto, and the atmosphere became ever more tense. In certain signs people saw a hint that a new misfortune was being readied. On 18 July, the *Chronicle* notes a report about an order to close the hospitals that were to be turned into workshops.[81] People saw a confirmation of this report in the closing of the large clinic on Zgierska Street on 4 August.[82]

On 25 August, by order of the German authorities, barracks began to be erected to which the hospitals were to be transferred.[83] Still earlier, around mid-July, barracks began to be put up at the Radogoszcz train station. It was claimed that they were designated for goods warehouses, but the *Chronicle* adds that it is possible they will also serve as concentration points before deportation.[84] The depressed mood in the ghetto became even more dejected from the shocking stories about the dreadful outrages during the deportations from a series of ghettos in the Łódź region, particularly the bloody deportation in Zduńska-Wola on 24–25 August 1942, about which the surviving remnants sent into the Łódź Ghetto spoke.[85] People did not understand this Nazi strategy of sending out and sending in, yet they sensed a new storm approaching. The ghetto drew analogies from the earlier deportation of January–March that was linked in the ghetto psyche with the "outsettlement" of nearly 20,000 Western European Jews (see chapter 7). Between May and August 1942, there were 14,441 Jews deported into the Łódź Ghetto from the liquidated ghettos of Pabianice, Ozorków, Brzeziny, Kalisz, Łask, Bełchatów, Turek, and other places.[86]

The fate of the Łódź Ghetto during the months of July and August teetered on the scales of the Nazi policy of extermination. In a letter dated 24 July 1942, addressed to the *Algemeine-Elektrizität-Gesellschaft* (AEG, General Electricity Company) that sought to order thin plates of mica (*plitn fun mika*) produced in the ghetto, the ghetto administration reckoned with the possibility that the situation in the ghetto could radically change in connection with the issue of "resolving the Jewish problem in general," and so it did not want to take on any commitments in regard to new orders for the ghetto.[87]

Apparently it was decided in the second half of August not to liquidate the ghetto for the time being—for the ghetto production was too important for the German war economy—but to turn it into a total labor ghetto, from which must be eliminated all unproductive, nonworking elements, namely, young children, the elderly, and the sick.

They began with the sick.

On Tuesday, the first of September, before daybreak, exactly on the third anniversary of the outbreak of war, military trucks drove up in front of the three hospitals on Wesoła, Drewnowska, and Łagiewnicka Streets and in a brutal manner the Germans loaded up all the patients they could catch. The ghetto population became alarmed and people began to gather in front of the hospitals. At first it was assumed that the patients were being transferred to the as-yet uncompleted barracks, but the brutal tossing of the patients into the trucks eliminated every doubt.

The Jewish ghetto police blocked all access routes to the hospitals and drove off the crowd. The SS-men could carry out their cold-blooded murder of the sick undisturbed by anyone. Dr. L. Szykier writes in his memoir: "The fashion in which the Germans took away the patients left no doubt at all regarding the fate of the unfortunates. They threw them down steps, they took them off of operating tables, they beat them and laid the patients one on top of the other in the trucks. No one knew where they were being taken, but for everyone it was clear that they were being taken to death."[88] In the writings of Joseph Zelkowicz, we find the following gruesome lines: "There was a terrible panic among the bedridden patients, who cannot even move. . . . They were just tossed as they were into the wagons, like calves to the slaughter."[89]

Patients who could move attempted to save themselves by jumping from the upper floors, climbing over fences, by hiding in the cellars, or by presenting themselves as hospital staff. At the fourth hospital on Mickiewicza Street, patients awoke from their beds and fled in their hospital garments before the trucks of the *Rollkommando* (transport unit) arrived. Some were caught, but the majority meanwhile escaped. In one children's preventorium in Marysin, where mildly ill children were kept, the management sent the children home to their parents.

According to Tabaksblat, 374 adults and 320 children were taken away to their deaths from the five hospitals and two preventoriums.[90] The authorities were left dissatisfied with such a small human catch and they insisted that all the patients who had fled from the hospitals must be delivered. The Jewish police received an order to search for the patients, who had hidden in their homes or with relatives. Those caught were sent to the central prison and the next morning, on 2 September, were loaded onto trucks and sent out of the ghetto.

But since not all could be found and since a certain number of escapees belonged to the favored group of those whom Rumkowski did not want to surrender, a deal was made with the authorities that instead of the escaped patients 200 others were to be delivered. These 200 scapegoats were gathered from among those who had once been hospital patients and were already long out of there, and even from people who had never yet been in the hospital, but had certificates from physicians to be admitted into a hospital and had reported their certificates.[91]

A deep desperation seized the ghetto population. It was sensed that this was only a beginning and people feared what must yet come. The question "Will it end with this?" gnawed at their minds. What people had feared during the last two months had become a tragic reality. On 2 September, people in the ghetto already knew that the authorities were demanding that (aside from the patients from the hospitals) children up to 10 years old and the elderly from 65 and up, altogether 20,000 souls, be sent out of the ghetto. It meant that Jews themselves must carry out this bloody operation on themselves. An Outsettlement Commission of five persons was formed, of the same composition as the previous one, to designate the candidates for deportation.

The building of the Labor Office was immediately besieged by hundreds of the elderly, the sick, and children, who because of their ages had not worked until now. They wanted to obtain a job card, a so-called "Rumkowski Rest-Pass" (*Rumkovskis ru-pas*), as a talisman against being sent away. But the Labor Office was closed. Also sealed was the Records Department's card file, in order to prevent any changes being entered in ages of those described.[92] Heartbreaking scenes were played out in the department's building.

With an entire staff of officials working all night, the Outsettlement Commission compiled lists of the population by streets and buildings.

Jewish police escort a group of Jews who have been seized for deportation in the Łódź Ghetto, 1942–1944. Photograph by Henryk Rozencwajg Ross. USHMM, courtesy of Sidney Harcsztark.

According to these lists, the number of children younger than ten years old and of the elderly over sixty-five totaled only about 13,000, that is, they alone could not fill the required contingent, and the difference of about 7,000 would have to be filled from another category—those unemployed and incapable of work. But this figure of about 13,000 also turned out to be uncertain, because children and parents of the Jewish policemen and firefighters who were supposed to carry out the murderous action, as well as children and parents of managers of the factories and offices, were exempted from the "outsettlement." Together, this amounted to a couple of thousand souls. Thus, the real difference between the demanded and the actual number of children and elderly "available" was even larger, and this gap could only be filled at the expense of the ghetto masses. Therefore, the danger of being deported hovered over each inhabitant of the ghetto (except the privileged).[93]

On the morning of 4 September, there was posted an announcement that at 4 P.M. Rumkowski and other high officials would speak at the Firefighters' Square about the recent events. Several thousand people came, yearning to hear an authoritative word about what was awaiting them. Both of the first two speakers, David Warszawski, the manager of the Tailoring *Centrala,* and S. Jakóbson, the chairman of the judicial court, clearly and unambiguously informed the crowd about the decree, that children up to age ten and the elderly from age sixty-five must be given up to the authorities to be sent out (the chairman of the court also mentioned the sick). They attempted to convince the desperate mothers and fathers that if the decree were carried out with their own hands, calmly and quietly, they would avoid the tragic events that took place during the deportations in other cities, where they were carried out by alien hands. The court chairman also stated that "in order to avoid misfortunes, in order to rescue the community," a ban on walking on the streets was being introduced during the entire time of the action.

Rumkowski spoke last. His speech was characteristic of his "rescue" ideology (see doc. no. 100 for excerpts, according to the text as noted down by Zelkowicz—perhaps literarily dramatized but correctly communicating Rumkowski's way of thinking).[94]

The crowd frequently reacted to the speeches with wailing and lamentation, particularly the mothers with small children in their arms.

On Saturday, 5 September, a general ban on walking in the streets (Yiddish *shpere,* from the German *Gehsperre*) was declared, from 5 P.M. until revoked, with the exception of firefighters, Transport Department workers, waste drivers, persons employed in fetching goods at Bałuty Marketplace and in Radogoszcz, as well as medical personnel. A permit to move about in the ghetto had to have the stamps of the Outsettlement Commission and of the Police Commandant (doc. no. 101).[95]

Until the ban went into force, the distribution points for food and vegetables were besieged by crowds of people who wanted to collect the eight kilos of potatoes per person that was then allotted by the Provisioning Department, in order to have a little food at home for the duration of the total curfew, whose length people could not foresee. In the workshops and offices, the workers and employees were already told on Friday that they were not to come to work the next day. Extraordinary panic and confusion engulfed the ghetto. Hurrying masses of people inundated the bridges connecting both parts of the ghetto. But at 5 P.M. the ghetto already looked like a ghost town. Only here and there did a policeman, a fireman, or a doctor appear.

Jewish police help an elderly Jew onto the back of a truck during the "Gehsperre" deportation action in the Łódź Ghetto, September 1942. Photographer unknown. USHMM, courtesy of Instytut Pamięci Narodowej.

Children from the Marysin colony, who were rounded up during the "Gehsperre" deportation action, march in a long column toward a deportation assembly point, September 1942. Photographer unknown. USHMM, courtesy of Instytut Pamięci Narodowej.

The Jewish police began the action on Saturday morning. From both homes for the elderly on Dworska Street and Gnieżnieńska Street (the latter for the resettled Western European Jews), their residents were led out, loaded onto wagons, and taken to the collection points. Here the Jewish police had an easy job; the human material was, so to speak, "ready."

The ghetto police also had an easy job in turning over to German hands the children from the orphanage and camp in Marysin. Rumkowski had ordered the woman supervisor to prepare the children, to bring them out to one place and wait for a further order. There were supposed to be nearly 850 children there on that day of deportation.[96] It seems that a certain number, who had parents or relatives in the ghetto, had earlier slipped away to them, with the silent agreement of the management or on their own. Biebow came to Marysin and received from the woman administrator the exact number of children. The Jewish police received the order to conduct the children into a former hospital. A wailing broke out among the children, who instinctively sensed what was awaiting them. Several hid themselves, but the diligent woman supervisor, it appears out of fear for the consequences, dragged out the children who were frightened to death.[97] The children were conducted to the collection point until late into the night. The next morning, the chief of the Gestapo came and counted them over. One child was missing. After lengthy searches a small boy was found hidden in a straw mattress. The Gestapo man made a gesture and freed the child.[98]

The inhuman task of the Jewish ghetto police became more difficult when they had to tear children from the arms of their fathers and mothers. Here they met resistance. Here they had to apply physical force. Joseph Zelkowicz records that a desperate father threw himself on the Jewish policemen with a knife or an axe.[99]

Also in another contemporaneous document, instances were noted when mothers threw themselves on the twentieth century *khapers*[100] (kidnappers), yelling: "Give away *your* kids, we will not give up *our* children" (*Git avek* ayere *nakhesn, mir veln* undzere *kinder nisht opgebn*).[101] A mother threw herself under the wheels of the wagon taking her child and was crushed to death. Mothers also voluntarily went along with their children.[102]

People also tried to conceal their children in cellars or attics.[103] Older children of six or seven attempted to save themselves from capture by climbing up onto the highest roofs, or managing to reach Marysin by back alleys, and there they hid among the potato fields.[104]

The results of this manhunt on the first day were very small and an inspection by the German ghetto administration and Gestapo determined that at such a rate the designated contingent of 20,000 would not be achieved within the foreseen deadline. Therefore, the authorities decided to take the action into their own hands. The ranks of the Jewish Order Service still had to carry out auxiliary work, reinforced with the firefighters brigade and the so-called "White Guard," that is, transport workers from the Provisioning Department and porters from Bałuty Marketplace. Like the Jewish policemen, these auxiliaries received a security guarantee for their own children and parents. As Zelkowicz reports, the "White Guard" voluntarily proposed its collaboration during the action "on the condition that they get the same that was promised to the police: bread, sausage and sugar and the exemption of their families."[105] There were also some officials who sought to get whatever employment on the margins of the action, in order to assure themselves the bread and sausage allocations instead of the workplace soups that they lost due to the total curfew.[106]

From the moment on 6 September when the German authorities led by Biebow took over the conduct of the action, the manner of taking victims changed entirely. Not only children, elderly, and hopelessly sick people, but anyone whom the SS-men did not like during the inspection in the courtyards was taken onto the wagon. Gestapo and SS-men, accompanied by their Jewish helpers, went from house to house, and a very few minutes after hearing the signal (generally a reckless revolver shot), all tenants had to present themselves for the selection. Here everything went at a lightning fast tempo. Fates were determined in a matter of seconds: a glance or a gesture with the hand (left or right). "Senseless and illogical: a swollen leg—up on the wagon; a high shoulder—onto the scrap heap; a red beard, can be without even one gray hair—taken."[107]

Oskar Singer in his mentioned reportage states that a young thirty-year-old wife of an official was "appraised for scrap" (*opgeshatst gevorn af shmelts*), because she became prematurely gray in the ghetto. She was saved by the intervention of her brother-in-law, who as a manager of a factory had the right to exempt his family.[108] In certain ghetto quarters, entire housing blocks were "outsettled" without distinction, even entire streets, while seriously ill people were shot on the spot.[109]

During the selection in the courtyards, victims died for no particular reason, from reckless shots. Everyone who displayed the slightest sign of resistance or who in the terrible confusion did not precisely adhere to the prescriptions of the hangman's rulebook was mercilessly shot on the spot.

A mother, among the remnants left of those deported from Germany, who stated during the selection that she would not voluntarily give up her four-year-old daughter, was shot together with the child before the eyes of all the tenants of the courtyard, after she had received three minutes to reflect.

Among those also shot were a young girl who showed her work card without being asked and a Jew who tried to cover his beard with an up-turned collar to appear younger.[110]

There also fell victims due to hunger and terror. As mentioned, all distribution points and warehouses were closed on 5 September before night, but many did not manage to collect their food allocations and in many homes an awful hunger prevailed. Only on the ninth was it permitted to issue the food portions in the southwestern section of the ghetto, in the part where the action was already concluded. In his file note (*Aktenvermerk*) of 9 September concerning this permission (with the reservation that the Gestapo would agree thereto), Biebow remarks that so long as the Gestapo finds itself left or right of the ghetto's chief artery (Hohensteiner Strasse-Zgierska Street) that traversed the ghetto's territory, no foodstuffs can be distributed.[111] It happened that when the Provisioning Department attempted to give out potatoes and big lines formed in front of the distribution points, the Germans opened fire and a couple dozen fell, dead and wounded.[112]

The exact number of deaths that were a result of the peculiar "outsettlement" methods during the "*Shpere*" is not known. No documents were found on many victims. They were photographed and the photographs marked with numbers because, due to the ban on entering the street, people could not even identify them (among some the faces were horribly disfigured). The highest number on one of them in the YIVO Archive is 571.[113]

In order to terrorize the desperate ghetto prisoners even more, the Germans also staged a hanging spectacle. On 7 September, they publicly hanged twenty-two (or twenty-one) Jews at Bazarowa Square; they were from Pabianice, among those who were sent into the Łódź Ghetto between May and August. They had been jailed for some time before the execution for certain transgressions. The gallows was prepared in the Carpentry Division (this was the only factory division working that day).[114]

In the course of the action, certain individuals were exempted due to intervention by leading ghetto authorities and officials, like for example the Central Bureau of Labor Divisions, the commandant of the *Sonderkommando* David Gertler, and the headquarters of the Order Service. Sometimes Richter, the German deportation commissioner, granted exemptions.[115] The exemption certificates were individual and had to have Biebow's stamp. In order to ensure that those exempted individuals and their families should not by error fall into the hands of the transport unit (*Rollkommando*) during the prevailing panic and disorder, two "asylums" were created for them: for children in the collection point on Łagiewnicka Street and for elderly people in Marysin. But even these "asylums" did not give any absolute security in the capricious atmosphere in the ghetto during the September Action.[116]

After negotiations with the authorities, the director of the labor divisions (*resortn*) managed to free 130 children among the older boys.[117]

A certain number freed themselves, even while already at the collection points, by bribing the Jewish police with valuable objects (gold watches, earrings) and dollars. Thus, through money and intervention with Biebow by high ghetto officials, a certain number of people were saved even though they were already on the wagons or in the collection points. There were also incidents when the Order Service man who went along with the wagon, or was guarding the collection point, released a relative or a friend of his without a bribe and then conducted him home.[118]

People also tried their luck by escaping from the wagon or by running over into the streets where the action was already concluded, even though victims were shot down.[119]

This orgy of murder continued for seven days (5–12 September). It swallowed 15,859[120] deportees and a minimum of 600 shot to death on the spot, altogether about 16,500 people. The designated quota of blood that the ghetto had to pay was thus more or less attained. Below (doc. no. 102), we bring a couple of longer excerpts from a contemporaneous description of the September Action.

On Saturday, 12 September, a decree from the ghetto administration, signed by Biebow, was posted in the ghetto, announcing that on the eleventh the action was concluded and that starting from the fourteenth all workshops and offices must be reopened and everyone must punctually show up for work, if they wanted to avoid "the most far-reaching unpleasantnesses." Biebow was apparently not sure whether the working masses, of whom it was rare for anyone not to have lost one or more of their nearest and dearest, would once again go to work for the Germans. He called on the workers to work diligently, in order to hasten the production that had been halted due to the "restbreak" (doc. no. 103).[121]

On the same day, Rumkowski announced that the ban on going about in the streets was withdrawn.[122] The next day, on the thirteenth, he announced the opening of the public kitchens, promising an improvement of the provisioning situation of the ghetto. He called on the population to turn in the food cards of the deportees, and he ordered building administrators and janitors to lock up their residences in order to protect them against theft and damage.[123] The final sentence of the announcement should be understood in connection with Greiser's secret decrees of 18 March and 1 May 1942, that the property of the deported Jews of Wartheland become the "legal" possession of the ghetto administration[124] and it was required therefore to see that this "inheritance" should remain whole and undamaged.

The summons to turn in the food cards of the deportees was repeated by Rumkowski in his announcement of 17 September.[125]

The September Action was the greatest shock that the ghetto had endured until then. There was almost no family that did not have to mourn a child or parents. Entire families were torn out by the roots. For long months people in the ghetto lived under the traumatic aftershock of that mass murder.

The Final Liquidation of the Ghetto
(June–August 1944)

After the bloody *Shpere,* the ghetto had a period of relative calm lasting almost two years. The situation more or less stabilized as the ghetto industry expanded mightily. Over four-fifths of the ghetto population remaining after September 1942 worked. In reality, the ghetto was transformed into a giant labor camp, only with a more moderate regime. The hunger situation in the ghetto also improved. People began to believe that things would stay this way until the end of the war.

Starting from the middle of 1943, the further existence of the Łódź Ghetto became the object of a behind-the-scenes struggle between Himmler and his *Wirtschaftsverwaltungshauptamt* (WVHA)[126] on one side, and the *Wehrmacht,* supported by *Statthalter* Greiser and the ghetto administration, on the other side. Odilo Globocnik, the Higher SS and Police Leader in Lublin District and chief of the so-called Reinhard Action in the Generalgouvernement, was very eager to take over the human and industrial potential of the Łódź Ghetto, to transfer the people and machinery into the Lublin region and integrate them into his huge SS camp combination.

In his letter to Rudolf Brandt, the chief of Himmler's personal staff, dated 21 June 1943, Globocnik writes that since a discussion was still going on about the fate of the Łódź Ghetto, he proposes to transfer skilled workers and machinery, as well as all of the war production, away from there into the concentration camps in the Lublin region that would be expanded for that purpose.[127] It would thereby be possible to liquidate the Łódź Ghetto, of whose 78,000[128] inhabitants only a fraction is employed in war production. He further complains that, in order to avoid an "outsettlement," the Łódź Ghetto has lately become overloaded (*vollgepackt*) with orders, which could be transferred to Lublin and thereby produce a production standstill in the ghetto.[129] To ease Globocnik's task, Himmler had already issued a decree on 11 June 1943 to transform the Łódź Ghetto into a concentration camp.[130]

In the first days of September 1943, a meeting was held in which the details of converting the ghetto into a concentration camp were discussed. Participating were Biebow, representatives of the City Administration and *Regierungspräsident,* and Kaltenbrunner's representative, Eichmann. Among other things, it was decided to deport all children, the elderly, and the sick as incapable of work.[131] But Himmler and Globocnik encountered opposition from the *Wehrmacht*'s Weapons Inspectorate (*Rüstungskommando*) and the Ministry for Armament and War Production, which did not want to release from their influence such an important center of supply for the *Wehrmacht*.[132]

In May, June, and July, a large number of commissions visited the ghetto from the army's *Rüstungskommando,* the *Oberbekleidungsamt* (Central Clothing Office), and the *Statthalter* in Poznań. Under the leadership of Gestapo chief Dr. Bradfisch and Biebow, they toured the ghetto workshops and collected statistical data about production. But the SS did not want to let such a juicy prize out of their hands. On 3 December 1943, Himmler again issued a secret order to Pohl, chief of the WVHA, to turn the ghetto into a concentration camp that would thereby come under Pohl's jurisdiction. Around the middle of December 1943, there came to Łódź Adolf Eichmann, the official over Jewish affairs in the *Reichssicherheitshauptamt* (RSHA), and Dr. Max Horn, chief of the SS's fictive corporation *Ostindustrie GbmH* (OSTI), an extension of WVHA. After inspection of the ghetto workshops, a conference with the leading figures of the Łódź organs of authority considered all the details involved in the transfer of the Łódź Ghetto into the domain of the SS as a concentration camp, and the necessity to reduce the ghetto substantially by deporting women, children, the sick, and elderly.[133] The SS officials were so certain that the Łódź Ghetto was falling into their hands that Horn ordered shipment into the ghetto of the machinery and equipment of a liquidated OSTI metal factory in Lublin, and ten people went from the Łódź Ghetto to collect the machinery.[134]

Horn came to Łódź in January 1944 in order to become personally familiar with the production possibilities of the Łódź Ghetto. In his very detailed report to Pohl of 24 January 1944, based on a prior report that he had compiled together with Eichmann, Horn placed the entire matter of taking over the ghetto through OSTI under a question mark. He asserted, among other things, that the productivity was very low due to the poor local working conditions and the lack of supervision by the Aryan factory management, and that the alleged profits that the ghetto administration showed were actually disguised losses. Takeover of the ghetto by OSTI could occur only under a series of conditions: the ghetto must be turned into a concentration camp. Management functions must be carried out by a qualified staff, sent in by OSTI, with a supplement of 200 German *Kapos* from German concentration camps. Finally, an additional loan must be obtained from private or government sources in the amount of 20 million RM.

Today, it is difficult to determine whether Horn's assertion that the production in the Łódź Ghetto was making no profit was objectively correct, or whether this was a shopkeeper's trick of minimizing the value of the item that one really wants to buy.[135]

But the SS made the calculation without the proprietor. Albert Speer, the Minister for Armaments and War Production, sent into the ghetto a series of commissions from the *Oberkommando der Wehrmacht* (OKW, Armed Forces High Command). In addition, it seems that Biebow went to Berlin in order to intervene personally on behalf of the status quo.[136]

The SS nevertheless did not want to resign from the opportunity to exploit for its own interests the slave labor and production of the Łódź Jews. The SS labor camps in the Lublin region alone employed 45,000 Jews. Two representatives from the WVHA's Office Group W (*Wirtschaftliche Unternehmungen,* Economic Enterprises), its chief, Hans Bayer, and Dr. Leo Volk, started negotiations with Greiser's representatives (*Oberregierungsrat* Reichschauer and Heusler). Greiser's representatives asked for recompense in the amount of 18–20 million marks, to which the SS negotiators cynically replied that actually the entire ghetto belonged to the Reich and if it came to payment, then pay the state treasury. They also refused to respond to the question of how long this concentration camp could exist within the city's boundaries. The discussion concluded with a proposal by Pohl's representatives, that WVHA would pay Greiser a certain sum for use of the machinery and the buildings and also a part of the revenues from the camp, subject to Himmler's agreement to this.[137]

In order to expedite the matter, Pohl himself with his juridical advisor Volk came to Łódź in February 1944.[138] In the same month, Himmler personally came to Poznań and arrived at the following agreement between him and Greiser:

a) The ghetto population would be reduced to a minimum and only as many Jews would remain as were unconditionally needed for the war production.

b) The ghetto would remain as a central ghetto (*Gaugetto*) of the province.

c) The reduction of the ghetto would be carried out by the *Sonder-kommando* of *SS-Hauptsturmführer* Bothmann, which was previously active in Wartheland (as *Sonderkommando Kulmhof,* Chełmno).[139] Himmler was to arrange to recall Bothmann and his unit, who were now in Croatia, and again place him at Greiser's disposition.

d) The use and sale of the ghetto's moveable property was in Greiser's domain.

e) After deportation of the Jews and dissolution of the ghetto, the entire ghetto terrain would revert to the city.[140]

Even though the ghetto was hermetically sealed, the ghetto leaders knew something about these negotiations. In the *Chronicle,* 14 February 1944, we read: "For a long time, people have been saying that the ghetto is supposed to leave the competence of the mayor and go under the jurisdiction of the SS. These rumors, it appears, are becoming a reality, and the ghetto, which is a component of the armaments industry sector will, it seems, be taken over by the so-called *Ostindustrie,* a quasi-state enterprise. The SS officer Dr. Horn is mentioned as a representative of OSTI."[141]

Under the date of 23 February, however, the *Chronicle* notes, "It is already certain that the negotiations among the Ostindustrie and the mayor, Gestapo, *Gauleiter,* and *Reichsstatthalter* (Greiser) produced no result—the ghetto remains with the previous management, as before."[142]

At the start of May 1944, it had been decided in the RSHA that the ghetto must finally be liquidated. We learn of this from a note of 5 May compiled in the Foreign Ministry on the basis of a report from the RSHA, where the topic is allowing the emigration of 5,000 Jewish children from German-occupied territory. The note asserts that such a number of children are available only in the Łódź Ghetto, "which will, however, soon cease to exist, according to a directive by Himmler."[143]

The circumstances radically changed in June 1944, as the Germans' military situation became ever more dangerous. The Soviet armies began their victorious offensive on the central front, and on 6 June, the Allied forces landed in Normandy. Himmler did indeed order the liquidation of the ghetto in the first half of June. The German Army's Weapons Inspectorate still sought to delay the deadline for the liquidation, while Speer also interceded. On 9 June, apparently fearing that a swift offensive by the Red Army could again put to naught the sacred task of annihilating the remnant of Łódź Jews, Greiser notified Himmler about these interventions. Greiser wrote to him that the Weapons Inspectorate had taken steps against his decree and that Speer had ordered his plenipotentiary to gather statistics about the state of employment and production of the individual enterprises in order to present them to the

Führer. Simultaneously, Greiser related that he had already completed all preparations for the "evacuation." In his reply to Greiser of 10 June, Himmler ordered him to go on with the liquidation of the ghetto.[144]

Frequent visits by various commissions naturally provoked fear in the ghetto. During only the first two months of 1944, the Łódź Ghetto had eleven such visits. The nervous mood further intensified when people learned at the start of January that the authorities were asking Rumkowski for a statistical list of the ghetto population by ages, gender, and employment. For this purpose, Rumkowski was summoned to the Gestapo and held for a full twenty-four hours (on 3 and 4 January). The managers of the factory divisions received a request from the Statistical Office to provide lists by ages and gender of those employed.

Rumkowski's announcement of 9 February 1944 came as a very familiar prelude to the approaching deportations. In it, he admonished the ghetto population not to take in strangers or relatives who were not registered in the relevant buildings.[145] On 12 February Rumkowski officially announced that 1,500 workers must leave the ghetto and that all persons who at one time reported for the medical examination by the physicians' commission must gather on 13 February in the Central Prison. A medical commission would examine the candidates, and those whose incapacity for work would be confirmed by the commission would be released. Failure to obey this order would be punished with confiscation of food cards from the entire family, with halting the issuance of dinners in the factories, and so on. At this occasion, Rumkowski reiterated the warning not to allow unregistered persons to spend the night in one's home (doc. no. 104).[146]

Since the request did not produce the desired results, on 18 February Rumkowski ordered a ban on going out into the street on Sunday the twentieth. All offices, work sites, and factories were to be closed on that day, aside from the two hospitals, two pharmacies, and the first aid service. All those employed (except children and old folk) would receive their identification forms at their workplaces, and they must also bring their dinner cards with them on the day of this *Shpere.* During the ban, all males (*mansparshoynen*) who could not identify themselves with the mentioned documents would be arrested. The closed cellars and attics must be opened at the demand of the Order Service (doc. no. 105).[147]

Sunday, 20 February, reminded the ghetto of the tragic days of the September *Shpere,* with the difference that only Jewish police were seen on the streets and there was no shooting. The result of the searches was negligible. In all, seventy persons among those designated to be sent away were caught. In addition, 400 people were arrested who had previously been rejected by the medical commission. The number of candidates for departure increased after this to 1,240 persons, including the sick and the weak. The German authorities, who until now had not publicly mixed into the "recruitment" campaign, conceded that the contingent could be filled out with women, and the Order Service immediately began to arrest women whose husbands, designated for departure, had not presented themselves.[148]

But all this did not help. The ghetto was now passively resisting to a greater extent than during previous deportations. People hid wherever possible. On 3 March, Rumkowski addressed a "final" warning to those in hiding, threatening that they would be caught anyway when they reported for food cards (as their old cards were annulled), and aside from this, they would be forced to reveal the persons with whom they found shelter and thus subject their benefactors to a serious penalty.[149]

The severe hunger and state of permanent terror compelled those who were resigned and desperate to leave their hiding places and report to the Central Prison. Starvation even created a peculiar trade in people. For two loaves of bread and 1 kilo of sugar, a substitute could be bought (they were called "Negroes" in the ghetto). And there were those who, for the price of being able to eat their fill for a single day, were induced to turn themselves over to Nazi hands for an undetermined fate, perhaps for death. So terrible was the hunger and so great the despair.[150]

Meanwhile, Biebow set himself to liquidation of the ghetto's Jewish administration through a large reduction of its office staff. He visited different offices and factory divisions, recording the names of the employees, not making any difference between higher and lower officials, personally removing them from their posts and sending them to physical work in the factories, or to build barracks in Radogoszcz, where cement plates (*plitn*) were produced for reconstruction of the bombed areas of Germany. A major reduction occurred in the Provisioning Office, as provisioning matters were already then in the hands of the German ghetto administration, and among personnel of the kitchens. The forty-nine public kitchens that employed 2,623 employees in March 1944 lost 677 workers. The Vocation and Control Commission (see chapter 4) was completely liquidated.

Biebow sent even high officials to labor in Radogoszcz, including judges and the director of the ghetto archive. They did not really need as many workers as Biebow sent there. The majority of those sent were unaccustomed to heavy physical labor (since they had been office workers for years) and many of them became ill due to the crowding and hunger. Some of the dismissed officials were also supposed to fill out the contingent of 1,500 persons designated for departure.[151]

Since the action to send out the 1,500 workers was dragging on, Mordecai Kliger, chief of the Jewish *Sonderkommando* ghetto police unit, took over the "recruitment effort" by order of the Gestapo. Kliger first dissolved the qualification commission that had been named by Rumkowski, and then the *Sonderkommando* energetically set to work. On the first of March, the designated contingent was increased to 1,600 and in the first ten days of March (on the third and tenth) two transports departed, one with 750 persons and the other with 850. They were sent to the ammunition factories in Skarżysko and Częstochowa (Radom district). In contrast to the previous transports in 1942, the treatment of those being sent out by the German police was correct. A physician from Prague even accompanied the transport. They took along a lot of baggage.

In the ghetto, naturally, the purpose of the trip was unknown. A rumor circulated that the Gestapo officer had supposedly told one of the workers that they were going to Częstochowa.[152]

The ghetto had its brief and final respite until June. A certain relaxation occurred. The behind-the-scenes game going on between Himmler and the *Wehrmacht* concerning the ghetto's fate had slowed the process of its liquidation.

Between the second half of March and the start of May, very small transports were sent out from the ghetto: On 16 March, 60 persons, a remnant from the Central Prison after the 10 March deportation, were sent away, as were about 200 more from May until the start of June. Rumkowski continued to call on the ghetto public to register voluntarily for departure.[153] It appears that he was being constantly pressured in that direction.

The ghetto's death warrant was finally signed on 15 June (after Himmler's telegram to Greiser of the tenth). On that day, a Gestapo commission led by its chief, Dr. Bradfisch, arrived in the ghetto and informed Rumkowski that groups of workers must be sent out to Germany in order to clear ruins caused by bombings. Meanwhile, 500 persons were needed and later it would be necessary to send 3,000 weekly.[154]

The very next morning, a new announcement by Rumkowski appeared. In order to motivate the stubborn public to obey, this time he attempted to trick them with "concessions" and rewards. First, whole families could travel together with their working-age children. Second, those reporting voluntarily would receive a set of clothing, shoes, and underwear and be able to take along 15 kilos of baggage. They would be permitted to write letters, and, finally, they would be able to pick up their food allotments without waiting in line (doc. no. 106).[155] Rumkowski also saw to it that the candidates for Chełmno or Auschwitz should be able to sell their last few possessions to his purchase points at prices determined by expert appraisers.[156]

According to a record made by Rumkowski's secretary on the basis of instructions from the Gestapo, every Monday, Wednesday, and Friday transports were to depart with 1,000 persons in each. The transports were numbered with Roman numerals; each person received a number, which was also to be on his baggage. The baggage had to include a small pillow and a blanket, while food for two to three days had to be taken along. A transport manager, taking on ten persons to help, was to be named for each transport. A physician or *feldsher* (barber-surgeon) and two or three health orderlies (*sanitarn*) were to be added to each transport. The families of the doctors and medical personnel must also go along.[157]

In order to reinforce the illusion that they were going to work, Biebow directed the Central Purchasing Office to pay for the household goods sold in German marks, "so that the money can be used in the German cities where they are going" and for this purpose allocated a half million RM. Each of those being sent out received 10 RM.[158]

While the ordained deportation had already deeply affected the productive, working element in the ghetto, the managers of the workshops were confronted with a serious and responsible task: to compile lists of their workers to be sent out. They held a conference about this, where several of the division managers declared that they would not bear the responsibility for what was happening in the ghetto. There were also various other suggestions. Finally, after a heated discussion, it was decided to form "an inter-divisional commission" of seven persons, to rule on who was to be sent out. The commission would compile lists to be sent to the Outsettlement Commission operating at the Central Prison. Certain criteria for qualifying to be sent out were also adopted: the lists were not to include people older than sixty or younger than fifteen; nor parents of children under age five; and minors were to be sent together with their entire family.[159] To consider appeals, a commission was formed of three members (the director of the Central Factories [*Resortn*] Bureau, the ghetto court chairman, and the director of the wood division in the ghetto).

A very real trade in people was played out behind the scenes of the "inter-factory commission." The factory managers had a silent agreement among themselves to do one another favors: "If you'll strike from your list a protégé of mine, I'll strike yours." Various bosses and commissioners thereby received an opportunity to get even with workers who had offended them in some way.[160]

Putting together the transports came with ever more difficulty. The total of 1,000 persons in each transport was never achieved. On 26 May 1944, Y. Hiler recorded in his diary: "They took people from their beds . . . including some who had weeks earlier ransomed themselves by providing another person."[161]

On 12 July, the ghetto *Chronicle* noted: "The situation is becoming ever more tense, since the [deportation] commission cannot deliver the required human material. The chairman therefore had to decide to adopt serious measures. People are forcibly gathered during night-raids. The units of the Order Service received lists, haul people from their beds, concentrate them in the precincts, and deliver them in the morning to the Central Prison."[162] Raids in the streets took place in broad daylight: "A street is closed and [the Order Service men] drive all the people that they came across to a designated place. There they had to identify themselves. The formalities are only completed in the precincts and this procedure takes until the late hours in the evening. The result is, however, negligible. Those actually in danger were already warned in time and hid out during the day, too."

The always careful *Chronicle* could not restrain itself here and adds: "A shameful and shocking image. Jews are hunting Jews as if after wild beasts. A true Jew-hunt, organized by Jews themselves." It appears that, in order to moderate the sharp accusation somewhat, it apologetically adds, "What should one do, there is no other way, the one who is summoned must present himself."[163]

For their participation in the preparation of the deportations, the Jewish police received a special daily allocation of products: 250 grams of bread, 3 soups, 30 grams of fat, and 50 grams of sausage.

The hunger and constant fear of being caught drove many Jews to turn themselves in for deportation. They thought that it could not be worse than it was in the ghetto. Many were soothed since the deportation summonses indicated that, in contrast to the prior deportations, people were traveling for work. Moreover, the fact that when one received a summons, the entire family went along, also increased the number of "voluntary" candidates.[164]

When the ghetto was threatened by a new deportation, two prominent representatives of the remaining Prague exiles, Dr. Oskar Singer and Dr. Karl Bondi, began an effort to rescue the group of intellectuals among the remnants of Western European Jews. It is told in the ghetto *Chronicle* that an understanding was reached about this with the commandant of the Jewish *Sonderkommando*. He played an important role during the final "outsettlement action" in the ghetto, and they found in him sympathy for this matter. Also helping was the head of the Department for the Resettled (*optayl far ayngezidlte*), attorney Henryk Neftalin, in whose records departments a group of intellectuals and academics from the Reich and Protectorate were employed. A list was compiled of about seventy favored people (*protezhirte*) who were supposed to be shielded from the danger of being sent out from the ghetto. At a special gathering with the seventy candidates, Rumkowski dealt with each case individually and accepted the presented list with but one exception (a woman who had concealed the fact that she had already received a summons to report).[165]

Earlier, on 17 June, a three-member delegation (Sh. Rozenshtayn, Y. Shpigel, and J. Zelkowicz) appealed in a letter to attorney Neftalin in behalf of the family of local writers and artists (at the time it still numbered, together with the "settlers" from Western Europe, over seventy persons), asking him "to take into protection our little literary family and shield it from further wandering, so that it can calmly do its work." Neftalin had evinced a warm attitude to the Jewish writers and artists in the ghetto and aided them in a time of need. He lobbied Rumkowski on behalf of the local writers group, as its letter of 17 July testifies, thanking him "for the great understanding that you have shown for our group, the remnant of the Jewish literature in former Poland." It is, however, not clear whether the review of 12 July also included the local writers and artists (the number seventy would speak for such an assumption), or whether their case was handled through Rumkowski in another fashion.[166]

In regard to the remnants from the West, aside from this group of intellectuals, no special question of Western European Jews existed. Those who were left in the ghetto after all the previous deportations were in their overwhelming majority integrated into the work divisions and shared with the ghetto residents their common fate.

About the mood that reigned among the various groups of Western European Jews during this final deportation, we read in a contemporaneous document:

> The mood this time is entirely not so panicked, as during the other [previous] actions, and this is due to many causes: (1) The [Western] settlers are accustomed to following the directions of the organs of power. They do not possess that vitality, conditioned by the environment, that is activated as soon as a danger approaches. (2) They do not have the experience and the connections to be able to protect themselves against the Jewish Order Service, as is the case among the local residents. (3) They are broken in a greater measure than the locals and are also more fatalistically inclined. (4) The still remaining Reichsdeutsche Jews live with the idea that they are finally going home. They still consider the ghetto as a greater evil than a collective camp life on German soil; and lastly, they believe that they will be able, in the event that the war ends, to cope more easily on home soil than in the ghetto.[167]

In this deportation, there was generally no discrimination regarding the remnants of Western European Jews. Just the opposite, the group of academics and intellectuals was placed in a privileged situation. Nevertheless, there were also cases when certain factory managers, who compiled the lists of candidates for deportation, placed on those lists all their "foreign" workers (after three years of being in the ghetto, they were still considered foreign).[168]

What was the ratio of the Western European exiles caught up in the deportation relative to the veteran ghetto residents? We have statistics only in regard to four transports, and they show that their percentage participation was higher than it would have been according to their number. Thus, for example, some 2,976 persons (1,094 men and 1,882 women) were sent away with the four transports that departed between 23 and 30 June. Among them were 362 Western European Jews (130 men and 232 women). This amounts to 12.1 percent of those deported, while at the time they numbered only something more than 6 percent of the total ghetto population (about 5,000 out of 76,400). It is possible that the proportion was different in the other six transports.

The first transport departed on 23 June and numbered a total of 560 persons; the second, on 26 June, with 912 people; the third on 28 June, with 799 people; the fourth on 30 June, with 700 people. The six transports (from the fifth to the tenth) dispatched from 3 to 14 July each numbered 700 souls. In the ten transports sent off by 15 July, a total of 7,196 people left, an average of 720 people per transport.[169] All the transports were accompanied by physicians from Western Europe, who had remained in the ghetto after the May deportation of the Western European Jews.

The deportation was suddenly halted on 15 July. An order came from the Gestapo to release the Jews not yet sent out. Rumkowski crisscrossed the ghetto in his horse-drawn droshky and told everyone the good news. The joy was boundless. People kissed and cried for joy. They began to believe that no more deportations would take place. The next day, Rumkowski called together all the managers of the factories and offices and read to them his program for reorganizing the ghetto industry: several divisions were to be liquidated, others to be merged, to reduce by 75 percent the administrative staffing, and so on.[170]

From the speech that Rumkowski delivered before the factory managers, one could infer that the danger had, at least temporarily, passed and that the 68,700 Jews remaining in the ghetto after 15 July could and should continue to work calmly, with even greater productivity than before. Rumkowski also ordered the unblocking of the food cards of those who had not reported. They were automatically entitled to collect all their products for the whole period of time.[171]

One can only guess about the reason for the sudden interruption in the deportation. Perhaps it occurred thanks to the intervention of the *Wehrmacht*'s Weaponry Inspectorate or of Speer's ministry, or of both together. It is symptomatic that during the two-week interruption in the action, the tailoring shops continually received goods for military projects, the furrier factory also received a large shipment of furs for processing, and the carpentry shops were fully employed in producing ammunition boxes. On 27 July, the ghetto *Chronicle* noted a visit in the ghetto by the *Rüstungskommando* (Armament and War Production Authority) from Berlin.[172]

The illusions, however, quickly melted away. On 17 July, Biebow directed the chief of the Records Department, at the order of the Gestapo, to compile a statistical overview of the ghetto population, according to gender, age, and capability for work.[173] The ghetto elite again declared that there was no cause for alarm.

On 21 July an announcement from Rumkowski was made public: all who were designated for departure and had already sold their household goods could ask for them back from the buyers, repaying the same sum or the quantity of products that they received. Refusal by the buyer needed to be reported at the Order Service's first precinct.[174] Rumkowski constantly inspected the ghetto workshops and held conferences with the leading personnel about reorganization. On 21 July, he announced issuance of the new coins ("hard money") worth 20 ghetto marks apiece.[175]

This could all be interpreted in the ghetto as signs of "stabilization." But in the sorely tested ghetto, which from bitter experience knew the dangerous significance of statistical compilations for the Gestapo, Biebow's request provoked a panic. People were again talking about a further deportation from the ghetto. Nor was Biebow's visit on 18 July to the commandant of the Jewish *Sonderkommando* and the long conversation with him capable of calming the mood.

Other signs indicated that the intermission signified only a pause before the liquidation of the ghetto.

On 19 July, the ghetto *Chronicle* noted that four pharmacies were ordered to compile an inventory of their stocks. Moreover, the ghetto was again reduced: cut from it was an area that included a number of housing blocks on Drewnowska, Stodolniana, and Podrzeczna Streets, taken over by the *Abbruchstelle* (Demolition Bureau) for demolition. In a single day, nearly 1,000 people lost the roof over their heads. On 26 July, the Criminal Police, with the aid of 200 Jewish policemen, searched the area of the cemetery in Marysin, probably in order to determine whether there were any secret hiding places and exits to the Aryan side there. A series of German firms, like for example one in Mannheim that had previously sent into the ghetto special machines for the corset factory (see chapter 4), now requested the Gettoverwaltung to return the equipment as well as the unfinished goods. The underwear and clothing division, the shoemakers division, and others also received an order from the ghetto administration to place at its disposal machinery sent into the ghetto.[176] The homework was halted at a series of workshops, like rugs, caps, and knitting. Naturally, the workshops from which the foreign machinery was removed also had to close, or in the best case sharply reduce their production. The Central Factories Bureau was moved, at Biebow's request, from the "neutral" area on Bałuty Marketplace into the ghetto, leaving behind only the chief and his secretary. The ghetto *Chronicle* explains these orders as intended to limit contact with Aryans to a minimum.[177]

All these signs, which did not bode any good, forged a mood in the ghetto of despair and helplessness, and the workers in the factories were less motivated to toil away.[178] Rumkowski on 28 July halted the disbursement of relief grants to the small number of persons who still benefited from them, as well as the issuing of loans. In this way, he wanted to compel even more to work.

On the other hand, all signs indicated that the war front was nearing Łódź. On Zgierska and Aleksandrowska Streets (the "Aryan" streets that cut through the ghetto) in the final days of July, people could observe an unceasing movement of military personnel and civilians toward the West.[179] Packing in the city had also already started. The carpentry division received an order to prepare boxes for the officials of the ghetto administration.[180] On 25 July, a total blackout was introduced and the air raid alarms repeatedly sounded ever more frequently. The ghetto had already been prepared earlier, in the first ten days of June, for air raid alarms. It was ordered that the fencing at the garden plots be removed and alarm bells installed.[181] If one put his ear to the ground, one could already hear reverberations from the explosions of artillery.[182] The Russian army was near Warsaw on 31 July 1944.

The ghetto even lived to see a squadron of Allied aircraft flying from East to West. To the disappointment of the ghetto inhabitants, the aircraft did not drop any bombs on the city.[183]

From the secret radio service that functioned in the ghetto the entire time (see below) and from reading between the lines of the *Litzmannstadter Zeitung* smuggled into the ghetto, people were precisely informed about the situation at the fronts.[184]

With an understandable caution, the mood in the ghetto was touched upon in the ghetto *Chronicle* in connection with the radical change of the strategic situation of Nazi Germany in July 1944. Under the date of 22 July, we find the following lines: "In the present situation, the Chronicler can by no means ignore the events that affect the entire world, and that naturally cannot remain without an influence on the ghetto. From here and there, newspapers and news do penetrate into the ghetto. The times are indubitably critical and the ghetto inhabitants go to meet the arriving hour with mixed feelings. All thoughts, considerations, hopes and fears are becoming forcused on one question: Will we be left alone?" And from 23 July the following: "A rosy mood reigns in the ghetto. All are full of hope for an immediate end of the war. But everybody is staying calm and thus will it hopefully also remain" (doc. no. 107).[185]

As Y. Hiler reports, the guards at the fence made such remarks: It's coming to an end; Jews will be freed, and they (German guards) will also go back home.[186]

These hopes dissolved a week later. On 2 August there appeared on the ghetto walls an announcement from Rumkowski: according to a decree by the mayor, the ghetto must be transferred to somewhere else (the "place" was, of course, not stated). All workshop and factory workers would leave the ghetto together with their families in closed units. The first transport was to depart on 3 August; 5,000 persons must report daily, while baggage up to 20 kilos can be taken along. The first transport was to include the workers of tailor workshops nos. 1 and 2 on Łagiewnicka Street. They were to present themselves on 3 August, at 7 A.M. in the barracks at the Radogoszcz train station.[187]

The results of this request were virtually nil. Almost none of the mentioned tailors reported. Educated by previous bitter experience with Nazi promises, people did not believe that, just when the fate of Nazi Germany was being decided on the fronts, the regime would have no other concern than transferring an entire ghetto with over 68,500 people, among them women, children, and the sick.

The first transport that, according to the plan, was supposed to leave on the morning of 3 August did not materialize. Rumkowski attempted to convince the stubborn Łódź tailors to leave the ghetto voluntarily and the same day called on all workers to come to a meeting, where he would explain what evacuation meant for the ghetto.[188]

What the head of the Łódź Ghetto said to his hungry and desperate subjects has not been preserved in the documentation of the Łódź Ghetto. It is, however, easy to surmise. Rumkowski remained loyal to the bitter end. Even at the final stage of the liquidation of the Łódź Ghetto, he loyally and diligently fulfilled the task that was placed upon him: to trick the Łódź Jews into the trap that the Gestapo set for them. In that fatal month of August, Rumkowski was tireless. From 2 until 24 August, he himself, or together with the ghetto administration and instructors and supervisors from the tailoring workshops, issued twenty-six appeals and warnings in which he attempted to influence Łódź Jews, with both carrot and stick, to report voluntarily to the rail wagons that were to take them to Auschwitz. There were days when he issued two and even more posted announcements. On 3 August, Y. Hiler recorded: "The fourth announcement today from Rumkowski has already appeared on the streets."[189] The written agitation to leave the ghetto was not enough for him, so he appeared in closed locales and on the public ghetto square with speeches. On the sixth, in his public speech on the firefighters' square, he repeated his old song: he did not want to allow "the Germans to be the ones who take people in the ghetto," and he boasted that he had seen to it that he alone would deliver the people. Thanks to his intervention, the Jews who had been caught at the Green Market that same day and were already waiting in the rail cars for departure were freed.[190]

On 7 August, Rumkowski appeared together with Biebow at a large gathering of the tailors, thereby giving a Jewish sanction to Biebow's mendacious and hypocritical speech before those who had to be tricked to Auschwitz. As if fearing that the exhausted ghetto Jews might sometime cease to produce with their last sweat, he called on the workers, whose factories had not yet been designated for deportation, to continue on with their work until their deadline would be announced.[191]

But none of this helped. People clung stubbornly to the last that remained—a roof over one's head and bedding for one's exhausted body. The reaction of the Germans to this stubbornness on the part of the Łódź Jews was not long in coming. Since the tailors of the aforementioned workshops (1 and 2) did not show up for the transport (according to Hiler, instead of the 5,000 that the plan foresaw, a total of 1,500 reported),[192] the mayor (who was simultaneously chief of the Gestapo) posted an announcement on 4 August in German and Yiddish that the food cards of the recalcitrant tailors were immediately blocked and anyone giving shelter or food to one of them would be punished with death (doc. no. 108).[193] The next day Rumkowski came out with an order to the tailors to report together with their families at the Central Prison.[194] On the fifth, a transport of 449 people was wangled together and the tension subsided somewhat. On the same day, Rumkowski also arranged for bread to be given out to the population.

The threat of death by starvation for the tailors and their families did not, however, suffice. Therefore the tactic of applying persuasion was attempted. On 7 August, a summons to leave the ghetto, addressed to tailor workshops nos. 3 and 4 and signed by Rumkowski and Biebow, expressed the conviction that after hearing out Biebow's speeches the tailors of factories 1 and 2 would also join in the transport.[195]

Biebow's speech, delivered that day in two tailor workshops on Młynarska and Jakuba Streets,[196] is so typical for the Nazi system of cynical and refined trickery, which was the chief method in their annihilation strategy toward the Jewish population, that we bring from it (see doc. no. 109) a large excerpt according to the text that has survived in the YIVO Archive.[197]

Biebow traveled about across the ghetto and spoke in various factories. In the metal works on 3 August, as Hiler states, he attempted to threaten the Łódź Jews with Soviet vengeance: "Do not assume that when the Russians arrive that you will be left here. They will send you away because for four and a half years you have worked for the German government." Here, too, he assured that "a hair will not fall from your head, I'm going with you. . . . Four and a half years I have been together with you and never did anything bad to you."[198] In one of his speeches, Biebow even affirmed that his only intention was to save the ghetto Jews, that "after the war, that we shall win, I will bring [you] back into the ghetto."[199]

Even Bradfisch, mayor and chief of the Łódź Gestapo, personally came into the ghetto in order to use pleasantries to influence the stubborn tailors. Among other things, according to Hiler, he promised them that "those who leave will not have it bad, not a hair will fall from their head, he will not employ any weapons and terror against the ghetto Jews. He guaranteed with his head in the event that, heaven forbid, anything will happen to one of us. Just the opposite, he wants to protect the Jews from air attacks, therefore it is better that Jews should go. Tomorrow [4 August] the first and second tailor works are leaving."[200]

Even a spectacle was arranged. Under the date of 6 August, Hiler notes:

> There came German Schupo police with Jewish policemen, who surrounded Yoyne Piltser's Square, where vegetables are given out. There pulled up automobiles with tractors, which packed up the people who had already collected the cabbage, left the cabbage with the sacks on the automobiles, and drove away. In the middle of the road Biebow arrived with Commissioner Fuchs from the 6th police precinct; they halted the automobiles and ordered everyone released. Before they were released, Biebow declared that if he wants, he has a way to compel the workshops to go, only he wants to convince them in a friendly fashion that they must leave. I release you, only go home to your acquaintances and tell them to leave.[201]

In order to raise an audience for the highly placed speakers, people were pulled in off the street, or the same workers were sent from one factory to the other. Nevertheless, both Bradfisch's gentle talk and Biebow's threats (the speeches of 3 and 7 August) made no impression on listeners who had lived since July with the well-founded hope for a speedy liberation and knew from bitter experience the trickery and inhumanity of the Nazis. "All the ghetto Jews among themselves were sure that a sheep was speaking that only yesterday was a wolf, and therefore nobody has any faith in the pretty talk. Everybody is surprised at why all of a sudden such beautiful words. We are not at all accustomed to hearing words of pleading," notes Hiler.[202] The rail wagons waited empty at the Radogoszcz station for their victims.

Meanwhile, the situation in the ghetto became ever more tense. The circumstance on 4 August can be described as follows: the distribution points and the few private shops were shut tight. Not the least thing was to be had, as money ceased to have any value. There were instances of looting bread from a bread warehouse. The garden plots were abandoned; whoever wanted could pull up the vegetables. The factories were empty; no one wanted to work. The Jewish policemen of the *Sonderkommando* and the Order Service searched with photographs of the tailors from the workshops.[203]

Convinced by the results until now that the workers would not let themselves be deported voluntarily, the Gestapo decided to take the operation into its own hands. On 8 August, various formations of German police marched into the ghetto and together with the Jewish policemen surrounded the entire residential area of Łagiewnicka, Zawisza, Brzezińska, and Młynarska Streets. They sealed off each entry to the buildings from which they pulled the people and transported them on wagons, by trolley or on foot directly to the train, where the long-ready railcars were already waiting. Again the ghetto recalled the nightmarish September days of 1942. Indeed, the public called the action of 8 August a "*Shpere*."[204]

On the same day, Rumkowski issued "a final warning" to the managers, workers, and office employees of eight listed tailoring workshops, who were to report voluntarily on the ninth in the morning at the Central Prison, so as to avoid further repetition of the day's events.[205] This method of forcible "evacuation" became a daily phenomenon and was applied until the end.

The next day, the ninth, Rumkowski also shifted from appeals to compulsion. In his poster of the day, he announced that starting from the tenth all workshops were being closed. At each worksite no more than ten workers could remain to pack up the goods and the inventory of machinery. All inhabitants of the western part of the ghetto—an area that included the right side of Zgierska from Podrzeczna, Drewnowska, Lutomierska, and Limanowskiego until Dolna and Piwna Streets—must move into the eastern part. No further food allocations would be issued in the western sector any more (doc. no. 110).[206] This decree put the residents of that excised ghetto region in a tragic state, for they lost the roof over their heads and the possibility of obtaining the meager food rations. For the majority of them, no other way out remained but for them to report to the Central Prison or the other collection point, in the former Culture House, that was opened on 10 August.[207]

A frightful panic broke out in the western part of the ghetto in the wake of Rumkowski's decree. People began to run, carrying a few necessary things, rushing to cross the pedestrian bridges where there was terrible congestion. They stood for hours with their baggage before they could make it over the high steps to the still "secure" eastern area. In the darkness, with the only light coming from the moon, multitudes stretched out like shadows across the ghetto streets. In the crowding, people fainted and were trampled.[208] On the fourteenth, the western ghetto region was entirely sealed. There remained only a few workers and Order Servicemen assigned to those workshops.[209]

Almost every day, Rumkowski's new calls appeared for the workers of different branches of the ghetto industry to report with their families to the "voluntary transports": on the eleventh and fourteenth, he addressed posters to the leather and saddlers' factories; also on the fourteenth to the underwear and clothing workshops; and on the twentieth to the remaining workers of the small appliances department, electricians, mechanics, and so on.[210]

On 13 August, Rumkowski came out with a fatherly "piece of advice" to the entire ghetto population to report voluntarily to the transports in order to avoid coercive measures. On the fifteenth, he posted an appeal that starts in the Yiddish text with the words: "Jews of the ghetto, come to your senses!" (*Yidn fun geto bazint zikh!*). He appealed for them to report to the transport, even throughout the night (accordingly, he canceled the curfew), in order to have the privilege of leaving the ghetto with baggage and together with their families[211] (doc. no. 111). All these constantly repeated demands, reminders, and pieces of advice had a negligible effect. People hid and they tried to resist against the hunger war that the German ghetto administration was conducting against these "disobedient Jews." An effort was made among the bakery workers to transfer their "bread consumption" for those whose food cards were blocked. The bakery workers had a right to a supplementary half kilo of bread daily that they could consume while at their work, aside from their normal ration. People ate vegetation from the virtually abandoned garden allotment plots.[212]

Indeed, the Germans could deliver to the transports only as many Jews as they managed to catch. The rail wagons were leaving half empty.

Rumkowski sought to enlist the political parties that still existed in the ghetto to come to his aid. As Jacob Nirenberg relates, he and another representative of the Bund were summoned to a meeting, apparently on 7 August, to which Rumkowski invited representatives of all the political parties. At this meeting he declared "that the ghetto is being liquidated, but he holds that a tactic of delay must be adopted. This can happen, in his opinion, under one circumstance: if the parties will take upon themselves to agitate and see that each day a minimum of 700–800 people leave. Then he would be able to persuade the Germans that he alone should conduct the action and the Germans should not come into the ghetto themselves to take [people], because then victims will fall and the liquidation will go faster."[213]

During the discussion, the representatives of the Bund spoke out against Rumkowski's proposal and suggested calling on the population to passively resist and hide themselves. Among the Zionists the opinions were divided, and the Communist representative declared that he must consult with his comrades.[214]

On 17 August, the German authorities again amputated a major portion of the ghetto. That day, the Gestapo issued a decree in Yiddish and German immediately designating another part of the ghetto as emptied.[215] The inhabitants of this area must leave their apartments and never return. Anyone found in that *Judenrein* area, as well as in the previously excised western part of the ghetto, would be punished with death. Exceptions applied to workers assigned to the factories and also for the hospital.[216]

Simultaneously, there also appeared an order from Rumkowski to the ghetto population to report all night long for the next day's transport. To add motivation, he promised that those who reported would be fed immediately at the collection point.[217]

Rumkowski harnessed the workers themselves into his agitation for leaving. On 19 August, there appeared on the ghetto walls an announcement signed by Rumkowski, two factory instructors, and by a supervisor from three clothing workshops, calling on all tailors still left in the ghetto to present themselves with their families and their baggage by 12 o'clock midnight to a general tailor transport. If not, they would be arrested at home or in the street and be mercilessly deported. This call also promised the starving tailors that they would be fed immediately when they reported.

The next day, 20 August, this warning was repeated and we again find, in addition to Rumkowski's signature, the signatures of three instructors, one supervisor, and two workers from six clothing factories.[218]

The area of the ghetto was again reduced on 22 August.[219] The Gestapo's decree that was posted a day later in Yiddish and German directed all the inhabitants of the emptied ghetto area to leave their apartments by 7 A.M. on the morning of the twenty-fifth. Anyone found in the excised area after that deadline would be punished with death (doc. no. 112).[220]

The remaining part of the ghetto where Jews were still allowed to stay included a small area, whose boundaries on the western side extended from the corner of Brzezińska-Łagiewnicka to the corner of Łagiewnicka-Dworska; in the east—from the corner of Brzezińska-

Marysińska to the corner of Marysińska-Dworska; in the south—from the corner of Łagiewnicka-Dworska to Dworska-Marysińska; and in the north—from the corner of Łagiewnicka-Brzezińska to the corner of Brzezińska-Marysińska.[221]

This ghetto island consisted of four streets with eighty-three houses, among which were located the enterprises with their included workers, two hospitals, the Central Prison, and the 4th Precinct of the Order Service.

After the designated deadlines concerning reduction of the ghetto, police and SS units raided the houses, tearing open doors, and searching in the attics and cellars and in all possible hiding places. Each person found was shot dead on the spot.

On the twenty-ninth, the hospital was cleared as the patients and medical personnel were led out to the transport.[222]

In the final days of August the ghetto became vacant, deadly still. The Germans carried out the deportation in the ghetto only by day. It appears that they were afraid to come into the ghetto at night. In the evenings there was a little movement. People crawled from their hiding places to look for food, to ask after relatives and acquaintances; they wanted to hear some news. They crept into former bakeries, searched in the closets, in the corners of the warehouses, and so on.[223]

For the last time, Rumkowski let people hear from him publicly on 24 August. On that day, he issued a decree concerning turning out the lights in the abandoned apartments and in the closed workshops.[224] He called on the Order Service, the Firefighters Brigade, and the neighbors of the vacated apartments to keep an eye out and unconditionally extinguish the lights; if not, they would be severely punished by the authorities.[225]

These were the final words that Rumkowski had to say to "his" last Łódź Jews, when they expected that any minute they would be sent to Auschwitz.

On the thirtieth, Rumkowski with his entire family also left with the transport of Metal Department Two to Auschwitz.

The deportation of the nearly 70,000 Łódź Jews in August 1944 concluded the final stage in the annihilation of Jewish communities on Polish soil.

In Table 17, we attempt to give an overall summary of the deportations from the Łódź Ghetto.

On 30 August 1944, two small groups of Jews remained in the ghetto. The first consisted of about five hundred laborers concentrated in a camp in the cleared out tailor workshop at Łagiewnicka 36, established by the director of the Central Factories Bureau.

Bendet Hershkovitsh, one of those who found himself in that camp together with his wife, tells about the creation of the camp as follows:

> The chief of all the work divisions, Vice Chairman Aaron Jakubowicz
> . . . asked Biebow to help him avoid Oshpitsin [Yiddish for Auschwitz].

Table 17[1]
Summary of the Deportations from the Łódź Ghetto, 1942–1944[2]

Period	Number of Trains	Number of Those Deported			To Where?	Remaining in the ghetto on the 1st of the next month	Per cent deported in relation to the population on the 1st of the given month
		Men	Women	Total			
						Jan. 1942 162,680	
1st Stage: 16–29 Jan. 1942	14	4,263	5,740	10,003	Chełmno	151,000	6.15
2nd Stage: 22 Feb.–2 Apr. 1942	40	12,847	21,226	34,073	Chełmno	110,806	29.52
3rd Stage: 4–15 May 1942	12	3,657	7,257	10,914[3]	Chełmno	104,470	9.85
Subtotal	66	20,767	34,223	54,990			
4th Stage: 1–12 Sept. 1942	—	—	—	ca. 16,500[4]	Chełmno	89,446	15.57
5th Stage: 23 June to 14 July 1944	10	—	—	7,190	Chełmno	68,516	9.37
6th Stage: August 1944	—	—	—	ca. 67,000[5]	Auschwitz	ca. 1,500	97.81
Overall Total Deported, 1942–1944				145,680[6]			

---

1. Ed. note: This table is incorrectly labeled Table 16 in the original Yiddish.
2. The table includes only the direct deportations to death, but not those sent out to labor camps, the overwhelming majority of whom also died.
3. This figure includes 10,161 people (3,290 men and 6,871 women) who were deported into the Łódź Ghetto from Central and Western Europe in the months Oct.–Nov. 1941, and 753 local residents; with the earlier transports 340 newcomers were deported, for a total of 10,501 newcomers.
4. During this action, 15,860 people were actually deported, but about 600 Jews were killed on the spot. We have also included these victims, who tragically died on the way to destruction.
5. A certain percentage of the deportees (young, healthy) were selected in Auschwitz as laborers and those who held out were evacuated from Auschwitz in January 1945 into German camps. A certain portion of them survived.
6. If we add to this the number of those who died in the ghetto (43,743), the total is 189,423 souls, while the maximum official number of ghetto inhabitants was no more than 163,623 (on 1 Dec. 1941). Thus, we have a surplus of 25,800 in our calculation. This surplus of over 25,000 can perhaps be explained by the following:
   a. Between May and September 1942, there arrived from the liquidated provincial ghettos an official total of 14,467 Jews (G.V. 81/44, not paginated—*Aktennotiz* of 9 Sept. 1942, no. 128/42), of whom the overwhelming majority stayed in the Łódź Ghetto only a short time and was caught up in the "outsettlement action" in September 1942. Perhaps due to reasons impossible to determine today (fear of subsequent deportations, etc.), they held it to be safer to disappear into the ghetto masses and not to register at the ghetto's Registry Bureau. Therefore, they did not figure in the official lists of the ghetto population.
   b. Due to the traditional Jewish fear of official population statistics, particularly when it involved statistics for the use of the Nazis, a certain percentage of the residents initially held it to be healthier not to register and therefore evaded the registration lists of the ghetto population, so that the real number of ghetto inhabitants was higher than the one officially reported. We encounter this phenomenon in many ghettos.
   c. A certain percentage of the surplus should also, probably, be ascribed to the inaccuracies and errors in the official ghetto statistics that were compiled in such extraordinary circumstances.

There was immediately found a German of the ghetto administration, a certain Seifert, who also sought an occupation, in order not to go to the front. With another German, Stenvers (who had connections in Nazi Party circles), he bought the factory for temporary housing [resort ba-helfshayzer][226] and decided to transfer it to Königswusterhausen, near Berlin. Workers were needed for it. Officially, the 500 people were all needed for production. In fact, there were 100 real workers and the rest were people whom Jakubowicz wanted to do a favor; the majority were managers with their families. Among the 500 persons were 30 children. . . . Thanks to the fact that I had worked at Bałuty Marketplace and was capable of work, I also had the privilege of getting in there. . . . Those barracked at Łagiewnicka 36 were supposed to ship out of Łódź all the factory's equipment, even the barracks where the construction panels were produced. All in all, 270 wagons with cargo departed for König-swusterhausen.[227]

The camp remained in the ghetto until 22 October 1944. Later, the men were sent to Sachsenhausen and the women to Ravensbrück. From Sachsenhausen, the 250 men (without a selection) were sent to König-swusterhausen and the women were sent from Ravensbrück into an-other camp.[228] The overwhelming majority of this group that avoided Auschwitz survived.

A second, larger group of a not precisely determined number of persons (the figures vary among 500, 850, and "nearly 1,000")[229] was concentrated on 27 August in two former tailoring workshops on Jaku-ba Street (men and women separate) as the Łódź Ghetto Cleanup Unit (*Aufräumungskommando, Litzmannstadt-Getto*). Its work consisted "of going about the buildings, closing the windows, taking apart all things and furniture left behind by the Jews who were sent out to their death. Also a lot of backpacks from the transports were returned to Łódź, in order to sort them and discover valuable items. We sorted the things in the barracks on Bałuty Marketplace."[230]

Biebow also took people to this work from the camp on Łagiewnicka, after shipping out the inventory of the factory.

The aforementioned Bendet Hershkovitsh writes about this: "We shuddered when we entered the apartments and found everything just as the people had left it, but in place of the owners there were mice and flies. There were cases when corpses were found in the beds. These were such as had hidden out during the deportation and later died from thirst or illness. In one place, an entirely bitten up body was found."[231]

About the tragic situation of those who had hidden, a survivor writes in her memoirs:

> The German goal was to have us so crowded together that whenever he would only stretch out his paw, he should bag us all. . . . But in spite of this, we defended ourselves with our last strength. . . . Like mice hidden away in attics and cellars, ruins. The worst [was] the terrible hunger that led to insanity. The Germans had already for many days not given [out anything] to eat. . . . Suddenly people found out that somewhere bread

was being given out. There immediately ran together 100 living skeletons, but right away shooting was heard. It was one of the innumerable provocations. They distributed a little bread in order to trick the stubborn Jews out of their hideouts.[232]

Y. Ayzikovitsh, who worked in the Cleanup Unit, relates that former people of the *Sonderkommando* and other "Jewish scoundrels" let their strong arms also be felt here, persecuted the camp inmates, and latched onto the offices of camp leaders. She also recounts that "many of them went away looking for concealed Jews in the ghetto and turned them over to Biebow, who put an end to their lives. Among the victims was Dr. Wajskopf"[233] (see below).

Biebow practiced his sadistic whims here, too (rapes of girls in the women's camp, savage outrages on captured Jews). From time to time, selections took place and the victims died.[234]

At the beginning of January 1945, Biebow ordered the digging of eight large trenches at the cemetery. On 17 January there was an order that everybody from the camp was to appear for roll call. From a secret radio, apparently concealed by one of the camp inmates, it was known that the Soviets were near Łódź and everyone hid wherever he could. Only fifty showed up. Biebow delayed shooting the Jews until all would report and ordered his Jewish helpers to find those in hiding. The remaining Germans, however, were already thinking about their own skin.

On 19 January, the Soviet army took Łódź and several hundred Jews who had been in hiding (together with those who had been concealed in bunkers the whole time) were saved.[235]

On 23 October 1944, a meeting had taken place about the work of the Clean-up Unit and the disposition of the collected Jewish property. Participants included the mayor, the director of the *SS-Ansiedlungsstab* (SS Settlement Headquarters), and Biebow, among others. It was decided that furniture, glassware, kitchenware, bedlinens, clothing, and underwear should be collected for the *SS-Ansiedlungsstab,* which was to pay for them at a price that remained to be fixed. Not even ovens and kitchens were forgotten. A decision was adopted that their moveable parts must be collected as quickly as possible and to ship them to the *Umsiedler im Gau* (i.e., for the civilian Germans who had fled from the lost territories).

All that remained not yet dealt with at the meeting was the matter of "managing the [Jewish] furs." Whether or not they also managed to regulate this portion of the bloody inheritance or, due to the swift change of the front situation in winter 1945, this very important matter was left unresolved—about this the documents are silent.[236]

Due to the lightning fast Soviet offensive in the second half of January 1945, the Germans also did not manage to make off with the huge quantities of goods and raw materials that remained in the factories and warehouses.

According to a protocol delivered to the Łódź provincial industry department on 21 March 1945 by the former manager of the Paper Division, who was named on 21 February to take over the inventory of the goods, the following equipment and other materials remained in the ghetto, in those areas of the ghetto that were left: the print shop and stamp-factory, large stocks (145,000 kilos) of various paper materials with the division's machinery; about 100,000 kilos of chemicals; a well-equipped tannery; 238,000 square meters of veneers; a couple of wagons with cement plates (*plites*); a couple dozen wagons with textile waste and rags; an oil and candle factory; 3–4 wagons of tar; nearly 150 motors; wagons with scrap iron; 10,000 pairs of straw shoes, and so forth. The Soviet military took over the paper warehouses.[237]

There also remained demolished and looted houses, with doors and windows ripped out. The Polish population in Łódź also had a hand in this; after the arrival of the Soviet army, they came into the ruined ghetto searching for hidden Jewish treasures.

Documents 96–112

No. 96: YI-55P

Report about brutal acts by the Volhynian Germans (no date). [in Polish]

Before the sealing of the ghetto, there was a transit camp for "Volhynians"[238] at 7 Mickiewicza Street in the ghetto, in the building where the home for the elderly is currently housed.

Daily in the morning hours, emissaries from this camp, lurking about in the entries of houses on Zgierska, Łagiewnicka, and side streets, threw themselves on singled out victims and took them to the aforementioned camp. They selected from among the Jews only the prosperously dressed and the like, from whom they could expect a certain ransom for being freed from labor. The labor was fictive because in fact nobody needed it, but it was made up expressly for ulterior ends.

If the one being led off for labor was fairly resourceful, he could free himself on the way to work; if he did not do this on the way, he could still free himself before the start of work. But woe to the one who did not figure out the situation before he started to work, for rarely did anyone get out of there without being roughed up. Most of those who fell into this trap got out of it for the price of even 1 mark, while others paid 10 marks and more each.

One of the most practiced tricks was extorting money, in a so-called collection for an overcoat supposedly stolen by a Jew the day before. They collected for the overcoat over the course of several weeks and exacted from people 5–10 and even 20 marks each, when someone did not contribute voluntarily and a personal search was carried out and whatever sum he had on him [was taken]. Initially, they collected for an "overcoat" and later on for supposedly stolen shoes.

No. 97: YI-473

Rumkowski's appeal to the ghetto population of 25 December 1941, concerning the shootings at the ghetto fences. [in Yiddish]

Appeal *To the Ghetto Population!* Sisters and brothers!

In connection with what has recently occurred, I make known in this way that at my intervention I have received the assurance that *such incidents will not be repeated,* with the exception, of course, of smugglers and any persons who leave the ghetto without permission. I therefore turn to you: absolutely preserve the calm and go, as hitherto, punctually to work. The workers and officials can go their way to work by day and by night and back home (also over the bridges) *without any hindrances!*

My slogan: "Work"! will, as before, be calmly maintained.

No. 98: YI-325

Rumkowski's announcement of 4 June 1941, concerning a ban against walking in the street, instituted as a punishment for a shot having been fired from the ghetto by an undetermined person. [in Yiddish]

On the night of 27 May 1941 at the corner of Piwna and Lutomierska, as well as at Modra Street, there was [a] shooting out from the ghetto and the bullet landed near the German guardpost. Who the shooter was has not been determined.

A portion of the ghetto population was supposed to be severely punished for this deed. At my efforts and interventions with the authorities, the execution of the penalty was established according to the following method:

From Friday, 6 June 1941, 9 o'clock P.M., until Saturday, 7 June 1941, 8 o'clock P.M., a general and strict *curfew* is declared.

That is, no one may leave his residence during this time. The public kitchens must be closed.

No one is to be found on the unenclosed courtyards, except when someone needs to go to the toilet.

People must strictly see to it that children also do not leave the residence for any reason.

The house watchmen must remain on the courtyard all day in order to see whether anyone leaves his apartment, or is simply loitering about. The gates must be locked. The house watchmen are personally responsible to me for all of this.

Not subject to the aforementioned ordinance:

1) Order Service personnel, firefighters, and chimneysweeps,
2) physicians,
3) first aid personnel, and
4) those persons who will, in exceptional cases, possess a special permit from the Order Service leadership. No other office is entitled to issue passes to walk in the street.

Due to this ban on leaving the residences, I have directed to provide the entire ghetto with a special physicians service.

The Order Service as well as the other officials designated by me will maintain careful watch on the entire area of the ghetto. In the event that medical care will be necessary somewhere in an urgent case, the house watchman must turn to the nearest control post and the latter will bring a doctor from the nearest location.

I draw attention again that only my Order Service leadership is entitled to issue passes and each pedestrian will be checked by it.

Whoever does not possess such a pass or will show another document will be immediately arrested on the spot.

I ask the ghetto population in its own interest to observe the ordinance strictly and warn expressly against any sort of transgressions.

Those who transgress this ordinance will be severely punished by me administratively.

No. 99: YI-415

Rumkowski's warning of 25 March 1942, to report to the deportation under penalty of being sent out through compulsion. [in Yiddish]

About *Deportation*.

I am told that rumors are being spread that the deportation [*aroysshikung*] has been halted. *These rumors do not correspond with the truth. The deportations are continuing to take place.*

Those persons designated for deportation must, therefore, as until now unconditionally punctually report at the appointed time at the stated meeting place. *If not, they will be dispatched without any baggage at all.*

No. 100: YI-54

Rumkowski's speech to the assembled crowd on 4 September 1942.[239] [in Yiddish]

[p. 17]

A severe blow has befallen the ghetto. They are asking from it the best that it possesses—children and old people. I have not had the privilege to have a child of my own and therefore I devoted the best of my years to children. I lived and breathed together with the children. I never imagined that my own hands would have to deliver the sacrifice to the altar. In my old age, I must stretch out my hands and beg: "Brothers and sisters, give them to me! Fathers and mothers, give me your children . . ." (Tremendous and dreadful weeping among the assembled crowd.)

I had the premonition that something was descending upon us. I anticipated "something" and I stood constantly on alert like a guard, in order to avoid that "something." But I could not do it, because I did not know what was menacing us. I did not know what is awaiting us.

That the sick were taken away from the hospitals, this was for me
[p. 18]
totally unanticipated. You have the best sign: I had my own kin and
near ones there and I could not do anything for them. I thought that
it would end with this, that after that we would be left in peace. This is
the peace for which I yearn so strongly, for which I have always worked
and striven, but it turned out that something different was predestined
for us. The luck of Jews is of course thus: always to suffer more and
worse, particularly in wartime.

Yesterday during the day, I was given a command to send twenty-
odd thousand Jews out from the ghetto; if not—"We will do it." And the
question arose: "Should we take it over and do it ourselves, or leave it
for others to carry out?" But being dominated not by the thought, "How
many will be lost," but by the thought, "How many can be saved," we, i.e.
I and my closest co-workers came to the conclusion that as difficult as
this will be for us, we must take into our own hands the carrying out of
the decree. I have to carry out this difficult and bloody operation. I must
cut off limbs in order to save the body! I must take children because, if
not, others could also, God forbid, be taken . . . (Frightful wailing).

I have not come today to console you. Nor have I come today to calm
you, but to uncover all your sorrow and pain. I have come like a robber
to take away from you the best from under your hearts! I tried with all
my abilities to get the decree revoked. After trying to get it revoked was
impossible, I attempted to moderate it. Just yesterday, I arranged a registration of all nine-year-old children. I wanted to rescue at least that
single year, from nine to ten years old. But they did not want to grant
this to me. One thing I succeeded at—to save the children from ten years
and up. Let this be our comfort in our great sorrow.

We have in the ghetto many sick with tuberculosis whose lives are
counted in days, maybe really in weeks. I don't know. Maybe it's a dev-
ilish plan, maybe not. But I cannot refrain from pronouncing it: "Give
me these sick and in their place healthy people can be saved." I know
how everyone cherishes a patient in his home, all the more so among
Jews. But at every decree, we must weigh and measure: Who should, can,
and may be saved? And common sense requires that saved must be that
which can be saved and has prospects of surviving, and not that which
cannot be saved anyway. . . .

We are living in the ghetto. Our life is so austere that we don't have
enough for the healthy, much less for the sick. Each of us feeds the sick
person at the expense of his own health: We give our bread away to the
sick person. We give him our bit of sugar, our piece of meat and the
result is not only that the patient becomes healthy from it, but also we
become sick. Of course, such victims are the handsomest and the most
noble. But in a time when we must choose: to sacrifice the sick person
who not only himself has not the least chance of recovery, but is also
likely to making others sick; or to save a healthy person—I could not

delve long into this problem and I had to decide it for the good of the healthy one. I have therefore in that sense instructed the physicians and they will be compelled to turn in all incurable patients in order to be able to rescue in their place healthy people who want and are able to live on. . . . (Terrible wailing.)

I understand you, mothers. I see your tears quite well. I also feel your hearts, fathers, that tomorrow, immediately after your child will have been taken away from you, you will have to go to work, while just yesterday you still played

[p. 19]

with your dear kids. I know all of this and I feel it. Since 4 o'clock yesterday, since I found out about the decree, I am entirely broken down. I am living with your grief and your pain torments me and I don't know how and with what strength I will be able to survive it. I must disclose to you a secret: 24,000 victims were demanded. Through eight days of three thousand people each day, but I succeeded in pushing the number down to twenty thousand, even less than 20,000, but on condition that there will be children up to ten years old. Children from ten years and up are secure. Since the children together with the elderly give only a number of approximately 13,000 souls, it will be necessary to fill the gap with sick people, too.

It is difficult for me to speak. I don't have any strength, I only want to say to you my request: Help me carry out the action! I am trembling. I fear that others will, God forbid, take over the implementation into their hands. . . .[240]

A broken Jew is standing before you. Don't envy me. It is the most difficult decree that I have ever had to carry out. I extend to you my broken, trembling arms and I beg: Give the victims into my hands, in order through them to avoid additional victims, in order to protect a congregation of a hundred thousand Jews. They promised me so: If we ourselves will deliver our victims, there will be calm. . . . (Yells are heard: "We'll all go"; "Mr. Chairman, no only-children should be taken—individual children should be taken away from those who have several!" . . .) These are empty phrases! I don't have any strength to conduct discussions with you! If someone will come from the authorities, no one will yell. . . .

I understand what it means to tear off a limb from the body. Yesterday, I pleaded on my knees, but it was no use. From small towns that possessed 7,000–8,000 Jews barely 1,000 have arrived here. What then is better? What are you asking for? To leave 80,000–90,000 Jews or, God forbid, to annihilate everybody? . . . Judge as you wish; my obligation is to take care of the remnant of Jews. I am not talking to hotheads—I am speaking to your reason and conscience. I have done everything and will also continue to do everything to prevent weapons being brought into the streets and that blood be shed. . . . The decree did not permit us to get it revoked; it only allowed itself to be reduced.

One needs the heart of a bandit in order to ask for what I am asking of you. But put yourself in my position and think logically and you yourself will come to the conclusion that you cannot act differently, because the number of the portion that can be saved is much larger than the part that must be surrendered.

. . . .

No. 101: YI-434

Rumkowski's announcement of 5 September 1942 concerning a general curfew (Yiddish "shpere"; German Gehsperre) in the ghetto. [in German]

Re: *General Curfew in the Ghetto.*
From Sunday, 5 September 1942, at 5 P.M. until revoked, there is a general curfew in the ghetto.

Hereby excluded are: Firemen, the Transport Department, fecal and garbage workers, reception of goods at Bałuty Market square and Radegast, physicians and pharmacy personnel.

Passes must be applied for at the Order Service executive—1 Hamburger Street.

All house watchmen are obligated to pay attention that no strangers managed to stay in the houses for which they are responsible, except the residents of the house itself.

Those found without passes on the street will be evacuated.

The building managers must *stand available with the house registers* in their block of houses.

Every house resident has to keep his work card with him.

No. 102: YI-54

From Joseph Zelkowicz's daily descriptions of the September Action, "In Those Nightmarish Days" (74 pp., not completed). [in Yiddish][241]

Wednesday, 2 September 1942
[pp. 2–3]
Not only from the hospitals
were patients removed and sent—God alone knows where and to what; also taken away were the children in the preventive care clinics; also taken away were all arrestees who were in the Central Prison and among these arrestees were also a mass of completely random people, like for example those who had to serve out an administrative penalty of twenty-four hours because their apartments were not blacked out according to regulation and a crack of light was visible in the evening, or provincial Jews who for lack of another place were meanwhile interned in the Central Prison, so the panic that this information evoked was indescribable. Everyone sees that evidently this is a decree that includes not only the sick and unemployed and . . . hearts pound with so much terror, with so much anxiety. . . .

[p. 4]

Meanwhile, the Jewish police go through Jewish houses and collect the sick patients, who yesterday had miraculously gotten out of the hospitals, and take them away. Horrible and heartrending scenes play out along the way. People cry, people plead, people kiss their hands, but can they help a bit? If it were known at least that the Molekh[242] will be satisfied with these victims, people would wipe away the tears, turn their hearts into stone, and would have given up on them like any corpse. . . . But nearly three years of ghetto have already trained the population and made it so accustomed to death, that for them it is more typical and more mundane than life. Yet the "Will it end with this?" is such a painful problem that not only does it pester the mind, but it simply turns the blood to water that freezes and becomes petrified in the veins beneath the cold of the violent outrage to which the ghetto populace is already so intensely accustomed. . . .

"Will it end with this?"—The provincial Jews, only recently arrived in the ghetto, laugh bitterly at the naiveté of this question. Oh, they already have experience, they know and they don't want to bring it to their lips: Everywhere, in the entire province, it began thus. First there was a period of "stamping," later patients were taken from the hospitals, after them—children and the old and only later they made ash of the rest: deported, shot, killed, dispersed on the seven seas, wives torn from husbands, husbands torn from wives, children from parents and parents from children—killed with several deaths, as if one death would have been too little for the weak and exhausted Jewish population. Oh, they already know the whole pattern very well, these provincial Jews! . . . Everywhere the tragedy was played out according to the same direction. So they don't reply to this question; they are afraid, they tremble to bring the words forth from their mouths. They only laugh bitterly. It's laughter of people who have nothing to lose. They, the provincial Jews, have already lost everything. This little bit of wretched life that they still haul about on their exhausted shoulders is for them only surplus ballast that they would willingly be done with. It's easy for them to laugh, but the local ghetto Jew, who until now had lived together with his family, with his friends and acquaintances—cannot laugh. His blood runs cold in the veins at the gall-filled chuckling of the provincial Jew.

The patients who had managed to escape from the hospitals and hid in their homes or with their relatives, but were found by the Jewish police and put in the Central Prison, were today loaded onto trucks first thing in the morning and sent away.

. . . .

[p. 8]

And the unfortunate little children who still know nothing. The little children who are unable to understand and do not comprehend how to take into account the sword of Damocles that is hanging over their innocent little heads. Perhaps they subconsciously sense the great danger that is hovering over them and they cling more firmly with both little arms to the skinny and strained necks of their fathers and mothers. . . .

You, mortal son of Adam, go into the street, watch, absorb the terror of the little infants, who are ready for the slaughter and be strong and don't cry! Be strong and your heart must not break, so that later you will with composure and in an orderly fashion only be able to describe barely a fragment of a fragment of what happened in the ghetto in the first days of September of the year thousandninehundredfortytwo! . . . Mothers are running through the streets. One foot shod, the other barefoot. The head combed up (*oyfgekemt*) but not properly combed (*derkemt*). The kerchief is half-hanging on her shoulder and it's half-dragging on the ground. They still keep their children with them. For now, they can still more rigidly, more tightly cuddle them to their wasted breasts. For now, they can still kiss their bright little faces and eyes. But what will be tomorrow, later, an hour from now?

People say: The children will be taken away from their parents this very day.

People say: The children will be sent away this Monday, they will be sent away—To where?!!

Sent away this Monday. To be taken away yet today. But in the meanwhile, now, in the present moment, each mother still has her child with her. Now she can still give the child everything. From the best that she possesses—the last bit of bread. Everything that she has beneath her heart, of the most cherished and best! . . . The child does not today have to wait for hours and cry until the father or mother had calculated that he can already be given a piece of his 25 deko of bread. Today the child is asked: "Maybe, dear soul, you want a piece of bread now?" . . . And the piece of bread that the child gets today, it receives not like always,
[p. 9]
dry and tasteless. It's smeared with margarine, if a bit was still left. . . . It's sprinkled with sugar, if there's still some here. The ghetto is living today without calculation. There's no more weighing and no more measuring. The sugar and margarine are no longer hidden, so that they should last for all ten days, until the next "ration." Today people in the ghetto are no longer living with the future. Today people are living with the present moment—and in the present moment each mother still has her child with her—her own heart, her own soul, if she could, would she not give those away? And children? What do children know?

They are naive creatures and if one has a little more sense, it only asks:

Mama, why are you giving me so much or so good to eat today, am I sick? . . .

Can the mother answer the child other than with tears? So the child chews the piece of bread and chokes on the bite. It doesn't know: "Yes, or not sick" and it comes to the conclusion: Probably sick. Because—if it were not sick, it would not have gotten so much and so good to eat. . . . Were it not sick, then [father] or mother would [not] have hugged it so strongly and so firmly. . . . If it were not ill, then father or mother would not have cried so intensely over it. . . . One thing only is difficult for the child to figure out: If sick, then why is she being dragged around through the streets? Why is he not allowed to rest in bed? Why don't they go with him to a doctor? . . .

Oh, they are very ill, the unfortunate little Jewish children. They are unfortunately very sick, the Jewish infants! Like sick birds they have their destination—slaughter.

But there are children who already comprehend. Ten-year-old children in the ghetto, for example, are already mature people. They already know and understand the fate that awaits them. Perhaps they do not yet know to what and for what they are being torn from their parents; this was perhaps not yet told them. For them, meanwhile, the fact is enough that they are being torn away from their faithful guardian, their father, and from their caring mother. It's already difficult to carry such children in one's arms, or to lead them by the hand. Such children already walk in the streets by themselves. Such children themselves already cry with their own tears. And their tears are so sharp and pointed, and they fall on the hearts like poisoned arrows. . . . But there are hearts become petrified in the ghetto. They miserably want to burst, but they cannot and this is perhaps the greatest, the harshest curse. This is perhaps the most terrible anguish that could have been thought up for the Jew: On the one hand a ghetto and on the other hand—a sensitive Jewish heart. . . .

. . . .

[p. 20]

Two fathers are standing with faces distorted from grief and they chat with each other: What are you thinking of doing? I won't give up my child. Meaning? I'll kill it with my own hands! So I'll at least know that it wasn't tormented in long agony, so I'll at least know where his remains ended up! . . .

The first one speaks more to himself than to the other:

I know that people give up a child to a grandfather, to a grandmother, to an uncle, to an aunt. It'll be worse for him there, or be better—anyhow, such things are understandable and it happens. But to give up children in such a fashion! To whom? Why? For whom? And to what?! . . .

These are the horoscopes that are being faced by Jewish fathers and mothers. But the mother refuses to utter that she will kill her child; she says, that first they'll have to kill her and only then will they be able to take her child away from her. The father is harder: He wants to kill the child with his own hands, so that it should not be worked to death and what afterward will become of him himself, what will happen to him, he does not think about that.

Still others attempt to comfort themselves and others:

It's just impossible that people would take thousands of children and for no good reason slaughter them!

They were bought off, the Jewish police. They became intoxicated. They were

[p. 33]

given hashish: Their children were exempted from the decree. . . . They were given one and a half kilograms of bread a day for the bloody bit of work—bread, then, to their fill and an addition of sausage and of sugar. . . . And for the sake of an idea they worked, these Jewish policemen— "With familiar, with cozy, with Jewish hands, is the molar ripped out, is the limb cut, is the body split, perhaps not so painfully done as with rough and coarse foreign hands." . . . It was heard thus explicitly in all three speeches, it was quite distinctly stated: "If you will not do this, we will do it" . . . and by this, their doing it, it was desired to prevent—It was preferable to do it themselves, so who should do it if not the Jewish police, who were simultaneously both bribed and intoxicated and ideologically convinced?

No. They had nothing for which to be envied, the Jewish police. But with black letters on the bloody page of this history should be recorded the so-called "White Guard," the porters from Bałuty Marketplace and from the Supply Office. This bunch, out of fear of losing their soups during the curfew, offered their voluntary assistance in the *Aktion,* on the condition that they should receive the same as was promised to the police: bread and sausage and sugar and the exemption of their families. Their offer was accepted—they voluntarily collaborated in the action. . . .

With black letters on the bloody page of this history should be recorded all of the officials who exerted themselves to have whatever employment around the *Aktion* and this only in order to receive the bread and sausage allowances instead of the soups that they would not have received sitting at home and . . .

Perhaps . . . Who then can know?—Who can evaluate a Jewish soul? Perhaps all of these were intent on doing something, to save something, if only it would be possible?

. . . .

The wagon is standing on Rybna Street. On the wagon are standing several forlorn children, with gaping eyes. They were already seized. They unfortunately don't know what was wanted of them. Why are so many people standing around them and staring at them so mournfully and troubled? Why are they crying, all these people? Why are they wringing their hands so desperately? They, the children, don't feel like crying. They are quite glad: They had been set on a wagon, so they'll go for a ride! . . . When did a ghetto child have an occasion to go riding around a little on a wagon? . . . If so many people weren't standing around them and crying, if mommy and daddy were not screaming and yelling so frightfully while they were being put on the wagon, they would have danced for joy! . . . They will go for a ride on a wagon . . . But the yelling, the screaming, the wailing—all of this makes them restless, it only disturbed their joy. They turn around on the long wagon, look around at the high walls like lost souls with gaping eyes: "What's happening here? What do they want from them? Why are they not being allowed to ride around a bit? . . .

. . . .

[p. 34]

In a corner of the wagon stands an old man and he is sobbing. An old man who was left alone in the world. He has nothing more to lose. All that he had he had already lost. His wife died still in the city. The unmarried daughter was killed on the road in her flight to Warsaw. One son, the married one, died in winter last year of tuberculosis. The other one, the youngest son, was taken away from the hospital a few days ago. He has nothing more to lose. But he is a believer, this Jew. He believes in the immortality of the soul and . . . he has not yet lost his soul. He still has it, the soul which will perhaps even today, perhaps in an hour, have to give an accounting of its deeds in the Other World and . . . this soul, the only one of them all, the last that still remains to him, this soul the old Jew does not want to lose. So he stands, this Jew, in a corner of the wagon and he totals up his deeds here in this world—he recites *Vidui,* the confession of sins. But can one in such sudden moments of panic remember all the details of his whole insignificant and long vain life? So he raps himself on the chest. He sobs and his tears, mature and earnest, fall on the floor of the wagon that is spread with filthy and trampled straw.

. . . .

[p. 38]

They are taking. The Jewish police are taking. They take with compassion, according to the regulations: children up to ten years old, elderly from sixty-five years old and patients that doctors affirm no longer have any prospect of getting well.

Taking are the Jewish police, with whom one can have a talk, onto whose conscience one can toss all the stones. One can at least cry before them, one can attempt to plead before them, to plead them into reversing the decision. And a mixed "commission" is taking: several Jewish policemen, several Jewish firemen, a physician (a mute figure who cannot have a say because no one asks his opinions), a nurse (a decorative figure), several porters from the White Guard,[243] whose task is to transport the "export goods" onto the wagon and . . . one fellow, a man in uniform with revolver in hand. . . .

They're taking. And this is the manner of taking:

The Jewish police arrive—a whole host. Police hats, firemen's hats, porters' hats. The house is besieged, the entrances are blocked—the house, where you lived the whole time and felt familiar and homey, suddenly is transformed into a prison for you. Each must be in his apartment—thus is the command called out in the courtyard. In this fashion the people are chased like mice into the mousetrap. The world becomes cramped. The apartment becomes cramped. The eye sockets become cramped for the eyes. The chest becomes too cramped for the heart—the eyes grow from fright and they protrude; the throat swells from anguish and wants to burst and the neck becomes stretched, not with a thin string, but with a thick rope that only chokes and suffocates and does not let one breathe, neither one way, nor the other—not permitting survival, not allowing death. . . .

The Jewish police have addresses. The Jewish police have a Jewish house watchman and the watchman has a house book. The addresses say: In apartment thus and so is a child that was born then and then. The addresses relate: In apartment this and this is an old man, who is so much and so much old. Into each home enters a doctor. He observes the residents; he sees who is healthy and who wants to pass for a healthy person. He had too much experience in the ghetto—he must be able to differentiate with a bare glance between the healthy and the mortally ill. . . .

And it's no use that the child is clinging with both little arms to the mother's neck. It's no use that the father throws himself down before the threshold and howls like a dying ox: "Only over my dead body will you take my child." It's no use that the old man clings with his bony arms to the cold walls and bed: "Let me die here quietly." . . . It's no [use] that the old woman falls at their feet, kisses their boots, and pleads: "I have grown grandchildren just [as old as you]." It's no use that the sick man buries his feverish head in the damp, sweat-covered pillow and there sobs out perhaps his last tears.

It's no use. The police must deliver their consignment. They must take. They must not have any mercy. They, the Jewish police, when they take, they take in an orderly fashion. They, when they take, are also crying, they are also groaning. They, when they take, attempt to comfort with shouts, to express the pain. Thus do earnest, conscientious physicians attempt to coax mortally ill patients into allowing a serious operation on their bodies. When the father or the mother turns the child over into their hands, perhaps they have, during the act, the sense that they have transferred the child into Jewish hands . . .

. . . .

[p. 39]

It appears completely different when others take!

They enter a courtyard and . . . the first thing is a wanton shot from a revolver and . . . all wings are already clipped. All blood is frozen. All throats are blocked with molten lead. Both the lead and the "*oy*" or the "*okh*" in him that did not manage to wrench itself from his throat congeal solid . . . with trembling . . . no, in order to tremble one has to have flowing blood and here the blood does not circulate in the bodies—it has become stiff like water in a frost!—People wait stiffly, with raw numbness; with mute helplessness they wait for what comes next and . . .

Then falls a hard, laconic and draconian command that is yelled out loudly and repeated by the Jewish police: "Within two minutes all must be in the courtyard. No one is allowed to remain in the apartment. The rooms must remain open!"

Who can describe, who can paint the insane and wild rush over the steps, flights of stairs and floors by the stiff and deathly people, rushing to carry out the order precisely? No one.

Old legs, deformed from sclerosis and rheumatism, stumble over crooked stairs and sharp stones. Young, flexible legs, fleet like gazelles, fly with birdlike swiftness. Clumsy and swollen legs of sick people and those agitated out from their beds stumble in their running. Swollen legs of starved people shuffle, groping like the blind. And all are running, all are hurrying, all are racing in the dash into the courtyard, because . . .

Woe to the one who's late. He will not walk his last road any more—he will have to swim it in his own blood. Woe to the one who on his way was bumped and fell—he will never more get back on his feet—he will again slip and fall in his own blood. Woe to the child who out of fear only wants to call out the single word, "Mama"—it will begin with "Ma" and not conclude with "ma." A brazen revolver shot will interrupt the word "Mama" in its throat: "Ma" will get out and "ma" will roll back in and will fall into the child's heart like a bird shot down in mid-flight. . . . The experience of the last two hours proved it with all its realism and vividness.

. . . .

[p. 40]

The row of people stands lined up in the courtyard. The colors of their faces are vague and faded. The fires in their eyes are extinguished and he . . . he has a revolver in his hand that fires wildly and wantonly and who will say to him: "This child turned thirteen years old in winter"? Who will say to him: "The woman with the gray head is not yet forty-five years old and she has been working without break for a year-and-a-half"? Who will say to him: "This one here with the swollen legs is only hungry—let him only get to eat his fill for two weeks and he will again become a fit and useful person"? Who will say this? No one! And in the end, the revolver is in a sure hand, in a hand that does not tremble and will not tremble when it knocks off even another hundred, another thousand of the "damned Jew rabble." . . .

. . . .

[p. 53]

They had to work today in the haberdashery division for fancy wooden articles. A fresh gallows was being finished up there. Twenty-two Jews will be hanged on it.

A gallows for twenty-two Jews and it was produced in the division for fancy wooden articles, where toys are produced for children . . . and— The balance tallies: The gallows are also no more than a toy. A toy for

the uncles of the same children for whom other toys are being produced.
. . . The gallows could not have been produced in any other division. Gallows are not an everyday item—they're a luxury item—a toy and it must be produced in the division where only toys are produced. . . .

"A gallows for twenty-two Jews" and you, son of Adam, turn around and choke on this news! Feel the rope around your own neck and simultaneously feel your powerlessness. Puny son of Adam, you can't even take your sharp fingernails and stick them into your neck, to tear chunk after chunk from it and toss them to the dogs!

—But you have no nails, nor are they sharp and you aren't even allowed to have a dog in the ghetto! . . . Puny son of Adam, you must remain quiet and impotent! You can no longer even howl and scream. You have already yelled out all your screams during the day. Nothing more is left to you, puny son of Adam, than to fry on the slow fire, unable to be incinerated.

. . . .

[p. 58]
And mothers who have only weak, maternal hearts, mothers who are completely incapable of persuading themselves to let their children be torn away from them, they refuse to entrust their children even into such a secure asylum for giving them up, mothers who yell: "As long as I live, I will not surrender any child from my hands." . . . And parents who do not have an "iron-clad letter" and cannot deliver their children into the "secure home," and old folks for whom no horse cabs came to drop them off in the "asylum" for old folks, and patients who are still trembling with their heart's final fever for the last weeks, last days, or only the last hours of their painful lives—

All of them want to hide. Mothers want to hide their children somewhere. Old people—want to bury their years somewhere. Sick people —want to conceal their illnesses somewhere.

. . . .

[p. 59]
Where? The mother runs with her infant up to the attic. She wants to burrow into the furthest corner. She wants to nestle her child into the depths of her heart. Not a peep should be heard from him. Trembling and quaking, she will stand there, until the commission will have departed from her house. . . . Everyone's skin crawls. A child is contraband. . . .

And the neighbors warn with deathly fear on their lips: "They're just as clever. . . . They, too, know where an attic is located . . . and God forbid—it must not [even] be said—if they find [them], not only are those in hiding playing with their lives, but together with them—the entire house, too, all the people. . . ."

The mother's wings are thus clipped. Clipped, but not yet burned. She wants to save the innocent, quivering life of her child, to whom she is linked and bound with thousands of heart threads. She places her clumsy feet on the steps of the stairs. She wants to go down, into the cellar. . . . She wants to burrow with her child into the farthest, into the wettest corner, and lie there, until after the house will have been "processed." The neighbors again admonish: "God forbid. The first place that will be searched is in the cellars!" . . .

And once again the desperate mother's wings are scalded. But as long as a single feather remains in them, as long as a single spark of hope still shines ahead, as long as her arm has not become stiff and it can still support the child, the Jewish mother will not lower the child and let it fall—so she will go with it into the small storeroom. Someone should lock her in there. Set the lock on the outside . . . a big lock that should be immediately conspicuous and everyone should see that the chamber is locked from the outside. . . . But people's skin crawls; they incessantly warn: "And what if, God forbid, may it not happen, if the child hears a shot, is frightened and bursts into tears? The whole building, all the people will be put at risk in such a case!" . . .

But the maternal wings are still not burned up. They cannot fly high. They can no longer fly far, but they are still able to hover in the air—She will hide with her child in the outhouse toilet. . . . In the toilet, they won't look there and even if they do, no one will be put at risk for her. . . . It can happen to everyone that he has to go into there . . . But—

There her wings collapse. The child tosses its head like a slaughtered chicken. . . . It becomes entirely blue. The tiny, weakened lungs don't have what to breathe there. It starts to suffocate and no mother will let her child be suffocated in her arms, so let them take it from her alive, not suffocated. . . .

. . . .

[p. 63]

She had held the child by the hand. Both of them smiled at each other. The child was glad that the mother had taken her out onto the court-yard. There is such a brightness today on God's world, such a delight-ful sun . . . and the mother . . . the mother had to smile, too. . . . One, of course, had to show a smiling face, that one is healthy, that one is capa-ble of working. . . . That one did not yet have to go to the scrap heap. . . . He noticed the freshness, the peaches-and-cream ruddiness of the little girl. As a good Party man, he was not allowed to delight in the beauty of a Jewish child. . . . As a good Party man, who was moreover born to annihilate all that is merely Jewish, he had to rule thus: "This bitch must get lost!" . . . But she, she was only a mother and—

No!—She will not give up the child. As long as she lives, she will not let the child be torn away from her and she continued to smile. What then was she supposed to do? Perhaps delight him with her tears? Make a free spectacle of her heart for his benefit and lay it out on her face? . . . So she smiled and she will not surrender the child anyway.
He also made a scornful grimace:

—No kidding? Really? She really seriously means to resist?

Yes. She may smile, but that does not at all keep her from being an earnest, devoted mother. She will not give up her child! And let him do what he wants. . . .

He was too well bred. In his chivalrous Junker school he was taught, it was pounded into his brain about courtesy in regard to women. But he did not know whether the general rules of courtesy applied in regard to Jewish women. He smiled disconcertedly and while smiling, he pulled her together with the little girl out of the line. The good schooling had won out. It was not without influence. He gave her three minutes to think it over. Three minutes on his watch.

Neighbors shook in convulsions. Neighbors who stood in the general big line, with tear-filled eyes covertly threw glances at these two in the separate [row] of those set aside, who were standing and smiling at each other; the child with gladness, that she was still with her mother who continued to hold it by the hand and the mother from gladness that she still had her child beside her and within herself. . . .

Precisely three minutes; not a second less, not a moment more.
[p. 64]

Well, how is it? What had she decided?

She had nothing at all to decide. Nothing had changed for her during the three minutes: As long as she lives she will not let go of the child. Nothing changed for her during the three minutes. Even the same smile.

Only his smile became darker, maybe more cowardly and this was perhaps the reason that he forgot the rules of courtesy toward women and he almost screamed out his command:

Turn to the wall!

With the same earlier smile, she turned to face the wall. Nothing else, though she more convulsively squeezed her hand around the childish little hand and this was perhaps the reason that the child jerked her little head upward to her mother. . . . The child probably wanted to complain at the small pain that the firm grip had caused her. . . . But the internal change was just a secret of the mother and the child—externally nothing was noticed in the mother, while one could clearly see how his smile trembled on his twisted face. He made an effort to keep smiling . . . and later, when he had done away with both of them, the mother and her child, with two shots from his small revolver, he did not have to exert any effort at all. The smile was frozen on his twisted mug; and if he were asked, why was he smiling, what his smile expressed: cowardice, bestiality, madness? Maybe he would not be at all aware that he was smiling, maybe he would not at all know that it can be true that just a moment ago he had so calmly, so politely and "*liebenswürdig*" (amiably) killed two people, a young, vibrant mother with her four-year-old child by the hand. He would perhaps yell the same thing that people will cry decades hence, when they will read about this event. He would perhaps himself cry out: "Lies"! "Nonsense."

[p. 69]

Those who returned relate:

Whoever does not lose his wits, whose brain still manages to think, still has a hope of making it through all seven circles of Gehenna and to emerge from them intact. Varied are the ways and means that open the doors even of collection points. The most proven and effective means is money; of course, not any *rumkes*.[244] But even *rumkes,* when one has a whole lot of them, are currency. Dollars are a very good currency, not to mention in gold! . . . German marks are also accepted tender. But one must have a lot of them. . . . Because not everybody who possessed even this valued coin at home had remembered and had the opportunity to bring it along with them into the collection point. Often decisive are valuable objects that the one caught had by chance on him or taken along. A gold watch, for example, of a good make . . . a pair of jeweled or diamond earrings . . . a ring, etc. Bread and other food products, however, are quite paltry merchandise. Firstly, the "liberator"—the Jewish policeman—is today not so very starved as usual. For his "work," he is getting another one and a half kilos of bread a day, aside from sausage, sugar and other things, in addition to his normal ghetto allotment. . . . Secondly, in such a case one has to deal, as they say, from hand to hand: You hand over the object and I will open the door for you. But with foodstuffs the liberator would have to take one's word. For no one had their food reserves with them! . . . It also happens that the policeman riding with the wagon or guarding the collection point finds a friend or a relative among those caught and he releases him without any payment and even conducts him on his way home, etc.

. . . .

[p. 70]

However, these categories of "liberated" individuals, as people who were not legally "liberated," mostly do not go back home. They hide out in other parts of the ghetto, where they are not known, where the fear does not arise that they will come for them again. That a begrudging neighbor will inform on them, etc. . . . One only knows that there are such freed persons, that they exist somewhere, but to converse with them directly, to hear them directly speak is not possible for the time being.

There are also, however, legally and totally kosher freed people. Among these, there are also two categories: To the first category belong those whose relatives managed, through money, intercession or influence, to obtain for their seized kin certificates of release and retrieved them from the collection point. To the other category belong plain lucky people: it happens that at the collection point an officer enters and he orders the release of this one or that one. Such cases are, in truth, rare, but they do occur.

. . . .

No. 103: YI-71

Announcement from the ghetto administration [Biebow] of 12 September 1942, concerning the just concluded action. [in German]

Reopening
of all factories and workshops *from Monday, 14 IX 1942.*

Since the outsettlement of population was concluded yesterday, from Monday, 14 IX 1942, *all workplaces of the ghetto will be put back into full operation.*

Every manager, worker, and employee is obligated to occupy his workplace punctually if he is concerned to protect himself from the greatest unpleasantness imaginable. The henceforth recognized workforce will be required to fulfill their tasks with the greatest diligence and take pains to make up as quickly as possible for the arrears caused by the rest break.

I will strictly supervise whether my directive is complied with completely.

No. 104: YI-449

Announcement by Rumkowski of 12 February 1944, that 1,500 workers must leave the ghetto. [in German]

Re: *Dispatch of 1,500 workers to outside of the ghetto.*

The summons immediately *to report on Sunday, 13.2.1944* from 8 A.M. *in the Central Prison* hereby applies to all persons who have reported to the commission at 40 Hamburger Street. Those who were found not suited for work outside the ghetto will be immediately released.

Those persons who for various reasons have not submitted themselves until the present day to the commission (Physicians Commission), in spite of the fact that they were obligated to do so, must report at the latest on Sunday, 13 February 1944, between 8 A.M. and 12 o'clock, at the 40 Hamburger Street clinic.

For all those others who do not immediately obey my summons, the following penal measures apply:

a) Stopping the bread and food ration cards for the entire family;
b) Stopping the dinners at the work sites (in the departments);
c) Penal measures—that are not dependent upon us.

I further refer to my Announcement no. 407 of 9.2.1944 and again finally warn against taking in family members or strange persons and letting [them] spend the night (all the same whether by day or by night).

Those who resist this directive have likewise to expect severe penal measures.

No. 105. YI-450

Announcement concerning the ban on walking in the street on 20 February 1944. [in Yiddish]

Concerning a total curfew, Sunday, the 20th of February 1944.

In connection with the action of dispatching 1,600 workers to work outside the ghetto, *a general curfew* is ordained on Sunday, 20 February 1944.

On that day, only [the following] will be in operation: Hospitals no. 1 and 2, the pharmacy at 8 Plac Kościelny, the pharmacy at 5 Rybna Street and the first aid stations. All other departments, as well as factories and workshops remain completely closed on that day.

There are to be in the factories on the aforementioned day only the firefighters and another two reliable people, who are designated by the manager. On the other hand, in the departments on the mentioned day there are to be the firefighters and another one senior reliable person designated by the manager.

I especially note that the kitchens will also be closed on Sunday, the 20th of February 1944.

However, all of those employed will already on Saturday, the 19th of February 1944, receive the soup for Sunday on control-card no. 2.

All other persons who will be in the factories or departments on that day will be arrested immediately.

The managers of the factories and departments must, after work on Saturday, hand out the identification cards with photographs, that are issued by the Ghetto Labor Office for Sunday, to all male workers (except children and old folks).

Identification cards, on which the photographs are lacking, must also be given out to the male workers.

Simultaneously, the persons who come into question need to have the main dinner card with them.

Monday, the 21st of February 1944, all male workers must return the identification cards at their work sites.

Male workers unable to present all the mentioned documents on Sunday, the 20th of 1944, will immediately be arrested.

The locked house cellars and attics must, at every request, be opened and the keys have to be located with the house watchman. Where there is no house watchman, the house residents have to single out from themselves a person who should keep the keys with him.

For the sake of orientation, there has to be a list posted in each corridor or at the entry into the house, where it should be precisely and clearly indicated with whom the keys are to be found.

Apartments that the Order Service recently sealed can be opened by the tenants in question in order to be able to stay there.

I note once again that on Sunday, the 20th of February 1944, all ghetto residents must be in their dwellings.

In exceptional cases, only I personally will issue any passes.

In order to avoid serious penalties, I advise every[245] ghetto resident to adhere strictly to this ordinance.

No. 106: YI-452

Rumkowski's request of 16 June 1944 to report to the transports, promising garments and allowances as incentives. [in Yiddish]

Attention! *Regarding a voluntary registration for work outside the ghetto.*

I hereby announce that men and women (also couples) can register for work outside the ghetto. When it involves families with children in *ages capable of work,* those children can also register together with their parents for work outside the ghetto.

All these persons receive full clothing, like a suit, shoes, underwear, and socks. Each person can take along with him a parcel of up to 15 kilos. Thereby, I want especially to note that for these workers postage will be free, so *that they will have the possibility to write letters.*

Moreover, I expressly point out that all those who register for work outside the ghetto will be able to collect their rations immediately without a line.

The mentioned registrations take place daily in the Labor Office at 13 Lutomierska from *Friday, the 16th of June 1944, from 8 o'clock in the morning until 9 in the evening.*

No. 107: YI-38

Notices in the ghetto Chronicle, *22 and 23 July 1944, concerning the mood in the ghetto. [in German][246]*

The question of restructuring has moved to some extent into the background due to the general situation. It appears as if the action could not be carried through with the original sharpness envisioned by the chairman. It also appears as if the question of homeworkers will not be solved as radically as the chairman had declared in his last speech. In other words, there is a certain relaxation to be noted that doubtless is to be traced back to the general world situation. At this point, the chronicler cannot possibly pass over the events that finally concern the whole world and that naturally cannot remain without influence on the ghetto. Here and there, newspapers or news penetrate into the ghetto. The times are unquestionably critical and the inmates of the ghetto look forward to the coming hours with mixed feelings. All thoughts, considerations, hopes, apprehensions culminate finally in the single principal question: Will we be left in peace?[247]

. . . .

The day passed calmly. The population is drawn as well as it can into the open air of Marysin, where the dignitaries made their summer residences again this year.[248]

The mood in the ghetto is rosy. Everybody is full of hope for a speedy end to the war. But everybody is staying calm and hopefully it will also remain so.

No. 108: YI-1371

Announcement by the mayor of Litzmannstadt of 4 August 1944, that the food cards are being blocked for the tailors of two shops and that the death penalty awaits those giving them shelter or food. [in Yiddish]

Concerning transferring the ghetto.

In as much as factories no. 1 and 2 (tailoring, 34–36 Łagiewnicka and 45 Łagiewnicka) have not carried out summons no. 417 of 2 August 1944, concerning transferring the ghetto, I direct the following with immediate effect:

1) The food allotments of those employed in factories no. 1 and 2 are immediately blocked. The issuance of food for those employed in the aforementioned plants takes place only at the Radegast train station.
2) Whoever conceals [in his residence], allows to spend the night, or gives food to those employed in plants no. 1 and 2 *will be punished with death.*

Signed:
The Mayor of Litzmannstadt

No. 109: YI-1283

Text of Biebow's speech before the Jewish tailors delivered on 7 August 1944. [in German]

The chairman (Rumkowski) speaks a few explanatory words and says that H.B. will address the transfer of the ghetto. Biebow says:

Workers of the Ghetto,

I have already spoken before on various occasions and hope that you will take what I have said until now to heart. The situation in Litzmannstadt has newly changed, specifically from midday today. It comes to a total evacuation of women and children on the German part. That means all the ethnic Germans must leave the vicinity. Whoever imagines that the ghetto is not confronting total dissolution is mightily mistaken. To the very last one, each must flee and will flee. A few will believe that it is better to remain as the last ones. Bombs have already fallen in the vicinity of Litzmannstadt; had they fallen in the ghetto, there would not be one stone on another any more.

The shifting of the ghetto should be carried out in calm, order, and quality and it is madness when plants 1 and 2 do not report: As a result, this will compel recourse to compulsory measures. . . . [I have] cooperated 4½ years, always striven to do the best. . . .

I give you the assurance that all of us will take pains to continue to do the best and through the shifting of the ghetto to maintain your life.

Now in the war, where Germany has been struggling of late, it is necessary to shift the workforce; since on the basis of Himmler's directive thousands of Germans are being sent out of the factories to the front, they must be replaced. I say it for your own good and assume that plants 3 and 4 will unanimously appear at the train station.

Mühl Street and 8 Neustadt are going in connection with this. These are according to the Eldest's statement 1,000 persons, including the family members at least 2,000 persons. Thus, if the wife works in the tailoring factory, but the husband at the time is in the carpet factory, he goes along. Whole families are going to the various camps that will be newly set up, where factories will be erected. The trifle of rug knotting and so forth is finally at an end here.

Workers are needed at Siemens, A. G. Union, Schuckert Werken, everywhere that munitions are made. In Czenstochau, where workers labor in the munitions factories, they are very satisfied and the Gestapo is also very satisfied with their production. You of course want to live and eat and you will have that. I am not standing here like a dumb kid, giving speeches and nobody comes. If you compel recourse to coercive measures then there will be dead and injured.

Care is being taken to deliver food into the wagons. The journey will last ca. 10–16 hours. Take along up to 20 kg in baggage. I have nothing against it if someone wants to travel along now, even though he works in a later scheduled tailoring plant. But the irksome behavior and negligence must cease, this I do say to you. I am not an itinerant speaker and blustering through the ghetto. If you do not accept reason, the ghetto administration withdraws and coercive measures will be applied. I implore you on this account to accept reason and heed my words and to obey; otherwise I have no more to add. This very morning, it was necessary to cram the people from the C[entral] P[rison] into the wagons. The machines are standing and there are no workers there.

In the camps, you will be paid in German Reichsmarks; the managers of the plants are Germans. The plant managers and instructors are going along; they are the first who have to report. Tomorrow after 12 o'clock in the C[entral] P[rison], if there is too little space in Schneider Street, or as the offices otherwise direct.

There is enough space in the train wagons. Sufficient equipment is being transferred. Come with your families and bring pots, drinking vessels, and eating utensils; we do not have such in Germany, for they are distributed to those harmed by bombings. I assure you again that you will be taken care of. Pack and present yourselves. If not and measures are applied, I cannot help any more.

No. 110: YI-458A

Rumkowski's announcement of 9 August 1944 that all inhabitants of the western part of the ghetto must move into the eastern part. [in Yiddish]

Ordinances concerning transferring the ghetto.

1) All plants are being closed
   From Thursday, the 10th of August 1944, all plants are being closed. In each plant there are to be at most ten persons, for packing up and shipping the goods.
2) Clearing of the western part of the ghetto
   From Thursday, the 10th of August 1944 on, the western part of the ghetto (the other side of the bridge) must be cleared of all inhabitants and workers. The inhabitants and workers there must all move over into the eastern part of the ghetto.

From Thursday, the 10th of August 1944, no food at all may be given out in the western part of the ghetto.

No. 111: YI-1377

Appeal by Rumkowski of 15th August 1944 to report to the transports in order to be able to leave the ghetto together with families and baggage. [in Yiddish]

Jews of the ghetto, be sensible!!!
Report voluntarily to the transports!
You thereby make the departure easier on yourselves.
Only those reporting voluntarily have the certainty of *traveling together with their family members and to take along baggage.*
I therefore advise you to report still tonight at the Central Prison or in the collection point at 3 Krawiecka Street.

No. 112: YI-1380

Demand by the Gestapo of 23 August 1944 concerning leaving the remaining ghetto area by the twenty-fifth under threat of the death penalty. [in Yiddish][249]

About reduction of the ghetto.
All ghetto areas, with the exception of those listed below, must be completely cleared out with immediate effect *by no later than Friday, 25 August 1944, 7 a.m.*
All the persons who reside in the closed areas must leave their dwellings by the mentioned deadline and may not set foot in the cleared areas again.
Whoever will not obey this ordinance and is found on Friday, 25 August 1944, after 7 o'clock in the morning in the closed areas will be punished with death.
Remaining as the residential area for Jews is the area that is bounded:

On the west side: Along Łagiewnicka Street from no. 1 to no. 27, i.e. from the corner Brzezińska-Łagiewnicka until the corner Łagiewnicka-Dworska.

On the south side: Along Dworska Street from no. 2/3 until no. 53, i.e. from the corner Łagiewnicka-Dworska until the corner Dworska-Marysińska.

On the east side: Along Marysińska Street from no. 8 until no. 30, i.e. from the corner Brzezińska-Marysińska until the corner Marysińska-Dworska.

On the north side: Along Brzezińska Street from no. 2 until 68, i.e. from corner Łagiewnicka-Brzezińska until the corner Brzezińska-Marysińska.

For special attention:

Remaining in the closed areas:

1) the plants housed in barracks,
2) the hospitals,
3) the Central Prison,
4) the 4th Order Service Department in Marysin.

Secret State Police.

VII

Internal Conditions

Housing Conditions

The area finally designated for the ghetto occupied 4.13 square kilometers on 1 May 1940. When a segment consisting of a series of streets on the ghetto's south side was cut off at the beginning of February 1941, it then occupied 3.851 square kilometers. During subsequent years, the ghetto's area changed somewhat (reduced in May 1941 to 3.743 square kilometers, but expanded in October 1941 to 3.82 square kilometers), until it stabilized in June 1942 at 3.82 square kilometers.[1]

Since the ghetto was bisected by two important arterial roads linking the city with the north (to Zgierz) and west (to Aleksandrów), these thoroughfares were excluded from the ghetto. The ghetto thus consisted of three separate sections (A, B, and C), whose connection was, starting in July 1940, over three wooden bridges constructed at the expense of the Jewish community (they cost around 60,000 RM). Two bridges crossed over Zgierska Street and a third crossed over Aleksandrowska Street. Ghetto A was the largest and together with Marysin occupied 3.07 square kilometers, while ghetto B was 0.52 square kilometers and ghetto C 0.23 square kilometers. The neutral strip on the Bałuty Marketplace was 0.01 square kilometers.[2]

Before the bridges were constructed, crossing from one part of the

ghetto to another was a real trial. The narrow passage gates were inadequate to let the dense crowds through during the few minutes that the gate guards allowed for this, and the guards would keep "order" by lashing out with leather belts. On 4 June 1940 this was eliminated and the traffic through the transit points took place all day without a break, initially until 5 P.M. and from 8 June until 8 P.M.[3]

At the beginning of 1941, the ghetto included 135 streets and alleys. The former Polish names of the streets were exchanged for German ones already in 1939.[4] But at the start of 1941, the German street names in the ghetto were changed to letters of the Roman alphabet: A, B, C, and so on, as well as combinations such as AB, AC, and AO, and also to numbers. According to a German map of the city of Łódź from 1942, there were 57 streets in the ghetto designated with letters, 54 with numbers, while the rest (mostly border streets) retained their German names. The color of the street signs was black on "Jew-color" (*Judenfarbe*) yellow.[5]

For a long time in 1940 there was no street lighting at all and the ghetto was sunken into darkness. The eventual street lighting at night was very meager, two or three lamps on each of the more important streets. Moreover, except for Rumkowski, the Order Servicemen, sanitation personnel, authorized officials, and old clothes collectors, nobody was allowed to appear in the streets. At first, the curfew hours were from 5 P.M. to 7 A.M., then from 16 May 1940 until 8 P.M. and from 4 October until 9 P.M.[6] The authorities would extend the curfew hours as a penalty. Thus, for example, a report spread in the ghetto on 2 July 1940 that the boundary between the Soviet and German occupation zones would be returned to the border of 1914.[7] Out of the joy that seized the ghetto population, people were in the streets until late into the night. As a penalty, on the order of the German authorities, Rumkowski immediately extended the curfew, starting from 6 P.M.[8] During the September Action of 5–12 September 1942, an absolute ban on walking in the street was imposed, the so-called "*Shpere.*"

The ghetto was also excluded from the municipal trolley system until 9 September 1941. Limited trolley service was reinstituted for transport of goods. In November 1941, the ghetto received five motor-wagons and twenty-four lorries. New trolley lines were laid out in the direction of Marysin and a series of lines were extended to different ghetto enterprises (leather warehouse, tailoring workshops).[9] At the beginning of May 1942, the trolley line to the rail siding station in Radogoszcz was completed.[10] The formerly independent Trolley Department was merged on 25 May 1942 with the Transport Department under one management.

From 1 June 1942, limited passenger service for workers was also introduced in the morning hours, until 7:30. One had to have a special permit to ride the trolley in later hours. About 3,500 people used the trolley daily in June 1942.[11]

The average population density in the ghetto at the very beginning is discussed in chapter 1. An average of more than 68,000 people inhabited each square kilometer, about 3.5 persons per room and 3.95 square meters per person.

During the transfer of nearly 7,000 people from the ghetto section excised in February 1941, the following proportion was adopted as a basis for housing the evacuees: "six people in one room, depending on its size; six to eight people in a room with a kitchen, depending on their size; and eight to twelve people in two rooms with a kitchen, depending on their size."[12] During the relocation that the Housing Department carried out in the second half of July 1942, in order to equalize the distribution of tenants, the rule of 3.5–4 square meters per person was adopted as a basis for the apportionment.[13]

These statistics are dry average figures and do not give a picture of the shocking housing conditions in the ghetto. We bring later (see doc. no. 113) a couple of descriptions of apartments where people lived, recorded by an inspector from the Relief Department during his visits.[14]

The severe winter of 1940–1941 ravaged the apartments and the courtyards. For heating fuel, people used double doors, double windows, interior walls, and even floors. Closets were ripped out, as well as the floors of the attics, "so that the residents of the floors beneath the attics were in constant danger that the ceiling over their heads would fall in, or that somewhere a neighbor woman who was just hanging out laundry would fall down on his head, as had already occurred in many such cases." It happened during a frosty night that someone took apart the wooden steps of the building and the occupants of the uppermost floors could not leave.[15] The wooden fences were torn away, so that whole streets became one big courtyard.[16]

In the hot summer months, the heat in the small, densely occupied stinking rooms, whose windows also had to be heavily curtained at night due to the mandatory blackout, would drive the exhausted people into the courtyards, where ghetto life concentrated (doc. no. 114).[17]

A German who visited the Łódź Ghetto in autumn 1941 describes in the following fashion the physical appearance of the ghetto and its people:

> The same picture catches the eye from both sides: Broken-down buildings in the construction style of the nineteenth century, clean streets—the only means to avoid an epidemic, remarked [the Order Service commandant] Rozenblat—dilapidated barracks, dim workshops with sweating, emaciated, yellowed, silent figures, who are working at an insane tempo . . . deeply creased, hungry faces. The rooms teeming with people, a couple of fields with vegetables, that had been torn out of the meager ground between demolished buildings, two half dried-out, bare trees on the Bałuty Market square, and above it all a sky whose cloudlessness and radiant blueness were more a curse than a blessing.[18]

Quite calamitous were the living conditions in the so-called "collectives," the shelters for the evacuees from the province and from Western Europe. People lived twenty to thirty in a room, sleeping for months on the bare earth. The second Prague transport of 1,000 people was housed in a building with a single pump in the yard and four toilets. There was not enough water, so they could not deal with the filth and lice infestation. The majority did not live long enough to get tolerable apartments. The deportation in the first half of May 1942, during which 10,161 "settlers" from the West were sent away, "solved" the problem of overpopulation and crowding in the collectives in a tragically radical way.[19]

Family Life, Children, and Old Folk

The ghetto conditions had a destructive influence on family life. First, many families were left without husbands and older sons, who had either been mobilized into the Polish army in August 1939 or had fled from the city during the days of panic in September 1939. The ratio of men and women was unbalanced, according to the census of 16 June 1940. Out of 156,402 Jews in all, there were 85,175 women and 71,227 men, i.e., there were 119.4 women for every 100 men.[20]

This disproportion was even greater among those "resettled" into the Łódź Ghetto in the months September-November 1941: among the deportees from Włocławek and its area, men were 28 percent (866 men out of 3,082 souls) and among the Western Europeans 41.5 percent (8,263 men and 11,690 women).[21]

According to the census of 1931, the ratio of men to women among the Jewish population in Łódź was 100:110. The number of men in the ghetto systematically declined due to the departures for labor outside the ghetto and due to higher mortality among men in comparison with women, who were as far as possible spared from heavy physical labor. In 1941, the ratio of men to women was 100:123, and by 1944 it was 100:137. In certain age groups this disproportion was even greater: Among those ages 30–34, the ratio of men to women was 100:151 in 1941, while according to the final ghetto census in March 1944 it had fallen to 100:196.[22] Of course, the absence of men meant that in quite a lot of families the wife had to bear the yoke of supporting herself and the smaller children.

The physical conditions and the crowding in the apartments, where people often had to live together with total strangers, negatively influenced family life, and familial intimacy vanished. Moreover, women were systematically recruited into the ghetto workshops, especially during and after the first outsettlement phase of winter and spring 1942. In April 1942, the number of employed women was almost as large as the number of working men—31,286 women and 32,985 men. However, by the end of 1943, the ratio was reversed, with 43,346 women and 30,436 men employed.[23]

The women, particularly the younger ones, became economically independent in the ghetto and, equally with the men, carried the heavy burden of ghetto life. The man was no longer able to support his family from his meager earnings alone. The so-called "family supplements" in the amount of 15 marks a month for each nonworking family member had very little value. Even the younger children in the family became more or less economically independent. In May 1942, there were 6,940 adolescents and children under age seventeen employed in forty-three ghetto workshops, but in the middle of August their number more than doubled to 13,881. On 1 March 1944, after a whole series of deportation actions had taken place, there were still 5,432 children and adolescents employed in the ghetto industry against the total of 72,786 adult workers.[24]

The ghetto family was thereby transformed into a sort of work cell, where each member, starting from children nine and ten years old, had to shift for his and her own existence and sustenance. This perforce had to result in weakening, or even completely abolishing, the position of the father as the head and provider of the family. His esteem and authority fell. There were even families where the children with their daring and inventiveness became the breadwinners, while the father who could not adapt to the radically changed ghetto conditions became the homebody and the failure. The sense of unity of the family members also became looser. Children recognized the bitter reality that their parents not only could not protect them, but were themselves helpless. The long workday caused people to meet only during very brief periods of time, in the morning, in the rush to the job and in the evening after work, when the exhausted body longed for rest. As a rule, common family mealtimes disappeared (except on days of rest); the chief meal, the soups, would be eaten in the workshops. The unceasing hunger caused an intensification of the instinct of self-preservation and weakened the feelings of familial solidarity. Close family members became alienated strangers.[25]

The meager food allocations were shared with a painful precision. Not infrequently this was a cause of flare-ups in the family. The small children who were driven by hunger to pick off bits of bread from the dreadful portions for the adults were also a cause for quarreling.[26] "In the area of food, great tragedies are occurring in homes. Whole families become angry at each other and no one can help at all," noted a Łódź Ghetto resident in his diary in January 1944.[27]

Small, nonworking children, whom people protected with great devotion in the ghetto, now became a heavy encumbrance. Parents either had to leave the home very early and abandon the little ones to God's mercy, or take them along with them into the workshops. It was easier in this respect when workshops, as already mentioned, introduced their own children's clubs where the children passed the day under the supervision of educators while the parents worked.

It is worth recalling here that, regardless of the September Action in 1942 that was essentially directed against children to age ten, people managed to save a large number of young children. According to the census of March 1944, the number of children up to age nine inclusive amounted to 5,287 or 6.6 percent of the total ghetto population (in 1941, they were 12.9 percent). Since the number of births from October 1942 until March 1944 did not amount to more than about 500, one can conclude from this that about 4,800 children up to age nine survived the September Action.

Difficult was the situation of the wife, who after a long workday had to wrack her brain and apply her entire culinary inventiveness in order to cook something for supper for her husband and children, who would come home hungry and exhausted from the job (if they still had a home of some sort).The nonworking wife filled her whole day with standing in lines in front of the food shops.[28]

The motives of attachment between husband and wife also changed. "People often married in the ghetto not out of one's hearty free will to wed, but through necessity of external circumstances, like a shared apartment, shared housekeeping and quite often on account of . . . wedding coupons"[29] (that Rumkowski would bestow on young couples).

Fictive marriages also occurred, especially during the deportations, when the family members of an employee in an important branch of the ghetto industry were spared in his merit. Lonely men and women, whose previous spouses had fallen victim to the deportations, also formed couples. Rumkowski and the Jewish court declared dead all those sent away and legally allowed the remaining spouses to remarry.[30]

Due to the constant state of hunger and heavy physical labor, normal sexual life was also disrupted: men became impotent and women would cease menstruating.[31]

Births in the ghetto were relatively rare events. They fell in comparison with the prewar period by more than two-thirds. In the years 1928–1939, the average number of Jewish births in Łódź was 260 a month, roughly 1.1–1.3 per thousand. During the five occupation years, the average was 46 a month, or 0.4 per thousand.[32]

Due to the abysmal housing conditions, sexual modesty also weakened. The housing conditions in the ghetto paired together in single rooms men and women of different ages. People slept crowded together, pressed together, frequently on the floor; a bed of one's own was a luxury in the ghetto. Total strangers of both genders were brought together under one roof. The permanent hunger evoked a general psychic negligence that blunted the instinct of shame.

In such conditions, children became sexually mature early (doc. no. 115).[33] Among the children in the ghetto there also developed a sort of practical intelligence. "Children in the ghetto take on themselves reasoning not according to their years and not according to their development—children in the ghetto are small adults with big worries," wrote a good observer of the ghetto conditions in his reportage.[34] On the other hand, however, due to poor nutrition, children would remain retarded in their physical development. It would happen that children ceased to grow, that young children would cease walking or talking.[35]

After the closing of the schools in October 1941, the majority of ghetto children were placed at risk of the destructive influences of street life. Of everything—of the home, of the school—only the street was left to the child. Children and adolescents occupied first place among the street peddlers. Street trade in the ghetto was strictly forbidden and more than one such "criminal" paid for this transgression with deportation. There were also a large number of children among the so-called "coal miners."

Hunger often drove children to snatch vegetables from a passing wagon and to other offenses. Rumkowski opened a special court and a separate prison for them.

Many children had been left half- or total orphans. In numerous cases their fathers had fallen in the war, were away in the Soviet Union, or were tormented or shot to death, or both their parents had been deported.

Children in the ghetto carried on their weak shoulders the entire burden of ghetto life. After a workday of four to eight hours (depending on their age), they would have to deal with the housekeeping (cleaning, making fire, preparing the meager meal, if there was what to prepare). They also had to stand long hours in the chaotic lines in front of the food shops, where they would sometimes be beaten by the ghetto policemen.

Total orphans were housed in orphanages, or they were given to

Children dig for fuel in an empty lot in the Łódź Ghetto, 1940–1944. Photographer unknown. USHMM, courtesy of Muzeum Sztuki w Łodzi.

relatives, or were placed with private persons. Such children were not infrequently helpless victims of exploitation. The better parts of their food rations would be taken away from them for the sick, or for one's own children, or they were wronged in another fashion. It also happened that families, after the loss of their children, took in a strange child and treated it as their own.[36]

In the workshops and other job sites, children and adolescents not infrequently ran into a heartless attitude from the management and the workers, particularly in periods when there was not enough work for everybody. The adults' talk in the workshops and their thieving would have a demoralizing influence on the adolescents. Women workers would treat these victims of modern child slavery much better, for they would take them under their protection.[37] Former teachers, who now labored in the workshops, also strove as far as possible to neutralize the harmful influences of the environment and clandestinely maintain among the children the desire to learn.

The ghetto's Guardians Commission for Adolescent Workers could do little. It had too few people and no authority. The commission was, for example, unable to eliminate in the workshops the dealing in the more expensive food rations (sugar, sausage) that went on among the employed children. The children felt justified in doing it due to lack of money and the small wages of their parents.[38] At the end of 1942, the Guardians Commission established collective residences for older adolescents.[39]

Children experienced all the horrors, social evils, and immoralities of ghetto life, and there grew up a younger generation about which a ghetto observer wrote with sarcasm: "On these 'natural treasures' of the ghetto state—in the 'coalmines'—is created the soil on which will grow the degenerate, the mutilated, and crippled Jewish generation that the enemies of the Jews want to see"[40]

Ghetto children and adolescents had a protesting and negative attitude to the world of the adults, a world that could not protect them and stood in sharp conflict with the ideal concepts that they had about it. Their innocent sense of justice was sharply assaulted by the wrongs and injustices that were a daily occurrence in the ghetto.[41] They would even collectively express their protest in the form of demonstrations (imitating the adults). A German police report describes a demonstration of several thousand "Jewish brats" (*Judenbälger*) in the ghetto as early as the start of August 1940.[42]

As Y. Nirnberg relates, in February 1941 a children's demonstration took place in front of the building where Rumkowski lived. Children carried a banner with the inscription: "Rumkowski, you are our misfortune." A speaker from SKiF (Socialist Children's League, the Bundist children's organization) gave a speech about the situation of the children in the ghetto, about the need, hunger, and great mortality among working children. When the march neared the Bałuty Market square, the Jewish police dispersed it.[43]

Among themselves, children in the ghetto evinced touching feelings of solidarity, such as giving up a part of their food for a sick friend, being concerned with a friend during illness, or in other serious conditions.[44]

Many children reacted to the new, extraordinary situation with fear, insecurity, withdrawal, and apathy. Jewish children were the first to whom the Germans denied the right to live. While the sense of the constantly lurking danger of death evoked among some children the strength for the stubborn struggle for their lives, among others there was a state of permanent terror and other neurotic symptoms. Among some children who were housed in the dormitories, the awareness that their parents could not, or would not, protect them from the danger of death, the feeling that they had no one on whom to count, evoked a hostile, aggressive attitude toward their parents and adults. Children in the ghetto knew that the chances of the parents to save themselves were in a certain measure dependent on whether they stayed together with their children or abandoned them. This situation naturally had to provoke suspicions in the child that could easily turn into a feeling of alienation and even open hatred.[45]

Older children often broke out of the ghetto and began a wandering life, hiring themselves out to peasants in villages, occupying themselves with smuggling, hiding out in the woods, joining groups of partisans, and going through all seven rings of the Gehenna of persecuted Jews.

During "actions" they would hide themselves, escape from groups being led to destruction, break out through the ghetto fences, and so on.

A group of young children play outside in the Łódź Ghetto, 1941–1943. Photograph by Mendel Grosman(?). USHMM, courtesy of George Kadish/ Zvi Kadushin. [The question mark after the photographer's name appears in the USHMM documentation for the photo.]

In addition to children, the category of superfluous people in the ghetto included the elderly. In the Nazi division of Jews into "useful" (until a certain time) and "harmful" (worthless bread eaters), the old belonged to the latter group. In the ghetto conditions, where only the working Jew had the right to exist, they were a burden for the ghetto and their own children. Old people had in still greater measure than children the feeling of being useless and defenseless. They lived in the shadow of constant danger of death.

In contrast to the children, the old could little adapt to the radically changed living circumstances. With their firmly fixed way of thinking and deeply rooted habits, they were incapable of it.

Nevertheless, Rumkowski even privileged old people until a specific period in the Łódź Ghetto, and promoted the biblical verse, "And you shall honor the face of the old man."[46] After arrival in the ghetto of nearly 20,000 Western European Jews, among whom the percentage of old people was very high, he established for them a special home for the aged. They were also favored in regard to monetary relief grants. In the first half of 1941, the elderly from age seventy received 14–20 marks a month (the amount increasing with age), while other age groups received only 10–15 marks (see chapter 2).

A certain number of old men and women were also employed in some ghetto crafts, like splitting mica and sorting objects brought into the ghetto.

When the deportations to destruction commenced, elderly people were the first victims. After the deportation of September 1942, a minimal number of old people remained in the ghetto.

Social Conditions

Intergroup Relations

The events of war and later the enclosure in the ghetto evoked far-reaching changes in the social structure of the Jewish population. The majority of wealthy Jewish bourgeoisie abandoned the city even before the sealing of the ghetto. Remaining were the middle class, the working masses, and the impoverished.[47] These social segments immediately lost the economic ground under their feet and tumbled ever deeper into the abyss of desolation. Their entire livelihood became dependent on the work that they were doing in the ghetto factories for the benefit of the German authorities.

But, as with every socioeconomic catastrophe, a certain class shift in the ghetto also took place. Being rich in the ghetto meant having one's fill of bread. Formerly more or less well-to-do segments were completely ruined. In contrast, certain individuals with their families worked themselves up economically and even became "*nouveaux riches*" thanks to speculative deals (when at first such were still possible) or thanks to their position in the ghetto hierarchy. "The wheel of fortune turned so that the former merchant and manufacturer could today tip his hat ten times to a nothing, a negligible personage, who before the war could [never and in no] way have such access to that rich man."[48]

The ghetto population was divided, first of all, into two chief groups: (1) Bałuters or residents of Old Town who were rooted in that soil for generations, and (2) city folk driven into the ghetto. The first group generally held on to their former household in the ghetto. They did not have to run into the ghetto, like the city folk, often with only the shirt on their backs. They had to share their apartments with those who came from town, but they retained their furniture and household furnishings. One could immediately differentiate between the apartment of a veteran resident of Bałuty or Old Town and that of a city fellow. While among the former, the residences were still more or less furnished residences of those "who can still allow themselves to have their worm-eaten closets, their wobbling dressers, their mirrors . . . their glass serving bowls with paper flowers and their photographs on the walls"; in contrast, "apartments of the newcomers echo with their emptiness, echo with the emptiness of their four walls."[49]

Of course, much of the furniture of the Bałuty residents also fell victim during the cold fall and winter months of 1940–1941. From the pale areas on the wall, one knew just where the burned furniture had stood. Generally, however, the local residents were better set up in regard to furniture and room furnishings than those who had come in from town. This difference between the Bałuters and the city folk found its expression in the ghetto language. A Bałuty resident was ironically and insultingly called a "*Reichsbałuter*" according to the pattern of "*Reichsdeutsche.*"[50]

Time was, before the war, that a well-to-do Łódź family was a bit embarrassed by their poor relatives in toiling Bałuty. The family contacts were very rare. In the ghetto, however, such a Łódź family was delighted with their Bałuty or Old Town relatives, who could assure them of a roof over their heads during the running and bundling into the ghetto. In time, these differences between the residents and the city folk, vivid in the first years of the ghetto, evened out into a universal poverty. By that time, the group differences formed on another basis: the position that a given individual occupied in the ghetto's social pyramid (see below).

Another differentiation arose in the fall of 1941, a division between ghetto residents and newcomers, after the arrival in the ghetto of over 23,000 Western European and provincial Jews.

First, however, a few words about the controversy that broke out among the Germans themselves in connection with the settlement of Western European Jews into the Łódź Ghetto. A bitter behind-the-scenes struggle between the Łódź administrative organs of power, supported by the Wehrmacht on one side and Himmler and Heydrich on the other side, played out in September–October 1941 about the planned expulsion of 20,000 Jews from the Reich and Protectorate, along with an additional 5,000 Gypsies.

On 24 September, the Łódź mayor sent to *Regierungspräsident* Uebelhör a memorandum, where he categorically opposed the deportation plan, pointing to the great crowding in the ghetto, an average of 5.8 persons per room that would become 7 people per room after the influx of 25,000 people. This could bring with it a huge danger of epidemic. Moreover, it would also harm the economic interests of the Wehrmacht, because it would be necessary to convert the laboriously constructed ghetto workshops into mass quarters for the newcomers.

On 4 October, Uebelhör sent a report about the matter to Himmler and three days later personally intervened at the Ministry of Internal Affairs. As he wrote in his second telegram to Himmler of 9 October, he there learned that Eichmann and the official for Jewish affairs in the Łódź Gestapo had, at a conference there on 29 September, given phony information that he, Eichmann, supposedly had received from him, Uebelhör, and from the director of the ghetto administration (Biebow) about the number of Jews in the ghetto. Eichmann had stated the number 120,000 when in fact the number of Jews in the ghetto on 1 September was 145,000. "I can only characterize the behavior of Eichmann and of the Jewish affairs specialist at the Gestapo as manners adopted from Gypsy horsetraders," wrote the *Regierungspräsident* in the telegram. He requested that both men be held to account and that the expelled not be sent into the Łódź Ghetto, which was operating in full shifts for the war economy, but into the Warsaw Ghetto "where there are still functioning dancehalls and bars" (doc. no. 115a.).[51]

The director of the ghetto administration also wrote a letter regarding intervention to General Thomas, chief of the *Wirtschafts und Bewaffnungsamt* (Office of Economy and Armament) of the Army High Command (OKW). Thomas requested Himmler on 11 October to send the *Reichsjuden* (German Jews) and Gypsies into another ghetto (mentioning Warsaw), giving the aforementioned motive of the harm to the economic interests of the Wehrmacht at war.

Nevertheless, as always in such cases, when the economic interests of the Reich came into conflict with the political principle of annihilation of Jews, the political principle won out. On the sixteenth of October the first transport of 1,000 Jews from Vienna arrived in Łódź.

Uebelhör, who dared to oppose the almighty SS and SD, received a severe rebuke both from Himmler and Heydrich: his stance on the question had very much impeded the deportation and "moreover demonstrated that he lacks the feeling of membership in the SS," in which Uebelhör had the rank of *Brigadeführer* (major general).

As for the Wehrmacht, in a personal letter to General Thomas of 22 October, Himmler reassured him that the workshops producing for the war industry would in no way be affected by the "resettlement." Himmler here still employed Eichmann's false statistic of 120,000 Jews in the ghetto.[52]

The nearly 20,000 Western European Jews, who constituted 13–14 percent of the local ghetto population (on 1 October 1941 there were 143,800 registered Jews living in the ghetto:[53] doc. no. 116), were a foreign element in the ghetto. With their very appearance, carriage, and clothing alone, they were differentiated from the "*Ostjuden*"[54] (doc. no. 117). Language was an important separation, as they spoke German or Czech. They looked down upon the Yiddish-speaking ghetto masses as a culturally backward element and referred to them coldly, as strangers, if not with contempt. The ghetto was not the right place to be able to create understanding and feelings of solidarity between two such differentiated groups of people, who differed in almost everything and were only united by their shared isolation.

The acclimatization and acculturation process was easier where the linguistic barrier was thinner. For example, the Praguers' knowledge of Czech enabled them to make themselves understood in Polish, while also some of the Viennese, among whom a large segment derived from Galicia, still understood and spoke a little Polish and Yiddish. Polish was the second official language, next to German, in the Jewish ghetto administration. Of all the Western European exiles, the Jews from Prague most easily took root in the ghetto and felt most at home there[55] (doc. no. 118).

Among certain more sensitive individuals, the Jewish catastrophe, the destruction of their heretofore human and Jewish faith, could evoke a drive to become closer to the Eastern European Jews, to their culture and way of life, as a sort of return to roots. But these were surely only individual cases, apparently so insignificant that they did not leave behind any traces in the quite rich documentation from the Łódź Ghetto, in the numerous reportages written by Western European Jews themselves. The Western European exiles, consisting mostly of older people with a firmly established way of thinking and strongly rooted habits, were generally incapable of such a far-reaching spiritual metamorphosis.[56]

It is easy to imagine the really catastrophic change that occurred in the life of these people from the moment they arrived in the Łódź Ghetto. Although in their hometowns they had also been persecuted, humiliated, and robbed, they had still not lived in ghettos. Their material conditions, in comparison with the living standard of a Łódź Ghetto, had been truly light-years away.

Both of these worlds, the ghetto inhabitants and the newcomers, little understood each other. The newcomers made no efforts in this direction. Like foreigners on foreign soil, they—with the exception of certain individuals—did not attempt to make themselves at home. Moreover, the objective conditions were very unfavorable for such a process. They dreamed of return to their *Heimat* from which they were so brutally expelled. They passively and obediently went to the deportations of May 1942 and June–August 1944, with the illusion that perhaps they were going back to Germany and would somehow hold out on homesoil. They instinctively resisted being equated with the local ghetto inhabitants. Just the opposite: they continually strove to underscore their difference and fed themselves with the hope that through this difference they would perhaps escape from the common fate. When they had to exchange the Jewish badge that they wore at home for the badge introduced in the Łódź Ghetto, many German Jews saw in this an act of social degradation.

Rumkowski's attitude toward the Western European Jews was ambivalent. On one hand, himself barely educated, he had great respect for their highly trained intellectuals, among whom there were scholars and artists of world renown. Examples included the famous cancer researcher Wilhelm Caspari, *Sanitätsrat* Dr. Ernst Sandheimt, the senior figure of the Berlin medical world, and the famous Frankfurt chemist Jakob Edmund Speyer.[57] Also among the evacuees were former parliamentary deputies, high government officials, and financial magnates; among the deportees from Prague was also the renowned economic historian Dr. Bernard Heilig. The second transport from Prague, a little ironically called the "VIP[58] or lawyers transport," numbered among its 1,000 deportees about 700 physicians, lawyers, and other members of the free professions.[59]

On the other hand, Rumkowski's domineering and despotic character could not tolerate the Westerners' bearing of independence and superiority, their critical attitude toward the ghetto in general, and toward the methods of the Rumkowski administration in particular. Rumkowski demanded from them, as from others, total subordination. It was also purely psychologically difficult for the Westerners to be subject to an *Ostjude*. They would have become more quickly reconciled with a purely German administration in the ghetto. Rumkowski categorically rejected any idea of taking representatives of the Western European exiles into the leadership of the ghetto.[60] He decided not even to assign the post of chief of the Department for Settlers (*Eingewiesene*) to a prominent representative from their ranks, but entrusted it to a Łódź Jew.

Of the approximately 500 legal practitioners who arrived in the ghetto, seven were assigned to the courts and four rabbis were co-opted to the fifteen-member College of Rabbis.[61] In addition, at the end of November and start of December 1941, nearly 100 newcomers, who were former officers of the German, Austrian, and Czech military, were admitted into the Order Service.[62]

On 8 November 1941, only the fourth day after the arrival of the last transport, Rumkowski delivered a speech at a revue performance in the ghetto theater, where he came out with sharp accusations directed at the newcomers:

> Some of the immigrants do not want to understand what a ghetto is and they exhibit a large measure of impertinence. It's enough for me to have to conduct wars with my own impertinent people and troublemakers, yet I now have to deal with my brothers from the Altreich, who want to

Mordechai Chaim Rumkowski delivers a speech to a crowd of Jews gathered in a public square on Lutomierska Street in the Łódź Ghetto, 15 June 1940. Photograph by Foto Kasprowy. USHMM, courtesy of Instytut Pamięci Narodowej.

bring order in their old style. They think that they are the smartest, the best, the top of the crop. . . . They're making a big mistake. . . . I'm telling you, watch your bones! In the event that you will not subject yourselves to my orders and decrees, I will have to calm you down. . . . I won't hesitate before the sharpest means, for that's why I have authority and power.[63]

Coupled with threats of severe repressions, Rumkowski reiterated accusations against the newcomers in his speech of 20 December[64] 1941 (doc. no. 119) that they were politicking, had a negative attitude to work, and so on. At Passover, during his speech in a synagogue on 23 April 1942, after 60 percent of the "settlers" had already left the ghetto on the way to their destruction, Rumkowski still complained "that the foreign Jews brought onto the ghetto many misfortunes and problems . . . so that it will take a long time until everything will return to equilibrium."[65]

There was no lack of objective and subjective causes of mutual embitterment, dissatisfaction, and lack of confidence. We will here mention the most important ones:

1. The exiles, consisting mostly of older and physically weak people, the overwhelming majority of whom had never done any physical labor, attempted (even more than the veteran residents) to wriggle out of the duty of forced labor. In Rumkowski's eyes, this was reckoned the greatest sin against the interests of the ghetto, as he understood them. Thus, for example, the *Chronicle* of 8 November 1941 recounts that Rum-

kowski ordered that 8 persons from each transport, in total 160 people, should report for work outside the ghetto. But instead of healthy and able-bodied workers, the newcomers picked out cripples that the German physicians rejected during the medical examination. Rumkowski compelled them to provide others in their place.

2. Rumkowski had hoped to bring into the ghetto a healthy, able-bodied element with a respectable percentage of skilled technical intelligentsia, who could be integrated into the ever-growing ghetto production.[66] Instead, he received a large percentage of elderly and sick folk, and a still greater percentage of people with such professions (professional intellectuals, merchants, manufacturers)[67] that they were only a burden for the ghetto. The newcomers experienced bitter disappointment, too. They were supposed to be going to a German industrial city for work, but had come to an Eastern European ghetto, where the heavy pressure of the double regime—Rumkowski on the one side and the Gestapo on the other—was unbearable.

3. Due to their bartering and trading, the price of food articles rose mightily on the free market. The illegal trade blossomed and there was inflation. This conflicted with Rumkowski's plan to turn the whole ghetto into a labor barrack, where need would compel people to work. At various occasions, Rumkowski blamed the newcomers for the great inflation in food product prices in the winter of 1941–1942.

4. The "settlers" quartered in private homes did not benefit from the public feeding in the collective kitchens. They attempted to evade the decree, deducting for the benefit of the collectives two-thirds of the remitted money that they received from the outside, principally through the mediation of the *Reichsvereinigung*.[68] Rumkowski wanted to impose on the "settlers" a strict collectivistic way of life in regard to housing, nutrition, and earnings. However, he encountered strong resistance to this attempt due to psychological reasons.

5. The newcomers sabotaged Rumkowski's decree to sell furs and other valuable items to the ghetto bank that paid negligible prices. They preferred trading them on the free market for food items.

6. Rumkowski, for whom remaining in power became a mania (see below), feared that one of the Western Europeans, who included a respectable number of capable, educated people with extensive administrative experience, might displace him from the office of *Judenälteste*. They stood much closer, particularly linguistically and culturally, to the German administration than he did. We hear this clearly from his speech of 4 November 1941, when he declared "that I am ready to go to war with those who propagate such a slogan and similar ones [concerning taking part in the ghetto management]."

7. Everyone in the ghetto knew, and Rumkowski underscored it in his speeches,[69] that due to the newcomers the already small enough bread ration was reduced (from 330 to 280 grams daily), and that they were to blame for the fact that the schools were closed.

8. Crafty local merchants, many of whom were little more than swindlers, engaged in widespread dealing with the often naive *"Yekes"* (Yiddish slang for German Jews) who knew little of the secrets of the black market; this naturally evoked among the Westerners not a little hatred for the *"ostjudische Gauner"* (Eastern Jewish thieves). This nasty exploitation took on such parameters that Rumkowski, in his speech of 3 January 1942, publicly branded these dealers hyenas and promised a war against them (see chapter 3).

9. The first deportation from the Łódź Ghetto in the winter months of 1942 had an unfortunate influence on the mutual relations between the expelled and the local population. The belief was widespread among the local population at the time that the arrival of the Western European Jews had provoked misfortune. "Many thousands had to leave their homes in order to make space for the infiltrators from the West," noted a contemporary source.[70] The newly arrived Westerners were then still in the role of sad onlookers; they were in the meantime in no danger.

10. Distrust of the German Jews also prevailed among the local population because of their loyal attitude to the German ghetto administration. People took a dim view of the fact that the Westerners were seeking pull with the Gestapo, and Rumkowski censured this—naturally because of other reasons—in one of his public addresses.[71] It was feared in the ghetto that Gestapo agents and informers would arise from the Westerners' ranks.[72]

All these factors combined to intensify still more the alienation and prejudices between the two groups and led to a deep embitterment and distaste, which had tragic results for the new ghetto inhabitants.

The approximately 250 Catholics and Protestants who arrived in the ghetto were a particularly complex problem, as apostates or children of apostates. These people felt that a great wrong was being committed against them. They or their parents had long ago cut every connection with the Jewish people. The complete alienation from the environment where they were brutally cast erected a high barrier between them and the ghetto population. It is clear that the ghetto masses could not have had any friendly attitude to this group. Some Jews perhaps had compassion for them, but on the other hand the ghetto inhabitants had a feeling of satisfaction that fleeing from the Jewish people had helped them little. The Jewish Christians were organized in a Christian Association and had a place in the ghetto where they held prayers. But Rumkowski rejected their request, made at the conference between Rumkowski and representatives of the "settlers" on 1 February 1942, to introduce religious instruction for their children and a separate cemetery. Rumkowski's explanation was that when the schools in the ghetto still existed the study of Jewish religion was also forbidden.[73]

Rumkowski also attempted to overcome Western European Jews' passive resistance through a more friendly and gentle attitude toward them. At the aforementioned conference of 1 February 1942 with 138 selected representatives of the deportees, after hearing out the opinions and statements from the delegates of the individual cities, he developed various plans of accommodating the exiles, like forming a group home for children ages seven to fourteen, two homes for the elderly, and so forth. He offered mild and reconciling words: "I am satisfied that we understand each other after three months living in the ghetto. The inflation prevailing in the ghetto is in the first place a result of the meager bread ration, aside from which many of our brothers have ratcheted up the prices. I am not making any charges against you." He also brought up the fact that, in contrast to their one-time sabotaging of the work, sixty persons had voluntarily reported for the very filthy work of removing waste from the ghetto. However, here too he did not forget to underscore that the Westerners should "promptly beat out of their heads the fantasy that they must get into the communal leadership."[74]

Officially, according to the protocol, the conference concluded in the friendliest mood. All the speakers from the "settlers" strongly praised Rumkowski, in the sycophantic tone of flattery that was adopted in the ghetto toward Rumkowski, for the aid that he had extended to them. Two of the co-opted Western rabbis even spoke, on the basis of quotations from the Bible and Midrash, about the "historic role in the history of modern Jewry that Providence had allotted to Rumkowski."[75]

But it is very doubtful whether these speeches of praise reflected the true opinions among the large mass of Western exiles. It must also be taken into account that the conference took place three days after the conclusion of the first stage of the deportation to Chełmno, when people looked with fear at the uncertain future.

Among the overwhelming majority of the "settlers," their stance and attitude to the new social environment was at best passive. The identification with the interests of this environment was quite weak and dictated throughout by self-serving motives.[76] They stood at a distance, foreign and deeply disappointed.

The majority of the exiles spent a total of six months in the ghetto, too short a time for a process of acclimation in such a diametrically different environment as the Łódź Ghetto. The remnants had enough time to lament their loved ones, who were torn away so suddenly and so brutally. But by now they possessed too little spiritual strength, in the constantly crushing process of physical and psychological forces in the ghetto, to become rooted in the soil constantly shaking beneath their feet.

Of course, even this brief cohabitation of the two population groups had to reduce somewhat the barrier that stood between them. The sources even note mixed marriages between residents and newcomers. The deportations especially led to a number of mixed marriages between "settler" women and privileged residents, and through this the women were saved from being sent out.[77]

On the other side, the exiles had a certain influence on the cultural life in the ghetto. Together with the mass of exiles, there arrived musicians, singers, and actors, like for example the Prague violinists Kraft and Weinbaum, the pianists Kurt Baer (Prague) and Leopold Birkenfeld (Vienna). At concerts and evenings of vocal music in the ghetto theater, they performed separately or together with local talents. The large number of Jewish doctors and nurses from Berlin, Vienna, Prague, and other cities, among whom were world-renowned figures, elevated the level of medicine in the ghetto. From time to time, scientific lectures were arranged for doctors and medical personnel on current diseases of the ghetto.[78]

Social Structure: M. Ch. Rumkowski

The social structure in the Łódź Ghetto had the form of a pyramid that narrowed very swiftly in the direction of its apex. At the very pinnacle stood the *Judenältester,* Mordechai Chaim Rumkowski.

As noted in chapter 2, the system of personal rule by the *Judenältester* was established in the ghetto from the very beginning. The entire internal ghetto regime with its division into different groups and segments was narrowly linked with this person and with the Nazi policy that he realized in the ghetto. His personal defects and qualities, his convictions and ideas, and his character and temperament had a decisive influence on the formation of the inner conditions in the ghetto. We must, therefore, be occupied in more detail with the person of *Judenältester* Mordechai Chaim Rumkowski and his role in the Łódź Ghetto.

Rumkowski was born in February or March 1877 in Vilna.[79] When he took office as *Judenältester* in Łódź in October 1939, he was sixty-two-years old.[80] Exactly when Rumkowski came to Łódź is not known. In Łódź, he worked himself up in time and became a well-to-do merchant and manufacturer, though he neglected his businesses due to his philanthropic-social activity. He was one of the founders and for many years director of the orphanage in Helenówek near Łódź. He finally became an insurance agent with quite a good income.[81]

Politically, he belonged to the Zionist camp and was elected from the Zionist list to the Jewish Religious Community's Board. However, when the Zionist members withdrew from the Jewish Community Board in 1937, as the Łódź Jewish Community fell under the hegemony of the Agudas Israel, Rumkowski did not submit to this decision and stayed on.[82]

Rumkowski's education was not more than a couple of years of elementary school. His intelligence was average. But he excelled—as a contemporary observer states—"with an extraordinarily quick grasp, outstanding memory and with a mighty appetite for honor."[83] This unsatisfied and discontented hunger for honor apparently drove him in the first weeks of the German occupation to seek with all sorts of means the nomination to the office of *Judenältester.*[84] He was already known before

Chairman Mordechai Chaim Rumkowski greets a child at a school ceremony in the Łódź Ghetto, 1940–1942. Photographer unknown. USHMM, courtesy of Zigi Levine.

the war as a person with a strong will and dictatorial inclinations. In the ghetto, with the passage of time, he turned into a despotic autocrat.

When the German authorities gave him the function of head of the Łódź Jewish community, his morbid ambition, bemoaned by enemies,[85] played itself out in his personality as a power complex. According to objective witnesses who survived the Łódź Ghetto, this striving to hold on to his power at any price and with all means turned into a mania with him.[86]

Rumkowski surely considered the dangers connected with his office. In the first weeks, he experienced on his own body the quality of Nazi brutality, when he came to intervene on behalf of the Jewish community secretary, Sh. Nadler, who had been seized for forced labor.[87] The lust to rule, however, overcame him, particularly since he was by nature not a coward and showed courage and self-control when he stood face to face with a death threat. On two different occasions this personal courage manifested itself.[88] In a speech on 1 November 1941, he declared that twice he was threatened with assassination attempts, but he did not tremble and faced his enemies when they menaced him with a knife.[89]

In those areas of ghetto life where the German supervisory authorities over the ghetto left the Jews free hands, Rumkowski's powers were like those of an absolute ruler. He truly became the master of life and death for over 150,000 Jews within the ghetto.

Rumkowski abolished the right of private property in the ghetto.[90] He himself decided about the different levels of the provisioning status for each individual in the ghetto. He had the unlimited right to allocate food coupons, which under the ghetto's conditions signified either giving someone a chance to hold on or condemning him to a gradual death from hunger. He hired and fired people from work. He took for himself the right of administratively punishing and rewarding. Finally, he took for himself the right to select candidates for deportations, both to work outside the ghetto and to destruction.[91] He did not tolerate any independent opinion or attitude around him. He did not tolerate expressions of social organization and activity and brutally suppressed them wherever they appeared.

Rumkowski had "a lucky break" ("*a glik*") when the members of the first *Beirat* (Advisory Council), which consisted of respected and independent people, were cruelly killed by the Gestapo.[92] Regarding the second *Beirat* that arose in February 1940, a contemporary document states that Rumkowski turned it into a council of "mere listeners."[93]

Three members of this "obedient *Beirat*" demonstrated virtue and civil courage and refused to play the role of yes-men. They were Engineer Lap, Dr. Leon Szykier, and M. Zażujer (for a certain time director of the Department for Social Aid). So Rumkowski removed them one at a time. With the removal of these last independent and morally untainted *Beirat* members, there disappeared the last glimmer whatsoever of organized society and the way opened for unlimited, uncontrolled, personal domination by the *Judenältester*.[94]

In order to suppress every independent social activity, Rumkowski liquidated the kibbutzim in Marysin in March 1941. Prior to this, in January, he shut down the Bundist youth collective there,[95] forbidding the activity of workers' delegates and dissolving them. For the same reason, in August he closed all public kitchens that had served, as mentioned, as a gathering place of political groupings in the ghetto. He did not refrain from persecuting to the bitter end everyone who had committed some transgression against him, not even refraining from using deportations to eliminate his opponents from the ghetto.

When nearly 20,000 Western European Jews were sent into the Łódź Ghetto, Rumkowski not only angrily ridiculed their demand to have a part in the ghetto administration, but even rejected a modest proposal by one of their representatives to establish a free loan fund from money to be collected among the more well-to-do exiles. Instead, he directed that a portion of the money for such an aid fund be deducted from arriving remittances and be made available "at my disposition."[96] In various sources, Rumkowski is accused of having been the initiator of the decree that banned receiving food parcels from outside (see chapter 2), because "receiving parcels makes a certain segment independent and therefore [it] must be abolished once and for all," and so the German authorities had only acceded to his request.[97]

In order to ensure for himself unlimited authority in the ghetto, he "chose as advisors and aides characterless people, blindly obedient, self-serving and criminal persons."[98] To one, known in Łódź as an underworld figure, he entrusted command of the ghetto prison and the management of the Marysin ghetto quarter.[99] He recruited people with a criminal past into the ghetto police assault unit (*Iberfal-komando*), hoping to combat one part of the underworld with another.

Rumkowski created around himself an atmosphere of real Byzantine sycophancy. The *Geto-tsaytung* (*GT*), the newspaper that he edited and censored in March–September 1941 (eighteen issues), was chiefly occupied with glorifying Rumkowski and exhibiting his great accomplishments for the ghetto.[100]

Artists painted works exalting Rumkowski. One picture, for example, portrays him spreading out his coat over the children and hungry of the ghetto, gazing up at him in adoration. Another painting depicts him hovering at night over the sleeping ghetto. The paintings are in the museum of the Jewish Historical Institute in Warsaw.

In the calendars published in the ghetto, among the dates noting the creation of all the different departments and workshops was the birthday of only one person—Rumkowski.

Every labor division or department considered it an obligation to present him with gorgeously produced albums at the celebrations of their establishment and at his birthday.[101] For Rosh Hashana 1942, the School Department presented him with a giant-size album bearing the signatures of 715 teachers and 14,587 children in honor of "*Adoneinu ha-Nasi*" (Hebrew: Our Lord the Chairman) and filled with panegyric poems and prayers, written by the children, presumably according to inspiration and directions from adults.[102]

Hundreds of letters arrived for Rumkowski, with songs and elaborate odes of praises from people who hoped in such fashion to obtain work or a food coupon.[103] Parades of children were arranged in his honor.[104]

Rumkowski considered himself a ruler in a sort of "Jewish state." One encounters this expression in the reports by officials of the ghetto administration (e.g., doc. no. 1220, p. 2). He himself employs a more modest expression—"autonomy" or "Jewish self-administration." He liked the external trappings of power. On 14 July 1941, like a governor, he reviewed a parade of 200 trained firefighters.[105] After his public speeches, he would leave the place, walking between two rows of Order Servicemen and firefighters standing at attention.[106] The judges and prosecutors would swear "in consciousness of [their] duty toward God, people and the *Judenältester*."[107]

After establishment of the Postal Department, Rumkowski had a couple of series of postage stamps printed with his picture on a background of ghetto symbols. However, they were not used. When finally, on Purim 1944, they were supposed to be put into use (coinciding with the chairman's birthday), Biebow confiscated them and ordered them destroyed.[108] For prayer services on Rosh Hashana and Yom Kippur, he came attired in "royal garments," wearing a large silver chain with a Star of David.[109]

He often displayed the unbridled temperament of a despotic ruler, cursing, ripping off medals, striking with his walking stick, and slapping.[110] Even when communicating with his officials, he would often behave brutally, as if he enjoyed intimidating everybody (doc. no. 120).[111]

On 16 April 1941, Rumkowski issued an order to the "chief of my Personnel Department" that "all dismissed officials may not hold any office or employment in various physical jobs."[112] This meant, in fact, imposing a death sentence on the dismissed person, because there were no other jobs than those managed by the ghetto administration.

Certain facts testify that he was completely caught up by a greed for power that finally turned him into an obtuse, heartless bureaucrat. In his speech on 3 January 1942, when the preparations for the first deportation were already in full swing and the ghetto was enveloped by fear and despair, he felt it important to devote a major part of his speech to . . . the question of reorganizing the accounting system in the direction of decentralization.[113]

At the end of July 1944, when the ghetto found itself in the stage of final liquidation, Rumkowski played with issuing his own coins in the value of 20 scrip-marks.[114] A similarly heartless and obtuse bureaucrat was his first deputy, the Order Service commandant L. Rozenblat. At the end of July 1944, Rozenblat, as the patron of the Free Loan Fund in the ghetto, halted the issuance of loans to workers with the explanation "that now, when the war is supposed to end shortly, how will we chase after our debtors?" The careful ghetto Chronicler could not here restrain himself, sarcastically adding: "He feared that the ghetto fences will fall and he will, heaven forbid, be left without *rumkes.*"[115] (The ghetto money was popularly called *rumkes* both in the ghetto and in town.)

It would, however, be too simple and perforce not correct if we were to view Rumkowski as merely a despotic autocrat, who did not stop at anything in order to still his hunger for power, or in order to save himself and his intimates at the expense of tens of thousands of others whom he sent to destruction. One of his opponents had to admit that before the war he had clean hands and was "one involved faithfully in the needs of the community."[116]

In the course of time, Rumkowski worked out a sort of ideology, a tactical program for how to save the Jews in the ghetto, or to save what could be saved. The program was based on three fundamental concepts. First, the useful work that the ghetto was carrying out for the German war industry was a firm basis for the existence of the ghetto. Second, to rescue at least some of the Jews, those who had more chances of holding out (the young, those who were working), had to agree to deliver up to the Germans the nonworking and the "harmful element," that anyway had little or no chance to survive at all. Third, the path of resistance would lead to nothing and could only bring misfortunes onto the ghetto.[117]

The idea of "rescue through work" found in Rumkowski its most fluent advocate. In innumerable instances, in all of his public addresses, he never tired of repeating in different variations this fundamental concept, that the ghetto based its existence on work that was useful for the German regime, and in all circumstances, even the most tragic, the ghetto must not lose this justification of its existence (doc. no. 121).

His slogans are known: "Labor is our hard currency," "Work is our guide."[118] In January 1944, he had to exchange this slogan for another. In one of his speeches at a conference with the representatives of the labor divisions on 18 January 1944, he stated "the three pillars on which the ghetto stands are cold, hunger and work." In comparison with his former self-confidence, this new slogan has its symptomatic and tragic point. Another symptomatic example: at the end of July 1944, when the final stage of the liquidation of the ghetto was in full swing, Rumkowski ordered a halt to the disbursement of monetary aid grants and loans, so that the workers would have to continue laboring for their picayune wages.[119] (There was a strong deflation in the ghetto at the time.) He carried through this principle of labor with an iron energy and consistency and created in the ghetto a multi-branched industry in which at the end of 1943 over 85 percent of the population worked.

He considered the nonworking portion of the ghetto population to be unneeded ballast, dependent upon public aid; it endangered the survival of the productive portion and one might sacrifice it—if necessary—in the name of keeping the working ghetto alive.

In the speech he delivered on 4 September 1942, during the action against the sick, the young children and the elderly, he expressed himself in favor of voluntarily surrendering these victims to the Nazi Molech with the reasoning that "at each decree, it must be weighed and measured: Who should, can and may be saved? And logical reason obliges that what is saved must be what can be saved and has prospects for survival, and not what cannot be saved anyway."[120]

Rumkowski went so far that he even argued that certain segments should indeed be deported. In a speech delivered on 3 January 1942 before officials of the ghetto administration, ghetto industry, and representatives of the Western European Jews, he announced that "on the basis of the existing autonomy, only that part of the population will be deported from the ghetto that, in my opinion, earned it." He boasted that he had managed to reduce the number of candidates for deportation from the 20,000 that the Germans initially demanded to 10,000.[121] Who were those who had earned this? Rumkowski listed them. First, they included all who had somehow sinned according to his severe penal code (in his eyes, even those who had stolen a couple of potatoes belonged to this category of "criminals").[122] In a speech presented on 20 December 1941, he explicitly announced that "he sees no other way [to combat the crimes in the ghetto] than through sending the undesirable elements out of the ghetto."[123] He also warned: "Remember that when a new contingent is demanded, I will include onto the list all black-market profiteers,"[124] that is, those not working, among whom were such that earned their meager livelihood from clandestine trade, often with their own food rations. To the category of speculators who should be sent out of the ghetto, he also reckoned parents of children involved in street trading (this was said when all schools in the ghetto had already been closed for two months and the ghetto workshops were not yet in a position to employ even all the adult men), as well as shopkeepers who purchased personal goods from the Western European Jews.[125]

He also reckoned among the undesirable, harmful elements that he would send out of the ghetto, though "after a serious inner struggle," those relief grant recipients "who made light of the obligation to work off the aid grant [fourteen days in the month]." He also threatened deportation for the least act of sabotage (doc. no. 112).[126]

When the second stage of the deportation took place, this time also affecting the families of the employed, Rumkowski came out openly on 2 March 1942 with the principle that "only working people can remain in the ghetto." He cast the blame for the new deportation on the "Jews of the ghetto who scoffed at him and lived to see a misfortune," though he himself admitted that there was not work for everybody. He again vented his total rage at the relief recipients who refused to be drawn into the reserve labor battalions. Sensing the weakness of his argumentation, he openly says "that the order must be carried out; if not, others will carry it out."[127] With total severity, Rumkowski applied the principle that "the order must be carried out" by his Resettlement Commissions during subsequent deportations (in September 1942 and June–August 1944).

Nevertheless, as domineering and inconsiderate as he was toward his ghetto subjects, so flattering and obedient was he toward the German authorities. One of his mottos was "to run ten minutes ahead of each German ordinance."[128] In a document from that period it is indeed said about Rumkowski that "with regard to the authorities he was always ready to obey all ordinances without discussion, even when it required of him very serious measures."[129]

Where did Rumkowski draw such inner strength that enabled him to take on himself the fateful responsibility to carry out all German decrees, even the most brutal? As we shall see from his speeches, Rumkowski believed that he had a great mission to fulfill, to rescue the part of the Łódź Ghetto that let itself be saved in accord with his rescue strategy and perhaps also on the basis of the hypocritical assurances by certain Nazi officials. That he had in this respect vague assurances by certain officials in the German ghetto administration is attested to by his statement on 17 January 1942, at the opening of the exhibition of underwear and clothing: "I have a firm hope on the basis of authoritative assertions that the fate of the expelled will not be as tragic as was foreseen in general in the ghetto. They will not be behind wires and to their portion will fall agriculture. . . . I guarantee with my head that not the least wrong will happen to the working person and I say this not only in my name, but also on the basis of promises on the part of the authoritative factors."[130]

Already in his first preserved speech of 30 August 1941 he stated: "With complete calm and a sense of responsibility before history, I confirm . . . that strength for the merciless struggle with the public troublemakers [those concealing their property, agitators, and loafers] is given me by my undisturbed awareness that there rests on me an obligation to give all of myself in order to give to the ghetto inhabitants a possibility to survive these times."[131]

At the end of his aforementioned speech of 3 January 1942, Rumkowski said: "I hope that, with your help, I will manage to realize my *mission*[132] to create such conditions that will make it possible to survive the present period, to maintain the life and health of broad circles of the ghetto population and its younger generations."[133]

Even earlier, he declared in his speech of 1 November 1941 that "he took over the office tearfully, believing that *Providence* will help him."[134]

Emanuel Ringelblum records in his ghetto notes:

> There arrived today, September 6th [1940], Rumkowski from Łódź, where he is called King Chaim, an old man of 70, a person with extraordinary ambitions and a little crazy [*a bisl a tsedreyter*]. He recounted miracles about the ghetto. There is [in Łódź] a Jewish state with 400 police with 3 prisons. He has a foreign ministry and all other ministries. To the question, why if it's so good, is it so bad, why is the mortality so great, he did not answer. He considers himself as divinely anointed.[135]

Rumkowski made a similar impression ("we have before us a sick person, he is a megalomaniac") on Mordecai Shvartsbard, co-worker of the Warsaw *Oyneg Shabes* clandestine ghetto archive. Shvartsbard also relates that during Rumkowski's second visit to the Warsaw Ghetto in May 1941, he socialized with the folk of the so-called "13th" (a Gestapo entity in the ghetto, led by Abraham Gancwajch), and that the "13th" posted an honor guard in front of the hotel where he stayed. In a speech he gave before the Łódź refugees in the Warsaw Ghetto, Rumkowski described in a self-confident, proud, and somewhat cynical tone the conditions there, bringing up his great accomplishments for the Łódź Ghetto, the trust that the authorities had for him, and his methods of suppressing opposition by the workforce. Exasperated at a series of questions that were asked about the situation of the Łódź Jews, he refused to reply.[136]

Rumkowski was subject to a megalomaniacal delusion of grandeur that came from his unlimited domination over 150,000 Jews. He convinced himself that he would go down in history as the one who managed to save from death tens of thousands of Łódź Jews. And who knows whether he would not have succeeded, if the Soviet army had not halted its offensive on the Polish front from August 1944 until January 1945?[137] There were still 68,500 Jews living in the ghetto on 1 August 1944.

When Hitler seemed to be succeeding, Rumkowski supposedly confided to his secretary that after Hitler's victory, when the task would arise to solve the Jewish question through setting the Jews of Europe up somewhere on a bit of land that Hitler would grant for this purpose, he—Rumkowski—would get authority over all Jews and organize a model state there, because he was highly esteemed by Greiser, the Gauleiter of Wartheland, and known in Berlin.[138]

He was without doubt infected by the Nazi *Führer Prinzip* (leader principle) due to his frequent contacts with the authorities. A contemporary document says about him "that he was already completely permeated with the mentality and ideology of the G[ermans]."[139]

On the other hand, Rumkowski untiringly devoted himself with all his limitless energy to the realization of his "rescue" program. He undoubtedly had organizational talent and he managed in a certain measure to realize some parts of his program, like "(1) bread, (2) work, (3) care for the sick, (4) supervision over the child, (5) calm in the ghetto,"[140] in the very most unfavorable conditions of a ghetto regime. He built up a network of factories and workshops, where the majority of the population found work, indeed heavy, exhausting work, but they could barely, though inadequately, feed themselves. With the help of the Jewish physicians, he set up the healthcare system in the ghetto on a relatively high level, establishing hospitals, outpatient clinics, preventoriums, first aid stations, and so on. Until the winter of 1942, when the hunger very much worsened in the ghetto, sick people benefited from special, better feeding. In the hospitals, nourishment and medical treatment were almost satisfactory until their liquidation in September 1942. Public assistance in the form of meager relief grants included tens of thousands of impoverished families that were either unable to work (elderly and children) or could barely earn anything from their work. A third of Rumkowski's monthly budget would be designated for this purpose.[141] His prewar public activity in the field of orphan care and his sentiment for children in general and orphans in particular (Rumkowski himself was childless) guaranteed that his program for child care was superlatively realized until the September 1942 deportation action (see chapter 2).

Tabaksblat, who was in general critically disposed regarding Rumkowski, nevertheless writes about his activity in this field: "We have to give Rumkowski his due. He cared for children generously. He was not satisfied only with the children of the schools, but he also looked out for them outside school . . . in the first place for orphans, who did not have anyone to raise them. . . . Here Rumkowski truly demonstrated his love and devotion to the child. He cared for them with everything that he could, not sparing any effort and material sacrifices."[142]

Surely it was one of the most tragic moments in Rumkowski's life when, during the September Action of 1942, he himself had to deliver to the Germans the thousands of children for whom he had cared more than for all others.

But even here he was true to himself and the principle that German edicts must be carried out. At a gathering of a huge ghetto crowd on 4 September 1942, he found in himself some sort of superhuman strength to ask for people voluntarily to give away to the Germans the children, the sick, and the old, so that the ghetto should continue to be able to exist. An eyewitness relates that Rumkowski burst into tears during the speech and could not conclude it.[143] Yet on the other hand, he sent policemen and firemen to tear children from their mothers' arms, and he ordered the woman director of the children's camp in Marysin to gather the children and prepare them for the transport.[144]

On 30 August 1944, Rumkowski *voluntarily* left with the final transport to Auschwitz, after he heard his brother's name called out among the deportees and his request to release him was rejected. Did he still believe Biebow's mendacious public assurances that the liquidation of the ghetto would be for the good of the ghetto Jews, who would thereby be protected from the Soviet bombs, that work and life was awaiting all of them in Germany?[145] That is hard to believe. He well knew that no trace remained of the approximately 75,000 Jews who had until then been sent out from the ghetto, that his words of consolation of 17 January 1942 (see above) were false and misleading.

There is no doubt that Rumkowski knew as early as spring 1942 about the tragic fate of those sent out. From the accounts of the remnants of the liquidated provincial ghettos that were sent into the Łódź Ghetto in May 1942, people knew clearly where the deportees were ending up. A deportee from Brzeziny brought a postcard from the rabbi in Grabowo (near Łęczyca), dated 19 January 1942, writing precisely about the Chełmno death camp. When Rumkowski was informed, he replied that he already knew about it somewhat earlier.[146] Perhaps he, like other ghetto leaders in that time, held that it was better that the victims not know about the fate awaiting them. That he consciously spread the illusion that the deportees were not going to their death is proven by the response that he gave a delegation of desperate mothers from the liquidated provincial ghettos, who were evacuated into the Łódź Ghetto: that he would intervene with the authorities to bring their children back to Łódź.[147]

Perhaps this voluntary accompanying of the last remnants of "his" Łódź Jews was an act of despair, after the realization that his entire miserable, bloodstained strategy of "saving" parts of the ghetto had so loathsomely failed. Or perhaps there was even in this a desire to redeem with his own life the serious, unforgivable sin that he had committed against his ghetto community, over which he had reigned with a strong arm for nearly five years. And maybe he really remained until the very last minute the insensitive bureaucrat and prideful "prince" of the Łódź Ghetto, who believed that his identification card as *Litzmannstadter Judenältester*, which he would show to the camp hangmen in Auschwitz,[148] would save him from death. It is difficult to give an answer to this today.

* * *

The second rank in the social pyramid was occupied by all sorts of directors of departments in the ghetto administration, managers of the work divisions, the ghetto police, the court, the firefighters, master craftsmen and instructors in the ghetto workshops, and the physicians and pharmacists. Their privileged provisioning status has already been discussed in chapter 3. Their unwritten juridical status also spared them until the end from deportations, except during the September Action of 1942, when their children and parents were also among the victims. The Jewish Order Service and the firefighters had a promise at the time that for their help in the action their families would still be spared.

These groups were externally differentiated from the ghetto masses with their uniform caps, ribbons of all sorts of colors, and badges.[149] This socially advanced group was composed of newly risen people whom Rumkowski had elevated to major and minor offices. In a contemporary document written by a member of the opposition, they are characterized as "people of whom no one had ever heard, no one had ever known them, half- and quarter-intellectuals, who were not linked with the sufferings and woes of the Jewish street."[150]

The social morality of this ghetto elite is best characterized by the fact that while the broad strata of the ghetto population sank into a sea of awful desolation and need, these people held it possible to set up for themselves in Marysin a boarding-house and summer residences[151] (doc. no. 123) and to hold jubilee balls in connection with dates of the establishment of ghetto workshops and at production exhibitions. About one such jubilee ball, the quasi-official ghetto *Chronicle* reports: "After the opening of the exhibition [of production] by five divisions that took place on 26 December 1942, to which were invited the five highest ghetto bigshots [*shpitsn*], the anniversary celebration organized on 1 July 1943 at the intellectuals' kitchen was especially rich and tasteful. Alongside different snacks ('dainty morsels'), wine was served and a real supper. The party only broke up around 2 o'clock in the morning. The population commented variously about this rare event."[152] It is not difficult to surmise the character of those comments.

Naturally, there were among them, "even among the very greatest ghetto stars," some people who maintained a moral stance in accord with the positions that they occupied in ghetto life,[153] but in light of the documents, they were likely among the rare exceptions.

Thus, there developed a deep moral and social chasm between this ghetto aristocracy ("*getokratye*") and the general ghetto population.

About the attitude of the broad masses to the ghetto elite, we read the following characteristic sentences in a monthly report (dated 23 June 1942) from the German Criminal Police Commissariate in the ghetto to the inspector of the Security Police and Security Service (*Sicherheitspolizei und Sicherheitsdienst*):

> Aside from the chronic distaste among the ghetto population for all that is German, there persists as before an express dissatisfaction among the working Jews with the reigning Jewish upper layers due to the insufficient allocation of foodstuffs. . . . The Jew basically despises the Germans less than his racial brothers ("*Artgenossen*") who rule over him, and he would gladly be rid of them. With time, this distaste changed into an incandescent hatred for the reigning Jewish circles without exception, especially for the *Judenältester*. The Jew cannot in any case be moved to commit a murder against another Jew, but in this case he would not refrain from such a deed, if he did not fear the German organs of power.[154]

General employees in the ghetto administration and the workers in the factories occupied the third spot on the hierarchical ladder in the ghetto. Their status in the provisioning system has already been discussed above. Until the final liquidation phase, their unwritten juridical status in regard to deportations was also more or less assured, particularly when technical specialists were involved. They, and partially their families, were generally spared during deportations and dispatch for work outside the ghetto. But during the final days of the September Action in 1942, the Gestapo no longer differentiated and also seized workers with labor cards in order to fill the quota of deportees.

A very small portion of workers and office employees could also benefit, starting in July 1942, from seven-day vacations in the two rest homes in Marysin, for which a special commission made selections (about fifty persons weekly, while office workers were fewer at twenty-three to thirty-six weekly). The food in the rest homes was much better (inter alia including 500 grams of bread and meat three times a week). Moreover, for the one "on whom fate had smiled," the family could pick up his food rations (except bread).[155] A survivor from the Łódź Ghetto remarks about the rest homes that they were "a bright point in the sad environment that was called Litzmannstadt Ghetto."[156]

On the bottom rung of the ghetto pyramid was the great mass of relief recipients and their families, the nonworking segment of the population. They were the first victims to fall, sooner and later, to hunger, cold, and sickness, and then—to the deportations. From the end of 1942 and start of 1943, they comprised a small percentage of the ghetto population.

As we see, the Rumkowski regime caused a marked and sharp social division of the ghetto population into different groups with different gradations of rights and chances of survival.

With his policy of economic leveling ("nationalization" of property, sharp struggle against private commerce, forcing everyone to go to work in the workshops), Rumkowski did not eliminate the social differences in the ghetto, though he strove for that.[157] In reality, he realized the Nazi program of dividing the Jews into useful and useless.[158] He applied the policy of "divide and rule" and fostered a sharp differentiation of the ghetto citizens of different categories.

Social ferment seethed all the time in the ghetto, fueled by the vivid contradiction between the indescribable need of the great majority and the relative well-being of a small privileged group, a part of which even managed to "make a living"—true, only for a short time—at the expense of the ghetto masses.

It must also be taken into consideration that people were struggling desperately for survival all during the ghetto's existence, and this created the red-hot soil. No civilized society until the Hitler period knew such a struggle between different classes, where the prize was naked life. In the ghetto conditions, the rescue of one person could occur *only at the expense of another*. This conflict for physical survival strongly influenced the intensity of the struggle between the social groups.

The German authorities helped to aggravate the social contrasts in the ghettos, creating an objective basis for those differences. This was, apparently, one of the means to disarm the ghetto population morally, to weaken the national solidarity, in order to have divided, quarreling, mutually loathing groups.

Political Life

The Worker Opposition

The Rumkowski regime's methods aroused against it both individual and collective opposition of varying levels of intensity, from passive to active struggle. There were, for example, some among the professional intelligentsia—attorneys, doctors, engineers, teachers—who did not want to take any part in the ghetto administration and changed their prewar occupation to become unskilled laborers. They did not want their names to be linked with the regime, and did not want to bear any responsibility for its deeds.[159]

Another form of opposition by certain groups was expressed in spontaneous actions against Rumkowski and his bureaucracy in various situations, when those groups presented specific demands or when they felt themselves wronged. Thus, for example, in March 1940, when the ghetto was formed, the Jewish war prisoners from the Polish army, who had been returned to their hometown, gathered on Pilicer's Square and demanded bread, work, and help for the needy. Rumkowski ordered them dispersed. They put up resistance and set off to his secretariat, located in another part of the ghetto. The German guards at the transit gate (there were no bridges yet) fired into the air and demanded that they leave. They stubbornly demanded to be received by the chairman, who finally agreed to receive a delegation. They obtained aid grants both in food and in cash.[160]

We have already alluded in chapter 3 to how the Jewish community's office was demolished in July 1940 by a hungry crowd. In summer 1940, tailors attacked Rumkowski with shears and other tools, after he issued the ordinance to confiscate tailors' sewing machines to equip the newly founded tailor workshops.[161]

The third and strongest form of opposition was active, organized resistance against Rumkowski and his ruling methods on the part of political groupings, particularly the worker parties. In the difficult summer months of 1940, when the dysentery epidemic raged in the ghetto and there was a dreadful hunger, mass meetings and demonstrations took place on the streets, conducted mainly by workers who belonged directly to or were under the influence of the worker parties and the trade unions. The bloody course of such hunger demonstrations on 10 and 11 August, ending with intervention by the Security Police and four injured on the workers' side, has already been discussed in chapter 3. On 12 August, Rumkowski issued an appeal for calm. He referred to the "irresponsible elements that want to bring agitation into our life" and promised to improve the provisioning in the ghetto. But emotions did not calm down. This was demonstrated by the written appeals that were posted about on 23–25 August, calling for people to come to designated streets and express their protest against the regime in power.[162]

How far the desperation among certain parts of the ghetto population had reached can be seen from an appeal dated 25 August and signed by "A Temporary Committee," calling for "dissolution of the Jewish Community [gmine] and immediately deliver ourselves into the hands of the German government, because we now have nothing to lose"[163] (doc. no. 124). The appeal of 23 August summoned "the hungry masses to a death march tomorrow at 8 A.M."[164]

Not yet feeling so powerful and essentially fearing that the demonstrations could undermine his esteem among the German supervisory authorities, Rumkowski convoked a conference with worker representatives of the various trades at the end of August or start of September 1940. There he was accused of being to blame for the bloody events in the ghetto. A delegate from the Bund (Esther Weinberg) demanded that the relief funds be turned over to the disposition of the worker delegates. This time Rumkowski gave in. Workers and their children received free soups and the distribution of provisions was turned over to the worker delegates who organized the distribution of meals at the Bundist and Poale Zion public kitchens. Several tearooms were also opened.[165] But in October 1940, when Rumkowski felt more secure in the saddle, he refused to recognize the competence of the worker delegates to hire and fire workers, and dissolved them. In a number of workshops, however, the delegates secretly continued to remain at their posts.[166]

Initially, Rumkowski encountered opposition during the consultations he convoked with representatives of the various social circles. At one such conference, held on 2 December 1940 during the strike by hospital personnel against the extension of the workday, all the directors of the departments of the ghetto administration and representatives of the ghetto workshops were present. One of the participants (Moyshe Lederman, representative of the Bund) "in a very sharp manner criticized the means [that are applied] to combat these or other phenomena of ghetto life and even the most recent strike," and "proposed to eliminate the police truncheon and the prisons and apply to the ghetto population the method of explanation and persuasion." Another delegate (Engineer Shiper) also submitted a proposal to create "an arbitration commission to be composed of people who have prior experience to negotiate with the worker world." Rumkowski sharply responded to his opponents, accusing the worker delegates of partisan motives in job hiring. As for the striking nurses, "whom he considers criminals . . . he, the dictator, will ruthlessly annihilate them through repressions against them and their families up to arrest and even dispatch to Radogoszcz [German penal camp]."[167]

Rumkowski kept his word. From a written appeal that was widely distributed in connection with the strike or was posted on ghetto buildings, we learn that thirty-five persons were arrested in the course of twenty-four hours and that even family members of the strikers were put into prison.[168]

It came to an intense contest between the worker opposition and Rumkowski in the final ten days of January 1941. The atmosphere in the ghetto was already tense at the start of January. Masses of people demonstrated on 11 and 12 January, demanding increased food rations and heating fuel. The crowd attempted to attack the wagons transporting food into the ghetto, but the Order Servicemen blocked them. The Order Service patrolled the streets all day and it became calm in the ghetto toward evening.[169] However, the unrest continued and the storm broke out on 23 January.

That day, two departments of the carpentry division halted work and declared a sit-down strike, presenting four demands: (1) a raise of 10–20 pfennig an hour for the four categories of workers; (2) half the salary to be paid out in food products; (3) an additional soup, not charged against the ration card; and (4) reinstatement of the 500-gram bread supplement (Rumkowski had just set a bread ration of 400 grams both for those working and for nonworkers). When the carpenters did not obey the division director's demand to leave the building, the Jewish Police Assault Unit (*Iberfal-Komando*), numbering seventy men, was summoned and forcibly removed the workers from the first floor and then from the second floor, where they had barricaded themselves. During the action, there were blows struck and several workers and Order Servicemen were injured, requiring the First Aid unit to be summoned. Arrests were made and the Order Service was placed in a state of emergency (doc. no. 125).[170]

These events disturbed the feelings of the workers in the remaining workshops where the special bread supplement and the soups had been eliminated. One sensed the approach of a general strike. Fearing further events, Rumkowski declared a lockout and closed all the ghetto workshops on 24 January (doc. no. 126).[171]

The strikers responded to his announcement about closing the workshops with an emphatic leaflet, reiterating their first three demands, but leaving out the demand for reinstating the special bread supplement that was not likely to win sympathy among the general populace.[172]

Rumkowski attempted to break the strike by subjecting the hungry workers to a great test. On 28 January, through one of his poster announcements (no. 203), he proclaimed the distribution among the workers of 850 grams of meat and 2 kilos of potatoes, but with the admonition that "only those who are now actually working" would benefit. He also ordered that all workers of the closed workshops should be paid their wages by mail, but not the striking carpenters.[173]

In the meantime, Rumkowski held three conferences with the instructors of the closed factories, on 24, 26, and 29 January, because the institution of worker delegates had already been abolished and the instructors *de facto* represented the worker side (whether with the consent of the workers is not known). But no compromise resulted.

At the consultations, Rumkowski threatened the instructors with retaliation for sabotage, and he managed to convince the instructors of the tailor workshops to persuade their workers to report to work. On the twenty-ninth, workers began to report to the factories. On the thirtieth, a poster was displayed in front of a tailor workshop announcing that all tailor workshops were resuming operation that day. The carpenters' strike committee (that perhaps also included other crafts) proclaimed them strikebreakers. On the same day, there appeared a leaflet from the woodworkers urging everyone in the name of worker solidarity not to enter the workshops. A gathering of the carpenters decided to set up strike pickets on the streets leading to the carpentry shops, in order to convince the workers to go home. But the strike was already broken. On the thirtieth, 270 carpenters were working and the next day 460 of about 600 woodworkers were as well. On 1 February, a meeting of the carpenters formally decided to halt the strike and announced this in a special leaflet that sharply censured the behavior of Rumkowski and his police. The next day, all the carpenters returned to work.[174]

Thus the great contest between Rumkowski and the worker opposition ended with Rumkowski's victory.

At the same time, on 26 January 1941, for the same reason, there broke out a short-lived strike of nearly 200 gravediggers. They rejected the demand by the director of the Cemetery Department to turn in their tools. Rumkowski ordered all of them arrested and held overnight. When a unit of Order Servicemen arrived at the cemetery, the gravediggers gave up the struggle.[175]

However, even after the failure of the carpenters strike, the worker opposition did not give up the struggle against Rumkowski. A short time later, on 6 March 1941, a street demonstration took place involving nearly 700 men. Proclamations were made against the ghetto administration and leaflets were distributed with demands to increase the food rations; to reduce their price; to abolish the *Beirat* allocations and Cooperative B; to permit food parcels from outside the ghetto; to increase the cash relief grants; and, finally, to establish free laundries and baths for the poor population. Leaflets in Polish and Yiddish were also posted, condemning the ghetto government. During the dispersal of the demonstrators by the Order Service, a couple of people were seriously beaten and two policemen were wounded. After this, numerous arrests occurred.[176]

Even earlier, on 12 February 1941, Rumkowski again closed the tailor workshops and decided to reorganize them. As a reason, the announcement pointed to a complaint by the German authorities about poorly done work (uniforms were missing buttons, holes, buckles, and so on).[177]

Rumkowski responded in his fashion to the stormy demonstration of 6 March: with police repression. A special brigade of the Order Service, directed by Prison Commandant Hercberg, carried out raids in the ghetto for three nights and arrested fifty men "among thieves, recidivists and inciters against the present order in the ghetto" with the aim of sending them out to work in Germany.[178] On 8 March, a medical commission qualified seventy-five prisoners in the ghetto prison for dispatch to work outside the ghetto (doc. no. 127).[179]

Another official act directed against the opposition activities by the political parties in the ghetto was, as mentioned, the closing of all public kitchens in August 1941. With this, the last institutions of a public character were liquidated in the ghetto.[180]

To grasp the extent of social tension engendered in the ghetto and that discharged itself in such a stormy fashion in demonstrations and strikes, it is enough to consider an account of the atmosphere of terror that prevailed in the ghetto under the dual government of Rumkowski on the one hand and the Gestapo on the other.

The opposition worker political parties (Bund, Right and Left Poalei Zion,[181] and Communist) attempted to coordinate their activity and formed a communication commission that for a certain time met for joint consultations. A delegation from the commission to Rumkowski after the August demonstration of 1940 succeeded, as already mentioned above, in getting him to agree to issue for each worker a certain quantity of food at the disposition of the separate parties. But no uniform worker front against Rumkowski was formed in the ghetto. The bloc collapsed and each party continued to operate on its own.[182] The cause of the breakdown in unity was apparently the effect of prewar traditions of party struggle, which could not be overcome even in the ghetto conditions. The worker parties battled against one another even in handwritten leaflets.[183] Particularly active in this area was the very energetic Communist group.

Certain forms of the former proletarian party traditions survived in the ghetto. In the workshops, where the official, later secret, delegates were Socialists or Communists, May Day was celebrated in a modest measure. Notes were distributed with a reminder about the date, work was interrupted for a short time, and revolutionary songs sung. On those days, or other socialist commemorative dates, people would gather in private apartments in small groups of active comrades and hold "holiday banquets" with poor ghetto foods.[184]

The Zionist groups also maintained their partisan traditions. Herzl-Bialik memorial programs were held on the twentieth day of the Hebrew month Tammuz, while a memorial program organized by the Revisionist kibbutz in Marysin took place at the conclusion of *shloshim* (thirty days after the death) of Jabotinsky in summer 1940.[185]

The majority of Zionist groups in the ghetto (General Zionists, Right Poalei Zion, Hitachdut, Mizrachi, and Jewish State Party) united into a federation "on the basis of negative attitude to the official ghetto representation and material aid for comrades." An executive was formed, including representatives of the listed groups.[186]

The Party Kibbutzim in Marysin

From a combination of public initiative and Rumkowski's administration, in May 1940 kibbutz farms and a youth collective were created in Marysin. Organizationally, they were subject to the Department for Gardening and Plantations, later the Agricultural Department. The kibbutzim were allotted areas for potato fields and gardens. The harvest was distributed among the kibbutzim themselves, the orphanages, camps, and day camps for children.[187] After a separate police precinct, the fifth, was formed for Marysin in summer 1940, the precinct commandant became the ghetto administration's supervisor over the kibbutzim. This was one of the factors that led to friction and to the kibbutzim's liquidation.[188]

The kibbutzim were formed on a partisan basis according to membership in a given branch of the Zionist movement. Thus, there were, among others, kibbutzim of Gordonia, Ha-Shomer ha-Tsair, Ha-Shomer ha-Dati, Mizrachi, and Revisionists. Officially, however, they did not bear any partisan label, but were designated with letters from the Roman alphabet. In addition, there were also agricultural collectives of the Bund and of the Bnos Poalei Agudas Israel (Daughters of the Workers of Agudas Israel).

All the Zionist kibbutzim (except the Left Poalei Zion one) were organized in *Ha-mazkirut shel vaad ha-meshutaf le-kibutsei he-hakhshara ha-haklait* (Hebrew: The Secretariat of the Joint Council of the Agricultural Preparatory Kibbutzim; abbreviated as *Vaad ha-kibutsim*, or Council of Kibbutzim), consisting of six or seven people.[189] Each party naturally favored its own kibbutzim. In all, there were twenty-one Zionist kibbutzim with 950 members.[190] These kibbutzim were also called *kibutsei ha-otiot* (Hebrew: kibbutzim of the letters), *bukhshtabn-hakhsharot* (Germanic-Hebrew compound: letters-preparatory farms), in contrast with another group of kibbutzim that were designated not with letters but with Roman numerals, whose official name on their rubberstamps was *Landarbeitsgruppen* (German: Agricultural Work Groups). In October 1940, there existed twelve such groups and they were also centralized in a secretariat (*Secretariat der Landarbeitsziffer-gruppen*, Secretariat of Agricultural Number Groups). They designated themselves in their correspondence as Zionist. These two groups did not get along. From the preserved documents it is not hard to discern the reason.

In their letters to the Council of Kibbutzim, the representatives of the "number groups" complain that their letters are not answered and they are being rejected.[191] In one such message of 23 September 1940, they admitted that they had "collaborated with elements, undesirable for the Zionist idea," on account of which a stigma had fallen on them.[192] Tabaksblat, who belonged to the executive of the Zionist federation in the ghetto (see above), states that Rumkowski, having his own intentions regarding the kibbutzim, "created alongside the Zionist kibbutzim a series of nonpartisan, so-called 'wild' [kibbutzim], lacking any [supervisory] control over them or discipline of an educational character, and therefore brought in demoralization and wantonness."[193] It is also recounted in the cited testimony about the Marysin ghetto quarter "that undesirable elements also crept in among the kibbutzim; whole groups, that supposedly bore the name of a kibbutz, but in fact was a group of smugglers . . . pickpockets [*tsipers*] and informers. . . . All of this did not bring any honor to the Council of Kibbutzim and it formed its own militia, MII, in order to annihilate the undesirable. It led to incidents."[194] Some of the "number groups" were apparently recruited from those elements and the Council of Kibbutzim did not want to have any contact with them.

Parallel with agriculture, the kibbutzniks were also employed in workshops created in Marysin by Rumkowski, such as the workshop for cloth house slippers (the first in the ghetto), a tailoring workshop, a carpentry shop, and a locksmith shop.[195] In addition, certain members of the kibbutzim were employed in projects of the Agricultural Department (for example, clearing land at the cemetery), and in other departments of the ghetto administration (unpaid).[196]

Young people aspired to leave the sad and hungry ghetto and enter the kibbutzim, where the atmosphere was freer, the air cleaner, and the food better (before introduction of the ration card system). People applied for admission both individually and collectively to the Council of Kibbutzim or to the *Brit ha-kibbutzim* (League of Kibbutzim, probably of the Revisionists). One collective application underscored that their motivation was not "*hazana*" (Hebrew: provisioning), but idealistic intentions.[197] Youth from the nearby town of Aleksander (Aleksandrów, from which the entire Jewish population was expelled to Łódź in summer 1940) applied, as did others.[198]

The Bundist youth and children's organizations, *Tsukunft* (Future) and *SKiF* (Socialist Children's Association), also founded an agricultural collective in Marysin, called Former Pupils of the Medem School. Forty adolescents and children moved into the collective. Initially, the Bund's committee fed them. Later, Rumkowski took over the feeding, but for only twenty-two children, so the food was divided among all forty.[199]

Political activity and cultural work were conducted both in the Zionist kibbutzim and in the Bundist collective, and they in fact became the cultural centers for all of Marysin. The agricultural collectives in Marysin could have become a healthy, dynamic force in the ghetto that would have been capable of positively influencing the public atmosphere, but Rumkowski did not tolerate any public force that was independent of him. He wanted to turn the kibbutzim into labor battalions under police supervision, and when this did not work out for him, he closed them down completely in March 1941.

The preparation for the liquidation is vividly expressed in the preserved correspondence between the Fifth Precinct's commandant (Chimowicz) and the Council of Kibbutzim. On 1 November 1940, the commandant sent a severe directive to the chairman of the Council of Kibbutzim that the Council had no competence at all in matters of the labor divisions in Marysin; its sole task was to deliver *halutsim* (Hebrew: pioneers) for work.[200] On 18 December 1940, the Council again received a sharp admonition from the Fifth Precinct's commandant not to sabotage the work that the *halutsim* must carry out at the cemetery. The Jewish police official ordered delivery of a full contingent of *halutsim* for the work; if not, then the *halutsim* would be removed from Marysin "due to their malevolent failure to show up for work" (doc. no. 128).[201] The commandant made continual complaints. The *halutsim* in the militia unit created in Marysin (MII) were not carrying out their obligations. In general, they were avoiding service in the militia.[202] He even made accusations that *halutsim* were stealing wood in Marysin, and so forth.[203]

Relations became ever more strained and at the start of March 1941, Rumkowski set himself to liquidating the kibbutzim; the Bundist youth collective had already been closed in January. On 9 March 1941, he inspected the *hakhshara* centers in Marysin, where there were still 360 kibbutzniks, men and women. As the ghetto *Chronicle* reports, Rumkowski determined that unsuitable elements had infiltrated into the *hakhshara* centers, and he ordered them immediately expelled from Marysin. He also ordained a reorganization to clean up the conditions there. As a result, the kibbutzim had to be liquidated. Enraged at the rebellious kibbutzniks, for a long time he did not admit them to any work and exposed them to hunger.[204]

* * *

Regardless of his merciless struggle with his opponents, Rumkowski could not realize the fifth point of his program—calm in the ghetto—and had to deal almost all the time with stronger or weaker expressions of spontaneous or organized opposition to his regime.

In a speech at Culture House on 3 January 1942, Rumkowski boasted that he had scotched the attempts to provoke a strike in the factories, and that he did it in his "characteristically firm fashion."[205] We already know that fashion: dismissal from work, that is, to be sentenced to starvation, and placing rebels onto the deportation lists.

During the Children's Action in September 1942, the opposition conducted agitation for passive resistance, not to give up the children, and for active resistance against the Jewish police if they came to take the children forcibly. This resistance by the desperate parents prevented the Jewish police and its helpers from carrying out the action, and on the third day it was taken over by the Gestapo and the German ghetto administration.[206]

The ghetto was relatively calmer in 1943 since the provisioning situation had improved and almost all were employed, but from time to time a secret hand distributed leaflets. Thus, for example, Biebow's deputy, Ribbe, on 17 January forwarded to Rumkowski a Yiddish leaflet for translation.[207]

In 1944, in the final year of the ghetto's existence, the struggle against Rumkowski by the worker opposition again intensified. In May and June of that year, the protest against the worsened provisioning situation in the ghetto and against the malevolent dismissal of people in some workshops took on the passive form of the so-called "soup strikes" that in the ghetto conditions amounted to a sort of hunger strike. The campaign, conducted mainly by adolescent workers, caught up nearly all the workshops where solidarity strikes took place. There was mutual assistance as soups were sent to the striking workshops from factories that were not being struck. Rumkowski reacted in his characteristic fashion and those who refused to take the soups were dismissed from work, but with their stance of firm solidarity the strikers managed to get those fired taken back.[208]

In the months July–August 1944, during the final liquidation phase of the ghetto, the Bund "conducted a broad propaganda not to go [with the transports] and to hide out as long as possible."[209] On 29 July, the ghetto *Chronicle* noted: "It is conspicuous that various elements are showing themselves in the divisions that until now had stayed in the background but now believe that their time has come. . . . These elements incite the workers, especially in the tailoring and shoemaking workshops. The production in the tailoring shops is sinking, and in the shoemakers' workshops [it is falling] at a rapid rate. The Chairman is doing everything to keep the factories at the proper level."[210]

In addition to these expressions of collective opposition, the documents note many cases of individual resistance against Rumkowski's ordinances and their executors from the Order Service. Thus, for example, Rumkowski announced on 23 August 1940 that he had punished two families with fourteen days of arrest and forced labor for resisting the Order Service and an official of the Tax Office engaged in the collection of rent and taxes.[211] Arrests on account of resistance are noted from time to time in the daily *Chronicle* and in reports by the Order Service's commandant.[212]

Attitudes of opposition against Rumkowski and the ghetto administration also found expression in ghetto humor. Biting jokes circulated about the ghetto rulers and their conduct, about swindles and social abuses, about the conditions in the workshops, and so on. In the ghetto theater's revue performances, people sometimes allowed themselves liberties in satiric sketches about the ghetto conditions.[213] These sketches were very popular and the songs were sung everywhere, at home and at work. There was in the ghetto a well-known street singer, Herszkowicz, who would sing his satiric songs that did not spare even Rumkowski himself, before an assembled audience (mainly near the transit bridges) to the accompaniment of a guitar, played by his partner, a Viennese Jew.[214] As the ghetto *Chronicle* of 5 December 1941 relates, these partners, a former Łódź tailor and a Viennese traveling salesman, were doing a brisk trade, and Rumkowski magnanimously treated the ghetto troubadour who performed songs about him. Humor was the only field in the ghetto over which Rumkowski with his police had no control, a field where the ghetto Jew could freely unload his dissatisfaction and embitterment with the sad situation.

Cultural Life

Cultural life in the ghetto had, of course, shrunk in comparison with its prewar scope. The Jew in the ghetto was too preoccupied with the difficult day-to-day material concerns that absorbed him completely to still have the mood and time to satisfy his intellectual needs. But in light of the meager documentation left about this aspect of ghetto life, one can assert that regardless of the terribly difficult material circumstances, often in the shadow of death, a strong need manifested itself in the ghetto for intellectual and esthetic experiences, so as to be free for a couple of hours from the depressing burden of the sad environment. The drive for culture, particularly for the artistic word and music, often came from the desire to escape from the gloomy reality. Moreover, cultural activity often served as a protective cover for conspiratorial work of the political parties. The cultural activity also played the role of intellectual self-defense against the methods of degradation and psychological humiliation that the Germans applied toward the Jews in the ghetto.

The first manifestations of a cultural life in the Łódź Ghetto were linked with the public kitchens, where the consumer would get sustenance not only for the body but for the spirit, too. The political parties that operated these kitchens arranged talks for their regular clients and guests on literary and social themes, interspersed with recitations and poetry. In the Zionist kitchens, the so-called *Oneg-Shabat* (Sabbath party) with song and declamations conducted by the youth became very popular.[215] The intellectuals' kitchen, located in a large space, would from time to time hold vocal musical evenings and concerts to raise funds and to support the unemployed artists. In summer 1940, the agricultural youth circle with the Polish name *Słońce* (Sun) formed a small string orchestra (eleven musicians) under the direction of Prof. Piaskowski. It was later expanded with wind instruments. On 27 July 1940, the orchestra gave its third symphonic concert and on 4 August, a fourth concert was held at the secondary school (the gymnasium) before a large audience.[216]

Through the initiative of the Bund, a Yiddish Culture Society was formed in October 1940. Among its leading members were activists of the Bund, ORT, Society of Friends of YIVO, writers, and artists. What united these people of various political inclinations was cultural activity in Yiddish. The charter of the society foresaw the founding of a library, a people's university, Yiddish courses for adults and teachers, a dramatic circle, sport activities, concerts, and so on. A lecturers' group was formed. The society's first program took place on 19 October, a lecture by the writer M. Wolman about cultural activity in Yiddish in the ghetto. On 24 October, there was a cultural program that was actually a camouflaged jubilee celebration of the Bund. Participants included the revived choir of the *Kultur-Lige* (Yiddish Culture League), conducted by the prewar director of the Łódź Philharmonia, Teodor Ryder, the dramatic studio *Awangard*, and a *Morgenshtern* (Morningstar) sport group. These two undertakings were repeated on 9 November.[217] At the end of November and beginning of December, two more lectures were presented by Dr. Volfson on "The Tasks of Social Medicine in the Ghetto" and by Engineer Shpiglman "Concerning Theories of Physics." Due to the cold in the unheated hall, attendance at the latter lecture was small. According to our information, the final event of the society (at the end of December or in January 1941) was an evening devoted to the young Jewish writers in the ghetto, where there appeared with their works A. Hofman, A. Joachimowicz, S. Shayevitsh, M. Wolman, Z. Shmul, A. Paciorek, and J. Zelkowicz.[218]

The society appears not to have been spared from Rumkowski's policy of liquidating everything in the ghetto that was an expression of independent public activity. Literary evenings, apparently organized by the writers themselves, were still held in March 1941.[219]

As already mentioned, there was also systematic cultural activity conducted in the kibbutzim and Bundist youth collective, whose primary goal was ideological education of their members. However, they also had a cultural influence on the ghetto through their work. The programs that they organized (e.g., Herzl-Bialik memorial meeting, Jubilee Assembly of the Bund) attracted a large audience from the ghetto. The singing of Yiddish and Hebrew songs was often heard there. The cultural activity of the kibbutzim also assisted the children's camp during its holiday programs.[220]

In October 1940, the very popular Łódź *Hazamir* (Hebrew: The Nightingale) music society resumed its activity. The choir was reactivated and expanded with the members of the *Shir* (Hebrew: Song) club. On 28 October, *Hazamir* used a poster to announce its first concert, with participation of the choir under the direction of Director Dargożański and a symphony orchestra conducted by Ryder. Seventy-five people participated in the choir. The symphony orchestra included twenty-five professional musicians and ten amateurs. Soloists also performed. Seven concerts took place by 7 December 1940 (doc. no. 129).

The *Hazamir* also planned to found a music school, although the plan was not realized. On 13 March 1941 (Purim), the *Hazamir* choir performed together with the symphony orchestra under the direction of David Bajgelman.[221] This is the final report about *Hazamir* in our documents. The *Hazamir* society was probably liquidated. Rumkowski correctly judged that his power in the ghetto would not be absolute as long as he did not also have cultural life under his control. It is, however, not to be excluded that Rumkowski liquidated the independent cultural institutions in the ghetto in accord with an instruction from the German supervisory authority, which through him had full control over the ghetto and refused to tolerate any Jewish activities that were not under the supervision of Rumkowski and his administration.

Whatever the decisive reason may have been, it is a fact that after February 1941 cultural life in the ghetto received an official imprint from Rumkowski's administration. Rumkowski had even earlier carried around the idea of taking cultural life in the ghetto under his control. On 24 November 1940, the director of the Labor Office, Akiva Sienicki, received from him an instruction to establish a Culture House.[222] The building at 3 Krawiecka Street was renovated. On 1 March 1941 Culture House opened and thenceforth remained under the management of the director of the Labor Office. It is not entirely clear whether there existed some sort of cultural desk at the Labor Office. From a document dated 8 July 1942 one could infer that at that time a cultural desk did exist within the framework of the ghetto administration.[223]

Two sorts of events took place at Culture House: symphonic concerts with soloists and revue performances by the *Awangard* (Vanguard) theater studio, which continued the tradition of the prewar Łódź *Kleynkunst-teater,* Ararat.

There remained in the ghetto such local artistic talents as the directors and composers Teodor Ryder and David Bajgelman. The latter was for many years linked with the Łódź Yiddish theatrical world. There were also the choral director M. Dargozański, the violinists Bronisława Rotsztat and Sh. Senior, and the singers Nikodem Steiman and A. Beyn. There were also the painters Maurycy Trębacz, Isaac Brauner, Israel Lejzerowicz, H. Schilis, and P. Szwarc.[224] There were scriptwriters and artists from Ararat (Moyshe Puławer et al.). After the *Einsiedlung* of the Western European Jews, the cultural life in the ghetto was enriched with a highly trained group of musicians, singers, and actors, like the pianist Kurt Baer, the violinists Weinbaum and Kraft (all three from Prague), the singers Rudolph and Lili Brandel, the pianist Leopold Birkenfeld (from Vienna), and the pianist Alfrieda Manteufel, the singer Amalia von Imhoff, the musician Philip Josef, and others (from Berlin). In accord with an ordinance by Rumkowski, Culture House registered all artistic talents among the new arrivals. By 6 December 1941, nearly sixty musicians, singers, and actors had already registered, as well as ten painters, among whom were two prominent Prague painters, Gutmann and Zdenek Golub. Writers and journalists were also among the new arrivals: Leon Deutsch and Oskar Rosenfeld from Vienna, Oskar Singer and the historian Bernard Heilig from Prague.[225] Some of the musicians, singers, and painters became involved in the cultural life of the ghetto.

The symphony orchestra, which included Jewish musicians from the prewar Łódź Philharmonia, initially gave concerts relatively frequently. On 31 December 1941, the one hundredth concert took place, indicating an average of ten concerts a month.[226] Later, in 1942, a tradition was introduced at Culture House of one concert each week, on Wednesdays.[227]

The symphony orchestra, which had a preponderance of string instruments, performed classical music under the direction of Teodor Ryder (doc. no. 130).[228] From time to time, there were also recitals by beloved violinists, quartets, and trios,[229] and concerts of light music, mostly folksongs, Hasidic motifs, and Jewish music under the direction of Bajgelman, who himself wrote music both for old lyrics and for lyrics composed in the ghetto by J. Zelkowicz, A. Joachimowicz, M. Wolman, Sh. Janowski, and others.[230] The symphony orchestra ceased to exist after the German authorities confiscated all musical instruments in January 1944.[231]

The previously mentioned *Awangard* theater studio, under the direction of M. Puławer, performed so-called revues, consisting of satiric sketches on ghetto themes, mood images of a vaudevillian character, and song and dance numbers. There was also a choreographic dance studio in the ghetto (doc. no. 131). The revue performances took place relatively frequently, two or three times a week. During 10 months of 1941 (March–December), two revues were performed eighty-five times.

One revue was still performed until June 1942. At the beginning of June, the premier of a third revue took place. Nearly 70,000 people attended concerts and performances during 1941 (from March).[232] Aside from the general audience, special performances were held for the workers of the ghetto factories.[233] The theater hall in Culture House could seat a maximum of 400 persons (twenty-five rows of sixteen seats each). Prices for the tickets were 30 pfennig to 1 mark for the general audience and 20–30 pfennig for the factory workers.

The scripts for the revue performances were both new, composed in the ghetto, and from the old repertoire of Ararat, like for example the numbers "*Yidn shmidn*" (Yiddish: Jewish blacksmiths) and "*Kloyznikes*" (Yiddish: Hasidic prayer hall denizens) by Moshe Broderson.[234] Very popular and beloved were stagings of poems by Itsik Manger.

The gymnasium students' choir also performed at the Culture House. On Purim, 17 March 1941, there was a musical-vocal performance by children from the ghetto schools.[235]

Rumkowski often exploited the performances at Culture House for his speeches. The performances were under his strict censorship. Shmerke Kaczerginski states that Rumkowski excluded two lullabies by the poet Isaiah Spiegel ("*Makh tsu di eygelekh*" [Yiddish: Close your eyes], "*Nisht keyn rozhinkes, nisht keyn mandlen*" [Yiddish: No raisins, no almonds]), because they expressed the great Jewish misfortune and the German terror. He threatened the poet with retaliation.[236]

For a short time, a marionette theater called "*Khad-gadye*" (Aramaic: One kid [from the Passover song of the same name]) existed in the ghetto, managed by the painter Isaac Brauner. This theater appears to have begun to function in January 1941. It is only known that on 11 December (1941?) the premier of "*Tsugedrikt*" (Yiddish: Squeezed) took place in Culture House. No further performances are known. The marionettes parodied popular ghetto personalities.[237]

As mentioned, a number of painters and sculptors remained in the ghetto; their number increased after the arrival of the Western European Jews. Some obtained work painting the scenery for the revue performances, in the Statistical Office and in the "Scientific" Department. A separate room was devoted in Culture House for the painters and sculptors. It was promised that the painters working there would receive free food coupons. There is a surviving report about an exhibition of pictures by Isaac Brauner and Joseph Kowner. Brauner tells of the exhibition's great success and that 21,000 people visited during six months.[238] After the war, paintings on ghetto themes were found, works by Y. Lejzerowicz, I. Brauner, M. Trębacz, H. Shilis, and others.[239]

A Writers Association was also active in the ghetto, grouped around the poet Miriam Ulinower. It included a couple of dozen poets, prose writers, and journalists, among them some quite young beginners.

Much was written in the ghetto: poems, stories, diaries, and reportages. After the war, literary creations from the ghetto period were found in the ghetto ruins. Some of them, like Szajewicz's deportation poem,

"*Lekh-lekho*,"[240] and diaries by Shlomo Frank, David Sierakowiak, and Jakub Poznański, have been published.[241] Several, like Y. Hiler's diary, have remained in manuscript.

Through the initiative of three directors of the Records Department, Statistical Office, and Archive, "higher lyceum courses" (popularly called *wszechnica* in Polish) were formed during August and September 1940. These were supposed to be the nucleus of a university. According to the plan, ten departments were foreseen (mathematics, physics, chemistry, biology, psychology, philosophy, pedagogy, philology, Judaica, and technical studies) with nearly thirty lecturers. From the second to the twentieth of September, twenty-seven lectures[242] took place in various fields: mathematics, psychology, pedagogy, chemistry, and physiology. Initially, 318 persons registered for the lectures, all with secondary education and even students who had been at universities. Average attendance at each lecture was 250.

Rumkowski initially permitted the lectures, but after a short time he ordered them closed. Later, a second registration took place, apparently in the hope that the program would be resumed. At that time, 116 students registered. It is worth noting that over two-thirds of the applicants were unemployed, which is a sufficient indication of the material situation of the young Jewish intelligentsia in the ghetto.[243]

Several former entrepreneurs of private vocational courses renewed their activity in the ghetto. Thus, for example, Henryk Lubiński, a prominent specialist and author of textbooks, resumed a business course he had formerly conducted. There were also language courses, among others.[244]

To complement the cultural picture in the ghetto, it is also worthwhile mentioning some data about libraries and sports. The contemporaneous "Ghetto Encyclopedia"[245] states: "Immediately after the establishment of the ghetto, before the Jews expelled from the city had managed to settle into their new living place, there arose among the 'People of the Book' a need to read."

Of all the prewar Jewish lending libraries that were liquidated in winter 1939–40 by the *Hauptpropagandaamt, Warthegau, Nebenstelle Lodz* (Main Propaganda Office, Warthegau, Łódź Office),[246] only Sonenberg's lending library remained.[247] It initially possessed 1,900 volumes, but by the start of 1944 it had 7,500 books with 4,000 readers. The subscription fee was initially 1 mark a month, later 2 marks. In addition, a private book peddler (Atlasberg) opened a lending library, numbering 2,000 books and 2,000 subscribers. There were also a number of smaller lending libraries functioning in private apartments, some of which possessed only Yiddish books and attracted the attention of those interested by displaying announcements. The majority of these libraries closed down in the course of time. Although the authorities generally tolerated these libraries, they were subject to the ban on keeping German war works, as well as books banned in the Reich.[248] The hunger for the printed word is attested to by a report in the ghetto *Chronicle* that there were "kilometer-long lines at Sonenberg's lending library, regardless of the high fee of 2 marks a month and 3 marks registration fee."[249] Private people had books, too.[250] In addition, in some of the shelters for the Western European expellees, for example in the Hamburg collective, lending libraries arose assembled from private gifts.[251] The political parties also maintained their own libraries.

When the deportations began, houses were left with stacks of abandoned books and sacred works that were sold as scrap paper (5 marks a kilogram) or used for various needs. Thanks to the initiative of the director of the Records Department, who also obtained the agreement of the Management (*Virtshaft*) Department, the house watchmen and administrators were directed to look through the vacant, sealed residences, attics, and cellars, to collect all books and bring them in to the Records Department. In such fashion, during 1942 and half of 1943 there accumulated in three rooms and in a cellar of the department about 30,000 different books, sorted and cataloged under the direction of Engineer Einhorn. The rich library of Łódź Rabbi Treistman also found its way into this book collection.[252] Also collected were several dozen Torah scrolls, *tfilin,* prayer shawls (*talitot*), *tfilin* straps, and other sacramental objects (doc. no. 132).[253]

From this stock of books, several hundred volumes were selected for young people. A couple of portable mini-libraries were formed, designated for institutions of child care and adolescent supervision. One mini-library of 150 books was sent to the convalescent home for adolescents.[254]

According to the "Ghetto Encyclopedia," aside from detective and adventure literature, the greatest demand was for books by Polish authors Żeromski, Strug, Orzeszkowa, Sienkiewicz, and Prus, and by the Russian writers Pilnyak, Ehrenburg, Gorki, and Aldanov. The Western European readers of German books inclined toward monographs, historical and philosophical works. Also much read were the classics of German literature, as well as Heine, Feuchtwanger, and Ludwig. Of the Yiddish writers, the most read were Y. L. Peretz and Sholem Asch.[255]

After the relative stabilization of life in the ghetto, the sport clubs began to revive. In September 1940, we hear about the existence of "an association for football in the ghetto." There were already then nine sport clubs, divided into two leagues. Between the fourteenth and nineteenth of September 1940, there were five matches in both leagues.[256] In addition to this association, there was the revived Bundist sport club *Morgenshtern* with its prewar coaches. Gymnastic groups from *Morgenshtern* appeared at cultural events.[257]

In a special announcement (no. 146) on 22 October 1940, Rumkowski proclaimed permission to organize a sport movement in the ghetto and to create a sport administration. Promising that he was taking over the supervision of sports in the ghetto, he urged the population to register in the sport association.[258]

A portrait of a Jewish couple in the Łódź Ghetto, printed as a Rosh Hashana New Year greeting card, September 1940. Photographer unknown. USHMM, courtesy of Żydowski Instytut Historyczny Instytut Naukowo-Badawczy.

Religious Life

The religious life of Łódź Jewry experienced serious shocks from the beginning of the occupation. First of all, there was a period of destruction of synagogues and chapels (*batei-medroshim*). Several were blown up according to the familiar pattern of *Kristallnacht*: the progressive *Synagoga*[259] on Aleje Kościuszki (existing since 1887; the explosion was so strong that neighboring buildings were damaged); the Voliner Synagogue on Wólczańska Street, the Wilker Synagogue with its chapel and study hall on Zachodnia Street, the Old Town Synagogue with its large *beit-midrash*, and other smaller synagogues. Some of the ruins of the synagogues were used for horse stalls (Wilker and Voliner synagogues). The site where the Synagoga had stood was turned into a station for hack-carriages. Left undesecrated was the site of the ruined Old Town Synagogue, because it was within the ghetto's perimeter. Of all these many synagogues, prayer houses, *batei midrash,* and Hasidic *shtiblekh* (small prayer houses) that Łódź had possessed, only the few *minyanim* (prayer quorums) and *shtiblekh* located in the ghetto itself were left. There was the synagogue and building of the Talmud Torah (elementary religious school) on Jakuba Street, where Torah scrolls rescued with devotion from the destroyed synagogues were transferred. Here prayed the former worshippers of the Old Town Synagogue.[260] Also surviving were the synagogue of the *Nosei-ha-mita* burial society on Brzezińska Street, the synagogue of the *Gmilut-Hasadim* free loan society on Kelma Street, and the Hasidic prayer halls of the Kozhenitsers (Łagiewnicka Street) and of the Aleksanderers (on Brzezińska Street and Marysińska Street). People would also gather in private residences and there pray collectively.

The High Holy Days of 5700 (1939) passed under the shadow of the invasion and Nazi terror. Prayers were conducted clandestinely, in cellars with shuttered windows and with watchmen outside to warn of danger. There was a ban on praying in groups in synagogues and private apartments. There was also an order from the authorities that all Jewish businesses and offices must be open on Yom Kippur. Many of the Jewish merchants sabotaged the decree by removing goods from their stores and hiding out in friends' apartments, while other Jewish merchants tried to obey the decree by opening their shops for a couple of hours. Pious office workers did not go to work. In a number of cases, SS personnel discovered private prayer groups and the worshippers were dragged out in their white prayer robes and led through the streets.[261]

Instances of public ridiculing of the religious feelings of the Jewish population occurred even earlier. Before the blowing up of the major synagogues, for example, the Germans ordered the Jewish community to provide 400 worshippers in prayer shawls and to conduct a prayer service there with the accompaniment of a choir. The prayer service was filmed. Afterward, the worshippers were murderously beaten. Some were chased across the city to a restaurant, where a large group of Germans awaited them. The Jews were ordered to sing and dance. This scene was also filmed. Afterward, the victims, under brutal blows, were compelled to perform hard labor.[262] Before the burning of the Voliner Synagogue, they commanded the Łódź assistant rabbi, Rabbi Segal, to come into the synagogue in *talit* and *tefilin* and there tear up the Torah scrolls.[263]

The situation changed in this regard during the High Holy Days of 5701 (1940). Prayer services were conducted undisturbed with the agreement of the municipal authorities, and there was even a visit by Nazi officers to *Kol Nidrei* in the *Bajka* (Polish: Fairy Tale) cinema hall, where a *minyan* was set up. They behaved respectably.[264] People prayed in many locations and even outdoors.

In 1940, Rumkowski publicly declared Yom Kippur an obligatory day of rest (doc. no. 133).[265] Two circulars from 30 September and 15 October also designated Rosh Hashana and Sukkot as days of rest in the offices and workshops.[266]

In subsequent years, Yom Kippur was a mandatory workday. Nevertheless, pious Jews took a risk. Those who could not free themselves from their jobs came in to the workshops and, where the director tolerated it, they stood at the machines and prayed there, even wearing *talitot*. Others stayed home and in concealment recited the prayers individually or in small groups.[267] In Marysin, a prayer group was set up in an uninhabited house. With closed doors and shutters, and having previously assured themselves of free access to the attic and cellar, people prayed clandestinely. Many of the ghetto elite also prayed there. When a suspicious sound was heard, the worshippers would silently leave, or hide in the attic. When receiving Torah honors (*aliyot*), the ghetto elite would pledge a few potatoes and vegetables for the poor worshippers.[268]

For Passover, *matsa* (unleavened bread) was baked in the ghetto mostly from rye flour (*kornmel*), but people could also collect regular bread on their ration cards instead of *matsot* (doc. no. 134).[269] The *matsa* ration (2.5 kilos for 8 days) was really barely enough to satisfy the minimum requirement. Due to suspicion of the presence of religiously prohibited *khomets* (leavened products) in the allocated foodstuffs, pious Jews fasted more than they ate during Passover. Rumkowski would hand out holiday coupons for favorites and clergy. Instead of wine, the juice of red beets sweetened with saccharine was used. "The only thing that was plentiful was *maror* (bitter herbs), not only on the table but in everyone's heart." At certain points in the *Haggada* (Passover Seder booklet) that discussed slavery and redemption, there would often be an outbreak at the table of "a wailing like on a former Yom Kippur day." All the traditional Passover dishes, like "fish" and *khremzlekh* (Passover pancakes), were made from turnips (*kileribn*)[270] and potatoes that the ghetto housewives learned to prepare artfully. "All of these dishes tasted of paradise." The prayer "*Shfokh hamatkha*" (Pour out Thy wrath), was recited with an especially contemporary intention.[271]

The period preceding Passover 1942 was disrupted, for the deportation from the ghetto was going on just then. But a miracle occurred in the ghetto on the first Seder night: A couple of hundred people were sent back from the rail station because the Christian Easter coincided with the Jewish Passover and the SS men left on vacation. So there was great joy, indeed, in the ghetto on the first day of Passover.[272]

As for the Sabbath, Rumkowski's announcement on the eve of Yom Kippur 1940 introduced Saturday as an obligatory day of rest in all ghetto institutions with the exception of certain facilities of public service (doc. no. 133),[273] but in 1941 this obligation was cancelled in regard to ghetto workshops and the question of Sabbath rest became dependent on the position of the individual workshop directors. A surviving instruction from March 1941, issued at Rumkowski's command for the carpentry factory, contains a prohibition on working overtime and on Saturdays, with the admonition that the factory managers have a right to repeal this ban.[274] What the situation was in this regard in other factories is not known, although probably the question of Sabbath rest was regulated there in a similar fashion. In any event, in later years, beginning from 1943, Sunday became the official day of rest. There were periods when there was no weekly day of rest in the ghetto at all.

In the first periods, before the whole male population was drawn into the ghetto production, people in the ghetto

> studied [Torah] day and night. . . . The young men did not tear themselves from the Talmud and studied in a building on the third floor . . . at no. 42 Kelma Street. The majority [studied] at night, so as not to be disturbed, also [in order] not to come to the attention of the frequent German commissions that were rife in the ghetto. . . . At the religious kibbutzim a prayer quorum was set up and [there] were a Torah scroll and many sacred books, where in free moments the religious youth studied a folio of Gemara, even kept to the daily folio schedule [*gelernt a blat gmore, afile opgehit dem daf yoymi*].[275]

After work in the summer, one encountered Jews sitting in the courtyards and studying Torah.[276]

Religious *khevres* (Yiddish: clubs, societies) also continued to exist in the ghetto (new ones also arose). They set themselves a goal of fighting against the destructive influences of the ghetto on religious life. The group *Bnei Horev* (Hebrew: Sons of Horeb), a sort of continuation of the Horeb Society that existed in Łódź before the war, was composed of followers of Rabbi Samson Raphael Hirsch's school of thought.[277] In the ghetto, they conducted propaganda efforts for Sabbath observance. Members of the group would intervene in the workshops in cases when a pious worker was harassed for refusing to work on the Sabbath. In the ghetto they conducted a Horeb school, around which the Łódź "Hirschians" grouped. When the *khedorim* (Yiddish: elementary religious schools) were closed in the ghetto, the *Bnei Horev* went to the children and privately studied with them. They also organized children's groups and taught them Hebrew, Jewish history, and religion. They would also seek out orphans, guide them into groups for prayer, and see that they recited the mourner's *kaddish*. On Friday nights, in private apartments, festive gatherings took place, where teachers would present sermons on topics of the day and children would chorally sing Sabbath hymns. On 28 March 1944, the society celebrated its fifth year of existence in the ghetto.[278]

In the second half of 1940, a religious association called *Pe Kadosh* (Hebrew: Sacred Mouth) arose in the ghetto. It set for itself the task of protecting the Jews of the ghetto from eating non-kosher food. Its members would stand in front of the meat shops and actively agitate among those standing in line not to buy the meat rations that consisted mostly of horsemeat. They conducted an open struggle against those who did not heed their moral reproof. The society's members would not admit them to prayer services, not allow them to be called up to the Torah, much less allow them to lead the service at the cantor's stand. On the eve of Rosh Hashana of 1941, they posted a leaflet at the entrances to the *minyanim*, where they warned in Hebrew that "a mouth that is tainted, may G-d preserve us, with non-kosher meat may not pray, much less be a prayer leader" (*ki ha-pe ha-meshukats ve-ha-metuav be-neveilot u-terei-fot rahmana litslan asur lo le-hitpalel u-mi-kol-she-ken li-heyot sheluha de-tsibura*). At the head of the association stood the Lutomirsker rabbinic judge, R. Mendel Lentshitski [Łęczycki?]. After a year of Quixotic struggle with their mightiest opponent, hunger, the society broke up in the second half of 1941.[279]

A society called *Shomrei Mezuzot* (Hebrew: Guardians of *Mezuzot*,[280] abbreviated as *ShM*) was formed in the ghetto on 1 May 1940. It operated from the assumption that, since only Jews lived in the ghetto, it was time to realize the commandment of affixing *mezuzot* on a major scale "on door and gate." The society did not settle for merely supplying kosher *mezuzot* in the buildings, particularly in those whose prior residents were Christians, but it would also hammer up *mezuzot* on the gates of buildings, in the soup kitchens, courtyard entries, and so forth. In connection with this, they came into friction with the Order Service. The society's founder, Avraham Meshngiser, agitated in the street and in the *minyanim* for his *mezuza* program, using proofs drawn from the Bible and Talmud to argue that the yellow badge decree was a punishment because Jews had not kept the commandments of *mezuzot* and *tsitsit*.[281] After the death of its founder, in the latter half of 1942, the group dissolved.[282]

The prewar religious association, *Ve-ahavta le-reiakha kamokha* (Hebrew: You shall love your neighbor as yourself), also continued its philanthropic activity in the ghetto. Until the introduction of bread rationing cards, the society maintained a bread-and-tea house especially for children, where they sold or gave away bread and coffee and promoted ritual handwashing and the blessings recited after eating. The founder of the society, the prominent Łódź activist Baruch Gelbart, would himself bring water to the children for washing their hands. The society also occupied itself with those expelled from the provincial communities and provided them with a night shelter, apartments, and household utensils. At the end of 1941, the society was also very active in the field of Torah study. It organized a number of *daf yomi* (daily Talmud folio) study groups.[283]

An Orthodox prewar journalist, Israel David Itzinger (literary pseudonym: Alter Shnur), issued a handwritten newspaper in Hebrew for nearly three years in the ghetto. In *Ha-mesaper* (Hebrew: The Narrator), with a literary supplement, *Min ha-meitsar* (From the Straits), he recorded the chronicle of the ghetto, wrote articles, ghetto songs, comic ghetto stories, and so forth. How far this newspaper reached in the ghetto is not known.[284]

The ghetto conditions in time caused far-reaching changes in the religious way of life. "Many customs, traditions and ancestral practices ceased, without noticing when and where. . . . [But] the peculiar rhythm and specific tempo in their course across the ghetto could extract no more than those ceremonies and traditions that were not deeply rooted in the people: almost all pre- and post-natal ceremonies, almost all ceremonies connected with funerals."[285] It was very difficult, almost impossible, to observe religious laws of kosher diet, family purity, group prayer, and so forth.

The marital ceremony was also reformed, becoming more similar to a civil marriage. First of all, the canonized text of the *ketuba* marriage document was edited to remove all aspects that had lost any practical meaning in the ghetto, like trousseau, the obligation to support the wife ("in the ghetto no one had and none could have any wealth," said Rumkowski). Also eliminated were the *khupa* and *yihud,* the canopy and the formal isolation together of bride and groom. What remained were the ring or other item of value with which one could wed (*mekadesh zayn*), the wording of the *kidushin* formula and the blessings. This occurred after Rumkowski abolished the Council of Rabbis in the wake of the September Action of 1942 (see chapter 6) and he himself took over the function of conducting wedding ceremonies as *mesader kidushin.* At a wedding, Rumkowski would address the couples (the practice was introduced of marrying multiple couples at a time)[286] and recite the Seven Blessings "loudly, but with a tone of sadness that reflects the mood of those present." Then the couples signed the marital documents. As wedding presents, Rumkowski would distribute special wedding coupons (at first for two breads and a half kilo of honey; this was later reduced) that he reinstituted after they were abolished in the hunger year 1942. These wedding coupons would sometimes be, as J. Zelkowicz sarcastically expresses it, the reason for getting married.[287]

The German authorities did not formally recognize civil marriages in the ghetto and thus the woman retained her maiden name. On the couple's personal documents, only the fact of having married was noted. In fact, the authorities recognized the marriage document to the extent that the children carried the name of the father. Divorces were issued by the Divorce Board at the *Standesamt* (Registry Office) that consisted of a judge and two rabbis. The parties had to appear before a public or closed court proceeding.[288]

Probably in response to a hint from the German supervisory authority, Rumkowski initiated a fight against the traditional Jewish costume, whose frequency in the ghetto had in any event strongly declined, and against beards and side curls (*peyot*). On 15 July 1941, in a *Geto-tsaytung* (no. 14) article ("Facts and Comments"), Rumkowski announced that he was introducing obligatory short garments[289] for all ghetto residents up to fifty years old, due to a shortage of new fabric arising from the large number of repairs of old garments in the tailor shop to be established for this purpose, and so that "the population should have . . . a proper external appearance in general." This ban on the traditionally long garments did not apply to rabbis and those who had rabbinic ordination. In exceptional cases, he would issue special permits for wearing a long garment. Rumkowski's article concluded with a threat to "all those who will not submit to my decision; I will compel them with all the means that are at my disposal."

In his speech on 1 June 1942, he again warned that within eight days beards and long *kapotes* (traditional men's kaftans) must vanish from the ghetto.[290] After this, he issued a circular that was displayed in all workplaces; those failing to shave off their beards would lose their jobs and only shaven people would be employed in the workshops. (In general, no pious Jews were employed in the ghetto administration.) On 13 June 1942, the Order Service carried out street "raids on beards." Those caught were forcibly taken to a barber and there shorn of beard and side curls.[291] Scenes from the times of Tsar Nicholas I and Tsar Alexander II were repeated in the Łódź Ghetto, with the difference that here Jews carried out the hunt for beards and *kapotes* at the command of a foreign power. Obstinate pious men would walk about with their faces wrapped as if due to toothache.[292]

Silent tragedies were played out in pious homes. The father strove to maintain *Yidishkayt* in his home. He would not want to consume meals from the public kitchens even at the price of starving. He tried to influence the children, particularly the grown sons, in that direction, but the children employed in the ghetto industry could not keep any rules of diet and Sabbath. Thus, the once pious home became divided into two worlds that were alien to each other.[293]

Deeply religious Jews, particularly mystically inclined Hasidim, looked on the ghetto as an earned punishment and accepted the suffering with love. They even attempted to see in this an *athalta de-geula* (Aramaic: beginning of redemption), a realization of a peculiar *kibuts galuyot* (Hebrew: gathering of the exiles; namely, the tens of thousands of Jews from Western Europe and from the provincial communities who were expelled into the ghetto).[294]

R. Simcha Treistman, the principal Łódź rabbi,[295] left for Warsaw in winter 1940. Officially, religious life in the ghetto was regulated by what was known in Yiddish as the *Rabonim-kolegye* (or in Hebrew as the *Vaad ha-rabanim etsel zaken ha-yehudim ba-geto litsmanshtat,* the Council of Rabbis at the Eldest of the Jews in Litzmannstadt Ghetto), consisting of fifteen rabbis, chaired by the venerable Łódź assistant rabbi Joseph Fajner. In December 1941, another four rabbis were co-opted from those deported from Germany (from Berlin, Hamburg, Buckshaven [?], and Oldenburg). On 25 November, together with another five rabbis, they had been examined by a commission of three Łódź rabbis, named by Rumkowski, and were certified as competent to conduct weddings.[296]

The rabbis were considered employees of the ghetto administration and their salary at the end of 1941 was 250 marks a month. They could conduct a wedding only on the basis of an authorization from the civil Registry Office. Rumkowski decreed that the fees charged for conducting a wedding (from 3 to 15 marks), which formerly belonged to the rabbis, should now go into the general ghetto treasury "for the public good." The rabbis were autonomous in all other matters. They ruled on questions of Jewish law and conducted courts according to the Torah (*din toyres*). However, Rumkowski strictly admonished them not to take on any *din toyres* in controversies concerning hard currency.

The rabbinical council faced the almost impossible task of finding a path between the strict requirements of the *Shulhan Arukh* (Code of Jewish law) and the hard, merciless facts of the ghetto reality. Such fundamental principles of religion as dietary laws, the Sabbath, and Passover restrictions could not be fulfilled in the circumstances of the ghetto. In our meager documentation about the activity of the Council of Rabbis, there remain traces that indicate how it struggled with these matters. Thus, for example, the council wrote to Rumkowski before Passover 1941 to arrange an analysis of a series of food articles, like citric acid, margarine, and saccharine, in order to find out whether they were permissible during Passover. The difficult conditions compelled the rabbis not to be too rigorous. In 1941 they permitted for Passover canned beets, margarine, and powdered saccharine (*krishtal sakharin*) supplied by the German ghetto administration.[297] On 27 February 1941 the council announced its ruling concerning who was allowed to eat non-kosher meat when kosher slaughter was strictly forbidden in the ghetto. Permitted such meat were women in childbirth, sick people, and "those who are losing a lot of their strength" for whom the doctors explicitly prescribed it. All fifteen rabbis signed the ruling (doc. no. 135).[298]

There was one official *mohel* (ritual circumciser) in the ghetto and an assistant, a superfluous indication of the state of the birthrate in the ghetto.[299]

Other clergy, like cantors, ritual slaughterers, and sextons, were formally assigned to the factory divisions so that they should not remain unemployed. Many of them were employed in the Cemetery Department.[300]

Due to the high rate of mortality, the issue of burial was a very painful issue in the ghetto. In periods of higher mortality, the gravediggers did not manage to bury all the dead and a large number of deceased collected in the mortuary (*tahare shtibl*). In January 1941, a minimum of three days and often even ten days elapsed until the dead could come to burial, even though the number of gravediggers in that month was nearly two hundred (before the war, there were twelve).[301] At the end of January 1942, the situation at the cemetery was such that over two hundred dead who could not be buried had accumulated in the mortuary (doc. no. 136).[302] The job of grave digging was given to sickly, weak people, while the healthy were sent to work outside the ghetto.

There were also difficulties with transferring the large number of dead to the cemetery, because a total of only three or four horses were assigned for this purpose. In order to be able to expedite the transportation of the deceased, starting in August 1942 a huge wagon began to circulate in the ghetto, consisting of a large platform where there was a box of unfinished boards that could contain up to thirty deceased at a time. "Sad—but a fact," as the *Chronicle* glumly comments.[303] Death became a commonplace matter in the ghetto, and funerals in their old-time form became a rarity.

At the demand of the German authorities, the no longer used original Jewish cemetery[304] was liquidated at the end of June 1942. The German ghetto administration ordained that the area of the cemetery should be turned into a lumberyard for the woodworking shops located nearby, and that the tombstones be used for paving the passageways. Since the decree could not be averted, a precise map of the graves was made by order of the rabbinate so that they could later be reconstructed.[305]

Criminality in the Ghetto

The difficult life of hunger in the ghetto weakened concepts of morality and ethics among a portion of the population and caused a growth of criminality. Since people could not survive for long on the meager food and heating fuel allotments and wages, people sought out all sorts of ways to smuggle home a little food, heating fuel, or money for buying something on the black market. The forms of the crimes committed were quite varied: using connections with the employees of the distribution cooperatives and public kitchens to collect double or even multiple food allotments and meals on the same ration card or coupon, stealing or counterfeiting food cards, shoplifting food from the food shops and warehouses, making off with accessories and goods from the workshops, money embezzling by officials, and so on. The thefts varied: they might include a board taken from a carpentry shop in order to be able to cook something at home, a couple of potatoes snatched from a wagon (mainly prevalent among children and adolescents), major quantities of flour taken from a food warehouse, or bread from bakeries. Food was stolen from homes and vegetables from the garden allotments. These sorts of thefts were a relatively widespread phenomenon, as a specifically ghetto form of struggle for physical survival. There were even a couple of cases of bloody assaults and murder motivated by hunger.

Embezzlements and swindles occurred relatively frequently in the departments of the ghetto administration. Having a very bad name in this respect was the Provisioning Department, often accused of corruption and predatory management (see chapter 3). There were cases when the wrongs committed were not in order to still one's own hunger and the hunger of one's family, but from a downright nasty desire to exploit the circumstances and procure for oneself illegal income.[306]

One of the factors in the growth of criminality in the ghetto surely was that the ghetto was established in the area of Bałuty where the Łódź Jewish underworld had been concentrated. Rumkowski's phony tactic of combating one part of the underworld by making another part the keepers of "calm and order" (as in the Hercberg case)[307] demoralized ghetto life. The ghetto had no small amount of trouble from this element. One of this bunch at the end of November 1941 carried out a daring theft in the building of the *Kripo* in the ghetto (two transmission belts worth 10,000 RM) and the ghetto was threatened with serious penalties (the arrest of all residents in the vicinity of the building and the shooting of every tenth person if the thief was not delivered). When the thief was caught after forty-eight hours, it turned out that he was a Bałuter with a prewar criminal past. In the ghetto he became a watchman (and an agent) at the same *Kripo* office. He carried out the daring theft under the *Kripo*'s nose when he was dismissed from his post. He escaped from prison but was finally captured. When his dead body was released from the *Kripo* prison, the cause of death listed on his death certificate was suicide.[308]

As mentioned, in his own fashion Rumkowski conducted an intense struggle against crime in the ghetto with the help of serious penalties (not only for the relevant person alone, but also for the family by confiscating from them the right to receive relief grants), even up to deportation to death. This sensitive question occupies the most prominent place in almost all of his numerous speeches. His opponents blamed him, holding him responsible for the corruption in the ghetto administration because he alone decided who would fill the positions. Rumkowski was also accused of conducting this struggle only against the "small people with small transgressions," while closing his eyes at the serious offenses of the ghetto "bigshots."[309]

The prevalence of crimes was dependent upon the situation in the ghetto in a given period, as we shall see from Table 18.

Table 18[1]
Crime in the Łódź Ghetto in Certain Time Periods, 1941–1944

Time Period	Thefts	Resistance	Various	Together	During the entire month[2]	Per 1,000 residents[3]
Jan. 1941	431	29	344	804	—	5.2
Feb. 1941	243	13	486	242	—	4.8
March (28 days)	388	53	464	905	970	6.5
Oct. 1941	181	?	?	615	—	4.3
Dec. 1941 (27 days)	142	8	102	252	285	1.7
May 1942 (21 days)	51	2	97	150	220	2.0
July 1942	113	1	50	164	—	1.9
Aug. 1942 (24 days)	111	1	81	193	250	3.0
June 1944 (17th–30th)	5	—	26	31	—	—
July 1944 (1st–12th)	4	—	14	18	—	—

1. Ed. note: This table is mislabeled Table 17 in the original.
2. The approximate numbers for the full months of March, December 1941 and May, August 1942 were obtained through adding the missing days, calculated according to the daily average. For the months June, July 1944, due to the negligible number of days, we could not derive any average monthly numbers. There is no statistical material for the year 1943. The figures are taken from the ghetto *Chronicle* and from reports by the Order Service.
3. Calculated according to the average ghetto population in a given month.

As we see, both absolutely and relatively the largest number of crimes committed in the ghetto was in the winter months of January–March 1941. Thefts ranged from 40 percent (in March) up to 54 percent (in January) of all the offenses committed. This fact is without doubt connected with the severe winter of 1941, when there was no heat and the taking of wood from half-ruined houses, lumberyards, and fences was very prevalent. The hunger then reigning in the ghetto also caused an increased number of cases of theft in the warehouses of raw materials, accessories (*tsudatn*), and heating materials, as well as theft in bakeries and from food transports. Rumkowski was moved by this to introduce the Summary Judgment Court (*Schnellgericht*) on 11 March (see chapter 2). According to a fragmentary list in the *Geto-tsaytung* of 21 and 28 March 1941, the Summary Court sentenced thirty-four persons to various terms of prison (from a month up to half a year) for such offenses.

On 28 March 1941, there were two hundred people in the ghetto prison (including fourteen women), while there were seventeen in the reformatory (*oysbeserung hoyz*) for minors in the same prison building.[310]

Two documents from that time (nos. 137 and 138) give us more details about the causes of crime in the ghetto in the mentioned period and a critique of the struggle that Rumkowski and the Summary Court waged against crime.

In the subsequent months, with the approach of spring and summer, the number of offenses committed fell. In the *Geto-tsaytung* (no. 14 of 15 July 1941), Rumkowski announced that "the number of matters arriving in the Summary Court is very small." Rumkowski stated this as a reason for dissolving the Summary Court. Another reason was the corruption that had infiltrated even into the court itself. On 13 May 1941, the chairman of the Summary Court was arrested after a search took place at his residence (*Geto-tsaytung,* no. 11 of 18 May 1941). The serious prison sentences on those convicted by the Summary Court and the no less serious administrative penalties that Rumkowski imposed for the least theft also apparently influenced the reduction in the number of offenses committed (doc. no. 139).

Table 18 shows us that the number of crimes in the ghetto fell from October 1941 until July 1942. In August 1942, it rose again (by 50 percent in comparison with May). On 21 August 1942, Rumkowski ordered distribution of a circular to all ghetto offices and workshops in which he asserted "that in the latest period the thefts are multiplying in factories, distribution points, and bakeries and kitchens." Therefore,

> my court will intensify the penalty for such crimes and [I] have ordered formation in the Central Prison of a separate section with an exacerbated regime. The prisoners will not have the right to leave the cells [or] have visits from relatives, [and] they will lose the right to work and therewith their food portions will be reduced. . . . In many cases the criminals were not punished because managers and their friends in the divisions concealed them. This also occurs due to interventions with the Order Service. [I warn] that persons who intervene [for the benefit of the wrongdoers] will be held responsible like the criminals themselves. Thus, the managers who intentionally concealed from the prosecutor a crime committed by one of their subordinates will be punished.[311]

In the months after the September Action, the number of thefts in the ghetto, particularly in the work divisions, so multiplied that Biebow himself on 9 October 1942 issued a severe public warning to the ghetto population, announcing that from that day on the Jewish *Sonderkommando* had taken into their hands the matter of thefts, for which punishment will be "with the most severe penalty possible."[312] It must be assumed that in these frequent thefts in the workshops, where Jews worked with German raw materials for the Nazi war machine, there was also an element of sabotage and a quiet form of revenge for the outrages committed during the last *Aktion.*

The most frequent thefts and frauds occurred in the institutions and offices that dealt with provisioning. Thus, for example, on 26 January 1941 ninety-one loaves of bread were stolen from a distribution point.[313] On 29 July 1942, a group of Order Service men, in partnership with night watchmen of a neighboring kitchen, attempted to steal a sack of bread from a bakery. They wanted to pull it into a nearby building with the aid of a rope.[314] On 12 December 1941, a scheme was uncovered in the public kitchen on Młynarska Street, consisting of about sixty dinners daily being picked up on forged coupons.[315] A case came before the ghetto court in January 1944 against a director of a tailoring division, two office employees, the records specialist (*referent fun der evidents*) in the division, as well as two managers of a kitchen, for fraud with meal coupons by which the director and the two office employees received double meals but paid for only one.[316] On 5 May 1943, a night watchman of Food Store no. 17 was sentenced to four months of severe incarceration for systematically stealing food during a lengthy period with the aid of a skeleton key.[317] In 1944, a case involved a couple of fellows who disguised themselves as Gestapo agents, entered residences, and told the shocked tenants to give them gold and jewels. In the end, they were satisfied with confiscating the bread rations.[318] People attempted to collect food allotments with coupons from various means, including stolen, forged, or lost food cards.[319]

The terrible hunger in the ghetto drove some to serious criminal acts and even to murder. Some examples:

A 17-year-old boy named Adler entered the ghetto illegally after he had escaped from a German labor camp in the Poznań area. Unable for this reason to get any work or a food card, he stole a 100 kilo sack of flour from a warehouse on 21 June 1942, after knocking out the elderly night watchman with strong blows. At his trial, he defended himself by saying that he was terribly hungry; on the same night, his sister had cooked up for him some of the stolen flour. Since he had another charge against him for escaping from a camp and sneaking into the ghetto in an illegal fashion, the German supervisory authorities were notified about the case. The fellow was still fortunate: He was sentenced to two and a half years of prison; the Germans usually hanged for escaping from a camp. His accomplices (three minors, one age fifteen) were sentenced to from one to three months in prison, although the penalty was suspended for all the accomplices.[320]

An elderly woman was murdered in a bestial fashion on 21 July 1942 while she was at home alone on Ceglana Street (*Tsiglgas*). A longtime neighbor woman of hers committed the murder with the aim of stealing food and money from her. As determined by the investigation, which was conducted initially by the German *Kriminalpolizei* (since all murder cases in the ghetto were in the competence of the *Kripo*) and later by the Order Service, the direct cause of the murder was hunger and envy. The murderess and her husband were unemployed and, for unknown reasons, ineligible for a relief grant, while the murder victim and her working daughter lived in better material conditions. The perpetrator became mentally ill after committing the murder and she was sent for a psychiatric examination. While she was sent to an institution for the insane, her husband died in the *Kripo* prison (doc. no. 140).

Only a few days later, on 23 July, another bloody assault was carried out on a seventy-two-year-old woman on Podrzeczna Street. In the unconscious woman's residence, the attacker stole her butter ration. The attacker was an employed carpentry worker and during his interrogation he stated "that he did not touch [the woman's] bread, he was only lacking butter to spread on his bread."[321]

Another instance of murder due to hunger occurred in April 1943. A young man from a Hasidic Łódź family strangled to death a thirteen-year-old girl while no one else was in the apartment and made off with four food coupons that belonged to the four sisters who occupied the apartment (the parents were no longer living). The murderer received the death penalty. A Jewish hangman and his Jewish assistants executed the sentence in the ghetto.[322]

In 1944 (on 19 June and on 3 July), two murder victims, a man and a woman, were found within the ghetto. The man was found in a well. Since no details are provided in the laconic police report, the motives in these two cases are unknown.[323]

Altogether, according to the available documentation, six cases of murder occurred in the ghetto, one of which, in December 1941, was a result of an argument between two Bałuty underworld figures. Concerning another murder (date unknown), only the fact is known that a father murdered his wife and son. He was tried by a German court and was hanged outside the ghetto.[324]

The rubric "Various" in Table 17 [18] includes a whole series of unspecified transgressions against the strict regulations of the ghetto codex. These included producing candies and other food items, frequently harmful to health, in clandestine little factories;[325] possessing German money or other foreign currency and fabrication of counterfeit ghetto marks;[326] concealing items subject to official confiscation;[327] not heeding the blackout rules at night (in the final days of August 1942, the majority of offenses in this rubric were of this kind); and so forth.

Cases like the following were also reckoned as "crimes": A German Jew deported to Łódź wrote a letter to a friend of his, an Aryan, about helping him out with money; the Jew received six weeks in prison. Another who wanted to let someone abroad know about himself came up with the idea of sending this person a fictive receipt for a sum of money that he had never received. For this, he was sentenced by the Gestapo to six days of arrest and additionally to fifteen lashes every third day from the Jewish Order Service.[328]

The motives for committed offenses were also sometimes quite specific. There was a case when a porter committed a theft before the eyes of a policeman and explained his deed by saying that he hoped in this way to get out of the ghetto into a labor camp in Germany; he had already gone voluntarily and he was better nourished there than in the ghetto.[329]

In general, it should be noted that within the systematic lack of rights and arbitrariness that the Germans imposed in the occupied territories, there could, naturally, not be any talk of legal norms that were obligatory toward the civilian population. The entire legal-administrative system that the Germans introduced into the ghettos was a mockery of the most elementary principles of legality, even in times of war.[330] Therefore, the concepts "crime" and "punishment" were very elastic in the ghetto and the penalty was often dependent not on the judges, but on a push from Rumkowski and his own overseers.[331]

The crimes under the rubric "Resistance" were mostly of a social-political character, particularly in the winter months of 1941, when they were the most numerous. These were arrests for demonstrations, strikes, and agitation to strike, in general for "inciting against the established order in the ghetto." They also included cases of resisting the Order Service when it came to make an arrest for other offenses, and so forth.

Crime among children and adolescents was a particularly grievous problem. The conditions in which children lived in the ghetto and the destructive influence on them from the negative sides of ghetto life have already been discussed above. Children and adolescents provided the largest contingent of those punished for street trading. The hunger and the desire to come to the aid of the hungry at home would drive them to commit petty thefts.

The case of seventeen-year-old Adler has been discussed above. In March 1943 on the docket of the ghetto court was a trial of three adolescents ages seventeen and eighteen (former schoolboys); they had attempted to extort 200 dollars in gold from the wife of a policeman by threatening her in a letter that they would inform the *Kripo* that he had been removed from his post because of shady deals and had gotten a job in a workshop. The court recognized that they were "sufficiently intelligent and intellectually developed to be responsible" and sentenced them to prison for a period of six weeks to three months. The author of the letter received the longest sentence. In the course of the trial, it became apparent that the whole "scam" was actually an adolescent prank by intelligent young men who had read too many detective novels, fallen under the demoralizing influence of the ghetto atmosphere, and sought an intense experience in the gray ghetto.[332]

As mentioned, at the end of July 1941 a separate court for adolescent criminals with a separate section in the prison was formed (see chapter 2). Previously, such adolescents were sent into the Central Prison, where a separate reformatory was reserved for them. In March 1941, there were seventeen prisoners there. In July 1942, this special prison for children and adolescents (outside the Central Prison, but in the same complex of buildings) held thirty-five children, among them twelve in the "improvement dormitory" (*oysbeserung burse*).[333] Children from the orphanage were also sent there for "stubborn [bad] behavior."[334]

It can be inferred from a report in the ghetto *Chronicle* of 5 July 1942 that imprisonment of adolescent "criminals" in the Central Prison (quotation marks are in the original) was halted for a couple of months in the first half of 1942, but at the end of June or beginning of July this procedure was resumed. As the *Chronicle* notice also relates, the conditions in the children's prison were much better than in the Central Prison for adults. The latter institution had a reputation in the ghetto as a place of torture, from which prisoners emerged as cripples. Whipping and other tortures were practiced there, particularly when its commandant was the underworld character Sh. Hercberg.[335] The prison for adolescents and children occupied a couple of houses with clean rooms. The children, sent over from the orphanage, slept in beds with clean bedding. The general prison kitchen cooked for them from the products that they received on their food cards. Those punished for habitual street peddling and petty thefts were in prison cells and slept on planks. In the morning, the young prisoners went out to their workplaces. The management for a time rested in the hands of a specially assigned Order Service functionary and of a woman from Frankfurt, who had for a long time worked in Germany in similar penal institutions for adolescent criminals (doc. no. 141).

Those designated for deportation, as well as workers who were sent back into the ghetto from the labor camps in the province (the latter, at the disposition of the Gestapo), were assembled in the ghetto prison.

Aside from the prisoners sentenced by the ghetto court, there were also in the ghetto prison people arrested by the German *Kriminalpolizei* or Gestapo. Thus, for example, on 7 December 1941, of 230 prisoners (including 44 women), 90 were at the disposition of the *Kripo* and 80 at the disposition of the Gestapo.[336] This was, moreover, in accord with the "guidelines" from the Senior State Prosecutor of 30 August 1941 "concerning penal prosecutions of Jews," where he indicated that no Jew need be transferred into a German prison. The German official stated the odd consideration "that imprisoning a Jew in a German penal institution does not mean anything bad for him, since he thereby is transferred into living conditions that are generally better than those that exist in the Jewish residential quarters . . . that in view of their character attributes, it can most certainly happen that the Jew will in such a fashion seek a way to get himself into a German penal institution in order to get out of the ghetto."[337]

As a rule, the Jewish courts judged all crimes in the ghetto. Exceptions were political crimes (like, for example, clandestinely listening to radio) and murder cases.

The German Criminal Police in Łódź had its own agency in the ghetto: the notorious "Little Red House." To it was attached a group of Order Servicemen, whose assignments were chiefly the delivery of summonses to report to the *Kripo* building to Jews, from whom the Germans wanted to extract their hidden wealth. With Nazi inquisitorial methods they always succeeded, and *Kripo* became a frightening word in the ghetto. It had in its service Jewish informers and agents who were principally recruited from the Bałuty underworld. They did their harmful work almost openly and were well known in the ghetto.[338] It is symptomatic for the moral atmosphere that the Germans created in the ghetto that the chiefs of the Jewish *Sonderkommando* (earlier David Gertler and later, after his disappearance, Marek Kliger) were the officially recognized agents and informers of the German police agencies[339] and had power and esteem in the ghetto.

Characteristic for the moral atmosphere was also "the plague of denunciations that spread in the ghetto."[340] Rumkowski's secretariat was flooded not only with requests and applications, but also with denunciations of employees in the ghetto administration and of private persons. Moreover, Rumkowski himself encouraged informing through his Announcement no. 275 of 30 May 1941, where he urged that "everyone who will discover whatever theft or abuse to the ghetto's loss, or will know about any sort of activity harmful to the ghetto, must unconditionally report this directly to the attorney Henryk Neftalin." Clearly, this opened a wide field for all sorts of malevolence and personal vengeance.

The ghetto had its major trials that agitated public opinion. In addition to the above mentioned murder cases, the trials about big scams uncovered in the institutions and facilities of the ghetto administration provoked excitement, like for example the trials concerning the frauds in the closed Department for Social Aid and in the wholesale tobacco outlet in February 1941; the affair in the carpentry workshops in March 1941; the frauds in the Meat *Centrala;* "the soup and waste racket"[341] (managers of the latter desk in the Economic Department took bribes to ascribe phony routes to the waste transporters, who for a lengthy period received unearned payments), and so forth. During his speech in the ghetto court at the trial concerning the "waste affair," an attorney exaggeratedly stated that "the future historian of the ghetto will not need to operate with dates of days and months. Rather, he will divide the ghetto into periods according to the swindles that took place in the given period. He will have a potato period [a trial concerning giving a prominent ghetto bigshot an overweight of 31 kilos of potatoes], a meat period, a waste period, and so forth."[342] Of course, this periodization is an attorney's rhetorical exaggeration, but abstracting the hyperbole from it, it does characterize in a great measure the criminal climate in the ghetto.

From certain facts it can be inferred that a sexual dissoluteness was prevalent among some ghetto officials. Stories were told about lovers of certain ghetto dignitaries. In the Order Service, there was a special *Sittensanitätsabteilung* (Moral Hygiene Department), whose task was to combat prostitution in the ghetto.[343]

Documents 113–141

No. 113: YI-55

J. Zelkowicz's depictions of living conditions in the Łódź Ghetto. No date. [in Yiddish][344]

[p. 37]

. . . and later, when your eye becomes accustomed to the weird darkness, you can immediately tell yourself:

"A dog that has an owner would not live in such a stall, and if the dog did not have an owner and were not crazy!—he would rather lay himself on the first best heap of rubbish and not here. . . . It would be softer for him there; rubbish would have been cleaner for him and—above all—he would have found the pile of rubbish reeked less . . ."

And here, in this very pit, that is not even similar to any doghouse, there lie living people, people who do not even think anymore with categories of homeless, but sane dogs.

You can't very quickly pick out the human faces from amidst the gloomy rot oozing down from the clayey and swollen walls!

. . . .

[p. 76]

People live in this utter darkness. People are breathing, in this home whose cellar is waterlogged both in summer and winter, with water that tears living chunks from the inanimate walls. Beneath the filthy, disgusting bedding on the rusted, rachitic iron bedsteads sleep people— living people with open eyes that once saw other sorts of lives. People who have mouths that can talk and scream and nevertheless they are silent and are expiring in quiet resignation, just like the flies that lazily slide on the walls, so that an hour later or the next day they give a final flutter of the wings and fall down lifeless on the dirty floor.

. . . .

[p. 83]

. . . .

And if you will have taught your eyes to look thus, you will discern that the seventeen people who are sitting around the table and eating do not comprise a single family. . . . The three loaves of bread sitting on the table will tell you this, the three plates with honey will tell you this, the three bowls with the finished coffee will tell you this. . . . Only they don't have any mouths, the breads, the plates, and the bowls. If they had mouths they would say that the seventeen people sitting at the table belong to three families . . . that their encounter in one home is only a factor of the ghetto conditions. . . .[345]

In the ghetto conditions, in the ghetto circumstances, it is not possible that three families comprised of seventeen souls, adults and little children, whom fate has stuffed into one room, can be housed under one roof, particularly since only three have a place to lay their heads;

in the best case—six, and in the very worst case—calculating even four in each bed, two at the head of the bed, two at the foot—there remain another five whole living people who do not have where to lay their heads down.
[p. 93]

. . . .

A courtyard in Bałuty. But it's not a courtyard that, according to the meaning of the word, should embrace house number so and so, yet it is a yard—a street. Last year's winter erased all the boundaries between yard and yard, between house and house. Now there is no "my" domain and "your" domain—it is a yard, public domain: all the fences and enclosures that had once divided yard from yard and house from house were burned on frosty days and extremely cold nights. The wooden wells lost their walls and covers. The toilets were taken apart and the wooden storage rooms—torn down. People ate so little and froze so intensely;
[p. 94]

. . . .

A courtyard in the ghetto: it's muddy and clayey like a dead-end road to a secluded Polish village. When you are in such a yard, you can never know whether or not beneath the mud and the clay there lies some pit, an open well, if not something still worse—a cesspit. . . .

No. 114: YI-49D

J. Zelkowicz's description of ghetto life in the courtyards of 6 August 1943. [in Yiddish]

[p. 1]
While daytime ghetto life is organized during working hours around the factories and offices and later on around the distribution points, the nighttime life of the ghetto, particularly in the hot days, [is organized] around the courtyards and . . . rubbish bins.

Ghetto apartments do not possess the calm, the homey, tranquil walls of the past. The ghetto apartments are by no means capable of nurturing their tenants. The walls of the ghetto in winter are permeated by cold and frost; in spring by hunger; in summer by lice and in autumn—with mold. Such walls are repulsive. It is impossible to live between such walls; it is impossible to breathe. Therefore . . .

Around nine in the evening, when the tired and exhausted ghetto body already has behind it an intensive 15-hour workday (the average worker in the ghetto cannot get up later than six in the morning), he only then begins his nocturnal life, the struggle for a bit of fresh air in a race with his lice.

Around nine in the evening, when curtaining the window and igniting the lights means settling down and bathing in one's own sweat; around nine in the evening, when the windows are opened up, to stay in the dark and lie down on one's bedding means letting yourself be eaten alive by stinking worms: around nine in the evening the ghetto commences its unique and special nightlife.

Husband and wife, kith and kin, like cursed souls, like homeless ghosts, seek salvation for the bodies that their tired, exhausted legs are already refusing to drag any more. The wooden steps groan. Unlubricated doors scream and grate. Clumsy feet stumble, severely dried out and scrawny lungs pant, hoarse throats wheeze nastily: this is the ghetto world looking for a bit of air, the foothold for their flickering souls in damaged bodies.

In the deserted rooms, lice crawl about on the stained and ruptured walls, while the ghetto yards are crawling with people. If there is a pump in the yard, it is instantly besieged around and around. Bodies lower themselves heavily on the wet boards, tired legs stretch out comfortably and unbuttoned breasts breathe more easily and freely, with sounds like a saw across sheet metal.

Happy are those who came in time and have found themselves a place. They are sitting. Their legs are stretched out. They can even cast off from their feet the wooden or leather shoes full of holes. They can more freely clear their throats. They can yawn more deeply and . . . they can now chat about the work in the factory, dream about supplemental rations and fantasize about a "ration" due to appear very shortly because he himself had heard from somebody that a guy had told him that a good friend of his works in Provisioning or at the vegetables place. . . . Happy are they

[p. 2]

but it is worse for those who have not managed to occupy a place around the well: They must search; they must detect by touch a free corner somewhere, that should also be clean enough that one should be able to lie down even on the bare earth. . . . The earth has the quality that it cools the feverish, overwrought body, but it has the defect that there remains no place where to stick the clumsy legs, unless the corner is located somewhere by a wall, to which one can press oneself. These corner- and on-the-ground-sitters are not as well off as the well sitters, but they do not have it so bad; their bodies do have support, they do not have to be continually hauled about by their rebellious legs. . . .

It's very bad for those whose kitchens smoked and thereby did not manage to cook up their meager night meals in time. They, like those who were delayed, also find no free corner. They have to drag themselves about on their feet, standing, or walking. These latecomers form little clumps on the yard. Clumps, that seem to be leaning one on the other, and if one would move from his place, the whole clump would collapse like a dilapidated building. . . .

. . . .

The yard rocks itself, humming like a beehive, and from the tremendous black spot runs the saliva from gaping mouths—the People of Israel delights itself with mind, the People of Israel delights itself with the reeking air that the nighttime pseudo-breeze chases out from the wide-open rubbish bins. . . .

Happy are those who have found a seat around the well! They, when they get tired of talking and listening, when their bodies heave from fatigue, without rocking on their bent and limp spinal cords, they can move themselves in a little deeper and lean their swaying bodies on the well wood and they can then allow themselves to shut an eye . . . —enough. Had enough until now of the hard, real ghetto day. . . . Now, when the rest of the crowd calms down and ceases chatting, it will be possible to grab a nap and maybe the dream will bring at least a little piece of the fantasized life of dreamland. . . . Happy are those who have a seat around the well.

Good for those who have found a corner on the ground and they can [p. 3] lean their wobbling shoulders against a cooled off wall. They too can permit themselves to shut an eye, take a nap and simultaneously have revenge on their lice. . . . Let them crazily search in the rooms, let them crawl there, bursting there. Today their bodies will not be sucked, not be bitten! Their lice will have a fast today. . . .

It's worse for those standing. Until now, they held their legs up with the force of inertia from the chats: People talked of good times, people talked of a "ration," people talked of the Messiah, of a heavenly wagon standing ready for his sake, like a ghetto horse cab before the door of a ghetto dignitary. . . . Until now, their legs still stood with difficulty, but still patiently stood. . . . Now, however, when strange, sour notes dropped into these conversations: a snore, a hiccup, or simply a yawn; these clumsy legs rebel and, indeed high time for them!—How much longer? sixteen hours, seventeen hours, they also have a right to a little, really, not a lot, but at least a drop of rest! . . .

. . . .

And later, trembling hands feel about in the dark dwellings. A hand finds a pillow, or a blanket, or a sheet. This is all brought into the yard, tossed down onto the first available free spot and the body stretches out. . . . Ah-ah-ah, wonderful! Rest for the tired and exhausted body. . . . Tranquility for the clumsy legs and—revenge on the lice!—Today they'll suck plagues, not any blood! . . .

Like lazy mice in an empty rubbish bin, the hours drag on through the ghetto night. The stones of the yard press themselves ever deeper into the shriveled bodies. Every side is sore from lying down. Among the well sitters, their heads hang down heavily. Among the corner-sitters, their bodies have bent crookedly. Among those lying on the ground, their skin is shivering from cold. The day is awaited, the day that will bring with it a warm sun, that will bring with it a factory soup, that perhaps will bring with it a fresh "ration," that should give strength to endure subsequent days and yet a lot of such subsequent summery nights. . . .

No. 115: YI-55

J. Zelkowicz's description of the weakened sense of shame in the ghetto. [in Yiddish]

[p. 14]
Wild animals and cattle carry out their physiological needs in the street, before the eyes of everyone and all gaze thereupon with indifferent eyes: that's how they were created. People, who live in animalistic conditions, people, from whom every cultural opportunity has been taken away, people, whose most elementary cultural needs are being malevolently and cynically ridiculed, are perforce turned into animals; they revert to what they were initially—people, born simply and naturally, with natural nakedness, for whom the sense of shame is alien. . . .

. . . .

[p. 28]
And when such a Moyshe or Khayim or Mendl becomes an official "coal miner," he becomes at the same time a loose person. The "coal mine" is not the home where modesty and nudity are still perhaps covered with the fragile spider web that holds on in the ghetto, even if only barely by the last thread. . . . Here, in the "coal mine" are sitting girls who have no more than the single dresses that they are wearing. They cannot, of course, sit in them in the mud. So these dresses are taken off and laid in a pile on a side and the naked bodies are anyway immediately covered with dust and mud. But dusty nakedness beckons still more . . . and draws even more attention to itself. . . . And eleven- or twelve-year-old boys and thirteen- or fourteen-year-old girls discover parental secrets here in the coal pit. . . . Here in the coal pit equality applies for everybody and all here perform their physiological needs, one under the other's nose—a waste of time [to go off a distance]. . . .[346]

. . . .

No. 115a: Police of Israel, Headquarters, 6th Department, doc. no. 1248

Telegram, dated 9 October 1941, from the Litzmannstadt Regierungsprä-sident to Himmler, opposing deportation into the Łódź Ghetto of 20,000 Jews and 5,000 Gypsies and accusing Eichmann of submitting false data to the Interior Ministry. [in German; original message text is entirely in upper case capital letters.]

REICH SECURITY MAIN OFFICE
News Transmission
Telegram—Radiogram—Teletype
Telephone

SSD . . . .
THE CHIEF OF POLICE. LITZMANNSTADT NR. 71 9.10.411425
TO THE R[EICHS]F[ÜHRER] SS AND CHIEF OF THE GERMAN
POLICE FUEHRER HEADQUARTERS

THROUGH THE REICH MINISTRY OF THE INTERIOR.
SUPPLEMENT FOR THE REICH MINISTRY OF THE INTERIOR:
PLEASE FORWARD I M M E D I A T E L Y.
REGARDING: DISPATCH OF 20,000 JEWS AND 5,000 GYPSIES INTO
THE LITZMANNSTADT GHETTO.
Pursuant to my report of 4.10.1941 I report:
At the Reich Interior Ministry I personally confirmed on 7.10.1941 that the official expert in this matter, SS-Sturmbannfueher *Eichmann* of the Reich Security Main Office, as well as the *official expert on Jews of the State Police Office Litzmannstadt,* through false statements at the meeting held on 29.9.1941 obtained the agreement of the representative of the Reich Interior Ministry.
Since I must accordingly accept that you also were not correctly informed, I report as follows:
[p. 2]
ROEM. 1.)
Explanation of SS-Sturmbannfuehrer Eichmann and my rectifications:
1.) *He discussed the execution of the measures with me in Litzmannstadt.* In reality SS-Sturmbannfuehrer Eichmann *did not report to me at all,* although he had to know that the total management of the ghetto lies only in my hands and I alone have the comprehensive supervision.

2.) States *The official charged with management for the ghetto expressly agreed with the dispatch. This man, in other respects not authoritative, firmly denies the emission of this statement.* He could also not have made it, since he is the author of report sent to you from the Mayor of Litzmannstadt of 24.9.1941. The director of the State Police Office Litzmannstadt, Regierungsrat Dr. S c h e f e, also confirms that this submission by SS-Sturmbannfuehrer Eichmann does not tally.

3.) *A reorganization of the ghetto has already been tackled for days,* that in the first line has the objective of assuring fulfillment of . . . Wehrmacht orders: The ghetto would be divided into a *labor ghetto* and a *welfare ghetto.* In the labor ghetto would be about 40,000 Jews for work on the Wehrmacht orders, all remaining Jews accommodated in welfare ghetto. Labor ghetto and welfare ghetto would be strictly separated by a clear lime strip,[347] trenches, fences, and guard team. After the future organization of the ghetto the fulfillment of the Wehrmacht's orders will also be even more guaranteed than until now. It is correct that the division into labor ghetto and welfare ghetto in practice cannot be realized, since the factories and workshops in which the major Wehrmacht orders are carried out lie scattered over the entire current ghetto. Even if one could shift the plants out of space prescribed by the Gestapo as welfare ghetto, the sending of the Jews incapable of work into this today already densely settled area would be impossible, since it comprises only 0.748 square kilometers, while the space proposed for the labor ghetto totals 3.162 square kilometers. A space lying between both parts is not at all available and also cannot be rounded up, because both of these parts are bisected by the major street on which the connection between the parts of the city that surround the ghetto must be maintained by streetcar and vehicular traffic. Preparations in this direction cannot and could not therefore be made.

ROEM. 2.

Statement of the official specialist on Jews of the State Police Office Litzmannstadt, and my correction: *No increase in the danger of epidemics occurs through the increase of 25,000 Jews.* The epidemics danger has already receded through a

[P. 3]

substantial reduction of the Jews living in the ghetto. In spring there were still around *185,000* Jews remaining in the ghetto. Their number presently amounts to *120,000.* It would thus grow through the deportation from the Reich to about *145,000* persons. It is correct that Regierungsrat SS-Sturmbannfuehrer Dr. Schefe notified me in writing on 29.9.1941 that after sealing of the ghetto on 30.4.1941 *160,000* Jews were located in the ghetto and that today around *145,000* Jews live in the ghetto. These numbers are also correct. *The information from the official expert on Jews*[348] *of the State Police Office Litzmannstadt in the meeting on 29.9.1941 I can only* describe *as deliberately misleading.* Although he knew that the living space in the ghetto has been substantially reduced in the course of city redevelopment and through putting into operation factories and workshops that were initially used as living space, the official expert on Jews of the State Police Office Litzmannstadt withheld this. Had he mentioned the correct number of 145,000 Jews now living in the ghetto, and the number of 170,000 after the possible settlement of Jews and Gypsies, thus 10,000 more Jews than at the sealing of the ghetto on 30.4.1940, the Ministry of the Interior would not have given its agreement concerning the danger of epidemics. The epidemics danger will thereby be increased, since the Altreich Jews, in contrast to the local Jews who are immunized through illness in youth, have no antibodies in their bodies, and through their illness in large numbers put at extreme jeopardy the Germans in the city Litzmannstadt. I can only characterize the practical [*sic!*] practices applied by SS-Sturmbannfuehrer Eichmann and the official expert of the State Police Office Litzmannstadt *as horse-trader ways adopted from the Gypsies.* Since the matter standing in question is extremely serious and therefore does not tolerate such practices, I must request *both of these men be called to account.* The admission of the Altreich Jews and especially the Gypsies into the ghetto Litzmannstadt working at full blast for the war economy cannot be responsible. The Warsaw ghetto, according to recent photo reports of the Berliner Illustrierte Zeitung, still has dance halls and bars. It can with ease admit the 20,000 Jews and 5,000 Gypsies, since over and above that there is no work there for the war economy and the war potential will not be endangered by the admission.

U E B E L H O E R REGIERUNGSPRAESIDENT UND
SS-BRIGADEFUEHRER

No. 116: YI-25

"Supplement to the report concerning arrival of the new population in the ghetto. November 1941." [in Polish]

[p. 8]

LIST OF ARRIVED TRANSPORTS

Transport	Number	Date of Arrival	Number of Persons
Vienna I	1	17 Oct. 1941	1,000
Prague I	2	18 Oct. 1941	1,000
Luxembourg	3	18 Oct. 1941	512
Berlin I	4	19 Oct. 1941	1,082
Vienna II	5	20 Oct. 1941	1,000
Frankfurt am Main	6	21 Oct. 1941	1,186
Prague II	7	22 Oct. 1941	1,000
Cologne I	8	23 Oct. 1941	1,006
Vienna III	9	24 Oct. 1941	1,000
Emden	10a	25 Oct. 1941	122
Berlin II	10b	25 Oct. 1941	912
Hamburg	11	26 Oct. 1941	1,063
Prague III	12	27 Oct. 1941	1,000
Düsseldorf	13	28 Oct. 1941	1,004
Vienna IV	14	29 Oct. 1941	1,000
Berlin III	15	30 Oct. 1941	1,030
Cologne II	16	31 Oct. 1941	1,006
Prague IV	17	1 Nov. 1941	1,000
Berlin IV	18	2 Nov. 1941	1,030
Vienna V	19	3 Nov. 1941	1,000
Prague V	20	4 Nov. 1941	1,000

In 20 transports from 17 October to 4 November 1941 there arrived 19,953 persons.

No. 117: YI-1198

Notice in the Ghetto Chronicle for October 1941 concerning the arrival of the West European Jews. [in German][349]

[p. 1]

The most significant event in October 1941 for the ghetto of Litzmannstadt was the arrival of 23,000 foreign Jews,[350] who until now have lived, relatively freely, amid their long familiar surroundings—their native places, with which they were very tightly linked and bound, often for generations, frequently for centuries. Knowing nothing different from this long familiar and quite naturally perceived environment, these tens of thousands of suddenly banished and deported Jews arrive, entirely without transition or preparation, into an environment and into a milieu of absolutely contrasting otherness in every respect: Right into the ghetto of Litzmannstadt, a creation whose uniqueness can and must be addressed.

When the contemporary ghetto chronicler on 16 October[351] calls the arrival day of the first transport of deported Jews (from Vienna) a historic moment in the history of the ghetto, this designation is apt. For nothing has so strongly influenced, yes, in part changed, the countenance and the inner structure of the "residential area of the Jews," as the forceful insertion of this large mosaic fragment into the otherwise homogeneous ghetto structure. Nevertheless, a sudden 15 percent increase in population, moreover of such utterly different type and essential difference from the main population, is an occurrence that cannot be accepted and swallowed unnoticed by the ghetto's everyday life. It had to have an effect and expand horizons. And at the same time: looking from the point of view of the old ghetto population, foreign "*datsche Juden*"[352] are arriving; they were above all different from the local people. And this erases or makes invisible to their eyes the great differences that contrast these German Jews from one another, if not perhaps separating them. It is well that they all come from the German Reich. Yet the long-resident Viennese Jew is not comparable in disposition and habits to the long-resident Hamburg, Berlin, or Düsseldorf Jews. Nor are the long-resident Prague Jews comparable to the Jews of Cologne, Emden, Frankfurt, or Luxembourg. Looked at from the ghetto: a unit of similar foreign Jews. But among one another, they are varied, essentially different Jews, linked (except for a portion of the Praguers) by the same language, related and loosely bound by the same, harsh fate: banishment without temporal limitation. A new contribution, a new chapter, for the much described problem of East and West has started on a soil that was, moreover, the bearer of this problem at least for a very long time: on the (old) Russian-Polish earth, on the soil of the East, not the opposite [in the West] as in the last four centuries.

. . . .

[p. 2]

And so we shall consider the minor and major events of this month in the ghetto, the typical and characteristic everyday events, this time under the shadow of the major event—the resettlement of the Western Jews. If we consider the [month of] January, hard and so extremely fateful for the ghetto populace, from the point of view of 'hunger and cold' and all that happened so that we could informally group these principal factors, the leitmotiv of this month is the arrival of the "newcomers." And we would now investigate which changes the ghetto milieu experienced and in which regard, in the weeks up to the arrival and during this time; which momentary situations the "newcomers" encountered, with which they must come to terms and with which they had to become accustomed—as far as October brought with it changes in relation to the earlier months. . . . .

No. 118: YI-1197

A reportage by a deportee from Vienna, entitled "How the Newcomer Works in the Ghetto." No date. [in German]

[p. 1]

How is the newcomer working in the ghetto?

". . . to a German industrial city, in which all receive work," they said to the sorely tested evacuees, laden with backpacks while standing ready for removal. Something conciliatory and consoling lay in these final words of the homeland: German city . . . , work . . . , wages . . . , set down roots again, to be able to stand on one's own feet!

Already on the next day, on 16[353] October 1941, the 1st transport from Vienna arrived in this German city, in LITZMANNSTADT. It tallied. Only they forgot to stress that here was involved the former Łódź with a Polish-speaking population and—moreover, they were brought not into the city itself, but rather into the strictly isolated "ghetto," surrounded with barbed wire—the residential area of the Jews.

In spite of this, the newly resettled—thus were the evacuees called here—were quartered in the holiday camp in Marysin, the rural suburb of the ghetto city, in small block houses; and in the individual rooms freshly fabricated wooden plank beds received the tired wanderers. First thing the next morning, lists were posted that registered the abilities and previously performed jobs of every individual, for the command here is: Everyone will and must work!

Skilled workers were especially sought after and electricians, carpenters, construction, and street workers, in short, artisans of all sorts, were immediately accommodated. At the same time, the many Poles who came from Vienna had it particularly good, since they speak the country's language. It was much more difficult, for example, for the office people in general, but particularly for the genuine, real Viennese, who had no idea of Polish and also had not provided themselves with that kind of means of communication, since it was said: into a German city! So what happened with him? Thus, for example: an award-winning, extremely dexterous woman machinist, a self-reliant and conscientious worker in every respect. Can she hold her own without the language here in the absolutely Polish atmosphere? And how does she, entirely without connections, at all get near to the high authorities?

. . . .

As secretary of the manager himself? But the telephone—*nie rozumię*[354] *po polsku,* I don't understand Polish—that will be impossible! The division was discussed. The many Praguers, who were in offices, had it easy for the Polish language is not so foreign to their Czech tongues and their ear comprehends almost everything. But the Germans!

After a couple of days, the remedy will be found. The ARCHIVE of the Eldest of the Jews in Litzmannstadt needs a trustworthy worker, who has to handle at the same time the German correspondence with the authorities and outside of the ghetto. So: "On the basis of the order of Mister Chairman you will transfer from 8.12.1941 from the Department for the Resettlers into the Records Departments, 4 Kirchplatz, and are assigned to the Archive in the function of independent female correspondent-machinist." So read the official text of the job assignment—called nomination.

. . . .

It is by far worse with the language. It is like sitting in a swarm of bees: Polish, Yiddish, Hebrew—only not German. One is fully isolated, has no sense of what was being said and would so like to take part in it. This costs nervous energy in colossal measure. One appears like an illiterate—why doesn't one know this language? . . . Inferiority complex?

The coworkers are amiable and polite, but—although almost all of them have command of the German language, even if often poorly and broken—they speak only in their mother tongue: Polish. One communicates with the bosses and managers, since what is not said in words is quickly guessed. There is no lack of intelligence. One attempts also to penetrate into the language but it is not easy. In spite of this: the *kierownik*, the manager, is satisfied. The jobs are correct, are *w porządku*, in order! So far, that the German woman machinist is even appointed to substitute for the ill Polish woman colleague in the secretariat.

New difficulties with the unfamiliar surroundings, with the foreign material. Internally, everything is conducted in Polish, the card files, the file cabinet, the reference books, the correspondence . . . but after a short time one gets worked in here, too. Here one knows what is going on, the ear becomes accustomed to the designations, one retains the words, even giving particulars in reply to questions asked in Polish—and the work booms and is satisfying everybody.

It costs a lot of energy to maintain oneself here, a lot of grit and diligent, indefatigable work, often until late into the evening. All "with a soup daily," since there is no longer any additional soup for jobs after four.

No. 119: YI-1221

A fragment from Rumkowski's speech of 20 December 1941, concerning the newcomers. [in Polish]

[p. 4]
One must not politicize. The walls have ears. This warning applies particularly to the newcomers. Newcomers, you discuss too much. In case of need, there will be
[p. 5]
arrests. Even the title of privy councilor[355] does not protect before these straitened circumstances. In today's times, titles do not play the least role. Bluntly, many of you relate negatively to work. You say to yourselves: Why do we have to work when it is possible here to live from the sale of things or from hoards of money brought along. I will teach you to work and to behave properly; I will break you of impertinence.

No. 120: YI-Diary: Leon Hurwitz[356]

A characterization of Rumkowki's behavior toward employees. [in Yiddish]

[p. 24]

... and the internal life in the ghetto recalls the feudal order of the Middle Ages, around some wealthy Russian boyar. All around, the court is deeply sunk in darkness and mud. The peasants, serfs for life of the rich lord, were only labor machines and they were born and live only so that the lord should draw both use and pleasure from them.

And the lord, also our lord, likes to display himself in his full glory before his subjects. Our lord is indefatigable. He jumps from one factory to the next. From one office to the next and everywhere he throws a scare, a terror into the officials, into the managers, into the lowly laborers and into the security guys and errand boys. And there is no reason to wonder [why], since only very rarely does it happen that someone does not suffer during such an "inspection," that an official is not slapped in the face or tossed out of his post without rhyme or reason, for no good reason, and become jobless for a very long time, if not until Rumkowski's dynasty ends or the barbed-wires of the ghetto fall. And Rumkowski performed these queer sadistic whims preferably in the presense of this or that "minister." Let them quake a little about their own fate.

. . . .

No. 121: YI-1220

A fragment from Rumkowski's speech of 1 November 1941 to the deportees from Western Europe. [in Polish]

[p. 7]

On the 6th of April 1940, I moved into the ghetto. I then notified the city's President that I was going to the ghetto because there is a gold mine there. To the astonished questions, I replied briefly:

"IN THE GHETTO I HAVE FORTY THOUSAND WORKING HANDS.

THIS IS MY GOLD MINE!"

As I organized work here, the authorities began to confer with me and to take me more and more into account. The first zeal of my efforts produced solutions for such questions as bread for everybody, considerate care for children, the sick and the elderly, organization of order and calm, etc. Intent on the above program, I started to work alongside my friends. At the very beginning, we set to organization of various branches of work. To the workers I cast the slogan of abandonment of factionalism. Politicizing, which is absolutely combated by me, at a certain moment threatened immobilization of factories that arose at the cost of the greatest effort. In the face of this danger, I resolved to close all enterprises for a short period of time. Today the number of fifty-two factories existing in the ghetto testifies to my attainments in the field of organization of work places. The highest representatives of the authorities often visited these factories. The inspectors were full of admiration. More than once they said to me that until now they knew only the figure of the Jew-merchant or broker, but they did not know that Jews could work productively. I will not forget the remark of one of the Berlin dignitaries, who at the sight of a unit of the Order Service patrolling the factory being inspected, thought that the policemen's role consists of daily forcing people into the factories. I corrected this gentleman's error, explaining to him that instead the policemen had to drive away applicants for work. By doing good work, the ghetto demonstrates that despite being an impoverished residential quarter, it does not ask for beggar's bread for itself. Work became the ghetto's advertising; created trust for the ghetto; multi-million credits are eloquent evidence of this trust.

[p. 8]

Over 2,000,000 marks monthly in wages flows into the ghetto. I am proud that I realize the full 100 percent payment for wages from the employers. In other centers, Jews receive only 50 percent of the normal remuneration. At first, it was difficult getting orders for the ghetto. With the passage of time, when the authorities and private clients became acquainted with the level of ghetto production—orders began to pour in to us from different lines of business. Today, the ghetto is not only a center of work, but also a city of production. In the ghetto everything is nationalized. From month to month, the productive range is increasing. In the ghetto one does not work with watch in hand. The effects are great: The more we are esteemed, the more we are consulted.

No. 122: YI-1221

A fragment from Rumkowski's speech of 20 December 1941 concerning whom he will deport from the ghetto. [in Polish]

[p. 3]

As usual in my addresses, I must turn to the field of struggle against crime. A regular court did not suffice, nor did it speedily perform its task. I myself sometimes do not know how to liquidate social wreckers. It turns out that even deportation does not frighten them. Rascals are growing like mushrooms after rain. I do not see any other way than dispatch of undesirable elements outside the ghetto. Only in this way can the evil be eradicated and entirely uprooted. Finally, if I do not do this, it will be done by someone else. . . . Nevertheless, I argued against dispatch. However, my plea,

[p. 4]

to the authorities perhaps came out too weakly. For I encountered from the deciding factors an argument difficult to demolish: "Whom are you defending? Bandits, thieves of the poor ghetto's public property?" In accord with authorizations I have and within the sphere of the ghetto's autonomy, I obtained the right to select candidates for dispatch, by which

I managed to reduce by half the contingent required for deportation, from 20 to 10,000 persons. A special commission comprised of my most trustworthy co-workers determined lists of candidates for dispatch. In return for those dispatched, I was promised the assignment to the ghetto of a desirable element: 10,000 good craftsmen and skilled workers. If this promise is realized I will be in a position to set in motion new enterprises by exploitation of the new work force. Aside from criminals I am sending out from the ghetto dole recipients who made light of the obligation to work off the dole grants. I have a tally that shows that of 100 dole recipients summoned to work, barely more than a dozen people reported. Those committing sabotage will be sent away! I will also send away shopkeepers occupying themselves with buying up things from newcomers. I commanded immediate arrest of persons who attempt to influence the decision of the committee for their favorites. They will share the fate of their protegés and any member of the commission who allows intervention will meet that same fate.

No. 123: Diary of Leon Hurwitz.[357] YI-Diary

Criticism of the summer residences of the ghetto elite in Marysin. [in Yiddish]

[p. 24]
Rumkowski also sought new emotions and an opportunity to show off before his dear guests at the boarding house, as well as before those chosen people who have received summerhouses in Marysin. It is not a joke: at the same time that people with lung diseases are sleeping with the healthy in one bed, spreading the germs from one to the other with frightful swiftness,
[p. 25]
at a time when hundreds and thousands of families are living in houses with broken doors, without windows or floors, when people are sleeping on the bare earth on a pile of rags instead of bedding—at this very same time summer dwellings were created in Marysin and it was also seen to it that the camarilla should have all that is necessary to be comfortable and should know how to be grateful and submissive to the master! Thus, two bigshots, Reb[358] Dovid and Reb Hersh,[359] are living in a well-renovated house with a fine little garden. Both each received two beds, a couch, a cabinet with a big mirror, tables and chairs and still more and more things which are necessary in the household and all of it delivered brand new from the furniture maker and other factories. How many summer dwellings or *datshes* were furnished in such or another fashion cannot be precisely determined, because Marysin is of course hermetically sealed off for the common masses.

But the number of *datshnikes* has recently grown so that together with the residents of the boarding house and also with the Saturday and Sunday guests who arrive packed five or six each on the communal *droshkies* continually coursing back and forth all day, they form quite a fine suite for His Majesty Rumkowski. And thus surrounded with these social prostitutes, Rumkowski reviewed the parade of the school youth.

No. 124: Franz Kurski Bund Archive [at YIVO]

Protest leaflet of 25 August 1940 against the ghetto regime. [in Yiddish]

Attention!

Today, Sunday, the 25/8, 12 o'clock noon, a large protest gathering is taking place against Rumkowski's 10,000 dinners with 100,000 worms that are being cooked at 26 Zgierska and against the Szczęśliwys, and the outrageous treatment [directed] against the worker masses.

Fellow Workers!

We call for the community to be dissolved and to give ourselves momentarily over into the hands of the German government, because we have no more to lose.[360] This will be our slogan at 4 Młynarska.

At the same time we notify all sausage shops and sweetshops to be closed today, Sunday the 25/8.

Simultaneously, we will demand bread and work not for individuals, but for whole families.

Simultaneously, we will protest against the worker-traitors who have sold their souls for the sake of a ribbon [of rank] on the right arm.[361]

Down with the traitors!

Long live the unity of the workers!

The Temporary Committee
Ghetto, 25/8 1940.

No. 125: YI-1241

Notes by J. Zelkowicz about the carpenters strike in January 1941. [in Yiddish][362]

[p. 1]

Noted on 24.1.1941.

Mr. Wolf Shtibl, employee in the carpentry shop at no. 3 Urzędnicza Street, where the mentioned events played themselves out yesterday, and the policeman Mr. Levi Gliksman relate the following about the events: Dissatisfaction has been simmering among the workers in the carpentry shop for a long time, arising from the fact that here in the carpentry shop all the workers each equally earn 30 pfennigs an hour, even though the carpentry trade was already divided before the war by a special craft commission into four categories: masters of luxury furniture, other carpentry masters, journeymen, and apprentices. Added to this comes the circumstance that with the introduction of the food cards, they were deprived of the soup that they had received once daily and finally—the taking away from them of the additional bread that they had received, as an equivalent for the withdrawn soup—all this forced them to put out four demands:

1) A wage supplement of 20 pfennigs an hour for workers in the first two categories and 10 pfennigs an hour for workers in the latter two categories;
2) Since, even after the supplement in the prevailing inflation, they will not be able to feed themselves, half of their earnings should be paid out to them in food products;
3) Due to the fact that they are not able in the current nourishment system to perform the difficult jobs that this trade demands, an additional soup should be given to them, aside from the food card; and
4) The supplement of the special bread ration that they have received until now is not to be canceled.

The manager of the carpentry division, Mr. B. Freund, conferred several times with the chairman concerning these demands and received a negative response from him regarding the latter three, [while] in contrast he promised to deal positively with the first point of the demands, after the NIK[363] will have determined that the carpentry enterprise brings in at least the most minimal revenue.

Yesterday (the 23rd) in the morning, the workers came into the first department of the furniture factory at no. 12 Drukarska Street and set themselves to work like always. The director of the division, Mr. Freund, discussed this by telephone with the chairman and he was given an instruction: "Whoever wants to work can proceed to work, and whoever does not want to—can go home."

Mr. Freund communicated this decision to the workers. With the exception of the mechanical workers (locksmiths, tinsmiths, electro-technicians, etc.) and the boiler workers, all the workers, approximately 200 men, took their tools and approached the other department of the carpentry division at no. 3 Urzędnicza Street in order to come to an understanding with those workers.

The police guard of the other department, which had in the meantime received a command from the division director not to admit the workers into the factory, halted those arriving at the gate. All the workers stayed calm.

[p. 2][364]

Waiting a little more time, he [Freund] crossed over to the first department in order from there to communicate with the Chairman. But from the first department he sent over representatives and through them asked the workers to leave the factory building in order not to force him to bring in police. And when the workers did not react to the warnings, he arrived with a police unit.

The police commandant, Mr. Rozenblat, and Commissioner Frenkel (flying squad) directed the police. When they arrived at the factory site, Commandant Rozenblat remained with the police unit outside and Commissioner Frenkel went in to the workers and called on the workers to leave the occupied area calmly within five minutes. Simultaneously,

Commandant Rozenblat ordered the police to put down their rubber clubs (the only weaponry of the Jewish police) and not to hit anyone. The workers of the ground floor hall (mostly older people) left the hall immediately after the demand. In contrast, however, the workers of the upper floors did not react to the police demand and then police were summoned, who were forcibly to remove the workers from the occupied area.

On the first floor, the police could not get in through the front door because it was barricaded and they had to make their way in through the rear entrance. When the police entered the hall, they again called on the workers to leave the building within five minutes. Some of the workers left but others in contrast bombarded the police with work tools and lumber. Thereby arose the clash between some of the police and some of the workers.

After the first floor was finally cleared, the police went up to the second floor where they encountered an entry barricaded both from outside and inside. The external barricade was removed, the door broken open and there the police again met active resistance by the workers, who threw clubs and lumber at them.

The police finally managed to gain control of the situation and to clear out the building.

During the action, several people were injured. Both by workers and by police. In one case, the first aid had to intervene and transport the severely injured worker home.

. . . .

[pp. 5–6]

Noted on 26.1.1941.

In worker circles, they tell about the events as follows: When the chairman telephoned to Commissioner Frenkel and tasked him with putting together a major group of police in order to clear the occupied area, Commissioner Frenkel supposedly said to him that in order to do that he needed no more than his people (the flying squad) and with them he would carry out the clearance, but he asked of the chairman that the reduction now being carried out in the police personnel not apply to his command. The chairman promised him that and that was the reason why the police behaved so aggressively toward the workers.

It is further told in the same circles that, while the police penetrated into the factory hall and the workers withdrew into the background, people looking through the factory windows that face out on Urzędnicza Street (the side that does not belong to the ghetto) saw German security policemen with automatic hand weapons arriving. The informants do not know, however, whether the arrival of the German police was in connection with the events or whether it was a pure coincidence.

On Friday, the 24th, alongside the mentioned poster announcement of the chairman,[365] leaflets were found at the entrances to the factories:

Shame on Rumkowski with his flying squad.

We communicate the following fact to the public in the ghetto.

For several months the carpentry workers in the ghetto, numbering 600, have been striving for a whole series of demands to enable them to carry out their work.

1) Increase the wage,

2) Some products instead of money,

3) In addition to the ration of bread, a soup outside the [ration] cards.

As an answer to these justified demands the Chairman sent in his fine lads and murderously beat up dozens of workers.

One more crime has been added to the bundle of Rumkowski's crimes and shameful deeds.

Workers!

Express your protest and embitterment.

A Group of Carpenters.

I did not see this leaflet in the original. It was supplied to me in a copied form just as I have recorded it here. Comrade Rozenshtayn (a co-worker of the Archive) states that he himself read this leaflet when it was pasted up in front of the entrance into the factory at no. 10 Dworska Street. Not having any paper on him, he went into his adjacent dwelling at no. 14 for paper in order to make of it a copy, and when he came out the appeal was already gone.

In town, people are saying that one of the injured workers supposedly died yesterday (Saturday, the twenty-fifth) and another is dying.

. . . .

[p. 11]

After the conference that the instructors of the tailor shops held yesterday with the chairman and he had promised them within the limits of his possibilities to see to a better feeding of the physical workers, the instructors of each shop held deliberations with their workers and it was decided immediately to set to work. On the basis of this decision the aforementioned announcement was hung out.

About the mood among the workers before the closing of the shop, Mr. Zbar[366] recounts:

Although the workers here did not present any direct demands at all, their mood was, nevertheless, depressed over the withdrawal from them of the bread supplement. In any event, the situation was uncertain and it is therefore understandable why the chairman found it necessary to close the work places as a preventive measure.

(As I am informed from official circles, the principal reason for closing the factories was this: Because several pieces of furniture were broken during the events among the carpenters, the chairman feared that if such events were to take place somewhere else, goods could be ruined which he would not be in a position to replace with any others. The situation would be catastrophic [as is known, the goods that are sent into the ghetto to be processed are German] and he therefore saw it necessary to prevent any damage that could cost something more than money and he therefore decided to close the factories.)

About a conference with the chairman at which he was also present, my interlocutor relates:

The chairman's situation was quite difficult. While recognizing in principle the hard conditions in which the laborer has to work and that they need to be better nourished than the nonworking element, on the other hand he nevertheless could not select a portion from among all ghetto inhabitants and privilege it, still more because all were willing to work. Officially, he also could not come [with such a proposal] to the authorities because it is much easier to demand in the name of 160,000 people than to plead in the name of 10,000. For this reason, he also rejected the proposal to deduct two and a half dkg of bread from the population for the benefit of the workers. However, he promised to exert himself concerning other products for the workers, like meat, sausage, etc., products that he cannot obtain in quantity for the entire population—and these he will from time to time share among the workers. After those present at the conference recognized the correctness of the Chairman's position, it was decided to set to work.

. . . .

[p. 14]
Noted on the 1.2.1941.

From worker circles I have been informed that today, Saturday, there took place a gathering of the furniture workers where it was decided to get to work and thereby to liquidate the strike.
Noted on the 2.2.1941.

The director of the furniture division, Mr. Freund, has informed me that all workers have reported to work. Work is proceeding normally in all the other factories in the ghetto. Thus, the strike can be reckoned as liquidated.

The standby alert for the police has been removed since the afternoon of Friday, January 31st.

No. 126: YI-461

Rumkowski's announcement of 24 January 1941, concerning closing the ghetto workshops. [in German]

Irresponsible people and provocateurs have attempted to disrupt the work in the factories and yesterday I had forcibly to expel the workers in one factory.

As is known to me, this occurrence was supposed to be repeated in other factories, too.

I have already repeatedly warned against these disruptions and thereby stated that the workers must take into consideration that work being done in the factories is chiefly for the Wehrmacht. I am responsible for all occurrences and for all damages in the factories and these transgressions by workers cannot be tolerated. I have therefore decided to close all factories.

The wages that were to be paid out today will be paid out to the workers in the course of

Friday,   24 January 1941
Saturday,   25 January 1941
Sunday,   26 January 1941

delivered at home through my postal department. Only the worker personally is entitled to receive the money. Thus, if the letter carrier finds a worker is not at home, the money will not be left behind. The worker must himself give a receipt for receiving the money.

I must once again observe that it was my entire concern to organize the factories so as to provide work and a serene possibility of existence to many people.

I will continue to provide for regular judicious supply of food. But it must be understood and taken into consideration that delivery of foodstuffs promised to me is not always possible due to the bad weather conditions and transport difficulties.

Wicked, irresponsible people exploit this. I have arrested some of them and I will undertake further arrests until I again establish calm in the ghetto, for this is my duty and I bear the responsibility for it.

No. 127: YI-24

Notice in the ghetto Chronicle *of 8 March 1941, concerning arrests and deportations. [in Polish]*

[p. 4]
DEPORTATION FROM THE GHETTO.
In his speech of 1 February, Chairman Rumkowski announced that the most rigorous methods of combat will be applied to persons making his work more difficult, particularly the criminal element; that is, troublemakers and notorious criminals, and thieves of public property will be eradicated from the ghetto by sending them to Germany for public works. In his speech, the chairman announced that he would be implacable in this, and only serious illness could shield anyone from deportation from the ghetto. The foregoing goal is already in the course of realization; namely, by the chairman's order a special brigade of the Order Service, under the command of Prison Commissioner [Salomon] Hercberg, has carried out mass arrests during the last three nights among thieves, recidivists and disturbers of the present public order in the ghetto. Altogether, over fifty persons were arrested. Arrestees will remain at the chairman's disposition. A medical review of eighty-six arrestees was conducted in the building of the Central Prison. This number also includes persons arrested during the last three days. Dr. Szykier presided over the medical commission. The chairman was also present during the examinations. The commission rated seventy-five persons as fit to be sent to work outside the ghetto.

No. 128: YI-719

Letter from the commandant of the Fifth Precinct (Marysin) to the Board of Kibbutzim ("Vaad Ha-Kibutsim") of 18 December 1940, where he threatens to remove from Marysin Halutsim[367] who do not report to work. [in Polish]

To the Secretariat of the Letter Groups
Marysin II

Confirming receipt of your letter of the seventeenth of this month, Nr. 243, we communicate the following:

The work of extraction of stumps at the cemetery at the order of the Eldest of the Jews is continuing and the Secretariat of the Letter Groups is neither authorized nor does it have the right to discontinue further work at the cemetery. We point out that workers from the city are also continuing to work.

Regarding the above, in accord with the Order of the Eldest of the Jews, I order the Secretariat to provide the full contingent of *halutsim* for the work of pulling stumps on the nineteenth of the current month at 7:45 o'clock and I underscore that if any of the *halutsim* does not report to work, he will be immediately removed from the area of Marysin II.

Simultaneously, we caution that in the event of non-appearance to whatever assigned work, members of the letter groups will immediately be removed from the area of Marysin II.

I will hold the Secretariat of the Letter Groups responsible in the event of further malicious non-appearance of *halutsim* for work.

Precinct Chief

No. 129: YI-945C

Program of the sixth and seventh symphonic concerts by the Hazamir Music Society in the ghetto, on 5 and 7 December 1940. [in Yiddish][368]

Hazamir Society
Thursday, 5 December 1940
Saturday, 7 December 1940
    VI and VII
Symphonic Concert

Program:
Compositions by F. Mendelssohn
    1) Overture of "Hebriden"
    2) Suite "Summer Night's Dream"
    a) Scherzo, b) Nocturne, c) Intermezzo, d) Dance, e) Wedding March.
    3) Overture "Athalia"
    4) "Walpurgisnacht" (fragments)

Participating: Mixed choir, soloists, and symphonic orchestra of Haza-mir.
Direction: Theodor Ryder.
Soloists: H. Korn (tenor),
        Y. Wiener (baritone).

No. 130: YI-953D

Reportage by Dr. Oskar Rosenfeld about the concerts and Culture House.
[in German][369]

[p. 1]

CONCERT IN THE CULTURE HOUSE

Through a suburban neighborhood, past dilapidated barracks, and open latrines, wanders the person who by chance, somewhere in the post office or the clinic or even in the gas kitchen, got the word about a "Concert on Wednesday," in the direction of Marysin, the villa quarter of the ghetto—a sort of cottage, where, alongside homes for children and orphans and the elderly, elegant little houses stand, that in the summer are inhabited by employees of the ghetto in need of recuperation, summer visitors, so to speak.

This neighborhood cannot be called a *datsche*[370] or a spa. But whoever can spend a couple of weeks resting there, far from the ghetto apparition, will be envied for this brief good fortune. . . . So now back on the way to the Wednesday concert, to the Culture House.

The gorgeous expression "Culture House" dies on the lips, when one actually sees the house. The word dies, but the house does not disappoint. A lengthy structure, one-story, with a flat roof, light gray and horizontally articulated like an early Greek temple of the ascetic Doric style representative of Hellenic culture. The house *represents* and therefore we would like to praise those who hit upon such a choice. The entrance does not lie in the middle of the front, but on the side, hard by a garden fence, open gutter, rubble and all around the desert of the ghetto in all its relentlessness.

Groups in front of the house. Mostly younger people, well-dressed natives, quite young girls and even children. At the house entrance opposite the box-office a hand drawn poster, in the Yiddish and German languages, presents the program. People glance over, read, many take note of the individual musical numbers, since there are no programs. Seats (only seats) for 1 mark, 75, 50, 30 pfennigs do not permit the burden of the expenditure for a program. A secretariat and a cloakroom are also present, not to forget the spacious, well-ventilated foyer with tall windows facing into a courtyard garden, that gives the impression of a metropolitan facility, particularly during intermissions, when cheerful smoking concert goers of both genders conduct earnest conversations in Yiddish, Polish, German, and even English, about the musical pieces just heard.

The hall resembles a theater. The musicians sit on the stage. Behind them, thus in the background, scenery partitions that unintentionally recall the Saturday revue performances, due to the sidewalls and the dismantled prompter's box. Below the ramp, a piano that very frequently has to take over the function of contrapuntal accompaniment. Twenty-five rows of sixteen seats each. Two dozen wall chairs fill the hall that altogether accommodates around four hundred people and is often sold out.

The members of the orchestra appear on the stage a few minutes after 6 P.M., in dark street suits, serious, silent, as befits such a type of person. Of course, most of them work daily in some factory—some producing straw shoes, or sorting stinking rags, or gluing soles, or serving another similar enchantment. There are mostly string players, i.e., violinists, cellists, violists. The flutist and the trombonist cannot, even together with the pianist, prevail against the bow playing majority, entirely irrespective of the conductor, whose delicate soul does not at all allow such a quarrel.

· · · · · · · · · · · · · · · · ·

[p. 2]

His[371] heart apparently belongs to Beethoven and the Romantics (Mendelssohn, Schumann, Schubert), although Bach, Handel, Haydn, and Mozart are not neglected. If he had access to musical material, he would doubtless also bring some Jewish music, pieces by Josef Achron, Gustav Mahler, Arnold Schoenberg, or even the Eastern Jews drawing from the Jewish people's soul, Weprik, Krein, Engel, Rosofsky. . . . But it makes no sense to daydream of such possibilities, to surrender to such illusions. Just as there is no egg or lemon in the ghetto, so there are also no musical notes, no instrumental voices, no full scores. Ryder conducts out of a small hand score, in which, of course, not all instruments, and thus not all entrances, are sketched, but the orchestra body functions so precisely that the few "jabs" with the conductor's baton suffice.

Four hundred people follow the playing on the stage. It does not irritate them; they accept it as something natural, fated, even willed by God, that before them in a dimly illuminated hall, hard by one of the grayest realities, through the gesticulation of a man with a yellow star on his back, Beethoven becomes audible and exactly that Beethoven, about whom so much was meditated and written and that is explained as the deepest revelation: the V Symphony.

It is not good for ghetto people to lose themselves in brooding. Time presses. The nerves demand solicitude. After the concert means finding one's way back to the daily soup (or to dry potatoes). Still, a singer demands a hearing. Rudolf *Bandler* from Prague is among the most in demand. His deep baritone leaves room for the gloomy, as well as the grotesque and the burlesque. He sings arias from the Italian operas, he sings them with enchanting Italian *parlando,* and when he sings Loewe ballads or Schubert *Lieder,* then even the souls born in the ghetto feel themselves at home, recall perhaps the poetry of Schiller and Heine, well known as among the favorite poets of Eastern Jewry, until their own *Yiddish* literature drove the German poets from the room.

Curt Behr (Prague), Leo Birkenfeld (Vienna), as well as Lili Bandler (Prague) are the pianists of the house. Miss B. Rotsztat, the violinist, represents the type of classical interpreters even when she reproduces the newer violin literature.

The composer David *Beigelmann* conducts the so-called lighter music. He is the shaper of the Yiddish folksongs. Born in Poland, grown up in musical space, a life-long propagandist of Yiddish music, he can take upon himself the whole responsibility for the popular program. His years of work in Yiddish theater and in Yiddish cabaret brought him the experiences that he needed in the ghetto Culture House.

Songs of a folksy type and Jewish art music formed the main part of the Jewish program. Both the songs and the orchestral compositions have the same melancholic keynote, like the major part of Jewish music, even where a more cheerful character would be in place. It is important that the public also perceives something of the creation of music that serves as typically, even representatively, Jewish or Hebrew, like Ernest Bloch's "Baal Schem" Suite and Jablon's "Hasidic Melodies." Beigelmann's songs go lightly into the ear, in part also by the power of the pleasing text. Here the modern lyricist *Itsik Manger* captures the first place. Texts like "Zog, Malkale di shayne," "Oyf der statsye Kolomey," are characteristic of Manger's folksong-like tone. Outside the ghetto,

[p. 3]

Itsik Manger, who derives from Galicia,[372] is known as the most original poet of Jewish ballads. To popularize him through song is a thankful task for everyone who takes part in Jewish cultural creation.

The general part of the program under the direction of Beigelmann includes familiar European names. Suppé and Waldteufel represent Austrian music and Verdi, Leoncavallo, Puccini, Grieg, Bizet, and Delibes European music.

The audience of the Culture House concerts has its favorite composers and favorite numbers. Troubadour, Bajazzo [German: Pagliacci], Rigoletto, and Butterfly are received with the smiling countenance of grateful recognition and are hummed right after the concert. Herein the ghetto public does not differ at all from those who attend the European concert houses. Truly, one can without exaggeration say that here nearly a hundred percent of the audience possess the necessary receptive maturity and intensity.

The "serious" program serves the great classics. Every concert is begun with them. As conclusion, however, a short clanging of instruments, some fantasy from "Mignon" or an overture by Mendelssohn, or a little bit of Smetana, if not even Jacques Offenbach, who regrettably is represented only with "Schoene Helena". Cooperating pianists must see to the orchestration of many pieces, like for example the young Praguer Kurt Behr, and so stands together a family endowed with the task every week of preparing two liberating hours for 400 sorely tried people. In this sense, the Culture House will do justice to its name and its mission.

No. 131: YI-29

Notice from the Ghetto Chronicle of 6 and 7 June 1942, about the premiere of Revue Number 3. [in Polish]

[p. 9]
PREMIERE OF REVUE No. 3

The promise of the premiere of a revue show evoked much interest in the ghetto. The premiere of the 3rd revue presented by the Culture House took place on Saturday, drawing the elite of local society with representatives of the communal authorities.

The Eldest of the Jews, together with his wife, honored the premiere with his presence.

The two-hour program consisted of fifteen choice numbers. Dance numbers predominated—solos and group. Meriting special distinction among the dance performances is the number in which the ghetto public's favorite Ruhe and the talented dancer Kacówna appeared within a quartet. The quartet performed oriental and burlesque dances with great success, amid musical sounds of jazz band and Jewish folk motifs. A quick waltz performed by the charming Lili Leder, the most capable pupil of the master director of the department of choreography, Halina Krukowska, enjoyed great recognition from the audience. As happened in previous revues, the star of the show was Wajnberg's performance in the monologue written by Janowski. Volleys of laughter, so rare among the Ghetto's residents, visibly erupted during the performance of this number. The punch line of the monologue was a parody of the behavior in the ghetto of newly arrived people. It is not possible to pass over in silence several very successful vaudeville-fantasy sketches, based primarily on Hasidic folk motifs. Master Bajgelmann conducted the orchestra in music that was in large part the conductor's own composition. Mr. Nelken led the narration as master of ceremonies. Szwarc[373] painted the scenery, masterful in his modernistic style. The whole makes an impression of a good revue spectacle. One completely forgets that this is a production starring total amateurs, aside from the director.

No. 132: YI-49C

Fragments from J. Zelkowicz's reportage, "In the Book Collection" of 5 July 1943. [in Yiddish]

[p. 1]
The ordinance of 8 February 1940 regarding the "systematic transfer of population" from the city into the ghetto, among others, also regulated

the things question: What could be taken along into the ghetto and what not. Thanks to this decree, the Jew found out that his whole bit of furniture, all of his movable possessions, for which he had labored hard and bitter a life long, is "property of the state" that he may not sell and not take with him. The Jew was officially allowed to take along with him, into exile, only the beds and . . . family pictures, that is, photographs. Beds and family pictures, these two sacred items that the Jew officially could take along with him into his modern exile of the twentieth century.

However, the piety and sanctity of family remembrance did not express itself in the paper picture or photograph among all segments of the Jewish population. For the ancient People of the Book that had always strictly regulated its life in all its phases according to its prescribed paragraphs and points, a photograph—when they even reluctantly tolerated it—was no more than a little paper picture that did indeed recall the external appearance of their near and dear, but this picture told him nothing about the inner essence of the relative—[it is] an inanimate object, no more. . . .

The People of the Book impressed its nearest and dearest into its memory in a different way: On the heavy covers of its cloth- or leather-bound *Vilner Shasn,* Vilna Talmuds; on the initial leaves of its small, but beloved Bibles, with permanent ink he sanctified the memory of his beloved and dear ones. Every commemoration became a monument— "*le-zikhron olamot*" ("in eternal memory)." . . .

. . . .

[p. 2]
Two desecrated sacred items and they had two different fates. In the hard winter of 1941, the profaned beds were broken and chopped up to use their ruins to warm up a little water for the youngest, for the weakest, for the most trembling child . . . and . . . the sacred books continued to be scattered about in mold and dust. The People of the Book does not burn their sacred books, except when they are burned and annihilated together with them. . . . A desecrated sacred object, a sacred book may not be burned—it must be brought to burial according to Jewish belief and according to Jewish law. . . .

The difficult year 1941 passed and there arrived the more difficult year 1942 that brought along: In January, an expulsion of 10,000 Jews; in February—7,000 Jews; in March—almost 25,000; and in April—over 2,000 Jews. Altogether, in the first months of 1942 precisely 44,076 Jews were sent out from the ghetto, an established fact of nearly 15,000 families. Familiar folk, kin. Where to?—That was not important—The "from where departed" dominated; one was not allowed to worry about the "to where sent." . . . Entire families were ripped out by the root and this without "*irgendwelches Gepäck,*" without any sort of baggage. . . . Not even a stick in the hand, much less a sack of sacred books on the shoulders, too. . . .

Abandoned, the sacred books then lay scattered about in the abandoned vacant dwellings. The Jewish Western [European] element, which had at that time already naturalized themselves in the ghetto, no longer had any reason to complain about the "scarcity of toilet paper." . . . Whole mountains lay scattered about, the mortified pages from desecrated sacred books in all the toilets of the ghetto: disgraced pages from prayer books; soiled pages from Bibles, profaned leaves from Mishnayot[374] and desecrated leaves from Zohars.[375] The large one-folio pages were used by wanton youths as cigarette paper, as packing paper, as paper for all sorts of uses—5 marks for a kilogram and . . .

[p. 3]

At that time, people only felt the emptiness of their stomachs. . . . The spring of 1942 was intensely hungry—[they did not feel] the emptiness of their minds and therefore it did not bother them that their hunger-swollen feet stumbled over desecrated holy things that lay scattered, abandoned in the streets. Only among individuals did their hearts shed their last blood:

"This is the fate of the People of the Book? Will they tread so long with their own clumsy feet on the wreckage of their own sacred things until they themselves will be stamped out? Or maybe it is possible to rescue what can still be saved in order thereby also to rescue what can be saved of the people itself? . . ."

Willingly and gladly, the director of the Records Departments, Attorney H. Neftalin, took up the initiative. Energetically, he demanded the telephonic connection with the Management Department of the ghetto and his instruction rang clearly:

—Enact that all administrators and house watchmen are obligated to look through the apartments, attics, cellars, and chambers left empty after the deported Jews, to gather together all books that are in them and bring them. . . . Where?—Let it be over here, to me, in the Records Departments . . . and—Thereby arose the Book Collection.

The initiative of an individual who understood the significance of the Jewish sacred book for the People of the Book was the cause of:

Thirty thousand different sacred books that have been collected until now and grouped in one place where they are tended, put in order, catalogued; several dozen Torah scrolls, tefilin,[376] prayer shawls, tefilin straps, and the like. The Jewish sacred book is not abandoned, it has an address, it has an owner—the head of the Jews.

Entering this book collection, which occupies three quite dark rooms and an even darker cellar, one has the impression of having fallen from the ghetto darkness into the deep swamp of Antiquity. . . . The space smells of dust from tattered old *sheymes*[377] pages and the stale odor from old *tefilin* straps, but no sooner have the electric lights been turned on for you and you perceive the tall book shelves, up to beneath the ceiling, that are stuffed from top to bottom with Jewish sacred books—organized according to sections and sub-sections by a good, old and powerful mind, and you become acquainted with the director of this institution, with the genial Eng. Einhorn, who leads with a trembling hand and caresses the leather spines of the big and heavy *seforim,* so it occurs to you that only a toiling father could thus stroke and caress with his callused hardworking hands the soft mind of his trembling only son. One can thus stroke and caress only a favorite and dear family ornament that is bequeathed from generation to generation. . . . And suddenly you find out:

"It is right this way. It cannot be different. Only and necessarily thus must treasures be concealed. . . . They must not be displayed in showwindows; they must be hidden in dark rooms, in deep cellars, on account of *maris ayin,* appearance. . . . It is healthier for them this way. . . ."

And the smell of Antiquity here is really a virtue: This is of course the strength of the old People of the Book—These are its old, deep roots, that extend from the most ancient Antiquity until and across the ghetto of the twentieth century! . . .

And the longer one is in this institution, the closer that one becomes acquainted with the different books, among which by the way are to be found several very significant antiques, the more one learns of the interest that the director of this institution displays in them, of the understanding that he has for [the collection], all the more one comes to the conviction that becomes a hundred percent certainty in you:
[p. 4]

As long as the Jews ground themselves in their old and deep roots and they also possess the modern minds of a Neftalin, an Einhorn and similar people, who comprehend the need to care for these roots and to avoid neglect, laziness, and the like, one can be calm about the fate of the old People of the Book—

No. 133: YI-185

Rumkowski's announcement of Yom Kippur Eve [11 October] 1940, that Yom Kippur (Saturday), as well as all subsequent Saturdays, are days of rest in the ghetto. [in Yiddish][378]

Announcement No. 134
To all residents in the ghetto! Saturday is the day of rest in the ghetto! I require, therefore, of all owners of businesses that their businesses and sales points should be unconditionally closed on Saturday. Street trade is in exactly the same way not permitted on Saturday.
There can only operate: The Health Office with all its departments, the Central Provisioning depot, the milk shops for children and the sick, and public kitchens.
All inhabitants in the ghetto must properly adapt to the aforementioned ordinance.

No. 134: YI-18

Rumkowski's announcement no. 242 of 3 April 1941, concerning allocation of matsot[379] for Passover. [in Yiddish]

Regarding Allocation of Matsot:
From Sunday, the sixth of April 1941, 2 ½ kilo of matsot will be issued for each person on coupons no. 1 and 2 of the bread card, for the period from the twelfth to the nineteenth of April inclusive (together eight days) for 3 marks 25 pfennig.

No. 135: YI-1268

Rabbinate's decision of 27 February 1941, concerning allowing certain categories of people to eat non-kosher meat. [in Yiddish and Hebrew]

Rabbinate Collegium at the Eldest of the Jews in Litzmannstadt
No. 25/41 With the help of God
To the Eldest of the Jews Here in Litzmannstadt
The Rabbinate at its plenary session of Sunday, 26 Shevat 5701 (23/2 1941) decided to formulate its opinion regarding the issue of eating meat in the following manner:

1) Pregnant women in the time before and after birth, who need—according to the opinion of the physicians—to benefit from meat are obligated to do it without any restraint;
2) People who feel that they are becoming significantly weaker need to turn to a doctor for an examination and after that apply to the Rabbinate (at the office of the Rabbinate Chancellory, 4 Miodowa Street, between 12 and 3 P.M.) or to a particular rabbi concerning a decision.

At the same time, we have the honor to request the chairman to alert the physicians to the significance of their decision in these matters that must be pronounced only in cases of possible *"pikuah nefesh,"* saving a life, and with complete professional seriousness!

With great honor,
Joseph Fajner—Eliezer Lipschitz—Zelig Rozenshtayn—Moshe Weiss—Abraham Silman—Shmuel David Laski—Yohanan Lipschitz—Aaron Bornshteyn—Akiva Eiger—Elijah Flayshhaker—Simcha Bunim Aberboym—Nechemia Alter—Shlomo Jakubowicz—Moshe David Domb—Hirshl Fischhof.[380]

No. 136: YI-27

Notice in the ghetto Chronicle *of 31 January 1942, concerning the situation at the cemetery. [in Polish][381]*

[p. 2]
INTERMENT DIFFICULTIES.
In connection with the record increase in mortality, over 200 unburied corpses had accumulated in the cemetery mortuary at the end of Janu-

ary. The Funeral Department arranged immediate measures with the aim of the speediest interment of the deceased. Special conferences with the rabbinate were initiated on this matter.

No. 137: Diary of L. Hurwitz. YI-Diary[382]

A diary fragment concerning the operation of the Summary Court. [in Yiddish]

[p. 6a]

After this, the court set to its normal work and right from the start they had a lot to do. Enough human material had already been collected at the [police] precincts and in the prisons and the court was bombarded with matters mostly of a criminal nature. The main matter dealt with concerned officials who committed small thefts or people from the street who took apart a fence or a stall and stole the wood. Here, however, there appeared an interesting psychological phenomenon. The broad public, that relates with scorn and has such a negative attitude to all community offices, was positively inclined toward the court right from the start and displayed this with its serious and dignified demeanor at the court deliberations. The phenomenon is still more noteworthy since it was well known in the ghetto that the court is not at all so free in its proceedings, that the will and the fist of Rumkowski intensely pressure the judges and that far from always will they be able to proceed according to their conscience. . . .

. . . .

[p. 7]

But it immediately became apparent that the number of criminal offenders in the ghetto is growing from day to day, that petty thefts have become a "normal" occurrence in the ghetto and that means must be adopted so that this pestilence that has penetrated into the ghetto organism can be combated and uprooted. And the ghetto psychologists and educators,—who not so long ago sought in the abnormal situation, in the terrible hunger and poverty an answer for the new ghetto sickness of mass thefts in the offices, in the factories and in the stores, committed by managers and minor officials, by master workers and laborers,—these people have suddenly made a double somersault and a 180 degree turn.

The matter has suddenly become clear to them. The regime does not bear the blame, nor do the natural living conditions into which we have been squeezed. At fault are the people in whom the disgusting instincts have taken root; for thievery and informing are in the blood and the Jews have indeed rightly earned the calamities that have fallen to them to endure and therefore summary courts must be introduced, to train the public and deter the officials and the workers through harsh punishments; but that they in fact have in themselves all the positive and negative national characteristics, this they do not want to recognize at all. I would stand all these moralists, who are living relatively very well in the ghetto, in front of a mirror—and let them look well into the mirror and immediately hold a summary court trial for the false mug peering out from the mirror! They should, however, be strict and issue a harsh punishment! But it's laughable! It's the relationship of a sated person to a hungry one, who cannot mutually understand each other.

. . . .

The situation is entirely different among us in the ghetto. Those who spoke up were mostly people who earlier stood quite far from Yiddish and Jewishness, who never considered and never sorrowed over the Jewish situation, who didn't grow up with the Jewish people. And therefore, when the ghetto was enriched with the new disease they also did not consider for a minute from where and why this epidemic originated. No prophylactic steps at all were adopted; they only became people's prosecutors, introduced summary courts and it is raining trials day in, day out, endlessly and it's hailing with the harshest punishments that are issued. If a tailor stole a spool of thread—two months severe imprisonment; if a tailor knew about it and kept quiet—two months severe imprisonment. Oh, it is known what sort of severe conditions the prisoners find in Rumkowski's prison, which the notorious commandant H[ercber]g has turned into an agency
[p. 8]
of the Angel of Death—What do the lawgivers of the ghetto care about this? They are indispensable, it's important to maintain them, but a tailor? There are enough tailors in the ghetto and we will teach them not to steal anymore.

No. 138: YI-55

J. Zelkowicz's notes about the issue of crime and punishment in the ghetto. [No date.] [in Yiddish]

[p. 104]

Serious sins were committed in the ghetto. The biggest sin was that people who cultivated themselves for decades in order to maintain their culture and civilization, that had cost thousands of years of labor, these people were turned into predatory beasts after a half-year of living in inhumane conditions. Over night, every sense of ethics, every sense of shame became foreign to them. The ghetto inhabitants stole and robbed at every opportunity that came their way, both what they needed and what they did not need. While on the one hand people died of hunger and people foraged in rubbish like pigs in order to find various spoiled food and dregs and eat it up on the spot, there were on the other hand some people who had the opportunities, [who] stole, robbed, gorged themselves and boozed.
[p. 105]

And there was theft right from communal property. There was stealing from the Provisioning storehouses, where people worked with their blood, with their sweat. From the Provisioning storehouses, that were supposed to feed the entire concentration-camp-ghetto—everybody equally.

On the one hand, there were people who harnessed themselves like common horses to carts and transported excrement and rubbish. They spent fourteen and sixteen hours a day at their wagons that stank from a distance of fifty cubits, in order to earn a few miserable pennies, not even enough to make themselves a satisfying meal after this difficult and bitter labor. On the other hand, there were people who loitered around, people who were employed in good and fat communal posts, who kept their hands in their pockets all day long. And their only work was to think up what and how to steal, so that the theft would not be so easily noticed.

Serious sins were committed in the ghetto. In the ghetto, people did not live according to the established human norm, but here the law of the jungle mattered, the right of "*man de-alim gavar*."[383] Whoever was stronger shoved the other, weaker one into the abyss and kept himself on the surface standing on the other's head.

So it's understandable that the sins had to be exterminated, without being picky about the means of extermination, at least through a summary court. Moreover, it's known that *es yidlt zikh, azoy vi es kristlt zikh*, Jews behave the same as Christians. . . .

But it is incomprehensible why the effort in the ghetto was always superficially broad and never in depth. Why did they suddenly take on the criminals so energetically and not the reasons that were the direct causes for these crimes?

It is understandable that someone was given a job in the ghetto, and thus could keep himself on the surface; if this employed person sought butter for his bread or fatty *geshmilts* shortening for his soup in a dishonorable fashion, and thereby harmed others—he had to be punished and even severely punished, in order to serve as an example for others.

What is incomprehensible is only: Why was it never thought to give the laborer or the employee in the ghetto the most minimal possibilities for existence, so that he should not need to steal?
[p. 106]
. . . What is incomprehensible is only: Why are the wives and children also sentenced to death by starvation together with the actual offenders?—Why did the summary court, with its severe verdicts imposed on the actual accused, in almost all cases also order a permanent ban from employment for the accused and ban his family from the relief dole?
It is understandable and the name "summary court" alone testifies that it was not possible to delve into the nature of the crime, like a normal court.

What is incomprehensible is only: Why was it that, right from the start, people were named to the Jewish summary court in the ghetto, who would with the best intent, even at the court session, be unable to penetrate into either the psychology of the criminal, according to which justice ought to be measured out, or into the essence of the committed sin? For the nominated "judges" of the summary court, that operated only at night like some revolutionary party cell, were of course employed all day at their normal jobs, and they perforce came to their night-work tired and overstressed. . . .

What is incomprehensible is that among the two young fellows who were named as judges of the summary court, there just had to be a youth to whom not only were the most minimal concepts of humanity and practical knowledge of life alien, but he was also lacking the most elementary principles of average intelligence.

What is incomprehensible is that the majority of the most serious cases of the summary court came into the hands of just that insolent and raw youth who measured out "justice" in his peculiarly criminal manner. . . .

What is incomprehensible is that the net that is spread out in the ghetto swamp, to catch every sort of crime committed against the essential interests of the ghetto public, caught only the minuscule, small-fry minnows, while letting through the big, fat, stinking pike fish that have swallowed hundreds of others in their swimming across the ghetto swamp. . . .

[p. 107]

. . . .

Offenses that were not detected and were perforce not judged by the summary court:

Managers of food stores who through their subordinate community employees sent to their own homes the handsomest and the best of what was designated for the entire population and later, so as to even out the gaps that they made with their thefts, they gave their "customers" false weights and measures.

These bandits and thieves swarmed and multiplied on the ghetto streets, but were tolerated by the directors of the summary court and not made to take any responsibility.

The directors of the Provisioning Department, from the largest to the smallest, intentionally allowed hundreds of tons of potatoes and other vegetables to rot, in order to be able to conceal their thefts and the storehouse [shortages] that the books ultimately had to reveal. . . . Hundreds of heavy wagonloads of potatoes were secretly taken out on dark nights and thrown into the rubbish trenches of the ghetto because they were rotten and spoiled. In the best case, this was the fault of the people who managed the ghetto administration and these people, though they have on their consciences so many hundreds of victims who died of hunger, were not tried by the summary court.

Protectors took bribes for arranging good posts for incompetents and loafers, while so many useful and healthy hands, so many good and clever heads did not have any employment and died of hunger . . . and these protectors were "*sheyne yidn*," fine fellows, and were not tried by the summary court.

The shops that had the finest and best goods lying in their show windows gouged [prices], [while their owners] bought flowers, diamonds, and jewelry at the expense of poor and sick folk, and those who propelled the ugly speculation in the most basic consumer goods,—these were eminent people in the ghetto who were not tried by the summary court. . . . And when once, by accident perhaps, the well-known and notorious potato affair arrived on the docket of the summary court in the ghetto, the insolent and shameless boy-judge took a bribe and acquitted all of the accused.

No. 139: YI-18

Verdict for a theft published in the Geto-tsaytung, *no. 13 of 20 June 1941. [in Yiddish]*

Those Sentenced by the Summary Court to the Pillory!
Moyshe Grinboym, twenty-two years old, son of Chaim and Elka, who resides at 20 Fefer Street, was sentenced to hard forced-labor because, while being employed as a laborer at the Bałuty Marketplace, he stole a bottle of soda water.

No. 140: YI-33

Notice in the ghetto Chronicle *of 19 August 1942, concerning a case of murder in the ghetto. [in Polish]*

ARREST OF A MURDERESS
On 21 July of this year, at 4 P.M., fifty-five-year-old Chana Rosenblit was murdered in a residence at no. 9 Ceglana Street. To the assassin's loot fell the weekly food allotment belonging to the murdered woman and her daughter, one loaf of bread, and 50 marks. For close to four weeks the local Order Service looked for the killer. During the last eight days nearly certain data was acquired that Mrs. Rosenblit's neighbor, sixty-five-year-old Mindla Gertner, committed the murder. From that time, she remained under discrete observation of the Investigation Service. From the moment of commission of the terrible act, Mrs. Gertner displayed symptoms of mental disturbance. She instinctively sensed that she was under investigation, which still more affected her psychological state. Now and then, she revealed her entire conscience and in just such a moment she confessed with contrition to a representative of the Order Service to having committed murder.

We have here a frequently encountered symptom, when pangs of conscience compel a murderer to reveal his secret. Her husband, Boruch Gertner, likely knew about the perpetrated act. For concealing this information from the authorities, he was arrested together with his wife. During a search, a large clod of ash from various burned things, among others sacks from food products belonging to the victim, was found in the stove. The killer also burned the stolen banknotes. Mrs. Gertner and her victim Mrs. Rosenblit had already resided in the house at 9 Ceglana Street for several years before the war. Despite being neighbors, they maintained no relations between each other. Mrs. Gertner continuously envied that her neighbor remained in the ghetto in a certain comfort; she envied that she was able to purchase all the allotments, while she herself together with her husband (they do not have children here) many a time did not collect the allotments due to lack of money. This couple was unemployed and they were not entitled to relief payments. Due to the mental illness into which Mrs. Gertner fell after the killing, it is now difficult to piece together the course and motives of the act. It seems most probable that the cause was hunger and envy. The act was committed during a fit of rage caused by a scuffle when, as is known from the primary investigation, the murdered woman defended herself against the theft of her products.

As we stated in the report after the discovery of the murder, the investigative authorities initially were completely convinced that the instrument of murder was a kilogram weight found near the corpse. Now it turned out that the murder was committed with the help of an axe. The instrument of the crime, discovered in Mrs. Gertner's dwelling, had apparently been scrupulously washed in the interim, since only with the help of microscopic examinations were traces of blood found on the axe. In accord with the relevant regulations binding in instances of murder in the ghetto, the German Criminal Police arrested the murderess with her husband. They were placed in the jail of the local branch of the Criminal Police. In the first phase of the currently conducted investigation, Mrs. Gertner will undergo psychiatric examinations for which local physicians were summoned.

No. 141: YI-30

Notice in the ghetto Chronicle *of 5 July 1942, concerning the penal institution for youthful offenders. [in Polish]*

[p. 1]
MINORS IN PRISON
After an interval of several months, juvenile "criminals" are again being put in the central prison. Minors are located in a completely different building than the rest of the prisoners. Cottages opposite the prison are designated for them. Today, the number of juveniles placed in the prison amounts to nineteen. Of this number, eleven are alumni of the dormitory located on Żydowska Street. In the dormitory reside predominantly orphans or half-orphans, ages from eleven to seventeen. Eleven children from the dormitory are placed on the terrain of the prison because of intractable behavior. In the cottage as opposed to the prison, the children were quartered in very clean, tidily arranged rooms. They sleep

in comfortable beds, made up with clean bedclothes. An expellee from Frankfurt takes care of them, an experienced educator who for more than a dozen years worked in similar institutions in Germany. A prison staff functionary, specially assigned to the section for juveniles, assists the directress in case of need. The children receive products on their food cards, while some of them benefit from supplemental coupons. The educator turns over all the products to the director of the prison kitchen, Dr. Familierowa, in daily proportion for preparation. This is the so-called Detention Chamber.

It is worth underscoring that the kitchen directress has been at her responsible post from the first moment of existence of the central prison, i.e., from 1 December 1940. She should be reckoned among those nameless, self-sacrificing, indefatigable workers, whose ideal is work for the good of others. When speaking of the kitchen, a recollection arises from the recent sad past. During the period of the deportation action, the prison kitchen, which had the task of feeding each deportee, became famous in the whole ghetto. And currently prisoners receive meals in the form of soups, in which regard they have no reason for complaint. Soups for the pupils of the dormitory are still better, since they are prepared, as already noted, from their own products.

[p. 2]

From the first moment that children were installed in the "black house," there prevailed between them and the management an atmosphere of hearty friendship, based on the children's great trust for their new superiors. In the morning, the children head off to their places of work. Aside from the children from the dormitory, the section for juveniles houses another eight children (six boys and two girls) serving out sentences of the court for minors. These children are placed in cells, where they sleep on plank beds. They were sentenced to short-term imprisonment for systematically engaging in street sale of saccharine, cigarettes, or petty thefts.

VIII

The Problem of Resistance

At the close of our book about the life and death of the Łódź Jews, it is still necessary to examine the question: Why was it that in the Łódź Ghetto, where there was concentrated a large Jewish community and a workforce with old traditions of struggle, no armed resistance occurred at least during the final liquidation phase, as happened in Warsaw, Częstochowa, Białystok, and in a number of smaller ghettos in the eastern territories?

To be able to give an answer, we must take into account that aside from the factors of a general character that determined the possibilities of armed resistance in the ghettos in general, there were also here a series of specific objective and subjective aspects that negated the possibility of armed resistance.

1. During the occupation period, the Germans transformed Łódź into a city with almost a purely German character. The ghetto found itself encircled by "Aryan" neighbors consisting of local Germans (about 9 percent of the prewar population)[1] and the thousands of Poles who overnight became ethnic Germans. In addition, the authorities in the first two years of the occupation systematically expelled Poles from whole quarters, concentrated them in the Chojny suburb, and in their place settled thousands of Germans from Volhynia and the Baltic lands. They expelled almost the entire Polish intelligentsia, the politically and

publicly active element, so that what remained was the petite bourgeoisie and the mass of workers. The Polish underground movement was little apparent during the whole occupation period.[2] "Calm and order" prevailed. The Łódź Ghetto was therefore absolutely cut off and isolated in respect to contacts with the external environment on whose sympathy and aid it could have reckoned during an eventual uprising. Not only could no assistance be expected from the Łódź population, but it would also have diligently collaborated with the police to stifle every sort of resistance. Isolated attempts to establish a link between the Bund and the Polish Socialist Party (PPS) in the city remained without result.[3]

Y. Tabaksblat relates an instance when a supposed trolley worker proposed, in the name of a Polish resistance group, that acts of sabotage be carried out in the ghetto through setting fire to the factories. But this was—as he states—a ruse by the Gestapo and the messenger was dismissed.[4]

There could, therefore, be no talk of bringing weapons in from the outside. "A revolver was an unattainable thing in the Łódź Ghetto," writes a survivor who was a professional activist in the ghetto.[5]

Such was the situation in regard to obtaining weapons and the "hinterland" for an eventual battle. This absolute isolation from the outside world and the sense of impotence could not summon any fighting spirit in the ghetto. There was also no success in making contact with the Jewish resistance movement in Warsaw. Two emissaries who were sent to Warsaw in the winter of 1942–43 never returned.[6]

2. The year 1943—a year of Jewish uprisings in Warsaw, Białystok, Treblinka, and Sobibór—was one of the calmest and relatively "best" periods in the history of the Łódź Ghetto. No deportations took place in that year and the provisioning situation improved, so the external stimulus toward an armed resistance was lacking.

3. The final liquidation "action" began as late as 2 August 1944. Thanks to the news from the secret radio receivers, people were feverish with the hope that very soon the Germans would have to leave the city and they would be delivered. The hope to hold on and to survive, a constant undercurrent in the ghetto in July–August 1944, began to sparkle with all the illusory or real possibilities. People still recalled the Germans' defeat in 1918 and they even imagined that the situation would repeat itself, "to be able to disarm our murderers, just as the Germans were disarmed on the 11th of November 1918."[7] It would, therefore, be psychologically impossible to motivate a mass that was caught up by such feelings to enter into a hopeless struggle that in the given circumstances could conclude in only one fashion—destruction with a heroic death. The masses would have considered any move against the Germans as a disruption of the last hope to safely live to experience the happy ending.

4. The ghetto population was already physically and psychologically exhausted from the five years of hunger and terror. Indeed, the Nazi annihilation strategy toward the Jewish population was that, after the

victims would be sufficiently "processed" for a lengthy time through hunger, terror, demoralization, and complete isolation from the outside, they would be powerless and allow anything to be done with them that would be demanded of them.

5. A factor that also strongly influenced the fighting capacity of the ghetto was the demographic composition of the population in 1944.

The young, healthy men were uprooted from the ghetto in large numbers with the transports to the labor camps. Together with the latest bloodletting of the ghetto—the dispatch in the first ten days of March of 1,600 relatively young and healthy people, of whom a substantial portion belonged to the more intellectual worker element—the deportations reduced the proportion between men and women. In March 1944 that proportion was 100:137, while for the ages 30 to 34 the ratio was 100:196 (see chapter 7). It is likely that in preparing for the final liquidation of the ghetto, the Gestapo in March 1944 intentionally removed the element from which it could expect resistance.[8]

6. The subjective readiness to put up resistance could also have been weakened by the news received from foreign radio stations, that the deportations of the Hungarian Jews were halted under the pressure of the Allies on Horthy, that the Germans were destroying the crematoria and the concentration camps,[9] and so on. Also contributing to this was the mendacious and misleading agitation by the Gestapo and Biebow, supported by Rumkowski and his clique that this time people were being sent for work and only for work. Thus, for example, Biebow sent a couple of workers from the ghetto's metal division out to Szamotuly (Poznań area), supposedly in order to make the necessary preparations for transferring the metal workshops there. The returned workers delivered good tidings: the treatment was humane, the new worksites were already being prepared there.[10] During the deportation of the tailors, work tools, like pressing irons and the like, were sent along in the railcars.

Letters from the deportees that arrived in the ghetto in the last days of July served to affirm this trickery. Under a characteristic heading, "Good tidings for the ghetto, postcards from Leipzig," the ghetto *Chronicle* of 26[11] July relates that "31 postcards have arrived from individuals who were recently sent out of the ghetto, all bearing the date of July 19th. It can be inferred from these postcards that they are doing well and mainly that the families are together. Some of the cards talk about good food. [. . .][12] People are overjoyed in the ghetto and they hope that similar letters will soon arrive from other deportees. It is confirmed, then, that the Old Reich needs workers."[13] A similar report about "good" letters from Częstochowa and other towns in Germany is presented in the *Chronicle* of 28 July 1944.

These cards—if they were not a cynical trick by the Gestapo that had coerced such calming letters (speaking for this well-founded assumption is the fact that all the postcards were of the same date and they mention families staying together)—were mailed by those who were sent in the first ten days of March into the local ammunition factories in Skarżysko and Częstochowa and also by those who, during the selections in Auschwitz, had been assigned to other German camps.[14]

These letters naturally evoked an optimistic attitude among many. Being condemned to destruction, they still could not accept the idea of the unavoidable end and they latched onto the least illusion.

There were, nevertheless, groups in the ghetto thinking that there must be preparation for the time when it would be necessary to put up resistance. Y. Nirnberg writes very laconically about "meetings concerning an eventual resistance in case of liquidation of the ghetto," and he adds that "all these consultations produced nothing concrete, because there were no weapons and no contact with the city."[15] Benjamin Frenkel, in his detailed memoirs about the Łódź Ghetto, also writes very obscurely "that at that time there were many organized groups to be able to take advantage of such a favorable moment, above all during an air attack, while the Germans ran about in fright. . . . Particularly the youth, coming together in a library or other gathering point, conducted their discussions in spite of the many informers."[16] The report in the 29 July 1944 ghetto *Chronicle* that elements that had until now stayed in the background had appeared in the ghetto workshops, and were inciting the workers, has already been discussed (chapter 7).

The memoirists do not tell us exactly what sort of projects and plans were brought out at these secret discussions. One can guess that they considered the state of the ghetto and the impossibility of imitating the heroic example of Warsaw in April 1943, about which people in the ghetto were well informed.[17]

According to an isolated source that regrettably finds no corroboration in other sources, there existed in the ghetto a conspiratorial group concentrated around the person of the popular physician Daniel Wajskop and his assistant, the teacher Sabina Witenberg. According to W. Karmiol, a survivor of the Łódź Ghetto, the group occupied itself with spreading radio reports (see below), with carrying out acts of sabotage (fires) in several factories in February and March 1944, and attempted to make contact (through a letter smuggled out with the help of Biebow's bribed chauffeur) with the Polish underground movement in the city and asked it to send weapons into the ghetto. No answer was received, and the swift liquidation action of August 1944 put an end to all daring plans.[18]

One thing these conspiratorial groups did do: they conducted a broad propaganda effort for people not to let themselves be deported and to conceal themselves as long as possible.[19] They also set up a secret radio monitoring service in the ghetto.

It is worthwhile to discuss this clandestine radio listening in a little more detail. During the five years of the ghetto's existence there was an active group of radio listeners who systematically, day in and day out, received news from the free world on sets constructed in the ghetto (all radio receivers had to be turned in to the authorities in December 1939) and spread the reports in the ghetto. To this group that put their lives on the line for five years belonged politically organized Zionists (Chaim Nathan Widawski), Bundists (five members of the Weksler family), nonpartisans (David or Moses Topel, the cantor of the Ohel Yaakov synagogue), and others. The builder of the receivers was the radio technician Wiktor Rundbaken. The chief monitor of the radio news was Topel.[20] He commanded several languages and received news from almost all the European capitals.

It is not hard to imagine the importance that this secret radio service had for the hermetically sealed ghetto, into which not even German newspapers were allowed. Under the date of 8 May 1944, Y. Hiler notes: "The little bit of news that reaches the ghetto is a support that lets the people not give up on everything."[21] The news about the Germans' defeats on the fronts, starting from the end of 1942, encouraged the fainting hearts in the ghetto and strengthened the hope for survival.

The ghetto was informed on the same day about all the events on the fronts and in the free world.[22] By means of the radio news, anniversaries were observed, like for example the first anniversary of the Warsaw ghetto uprising and the first anniversary of Shmuel Zygielbojm's death. Through the London radio, the encouraging words of the Bundist representative in the Polish National Council in London would reach into the desperate ghetto.[23] Hunger was forgotten in the fever over the radio news.

Who the actual listeners and relayers of the good tidings were was known in the ghetto, but during the entire time there were no instances of denunciation. Even the Jewish official informers were themselves eager to hear the radio news. But at the beginning of June 1944 an informer was found who told the *Kripo* about it. In the course of three days, from 6 to 8 June, the *Kripo* arrested almost all the radio listeners, according to the indications of the informer. Topel was caught at his radio, while the Wekslers managed to remove the receiver though they stayed and were arrested. Also arrested were the Viennese former editor Richard Baer, who was discovered with copies of political reports, and distributors of contraband German newspapers. Widawski succeeded in evading arrest, but after only a couple of days he committed suicide by taking poison. Physically a very weak person, he feared that he would not be able to withstand the Gestapo torture and would break, revealing the others involved. Those arrested were tried in town. It was not possible to find out what sort of verdict they received. It was rumored that some were sentenced to death and some to be deported to a concentration camp. In the ghetto, people continued to fear for a long time that the arrests might bring serious repercussions.[24]

It appears that not all of the secret radio receivers were caught at the time. Under the date of 20 July, diarist Y. Hiler notes the report about "an assassination attempt on six generals and on F[ührer]." Also the *Aufraumungskommando* (Cleanup Unit) received news from some sort of secret device. Moreover, there were also individuals in the ghetto who, regardless of the danger, had concealed their receivers and secretly distributed the news.[25]

There were also a couple of instances recorded of individual resistance during and after the liquidation of the ghetto. B. Frenkel refers in his memoirs to the fact that already at the rail station a certain Zonenberg, who had kept with him his brother's rescued child, turned to Biebow in an agitated state with the words: "Shoot, murderer. Your end is near. The world will take vengeance on you, I am no longer afraid." Fearing that this incident could lead to a general upsurge from the large crowd gathered at the transport, the Germans did not use any weapons but only directed the Jewish rail workers to isolate him in a rail wagon and leave him in the ghetto overnight, in order to determine whether he was out of his mind. The next day the same thing repeated itself. Biebow ordered that he be shoved into a wagon and he departed together with others for Auschwitz.[26] The aforementioned Dr. Daniel Wajskop, with his family and others, was concealed in a bunker for some time after the liquidation of the ghetto. On 6 November 1944, the bunker was discovered through Jewish informers from the Cleanup Unit. Biebow was summoned and arrived with his aide, Schwind. When the bunker was opened, Dr. Wajskop, who was a physically strong person, threw himself on the informer. Biebow came over and got involved in the scuffle. Wajskop bloodied both of them and began to strangle Biebow. The latter was saved when a German gendarme shot Wajskop (according to another version, Biebow himself fired). Bleeding to death, Wajskop is supposed to have cried out: "Germans, your end is near."[27]

IX

Conclusions and Summations

From all the facts and observations, it seems quite clear that the Łódź Ghetto was unique in a number of aspects: the role and position of Rumkowski, the pretense of ostensible "autonomy," the social atmosphere, and the role that the Łódź Ghetto played in the German war economy.

In no other ghetto did the Nazi *Führerprinzip* or authoritarian principle adapted to the ghetto conditions take on such proportions as in Łódź. Nowhere else was the Jewish council, as a collective representative body of the ghetto population, so degraded to such a miserable role of servile figureheads as in the Łódź Ghetto.

In ghettos such as Warsaw, Vilna, Białystok, and many others, the members of the councils represented in a smaller or larger measure certain political and communal groupings and constituted definite communal forces with which the most authoritative ghetto representatives had to reckon, whether willingly or unwillingly. It was different in Łódź. After the tragic end of the first *Ältestenrat* (*Beirat*) and after the removal of the last members with an independent opinion from the second *Beirat,* the sole rule of one person was instituted, of the *Judenältester* Mordechai Chaim Rumkowski.

Such one-man rule in the ghetto was very convenient for the German supervisory authority. In its relations with the ghetto population, the Nazi administration in the occupied areas always preferred to deal with one person, rather than with collective representative bodies. He would be responsible for everything and could more easily be broken and turned into an obedient instrument. In the soil of the Łódź Ghetto, this calculated tactic of the German authorities coincided with Rumkowski's insatiable appetite for power and in result produced the bizarre phenomenon of a ghetto dictator who was servile toward his masters and imperious toward his "subjects."

Another phenomenon, very characteristic for the Łódź Ghetto, was the hyper-organization, the immense branching out of the structure of the Jewish ghetto administration. As in every dictatorship, where every corner of social and even private life is regulated by a powerful bureaucracy, so too was all of life in the Łódź Ghetto embraced by a large network of departments, divisions, and secretariats with thousands of employees.

To be sure, we find this phenomenon in all the Nazi-imposed ghettos. This was an objective result of the fact that the ghetto was excluded from the municipal organization and was thus compelled to deal with all functions of an organized social unit (provisioning, economic administration, communication, public security, and order). In Nazi propaganda, the ghetto was supposed to comprise an "autonomous" unit, a sort of Jewish town. But in no other ghetto did the organizational structure take on such dimensions. The Łódź Ghetto even had its own currency-issuing "bank" with its own "money."[1] The Nazi fiction of Jewish "autonomy," it seems, attained its pinnacle here.

In connection with these specificities also stands the fact that in no other ghetto was the fate of the individual dependent to such an extent on the activity and the social politics of the Jewish Council, nor was the individual's initiative as fettered as it was in Łódź. Here, only Rumkowski decided who should get work and bread. All other sources of livelihood were closed, smuggling interdicted, private property confiscated ("nationalized"), illicit trading forbidden and suppressed. In other ghettos (for example, Warsaw, Vilna, Białystok et al.), the individual still retained a little free space for his own initiative, and he could attempt somehow to keep himself from going under with his own strength, independent of the ghetto administration that was not the sole internal factor that determined his day-to-day life.

In other ghettos, private commerce "blossomed" in certain periods with goods smuggled in, in large measure made possible thanks to the work assignments outside the ghetto (Jewish *Aussenkommandos*). None of this occurred in the Łódź Ghetto. Rumkowski strove to have in his hands total control over all aspects of internal ghetto life and he succeeded in this to a large degree.

The Łódź Ghetto was also different in regard to the target against whom the population directed its collective protest. Since in other ghettos the individual did not feel the direct pressure of the Jewish ghetto administration so intensely, his protest was therefore more directed against the external deciding factor—the Nazi oppressor—in whom he saw the cause of all his troubles and misfortunes. In the Łódź Ghetto there was a single address to which the social protest was directed: this was Rumkowski. He was the one who in large measure created the day-to-day conditions for the Jew in the ghetto.

There was also a difference in the forms by which the opposition came to be expressed. If we take, for example, the Warsaw ghetto, the opposition there could speak out in a more or less legitimate fashion in the political parties, in the communal institutions for social aid and for cultural work, and in the house committees where people openly and even sharply criticized the activity of the *Judenrat.* The Jewish Society for Social Aid (Ż.T.O.S.), the communal sector of the Jewish Social Self-help (Ż.S.S.) organization, where esteemed communal and cultural activists were grouped, had such social prestige that the *Judenrat,* whether it wanted to or not, had to reckon with their position. The oppositional attitudes of the communal-political activists of the ghetto population against the *Judenrat* and its policies in the Warsaw ghetto could be expressed in the multifaceted underground press that as a rule adopted a stance of explicit opposition toward the *Judenrat.* Thus, public channels existed in the Warsaw ghetto through which protest against the *Judenrat* could be made public. In the Łódź Ghetto, the *Judenältester* ruthlessly suppressed communal-political life, which could not hide under the cover of various relief and cultural institutions. It thus vanished from the surface. Therefore, collective protest here had to adopt a form that is possible in a dictatorial regime: clandestinely organized street demonstrations of masses driven to the brink of despair. Here the opposition had to operate in deep conspiracy and could break through to the public only with major difficulties.

A further characteristic that adversely separates the Łódź Ghetto from other well-known ghettos is the role played there by corrupted, socially inferior elements, some of which originated from the underworld.

To be sure, in many other ghettos there were also prominent figures, whose open or disguised contacts with the *Gestapo* were not a secret to anyone. Frequently, the Jewish councils themselves, in their negotiations with corrupt officials of the German supervisory organs, had to employ such figures as intermediary "brokers," in delivering bribes, gifts, or other favors for them. The Warsaw *Judenrat* made use of such a figure to deliver gifts and the like for the wife of General-Governor Hans Frank and for Warsaw Governor Fischer.[2] There were special officials in the ghettos whose job was to maintain contacts with German bodies like the Labor Office or Gestapo, and it was natural that the ghetto inhabitants did not have much confidence in such officials. "The authorities require of us dirty work that must be carried out under the pressure of those in power. Not everyone is capable of carrying this out and we must, willingly or unwillingly, have recourse to the underworld people," wrote Dr. J. Milejkowski, chairman of the Health Department at the Warsaw *Judenrat,* in his response to a survey by *Oyneg Shabes.*[3]

But no other ghetto is known to us where such open agents of the Gestapo, like for example David Gertler and Mordecai (Marek) Kliger, played such a leading role and had under their control such important areas of ghetto life as was the case in Łódź.

This negative phenomenon in the life of the Łódź Ghetto was a result of Rumkowski's tactic of not being particular about means if they only served his power politics. Accordingly, he did not refrain from involving even notorious underworld figures in the ghetto bureaucracy.

Other characteristic traits can be explained by the economic aspect and role that the authorities designated for the Łódź Ghetto in the German war economy. The Łódź Ghetto was a classic example of a Nazi "labor ghetto" whose industrial production and potential occupied an evident place in the plans of the Nazi war economy.

The Łódź Jewish population possessed a substantial percentage of skilled workers and craftsmen in various fields, especially in such important industries as textiles and metal. The Łódź Ghetto therefore was, on one hand, the most favorable soil for the "rescue-through-work" ideology consistently advocated by Rumkowski; on the other hand, the ghetto with its rich industrial potential occupied a special position in the calculations of various German administrative, SS, and military offices, and became an object of rivalry among them when its final fate had to be decided (see chapter 6).

These two considerations were in large measure the cause of the lon-

View of the Łódź Ghetto after liberation, January 1945. Photographer unknown. USHMM, courtesy of Instytut Pamięci Narodowej.

gevity of the Łódź Ghetto that was liquidated only at the end of August 1944, when nowhere else in occupied Europe was there an organized Jewish community (aside from Theresienstadt).

The last, nearly 70,000 Łódź Jews shared the fate of all Polish Jews, but they had a feeling of consolation: in August 1944, they could see from the Łódź Ghetto bridge with their own eyes how the end of Hitler's rule was approaching—German military units, officials, civilians, and their helpers from among the local population were fleeing westward in panic along Zgierska and Aleksandrowska, the streets that bisected the ghetto. This sight probably eased their way to their final destination—to Auschwitz.

Chapter I

1. Decree of Kalisz Regierungspräsident Übelhör, 14 November 1939, ordering all Jews without distinction of sex or origin to wear a yellow armband under penalty of death.

Note: A second decree of the Regierungspräsident, 12 December 1939, replaced the armband with a yellow Star of David, ten centimeters across, to be worn on the chest and back.

2. Order of the Municipal Commissioner governing the identification of Jewish stores by means of a yellow sign with the inscription "Jew."

3. Decree of Wilhelm Koppe, Higher SS and Police Chief in Wartheland, 13 November 1939, forbidding Poles and Jews to leave their homes.

4. Confidential memorandum by Übelhör, 10 December 1939, on the establishment of a ghetto for Jews in Łódź.

5. Warning by Łódź Chief of Police Schäfer, issued on 9 January 1940, to avoid contact with the Jewish section as a source of epidemics.

6. Decree of Chief of Police Schäfer, 8 February 1940, ordering the establishment of a ghetto.

7. Regulations governing the decree of the Chief of Police of 8 February 1940.

8. Announcement by the Chief of Police, 1 March 1940, of the arrest of a large number of Jews for maintaining contact with the city.

9. Request on the part of the Chief of Police to Rumkowski, 2 March 1940, for the payment of the fine and provisions for the imprisoned.

10. Letter of Łódź branch of the Office for the Settlement of the Balts at the Higher SS and Police Chief Warthe[land] to Rumkowski, 2 February 1940, concerning property left by Jews expelled from their residences.

11. Letter from the same office to Rumkowski, 13 February 1940, concerning contact with the new occupants of Jewish residences.

12. Police decree of 7 March 1940, voiding all temporary permits for passing through the streets outside the ghetto.

13–14. Second and third regulations, of 15 March and 3 April 1940, prohibiting Jews from staying in certain western and southern sections of the city.

15. Decree of the Chief of Police, of 8 April 1940 [fourth regulation governing the decree of 8 February 1940], modifying and slightly enlarging the area of the ghetto.

16. Letter of the Municipal Health Bureau to Rumkowski, 11 April 1940, about an outbreak of typhus in the gathering camp of the ghetto.

17. Letter of Rumkowski to the Resettlement and Residence Bureau, 30 March 1940, petitioning for the delivery of the keys to a locked house in the ghetto.

18. Rumkowski's order no. 13, 8 April 1940, prohibiting people from arbitrarily occupying residences in the ghetto.

19. Rumkowski's announcement of 3 May 1940, permitting people to occupy single rooms in the expanded ghetto.

20. Letter of the Chief of Police to Rumkowski, 17 April 1940, ordering the ghetto police (Ordnungsdienst) to assume responsibility for guarding the ghetto enclosure.

21. Announcement of the Chief of Police, 19 April 1940, about the possibility of the total isolation of the ghetto.

22. Fifth and last regulation of the Chief of Police, 7 May 1940, governing the decrees of 8 February and 8 April 1940, about the final isolation of the ghetto.

23. Plan of the Łódź Ghetto (enlarged area).

Note: nos. 24, 25 not used

Chapter II

26. The Łódź Municipal Commissioner appoints Mordechai Chaim Rumkowski as chief (Älteste) of the Jews in Łódź, 13 October 1939.

27. Decree of the Municipal Commissioner of 14 October 1939, ordering the dissolution of all institutions and administrative bodies of the Jewish community.

28. Rumkowski's letter to Sicherheitsdienst in Łódź, 5 February 1940, about the second auxiliary council (Beirat).

29. The Oberbürgermeister authorizes Rumkowski, 30 April 1940, to organize the life of the ghetto.

30. Rumkowski appoints on 17 January 1941 Dr. Leon Szykier, chief of the Health Department, as his assistant.

31. Rumkowski dismisses Dr. Szykier on 12 June 1941.

32. Rumkowski nominates two deputies.

33. Letter of the chief of the civilian administration at the Armee Oberkommando, 15 October 1939, ordering a daily supply of 600 Jews for compulsory labor.

34. Internal memorandum on compulsory labor in 1939–1940 (n.d.).

35. List of divisions and shops of the ghetto administration.

36. Announcement no. 71, 24 June 1940, concerning the introduction of "mark receipts" as legal tender in the ghetto.

37. Announcement no. 158, 6 November 1940, concerning the establishment of the Highest Control Office.

38. Rumkowski's circular of 16 August 1942, appointing new members to the Highest Control Office.

39. Rumkowski's circular of November 1942, dissolving the Highest Control Office.

40. Announcement no. 30, 1 May 1940, concerning the ghetto police.

41. Order of the day of the commandant of the ghetto police, 1 March 1943.

42. Letter of the ghetto police, second precinct, to Rumkowski, 14 August 1940, petitioning for the admission of five agents into the political secret service on the basis of the recommendation of the Sonderkommando.

43. Announcement no. 233, 15 March 1941, concerning the establishment of a Court Extraordinary.

44. Announcement no. 275, 30 May 1941, governing the report of thefts, offenses, and frauds.

45. [Procedure] of criminal jurisdiction in the ghetto [1940].

46. Announcement no. 81, 12 July 1940, concerning the introduction of censorship of outgoing mail.

47. Announcement no. 221, 26 February 1941, concerning confiscation of all food parcels arriving in the ghetto.

48. Announcement no. 35, 9 May 1940, concerning the obligation to register in the newly created registration bureau.

49. Letter of the Oberbürgermeister to Rumkowski, 24 April 1940, appointing him commissary administrator of the real property in the ghetto.

50. Financial report of the activities of the Jewish community for the period of 1 January–27 July 1940.

51. Announcement no. 105, 13 August 1940, concerning the opening of trading exchange.

52. Announcement no. 179, 17 December 1940, ordering the compulsory sale of all furs and tippets.

53. Announcement no. 350, 6 January 1942, ordering the compulsory sale of men's skiing and mountain-climbing shoes.

54. Announcement no. 368, 2 March 1942, concerning the sale of furniture and household articles of persons selected for deportation.

55. Rumkowski's petition to the Oberbürgermeister, 5 April 1940, to establish shops in the ghetto working for the German authorities.

56. The Municipal Commissioner's authorization of Rumkowksi, 25 October 1939, to assume the administration of the Jewish elementary schools.

57. Anonymous report on the school system in the Łódź Ghetto for 1939–1941.

58. Decree no. 171, 3 December 1940, ordering the subordination of the entire medical personnel in the ghetto to the authority of the representative of the Health Department.

59. Monograph on the organization and activities of the Social Welfare Department by [Józef Zelkowicz].

60. Announcement no. 123, 20 September 1940, concerning the introduction of a relief system.

61. Anonymous report on the activities of the Relief Division for September 1940 September 1941.

62. Announcement, 30 July 1940, concerning the establishment of day camps for children between the ages of four and seven.

63. Statistical table: The ghetto population on 12 July 1940, according to occupation, sex, and age.

64. Graphic representation of the labor divisions and internal administration of the ghetto, Litzmannstadt Ghetto, August 1943.

Chapter III

65. Permission granted by the Chief of Police, 2 March 1940, to open three grocery stores for the Jewish population in the ghetto.

66. Announcement no. 186, 27 December 1940, concerning the distribution of food to the holders of the newly introduced ration cards.

67. Report of the organization and activities of the Division of Groceries and Bread [1942].

68. An item in the ghetto *Chronicle*, 12 January 1941, about the demonstrations in the streets of the ghetto. Note: the item gives the ghetto administration's official version of the demonstrations.

68a. Announcement no. 203, 28 January 1941, concerning supplementary food coupons for workers, janitors, police, firemen, and chimney sweeps.

69. Announcement of 3 April 1942, concerning the distribution of food for the general population and the possessors of supplementary food coupons.

70. An announcement of the German ghetto administration [n.d., early November 1943] that it had assumed the supervision of provisioning in the ghetto.

71. Announcement of 11 February 1942, concerning the distribution of food for those who did not eat in the public kitchens.

72. Announcement of 26 July 1942, concerning the distribution of food for people who cooked at home and for those who ate in the public kitchens.

73. Report on the activities of the Division of Public Kitchens in the bulletin of the daily ghetto *Chronicle* of 29 January 1941.

74. Item in the ghetto *Chronicle* of 2 July 1942, about spoiled food delivered to the ghetto.

75. Item in the ghetto *Chronicle* of 16 May 1942, about the great demand for potato peels.

76. Fragment of a reportage by Józef Zelkowicz, 8 July 1943, concerning the disorders and abuses attendant on the distribution of vegetables.

77. Items in the ghetto *Chronicle* of 6 and 14 May 1942 about the abuses and corruption of the ghetto's public kitchens.

78. Announcement of 7 March 1941, concerning the lease of planting parcels for 1941.

79. Item in the ghetto *Chronicle* of 27 May 1942, about conditions in soil cultivation.

80. Item in the ghetto *Chronicle* for November 1941, about the inflation and speculation in food in the ghetto following the "arrival" of the Western European Jews.

81. Items in the ghetto *Chronicle* for 9, 10, and 11 May 1942, about the trade fever and inflation in the ghetto during the deportation of the Western European Jews.

82. Reportage by Józef Zelkowicz (n.d.) about distribution of wood in the winter of 1941.

83. Diary entry by [Joseph] Hurwitz [Klementynowski], dated August 1941, about "miners" in the ghetto.

Chapter IV

84. J. Zelkowicz's reportage, "In the Transmission Belts Repair Shop," dated 10 August 1943.

85. From J. Zelkowicz's reportage, "In the Paper Factory," dated 26 and 28 June 1943.

86. From an address at the exhibition of the products of five factories, 26 December 1942.

87. Items in the bulletin of the ghetto *Chronicle* for 13 and 14 May 1942, about the causes of decline in productivity in the factories.

88. Reportage of O[scar] S[inger] on the state of the sick workers in the ghetto, 14 July 1942.

89. From Dr. Philip Friedman's Collection. "Notes" of Alfred Ball, authorized by the Municipal Administration to organize the utilization of Jewish artisans for the economy [n.d., 1940].

90. Letter of Biebow to Rumkowski, 9 November 1942, forbidding the delivery of goods or the acceptance of orders from officials of the German administration without his permission.

91. From J. Zelkowicz's reportage, "Impressions of a Visit in the Electric Works Division," 19 July 1943.

92. From an anonymous reportage on children in the Electro-Technical Division, 8 April 1943.

93. Rumkowski's announcement no. 250, 16 April 1941, concerning registration of men and women for work outside the ghetto.

94. Order of Governor Greiser, 25 June 1942, governing employment of Jewish workers.

118. A reportage by a Viennese deportee, titled "How Does the New Arrival in the Ghetto Work."

119. Fragment of Rumkowski's address, 20 December 1941, about the new arrivals.

120. Diary of Leon Hurwitz. Rumkowski's conduct toward subordinates.

121. Fragment of Rumkowski's address, 1 November 1941, to the deportees of Western Europe.

122. Fragment of Rumkowski's speech, 20 December 1941, on those who would be sent out of the ghetto.

123. Diary of Leon Hurwitz. Criticism of the summer residences of the ghetto elite in Marysin.

124. A call of protest against the ghetto regime, 25 August 1940.

125. J. Zelkowicz's notes on the carpenters' strike in January 1941.

126. Rumkowski's announcement on 24 January 1941, of the closing of the ghetto shops.

127. Item in the bulletin of the ghetto *Chronicle*, 8 March 1941, about arrests and deportations.

128. Letter of the commandant of the fifth precinct (Marysin) to the *Vaad Hakibutzim*, 18 December 1940, threatening to send out of Marysin *Halutzim* who fail to report to work.

129. Program of the sixth and seventh symphonic concerts of the Hazamir in the ghetto, 5 and 7 December 1940.

130. Reportage of Dr. Oskar Rosenfeld on the concerts in the Hall of Culture.

131. Items in the bulletin of the ghetto *Chronicle*, 6 and 7 June 1942, about the first performance of Revue no. 3.

132. Fragment of J. Zelkowicz's reportage, titled "In the Book Collection," 5 July 1943.

133. Rumkowski's announcement on the eve of the Day of Atonement, 1940, that the following day, Saturday, as well as other Saturdays will be days of rest in the ghetto.

134. Rumkowski's announcement no. 242, 3 April 1941, concerning distribution of *matsa* for Passover.

135. The decision of the rabbinate, 27 February 1941, to permit the eating of non-kosher meat for certain categories of Jews.

136. Item in the ghetto *Chronicle*, 31 December 1942, about conditions at the cemetery.

137. Diary of Leon Hurwitz. Fragments dealing with the activity of the Summary Court.

138. J. Zelkowicz's notes on crime and punishment in the ghetto.

139. Sentence of a thief announced in the *Geto-tsaytung*, no. 13 (20 June 1941).

140. Item in the bulletin of the ghetto *Chronicle*, 19 August 1942, about a case of murder in the ghetto.

141. Item in the bulletin of the ghetto *Chronicle*, 5 July 1942, about the reformatory for juvenile delinquents.

German Name	Polish Name	Polish Name	German Name
Ackerweg	Lewa-Kielma	Bałucki Rynek	Baluter Ring
Alexanderhofstrasse	Limanowskiego	Bazarowa	Basargasse
Alt-Markt	Stary Rynek	Berka Joselewicza	Brunnenstrasse
Am-Bach	Podrzeczna	Bracka	Ewaldstrasse
Am-Quell	Źródłowa	Brudzińskiego	Edmundstrasse (Heilrunnenweg)
Arminstrasse	Miarki Karola	Brzezińska	Sulzferderstrasse
Baluter Ring	Bałucki Rynek	Ceglana	Steinmetzgasse
Basargasse	Bazarowa	Chłodna	Kuhle Gasse
Bernhardtstrasse	Zagajnikowa	Chopina	Müllerstrasse
Bertholdstrasse	Jagiellońska	Ciemna	Dunkle Gasse
Bertramstrasse	Jonschera	Ciesielska	Bleicherweg
Bierstrasse	Piwna	Czarnieckiego[2]	Schneidergasse
Blattbindergasse	Lotnicza	Dekerta	Oskarstrasse
Blechgasse	Towiańskiego	Dolna	Talweg
Bleicherweg	Ciesielska	Drewnowska	Holzstrasse
Bleigasse	Mianowskiego	Drukarska	Zimmerstrasse
Braune Gasse	Lwowska	Dworska	Matrosengasse
Breite Gasse	Szeroka	Dzika	Stolpergasse
Bretgasse	Zbożowa	Flisacka	Hausierergasse
Brunnenstrasse	Berka Joselewicza	Franciszkańska	Franzstrasse[3]
Buchbinderstrasse	Goplańska	Garbarska	Gerberstrasse
Buchdruckergasse	Okopowa	Gęsia	Gänsestrasse
Cranachstrasse	Żydowska	Głowackiego	Konradstrasse
Dunkle Gasse	Ciemna	Gnieźnieńska	Gnesenstrasse
Edmundstrasse	Brudzińskiego	Goplańska	Buchbinderstrasse
Ewaldstrasse	Bracka	Grabinka	Mehlstrasse
Fischstrasse	Rybna	Hoża	Frohe Gasse

German Name	Polish Name	Polish Name	German Name
Franzstrasse	Franciszkańska	Hutnicza	Huttenwinkel
Frohe Gasse	Hoża	Inflancka	Gartnerstrasse
Froschweg	Żabia	Jagiellońska	Bertholdstrasse
Gänsestrasse	Gęsia	Jakuba	Rembrandtstrasse
Gartnerstrasse	Inflancka	Jerozolimska	Rubenstrasse
Gerberstrasse	Garbarska	Jonschera	Bertramstrasse
Gewerbstrasse	Przemysłowa	Koszykowa	Korbgasse
Gnesenstrasse	Gnieźnieńska	Kościelna	Kirchgasse
Goldschmiedegasse	Tokarzewskiego	Koziołkiewicza	Idastrasse
Halbe Gasse	Niecała	Krawiecka	Schneidergasse
Hamburgerstrasse	Lutomierska	Krótka	Kurze Gasse
Hanseatenstrasse	Łagiewnicka	Krótko-Lwowska	Sackgasse
Hausierergasse	Flisacka	Krzyżowa	Kreuzstrasse
Hertastrasse	Staszica	Lekarska	Kramergasse
Hirtenweg	Pasterska	Lewa-Kielma	Ackerweg
Hofgasse	Podwórzowa	Limanowskiego	Alexanderhofstrasse
Hohensteinerstrasse	Zgierska	Lotnicza	Blattbindergasse
Holzstrasse	Drewnowska	Lutomierska	Hamburgerstrasse (Telegrafenstrasse)
Honigweg	Miodowa	Lwowska	Braune Gasse
Huttenwinkel	Hutnicza	Łagiewnicka	Hanseatenstrasse (Sonnleite)
Idastrasse	Koziołkiewicza	Majowa	Maienstrasse
Inselstrasse	Zawiszy Czarnego	Marynarska	Kelmstrasse
Kachlergasse	Sukiennicza	Marysińska	Siegfriedstrasse
Kelmstrasse	Marynarska	Masarska	Storchengasse
Kirchgasse	Kościelna	Mianowskiego	Bleigasse
Kirchplatz	Plac Kościelny	Miarki Karola	Arminstrasse
Konigsbergerstrasse	Wrześnieńska	Mickiewicza	Richterstrasse
Konradstrasse	Głowackiego	Miodowa	Honigweg
Korbgasse	Koszykowa	Młynarska	Mühlgasse
Korngasse	Żytnia	Moskulska	Paulastrasse
Kramergasse	Lekarska	Mroczna	Nebengasse
Kranichweg	Żurawia	Nad Łódką	Tizianstrasse
Krautergasse	Zielna	Niecała	Halbe Gasse
Kreuzstrasse	Krzyżowa	Niemojewskiego	Waldemarstrasse
Krimhildstrasse	Starosikawska	Nowomiejska	Neustadtstrasse
Kuhle Gasse	Chłodna	Oblęgorska	Leibstrasse
Kurze Gasse	Krótka	Okopowa	Buchdruckergasse
Leere Gasse	Próżna	Otylii	Ottilienstrasse
Leibstrasse	Oblęgorska	Pasterska	Hirtenweg
Lindwurmstrasse	Smugowa	Pawia	Pfauenstrasse

German Name	Polish Name	Polish Name	German Name
Lustige Gasse	Wesoła	Pieprzowa	Pfeffergasse
Maienstrasse	Majowa	Piwna	Bierstrasse
Matrosengasse	Dworska	Plac Kościelny	Kirchplatz
Maxstrasse	Plater Emilii	Plater Emilii	Maxstrasse
Mehlstrasse	Grabinka	Podrzeczna	Am-Bach
Mühlgasse	Młynarska	Podwórzowa	Hofgasse
Müllerstrasse	Chopina	Północna	Nordstrasse
Nebengasse	Mroczna	Próżna	Leere Gasse
Neustadtstrasse	Nowomiejska	Przelotna	Richardstrasse
Nordstrasse	Północna	Przemysłowa	Gewerbstrasse
Oskarstrasse	Dekerta	Pucka	Putziger Strasse
Ottilienstrasse	Otylii	Rawicka	Tirpitzstrasse
Packerstrasse	Żabia	Roberta	Robertstrasse
Paulastrasse	Moskulska	Rozwadowskiego	Udostrasse
Pfauenstrasse	Pawia	Rybna	Fischstrasse
Pfeffergasse	Pieprzowa	Rymarska	Riemergasse
Putziger Strasse	Pucka	Smugowa	Veit-Stoss-Strasse (Lindwurmstrasse)
Rauchgasse	Wolborska	Sołtysówka	Schulzenstrasse
Reigergasse	Spacerowa	Spacerowa	Reigergasse
Reiterstrasse	Urzędnicza	Starosikawska	Krimhildstrasse
Rembrandtstrasse	Jakuba	Stary Rynek	Alt-Markt
Richardstrasse	Przelotna	Staszica	Hertastrasse
Richterstrasse	Mickiewicza	Stefana	Wirkerstrasse
Riemergasse	Rymarska	Stodolniana	Scheunenstrasse
Robert-Koch-Strasse	Sterlinga	Sukiennicza	Kachlergasse
Robertstrasse	Roberta	Szeroka	Breite Gasse
Rubenstrasse	Jerozolimska	Szklana	Trodlergasse
Runde Gasse	Wincentego	Ślusarska	Schlosserstrasse
Rungestrasse	Widok	Środkowa	Winfriedstrasse
Sackgasse	Krótko-Lwowska	Tokarzewskiego	Goldschmiedegasse
Sattlergasse	Wawelska	Towiańskiego	Blechgasse
Scheunenstrasse	Stodolniana	Urzędnicza	Reiterstrasse
Schlosserstrasse	Ślusarska	Wawelska	Sattlergasse
Schneidergasse	Krawiecka	Wesoła	Lustige Gasse
Schneidergasse	Czarnieckiego[4]	Widok	Rungestrasse
Schulzenstrasse	Sołtysówka	Wincentego	Runde Gasse
Siegfriedstrasse	Marysińska	Wolborska	Rauchgasse
Sperlinggasse	Wróbla	Wrocławska	Sudetenstrasse
Steinmetzgasse	Ceglana	Wróbla	Sperlinggasse
Stolpergasse	Dzika	Wrześnieńska	Konigsbergerstrasse
Storchengasse	Masarska	Zagajnikowa	Bernhardtstrasse

German Name	Polish Name	Polish Name	German Name
Sudetenstrasse	Wrocławska	Zawiszy Czarnego	Inselstrasse
Sulzferderstrasse	Brzezińska	Zbożowa	Bretgasse
Talweg	Dolna	Zgierska	Hohensteinerstrasse
Telegrafenstrasse	Lutomierska	Zielna	Krautergasse
Tirpitzstrasse	Rawicka	Źródłowa	Am-Quell
Tizianstrasse	Nad Łódką	Żabia	Froschweg (Packerstrasse)
Trodlergasse	Szklana	Żurawia	Kranichweg
Udostrasse	Rozwadowskiego	Żydowska	Cranachstrasse
Veit-Stoss-Strasse	Smugowa	Żytnia	Korngasse
Waldemarstrasse	Niemojewskiego		
Winfriedstrasse	Środkowa		
Wirkerstrasse	Stefana		
Zimmerstrasse	Drukarska		

The work of translating Isaiah Trunk's book on the Łódź Ghetto commenced more than thirty years ago, when I had the privilege of studying with him at the YIVO Institute for Jewish Research. With YIVO's material support, I was able to pursue my doctoral research on the Jewish community of Łódź, with the advice and guidance of my principal teacher, the late Dr. Lucjan Dobroszycki. Years later I was given the opportunity to undertake the translation of Trunk's book by Benton Arnovitz, director of Academic Publishing at the U.S. Holocaust Memorial Museum, who was acting on the recommendation of Prof. Raul Hilberg, that Trunk's work must be made accessible to the English-reading public. Paul Shapiro, director of the USHMM's Center for Advanced Holocaust Studies, supported the project and gave me several opportunities to lecture about Łódź and to chair the research workshop on the Łódź Ghetto that brought together an energetic international group of scholars. Special thanks must go to Isaiah Trunk's son Gabriel who preserved his father's papers and worked assiduously to bring his father's work to the attention of a new generation of readers. It is a pleasure to acknowledge the professional efficiency and care of Indiana University Press, whose director Janet Rabinowitch and her staff have had to contend with the production of a very complex work. Judy Cohen of the Photographic Archive at the USHMM contributed the selection of photographs that illustrate the book. More personally, I must acknowledge my wife Rena who has had to contend with this and other projects that have diverted my attention. From my parents, Fela and Sender Shapiro, natives of Poland and survivors of the ghettos in Chrzanów and Sosnowiec, as well as the Nazi German camps at Auschwitz, Blechhammer, Flossenburg, and Bergen-Belsen, I acquired more than I can express.

Robert Moses Shapiro / Ruvn-Moyshe Szpira
March 2006

Major Tables, Charts, and Maps

1. Editor's note: The number 14 corresponds to the sequence of tables in original source document no. 59.

2. Editor's note: Trunk, 94, no source cited, although it was likely part of the previous Zelkowicz report, document no. 59.

3. Editor's note: This table is mislabeled Table 16 in the original.

4. Editor's note: This table is mislabeled Table 17 in the original.

Translator-Editor's Introduction

1. Biographical information about Isaiah Trunk is taken from Isaiah Trunk, "The Historian of the Holocaust at YIVO," in *Creators and Disturbers: Reminiscences by Jewish Intellectuals of New York*, ed. and comp. by Bernard Rosenberg and Ernest Goldstein (New York: Columbia University Press, 1982), 61–74; Rita Delfiner, "Daily Closeup," *New York Post*, May 4, 1973; *News of the YIVO/Yedies fun YIVO* no. 156 (Spring 1981): 1–2 (Yiddish and English).

2. *Jewish Responses to Nazi Persecution* (New York: Stein and Day, 1979).

3. See the bibliography for full citations.

4. Some of the color images have been published in *Unser einziger Weg ist Arbeit . . . : das Getto in Łódź, 1940–1944: eine Ausstellung des Jüdischen Museums Frankfurt am Main*, ed. Hanno Loewy and Gerhard Schoenberner (Vienna: Löcker in cooperation with Yad Vashem, 1990); Alan Adelson and Robert Lapides, eds., *Łódź Ghetto* (New York: Viking, 1989); and *The Last Ghetto: Life in the Łódź Ghetto, 1940–1944*, ed. Michal Unger (Jerusalem: Yad Vashem, 1995). The U.S. Holocaust Memorial Museum has a large collection of the color images, as well as of the many monochrome photographs from Łódź.

5. *"Les Vrais Riches," Notizen am Rand: ein Tagebuch aus dem Ghetto Łódź (Mai bis August 1944)*, ed. Hanno Loewy and Andrzej Bodek (Leipzig: Reclam, 1997).

6. Oskar Rosenfeld, *In the Beginning Was the Ghetto: Notebooks from Łódź*, ed. Hanno Loewy, trans. Brigitte M. Goldstein (Evanston, Ill.: Northwestern University Press, 2002); based on *Wozu noch Welt: Aufzeichenungen aus dem Getto Lodz*, ed. Hanno Loewy (Frankfurt am Main: Verlag Neue Kritik, 1994).

7. *Unser einziger Weg ist Arbeit.*

8. Jakub Poznański, *Dziennik z łódzkiego getta* (Warsaw: Bellona and Jewish Historical Institute, 2002).

9. *The Last Ghetto* (Jerusalem: Yad Vashem, 1995); *Lodz: The Last Ghetto in Poland* (Hebrew) (Jerusalem: Yad Vashem, 2005).

10. *Kronika getta łódzkiego,* 2 vols., ed. Danuta Dąbrowska and Lucjan Do-broszycki (Łódź: Wydawnictwo Łódzkie, 1965–1966).

11. Lucjan Dobroszycki, ed., *The Chronicle of the Łódź Ghetto 1941–1944* (New Haven, Conn.: Yale University Press, 1984).

12. *Kronika shel geto lodzh,* translated into Hebrew and annotated by Arye Ben-Menachem and Joseph Rab, 4 vols. (Jerusalem: Yad Vashem, 1986–1989).

13. The text of Gutman's introduction is reprinted in the present volume.

14. *Żółta gwiazda i czerwony krzyż* (Warsaw: Państwowy Instytut Wydawni-czy, 1988).

15. Lucille Eichengreen, with Harriet Hyman Chamberlain, *From Ashes to Life: My Memories of the Holocaust* (San Francisco: Mercury House, 1994); Lucille Eichengreen, with Rebecca Camhi Fromer, *Rumkowski and the Orphans of Lodz* (San Francisco: Mercury House, 2000).

16. Oskar Singer, *"Im Eilschritt durch den Gettotag . . . ": Reportagen und Es-says aus dem Getto Lodz,* ed. Sascha Feuchert, et al. (Berlin: Philon, 2002); Oskar Singer, *Herren der Welt: Zeitstück in drei Akten,* ed. Sascha Feuchert (Hamburg: University of Hamburg, 2001). *"Im Eilschritt . . . "* was published in Polish as *Przemierzając szybkim krokiem getto—: reportaże i eseje z getta Łódzkiego,* trans. Krystyna Radziszewska (Łódź: Oficyna Bibliofilów and Archiwum Państwowe w Łodzi, 2002). Also see Sascha Feuchert, *Oskar Rosenfeld und Oskar Singer: Zwei Au-toren des Lodzer Gettos Studien zur Holocaustliteratur* (Berlin: Peter Lang, 2004).

17. Helene J. Sinnreich, "The Supply and Distribution of Food to the Łódź Ghetto: A Case Study in Nazi Jewish Policy, 1939–1945" (Ph.D. diss., Brandeis University, 2004).

18. Julian Baranowski, *The Łódź Ghetto 1940–1944/ Łódzkie Getto 1940–1944: Vademecum* (Łódź: Archiwum Państwowe w Łodzi and Bilbo, 1999). Compare the inventory of the Zonabend Collection compiled by Marek Web at YIVO: *The Documents of the Łódź Ghetto: An Inventory of the Nachman Zonabend Collec-tion,* compiled by Marek Web, preface by Lucjan Dobroszycki (New York: YIVO, 1988).

19. Icchak (Henryk) Rubin, *Żydzi w Łodzi pod niemiecką okupacją 1939–1945* (London: Kontra, 1988).

20. Ibid., 61–62.

21. Rubin exclaims (19):

The world, the goyish world prepared this fate for the Jews! And let no goy, neither those who made it possible, nor those who murdered or helped the murderers, nor those who benefited by it, nor those who "didn't notice" and don't notice it, nor those who were and are "neutral" or apathetic, nor finally those who concealed and are concealing the truth about it, [who] falsified and continue to falsify, let none of them wash their hands of this, but declare only that they are unclean.

22. Ibid., 41–47. Trunk expressed his own attitude in a posthumously pub-lished interview: "You have to distinguish between collaboration and coopera-tion. . . . Without the Judenrat the situation would have been worse. . . . Look, they gained time . . . They managed to forestall, to alleviate the worst for a while, to save people." See Isaiah Trunk, "The Historian of the Holocaust at YIVO," 71–72.

23. Rubin, *Żydzi w Łodzi pod niemiecką okupacją,* 307–308.

24. Dobroszycki, *Chronicle,* xxviii, n59.

25. Rubin's criticisms of Trunk are in *Żydzi w Łodzi pod niemiecką okupacją,* 41–47, 54, 208–209, 322, 356–359, and 366–367.

26. Ibid., 54.

27. Ibid., 322.

28. Ibid., 356–359.

29. Ibid., 366–367.

Isaiah Trunk

1. Editor's note: foreword to Trunk's posthumously published *Geshtaltn un gesheenishn (naye serye)* (Tel Aviv: Farlag Y.L. Perets, 1983), 7–16.

2. *Bleter far Geshikhte* 1, nos. 1–2 (1948).

3. *Bleter far Geshikhte* 2, nos. 1–4 (Jan.–Dec. 1949): 64–166.

4. In *Dapim le-heker ha-shoa ve-ha-mered*, second series, 1 (1969): 119–125.

5. *Kovets mekhkarim Yad Vashem* 7 ([1968]): 137–153.

6. In the collection *Ha-Amida ha-yehudit be-tekufat ha-shoa—diyunim be-kinus hokrei ha-shoa, Yerushalaim, 9–13 be-nisan 5722—7–11 April 1968* (Jerusalem, [1970]), 160–180.

7. New York: Macmillan, 1972; Hebrew translation published by Yad Vashem in 1979.

8. In *Dapim le-heker ha-shoa ve-ha-mered*, second series, vol. 2 (1973), 7–22.

9. See *Defusei ha-hanhaga ha-yehudit be-artsot ha-shlita ha-natsit 1939–1945: Hartsaot ve-diyunim* (Jerusalem, [1980]), 11–22.

10. *Geshtaltn un gesheenishn—historishe eseyen* (Buenos Aires: Tsentral Farband fun Poylishe Yidn in Argentine, 1962).

11. Editor's note: Trunk's posthumously published *Geshtaltn un gesheenishn: naye serye* (Tel Aviv: Farlag Y.L. Perets, 1983).

12. Editor's note: originally published in Yiddish in the anthology *Studies on Polish Jewry, 1919–1939,* ed. Joshua Fishman (New York: YIVO, 1974).

Introduction

1. Editor's note: This essay was originally published in Hebrew as an introduction to *Kronika shel geto lodzh,* translated and annotated by Arye Ben-Menachem and Joseph Rab (Jerusalem: Yad Vashem, 1986), vol. 1: xxxxii–lxxii. The text was reprinted in both Hebrew and English, without footnotes, in *The Last Ghetto: Life in the Łódź Ghetto, 1940–1944,* ed. Michal Unger (Jerusalem: Yad Vashem, 1995), 19–34. The present version is based (with minor revisions) on the English translation of the main text from *The Last Ghetto,* with footnotes translated by R. M. Shapiro from the original Hebrew version. In some instances, source references have been updated. It is reprinted here with the gracious permission of Israel Gutman and of Yad Vashem.

2. A. Z. Eshkoli, *Kehilat lodzh: Toldot ir ve-em be-Israel* (Jerusalem, [1948]), 7. See also *Pinkas ha-kehilot, Polin,* vol. 1: *Lodzh ve-ha-galil* (Jerusalem, [1976]), 1–11 (hereafter *Pinkas ha-kehilot, Lodzh*).

3. A. Eisenbach, ed., *Dokumenty i materjały do dziejów okupacji niemieckiej w Polsce,* vol. 3: *Getto Łódzkie* (Warsaw, 1946), 167.

4. Ibid., 26.

5. Ibid., 117. [Editor's note: The page cited does not include the mentioned document.]

6. See Reinhard Heydrich's *Schnellbrief* of 21 September 1939 to the commanders of the *Einsatzgruppen* in the matter of policy and the taking of measures regarding Jews in the conquered territories. Inter alia, the following is stated in this letter: "For reasons of general police security, the concentration of the Jews in the cities probably will call for regulations in these cities that will forbid their entry to certain quarters completely and that—but with due regard for economic requirements—they may, for instance, not leave the ghetto, nor leave their homes after a certain hour in the evening, etc." Many want to see in these sentences an instruction in regard to establishment of the ghettos. But this is not accurate: There is no doubt that with the term "ghettos" the intention in this case is to quarters in various Polish cities that were densely occupied by Jews. In Central and Western Europe, it was common to refer to Jewish quarters by the term "ghettos."

Heydrich's letter appears in *Documents on the Holocaust: Selected Sources on the Destruction of the Jews of Germany and Austria, Poland, and the Soviet Union,* 8th ed., ed. Y. Arad, I. Gutman, and A. Margoliot, trans. Lea Ben Dor (Lincoln and Jerusalem: University of Nebraska Press and Yad Vashem, 1999), 173–178; the quotation appears on 175.

7. Delegations arrived in Łódź from various places and the German Ghetto administration (*Gettoverwaltung*) served as a model for occupation authorities in their effort to organize a framework of mutual relations in other large ghettos. On 13 September 1940, a delegation of fifteen officials from the district of Warsaw visited Łódź in order to study the administration of the ghetto in Łódź in preparation for the ghetto to be established in Warsaw. In February 1942 there also arrived a delegation from Białystok in order to study the organizational and management system of the *Gettoverwaltung* in Łódź. See Trunk, *Judenrat: The Jewish Councils in Eastern Europe Under Nazi Occupation* (Hebrew) (Jerusalem: Yad Vashem, [1979]), 261.

8. Eisenbach, *Dokumenty,* vol. 3, *Getto Łódzkie,* 35–49.

9. Ibid., 84, 86.

10. On 15 November 1941, Hans Frank, ruler of the Generalgouvernement, issued a directive forbidding Jews, under pain of death, to leave the Jewish quarters (ghettos). One can assume that this directive by Frank was linked with the preparations for carrying out the "Final Solution," an intent apparently already known to Frank at that time. See *Dziennik Rozporządzeń Generalnego Gubernatorstwa,* 1941, no. 99.

11. Eisenbach, *Dokumenty,* vol. 3, *Getto Łódzkie,* 84.

12. See Heydrich's famous 21 September 1939 *Schnellbrief* instruction on establishment of the Judenrats in occupied Poland (Arad, *Documents on the Holocaust,* 174–175). Also see Governor Frank's 28 November 1939 instruction on formation of the Judenrats in the Generalgouvernement (*Dziennik Rozporządzeń Generalnego Gubernatorstwa,* 1939, no. 9).

13. Editor's note: The Polish term *prezes* can be rendered variously as president or chairman.

14. Editor's note: For the prewar history of the Jewish Community Board of Łódź, see R. M. Shapiro, "Jewish Self-Government in Poland: Łódź, 1914–1939" (Ph.D. diss., Columbia University, 1987).

15. Philip (Yeruham Fishel) Friedman, "Goalei-sheker be-gitaot polin," *Metsuda* 7 (London, 1954), 605.

16. See the *Min ha-meitsar* newspaper report that was found in the ruins of the Łódź Ghetto in January 1945, *Dapim le-heker ha-shoa ve-ha-mered* 1 ([1951]), 121.

17. Editor's note: Near the Western Dvina River in the Russian *Gubernia* of Vitebsk. Dobroszycki, *Chronicle,* 99n107.

18. See Friedman, "Goalei-sheker be-getaot polin," 604: "His enemies accused him of having excessively close relations with female pupils and teachers." Also note 2 on the same page. [Editor's note: See also Lucille Eichengreen with Rebecca Camhi Fromer, *Rumkowski and the Orphans of Lodz* (San Francisco: Mercury House, 2000).]

19. Among the works of fiction at whose center stands the image of Rumkowski, see Adolf Rudnicki, *Kupiec Łódzki* (Warsaw, 1963), 8–51; Chava Rosenfarb's comprehensive Yiddish trilogy, *Der Boym fun Lebn* (Tel Aviv: ha-Menorah, 1972), in Hebrew as *Ets Ha-hayim* (Tel Aviv, [1978–1980]), and abridged in one volume in English as *The Tree of Life* (Melbourne: Scribe, 1985); and Leslie Epstein, *King of the Jews* (New York: Coward, McCann & Geoghegan, 1979).

20. Trunk, *Judenrat,* 25.

21. Ibid., 26.

22. Ibid., 26–27.

23. E. Ringelblum, *Ksovim fun geto* 1: *Togbukh fun varshever geto (1939–1943)* (Warsaw, 1961), 137.

24. A. Czerniaków, *Yoman geto varsha, 6.9.1939–23.7.1942,* ed. Nahman Blumental et al. (Jerusalem, [1969]), 184.

25. N. Eck (Ekron), *Ha-toim be-darkhei ha-mavet: havay ve-hagahot be-yemei ha-kilayon* (Jerusalem, [1960]), 13.

26. J. Poznański, *Pamiętnik z getta lódzkiego* (Łódź, 1960), 101.

27. Isaiah Trunk, *Lodzher geto* (New York: YIVO Institute for Jewish Research, 1962), 359, 369.

28. Philip (Yeruham Fishel) Friedman, "Goalei-sheker ba-getaot polin," *Metsuda* 7 (London, 1954), 602. [Editor's note: See the English translation in Philip Friedman, *Roads to Extinction: Essays on the Holocaust,* ed. Ada June Friedman (Philadelphia: Jewish Publication Society, 1980), 333–334.]

29. Friedman, "Goalei-sheke ba-getaot polin," 602. It is worth noting a passage of memoirs by Jacob Nirenberg, a Bundist, writing on the basis of declarations by a secretary who worked with Rumkowski. Nirenberg states that the chairman expressed his faith in the Germans' victory in the war, that he spoke about his closeness to Greiser, that he was thus known in Berlin and designated to rule over all the Jews and to direct a state. Friedman relies on these words, but in light of Nirenberg's hostile and tendentious attitude to Rumkowski, it is possible to cast doubt on the whole story. See Y. Nirenberg, "Di geshikhte fun lodzher geto," *In di yorn fun yidishn khurbn* (New York, 1948), 236–237.

30. Editor's note: A diametrically opposed assessment of Rumkowski is presented in the heated prose of Icchak (Henryk) Rubin's *Żydzi w Łodzi pod niemiecką okupacją 1939–1945* (London, 1988), that portrays the leader of the Łódź Ghetto as a tragic heroic figure. Based on extensive archival research, Rubin's book is flawed by its author's barely controlled rage at many enemies, starting with the brutal Nazi German occupiers of Poland. Nevertheless, the book deserves serious examination.

31. See Y. Trunk, "Ha-yudnratim ve-yahasam le-baayot ha-meri ha-mezuyan neged ha-natsim," in *Shoat yehudei eyropa: reka-korot-mashmaut,* ed. I. Gutman and Livia Rothkirchen (Jerusalem, [1973]), 310.

32. See Auerswald's letter of 24 November 1941 in the appendix to the diary of Czerniaków in the English-language edition (New York: Stein and Day, 1979), 402. In this letter it is said, among other things: "When deficiencies occur, the Jews direct their resentment against the Jewish administration and not against the German supervisors."

33. This indictment accused Rumkowski: that he "named as manager of a new workshop a man other than the one expressly recommended by the German ghetto administration; that he printed his orders in Yiddish next to the German . . . ; that without the knowledge of the ghetto administration he founded a hospital for the mentally ill in the ghetto and there were 450 patients lacking treatment." See Trunk, *Judenrat,* 257.

34. The Ringelblum Archive contains diary entries by Mordechai Shvartsbard of Warsaw. On 16 April 1941, Shvartsbard wrote in his diary: "Yesterday on the 16th [15th] I was at a conference with the head of the Jews in Łódź, Rumkowski. He wanted to communicate how things look in Łódź. Former Lodzhers were present. He said: It was bad in the ghetto. If now is good—he does not know. 'I did not want to take on the post, it's not for my age, not for my education and not for my health.'" See M. Shvartsbard, "Notitsn fun geto," *Bleter far geshikhte,* nos. 3–4 (Warsaw, 1955), 129.

35. Y. Shulman, "Rumkowski—der elteste der yuden," *Yediot bet lohamei ha-getaot al shem Yitshak Katzenelson,* no. 20 (April 1958), 75.

36. Y. Tabaksblat, *Khurbn lodzh: 6 yor natsi gehenem* (Buenos Aires, 1946), 33.

37. Ibid., 27, 61.

38. Shulman, "Rumkowski," 69, 74.

39. Trunk, *Lodzher geto,* 370–371.

40. Ibid., 370.

41. J. Robinson, *Nituk o retsifut be-vaadei ha-kehilot be-tekufa ha-natsit* (Jerusalem, [1967]), 35 (Shazar's remarks in response to the lecture.)

42. Editor's note: A term adopted into the Łódź Ghetto's jargon for workshops, divisions, and factories of all kinds, from the German *Arbeitsressorts* and Polish *resorty pracy.* Dobroszycki, *Chronicle*, 9n14.

43. See, for example, M. Checinski, "How Rumkowski Died," *Commentary,* May 1979.

44. P. Fode, "Hirhurim al yihuda shel ha-mahteret be-geto lodzh," *Yalkut Moreshet* 11 (November 1969), 65.

45. Trunk, *Lodzher geto,* 371–372.

46. See *Pinkas ha-kehilot, Lodzh,* 27.

47. Tabaksblat, *Khurbn lodzh,* 76–77.

48. *Proces Artura Greisera przed Najwyższym Trybunałem Narodowym,* (1947), 157.

49. *Pinkas ha-kehilot, Lodzh,* 27–28.

50. B. Hershkovitsh, "Litsmanshtat-geto," *Yivo-bleter* 30, no. 1 (Fall 1947): 47.

51. Ibid.

52. A. Eisenbach, *Hitlerowska Polityka Zagłady Żydów* (Warsaw, 1961), 231.

53. See the document appended to Trunk, *Lodzher geto,* 437.

54. *Kronika getta łódzkiego,* ed. D. Dabrowska and L. Dozroszycki, vol. 1 (Łódź, 1965), 48. [Editor's note: Emphasis in original. See entry in the *Chronicle* dated 1 February 1941 (Hebrew edition, vol. 1, 45).]

55. Eisenbach, *Dokumenty,* vol. 3, *Getto Łódzkie,* 182.

56. Hershkovitsh, "Litsmanshtat-geto," 46.

57. Eisenbach, *Dokumenty,* vol. 3, *Getto Łódzkie,* 177–178.

58. Eisenbach, *Hitlerowska Polityka,* 539–540.

59. See the broad overview of this topic in Eisenbach, *Hitlerowska Polityka,* 558–560.

60. Ibid.

61. See the text of the statement in Arad, *Documents on the Holocaust,* 433–434.

62. Tabaksblat, *Khurbn lodzh,* 122.

63. Eisenbach, *Dokumenty,* vol. 3, *Getto Łódzkie,* 217.

64. Tabaksblat, *Khurbn lodzh,* 123–124.

65. Nirenberg, "Di geshikhte fun lodzher geto," "Di geshikhte fun lodzher geto," 59; A. Volf Yasni, *Di geshikhte fun yidn in lodzh in di yorn fun der daytsher yidn-oysrotung,* 1 (Tel Aviv, 1960), 454.

66. Ibid., 453–454.

67. Editor's note: Jasny (Yasni), *Di geshikhte fun yidn in lodzh,* vol. 1, 454.

68. Sh. Esh, *Iyunim be-heker ha-shoa ve-yahadut zmaneinu* (Jerusalem, [1973]), 296–316.

69. His testimony was known in London in June 1942. Yad Vashem Archive, JM 2713. [Editor's note: See the English translation of Grojanowski's testimony in the Archive of the Jewish Historical Institute (Warsaw) published in Martin Gilbert, *The Holocaust* (New York: Henry Holt, 1985), chap. 16, 252–279.] In publications by survivors from Łódź, there are scattered references to one or more emissaries who were sent from Łódź in order to warn Warsaw. There are among them those who think that information about Chełmno arrived by means of one or more of these emissaries (see among others the article by Riva Kwiatkowska in the periodical *Nasze Słowo,* nos. 6–7 (1948), subsequently reprinted in the *Biuletyn Żydowskiego Instytutu Historycznego* [*BZIH*] 54 [Warsaw, 1965], 125). It appears that the story is entirely based on rumor; there is no evidence whatsoever

that representatives from Łódź bearing information about Chełmno ever reached Warsaw.

70. See *Itonut 'gordonia' va-mahteret geto varsha* (Hulda, 1966), the journal *Slowo Mlodych,* Warsaw (February-March 1942), the article "Shkiat ha-yahadut shel ha-mahoz ha-karui 'Vartbrikn,'" 204.

71. Chaika Klinger, *Mi-yoman ha-geto* (Merhavia, 1959), 60.

72. Ringelblum, *Ksovim fun geto* 1, 376–377.

73. Trunk, *Lodzher geto,* 374. Trunk relies on the testimony of the Bundist Nirenberg, who claims in his memoirs (261–262) that he informed Tabaksblat about the postcard that arrived from the rabbi of Grabów with details about Chełmno. According to him, members of the Bund turned to the Zionist Tabaksblat and asked him to tell Rumkowski about the matter, but Rumkowski "already knew about it from other sources sometime earlier." Nirenberg's writing is very critical of Rumkowski and bears a partisan apologetic character. Thus, for example, it is stated in Nirenberg's account that in the postcard from the rabbi of Grabów that was received through a Jew from Brzeziny, the information is based on three witnesses, and it was passed on to Tabaksblat so as to bring the truth through him before Rumkowski. In Tabaksblat's book, nothing is said about contact with Bundists or about a conversation with Rumkowski. Nevertheless, his book presents the content of the postcard from the rabbi of Grabów, bearing the date 19 January 1942 (didn't the rabbi use the Hebrew calendar?!). The postcard is detailed, but it is not based on three witnesses, but on *one witness* (124). There is a segment in Tabaksblat's book that also talks about how emissaries were sent twice from Łódź to Warsaw in 1942, but no answer arrived from there (177–178). Who these people were is not stated, nor what they had to communicate, or what response they expected from Warsaw. Also see the words of Shlomo Uberbaum in the work of Sh. Hupert, "Melekh ha-geto: Mordechai Chaim Rumkowski," *Mehkarei Yad Vashem* 15 ([1985]), 114–115.

74. A Polish version of the letter of the rabbi of Grabów that matches up with the version of Tabaksblat appears in *Dokumenty i materjaly z czasów okupacji niemieckiej w Polsce,* vol. 1: *Obozy* [*Camps*], ed. N. Blumental, with an introduction by [Ph]ilip Friedman (Łódź, 1946), 233. However, in this place the name of the rabbi is given as Jacob Szulman and not J. Silman. On 232 in this collection there appears additional content of the postcard on Chełmno, so it is difficult to determine its documentary reliability. [Editor's note: The translation given in the present essay varies from the Polish text published in 1946. A fuller English translation of the Polish version of the originally Yiddish missive is published and discussed by Lucjan Dobroszycki, *Chronicle,* xx–xxi and xxi, n32.]

75. Editor's note: Compare with the 14 September 1942 *Chronicle* entry in Dobroszycki, *Chronicle,* 250–251.

76. Trunk, *Lodzher geto,* 311. [Editor's note: This refers to doc. no. 100 (YI-54).]

77. Tabaksblat, *Khurbn lodzh,* 156.

78. See Hupert, "Melekh ha-geto," 116.

79. Barbara (Hinda) Beatus, "Lewica Związkowa w getcie łódzkim," *BZIH* 54 (1965), 49.

80. Trunk, *Lodzher geto,* 464.

81. On this, see the various articles in *BZIH,* no. 54.

82. Ibid. See the article by Gershon Fogel, 104–112.

83. See, for example, Fode, "Hirhurim al yihuda shel ha-mahteret be-geto lodzh," 64.

84. See *BZIH,* no. 54: 47, 53, 70, 85, 92, 95, 99, 121; and also in Fode, "Hirhurim al yihuda shel ha-mahteret be-geto lodzh," 66–67.

85. Fode, "Hirhurim al yihuda shel ha-mahteret be-geto lodzh," 65.

86. See the article by Halina Najduchowska in *BZIH* 54: 102.

87. The article by "Bona" (Binem Wiener, an active Bundist who survived the war and lived for many years in Australia), ibid., 115. [Editor's note: Tsukunft and SkiF were the youth and children's organizations of the Bund.]

88. The article by Riva Kwiatkowska, who survived the war and resided many years in Israel; ibid., 119.

89. A few issues of this publication survive in the Moreshet archive at Givat-Haviva.

90. About the story of the radio receivers and those arrested, see appendices nos. 37–40 in *BZIH* 54: 33–36; and also Trunk, *Lodzher geto,* 469–471.

91. Editor's note: See *The Documents of the Łódź Ghetto: An Inventory of the Nachman Zonabend Collection,* compiled by Marek Web (New York, 1988).

92. Editor's note: See Pinchas Shaar, "Mendel Grossman: Photographic Bard of Ghetto Łódź," in R. M. Shapiro, ed., *Holocaust Chronicles* (Hoboken, N.J.: Ktav, 1999), 125–140.

93. See Tabaksblat, 177–178; Nirenberg, "Di geshikhte fun lodzher geto," 292–293; and appendix no. 72 in *BZIH* 54: 132–133.

94. On those who went into hiding, see appendix no. 71 in *BZIH* 54: 130–131. [Editor's note: Also see the diary by Jakub Poznański (1960), who was with a group in hiding for several months, until the arrival of the Soviet military.]

Foreword

1. Editor's note: Translated by Dr. Shlomo Noble with minor editorial changes.

2. *Dokumenty i materiały do dziejów okupacji niemieckiej w Polsce,* vol. 3: *Getto Łódzkie,* ed. Artur Eisenbach (Warsaw: Towarzystwo Przyjaciol Centralnej Zydowskiej Historycznej w Polsce, 1946), 300 pages, map.

3. *Dziennik Dawida Sierakowiaka,* ed. Lucjan Dobroszycki, with a foreword by Adolf Rudnicki (Warsaw: Iskry, 1960), 225 pages.

4. Jakub Poznański, *Pamiętnik z getta Łódzkiego* (Łódź: Wydawnictwo Łódzkie, 1960), 285 pages.

5. Shlomo Frank (Frenkl), *Togbukh fun Lodzher geto,* introduction by Nahman Blumental (Buenos Aires: Tsentral farband fun poylishe yidn in argentine, 1958), 335 pages.

6. Y. L. Girsht, *Min ha-meitsar. zikhronot mi-yemot ha-ayemim ve-ha-shoa ba-geto Lodzh u-mahanot ha-hesger* (Jerusalem, [1949]) [Editor's note: Girsht's book is a memoir and not a diary.].

7. Yisroel Tabaksblat, *Khurbn-Lodzh. 6 yor natsi-gehenem* (Buenos Aires: Tsentral farband fun poylishe yidn in argentine, 1946), 203 pages.

8. A. Volf Yasny [A. Wolf Jasni], *Geshikhte fun yidn in Lodzh in di yorn fun der daytsher yidn-oysrotung* (Tel Aviv, 1960), 516 pages, illus. [Editor's note: The second volume of Yasny's work appeared in Tel Aviv in 1966.]

9. We have mentioned here books and not articles in periodicals or publications of *landsmanshaftn.* [Editor's note: For a discussion of diaries in the Łódź Ghetto, see R. M. Shapiro, ed., *Holocaust Chronicles* (Ktav, 1999), 93–124.]

Author's Preface

1. Editor's note: Translation by Dr. Shlomo Noble with minor editorial changes.

2. Editor's note: In the wake of the 1968 "anti-Zionist" campaign, the bulk of the Łódź Ghetto documentation was transferred from the JHI in Warsaw to the State Archive in Łódź.

3. A. Eisenbach published a collection of documents from these archives in 1946, under the title *Getto Łódzkie.*

I. Establishment of the Ghetto

1. *Yivo-bleter,* 30, no. 2 (1947): 164. [Editor's note: Heydrich's order of 21 September 1939 established the basics of Jewish policy for the German police and security units in newly conquered Poland. Although Heydrich does not refer to ghettos, he does direct appointment of Jewish councils in each locality, with primary responsibility for obedience to German orders, to conduct a census of Jews, and to facilitate the transfer and housing of Jews moved into the cities. See Isaiah Trunk, *Judenrat: The Jewish Councils in Eastern Europe under Nazi Occupation* (New York: Macmillan, 1972), 1–3.]

2. The very first Nazi German ghetto in Poland arose in Piotrków-Trybunalski (October 1939). It was officially designated a ghetto in the *Stadtkommissar's* ordinance of 1 December 1939. Text published in *Exterminacja żydów na ziemiach polskich w okresie okupacji hitlerowskiej* (Warsaw: ZIH, 1957), 75.

3. TA: *Lodzer Zeitung,* 16 November 1939. Editor's note: Trunk annotations (TA) are taken from handwritten notes on Trunk's personal copy of his book. It appears that he may have wanted to revise the book by replacing some of the document extracts with simple footnotes.

4. TA: *Lodzer Zeitung,* 30 November 1939.

5. TA: *Lodzer Zeitung,* 15 November 1939.

6. TA: A. Eisenbach, [*Dokumenty i Materiały do dziejów okupacji niemieckiej w Polsce,* vol. 3], *Getto Łódzkie,* part 1 (1946), 31.

7. Editor's note: The region of western Poland that was annexed to the Reich, not including the region of Polish Silesia.

8. Ibid., 32–33; also see Stanislaw Wasiak, "Bilans Walki narodowościowej rządów Greisera," *Przegląd Zachodni,* no. 6: 492. [TA: *Eksterminacja żydów na ziemiach polskich w okresie okupacji hitlerowskiej* Warsaw; *BZIH,* 1–32.]

9. Editor's note: Karl Litzmann was a German general killed in combat near Łódź in 1915. Lucjan Dobroszycki, ed., *The Chronicle of the Łódź Ghetto 1941–1944* (New Haven, Conn.: Yale University Press, 1984), xxiii.

10. A. Eisenbach, ed., *Dokumenty i materiały do dziejów okupacji niemieckiej w Polsce,* vol. 3, *Getto Łódzkie,* part 1 (1946), 177.

11. Anonymous notice from December 1939, in *Eksterminacja żydów na ziemiach polskich,* 36–37.

12. Ibid., 47; also see Isaiah Trunk, *Shtudye tsu der geshikhte fun yidn in varteland in der tekufe fun umkum (1939–1944)* (Warsaw, 1950), 82–90; [reprinted in Y. Trunk, *Shtudyes in yidisher geshikhte in poyln* (Buenos Aires, 1963), 171–289]. Greiser made further efforts so that an exception would be made at least for Łódź. At the conference in Berlin, held on 1 April 1940 (whose participants included, inter alia, representatives from Goering, from the ministries of Finance and Supply, and Greiser), it was decided to turn to Goering and to General-governor Hans Frank about this. See the notice about the meeting, in *Eksterminacja żydów na ziemiach polskich,* 46–47.

13. Editor's note: Ethnic Germans from the Baltic countries were to be resettled within the Reich, presumably into housing cleared of Jews and Poles.

14. TA: Doc. no. 621/6.

15. TA: Doc. no. 621/11.

16. TA: *Lodscher Zeitung,* 10 January 1940.

17. TA: Ibid., 9 February 1940.

18. TA: Ibid.

19. TA: Ibid. [illegible], 1 March 1940.

20. TA: Doc. no. 621/49.

21. *Biuletyn Głównej Komisji Badania Zbrodni Hitlerowskich w Polsce,* vol. 12 (1960), doc. no. 25, 98F.

22. Doc. no. 81 [Editor's note: In the Zonabend Collection, YIVO].

23. Doc. no. 1002 [Editor's note: In the Zonabend Collection, YIVO].

24. Yisroel Tabaksblat, *Khurbn lodzh, 6 yor natsi-gehenem* (Buenos Aires, 1946), 38; Eisenbach, *Dokumenty,* vol. 3, *Getto Łódźkie,* part 1 (1946), 33.

25. TA: *Lodscher Zeitung,* 9 March 1940.

26. Tabaksblat, *Khurbn lodzh,* 38.

27. TA: *Lodscher Zeitung,* 19 March and 9 April 1940.

28. TA: *Litzmannstädter Zeitung,* 9 April 1940.

29. Doc. IT: 16, 19, 20, from an anonymous monograph about the Łódź Ghetto, apparently composed by one of the German Jews who was deported there.

30. Doc. no. 103.

31. Doc. no. 104.

32. TA: Doc. no. 762.

33. TA: *Litzmannstädter Zeitung,* 20 April 1940. Editor's note: Trunk's annotations to this paragraph also refer to Docs. nos. 621/86, 621/68, 92 and 103 (?).

34. Eisenbach, *Dokumenty,* vol. 3, *Getto Łódzkie,* 102–104.

35. Editor's note: References to the YIVO Archive Zonabend Collection are according to the enumeration used by Trunk. In 1987 the collection was reorganized, as described in the finding aid, *The Documents of the Lodz Ghetto: An Inventory of the Nachman Zonabend Collection* (Record Group No. 241), compiled by Marek Web (New York: YIVO, 1988). A conversion table reconciling the old and the new folder numbers has been compiled and is kept in the YIVO Archives. The original folder numbers remain valid for finding documents on the microfilm copies of the Zonabend Collection.

36. Another Regierungspräsident decree, dated 12 December 1939, replaced the armband with a ten-centimeter yellow Star of David to be worn on the breast and back. See Eisenbach, *Dokumenty,* vol. 3, *Getto Łódzkie,* 23.

37. Editor's note: Ellipsis indicates that material has been left out by Trunk or by the original author of the quoted document. Ellipsis in brackets [. . .] indicates material left out by the translator.

38. Editor's note: The Germans initially referred to the city as Lodz and Lodsch before renaming it Litzmannstadt.

39. Editor's note: Compare the English translation in *Documents on the Holocaust,* ed. Y. Arad et al., 3rd ed. (Jerusalem, 1988), 192–194.

40. Editor's note: Emphasis in original, *"nicht moeglich ist."*

41. Editor's note: Plac Wolności.

42. Editor's note: The omitted segment consists of the following listing of the Judenrat's tasks. This is taken from J. Noakes and G. Pridham, eds., *Nazism A History in Documents and Eyewitness Accounts, 1919–1945,* vol. 2 (New York: Schocken, 1988), 1062.

1. *Food Department:* Establishment and maintenance of communal kitchens. Utilization of the food supplies available in the ghetto and those delivered by the city administration.

2. *Health Department:* Deployment of the available doctors. Supervision of pharmacists. The establishment of one or more hospitals as well as epidemic centers, provision of drinking water, lavatories and sewage disposal, burial arrangements.

3. *Finance Department:* The financing of food supplies.

4. *Security Department:* The establishment of a police force. The establishment of a fire service.

5. *Accommodation Department:* Distribution of the available rooms. Erection of barracks. The provision of beds for the ghetto inhabitants.

6. *Registration Department:* Registration of all persons in the ghetto and control over those moving to and from it.

43. The newspaper had in the meantime changed its name to reflect the new German name of the city.

44. There is another warning about the same matter, dated 25 April 1940 (doc. YI/103).

45. The map is located between pages 46 and 47 in the 1962 Yiddish edition.

II. Organization of the Ghetto

1. Editor's note: See Isaiah Trunk, *Judenrat: The Jewish Councils in Eastern Europe under Nazi Occupation* (New York: Macmillan, 1972).

2. Editor's note: Ibid., 3–4.

3. Editor's note: On the prewar Jewish Religious Community of Łódź and Rumkowski's activities, see R. M. Shapiro, "Jewish Self-government in Poland: Łódź, 1914–1939" (Ph.D. diss., Columbia University, 1987), esp. chaps. 3, 5, and the conclusion. Also see R. M. Shapiro, "Aspects of Jewish Self-Government in Łódź, 1914–1939," in A. Polonsky, ed., *From Shtetl to Socialism* (London: Littman, 1993), 296–317; and R. M. Shapiro, "The Polish *Kehillah* Elections of 1936: A Revolution Re-examined," POLIN, vol. 8 (London: Littman, 1994), 206–226.

4. TA: Doc. no. 1201. Editor's note: On Rumkowski's role in the Łódź Ghetto, see Rafael F. Scharf, "Rola Ch. Rumkowskiego w Łódzkim Getcie," in W. Puś and S. Liszewski, eds., *Dzieje żydów w Łodzi 1820–1944* (Łódź, 1991), 301–310.

5. TA: Doc. no. 1202.

6. Editor's note: See the list of names in I. Rubin, *Żydzi w Łodzi pod niemiecką okupacją 1939–1945* (London: Kontra, 1988), 171–172.

7. Testimony of one of the surviving members of the council: *Sefer ha-zevaot* (Jerusalem, 5705), 65. In the camp there were also leaders of the Bund, Left Poalei Zion, and other public activists who had been arrested on 11 November 1939. Some were tortured to death, while others were deported to German concentration camps where they died. [Editor's note: Also see Rubin, *Żydzi w Łodzi*, 174–175.]

8. TA: Eisenbach, *Dokumenty,* vol. 3, *Getto Łódzkie,* 21–22.

9. Tabaksblat, *Khurbn lodzh,* 34. [Editor's note: See the list of second Beirat members in Rubin, *Żydzi w Łodzi* , 175.] A similar, still sharper assessment of the second Beirat is in Engineer [Leon Hurwicz]'s diary, written in the Łódź Ghetto (YIVO Archive, 15). [Editor's note: Both Lucjan Dobroszycki and I. H. Rubin reject Trunk's identification of Hurwicz (Hurvits, Hurwitz) and Józef Klementynowski as one and the same person. Hurwitz was an engineer about whom there is much documentation, while the attorney Józef Klementynowski was well known, having served as the first director of the ghetto archive and then in other positions in Rumkowski's administration. Moreover, the handwriting in the manuscripts left by each man is clearly different. Dobroszycki, ed., *The Chronicle of the Łódź Ghetto, 1941–1944* (New Haven, Conn.: Yale University Press, 1984), xxviiin59; Rubin, *Żydzi w Łodzi*, 41, 307–308.]

10. TA: Doc. no. 1204.

11. TA: Doc. no. 54A.

12. TA: *Geto-tsaytung,* no. 13 (20 June 1941).

13. TA: Ibid., no. 17 (14 September 1941).

14. Editor's note: In prewar Łódź, over 15,000 Jewish pupils comprised nearly 30 percent of public elementary school students, while about 6,000 Jewish pupils attended private elementary schools. Shapiro, *Jewish Self-government in Poland*, 393n258.

15. Editor's note: A Talmud Torah was traditionally a free Jewish religious elementary school operated for the benefit of poor children.

16. Eisenbach, *Dokumenty,* vol. 3, *Getto Łódzkie,* 77–79.

17. TA: Ibid., 19.

18. TA: Doc. no. 630.

19. Rumkowski's speech, presented at the end of January or start of February 1941 (doc. no. 1213).

20. Tabaksblat, *Khurbn lodzh*, 57; doc. no. 26: 12; doc. no. 33: 1. [Editor's note: References to doc. no. 26 and doc. no. 33 presumably refer to the document numbers in the Zonabend Collection at YIVO. References in the body of the text are clearly to the appended 141 documents published to supplement the chapters of the present book.]

21. TA: Doc. no. 1207.

22. Doc. no. 1200, a circular forbidding further issuance of separate payrolls of the newly arrived. The department, however, continued to operate perfunctorily until the end.

23. Editor's note: The Rumkowski Archive at the Łódź State Archive includes tens of thousands of petitions and applications submitted to Rumkowski, along with proposals and plans that the chairman solicited for improving the ghetto's administration. Rubin, *Żydzi w Łodzi*, 35.

24. TA: Doc. no. 130.

25. *Geto-tsaytung*, no. 13 (20 June 1941).

26. TA: Doc. no. 208.

27. *Geto-tsaytung*, no. 14 (14 July 1941).

28. TA: Doc. no. 609.

29. TA: Doc. no. 615.

30. Doc. no. 607; circulars 678, 858, 976.

31. Doc. no. 762, *Geto-tsaytung*, no. 2 (14 March 1941).

32. TA: Doc. no. 150a.

33. ZIH Archive, Rumkowski Archive, file IV/84: 41.

34. Doc. no. 816. [Editor's note: This is an example of how, sometimes, Trunk simply gives the archival signature without describing the document as such. One assumes that the data presented here is taken from the cited Zonabend Collection document.]

35. TA: Doc. no. 788.

36. TA: Doc. no. 808B.

37. Editor's note: The Isaiah Kuperstein Collection at YIVO includes more than six hours of interviews with former *Sonderkommando* head David Gertler, conducted in Munich in 1974 by Isaiah Kuperstein. The interviews have not yet been transcribed.

38. Testimony of B. Frenkel, manuscript, ch. "Lodzher marishin ghetto," 21.

39. Doc. no. 862A.

40. *Geto-tsaytung*, no. 14 (15 July 1941).

41. TA: Doc. no. 279.

42. *Geto-tsaytung*, no. 13 (20 June 1941).

43. TA: Docs. nos. 18, 322.

44. *Geto-tsaytung*, no. 14 (15 July 1941).

45. Ibid., nos. 15 (1 August 1941) and 16 (17 August 1941).

46. TA: Doc. no. 862A.

47. TA: *Geto-tsaytung*, no. 18, eve of Rosh Hashana (21 September 1941); and doc. no. 26: 19. [Editor's note: Presumably this refers to doc. no. 26 in the Zonabend Collection; it is not a reference to doc. no. 26 appended to the present book.]

48. *Geto-tsaytung*, no. 8 (25 April 1941). Y. Nirenberg mentions the names of four such judges ("Geshikhte fun Lodzher geto," *In di yorn fun yidishn khurbn* [New York, 1948], 235–236). In contrast, Jakub Poznański names ten such judges and prosecutors in *Pamiętnik z getta łódzkiego* (Łódź, 1960), 60. [Editor's note: cf. Rubin, *Żydzi w Łodzi*, 321.]

49. Doc. no. 621/120.

50. Docs. nos. 118, 119. Mainly food would be sent into the ghetto in exchange for the goods that were sent out.

51. TA: Doc. no. 139.

52. Docs. nos. 141, 144, 172. Only postcards and letters up to twenty grams could be mailed out. Monetary traffic was restricted only to the ghetto itself.

53. TA: Doc. no. 267.

54. Docs. nos. 396, 1175.

55. The Statistical Department compiled statistical annuals as well as jubilee albums for various branches of the ghetto administration. A number of albums have survived; for example, "Educational Services in Litzmannstadt Ghetto" (doc. no. 1464), "Educational Services in Marysin" (doc. no. 1465), "Health Department" (doc. no. 1496), an album presented to Rumkowski by the school department (doc. no. 1466), major fragments of albums from the Welfare Department (doc. no. 1470) and from the Textile Department (doc. no. 1432), as well as the first part (May 1940–June 1942) of a comprehensive statistical monograph in the form of tables about all the branches of the ghetto administration (doc. no. 58).

56. Doc. no. 1252. Application by Rumkowski to the mayor about organizing a civil records office.

57. Doc. no. 55ii.

58. *Geto-tsaytung,* no. 5 (4 April 1941).

59. Editor's note: See the introduction to Dobroszycki, *Chronicle of the Łódź Ghetto,* ix–lxviii.

60. *Geto-tsaytung,* no. 4 (28 March 1941).

61. Ibid., no. 10 (11 May 1941); doc. no. 313. Around September 1941, another ten distribution points for sausage were added to the network.

62. Doc. no. 289.

63. TA: Doc. no. 621/161.

64. Y. Tabaksblat, *Khurbn lodzh,* 49.

65. Docs. nos. 93–99, all dated 24 April 1940.

66. Doc. no. 621/81.

67. Doc. no. 621/80. Letter to Rumkowski, 5 June 1940.

68. Doc. no. 1141. Letter to Rumkowski, 23 March 1940.

69. Docs. nos. 1001, 1470.

70. Doc. no. 1220. Ghetto *Chronicle* of Nov. 1941. [Editor's note: The issues dated November 1941 and November 28, 1941, contain no reference to two million RM. See *Lodz Ghetto Chronicle* Polish edition (1965), English edition (1984), and Hebrew edition (1986).]

71. TA: Doc. no. 40.

72. Doc. no. 1002: 2–3. The exchange rate for the złoty was set at 2 zł. = 1 RM.

73. Doc. no. 41[: 3, though not paginated].

74. Doc. no. 150. The exemption was retroactive to 1 April. [Editor's note: Once again, Trunk does not describe the specific document he cites in a footnote, presumably assuming that the reader will accept that the document contains the relevant data.]

75. Docs. nos. 1149, 1151, 1156.

76. Doc. no. 207.

77. Doc. no. 621/56, 60–63; doc. no. 1011.

78. Doc. no. 621/141–145, 148, 149.

79. Doc. no. 777.

80. "Encyclopedia of Łódź Ghetto" [Hebrew], *Yediot beit lohamei ha-getaot,* no. 14–15 (April 1956): 67.

81. Doc. no. 664.

82. Doc. no. 621/30.

83. Doc. IT: 24–25. Until then, ghetto residents could cross the two "Aryan" streets under guard at seven designated times between 8 A.M. and 4:30 P.M. From June 1940, crossing those streets was allowed until 5 P.M. without interruption (Doc. IT: 23–24).

84. Doc. no. 965.

85. Doc. no. 30; *Ghetto Chronicle*, 11 July 1942.

86. Doc. no. 621/43, 44.

87. Announcement no. 225 of 3 March 1941. A police order of 14 October 1940 had forbidden the use of electricity and gas after 8 P.M. After introduction of the restrictions of 3 March, the police order became moot.

88. Bendet Hershkovitsh, "Litsmanshtat-geto," *Yivo-bleter* 30, no. 1 (1947): 39.

89. Goering's decree of 17 September 1940 (*RGBl* N-170), "Ueber Behandlung von Vermoegen der Angehoerigen des ehemaligen polnischen Staates," ordained full-scale confiscation of both immovable and movable property of Jews (with the exception of objects of personal use), as well as cash, banknotes, and stocks and bonds, whose value exceeded 1,000 RM.

90. Eisenbach, *Dokumenty,* vol. 3, *Getto Łódzkie,* 112. The *Gettoverwaltung* was almost the sole master over all the goods and valuables in the ghetto.

91. TA: Doc. no. 159.

92. Docs. nos. 154, 168, repeated on 16 October (doc. no. 193).

93. TA: Doc. no. 228.

94. TA: Doc. no. 394.

95. TA: Doc. no. 44 (?).

96. Docs. nos. 431, 442, 448, 487: Rumkowski's appeals during 1942–1944.

97. TA: Doc. no. 1212.

98. Doc. no. 631.

99. Doc. no. 55K.

100. Editor's note: The Yiddish term *arbet-resortn* originated from the German *Arbeitsressorts,* meaning work departments, that came to be applied to ghetto workshops and factories in general. See *Nazi Deutsch/Nazi German,* eds. Robert Michael and Karin Doerr (Westport, Conn.: Greenwood, 2002), 71. Within the bureaucratic language of Rumkowski's ghetto administration, the term "ressort" was used to refer to major divisions of the overall ghetto industry.

101. TA: Doc. no. 931/2.

102. Doc. no. 1/931. On 1 November, Rumkowski issued a circular to all the principals of the state elementary schools for Jewish children, announcing that according to the decree of the German authorities he was taking over the administration of the schools and introducing a school fee of 4 złoty a month (doc. no. 1464: 7).

103. Doc. no. 1464: 11. [Editor's note: Secondary schools included a gymnasium with 508 students and a lycée with 125.]

104. TA: Doc. no. 959.

105. Doc. no. 1464,: 22, 23: Rumkowski's announcements nos. 69 and 73 from 20 and 28 June 1940.

106. Doc. no. 1464: 73; doc. no. 933.

107. Doc. no. 1213.

108. Doc. no. 1464: 5.

109. Y.L. Gersht, "Lererkursn far yidish in *lodzher* geto," *Yivo-bleter* 30, no. 1: 152–155; doc. no. 959: 24.

110. Doc. no. 940.

111. Doc. no. 30, *Ghetto Chronicle* of 31 July 1942. The Germans were already then apparently preparing for the "Children's Action" of September 1942.

112. Docs. nos. 729, 747.

113. Doc. no. 730.

114. Editor's note: This probably refers to the *Linat Ha-holim* clinic at 19

Południowa Street, where in 1989 one could still make out the Hebrew inscription over the entrance.

115. Editor's note: Located in the former mortuary building at the original Jewish cemetery on Wesoła [Happy] Street.

116. Doc. no. 621/73.

117. Doc. no. 621/76.

118. Doc. no. 770.

119. Doc. no. 621/112, 115.

120. Docs. nos. 58, 1469.

121. Editor's note: *Feldshers* = barber-surgeons without formal medical training.

122. TA: Doc. no. 221.

123. Doc. no. 50A.

124. Docs. nos. 152 and 1469, photograph no. 47.

125. Doc. no. 135, *Geto-tsaytung,* no. 6 (11 April 1941); Doc. no. 58: 56.

126. Doc. no. 58: 48–53.

127. For more detail about this, see chapter 5.

128. Y. Tabaksblat, *Khurbn Lodzh*, 73.

129. TA: Doc. no. 1002.

130. Doc. no. 1002: 68, 69.

131. See chapter 3.

132. TA: Doc. no. 1470.

133. Doc. no. 177. [Editor's note: This pattern is similar to the reform introduced into the public assistance operations of the prewar Łódź Jewish Religious Community. See Shapiro, "Jewish Self-government in Poland," 344–363.]

134. TA: Doc. no. 1001.

135. Docs. nos. 245, 388. *Geto-tsaytung,* nos. 13 (20 June 1941) and 17 (14 September 1941). The increase of the relief sum in January 1941 was made possible by a surplus of about 340,000 marks that was saved due to the free labor of the recipients (doc. no. 1001: 14).

136. Doc. no. 1001: 61.

137. Editor's note: Mordechai Chaim Rumkowski was the longtime director of the Helenówek orphanage. TOZ was the Polish acronym for the Jewish Society for the Protection of Health.

138. Doc. no. 1010: 9–10.

139. Yeshaye Trunk, "Mayrev-eyropeishe yidn in mizrekh-eyropeishe getos," *Goldene keyt* (April 1953): 86.

140. Doc. no. 49H.

141. Doc. no. 1464: 59. Diagram about the expenditures to maintain the camp.

142. TA: Doc. no. 938.

143. *Yediot beit lohamei ha-getaot,* no. 14–15 (April 1956): 70.

144. Editor's note: The director was Rabbi Prof. Emanuel Hirschberg. Oskar Rosenfeld describes the department's work in one of his notebooks. Oskar Rosenfeld, *In the Beginning Was the Ghetto,* ed. Hanno Loewy, trans. Brigitte M. Goldstein (Evanston, Ill.: Northwestern University Press, 2002), 305–307 n12.

145. *Yediot beit lohamei ha-getaot,* no. 14–15 (April 1956): 69–70. A number of examples have survived and are today located in the museum of the Jewish Historical Institute in Warsaw.

146. Nos. 24 and 25 were not used.

147. Eisenbach, *Dokumenty,* vol. 3, *Getto Łódzkie,* 21–22.

148. *Geto-tsaytung* no. 13 (20 June 1941).

149. Editor's note: The German term was used in the original Polish text.

150. Editor's note: Compare the list based on the Łódź Jewish Council's organizational chart of 20 August 1940, presented in Raul Hilberg, *The Destruction of the European Jews* (Chicago: Quadrangle Books, 1967), 154–155.

151. At the beginning of August 1942, Rumkowski issued a proposal to replace the SCO with a Chairman's Council (Yiddish: *prezidialer rat*) as the supreme administrative and supervisory council in the ghetto with the chairman of the SCO at its head (doc. no. 33: 5, 10). It appears that nothing came of the proposal.

152. In the report that Rumkowski presented in Warsaw during his second visit in the middle of May 1941, he boasted of his secret police that attended all meetings and informed him about what was being discussed (M. Shvartsbard, "Notitsn fun geto," *BlfG* 8, no. 3–4 [1955]: 129).

153. [Added in pencil on the document:] "(Unpaid compuls[ory] labor for communal purposes)."

154. Announcement no. 224 of 1 March 1941 calls on the ghetto population to write to relatives to send no more parcels (doc. no. 270).

155. Rumkowski published the contents of this letter in his Announcement no. 26 of 24 April 1940 (doc. no. 102).

156. Editor's note: The original of this financial summary is laid out in five columns that would facilitate noting both spending and income entries for each numbered rubric.

157. The same was repeated during the outsettlement of June–August 1944 (doc. no. 1370).

158. Editor's note: This seems to refer to the gymnasium or secondary school established for teenagers in the ghetto.

159. Editor's note: See the nineteen vignettes by Zelkowicz describing his visits to relief applicants' homes as an inspector for the Relief Grants Department. Josef Zelkowicz, *In Those Terrible Days,* ed. Michal Unger (Jerusalem, 2002), 31–178.

160. Editor's note: *Opieka Społeczna* is Polish for Social Aid or Social Welfare.

161. Editor's note: *Tomkhey Orkhim* (Hebrew, *Tomhei Orhim:* Supporters of Wanderers) and *Noysen Lekhem* (Hebrew, *Noten Lehem:* Giver of Bread) were traditional Jewish charitable organizations of long standing.

162. Editor's note: This document reflects the very heavy influence of German over Rumkowski's Yiddish. One suspects that the announcement was drafted in German for official prior approval and then translated into Yiddish.

163. Editor's note: Yiddish *arbetsresort*.

164. Editor's note: 25 September 1940.

165. Letters P, O, S, R, and L are taken from Polish and German terms: *pewne, odmowne, sprawy, różne, Lohnlisten.*

166. *Obrona przeciwlotnicza:* Polish for anti-aircraft defense.

III. Provisioning

1. Editor's note: Artur Eisenbach (*Dokumenty i materiały do dziejów okupacji niemieckiej w Polsce,* vol. 3, *Getto Łódzkie,* part 1 [1946], 59–68) presents an array of decrees issued by the German authorities regarding confiscation of a wide range of property in Łódź.

2. Doc. no. 1021: 2.

3. Doc. no. 51A: 16–19.

4. Doc. no. 1021: 4–5

5. Doc. no. 621/7, 8, 9. [TA: Doc. no. 621: 51.]

6. Doc. no. 82.

7. Doc. no. 1021: 10.

8. Doc. no. 1/115.

9. Doc. no. 117. Announcement no. 51 (2 June 1940) contains a list of the products for a week for one person: 250 grams each of sugar and rye-meal, 500 grams cereal (*kashe*), 100 grams salt, 30 grams bicarbonate of soda and chicory, 100 grams synthetic honey, 50 grams each of coffee mix, canned onion, 20 grams oil, and 5 kilograms of coal. For children up to three years old: a quarter liter of

milk daily, two eggs, 250 grams farina, and one piece of soap. In addition, the house committees received cucumbers, lemon vinegar, and methylated spirits to distribute according to their own discretion.

10. Doc. no. 1021: 14.

11. Docs. nos. 233, 234: announcements of 24 and 27 December 1940. Poor tenants encountered unfairness and cheating during the distribution through the house committees.

12. Doc. no. 1021: 19. The thirteen sub-departments were the central bureau, bookkeeping of the house committees, Bałuty Marketplace, warehouses, bakeries desk, distribution points desk, milk points desk, assigned commissioners, department for vegetables, coal, milk products, meat headquarters, and tobacco.

13. Ibid., 24.

14. Ibid., 14, 25.

15. Archive of the German ghetto administration (*Gettoverwaltung*), ZIH, G.V. 18/3: 148. It is, however, worth noting that, during the first months after the sealing of the ghetto (until 27 August 1940), over 5 million RM in cash was signed over to the nutrition account of the *Gettoverwaltung,* aside from thousands of pieces of jewelry and furs. (Eisenbach, *Dokumenty,* vol. 3, *Getto,* 120–121.) [Editor's note: The huge archive of the German ghetto administration was transferred from the Jewish Historical Institute in Warsaw to the State Archive in Łódź in 1968, in the wake of the notorious "anti-Zionist" campaign.]

16. Eisenbach, *Dokumenty,* vol. 3, *Getto,* 143.

17. Yeshaye Trunk, "Shtudye tsu der geshikhte . . . ," *Bleter far geshikhte* 2: 107.

18. Ibid., 108. According to the 9 July 1941 *Landesernährungsamt* (Regional Food Office) circular to all organs of the state administration, the same norms as Polish prisoners or concentration camp inmates receive are foreseen for the non-working Jewish population in the ghettos (to this category the circular also reckons those who were employed in working for the benefit of the *Gettoverwaltung,* such as street cleaners and the like) (ibid., 107–108).

19. Doc. no. 50A: 3; doc. no. 200a; Announcement no. 150, 30 October 1940.

20. Eisenbach, *Dokumenty,* vol. 3, *Getto,* 244.

21. Doc. no. 1002: 37. A couple of months earlier, an embittered hungry crowd demolished the office of the administrator of the Provisioning Department and threatened him (doc. no. 1021: 18).

22. Doc. no. 158; Tabaksblat, *Khurbn lodzh,* 53–54. [TA: According to a secret report from "Forschungsstelle A" in Łódź, dated 10 August, citing a communication from the Gestapo, after August 8th there occurred a demonstration against Rumkowski and the Order Service that was dispersed by the German police with weapons. No casualties are mentioned. Yad Vashem Archive, file 3–4 [illegible], p. 207. (Editor's note: End of TA is illegible).]

23. Doc. no. Occ-E-2–96 in the YIVO Archive: Report from the chief of the German police (*Ordnungspolizei*) to the Propaganda Ministry of 7 October, where it is recounted that due to insufficient food supply there were disturbances in the ghetto, that weapons were used nineteen times and in result two Jews were killed and four wounded. Cf. also Tabaksblat, *Khurbn lodzh,* 54.

24. Doc. no. 28: 9. No detailed information about the *Beirat* supplements survived. The reason is clear: it was more comfortable for this group not to reduce to writing its privileged status. They are only mentioned in passing in a series of documents, like doc. no. 43: 1, docs. nos. 907, 834, 1036, and so on.

25. Doc. no. 699: circular of Supreme Control Office (HKA) of 30 August 1942.

26. Doc. no. 444, announcement no. 402 of 5 November 1943.

27. Diary of [Leon Hurwitz], 47.

28. Docs. nos. 239, 251, 1089, 1112, 1123; doc. no. 46: 101. In 1941, this category received, inter alia, 4.04 kilograms more meat, 800 grams more sausage,

and 2 kilograms more potatoes than the rest of the population. There were eight different gradations in the coupons in regard to quantity, quality, and length of validity. In a circular from the Supreme Control Office of 28 August 1942, there is still mention of a "supplemental coupon" H (doc. no. 698).

29. Docs. nos. 29, 30, 599. Still earlier, due to a shortage of potatoes and cereal (*kashe*) in May 1941, Rumkowski temporarily introduced giving out bread, sausage, and coffee to the workers instead of soups (*Geto-tsaytung*, nos. 11–12 [18 May 1941]).

30. See also doc. no. 1361.

31. Doc. no. 445. From 4 March 1944, the so-called "long- and hard-working" began to be issued special coupons marked with the letters L and S. About 22,500 workers benefited from them (Y. Hiler's diary, in the Franz Kurski Archive [Editor's note: Now at YIVO], 163).

32. Doc. no. 24, p. 18.

33. ZIH, Rumkowski Archive, file "Tsirkularn"; doc. no. 1031.

34. Doc. no. 29.

35. Docs. nos. 23, 505, 28: 4–5; 29: 1; 30 (*Chronicle*, 1 July 1942). The intelligentsia kitchen was considered the best in the ghetto in regard to quality and sanitary-esthetic conditions. It was under the patronage of Rumkowski's sister-in-law, the wife of Joseph Rumkowski (doc. no. 28: 9).

36. Docs. nos. 1021: 17; 25: 11; 30: 36.

37. Docs. nos. 243, 43: 10.

38. Tabaksblat, *Khurbn lodzh*, 61.

39. Editor's note: The German civilian administrative unit embracing the Baltic countries and parts of Poland and Belorussia.

40. Doc. no. 137; IT: 3, 6; 788; 225.

41. Testimony of B. Frenkel: "Lodzher marishin-geto," 8–9.

42. Doc. no. 136.

43. Doc. no. 55B.

44. Eisenbach, *Dokumenty*, vol. 3, *Getto*, 241–242.

45. Tabaksblat, *Khurbn lodzh*, 57, 58, 60, 67. In one of the documents from that time, the reason given for the freezing of large stocks of vegetables was that, during the deportation of the Western European Jews to Łódź during the autumn months of 1941, all transport was occupied with transferring their baggage and because of this the vegetables set aside for winter froze in Marysin (doc. no. 28: 8).

46. Doc. no. 30: 34. The vegetable distribution points owed the consumers 130,000 kilograms of vegetables for April and May 1942 (doc. no. 28: 8).

47. Doc. no. 1/29: 1.

48. Docs. nos. 178, 181.

49. Doc. no. 43.

50. Doc. no. 425.

51. Docs. nos. 888–890. An issue also came out on 2 July 1943 (doc. no. 21).

52. Doc. no. 28: 9, 19.

53. Doc. no. 28: 29.

54. Doc. no. 1/29 (*Chronicle*, 13 June 1942). At the start of June 1943, Rumkowski banned sales of privately cultivated vegetables to traders or by public sale in the streets (doc. no. 1129).

55. Doc. no. 49B.

56. *Geto-tsaytung*, no. 10 (11 May 1941).

57. Doc. no. 33: 27.

58. Doc. no. 28: 9.

59. Ibid.; doc. no. 1199.

60. Doc. no. 28: 9.

61. Doc. no. 28: 33.

62. Docs. nos. 434, 435, 1397.

63. Doc. no. 449.

64. Doc. no. 1368.

65. Doc. no. 1076.

66. An announcement from the *Gettoverwaltung,* 4 August 1944, threatened the death penalty for anyone who allowed workers of two tailoring factories (who had not reported for deportation) to stay overnight or gave them food (doc. no. 2/453).

67. Doc. no. 452.

68. Doc. no. 1/458.

69. Doc. no. 2/114. For each kitchen (family), 25 kilograms of coal was issued.

70. Doc. no. 57A (22). [Editor's note: *Tsholnt* bakeries refers to bakeries to which people without hot ovens could bring food to be slow cooked in the remaining heat, traditionally the way in which Jewish families would have a hot dish for Sabbath lunch.]

71. Doc. no. 244.

72. Doc. no. 43: 1.

73. Doc. no. 43: 11.

74. Doc. no. 55: 122–124; Tabaksblat, *Khurbn lodzh,* 67; Shlomo Frank, *Togbukh fun lodzher geto* (Buenos Aires, 1958), 36.

75. Docs. nos. 179, 299; *Geto-tsaytung,* no. 4 (28 March 1941).

76. "Tsum shandslup," *Geto-tsaytung,* nos. 3, 4, 6, 8, 9, 13, 14 (March–July 1941).

77. Docs. nos. 1052, 269, 280.

78. Doc. no. 873. At that, one was not allowed to make use "of [even] the smallest handcart" but had to carry the briquettes oneself from the lumberyard in Marysin (docs. nos. 377, 383).

79. Docs. nos. 878, 879, 880, 881.

80. Notice in *Geto-tsaytung,* no. 13 (20 June 1941).

81. ZIH archive, *Chronicle,* 22 April 1944; Y. Hiler (Diary, 150) tells of deaths due to eating these decayed vegetable remnants, and about the use of painter's glue (*moler-kley*) for cooking (303).

82. Information about this in many daily *Chronicles.*

83. Should be Pływacka. [Editor's note: Regina Pływacka was an attorney whose father was chairman of the Jewish Community Board during the first weeks of the German occupation. After the ghetto was sealed, she used a forged pass to enter the city and arranged for transfer into the ghetto of medical and x-ray equipment from the former apartments and offices of Jewish physicians. Through informants, the Kripo learned of the scheme, arrested Pływacka on 22 May 1940, and confiscated the medical equipment. Rumkowski appealed to the German authorities, including chief municipal physician Obermedizinalrat Dr. Merkert, requesting Pływacka's release and return of the equipment. The German authorities allowed Rumkowski to obtain the equipment after payment of 1,815 marks. According to one source, Pływacka was not released, but held in the jail in Poznań for a year, after which she was sent to Auschwitz, where she died. On the other hand, the ghetto *Chronicle* of 24 December 1941, in describing the first murder trial in the ghetto, identifies the defense attorney as a woman named Pływacka. Icchak (Henryk) Rubin, *Żydzi w Łodzi pod niemiecką okupacją 1939–1945* (London, 1988), 203.]

84. Editor's note: Refers to rations for individuals.

85. Editor's note: *Wydziału Towarów i Chleba.*

86. This notice presents the ghetto administration's official version about the disturbances.

87. Editor's note: Compare the somewhat different translation in Dobroszycki,

Chronicle, 18–20, once again likely reflecting the minor variations of the various typescripts of the *Chronicle*, as well as variations in rendering the original into English.

88. Editor's note: The five central community soup kitchens were located at 30 Mlynarska, 26 Zgierska, 10 Ceglana, 10 Jakuba, and 19 Lagiewnicka streets (Dobroszycki, *Chronicle*, 19).]

89. Editor's note: At 10 Ceglana (ibid.)

90. Editor's note: Cf. ibid., 218.

91. Editor's note: It is interesting how often there are divergences between the *Chronicle* texts in Trunk when compared with Dobroszycki's 1984 Yale edition. Dr. Sascha Feuchert of the Holocaust Literature Program at the University of Giessin and one of the editors of the forthcoming complete German-Polish edition of the Łódź Ghetto *Chronicle* notes that there are often differences between *Chronicle* entries reflecting interim editing and self-censorship (USHMM Łódź Ghetto Workshop, Aug. 2002). Another factor may be the effects of editing and translation decisions.

92. Editor's note: This is another instance of variation between versions of the text. In the 1984 Yale edition, it is rendered:

> The demand for potato peels, obtainable with medical certification, has recently been so great that the director of the Department of Health was forced to forbid doctors to issue any more such certificates. However, it is not always possible to refuse to give people cards. By Friday, the Department of Soup Kitchens had given out 350 authorizations for potato peels at various public kitchens. Control of the potato peels in workshop kitchens, which are exclusively for the workers employed in those enterprises, has been left to the directors.

The 1986 Hebrew edition agrees with this rendering, but not with the document published by Trunk.

93. Editor's note: These vegetables were distributed as extra items not so strictly rationed as bread, meat, and other staples. They were additions to the ghetto diet that could be bought in a given quantity for a fixed price by each person with an official ghetto identification card.

94. Editor's note: Compare the full texts in the Hebrew edition of the *Chronicle* (1986), 1: 467–468 and 1:501–502.

95. *TRóJGŁOS.*

96. Editor's note: Pagination according to Trunk, with 4 following 5.

97. Editor's note: According to the Hebrew ed., 1:467, this entry is signed BO for Bernard Ostrowski.

98. Editor's note: This segment appears in the Hebrew ed., 1:501–502, under the date 14 May 1942.

99. Editor's note: Hebrew ed., 1:554–556.

100. Editor's note: 1984 English ed., 80–81; 1986 Hebrew ed., 1: 249–250.

101. Editor's note: Satiric Yiddish slang for German Jews.

102. Editor's note: 1986 Hebrew ed., 1: 484–485.

103. Editor's note: At this point, the Hebrew edition has seven additional lines of text:

> The people descend like wild animals on the refugees selling their possessions. This really constitutes exploitation of human distress. A sort of epidemic broke out of petty self-enrichment at another's expense. Base scenes are playing out in the final stages—adjacent to the prison and in Marysin. People greedy for possessions, lacking a speck of morals and conscience, circulate in that quarter day and night and insist to the refugees that they sell to them something else or even to give them a present from the possessions

they have left for the journey, because its further fate obviously depends on luck or lack of luck during the boarding of the train.

104. Editor's note: Following the opinion of A. Wolf Jasny, Trunk holds that Hurwitz is only a pseudonym used by Dr. Józef Klementynowski, the first head of the ghetto archive. However, Lucjan Dobroszycki demonstrates that they were two separate individuals who left numerous handwritten documents that are clearly by different people. The original Hurwitz diary is at the Jewish Historical Institute in Warsaw, Rumkowski Records, no. 11. Dobroszycki, *Chronicle*, xxviiin59; Jasny, *Geshikhte fun yidn in Lodzh in di yorn fun daytsher-oysrotung* (Tel Aviv, 1960), 222, 325–326.

105. Editor's note: Compare the description of ghetto coal miners by Josef Zelkowicz, *In Those Terrible Days* (Jerusalem, 2002), 64–69.

106. Editor's note: Ironically comparing Rumkowski's summer cottage at Marysin with the Tsarist palace at Tsarskoye Selo.

IV. Forced Labor

1. Editor's note: The term *Ressort* was derived from German and commonly used in the ghetto to refer to large factories, workshops or divisions of the ghetto industry.

2. Doc. no. 55K.

3. Eisenbach, *Dokumenty* vol. 3, *Getto Łódzkie,* 102.

4. Ibid., 114–116.

5. Doc. no. NG-5340, cited by Raul Hilberg, *The Destruction of the European Jews* (Chicago: Quadrangle Books, 1961), 305–306.

6. Doc. no. 738: 15.

7. Doc. no. 199.

8. Doc. no. 217.

9. Doc. no. 33, *Chronicle*, 27 August 1942.

10. Doc. no. 41F: 3.

11. Doc. no. 758A.

12. Doc. no. 738: 6–7.

13. Doc. no. 30; *Chronicle*, 3 July 1942.

14. Doc. no. 157.

15. Doc. no. 55K.

16. Doc. no. 742, Part 1: 7.

17. ZIH Archive: G.V., file 168, p. 54. [Editor's note: Trunk actually states 87 percent.]

18. Tabaksblat, *Khurbn lodzh*, 79.

19. Doc. no. 58: 5.

20. Doc. no. 55K.

21. Doc. no. 41D.

22. Doc. no. 738: 4.

23. Ibid., 21. This basic idea was repeated in almost all the speeches (ibid., 13–21).

24. Ibid., 28.

25. Doc. no. 734.

26. Doc. no. 738: 19.

27. Ibid., 7

28. Doc. no. 1157.

29. Doc. no. 1027; doc. no. 28, *Chronicle*, 19 May 1942: list of the old and new prices.

30. Doc. no. 690.

31. Doc. no. 1157; doc. no. 1156 (circular from the Central Treasury of 28

January 1941) also refers to various types of taxes, including a "headtax," that was, it appears, later abolished.

32. Doc. no. 35, *Chronicle*, 6 January 1943.

33. Doc. no. 758A.

34. Tabaksblat, *Khurbn lodzh*, 82–83.

35. Doc. no. 33, *Chronicle*, 11 August 1942.

36. Diary (MS), 93.

37. Doc. no. 304, announcement of 23 April 1941 (no. 251); doc. no. 569.

38. Doc. no. 1616; Eisenbach, *Dokumenty*, vol. 3, *Getto Łódzkie*, 245. The mayor himself mentions in his memorandum of 24 September 1941 that the ghetto workers labored ten hours and more.

39. Doc. no. 754.

40. Doc. no. 29, *Chronicle*, 26 June 1942. The metal department had at the time taken on a large order for nails of a special type. The nails factory employed boys younger than seventeen years old (Doc. no. 29). The order was apparently not fulfilled in time.

41. Doc. no. 758A.

42. Docs. nos. 758A, 55K.

43. *Geto-tsaytung*, no. 11 (18 May 1941). The description is probably exaggerated.

44. Himmler Files, reel no. 9, exp. 90402.

45. Eisenbach, *Dokumenty*, vol. 3, *Getto Łódzkie* , 244. He writes, inter alia: "Jeder der die Verhältnisse im Getto kennt, weiss dass die Werktätigen buchstäblich an ihren Arbeitsplätzer wegen Entkräftigung zusammenbrechen" (Everyone familiar with the conditions in the ghetto knows that those working literally collapse at their work places due to debilitation).

46. Ibid., 245–246.

47. ZIH Archive, G.V., file 229: 514.

48. *Chronicle*, 2 August 1942.

49. Ibid., 20 June 1943.

50. "Entsiklopedia shel geto Łódź," *Yediot*, no. 9–10 (April 1955): 34–35; Hiler, Diary, 126.

51. Eisenbach, *Dokumenty*, vol. 3, *Getto Łódzkie*, 246.

52. Doc. no. 738: 20.

53. Eisenbach, *Dokumenty*, vol. 3, *Getto Łódzkie*, 131–132. The foreseen reduction of a series of Jewish income sources (remittances from outside, participation by the *Gettoverwaltung* in the profits from Jewish labor in the labor camps) is apparently in connection with the extermination of the Jewish population in the occupied territories and in the labor camps.

54. Yeshaye Trunk, *Shtudye tsu der geshikhte*, 113–114; memorial from *Oberfinanzpräsident beim Statthalter* in Poznań to the Reichsminister for Internal Affairs, of 18 May 1942.

55. Rumkowski Archive V/39, 593; Himmler Files, reel no. 9, exp. 90401. In that month, working for the German army were 36 factories with 11,666 workers, while 35 factories with 5,120 workers and 9,000 home workers labored for private firms.

56. Doc. no. 26, *Chronicle*, end of December 1941; doc. no. 33, *Chronicle*, 11 August 1942.

57. Doc. no. 33, *Chronicle*, 11 August 1942. [Editor's note: Cf. Dobroszycki, *Chronicle*, 240.]

58. Docs. nos. 758A, 735.

59. ZIH Archive, G.V., III/45.

60. *Proces Artura Greisera przed Najwyższym Trybunałem Narodowym* (stenogram), 1947, 157.

61. Trunk, *Shtudye tsu der geshikhte*, 115.

62. Tabaksblat, *Khurbn lodzh,* 160. [Editor's note: See the photographs in *The Last Ghetto,* ed. Michal Unger (Jerusalem, 1995), 175.]

63. Doc. no. 29, *Chronicle,* 4 June 1942.

64. *Chronicle,* January–February 1944, etc.

65. Doc. no. 727.

66. G.V., III/18: 192.

67. Doc. no. 51C.

68. Doc. no. 758A.

69. Doc. no. 41G.

70. Doc. no. 41C.

71. Doc. no. 758A.

72. In many reports from the workshops.

73. Doc. no. 24.

74. Doc. no. 26.

75. Doc. no. 30. In Marysin, 300; in the actual ghetto, 230.

76. Hiler, Diary, 177, 193.

77. Docs. nos. 273 and 416. Announcements from 7 March 1941 (no. 227) and 3 April 1942 (no. 273).

78. Doc. no. 26.

79. Doc. no. 750.

80. Editor's note: *"Bau mayim ad nefesh"* is quoted from Psalms 69:2; here as translated in *The Writings: Kethubim* (Philadelphia: Jewish Publication Society, 1987), 87. An alternate rendering is "for the waters threaten to engulf me," in *The Living Nach: The Sacred Writings* (New York: Moznaim, 1998), 125, which also notes that the eleventh-century Jewish commentator Rashi interprets the word "waters" as an allusion to the nations of the world.

81. Doc. no. 51A: 7–8. The public willingly exchanged the ghetto marks for garments and underwear. Rumkowski, who saw in this an expression of distrust for the ghetto currency, scolded this phenomenon in one of his speeches.

82. Doc. no. 30, *Chronicle,* 21 July 1942.

83. Doc. no. 1027.

84. Doc. no. 41C.

85. Doc. no. 758A; doc. no. 28, *Chronicle,* 15 May 1942.

86. Doc. no. 736.

87. Doc. no. 688.

88. Doc. no. 687.

89. Yeshaye Trunk, "Yidishe arbet-lagern in varteland," *BfG* I, nos. 1–2 (1948), 120.

90. Ibid., 119, 200. Sources known until now enumerate a total of 173 labor camps in Wartheland.

91. Ibid., 120.

92. ZIH Archive, G.V., files nos. 233 and 234.

93. Doc. no. I/29.

94. Ibid., *Chronicle,* 8 and 9 June 1942. The chronicler saw with satisfaction in this case a confirmation of Rumkowski's fundamental premise, that "work is our security passport" (ibid.).

95. G.V., VI/17: 102–114; Hiler, Diary, 177, states the number 1,500.

96. Jakub Poznański, *Pamiętnik z getta łódzkiego* (Łódź, 1960), 251. The author, who hid out after the liquidation of the ghetto, was in contact with this group until their departure. [Editor's note: The designer-artist Pinchas Szwarc/Shaar was part of this group, together with ghetto photographer Mendel Grossman. See Pinchas Shaar, "Mendel Grossman: Photographic Bard of Ghetto Lodz," in R. M. Shapiro, ed., *Holocaust Chronicles* (New York: Ktav, 1999), 128–130.]

97. Doc. no. I/29, *Chronicle,* 8, 9, and 14 June 1942; Doc. no. 35, *Chronicle,* 8–10 January 1943.

98. *Di dray feyen:* Yiddish slang abbreviation for *furmanes, fleyshers, fishers,* "the three Fs."

99. Doc. no. 24, *Chronicle,* July 1941; Sh. Frank, *Togbukh fun lodzher geto,* 63.

100. Doc. no. 25.

101. Paragraph 3 of the decree foresees that those who earn more than 84.50 marks a month must pay "wage tax and social security tax" (*soziale ausgleichsabgabe*), versus those earning between 45.50 and 84.50 marks a month who are required to pay only the social tax. This cynical paragraph, which compels Jewish workers to pay the social tax, even though they could not benefit from the sickness and unemployment insurance, even provoked criticism from Biebow, who writes in the memorandum from the *Gettoverwaltung* of 1 September 1941 that "the 15 percent reduction is incomprehensible, because the institutes of social insurance do not interest themselves in any form with Jews who are sick or unable to work" (G.V., file IV/28, 64). This paragraph is still more remarkable in that an explicit decree of the Reichsminister for Internal Affairs of 24 December 1940 (*RGBl* I, 1666) excludes Jews of Wartheland and other "incorporated eastern territories" from the obligation to pay the social tax.

102. G.V., IV/28, 61–64. On 14 September, in a memorandum to Greiser, Uebelhoer demands elimination of this decree, reiterating Biebow's arguments (Beit Lohamei Ha-Getaot Archive, doc. no. 393).

103. G.V., IV/28: 65–69. The sum of 64,380 RM is stated in the memorandum cited in the previous note.

104. G.V., IV/21: 445; IV/6: 63, 133.

105. G.V., IV/28: 61. Sick workers sent back from the camps would still arrive as late as March 1943: around mid-March, a transport of 850. See Poznański, *Pamiętnik,* 51.

106. Testimony of David Khentshinski [Chęcinski], who at the end of March 1941 was sent out with a transport of Łódź Jews to Nenkau (near Danzig), 2. Unpublished testimony at YIVO.

107. G.V., IV/28: 68.

108. Ibid., IV/27: 228.

109. Ibid., IV/12: 230.

110. "Die Judenausrottung in deutschen Lagern. Augenzeugenberichte," Geneva, 1945 [mimeograph].

111. G.V., IV/21: 494; IV/14: 365.

112. Ibid., IV/21: 217, 218, 220; IV/12: 143.

113. Ibid., IV/11: 476.

114. The following detail testifies concerning this: in the weekly reports (*Nachweisen*), a large number of those sick appears mostly on Sunday, often exceeding the number of those healthy (for example: 17 March 1943 saw 33 healthy and 55 sick; on 4 April, 19 healthy and 41 sick). But the next day, Monday, a "miracle" occurs and the number of the sick falls to a minimum. On 18 March (Monday), the number of sick, according to the status report (*Veränderungsnachweis*), fell from 55 to 6, and the number of healthy shot up from 33 to 83. The same "miracle" happened at the Kreising construction site: On 7 July 1943 (Sunday), among 193 workers, there were 129 sick; and the next day only 9 sick (G.V., IV/14, 480). Under the regime that reigned in the camps, it is impossible to imagine that such a conspicuous number of workers could be able to simulate an illness. The "'miracle'" can only be explained thus: on Sunday the camp regime was milder and the sick were not chased to work, but the next day, after the sick "got well" in a spectacular fashion, they were again driven from the barracks.

115. Yeshaye Trunk, *Yidishe arbet-lagern,* 160.

116. G.V., IV/27: 108–111.

117. Ibid., IV/14: 284–492.

118. Ibid., IV/14: 211.

119. Ibid., IV/13: 642–647. Biebow also asserts this in his aforementioned memorandum of 1 September 1942.

120. "Die Judenausrottung in deutschen Lagern," 3, 4, 6, 7.

121. Kwestionarjusze Instytutu Pamięci Narodowej (Warsaw), no. 7; G.V., V/16: 287; IV/23: 26.

122. ZIH Archive: Kwestionarjusze Instytutu Pamięci Narodowej (Warsaw), no. 2.

123. Doc. no. 30, *Chronicle,* 22 July 1942; G.V., IV/14: 161.

124. "Die Judenausrottung in deutschen Lagern," 16.

125. There were three categories: *Siegesentscheidene* (decisive for victory), *Kriegswichtige* (important for war), and *Lebenswichtige* (vitally important), according to Hoess's statement at his trial in Warsaw.

126. G.V. 33/3, 44/81, not paginated.

127. Yeshaye Trunk, *Yidishe arbet-lagern,* 180–185.

128. Editor's note: Ellipsis of three or four periods (. . . .) indicates that the document's author left out material. Ellipsis of ten or more periods (. . . . .) indicates that Trunk decided to leave out a portion of a document.

129. A camp near Pabianice, where the personal possessions of the liquidated provincial ghettos were collected and sorted.

130. Editor's note: The report is dated in 1942 by Michal Unger. Compare the translation in Josef Zelkowicz, *In Those Terrible Days: Notes from the Lodz Ghetto,* ed. Michal Unger (Jerusalem, 2002), 240–248.

131. Mordechai Bajgelman, manager of the paper factory.

132. Editor's note: Traditional Jewish religious primary school.

133. Editor's note: The site of offices of the German ghetto administration and Rumkowski's administration.

134. White camouflage dress for the Eastern Front.

135. Editor's note: See the Hebrew ed., 1: 498–499.

136. Editor's note: This refers to the ten-day periods between ration distributions.

137. The Jewish cemetery was located in the vicinity of Marysin.

138. Editor's note: Philip Friedman, born in Lwów in 1901, was a teacher and historian in prewar Łódź who survived the German occupation of Poland. From 1944 to 1946, he was the founding director of the Central Jewish Historical Commission in Poland. From 1948, he resided in New York City, where he lectured at Columbia University and at other institutions, and joined the staff of YIVO. See his *Roads to Extinction: Essays on the Holocaust,* ed. Ada June Friedman (Philadelphia: Jewish Publication Society, 1980). He died in 1960.

139. Editor's note: It would appear that Hall was to serve as an intermediary agent for the contracting of Jewish labor and production.

140. Editor's note: Aron Jakubowicz was the director of the Central Workshop Bureau and one of Rumkowski's two chief deputies. Dobroszycki, *Chronicle,* 31n43.

141. Glimmer = mica.

142. "*Baklepsidrete.*" *Klepsydra* is Polish for a public obituary notice or poster.

143. The enactment has not been preserved.

V. Diseases and Mortality

1. Mark Dvorshetski [Dworzecki], "Patalogye fun hunger in di getos," *Folksgezunt* no. 54–55 (1955); cf. Yeshaye Trunk, "Milkhome kegn yidn durkh farshpreytn krankaytn," *Yivo-bleter* 37 (New York, 1953).

2. G.V., no. 117: 365.

3. ZIH Archive: Rumkowski Archive, Statistical Department, file no. 2.

4. G.V., no. 108: 598. During the months July–December 1940, of 31 children

up to one year of age who were admitted to the hospital, 21 died; of 131 children from 1 to 8 years old, 25 died; and of 382 elderly over 60 years old, 192 died. In general, during this same period, of 2,166 newly arrived dysentery patients in the hospital, 551 died, or 25.4 percent, and in 1941 of 1,020 patients, 106 died, or 16.3 percent. As we see, the mortality in the hospital was greater than among the sick who remained at home, because on average the mortality among both types of patients amounted to no more than 11.8 percent.

5. Ibid., no. 108: 598–627.

6. Thus, for example, on 4 June 1941, the Jewish *fekalist* [excrement remover] Grinboym was shot to death on the field very close to the ghetto. G.V., 229: 159.

7. G.V., 117: 353–356, a report by Biebow about his night inspection of this work.

8. Ibid., 117: 376–377, notice about a conference on 25 June 1940 on ghetto affairs, with participation of representatives of the administrative police and sanitation authorities. At a previous conference on 21 June, Dr. Melkert reported about the police-president's refusal.

9. Ibid., no. 117: 365.

10. Ibid., no. 117: 349–352.

11. Ibid., no. 109: 86.

12. In the months November–December 1941 and January 1942, an intense epidemic of typhus raged and caused a disaster in the Gypsy camp that was located on the terrain of the ghetto. For a certain time the Gypsy camp was under the control of the Jewish ghetto administration for food and medical care. There was danger that the epidemic would extend to the Jewish population too. (Two Jewish doctors from Prague and Vienna became infected in the camp and died.) Due to the energetic sanitary resistance campaign by the Health Department, the danger was avoided at the time.

13. *Chronicle*, 2 March 1942.

14. Ibid., 20 May 1942, 190.

15. Rumkowski Archive, file no. 5.

16. *Chronicle*, July 1942.

17. Ibid., March 1944.

18. Trunk, "Milkhome kegn yidn durkh farshpreytn krankaytn," *Yivo-bleter* 37 (1953): 74–91.

19. *Chronicle*, 2 September 1942. In a certain contradiction to this, one finds the decree of the Health Department of 26 August 1942, reiterated on 24 September, that the obligation is to report every case of fever with an unknown diagnosis on the fifth or sixth day, in order to send these patients to the infection hospital (Rumkowski Archive, file no. 13).

20. *Chronicle*, 25 September 1942 [Editor's note: Dobroszycki, *Chronicle*, 261.]

21. Trunk, "Milkhome kegn yidn durkh farshpreytn krankaytn," *Yivo-bleter* 37 (1953): 100.

22. In the Warsaw Ghetto the increase in deaths from tuberculosis from 1940 to 1941 was even greater. In 1940 the average number of deaths from tuberculosis was 62.8 per month and in the first months of 1941 reached 325 a month, an increase of more than five times. If in 1940 consumption occupied its normal position in the mortality table (8.3 percent), in the first two months of 1941 it became the leading cause of death with 33.7 percent (ibid.).

23. Rumkowski Archive, file no. 5.

24. Ibid.

25. Ibid.

26. Ibid.

27. Editor's note: For a fuller, alternative translation, see Dobroszycki, *Chronicle*, 335.

28. On the night of 29–30 March 1943, the Jewish ghetto police dragged

nearly ninety sick people from their dwellings, as well as a certain number of cripples from the hospital on Dworska Street, and transferred them to the central prison from which they were shipped in "an unknown direction." The *Chronicle* adds "that only cases of open tuberculosis are designated by the commission for resettlement" (30 March 1943).

29. About the catastrophic spread of tuberculosis in the final year of the ghetto, see also the memorial by Dr. Moshe Feldman to Rumkowski, 16 June 1944, published in *Yediot beit lohamei hagitaot*, no. 13 (1956): 13–16.

30. *Chronicle,* April 1943.

31. *Chronicle,* July 1942.

32. Rumkowski Archive, no. 31. The statistics we have for 1941 testify about the ever-growing number of tuberculosis patients who reported to the tuberculosis station for X-rays: in March 501 patients were admitted there, and in December their number reached 4,813, almost tenfold more.

33. Rumkowski Archive, file no. 5. From an unknown author's introduction to a collection of statistical material on the problem touched upon (in Polish).

34. See Y. Trunk, "Shtudye tsu der geshikhte fun yidn in varteland," *BfG* 2 (1949): 86.

35. By the way, one of the Prague physicians, Dr. Boehm, died on 29 December 1941, a victim of his profession. *Chronicle,* December 1941.

36. Rumkowski Archive, file no. 5: 13, according to a table compiled in the ghetto by Dr. E. Fogel.

37. As an example of the situation in the Berlin "collectives" or dormitories, we can take Berlin Collective III, where 980 people lived (of 1,100). Of this number, during the course of seven months (by June 1942), 74 died on the spot, 78 were transferred to hospital, and 155 were deported from the ghetto. Of the remaining 673 Berliners, "330 [were] sick, swollen, and incapable of work" (Beit Lohamei Ha-Getaot Archive, doc. no. 89: 1–2; no. 658: 1). In January 1942, of 570 deaths among the deportees from Western Europe, 228 (44.6 percent) were Berliners, although they composed no more than 20 percent of the total number of Western European "settlers."

38. The deportation campaign to Chełmno in 1942 also had an influence on the large number of deaths in the months January–March 1942. In the course of time, over 44,000 people were deported. In addition to direct victims at the extermination camps, each deportation action also caused a certain number of deaths on the spot in the ghetto.

39. Editor's note: Tables 14A, 14B, and 14C are actually part of a single Table 14 in Trunk.

40. For comparison: in Warsaw the number of deaths among Jewish infants in 1936 was only 8.5 percent (L. Hersh, "Yidishe demografye," *Algemeyne Entsiklopedye, Yidn,* vol. 1: 363).

41. *Chronicle* of 19 August 1942 [Editor's note: Trunk gives 28 August]. Compare J. Poznański, *Pamiętnik z getta Łódźkiego* (1960), 156. [Editor's note: Cf. Dobroszycki, *Chronicle,* 242; *Kronika Getta Łódzkiego* (1965), 2: 215.]

42. Trunk, "Milkhome kegn yidn durkh farshpreytn krankaytn," *Yivo-bleter* 37 (1953): 92.

43. Ibid., 100.

VI. Persecutions, Murder, and Deportations

1. YIVO Archive, testimony of Kh. L. Fuks.

2. TA: Doc. no. 55b.

3. Tabaksblat, *Khurbn lodzh,* 21–23. Another source (testimony in *Sefer Ha-Zevaot,* 60) states that the number of those arrested was forty and the number shot to death was fifteen.

4. *Undzer Lodzh,* no. 4. A large number of reports about the torments of the Łódź Jews in the first months of the occupation are published in *Sefer Ha-Zevaot.*

5. Doc. no. 630.

6. Shlomo Frank, *Togbukh fun Lodzher geto* (Buenos Aires, 1958), 10.

7. Doc. no. 643.

8. Testimony of Kh. L. Fuks.

9. Doc. no. 1021: 3.

10. According to these decrees, the following had the right of confiscation: Himmler as the Chief of the SS and Police and *Reichskommissar* for the Fortification of the German Race; and the police organs that were subject to him; the Eastern Commander (*Der Befehlshaber Ost*) and his plenipotentiary for confiscation of raw materials and half-fabricated products, Major-General Biermann; and the *Haupttreuhandstelle Ost.*

11. Testimony of Kh. L. Fuks, 25.

12. Eisenbach, *Dokumenty* vol. 3, *Getto Łódzkie,* 62–68.

13. Stenogram of Greiser's trial, 27.

14. Y. Nirenberg, "Geshikhte fun Lodzher geto," 220. A group of Jewish tanners still worked in town until 2 June 1942 (doc. no. A/29, *Chronicle,* 2 June 1942).

15. Editor's note: Christopher Browning describes the Hamburg Reserve Police Battalion 101, based for several months in Łódź in 1940 and involved in deportations and guarding ghettos. See *Ordinary Men: Reserve Police Battalion 101 and the Final Solution in Poland* (New York: HarperCollins, 1993), xvi, 39, 41–44, 50, 92, 148.

16. Doc. no. 55B; YIVO Archive, testimony of B. Frenkel: "Lodzher marishin-geto," 14–15. This mass murder by an ethnic German was an act of revenge against a Jewish customer who did not pay him for twelve chickens that were smuggled into the ghetto with his help, because they were confiscated by the Jewish police. His calculation was two Jews for each unpaid chicken. Another guard with a treacherous enticing voice shot dead eleven Jews.

17. Doc. no. 794. According to a 10 May 1940 decree by the police-president, the ghetto guards were authorized to fire without warning at any Jew attempting to leave the ghetto (Eisenbach, *Dokumenty* vol. 3, *Getto Łódzkie,* 83–84). Tabaksblat (*Khurbn lodzh,* 110) states that two German physicians came into the ghetto with the purpose of "hunting hares and two old Jews fell dead."

18. Doc. no. 26. The cases of murder were noted in the *Chronicle,* 3, 5, 7, 21, 24, and 29 December 1941.

19. TA: Doc. no. 473.

20. Doc. no. 26. *Chronicle,* 29–31 December 1941.

21. Doc. no. 392.

22. *Chronicle,* various dates.

23. Docs. nos. 29, 33: 18. *Chronicle,* 22 June and 18 August 1942, et al.

24. Doc. no. 28, *Chronicle,* May 1942.

25. Docs. nos. 28 and 29, *Chronicle,* 28 June 1942, 17 July 1944, et al.

26. TA: Doc. no. 325.

27. Statements by Avraham Levkovitsh (Lewkowicz), printworker in the ghetto, now in New York.

28. *The Persecution of Jews in German-Occupied Poland,* no. 2 (May 1940): 18.

29. Doc. no. 1399, Announcement no. 356.

30. Doc. no. 27, combined *Chronicle,* 14–31 January 1942.

31. *Chronicle,* the last ten days of February 1942. [Editor's note: Also see the entry describing the execution in the published notebooks of the *Chronicle* staff writer, Oskar Rosenfeld, *In the Beginning Was the Ghetto,* ed. Hanno Loewy,

trans. Brigitte M. Goldstein (Evanston, Ill.: Northwestern University Press, 2002), 81–84.]

32. Doc. no. 430, Announcement no. 387 of 27 June 1942. The announcement reminds the ghetto residents that this obligation, which apparently was introduced earlier, is not being fulfilled. The prior announcement has not been found. Still earlier, on 19 June, Rumkowski had issued a circular about this to all departments and workshops, instructing about how to behave during visitations by German commissions (doc. no. 29, *Chronicle,* 21 June 1942). Announcements about the obligation to salute are reiterated on 6 January and on 10 February 1944 (docs. nos. 1363 and 1365). [Editor's note: The salute had to be given by Jewish pedestrians to Germans in passing vehicles as well.]

33. Documents from Greiser's trial, photocopy of document in *B.G.K.B.Z.H. w Polsce,* vol. 13: 28F–29F.

34. W. Bednarz, *Obóz straceń w Chełmnie nad Nerem,* 13.

35. *Chronicle* from the end of July 1941; doc. no. 1463; Tabaksblat, *Khurbn lodzh,* 117 and 154. The date cited by Tabaksblat on page 154 is incorrect. The system of murdering the chronically and mentally ill, as well as the handicapped, had already been applied by the Nazis much earlier. In Łódź, the department for the mentally ill (*nervn-kranke*) of the Poznański Hospital was "evacuated" in March 1940 (doc. no. 54: 1). In Kalisz, on 27 and 28 October 1940, three groups of patients and elderly people were "outsettled." They numbered 250 people who were calmed with promises that they were traveling to be "treated" in a sanatorium. They all died in a nearby wood (ZIH Archive, testimony no. 567).

36. "Erlass die Entjudung des Warthegaues betreffend vom 2.I.1942/1/50, 142/.g[eheim]." The decree has not been found. We learn about it from his letter to the Łódź mayor, dated 13 December 1942 (G.V. 40/41, not paginated.)

37. *B.G.K.B.Z.H.,* vol. 3: 24–26.

38. Ringelblum Archive, I, no. 1256.

39. Doc. no. 46: 97.

40. Doc. no. 1221.

41. *Chronicle* for January, cited by A. Volf Yasni, *Di oysrotung fun Lodzher yidn* (Tel Aviv, 1950), 8.

42. Tabaksblat, *Khurbn lodzh,* 122.

43. Doc. no. 391, Announcement no. 347.

44. Doc. no. 399, Announcement no. 355.

45. Frank, *Togbukh fun Lodzher geto* (Buenos Aires, 1958), 230.

46. Tabaksblat, *Khurbn lodzh,* 122–123.

47. Doc. no. 411. This procedure is first documented in Announcement no. 368 of 2 March 1942, but it was applied, as is known, from the very start.

48. *Chronicle* (January 1942): 37, cited by Yasni, *Di oysrotung fun Lodzher yidn,* 10–11.

49. ZIH Archive. File "Statistics" in the Rumkowski Archive. Among the 10,103 deported were 4,263 men and 5,740 women.

50. In the above-cited diary by Sh. Frank (*Togbukh fun Lodzher geto*), it is told that on 4 February Rumkowski was informed by the Gestapo that the deportation action was to be renewed, but under the date of 11 February the author noted that in a second notice from the Gestapo the action was temporarily halted due to the ordained suspension of train service (*banshpere*) in Wartheland (253–254).

51. File "Statistics" in Rumkowski Archive. [Editor's note: It is unclear if the figures do not include 9,000 children or if the total is a typographic error.]

52. Doc. no. 46.

53. TA: Doc. no. 415.

54. Doc. no. 46.

55. Doc. no. 417.

56. Docs. nos. 419–423. Sh. Frank (*Togbukh fun Lodzher geto*, 255) states that on 26 April a call was published "that all physically healthy people in the ages from 10 to 60 were to report to a special labor commission. Those whom the commission would determine are not capable of any work will have to leave the ghetto. On their bread cards will be a stamp 'Incapable of any work.'" This fact is not confirmed in light of the documentation about the stamp decree in the YIVO Archive; the announcement of 23 April bears the number 377, the one from 27 April is labeled no. 378, i.e., between both of these dates no other new announcements were issued. The announcement of 27 April does not know of any changes in the procedure heretofore and continues to call on all who had not reported by that date to appear before the medical commission. The reason why the commission's stamping was halted on 26 January is quite simple: it was a Sunday and the commission was not active that day.

57. Doc. no. 423.

58. Doc. no. 1/423. By 2 May, the final day to report to the commission, over 11,000 people were stamped with the letters A and B (*Chronicle*, 4 May 1942).

59. Beit Lohamei Ha-Getaot Archive, doc. no. 70: 2–3.

60. Doc. no. 1199.

61. Y. Trunk, "Mayrev-eyropeyishe yidn in mizrekh-eyropeyishe getos," *Di Goldene keyt* (1953), 98.

62. In his speech delivered at the exhibition of the underwear and clothing division on 17 January 1942, Rumkowski expressed words like the following about the Western European exiles: "I will strive to settle accounts with them, too, with the German Jews. Their luck is that the outsettlement has come along; their own judgment day will yet come" (Beit Lohamei Ha-Getaot Archive, doc. no. 88).

63. In a speech that Rumkowski gave at the celebration of the first twenty-five marriages among the deportees, he admitted that he was not prepared for such a large number of Western European Jews as arrived.

64. Doc. no. 28, *Chronicle*, 16 May 1942; Rumkowski Archive, file V/39: 262–267, 270. Here the number cited is 279.

65. Ibid., *Chronicle*, 6 May 1942.

66. Beit Lohamei Ha-Getaot Archive, doc. no. 88: 24.

67. Ibid., doc. no. 658.

68. Ibid., doc. no. 89.

69. Ibid., doc. no. 88: 24.

70. Ibid., doc. no. 88: 9–10.

71. *Chronicle*, May 1942.

72. Beit Lohamei Ha-Getaot Archive, doc. no. 88: 31.

73. Ibid., doc. no. 88: 18.

74. Rumkowski Archive, file "Statistics." The *Chronicle*, 17 May 1942 states that about 300 persons from the local population voluntarily reported for deportation in a vivid indication of the desperate mood in the ghetto.

75. Doc. no. 28, *Chronicle*, May 1942.

76. Doc. no. 28, *Chronicle*, 9–11 May 1942. [Editor's note: Cf. Dobroszycki, *Chronicle*, 168. There were several hundred "non-Aryan" Christians in the ghetto, considered Jews under the Nuremburg laws.]

77. Doc. no. 29. Even an official of the Central Accounting Office was arrested for spreading the "false" rumors.

78. Ibid., *Chronicle*, 6 and 7 June 1942.

79. Doc. no. 30, *Chronicle*, 2 and 21 July 1942.

80. Ibid., *Chronicle*, 3 July 1942.

81. Ibid., *Chronicle*, 18 July 1942.

82. Ibid., *Chronicle*, 4 August 1942.

83. Doc. no. 33, *Chronicle*, 25 August 1942.

84. Doc. no. 30, *Chronicle*, 11 July 1942.

85. Doc. no. 33, *Chronicle,* 28 August 1942. Biebow took an active part in this bloody action, during which several hundred people were shot at the cemetery (Tabaksblat, *Khurbn lodzh,* 147–148).

86. G.V. 44/81, not paginated. Protocol from the start of September 1942 of the conference between *Obersturmführer* Melhorn, *Regierungsrat* Heusler and two representatives of the German ghetto administration.

87. G.V. I/55: 252, 255, cited in Eisenbach, *Hitlerowska polityka eksterminacyjna,* 311–312. In July 1942, Himmler predicted "the elimination of the Jewish population from the occupied territories" (see *Trials of War Criminals before the Nuremberg Military Tribunals,* vol. 14: 1011.)

88. See Yasni, *Di oysrotung fun Lodzher yidn,* 21.

89. Doc. no. 54, Y. Zelkowicz, "In yene koshmarne teg," 2.

90. Tabaksblat, *Khurbn lodzh,* 155–156.

91. Zelkowicz, "In yene koshmarne teg," 4, 5.

92. Ibid., 11.

93. Ibid., 12.

94. TA: Doc. no. 54: 18–19.

95. TA: Doc. no. 434.

96. Y. Nirenberg, "Geshikhte fun Lodzher geto," 270. Tabaksblat cites the figure of about 1,000.

97. Tabaksblat, *Khurbn lodzh,* 158.

98. Nirenberg, "Geshikhte fun Lodzher geto," 270. [Editor's note: Cf. Yankl Nirenberg, *Zikhroynes fun Lodzher geto* (Buenos Aires, 1996), 84.]

99. Zelkowicz, "In yene koshmarne teg," p. 47.

100. Editor's note: *Khapers* were notoriously employed by some Jewish community leaders in Tsarist Russia when forced to provide young boys and men as conscripts in the time of Nicholas I, 1827–1855.

101. Reportage by Oskar Singer about the September Action, cited by J. Kermisz, ed., *Dokumenty i materiały do dziejów okupacji niemieckiej w Polsce,* vol. 2, *"Akcje" i "Wysiedlenia"* (Łódź, 1946), 246.

102. Tabaksblat, *Khurbn lodzh,* 156.

103. At the start of March 1943, during the dismantling of a house in the ghetto, the little bodies of three children were discovered in a cellar, where they had been hidden by parents who died during the action. [Leon Hurwitz], Diary, 43.

104. Zelkowicz, "In yene koshmarne teg," 59.

105. Ibid., 33.

106. Ibid.

107. Ibid., 40.

108. Kermisz, *Dokumenty i materiały,* 249.

109. Ibid., 249–250.

110. Zelkowicz, "In yene koshmarne teg," 41.

111. Doc. no. 1397.

112. Y. Nirenberg, "Geshikhte fun Lodzher geto," 241; Y. L. Girsht, *Min ha-meitsar,* 28.

113. Photograph no. 241.

114. Zelkowicz, "In yene koshmarne teg," 53. Nirenberg states that twenty-one were hanged. The carrying out of the public execution spectacle by hanging shortly before or during the "outsettlement" actions was part of the German hangman's style. Such public executions took place in February 1942 in Wieluń (ten people); in Brzeziny in March (ten people); ten victims each in Zduńska-Wola, Łęczyca, and Bełchatów, and five in Podembice. In April, two Jews were hanged in Piątek, eight Jews in Ozorków, and, in June 1942, ten Jews in the village ghetto in Nowy Ciachulec (?) (Turek district). ZIH Archive: Ringelblum Archive I, no. 41; questionnaires of the Polish Institute of National Memory, no. 7; manuscripts of towns no. 151: 218.

115. Zelkowicz, "In yene koshmarne teg," 57.

116. Ibid., 58.

117. Nirenberg, "Geshikhte fun Lodzher geto," 270–271.

118. Zelkowicz, "In yene koshmarne teg," 69–70.

119. Nirenberg, "Geshikhte fun Lodzher geto," 269.

120. According to the compilation by Dr. Edward Rosset, director of the Statistical Office at the Łódź City Administration; see Yasni, *Di oysrotung fun Lodzher yidn,* 29. According to a calculation by the German ghetto administration, between 2 and 12 September there were 15,685 people deported, among them 1,253 patients (on 2 September). See G.V., 168: 63–64.

121. TA: Doc. no. 71.

122. Doc. no. 435.

123. Doc. no. 436.

124. G.V., V/16: 108; IV/25: 192–193. The contents of the decree of 18 March was published in Eisenbach, *Dokumenty* vol. 3, *Getto Łódzkie,* 209–210, according to Biebow's circular of 20 April 1942. By error, the date given there is 23 March.

125. Doc. no. 437.

126. Editor's note: Economic Administrative Main Office, headed by SS General Oswald Pohl, which administered concentration camps and operated the SS business enterprises in camps and ghettos.

127. Editor's note: The Yiddish text seems to be missing words here. The translation reflects Trunk's handwritten correction on his own copy of the book.

128. In fact, the ghetto on 1 June 1943 numbered 84,887 souls. See A. Melezin, *Przyczynek do znajomości stosunków demograficznych wśród ludności żydowskiej w Łodzi,* (Łódź: Central Jewish Historical Commission, 1946), 44.

129. Doc. no. NO-485.

130. Doc. no. NO-519, copy of a letter from Pohl to Himmler, dated 9 February 1944.

131. Doc. no. 943 of the Eichmann documents provided by the Israel Police for his trial.

132. About a conference at Weapons Inspectorate XXI (Poznań District) on 30 November 1943, concerning retaining the Łódź Ghetto for the needs of the *Wehrmacht,* see Raul Hilberg, *The Destruction of the European Jews* (Chicago: Quadrangle Books, 1961), 333.

133. Doc. no. NO-519, handwritten short protocol of the meeting; cf. Eisenbach *Dokumenty* vol. 3, *Getto Łódzkie,* 383. A visit by Eichmann to Łódź was already announced in a telegram from Kaltenbrunner of 30 June 1943 (verdict in Eichmann trial, mimeographed, par. 133).

134. Eisenbach, *Hitlerowska polityka eksterminacji Żydów,* 383.

135. Doc. no. NO-519. That somebody did well from the Jewish slave labor in the ghetto can be seen from Horn's own determination in the same report: in the single year 1943 Jewish workers did not receive a sum of 18 million marks that flowed into the coffers of the German ghetto administration, *Statthalter* Greiser and German weapons concerns (ibid.).

136. *Chronicle,* 18 February 1944.

137. Doc. no. NO-519, file note compiled by Dr. Volk on 9 February 1944.

138. *Trials of War Criminals before N.M.T.,* vol. 5: 1049.

139. After an interruption in the operation of the Chełmno death factory from 11 April 1943, the Chełmno camp resumed its activity in spring 1944, with almost the same staff. See W. Bednarz, *Obóz straceń w Chełmnie n/Nerem* (1946), 36.

140. Doc. no. NO-519, copy of Greiser's letter to Pohl of 14 February 1944.

141. Eisenbach, *Hitlerowska polityka eksterminacji Żydów,* 389. [Editor's note: Cf. the differences with Dobroszycki, *Chronicle,* 452. Clearly, Trunk did not always have access to the original *Chronicle* texts. Some of the differences may also be attributed to the style of editing in the Yale edition.]

142. Yasni, *Di oysrotung fun Lodzher yidn,* 41. [Editor's note: Cf. Dobroszycki, *Chronicle,* 459, which varies from this text. Trunk was dependent on Yasni's version that appears to be more of a summary than a full translation.]

143. Doc. no. 1389 in the documents of the Eichmann trial in Jerusalem. Photocopy in YIVO Archive.

144. Documentation Centre, Berlin, docs. nos. 334, 335, cited by Eisenbach, *Hitlerowska polityka eksterminacji Żydów,* 392.

145. Doc. no. 447.

146. TA: Doc. no. 449.

147. TA: Doc. no. 450.

148. *Chronicle* from end of February 1944.

149. Doc. no. 1368.

150. Hiler, Diary, 172.

151. Ibid., 177–179.

152. Ibid., 293.

153. Doc. no. 488, announcement of 9 June 1944.

154. *Chronicle,* June 1944, cited by Yasni, *Di oysrotung fun Lodzher yidn,* 48–49.

155. TA: Doc. no. 452.

156. Doc. no. 1370, announcement of 18 June 1944.

157. *Chronicle,* June 1944, cited by Yasni, *Di oysrotung fun Lodzher yidn,* 49.

158. Yasni, *Di oysrotung fun Lodzher yidn,* 50 (according to the daily *Chronicle*); Hiler, Diary, 414, 416–418.

159. Yasni, *Di oysrotung fun Lodzher yidn,* 50 (according to the *Chronicle*); Hiler, Diary, 411, 436–437.

160. Hiler, Diary, 417–418.

161. Ibid., 349.

162. Doc. no. 38, *Chronicle* [12 July 1944].

163. Doc. no. 38, *Chronicle,* 13 July 1944.

164. Hiler, Diary, 414, 417, 446.

165. Doc. no. 38, *Chronicle,* 12 July 1944.

166. A. Eisenbach, "Di yidishe literarish-kinstlerishe mishpokhe in Lodzher geto (in der helft 1944)," *Undzer Lodzh* (Buenos Aires) no. 2 (November 1951), 60–62.

167. *Chronicle,* 18 July 1944; Hiler, Diary, 417, 448.

168. *Chronicle,* 19 July 1944.

169. Doc. no. 38, *Chronicle,* 12 and 29 July 1944. Hiler (Diary, 431) noted that in addition to the 560 people of the first transport, 50 were sent to Aleksandrów near Łódź and 100 were sent into the city. He also recounts that before the departure of the first transport Gestapo Commissioner Fuchs assured the crowd in a speech that they were going to Munich for work.

170. Doc. no. 38, *Chronicle,* 16 July 1944; YIVO Archive, testimony of Binyomin Frenkel, "Likvidatsye fun der Lodzher geto—summer 1944," 5. Inter alia, the blanket factory was liquidated (liquidation document of 19 July 1944, doc. no. 733).

171. Doc. no. 38, *Chronicle,* 16 July 1944.

172. Doc. no. 38, *Chronicle,* 19, 25, and 27 July 1944.

173. Ibid. At Neftalin's observation that his department did not maintain a rubric of capability of work and therefore could not provide such material, Biebow replied that he would obtain this data at the Health Department.

174. Doc. no. 491; doc. no. 38, *Chronicle,* 21 July 1944.

175. Doc. no. 38, *Chronicle,* 21 July 1944.

176. Doc. no. 38, *Chronicles* under the respective dates.

177. *Chronicle,* 20 July 1944.

178. Editor's note: "*un bay di arbeters in di varshtatn hobn zikh di hent nisht gehoybn tsu der arbet.*"

179. *Chronicle,* 30 July 1944.

180. *Chronicle,* 21 July 1944.

181. Hiler, Diary, 391–392.

182. Testimony of B. Frenkel, "Likvidatsye fun der Lodzher geto," 5; *Chronicles* of 25 July and following; Hiler, Diary, 295ff.

183. Testimony of B. Frenkel, "Likvidatsye fun der Lodzher geto." 4; Hiler, Diary, 424.

184. News of the Normandy landings was known in the ghetto on the same day (6 June 1944), as was news of the fall of Rome. Hiler often cites news about the German defeats (e.g., Diary, 306, 317, 343, 378, 379). He comments about the news with political assessments apparently taken from the London radio.

185. TA: Doc. no. 38.

186. Hiler, Diary, 415.

187. Doc. no. 453.

188. Doc. no. 45A.

189. Hiler, Diary, 563.

190. Doc. no. 492; Hiler, Diary, 574. It was, it turns out, an empty boast, because the story that Biebow and the Gestapo commissioner released the captured Jews was no more than a well-directed spectacle to win trust among the victims. Hiler also noted "that Biebow says that it's his bit of work" (575).

191. Doc. no. 1386.

192. Hiler, Diary, 568.

193. TA: Doc. no. 1371.

194. Doc. no. 454.

195. Doc. no. 457.

196. Hiler, Diary, 577.

197. TA: Doc. no. 1283.

198. Hiler, Diary, 562.

199. Ibid., 568.

200. Ibid., 561.

201. Ibid., 573.

202. Ibid., 562.

203. Ibid., 569, 571.

204. Ibid., 574.

205. Doc. no. 493.

206. TA: Doc. no. 458A.

207. Doc. no. 1390.

208. Testimony of B. Frenkel, "Likvidatsye fun Lodzher geto," 7.

209. Doc. no. 459.

210. Docs. nos. 494, 495, 497, 1393.

211. Doc. no. 1392. [Editor's note: YIVO Archives, Zonabend Collection, Folder 568].

212. Hiler, Diary, 578.

213. Nirenberg, "Geshikhte fun Lodzher geto," 291–292.

214. Ibid.; YIVO Archive, testimony of Mordkhe Goldshteyn, 2.

215. [TA: This note is crossed out by Trunk.] The boundaries of this eliminated area were: on the south side—corner of Bałuty Marketplace and Łagiewnicka to the corner of Bałuty Marketplace and Zgierska Street; on the west side—corner of Bałuty Marketplace and Zgierska to the corner of Zgierska and Goplańska Street in the direction of the corner Brzezińska to Zgierska at the church, down to the corner of Nowomiejska and Nad Łódką; on the north side—from the last point to the corner of Goplańska and Żurawia, from there to the corner Żurawia-Stefana, along Żurawia, Stefana, to the corner of Stefana-Łagiewnicka; on the east side—from the corner of Bałuty Marketplace and Łagiewnicka to the corner of Łagiewnicka and Stefana.

216. Doc. no. 1387.

217. Doc. no. 1394.

218. Docs. 1395; 497A.

219. [TA: This note is crossed out by Trunk.] The boundaries of this again reduced area were: in the west—from the corner of Brzezińska-Marysińska to the corner of Marysińska-Roberta; in the south—from the latter point to the corner of Roberta and Emilii Plater; continuing along Bracka to the ghetto fencing; in the north—through Środkowa Street along the ghetto enclosure.

220. TA: Doc. no. 1380.

221. Doc. no. 1380. [Editor's note: In Trunk's annotated copy, the description of the rump ghetto's boundaries is crossed out.]

222. Yasni, *Di oysrotung fun Lodzher yidn*, 64–65.

223. Hiler, Diary, entries from 6–8 August 1944.

224. When leaving their apartments, people intentionally did not turn off the electricity, hoping that this could perhaps attract Allied pilots at night (testimony of B. Frenkel, "Likvidatsye fun der Lodzher geto," 9).

225. Doc. no. 498.

226. This factory produced cement sheeting (*plites*) in Radogoszcz for replacement housing in the bombed German areas.

227. Bendet Hershkovitsh, "Litsmanshtat-geto," *Yivo-bleter* 30, no. 1 (1947), 57–58. [Editor's note: Cf. Bendet Hershkovitsh, "The Ghetto in Litzmannstadt (Łódź)," *YIVO Annual of Jewish Social Science* 5 (1950), 121.]

228. Hershkovitsch, "Litsmanshtat-geto," 57–58.

229. Eisenbach, *Dokumenty,* Vol. 3, *Getto Łódzkie,* 266; J. Kermisz, *Akcje i Wysiedlenia* (Łódź, 1946), lxvii–lxviii; YIVO Archive, testimony of Yehudis Ayzikovitsh, 5.

230. Testimony of Yehudis Ayzikovitsh, 3.

231. Hershkovitsh, "Litsmanshtat-geto," 58.

232. Lonye Bimko, "Mayn rayze fun Lodzher geto tsum farnikhtung lager oyshvits," *Undzer Lodzh,* no. 3: 57. She herself could not withstand the hunger and "voluntarily" reported to the transport in Marysin on 25 August.

233. Testimony of Yehudis Ayzikovitsh, 3. After the arrival of the Soviets, several former ghetto policemen and other scoundrels were tried and banished into the Soviet Union.

234. Ibid., 4. Cf. also J. Poznański, *Pamiętnik z getta Łódźkiego*, 257–269, which contains many unknown details about the life of these last groups of Łódź Jews before the liberation.

235. Testimony of Y. Ayzikovitsh, 5.

236. Eisenbach, *Dokumenty,* Vol. 3, *Getto Łódzkie*, 275–276.

237. Franz Kursky Archive of the Jewish Labor Movement [Editor's note: Now at YIVO], "File Beyglman."

238. Editor's note: *Wołyniaków,* ethnic Germans or *Volksdeutsche* from Volhynia in northern Ukraine.

239. Editor's note: Compare with the version in Zelkowicz, *In Those Terrible Days,* 280–283.

240. Editor's note: Three or four dot ellipsis (. . .) in the text reflects the original text. Omission of material by Trunk's selection is indicated by a row of dashes or ellipses (. . . . .).

241. Editor's note: See the full text in Zelkowicz, *In Those Terrible Days*, 251–381.

242. Editor's note: Biblical name for a god or idol to whom living people were sacrificed.

243. Editor's note: The White Guard was the nickname for the teamsters and porters who transported flour and other bulk items in the ghetto.

244. Editor's note: Slang, after Rumkowski, for the ghetto money that was worthless outside the ghetto and could buy little within the ghetto.

245. Editor's note: Typographic error in Yiddish "*dat;*" should be "*rat.*"

246. Editor's note: Trunk has here combined selections from two different issues of the *Chronicle*.

247. Editor's note: Ghetto *Chronicle*, 22 July 1944. Perhaps this is an allusion to the attempt on Hitler's life on 20 July 1944, or to the establishment on 21 July in the USSR of the Soviet-backed Polish government in the USSR; or to the Red Army's liberation of Chełm Lubelski on 22 July. Compare Dobroszycki, *Chronicle*, 531–532 and n. 24; and Hebrew *Chronicle* (1989), 4:512 and n. 91.

248. Editor's note: *Chronicle*, 23 July 1944. Cf. Dobroszycki, *Chronicle*, 532; and Hebrew *Chronicle* (1989), 4:514.

249. Editor's note: Compare the somewhat different German text of *Bekanntmachung* Nr. 428 (YIVO: Zonabend 563; and published in Hanno Loewy et al., eds., *Unser einziger Weg ist Arbeit . . . eine Ausstellung des Jüdischen Museums Frankfurt am Main* [Vienna: Löcker, 1990], 272).

VII. Internal Conditions

1. Doc. no. 58: 3, table by Statistical Office.

2. Ibid.

3. Doc. no. 1212.

4. Editor's note: See the alphabetical list of Polish street names with alternate German names in the appendices to this book.

5. Doc. IT.

6. Doc. no. 184A.

7. Editor's note: This would have put Łódź under Soviet rule.

8. Doc. no. 133.

9. Doc. no. 25: 12.

10. Doc. no. 28: 9.

11. Doc. no. 30, p. 20; doc. no. [?], *Chronicle,* 5 June 1942.

12. Doc. no. 14, p. 15. The author of a diary written in the Łódź Ghetto relates that there were eleven persons in the room where he lived with his family, including couples with children. Hiler, Diary, 58, recorded on 14 January 1944.

13. Doc. no. 30: 30.

14. TA: Doc. no. 55: 37, 76.

15. Doc. no. 23: 2.

16. Doc. no. 14: 18.

17. TA: Doc. no. 49D.

18. Friedrich Hielscher, *Fünfzig Jahre unter Deutschen* (Hamburg, 1954), 361.

19. Testimony of Margit Galat from Prague, 7–8; Trunk, "Mayrev-eyropeishe yidn," *Goldene Keyt* (April 1953): 89.

20. Doc. no. 58, Table 5.

21. Doc. no. 58, Table 11; cf. Trunk, "Shtudye tsu der geshikhte," 86.

22. A. Melezin, *Przyczynek do znajomości stosunków demograficznych wśród żydowskiej . . . podczas okupacji niemieckiej* (Łódź, 1946), 21–22.

23. Tabaksblat, *Khurbn lodzh*, 79. On 17 June 1944, there were 42,486 women and 28,945 men employed in all the ghetto's workplaces, i.e., men were only a bit more than two-fifths of all those employed. G.V. 168: 167–168.

24. Melezin, *Przyczynek*, 24–25. [Editor's note: There are some minor discrepancies between the figures cited by Trunk and those on the cited pages of Melezin.]

25. Doc. no. 55: 25. We bring from there a characteristic quotation about a family situation: "She [the wife] sleeps in her bed, I [the husband] on my settee, she still has her bedding, I have already sold mine. Therefore she raises a child, she sits in her corner, I in mine. . . . She eats her bread, I mine, I have a cup for my soup—she for her soup. . . . I didn't make life this way, she didn't make it this way."

26. Docs. nos. 46C, 49A.

27. Hiler, Diary, 8.

28. Doc. no. 55: 27.

29. Doc. no. 1255: 14.

30. Testimony of Binyomin Frenkel, 39.

31. Doc. no. 55: 17.

32. Melezin, *Przyczynek*, 15–16. During the entire year of 1943, a total of 210 births were recorded in the ghetto—2.6 per thousand in comparison with 14.8 per thousand in the years 1929–1938. A curious phenomenon in connection with births, which reflects the tragic situation in the field of provisioning in 1944, was noted by Poznański (*Pamiętnik,* 168): in the spring months of 1944, there were registered three times as many births as in the previous three months, and the author explains this phenomenon with the fact that a child immediately gets a food card as soon as it is born, in addition to supplemental food for the mother and child; "a clean profit and a good deal without risk," comments the diarist Poznański.

33. TA: Doc. no. 55: 14, 28.]

34. Doc. no. 55: 12.

35. Ibid., 130.

36. Doc. no. 736: 3–4. [Editor's note: See the diary excerpt about the adoption of a young child in the Łódź Ghetto in summer 1942, quoted in Robert M. Shapiro, ed., *Holocaust Chronicles*, 108–109.]

37. Doc. no. 736: 3.

38. Ibid.

39. Ibid., 4.

40. Doc. no. 55: 28.

41. Editor's note: A young girl named either Esther or Minia wrote in her brief diary in the Łódź Ghetto, "There is no justice. And even less in the ghetto." Lucjan Dobroszycki, ed., "Polska Anna Frank nazywała się," *Mówią Wieki*, no. 7 (1958). Marian Turski, "Individual Experience in Diaries from the Łódź Ghetto," in Shapiro, *Holocaust Chronicles,* 120–121, publishes some extracts from Esther/Minia's diary:

> You can fall down and nobody will lift you up; a human life is of no value. Hundreds of human lives are of no consequence. Each looks out for himself. Lately, I have become more hardened so that nothing, even the worst suffering, moves me. This is what mankind has taught me. . . .
>
> The hunger is getting worse. In the morning, I wish that my father would leave—since then I can jump from bed and eat the piece of bread my mother left me for the whole day. Oh, God. What has become of me! I cannot contain myself and then I am hungry for the whole day. How I wish I were different! God have pity on me. . . .
>
> It appears I have no more heart. I have no more pity. I eat anything I have in front of me. Today I quarreled with my father. I verbally abused him and even cursed him for the following reason: After I weighed 20 dkg of farfel, the next day I took just a spoonful of it, and in the evening when my father came he weighed it once more and, of course, there was less. My father complained. He was right. Am I entitled to eat this individual dkg that our Chairman [Rumkowski] gave us to cook? I got upset and cursed my father. What did I do! I am sorry for what happened, but what is done cannot be undone. My father will never forgive me. I will not be able to look him straight in the eye. He stood at the window and started crying like a small child.

42. ZIH Archive, G.V., VI/53: 295. This children's demonstration was probably influenced by the workers' agitation conducted against Rumkowski that caused two street demonstrations in the same month (see below).

43. Nirenberg, "Geshikhte fun Lodzher Geto," 249. D. Dąbrowska, "Zagłada skupisk żydowskich w 'Kraju Warty' w okresie okupacji hitlerowskiej," *BZIH,* no. 13–14: 150. Here the month of the demonstration is given as January.

44. Doc. no. 796.

45. Rene Fodor, "Di virkung fun der natsisher okupatsye fun poyln af di bat-siungen tsvishn muter un kind bay yidn," *Yivo-bleter* 40 (1956): 162–163; Rene Fodor, "Agresye fun kinder in a toyt-sakone," *Yivo-bleter* 37 (1953): 248–250.

46. Editor's note: "Before the hoary head you shall rise up, and you shall honor the face of the old man, and you shall fear your God: I am the Lord." (Leviticus 19: 32).

47. Doc. no. 1213: 2.

48. Testimony of B. Frenkel, "Lodzher marishin-ghetto," 87.

49. Doc. no. 55: 121.

50. "Entsiklopedia shel geto Lodzh," *Yediot bet lohamei ha-getaot,* no. 14–15: 63. According to a compilation by the Statistical Office, at the sealing of the ghetto its Jewish population consisted of 38.5 percent local residents, 58 percent people who had arrived from elsewhere in the city, and 4 percent from the province (Doc. IT: 16).

51. TA: Doc. no. 1248 from the document collection for the Eichmann trial.

52. The memorandum from the mayor is reprinted in Eisenbach, *Dokumenty* vol. 3, *Getto Łódzkie,* 197–200; Übelhör's telegram to Himmler of 9 October is doc. no. 1248 of the police documents of the Eichmann trial in Jerusalem; General Thomas's letter to Himmler of 11 October is doc. no. 1545 of the Eichmann trial documents; Heydrich's *Schnellbrief* to Himmler of 19 October where he cites the text of the rebuke he sent to Übelhör, and Himmler's letter to General Thomas of 22 October, where he also mentions his instructions for Übelhör, are docs. nos. 1544 and 1546 of the Eichmann trial documents.

53. TA: Doc. no. 25: 8.

54. TA: Doc. no. 1198.

55. TA: Doc. no. 1197.

56. A characteristic detail is recounted in a contemporaneous reportage about the old age home for the "settlers" from Western Europe; namely, that the apostates who lived there were "the keenest synagogue goers. . . . They came earliest and left latest. . . . With greatest attention they listened to the preacher and bowed lowest at [the prayer] *Modim*" (doc. no. 49H: 5). It is difficult today to say whether this was a result of an inner spiritual change, or of an inborn sense of discipline and a desire to find favor with the Jewish administration in order to avoid eventual discrimination.

57. Doc. no. 1192: 3, 6; doc. no. 26: 16; doc. no. 28: 18. They died in the Łódź Ghetto: Caspari on 21 January 1944 (conducted research in the ghetto until the liquidation of the main hospital in September 1942); Sandheimt on 12 December 1941; Speyer on 5 May 1942.

58. Editor's note: *Prominenten.*

59. Doc. no. 25: 4. Bernard Heilig died in the ghetto on 5 May 1942.

60. Doc. no. 1220. Rumkowski's speech to the nearly 400 representatives of the newcomers on 1 November 1941: "You must beat out of your head sick aspirations to get leading posts."

61. Doc. no. 26: 4–5. A small number of intellectuals from the newcomers were engaged in the ghetto archive. Of course, they were also employed in the internal administration of the "collectives" (as managers, officials, and so on).

62. Doc. no. 24: 4.

63. Beit Lohamei Ha-Getaot Archive, doc. no. 104: 134.

64. TA: Doc. no. 1221: 4–5.

65. Doc. no. 28: 28.

66. Beit Lohamei Ha-Getaot Archive, doc. no. 88.

67. Among 3,359 *Eingesiedelte,* about whose occupation we have information, manufacturers, merchants, and bankers amounted to 11.3 percent (among the Frankfurters, 17 percent), business and office employees were 6.8 percent, free professions 5.6 percent, workers and domestic servants 16 percent, craftsmen 7 percent, children and school pupils 3.9 percent, and those under the rubric "without occupation" were 47 percent. The latter category apparently included widows, invalids, poor folk who lived from communal aid grants, as well as those who had lost their former businesses and professions and lived from the remnants of their former capital or had fallen to the level of paupers. As we see from the above figures, not quite a fourth (workers and artisans, together 23 percent) could, if their age did not impede them, be drawn in time into the ghetto industry. Among the overwhelming majority this was virtually precluded, both because of their age (children up to age seven and adults over age fifty composed 55.8 percent of all the "settlers") and because of their professional unsuitability. Cf. Trunk, "Mayrev-eyropeyishe yidn in mizrekh-eyropeyishe getos," *Goldene keyt* (April 1953): 87–88.

68. *Reichsvereinigung der Juden in Deutschland* (Reich Association of Jews in Germany).

69. In his speech of 3 January 1942 (doc. no. 27), Rumkowski said that if not for the newcomers, he would have been in a position to maintain the bread allocation of 400 grams per person. This was, by the way, not true, because even before the arrival of the expellees the bread ration was only 330 grams per person daily and, on 4 November 1941, was reduced to 280 grams (cf. chapter 3).

70. Beit Lohamei Ha-Getaot Archive, doc. no. 70.

71. Doc. no. 1220: 9–10.

72. The attitude was similar in the Warsaw and Riga ghettos. See E. Ringelblum, *Notitsn fun varshever geto,* May 1942; and M. Kaufmann, *Destruction of Latvia* (German), 184.

73. Doc. no. 1192: 9.

74. Ibid.

75. Doc. no. 1192: 5.

76. The *Chronicle* of 19 March 1942 reports conversations among the exiles, where an awaited deportation is assessed from the standpoint of the prices on the black market.

77. *Chronicle* of 13 February 1944 (in ZIH Archive) relates, among other things, that a Łódź young man literally pulled his future wife down from the wagon where she already sat together with her parents, ready for deportation.

78. Trunk, "Mayrev-eyropeyishe yidn in mizrekh-eyropeyishe getos," *Goldene keyt* (April 1953): 96.

79. Doc. no. 26: 26. In the document, the town Ilno in Russia is stated. This is certainly a writing error and it should be Vilna. In the Ghetto Encyclopedia, the date of his birth is given as 17 March. [Editor's note: Lucjan Dobroszycki (Introduction to *Chronicle,* xlv) writes that Rumkowski was born in the village of Ilino, not Vilna.]

80. Editor's note: The original erroneously says that Rumkowski was sixty-three when he took office "in the ghetto in October 1939." Of course, the ghetto was not introduced in Lodz until February 1940, although he was named *Judenältester* in October 1939.

81. Doc. IT: 30.

82. Philip Friedman, "Goalei sheker ba-getaot polin [False Messiahs in Poland's Ghettos]," *Metsuda* (5714), 604. [Editor's note: Also see R. M. Shapiro, "Jewish Self-Government in Poland: Łódź, 1914–1939" (Ph.D. diss., Columbia University, 1987), 216–221.]

83. Doc. IT: 30.

84. In contradiction to this generally accepted opinion (e.g., Hurwitz, Tabaksblat) stands his own declaration in a speech he gave during his second visit to

Warsaw, on 15 May 1941, that he "cried and with tears in my eyes asked to be released from the deal," because he did not feel himself capable of taking over such a responsible office (doc. no. 17 of the Warsaw Collection, YIVO Archive).

85. His opponents in prewar Łódź did not spare him. A couple of years before the war, a brochure by a certain Doctor Preger, or Peker, came out in Łódź that openly accused him of suspicious relations with schoolgirls and women teachers in the Helenówek institution. See Friedman, "Goalei sheker ba-getaot polin," 604. [Editor's note: Lucille Eichengreen, born Cecilia Landau and expelled from her native Hamburg to the Łódź Ghetto with her mother and sister in 1941, has published two volumes of memoirs in which she alludes to sexually abusive behavior by Rumkowski, both on the basis of hearsay and her own experience. As far as I am aware, Eichengreen's second memoir is unique as a first-hand, eyewitness testimony that Rumkowski was, in fact, a sexual predator. Lucille Eichengreen, with Harriet Hyman Chamberlain, *From Ashes to Life: My Memories of the Holocaust* (San Francisco: Mercury House, 1994); and Lucille Eichengreen, with Rebecca Camhi Fromer, *Rumkowski and the Orphans of Lodz* (San Francisco: Mercury House, 2000).].

86. Tabaksblat, *Khurbn lodzh*, 27–28; Y. L. Girsht, *Min ha-meitsar* (Jerusalem, 5709), 87.

87. The soldiers threw him into a tub of water, pulled him out, and then beat him. Tanye Fuks, *A vanderung iber okupirte gebitn* (Buenos Aires, 1947), 36.

88. Fuks (ibid.) relates that Rumkowski answered a German: "What can you do to me? I am seventy years old and I have already outlived my [loved ones]." A second instance is in *Dapim le-heker ha-shoa ve-ha-mered*, vol. 1: 122, according to which Rumkowski refused to point out rich Jews to the Germans with these words: "I am a widower. I don't have any children and nobody in the world. I am ready to die."

89. Doc. no. 1220: 6. After an attack on him by tailors, embittered by the confiscation of sewing machines in October 1940 (announcement of 26 October 1940, doc. no. 199), his residence in Marysin was protected by a bodyguard of three Jewish policemen. Testimony of B. Frenkel, "Geto Lodzh," 42.

90. Doc. no. 1220: 7: "The Jewish property in the ghetto lost the status of individual possession. I can dispose of it without restriction, the same goes for the buildings, the rent, the machines, materials and raw materials, costly objects, foreign currency, gold and so forth" (from Rumkowski's speech delivered on 1 November 1941 before 400 representatives of the "resettled" Western European Jews). He justified the confiscation of hidden possessions with anti-capitalistic phraseology: "As long as I will be at my responsible post, I will not allow individuals to possess great fortunes, while others are dying from hunger. . . . I administer [that wealth] for the needs of the whole community" (doc. no. 1220: 7). In fact, the confiscated Jewish property served to pay for the delivery of food into the ghetto.

91. Doc. no. 1221: 2. From Rumkowski's speech on 20 December 1941: "In accord with the authorization that I possess within the framework of the ghetto autonomy, I obtained the right personally to select the candidates for being sent out."

92. Ph. Friedman ("Goalei sheker ba-getaot polin") raises the question about the role that Rumkowski may have played in the tragic end of the first *Beirat* by "complaining to the Gestapo about the insubordination of the *Beirat* members," and he says that this question cannot be answered due to the lack of trustworthy documents. It seems to me that, in light of contemporary documents, Rumkowski can be cleared of this suspicion. In *Min ha-meitsar,* a literary supplement to *Hamesaper* (handwritten fortnightly that came out in the ghetto, no. 1 of 8 July 1941, published in *Dapim le-heker ha-shoa ve-ha-mered,* vol. 1: 120–121), it is recounted that there was a meeting at the Jewish community, on the same day when the *Bei-*

rat members were arrested. Taking part were both the unarrested and released members of the council, as well as representatives of different political and social organizations in the city. Rumkowski requested, after he was pistol-whipped by the Gestapo representative to the Jewish community, that all those arrested be released. Ch. M. Pik, one of the five members of the arrested *Beirat* who survived the torments in the Radogoszcz camp and was sent out with a transport of expelled Łódź Jews to Kraków, states that among them was also an unnamed brother-in-law of Rumkowski (see *Sefer ha-zevaot,* 68). Rumkowski's very sharp critic, Engineer [Hurwitz], the author of the above-cited diary, does not raise this suspicion against Rumkowski when he writes about the end of the *Beirat*. He only says that Rumkowski had "a lucky break" (*a glik*) with it.

93. Doc. IT: 30; doc. no. 54: 17.

94. [Hurwitz], Diary, 16.

95. Y. Nirenberg, "Di geshikhte fun Lodzher geto," 226.

96. Doc. no. 1192: 6.

97. [Hurwitz], Diary, 41–42. The same reason for not admitting parcels into the ghetto is stated in the diary of Mordecai Shvartsbard, a coworker of *Oyneg Shabes* in the Warsaw ghetto, *BfG* 8, no. 3–4: 118.

98. Tabaksblat, *Khurbn lodzh*, 90.

99. *Geto-tsaytung,* no. 13, 20 June 1941. This figure came to a sad end. The German *Kriminalpolizei* searched his residence and discovered a large quantity of garments, underwear, leather, cameras, jewelry, and so on (docs. nos. T14, T15). He and his family were deported from the ghetto in March 1942. [Editor's note: On the fate of the former prison commandant, see entry dated "The Month of March, 1942," in Dobroszycki, *Chronicle,* 136–138 and n27.]

100. It is worthwhile citing some headlines from articles: "The Most Beautiful Gift For the Chairman at His Birthday—Honest and Useful Work" (*Geto-tsaytung* no. 3 [21 March 1941]) and "My Concern for the Workers" (*Geto-tsaytung* no. 12 [18 May]). In a reportage about Bałuty Market square, the nerve-center of the ghetto, we find such bouquets: "It not infrequently happens, however, that the chairman is in a good mood and this can be observed immediately: His countenance then has a mild appearance; warm love and good-naturedness stream from his eyes. . . . He is then like a quiet, tame dove, that gently flaps its wings, warming and caressing the little doves" (*Geto-tsaytung* no. 5 [4 April]). A sort of "court poet," a well-known prewar journalist in Łódź, published panegyric poems about the chairman in a number of issues of the newspaper. Yani Shulman, in his ghetto notes, also mentions the sycophantic atmosphere around Rumkowski (*Yediot beit lohamei ha-getaot,* no. 20 [1958], 79).

101. Docs. nos. 1432, 1464, 1465, 1469, 1470.

102. Doc. no. 1466.

103. They are in the Rumkowski Archive in the Jewish Historical Institute in Warsaw (File VI/48: 97, 298, 475, etc.). For his wedding on 27 December 1941, he received 600 telegrams with greetings (doc. no. 26: 28). It is symptomatic that in connection with Rumkowski's wedding the population hoped for better food allotments (ibid., 26).

104. [Hurwitz], Diary, 25.

105. Ibid., 20.

106. Doc. no. 1219: 7. A selected anthology of his speeches was even prepared (doc. no. 25: 4). Whether it was published is not known.

107. Doc. no. 26: 4.

108. "Entsiklopedia shel geto Łódźh," *Yediot beit lohamei ha-getaot,* November 1954: 16.

109. Girsht, *Min ha-meitsar,* 43; Ph. Friedman, "Goalei sheker ba-getaot polin," 607. The chain has survived and is in private possession.

110. [Hurwitz], Diary, 30; Solomon F. Bloom, "Dictator of the Łódź Ghetto," *Commentary* 7, no. 2 (1949): 116. At the end of August 1941, Rumkowski introduced whipping as a punishment (doc. no. 1216: 4).

111. [TA: Klementynowski, op. cit., p. 24. Editor's note: Trunk erroneously ascribed the diary of Leon Hurwitz (JHI Rumkowski Records no. 11) to Józef Klementynowski, first director of the Łódź Ghetto archive. See Dobroszycki, *Chronicle,* xxviii, n59.] The fright that Rumkowski would throw into everybody is also mentioned in the testimony of B. Frenkel, "Lodzher marishin-geto," 82.

112. *Geto-tsaytung,* no. 7 (17 April 1941).

113. Doc. no. 27: 16.

114. Doc. no. 38: 10.

115. Doc. no. 38: 17. [Editor's note: The ghetto "Chronicler" is Trunk's reference to the author of the ghetto *Chronicle*'s entries. It is an echo of the term used for the author of the biblical Book of Chronicles.]

116. Notes of Yani Shulman, written in the ghetto and found by N. Blumental in March 1945 among the ghetto ruins, published in *Yediot beit lohamei ha-getaot,* no. 20 (1958): 73. [Editor's note: The quote is an allusion to a Hebrew phrase in the Sabbath morning prayers after the Torah reading: see *The Complete ArtScroll Siddur,* 2nd ed. (Brooklyn: Mesorah Publications, 1988), 451.]

117. This Jewish Council ideology was also preached by Ephraim Barash, head of the Białystok ghetto, and Jacob Gens, chief of the Vilna ghetto. See Chaika Grossman, *Anshei mahteret* (1950), 163–164; Mark Dworzecki, *Yerushalayim de-lite in kamf un umkum* (1948), 308–309. [Editor's note: Also see Yitzhak Arad, *Ghetto in Flames: The Struggle and Destruction of the Jews in Vilna in the Holocaust* (New York: Holocaust Library, 1982).]

118. Doc. no. 1192 [TA: Doc. no. 1220]. These slogans were displayed in big print during the exhibitions of the ghetto production, in certain workshops, at gatherings, and the like.

119. Doc. no. 38: 17.

120. Doc. no. 54: 18–19.

121. Doc. no. 27: 16. In fact, less than a month after the end of the January deportation, a second, much larger deportation began on 22 February 1942, that by 2 April swallowed 34,073 victims.

122. Doc. no. 1213: 6.

123. Doc. no. 1221: 2.

124. Ibid.; doc. no. 27: 17 [3].

125. Doc. no. 1221.

126. TA: Doc. no. 1221: 3–4.

127. Doc. no. 1224: 2.

128. *Chronicle,* 18 January 1944: Rumkowski's speech at the conference with the managers of the divisions.

129. Doc. IT: 30; Girsht, *Min ha-meitsar,* 26.

130. Doc. no. 1218: iv; doc. no. 27: 3.

131. Doc. no. 1216: 2.

132. Editor's note: Polish *posłannictwo,* with emphasis in original.

133. Doc. no. 27: 18.

134. Doc. no. 1220: 6.

135. Emanuel Ringelblum, *Notitsn fun varshever geto* (Warsaw, 1952), 41.

136. M. Shvartsbard, *BfG* 8, no. 3–4: 129–133.

137. Rumkowski sometimes adopted a tone of feigned modesty and humility. In his speech to the Western European Jews on 1 November 1941, he expressed himself: "In essence, I am not your boss but only an honorable guardian, who unceasingly keeps watch in order that all should be able to sleep." He liked to designate himself "as a soldier on guard, who never falls asleep at his post" (docs. nos. 1214, 1220). He even once admitted "that he is not sure of himself [*iz nisht*

ayngegleybt in zikh] and that he made various mistakes." He found, however, a justification in the well-known saying that the only one free from mistakes is the one who does nothing (doc. no. 1214).

138. Nirenberg, "Geshikhte fun Lodzher Geto," 236–237. Also Hurwitz (Diary, 23) speaks about the fact that "Rumkowski imagines even the postwar new order differently than most Jews do . . . when he will become ruler over all Jews." In a November 1941speech, he said: "The war will still last a long time. . . . The ghetto will also exist for a good number of years after the war and I will continue to remain the Eldest of the Jews" (ibid., 47).

139. [Hurwitz], Diary, 16.

140. Rumkowski's programmatic article in the first issue of the *Geto-tsaytung* (doc. no. 18).

141. Doc. no. 1216. The monthly budget amounted to 3.2 million marks.

142. Tabaksblat, *Khurbn lodzh*, 69–70; Yani Shulman similarly assesses Rumkowski's work in the field of child welfare (in *Yediot beit lohamei ha-getaot*, 78).

143. Doc. no. 54: 17.

144. Nirenberg, "Geshikhte fun Lodzher Geto," 270.

145. Doc. no. 1283: Biebow's speech to the assembled workers on 7 August 1944. Rumkowski came out with a declaration about the situation in the same sense (Eisenbach, *Dokumenty*, vol. 3, *Getto Łódzkie*, 267–268).

146. Nirenberg, "Geshikhte fun Lodzher Geto," 261–262. Nirenberg also cites other sources of information about Chełmno in the Łódź Ghetto.

147. Doc. no. 28, *Chronicle* from end of May 1942.

148. In a testimony by Abraham Bialkower, who was sent out to Auschwitz on the same day, it is told that the camp officials received him politely, made a serious face, led him onto a hill, and let the thousands of Jews being led into the gas chambers march past him. When the procession ended, there came an order that he should join in the line (A.Volf Yasni, *Di oysrotung fun Lodzher yidn* [Tel Aviv, 1950], 67). [Editor's note: Lucjan Dobroszycki (*Chronicle*, lxvn164) argues that there are no reliable sources on Rumkowski's last days, both before leaving the ghetto and after his arrival at Auschwitz where he died. Icchak (Henryk) Rubin accepts that Rumkowski was directed immediately to the gas chambers like every elderly Jew arriving at the ramp at Auschwitz (*Żydzi w Łodzi pod niemiecką okupacją 1939–1945* (London: Kontra, 1988), 466. A lurid version of Rumkowski's end is presented by Michael Chęciński, "How Rumkowski Died," *Commentary* (May 1979): 63–65.]

149. [Hurwitz], Diary, 36.

150. Ibid., 23–24.

151. Doc. no. 1/30: 1–2; doc. no. 38: 12; *Chronicle*, July 1944: "This year, too, the dignitaries established their summer residences there [in Marysin]." In the ghetto, Rumkowski's summer residence in Marysin was ironically called "Tsarskoye Syelo" [Editor's note: after the Tsar's vacation residence]. Cf. also J. Poznański, *Pamiętnik*, 88. [TA: and J. Klementynowski, op. cit., 24–25.]

152. Doc. no. 35: 8.

153. [Hurwitz], Diary, 4. It is worth noting the fact that four doctors in May 1942 resigned from their special food allocations to benefit the sick (doc. no. 28, *Chronicle*, May 1942) [Editor's note: Dobroszycki, *Chronicle*, entry dated May 9–11, 1942, 169]).

154. Beit Lohamei Ha-getaot Archive, doc. no. 388. This hatred is also discussed in the *Kripo* report of 28 July 1942 (doc. no. 388).

155. Doc. no. 1/30: 1–3; doc. no. 33: 17. Instead of vacation in Marysin, one could get a free food coupon whose value was about 6 marks at the official prices. As the *Chronicle* of 13 January 1942 noted, the overwhelming majority of workers preferred to receive the food coupons, probably so that the family could also benefit from them (doc. no. 33: 17).

156. Nirenberg, "Geshikhte fun Lodzher Geto," 276.

157. Doc. no. 1220: 3.

158. In the above cited report from the Criminal Commissariate to the inspector of the *Sicherheitspolizei* of 28 July 1942 [Editor's note: Beit Lohamei Ha-getaot Archive, doc. no. 388], the author of the report proposes to improve the provisioning condition of the working Jews: "They will be in whatever form separated from their parasitic relatives . . . and take control over their feeding, because working Jews can be found who are very useful to the state, but due to the poor nutrition they are on the verge of a starvation death, or die."]

159. Testimony of Binyomin Frenkel, "Lodzher marishin-geto," 40.

160. Ibid., 88–91.

161. Ibid., 91.

162. The appeals are in the Franz Kurski Bund Archive [at YIVO], folder "Łódź Ghetto."

163. [TA: Ibid.]

164. Ibid.

165. Tabaksblat, *Khurbn lodzh*, 54; Nirenberg, "Geshikhte fun Lodzher Geto," 228–229.

166. Doc. no. 196, announcement of 20 October 1941 [*sic*] (no. 145); Nirenberg, "Geshikhte fun Lodzher Geto," 246.

167. Doc 50A. Carbon copy of a protocol of the meeting.

168. Leaflet reproduced in *BfG* 1, no. 3–4 (1948): 221. Nirenberg writes about brutal repressions against the striking hospital personnel ("beatings, families thrown out of their residences, their food cards confiscated and put in prison") in "Geshikhte fun Lodzher Geto," 246. Also see Shlomo Frank, *Togbukh fun Lodzher geto,* 90–93.

169. Doc. no. 23, *Chronicle* under the relevant dates.

170. TA: Doc. no. 1241, notes by J. Zelkowicz about the carpenters strike in January 1941, 1–2.

171. TA: Doc. no. 461.

172. Text of the leaflet in doc. no. 1241 [TA: 6].

173. Docs. nos. 251, 1241.

174. Doc. no. 1241 [TA: 11–14]; G. Fogel, "Tsum yortsayt fun stolyar-shtrayk in Lodzher geto," *Dos Naye Lebn,* no. 10 (Nov. 1947); also see the wall poster addressed to the striking carpenters in the ZIH Museum in Warsaw.

175. Doc. no. 1241.

176. Doc. no. 24: 6. One of the leaflets is in the Bund's Franz Kurski Archive [at YIVO], file "Geto Lodzh."

177. Doc. no. 462. Rumkowski threatened the instructors with repression for sabotage. See the illegal bulletin of the Bund in the ghetto, no. 7 (20 February 1941), in the Bund's Kurski Archive, file "Geto Lodzh."

178. Doc. no. 24: 5. Among those arrested were six Bundists. The Bundist group in the ghetto let Rumkowski know that in the event that he dared to send any of them out it would not be silent and he would bear the responsibility. The arrestees sat in prison for six weeks and were amnestied at Passover. They were required to sign a declaration that they would not take any job in the ghetto (Nirenberg, "Geshikhte fun Lodzher Geto," 248).

179. TA: Doc. no. 24: 4.

180. Tabaksblat, *Khurbn lodzh*, 97; Nirenberg, "Geshikhte fun Lodzher Geto," 249.

181. Editor's note: "Workers of Zion," i.e., Labor Zionists. The Poalei Zion had split in the 1920s over identification with the Bolsheviks and the new Soviet Union.

182. Tabaksblat, *Khurbn lodzh*, 100–101. Nirenberg ("Geshikhte fun Lodzher geto," 229, 248) states that the understanding indeed was supposed to include only

the Bund, Left Poalei Zion, and Communists, but due to the fact that "among the Left Poalei Zion there were people who stand quite close to Rumkowski," there was an understanding only between the Bund and the Communists. But it, too, did not last long.

183. Partially preserved in the Bund Archive, file "Geto Lodzh," and in the ZIH Archive in Warsaw. Some are reproduced in *BfG* 1, no. 3–4 (1948): 215–221.

184. Nirenberg, "Geshikhte fun Lodzher Geto," 240–241; Hiler, Diary; Dawid Sierakowiak, "Dziennik z getta łódzkiego," *BZIH*, no. 28 (1958): 92.

185. Testimony of B. Frenkel, "Lodzher marishin-geto," 13.

186. Tabaksblat, *Khurbn lodzh*, 99.

187. File no. 719, folios 2715, 2716. [Editor's note: This presumably refers to the Zonabend Collection.]

188. Editor's note: Similar Zionist collective agricultural training groups were created in the Warsaw ghetto, where the members played a significant role in the organization of armed resistance. See Israel Gutman, *The Jews of Warsaw 1939–1943: Ghetto, Underground, Revolt* (Bloomington: Indiana University Press, 1982).

189. File no. 719, folio 2707, lists six names. Tabaksblat, *Khurbn lodzh*, 91, gives seven.

190. Tabaksblat, *Khurbn lodzh*, 91.

191. File no. 719, folio 2719. Letter to the Council of Kibbutzim from the 12 "Number *Hakhsharot*."

192. Ibid., folio 2713.

193. Tabaksblat, *Khurbn lodzh*, 92–93.

194. Testimony of Frenkel, "Lodzher marishin-ghetto," 8.

195. File no. 719, folio 2642.

196. Ibid., folio 2695.

197. Ibid., folio 2737. Application of the agricultural group CH, dated 16 Av 5701 (9 August 1940 CE).

198. Ibid., folio 2726, 2727. Applications from the end of August 1940.

199. Nirenberg, "Geshikhte fun Lodzher Geto," 224–225.

200. File no. 719, folio 2623.

201. TA: Doc. no. 719.

202. Ibid., folio 2706. Letter of 2 October 1940; folio 2652, letter of 16 December 1940.

203. Ibid., folio 2697. Due to the tragic heating fuel situation in the ghetto in winter 1940–1941, adolescents and children would carry home under their clothing a board or a piece of roofing, so as to be able to cook something for a sick relative. For such a transgression, they would be expelled from the kibbutzim and from the children's camp (see Frenkel testimony, 18). The kibbutz militia studiously ignored such "criminals," whence came the rage of the Marysin police commandant.

204. Doc. no. 24, *Chronicle* of 10–24 March 1941; Tabaksblat, *Khurbn lodzh*, 93, erroneously gives the date of the liquidation of the kibbutzim as February 1941. With the dissolution of the kibbutzim, the activity of the Zionist-pioneering *Haluts* youth did not, however, end. A discovered diary tells of political-educational activity of the Zionist youth in the ghetto from August 1941 until 1 October 1943. Another diary, which included the period from 20 July, was lost (see Dr. A. Bauminger, "Hazit dor bnei midbar—tnuat noar tsioni be-geto lodzh [Front of the Desert Generation—a Zionist Youth Movement in the Lodz Ghetto]," *Yediot Yad Vashem*, no. 12 [January 1957]: 9–10). A Communist youth group was also active in the ghetto (see David Sierakowiak's diary, *passim*.)

205. Doc. no. 27: 17 [3].

206. Nirenberg, "Geshikhte fun Lodzher Geto," 266. Also during the September Action, a hungry crowd looted a warehouse of vegetables. The SS shot and

killed a number of people (Girsht, *Min ha-meitsar*, 28). [Editor's note: On the September Action, see chapter 6. During the notorious "Gehsperre Aktion" or "Curfew Action" (referred to as the "Shpere" in Yiddish), between 5 and 12 September 1942, children under ten years of age, as well as the elderly and the sick, were hunted down and rounded up by the Germans with the collaboration of members of the Order Service and some other employees of Rumkowski's administration. About 16,000 Jews were deported to death, including more than 5,000 children. Also see I. H. Rubin, *Żydzi w Łodzi*, 376; and Michal Unger, *Lodzh: aharon ha-getaot be-folin* (Jerusalem: Yad Vashem, 2005), 299–310.]

207. ZIH Archive, file III/36: 359. The content of the leaflet is unknown.

208. *Chronicle*, 6 and 15 May and 6 June 1944. Hiler, Diary, 278, 280.

209. Nirenberg, "Geshikhte fun Lodzher Geto," 292.

210. Doc. no. 38: 18.

211. Doc. no. 164.

212. Doc. no. 23, *Chronicle*, 23 January 1941 ("33 Arrestees for Resistance"), etc.

213. Docs. nos. 47, 955A, 955C, 956A.

214. Doc. no. 26: 8; *Chronicle*, 5 December 1941; doc. no. 55: 35: "*Prezes khayim / vos teylt mit / un git undz klayen.*" Yerakhmiel Bryks (manuscript about Sh. Yanovski in YIVO Archive) gives a longer version. See also doc. no. 51A: reportage by Y. Zelkowicz, "Vos in geto kon alts pasirn." [Editor's note: See also Gila Flam, "The Role of Singing in the Ghettos: Between Entertainment and Witnessing," in Shapiro, *Holocaust Chronicles*, 141–153; and Gila Flam, *Singing for Survival: Songs of the Łódź Ghetto* (Urbana: University of Illinois Press, 1992). Herszkowicz survived the war and recorded several of his songs; the tape is available at YIVO. Recent renditions of several of Herszkowicz's ghetto songs are performed by Adrienne Cooper and Zalmen Mlotek on the CD *Ghetto Tango* (New York, 2001).]

215. Doc. no. 24: 1 (the fifth *Oneg Shabat* took place on 1 March 1941). Tabaksblat, *Khurbn* lodzh, 97; Nirenberg, "Geshikhte fun Lodzher Geto," 239.

216. Doc. no. 24: 7; doc. no. 945.

217. Tsvi Shner, "Le-toldot ha-haim ha-tarbutiim ba-geto lodzh," *Dapim leheker ha-shoa ve-ha-mered*, vol. 1 (1951): 92–93. This work is based on a document from the Łódź Ghetto Archive that is in the Beit lohamei ha-getaot Archive; Nirenberg, "Geshikhte fun Lodzher Geto," 240.

218. Ts. Shner, "Le-toldot ha-haim ha-tarbutiim ba-geto lodzh," 93; inter alia, Zelkowicz lectured about Jewish humor (doc. no. 43: 12).

219. Doc. no. 24: 1, 17.

220. Testimony of B. Frenkel, 13–17; Nirenberg, "Geshikhte fun Lodzher Geto," 225; Tabaksblat, *Khurbn lodzh*, 91–92; file no. 719, folio 2204.

221. Doc. no. 24: 13.

222. Doc. no. 26: 30. Tsvi Shner erroneously gives the date of 1 February 1941 (Shner, "Le-toldot ha-haim ha-tarbutiim ba-geto lodzh," 96). The error is apparently in the document that is not based on official data, but on interviews with former public activists in the ghetto.

223. Doc. no. 944A bears the heading *Kultur-Referat*.

224. Editor's note: Pinchas Szwarc survived the war and continued his artistic career under the surname Shaar. See his memoir: Pinchas Shaar, "Mendel Grossman: Photographic Bard of the Lodz Ghetto," in Shapiro, *Holocaust Chronicles*.

225. Doc. no. 24: 9; Isaiah Trunk, "Deportatsye, lebn un umkum fun korev 20,000 mayrev-eyropeyishe yidn in Lodzher geto," manuscript, 84–85.

226. Doc. no. 26: 30.

227. Doc. no. 30, *Chronicle*, 19 July 1942. The orchestra would, inter alia, also perform music of German and Austrian composers, like Beethoven, Bach, and Haydn, that was forbidden in other ghettos, for example in Warsaw (see Jonas Turkow, *Azoy iz es geven* [1948], 213).

228. TA: Doc. no. 953 D.

229. Doc. no. 26: 17; doc. no. 949C.

230. Doc. no. 29, *Chronicle*, 6 and 7 June 1942; docs. nos. 948A, 955, 956A.

231. Poznański, *Pamiętnik,* 140.

232. Doc. no. 26: 30.

233. Docs. nos. 29 A; 24: 13.

234. Doc. no. 950A.

235. Ts. Shner, "Le-toldot ha-haim ha-tarbutiim ba-geto lodzh," 98; V.H. Ivan in *Dos naye lebn* (Warsaw), 3 September 1948 (according to archival materials of ZIH).

236. Szmerke Kaczerginski, *Lider fun di getos un lagern* (New York, 1948), 93. [Editor's note: Also see Cooper and Mlotek, *Ghetto Tango,* CD-ROM.]

237. Docs. nos. 960A; 43: 12. [Editor's note: The marionette theater presumably echoed Moshe Broderson's prewar Yiddish Chadegadia Puppet Theater. Pinchas Shaar, "Mendel Grossman ," 125.]

238. Ts. Shner, "Le-toldot ha-haim ha-tarbutiim ba-geto lodzh," 99.

239. A large number are in the museum of the ZIH in Warsaw. Trębacz died in the ghetto on 29 January 1941, at the age of eighty.

240. Editor's note: See the translation in David Roskies, ed., *The Literature of Destruction* (Philadelphia: Jewish Publication Society, 1989), as well as the translation in Alan Adelson et al., eds., *Łódź Ghetto Inside a Community under Siege* (New York: Viking, 1991), 126–130.

241. Editor's note: See the bibliography. Regarding other published diaries, see Shapiro, "Diaries and Memoirs from the Łódź Ghetto in Yiddish and Hebrew," in Shapiro, *Holocaust Chronicles*, 95–116; and Marian Turski, "Individual Experience in Diaries from the Łódź Ghetto," in Shapiro, *Holocaust Chronicles,* 117–124.

242. The already mentioned "Ghetto Encyclopedia" states that only "more than ten lectures" took place (see *Yedlot Beit lohamei ha-getaot,* no. 9–10: 35).

243. Ts. Shner, "Le-toldot ha-haim ha-tarbutiim ba-geto lodzh."

244. Docs. nos. 941, 942.

245. "Entsiklopedia shel geto lodzh," *Yediot,* no. 9–10: 35: s.v. Leihbibliotheken.

246. There was also a circular about this matter from the Kalisch *Regierungspräsident* of 22 January 1940 to all *Landraten* of the district and to the Łódź police-president about confiscation of artistic and cultural-historical objects, including books (see Eisenbach, *Dokumenty* vol. 3, *Getto Łódzkie,* 65–66).

247. Editor's note: cf. Dobroszycki, *Chronicle*, 201–202, for 9 June 1942.

248. "Entsiklopedia shel geto lodzh," *Yediot,* no. 9–10: 35.

249. Doc. no. 29A, *Chronicle*, 9 June 1942. [Editor's note: Cf. Dobroszycki, *Chronicle*, 201–202, where the text differs somewhat.]

250. Hiler, Diary, 89.

251. Beit Lohamei Ha-Getaot Archive, doc. no. 594. Sonenberg introduced a rule in May 1942 that any German Jew desiring to register with his library had to donate a German book to the library in lieu of the registration fee. With time, the number of German books grew to 800.

252. Doc. no. 943.

253. TA: Doc. no. 49C. [Editor's note: R. Ephraim Oshry was in charge of a comparable repository of abandoned Jewish books in the Kovno Ghetto. See his memoir, *The Annihilation of Lithuanian Jewry* (Brooklyn: Judaica Press, 1996), 71–77.]

254. Doc. no. 30, *Chronicle*, 23 July 1942.

255. "Entsiklopedia shel geto lodzh," *Yediot,* no. 9–10: 35.

256. Doc. no. 958. Printed poster about the matches.

257. Nirenberg, "Geshikhte fun Lodzher Geto," 239–240.

258. Doc. no. 197.

259. Editor's note: Its spiritual leader, Dr. Markus Mordecai Zeev Braude (1869–1949), had been a senator, a city councilman, and president of the Institute for Judaic Studies in Warsaw, whose building today houses the Jewish Historical Institute of Poland. He founded a network of elite bi-lingual Polish-Hebrew secondary schools. Within the first months of the occupation, Braude and his wife, sister of the philosopher Martin Buber, succeeded in fleeing Poland and making their way to Palestine. *Encyclopaedia Judaica* (1972), vol. 4: 1314–1315.]

260. Doc. no. 1266.

261. Girsht, *Min ha-meitsar*, 39–41.

262. *The Persecution of Jews in German-Occupied Poland,* Free Poland Pamphlet, no. 2 (London, n.d.), 18.

263. Tabaksblat, *Khurbn lodzh*, 24.

264. Testimony of B. Frenkel, "Lodzher geto," 57–61. To set up a prayer group required a permit from Rumkowski (doc. no. 160).

265. TA: Doc. no. 185.

266. Docs. nos. 542, 548.

267. Girsht, *Min ha-meitsar*, 44–45.

268. Testimony of Frenkel, "Lodzher geto," 64–66.

269. TA: *Geto-tsaytung,* no. 5 (4 April 1941).

270. Editor's note: Also known in Polish as brukiew, kalarepa, and karpiel, and known in English as "turnip cabbage" and kohlrabi, which are all in the same family of vegetables.

271. Testimony of Frenkel, "Lodzher geto," 68–69.

272. Ibid., 66. For the first days of Passover 1944, the German ghetto administration let workers have a day and a half off from work (Hiler, Diary, 255).

273. TA: Doc. no. 185.

274. Doc. no. 24: 13.

275. Testimony of Frenkel, "Lodzher marishin-geto," 7–8. [Editor's note: The following Hebrew prayer by an unknown author was displayed in the prayer room at Podrzeczna 8 for the High Holy Days of 1941 (5702):

> May it be Your will, You who hear the beseechings of Your petitioners, to hearken unto the heartfelt sighs and pleadings that emanate from our hearts each and every day, evening, morning, and afternoon. Our endurance is under strain; we have neither a leader, nor source of support, nor anyone to turn to and rely on, save for You, our Father in Heaven. Our Father, merciful Father, You have visited upon us a daily torrent of retribution, famine, sword, fear, and panic. In the morning we say, "If only it were evening," and in the evening we say, "If only it were morning." No one knows who among Your people Israel, Your flock, will survive and who will fall victim to plunder and abuse. We beg of you, our Father in Heaven, restore Israel to their precincts, sons to their mothers' embrace, and fathers to sons. Bring peace to the world and remove the evil wind that has come to rest upon Your creatures. Unlock our shackles and remove our tattered, befouled clothing. Return to our homes those who have been abducted, deported, and captured. Have mercy upon them and protect them, wherever they may be, from all evil afflictions, disasters, disease, and all manner of retribution, and extricate us from woe to relief, from darkness to great light, so we may serve You with our hearts and souls and keep Your holy Sabbath and festivals joyously and happily. Illuminate us in the light of Your countenance and make Your signs evident, so that we may witness plainly as the Lord returns the captivity of his people. Then Jacob will rejoice, and Israel will take delight, and may all who seek refuge with You experience neither shame nor disgrace. May God redeem the righteous summarily, promptly, and speedily, and let us say: Amen.

Collected by Yerachmil Breiman, a contributor to the ghetto *Chronicle.* See the photograph of the Hebrew text and English translation in Michal Unger, ed., *The Last Ghetto: Life in the Łódź Ghetto, 1940–1944* (Jerusalem: 1995), 150–151.]

276. "Entsiklopedia shel geto Łódźh," *Yediot*, no. 14–15: 69.

277. Editor's note: Hirsch (1808-1888) was a prominent rabbi in Frankfurt am Main who developed a philosophy of Neo-Orthodox Judaism that emphasized strict Jewish religious observance while accepting the value of secular education and superficial acculturation.

278. *Yediot beit lohamei ha-getaot,* no. 7: 15.

279. Ibid., no. 11–12: 31.

280. Editor's note: *Mezuzot* are containers holding biblical texts (Deuteronomy 6:4–9 and 11: 13–21) written on parchment, traditionally placed on the doorposts of Jewish homes.

281. Editor's note: *Tsitsit* are the ritual fringes attached to rectangular garments worn by men. Like *mezuzot,* they are a form of public display of Jewish identity and traditional observance.

282. *Yediot beit lohamei ha-getaot,* no. 14–15: 64.

283. Ibid., 69.

284. The literary supplement *Min ha-meitsar,* no. 1, of 8 July 1941, for no. 120 of *Ha-mesaper,* as well as a fragment of *Ha-mesaper,* dated "Fast of Gedalia 5702," were published in *Dapim le-heker ha-shoa ve-ha-mered,* vol. 1: 115–147, and vol. 2: 87–90. [Editor's note: See the photograph of a page from *Min ha-meitsar* in Unger, *The Last Ghetto,* 46.]

285. Doc. no. 1255, p. 3.

286. Thus, for example, in the building of the *Standesamt* (Registry Office), on 6 May 1942, there took place forty-two weddings, among them twenty among the Western newcomers; on 4 July 1944, nineteen marriages took place, and on 6 July there were eleven weddings (docs. nos. 28: 5; 1259; 1260).

287. Doc. no. 1254.

288. Docs. nos. 845; 44: 2. The board was formed in February 1941.

289. Editor's note: In lieu of the traditional long gaberdine *kapotes* and *bekishes,* the coats worn by Hasidim and rabbis instead of short suit jackets or sport coats.

290. Doc. no. 29: 1.

291. Doc. no. 29A, *Chronicle,* 14 and 18 June 1942.

292. Testimony of B. Frenkel, "Lodzher marishin-geto," 8.

293. Doc. no. 55: 114–116. Although there were two kosher kitchens, and from August 1941 three for religious Jews in the ghetto, strictly pious Jews did not want to take advantage of them. Moreover, their "menu" was for understandable reasons very limited (meat was precluded). [Editor's note: See Joseph Zelkowicz's reportage, "The Messiah Is Taking Too Long," in Zelkowicz, *In Those Terrible Days Notes from the Lodz Ghetto,* ed. Michal Unger (Jerusalem, 2002), 139–149.]

294. Ibid., 112–113.

295. Editor's note: Simcha Treistman was actually general secretary of the Łódź Rabbinate in the 1930s. There was no chief rabbi in Łódź since the death of R. Treistman's father in 1921. Efforts to elect a new chief rabbi failed, although the son of the late R. Treistman was a serious contender for the post. See R. M. Shapiro, "Jewish Self-Government in Poland: Lodz, 1914–1939," 301–305.

296. Doc. no. 26: 5–6.

297. Doc. no. 1267; *Geto-tsaytung,* nos. 4 (28 March 1941) and 5 (4 April 1941).

298. TA: Doc. no. 1268.

299. Doc. no. 55–0. Fragment from a protocol of a session of the Council of Rabbis with Rumkowski and the director of the Records Department, Neftalin.

300. Testimony of B. Frenkel, "Lodzher marishin-geto."

301. Doc. no. 23, *Chronicle,* 14 January 1941.

302. See [TA: Doc. no. 27: 2; and] doc. no. 30: 42, about the situation in July 1941. In order to speed the procedure, the Cemetery Department published on 28

January 1941 an announcement about the duty of the family to provide shrouds and boards on the same day that the deceased is conducted out to the cemetery (doc. no. 1262A).

303. Doc. no. 33, *Chronicle,* 6 August 1942.

304. Editor's note: The original Jewish cemetery in Łódź was established in 1809, located on the ironically named Wesoła (Happy) Street. The official Jewish Religious Community in Łódź had a monopoly on operating the Jewish cemetery. After 1945, the postwar authorities in Łódź cleared the site to rearrange the street grid and construct new apartment buildings, so no trace of the former cemetery remains visible on the surface.

305. Doc. no. 29A, *Chronicle,* 26 June 1942.

306. Doc. no. 23, *Chronicle,* 17 January 1941; *Geto-tsaytung,* no. 6 (11 April 1941).

307. Editor's note: Salomon Hercberg was a native of Bałuty with a shady past who became a high officer in the Order Service and director of the ghetto's Central Prison. In March 1942, he was arrested by the German Police, who confiscated huge amounts of loot from his apartments. He and his family were deported from the ghetto to an unknown destination. See Dobroszycki, *Chronicle,* entry for March 1942, 136–138.

308. Doc. no. 26: 11–12.

309. [Hurwitz], Diary, p. 8.

310. Doc. no. 24: 16. In February there were only 104 arrestees in the prison, among them 13 women (doc. no. 44).

311. Doc. no. 33, *Chronicle,* 21 August 1942.

312. Doc. no. 1398.

313. Doc. no. 43: 6.

314. Doc. no. 30, *Chronicle,* under the same date. It often happened that the loaves of bread brought from the bakery had been picked at and so were short in weight (doc. no. 806).

315. Doc. no. 26: 15.

316. Doc. no. 49G.

317. Doc. no. 840.

318. Hiler, Diary, 156.

319. Docs. nos. 804; 24: 14.

320. Doc. no. 29, *Chronicle,* 21 June 1942; doc. no. 893 (reportage about the trial).

321. Doc. no. 30, *Chronicle,* 30 July 1942.

322. *Chronicle,* 26 April 1943; testimony of B. Frenkel, "Geto Lodzh," 25. Frenkel gives inaccurate details about the basic fact.

323. Doc. no. 808, Police Reports. Hiler relates in his diary (474–475) that the man found in the well was the *Vakhmayster* (Guard Captain) Fridman who was killed at his garden parcel.

324. Docs. nos. 837; 30, *Chronicle,* 25 July 1942.

325. Docs. nos. 793; 28, *Chronicle,* 27 May 1942. On that day, the Order Service liquidated a little factory that produced a *"sałatka"* from rotten vegetables pulled from waste bins. Two families were arrested.

326. Docs. nos. 802; 25: 13. From fall 1940 until June 1941, the counterfeiter issued phony two-mark banknotes worth 5,500 marks. He was sentenced to one year at hard labor and a fine of 300 marks.

327. Docs. nos. T11; 33, *Chronicle,* 27 August 1942.

328. Doc. no. 30, *Chronicle,* 5 July 1942; doc. no. T9.

329. Doc. no. 28, *Chronicle,* May 1942.

330. Y. Trunk, *Shtudye tsu der geshikhte,* 71–75.

331. [Hurwitz], Diary, 6a. There were also isolated cases when judges found in themselves the courage to oppose Rumkowski's desire, like for example in his at-

tempt to introduce the death penalty, or during the trial concerning the swindles in the Department for Social Aid (Diary, 8).

332. Doc. no. 55H.

333. Doc. no. 30, *Chronicle,* 21 July 1942.

334. Doc. no. 30, *Chronicle,* 5 July 1942.

335. *Chronicle,* Bund, no. 7, dated 20 February 1941; [Hurwitz], Diary, 7–8; Tabaksblat, *Khurbn lodzh*, 52.

336. Doc. no. 26: 10.

337. Cf. Trunk, *Shtudye tsu der geshikhte,* 97.

338. Tabaksblat, *Khurbn lodzh*, 108; Nirenberg, "Geshikhte fun Lodzher Geto," 244–245.

339. Doc. no. 1398. [Editor's note: See the interviews with David Gertler recorded in 1974 by Isaiah Kuperstein and stored at the YIVO Sound Archive.]

340. Doc. no. 23, *Chronicle,* 16 January 1941.

341. Doc. no. 24, summary *Chronicle* of 10–24 March 1941; [Hurwitz], Diary, 6a; *Geto-tsaytung,* no. 2 (14 March 1941); docs. nos. 49G, 834, 838.

342. Doc. no. 838: 7.

343. Hiler, Diary, 235; Rumkowski Archive, file "Ordnungsdienst": report about the activity of this department for the period from 5 March until 31 December 1941.

344. Editor's note: This selection of extracts are from a series of vignettes written by Zelkowicz, who recorded his impressions and observations from visits to homes of applicants seeking aid from the Jewish ghetto welfare department for which Zelkowicz worked as a home inspector. See the nineteen vignettes published in Zelkowicz, *In Those Terrible Days,* 33–178.

345. Editor's note: Ibid., 116–117.

346. Editor's note: Compare this account of the ghetto coal miners with the version published in Zelkowicz, ibid., 66–67.

347. Editor's note: *Klorkalkstreifen.*

348. Editor's note: *Judensachbearbeiter.*

349. Editor's note: This entry does not appear in either the English or Hebrew published editions of the *Chronicle*, although portions of other entries for October 1941 have survived. See the editors' notes in the 1984 English edition (78n92) and in the 1986 Hebrew edition (vol. 1: 245).

350. This figure includes the more than 3,000 Jews deported from Włocławek and vicinity.

351. Editor's note: The correct date of the arrival of the first transport is 17 October 1941.

352. Editor's note: This is a play on the Łódź Yiddish pronunciation of "German Jews," *datshe yidn.*

353. Editor's note: Correct date is 17 October 1941.

354. Editor's note: Correct Polish: *rozumiem.*

355. Editor's note: "Tajnego radcy," which is equivalent to the German title, *Geheimrat.*

356. Editor's note: Following the opinion of A. Wolf Jasny, Trunk holds that Hurwitz is only a pseudonym used by Dr. Józef Klementynowski, the first head of the Ghetto Archive. However, Lucjan Dobroszycki demonstrates that they were two separate individuals who left numerous handwritten documents that are clearly by different people. The original Hurwitz diary is at the Jewish Historical Institute in Warsaw, Rumkowski Records, no. 11. Dobroszycki, *Chronicle,* xxviii, n59; Jasny, *Geshikhte fun yidn in Lodzh in di yorn fun daytsher-oysrotung,* 222, 325–326.

357. See n. 356.

358. Editor's note: Traditional Yiddish honorific title prefixed to a man's first name, here having an ironic tone.

359. David Warszawski and Hersz Szczęśliwy (Shtshenshlivi). The latter was director of the Provisioning Department. According to TA, David Warszawski was manager of the Tailor Ressort.

360. This sentence and the entire phraseology of the appeal indicate its Communist origin.

361. Editor's note: Alluding to the armbands worn by the members of the Order Service.

362. Editor's note: See the full translation in Zelkowicz, *In Those Terrible Days*, 205–232.

363. Editor's note: Najwyższa Izba Kontroli (Polish: Supreme Control Chamber) that audited and inspected all ghetto institutions and programs.

364. Editor's note: The 2002 Zelkowicz edition of *In Those Terrible Days*, 207, here has a paragraph that is missing from Trunk's version.

365. See doc. no. 126.

366. Editor's note: Manager of the needlework factory at 45 Łagiewnicka Street, whom Zelkowicz interviewed on 30 January 1941. See Zelkowicz, *In Those Terrible Days*, 224–225.

367. Editor's note: Hebrew for pioneers, that is, members of the kibbutzim.

368. Editor's note: See the photograph of a trilingual poster announcing first symphony concert of the Hazomir [*sic*] Society: Julian Baranowski, *The Łódź Ghetto 1940–1944 / Łódzkie Getto 1940–1944 Vademecum* (Łódź, 1999), 58.

369. Editor's note: Compare the translation in Oskar Rosenfeld, *In the Beginning Was the Ghetto: Notebooks from Łódź*, ed. Hanno Loewy, trans. Brigitte M. Goldstein (Evanston, Ill.: Northwestern University Press, 2002), 78–81. Note that the document Trunk here presents is somewhat different and longer than the selection from Rosenfeld's notebooks edited by Loewy. Presumably, the document in the Zonabend Collection at YIVO is a text based on Rosenfeld's notebook draft.

370. Editor's note: Russian for weekend home.

371. Editor's note: The conductor is Theodor Ryder.

372. Editor's note: Manger (1901–1969) was a native of Czernowitz, Romania, who became popular in interwar Poland.

373. Editor's note: Pinchas Szwarc (later Shaar) was employed as a graphic artist in the ghetto's Statistical Office. See his memoir in Shapiro, *Holocaust Chronicles*, 125–140. He created reproductions of ghetto stage scenery for Yad Vashem's exhibition on the Łódź Ghetto: Unger, *The Last Ghetto*, 156–157.

374. Editor's note: Volumes of the Mishna, the codification of Jewish law compiled in Roman-ruled Palestine, the Land of Israel, by Rabbi Judah the Prince, ca. 200 C.E.

375. Editor's note: The *Zohar* or Book of Splendor is a fundamental work of Jewish mysticism, traditionally attributed to second-century C.E. Rabbi Shimon bar Yohai and revealed by R. Moses de Leon in thirteenth-century Spain.

376. Editor's note: *Tefilin* are small boxes containing sacred Biblical texts, worn by Jewish men during weekday morning prayers, attached to the arm and head with leather straps.

377. Editor's note: Hebrew "names," referring to documents or fragments of sacred books written in Hebrew characters that might include the name of God or Scriptural passages and therefore require respectful burial.

378. Rumkowski's circular announcing that the decree concerning Sabbath rest also applied to offices, ghetto institutions, and workshops was issued only on 13 November 1940 (doc. no. 547).

379. Editor's note: Hebrew plural of *matsa* (matzah, matsoh), the unleavened bread eaten during Passover.

380. Editor's note: Note that spellings of Jewish surnames vary, depending on whether German or Polish or phonetic Yiddish rules are applied.

381. Editor's note: Compare the entry for 14–31 January 1942, in Dobroszycki's 1984 English edition of the *Chronicle* (124).

382. See n. 356.

383. Editor's note: A Talmudic expression based on "*kol de-alim gavar*" (Whoever is stronger prevails), Babylonian Talmud, Gitin 60b and Baba Batra 34b, according to Yitzhak Frank, ed., *The Practical Talmud Dictionary*, 2nd ed. (Jerusalem, 1994), 29, s.v. *alim*.

VIII. The Problem of Resistance

1. Editor's note: Original text erroneously says local Germans were a third of the prewar population. According to the 1931 census, those declaring German as their mother tongue numbered about 53,500 or 8.8 percent of the city's population. *Concise Statistical Year-Book of Poland September 1939–June 1941* (Glasgow: Polish Ministry of Information, 1941), 17, Table 26.

2. Irena Tarłowska, *Łódź w walce o wolność* (Warsaw, 1947).

3. Nirenberg, "Di geshikhte fun Lodzher geto," 289–290.

4. Tabaksblat, *Khurbn lodzh*, 178. [Editor's note: During the August 2002 Research Workshop on the Łódź Ghetto at the U.S. Holocaust Memorial Museum, Dr. Michael Thaler described his research into the correspondence between German insurance companies and the Gettoverwaltung over the necessity to equip the ghetto firefighters with a working fire engine, in view of the danger of fires in ghetto warehouses and workshops.]

5. G. Fogel, "Di geto fun litsmanshtat," *Tsukunft*, no. 4 (April 1958): 176.

6. Tabaksblat, *Khurbn lodzh*, 104. In a secret report by the Jewish National Committee in Warsaw, dispatched to London on 24 May 1944, we read: "Łódź ghetto is still hermetically sealed. In spite of our repeated efforts to establish contact with the Jews in Łódź—it did not succeed. Both our independent attempts and those made with the aid of the Polish underground organizations did not bring the desired result—to get into the Łódź ghetto. It is an island cut off from the whole world" (Melekh Nayshtat, *Khurbn un oyfshtand fun di yidn in varshe*, vol. 1 [1948], 192).

7. Hiler, Diary, 536.

8. Cf. *Chronicle*, March 1944.

9. Editor's note: Were there broadcasts in spring or summer 1944 that the Germans were destroying the concentration camps and the crematoria? Horthy was the regent of Hungary.

10. Testimony of B. Frenkel, "Likvidatsye fun der lodzher geto, zumer 1944," 5–6.

11. Editor's note: Dobroszycki, *Chronicle*, 534, gives the date 25 July. On the other hand, the unabridged Hebrew edition dates the entry to 26 July (*The Chronicle of the Łódź Ghetto*, vol. 4, trans. and annotated by Arie Ben-Menachem and Joseph Rab [Jerusalem, 1989]: 520–523.)

12. Editor' note: A couple of lines are missing in comparison with Dobroszycki, *Chronicle*, 534, and the Hebrew edition (1989), vol. 4: 521.

13. Doc. no. 38; Hiler, Diary, 510.

14. The tactic of letting upbeat letters come into the ghetto from those sent out into the Poznań labor camps had already been applied by the Gestapo previously (see *Chronicle*, 28 May and 24 July 1942). One of the small number of those rescued from the Jewish burial brigade in Chełmno, Mordecai Żurawski, testified at Greiser's trial in Poznań in 1946 that from each transport eight to ten people were compelled to write letters to their relatives, that they were in Leipzig, or in Munich, that they were doing well, and so on. As a reward, they were shown "kindness" and not killed in the gas truck, but shot at the crematorium ovens (Protocol

of interrogation, recorded by the investigative judge Władysław Bednarz on 31 July 1945, quoted in his *Obóz Straceń w Chełmnie nad Nerem* [1946], 60). Also compare the statement, concerning sending out such "good" letters from Auschwitz, that the camp's commandant Höss presented at his trial before the Polish tribunal (*BGKBZH* vol. 13, p. 173).

15. Nirenberg, "Di geshikhte fun Lodzher geto," 289.

16. Frenkel, Testimony "Likvidatsye fun der lodzher geto, zumer 1944," 4–5.

17. Hiler, Diary, 289; testimony of Mordecai Goldshteyn, 3.

18. Betti Ajzensztajn, *Ruch podziemny w ghettach i obozach* (Warsaw-Łódź-Kraków, 1946), 79–80.

19. Nirenberg, "Di geshikhte fun Lodzher geto," 292; testimony of Mordecai Goldshteyn, 2.

20. Editor's note: See Dobroszycki, *Chronicle*, 499, that refers to Mojżesz Tafel, as does the 1989 Hebrew edition of the *Chronicle,* vol. 4: 405.

21. Hiler, Diary, 289.

22. Hiler, Diary; Sierakowiak, Polish edition (1958), 82, 83, 95 et al.

23. Hiler, Diary, entries under the dates of 14 May and 30 June 1944.

24. *Chronicle,* 7 July 1944; Hiler, Diary, 382–384, 386, 388, 392; Nirenberg, "Di geshikhte fun Lodzher geto," 286–288; Tabaksblat, *Khurbn lodzh,* 106–108. Hiler gives another version of the failure: "It originates from the ghetto big shots. They saw that the workers are starting to be a bit recalcitrant and this could lead to smaller production and they decided to notify [the authorities] themselves about it." This version is nowhere corroborated. The informer received his own terrible verdict. In Auschwitz the "Canadians" [Editor's note: the *Sonderkommando* members employed in the warehouses of possessions confiscated from arriving Jews] who originated from Łódź beat him to death on the spot.

25. J. Poznański, *Pamiętnik*, 150.

26. Testimony of Frenkel, "Likvidatsye fun lodzher geto, zumer 1944," 11–12.

27. Testimony of Yehudis Ayzikovitsh, 3; "Di letste minutn fun Dr. Wajskop," *Undzer lodzh,* no. 1 (1950): 27; Beit Lohamei Ha-gitaot Archive, testimonies nos. 616, 672; J. Poznański, *Pamiętnik,* 257–258; Betti Ajzensztajn, *Ruch podziemny,* 81.

IX. Conclusions and Summations

1. This was also the case in Theresienstadt, which in its organization has certain similarities to the Łódź Ghetto. See H. G. Adler, *Theresienstadt 1941-1945. Das Antlitz einer Zwangsgemeinschaft,* 2nd ed. (Tübingen, 1960), 223, 249, 250.

2. Letter from the *Transferstelle* to Czerniaków, Chairman of the *Judenrat,* dated 22 July 1941.

3. *BfG,* 1, no. 3–4, (1948): 289–290.

Documents Arranged by Chapter

1. Translation by Dr. Shlomo Noble with minor subsequent editorial changes.

Street Names in the Łódź Ghetto

1. See lists of street names in Dobroszycki, *Chronicle*, 537-539; Julian Baranowski, ed., *The Łódź Ghetto1940-1944/ Łódzkie Getto 1940-1944: Vademecum* (Łódź: Archiwum Państwowe w Łodzi and Bilbo, 1999), 112-114; and *The Chronicle of the Łódź Ghetto*, trans. Arie Ben-Menachem and Joseph Rab (Hebrew; Jerusalem: Yad Vashem, 1986), vol. I, after 569.

2. Extension of Krawiecka Street.

3. To Tokarzewskiego Knüpfergasse, from Tokarzewskiego Schlosserstrasse.

4. Extension of Krawiecka Street.

Note: *This bibliography combines sources referenced by Isaiah Trunk in the Yiddish original and by Robert Moses Shapiro in this translation.*

Adelson, Alan, et al., eds. 1991. *Łódź Ghetto: Inside a Community under Siege.* New York: Viking Penguin.

Adler, H. G. 1960. *Theresienstadt 1941–1945: Das Antlitz einer Zwangsgemeinschaft.* 2nd ed. Tübingen.

Akcje i Wysiedlenia. 1946. See J. Kermisz.

Ajzensztajn, Betti, ed. 1946. *Ruch podziemny w ghettach i obozach.* Łódź.

Arad, Yitzhak. 1982. *Ghetto in Flames: The Struggle and Destruction of the Jews in Vilna in the Holocaust.* New York: Holocaust Library.

Arad, Yitzhak, Israel Gutman, and A. Margoliot, eds. 1999. *Documents on the Holocaust: Selected Sources on the Destruction of the Jews of Germany and Austria, Poland, and the Soviet Union.* 8th ed. Trans. Lea Ben Dor. Lincoln: University of Nebraska Press; Jerusalem: Yad Vashem.

Baranowski, Julian. 1999. *The Łódź Ghetto 1940–1944 / Łódzkie Getto 1940–1944: Vademecum.* Łódź.

Bauminger, Dr. A. 1957. "Hazit dor bnei midbar—tnuat noar tsioni be-geto lodzh [Front of the desert generation—a Zionist youth movement in the Łódź ghetto]." *Yediot Yad Vashem,* no. 12 (January): 9–10.

Beatus, Barbara (Hinda). 1965. "Lewica Związkowa w getcie łódzkim." *BZIH* 54.

Bednarz, Wladyslaw. 1946. *Obóz straceń w Chełmnie nad Nerem.* Łódź-Warsaw-Kraków.

Bernstein, T., A. Eisenbach, and A. Rutkowski, eds. 1957. *Exterminacja żydów na ziemiach polskich w okresie okupacji hitlerowskiej.* Warsaw.

Bimko, Lonye. 1953. "Mayn rayze fun Lodzher geto tsum farnikhtung-lager oyshvits." *Undzer Lodzh,* no. 3. Buenos Aires.

Biuletyn Głównej Komisji Badania Zbrodni Hitlerowskich w Polsce. 1950–1960. Vols. 3 and 13. Warsaw.

Biuletyn Żydowskiego Instytutu Historycznego. 1965. *Podziemne życie polityczne w getcie łódzkim (1940–1944),* no. 54 (April–June). Warsaw.

Bloom, Solomon F. 1949. "Dictator of the Łódź Ghetto." *Commentary* 7, no. 2.

Blumental, N., ed. 1946. *Dokumenty i materjaly z czasów okupacji niemieckiej w Polsce,* vol. I: *Obozy* [Camps]. Introduction by [Ph]ilip Friedman. Łódź: Central Jewish Historical Commission.

Browning, Christopher. 1993. *Ordinary Men: Reserve Police Battalion 101 and the Final Solution in Poland.* New York: HarperCollins.

Chęciński, Michael. 1979. "How Rumkowski Died." *Commentary* (May): 63–65.

The Chronicle of the Łódź Ghetto. 1986–1989. Unabridged Hebrew ed., trans. and annotated by Arie Ben-Menachem and Joseph Rab. 4 vols. Jerusalem: Yad Vashem.

Concise Statistical Year-Book of Poland September 1939–June 1941. 1941. Glasgow: Polish Ministry of Information.

Cooper, Adrienne, and Zalmen Mlotek. 2001. *Ghetto Tango.* CD-ROM. New York: Traditional Crossroads.

Czerniaków, Adam. 5729 [1968]. *Yoman geto varsha, 6.9.1939—23.7.1942.* Ed. Nahman Blumental et al. Jerusalem.

———. 1979. *The Warsaw Diary of Adam Czerniaków.* Ed. Raul Hilberg et al. New York: Stein and Day.

[Czerniaków, Adam]. 1983. *Adama Czerniakowa dziennik getta warszawskiego.* Ed. Marian Fuks. Warsaw.

Dąbrowska, D. 1955. "Zagłada skupisk żydowskich w 'Kraju Warty' w okresie okupacji hitlerowskiej." *BZIH,* nos. 13–14.

Dąbrowska, Danuta, and Lucjan Dobroszycki, eds. 1965–66. *Kronika getta lodzkiego.* 2 vols. Łódź.

Dapim le-heker ha-shoa ve-ha-mered. 5711 [1951]. Vols. 1 and 2. Tel Aviv.

Delfiner, Rita. 1973. "Daily Closeup." *New York Post,* May 4.

Dobroszycki, Lucjan, ed. 1958. "Polska Anna Frank nazywała się." *Mówią Wieki,* no. 7.

———, ed. 1984. *The Chronicle of the Łódź Ghetto 1941–1944.* New Haven: Yale University Press.

The Documents of the Łódź Ghetto: An Inventory of the Nachman Zonabend Collection. 1988. Comp. Marek Web. Preface by Lucjan Dobroszycki. New York: YIVO.

Dworzecki, Mark. 1948. *Yerushalayim de-lite in kamf un umkum.* [Paris.] 308–309.

———. 1955. "Patalogye fun hunger in di getos." *Folksgezunt,* no. 54–55.

Dziennik Rozporządzeń Generalnego Gubernatorstwa. 1939, no. 9; 1941, no. 99.

Eck (Ekron), N. 5720 [1960]. *Ha-toim be-darkhei ha-mavet: havay ve-hagahot be-yemei ha-kilayon.* Jerusalem.

Eichengreen, Lucille, with Harriet Hyman Chamberlain. 1994. *From Ashes to Life: My Memories of the Holocaust.* San Francisco: Mercury House.

———, with Rebecca Camhi Fromer. 2000. *Rumkowski and the Orphans of Lodz.* San Francisco: Mercury House.

Eisenbach, A., ed. 1946. *Dokumenty i materiały do dziejów okupacji niemieckiej w Polsce,* vol. 3, *Getto Łódzkie,* part 1. Łódź: Central Jewish Historical Commission.

———. 1951. "Di yidishe literarish-kinstlerishe mishpokhe in Lodzher geto (in der helft 1944)." *Undzer Lodzh,* no. 2 (November). Buenos Aires.

———. 1953. *Hitlerowska polityka eksterminacyjna* [Editor's note: It is unclear if the work referred to is *Hitlerowska polityka eksterminacji Żydów w latach 1939–1945 jako jeden z przejawów imperializmu niemieckiego.* Warsaw].

———. 1961. *Hitlerowska polityka zagłady Żydów.* Warsaw.

"Encyclopedia of Łódź Ghetto" [Hebrew]. November 1954–April 1956. *Yediot beit lohamei ha-getaot,* no. 9–15.

Epstein, Leslie. 1993 [1979]. *King of the Jews.* New York: Coward, McCann & Geoghegan.

Esh, Shaul. 5733 [1973]. *Iyunim be-heker ha-shoa ve-yahadut zmaneinu.* Jerusalem.

Eshkoli, A. Z. 5708 [1940]. *Kehilat lodzh: Toldot ir ve-em be-Israel.* Jerusalem.

Feuchert, Sascha. 2004. *Oskar Rosenfeld und Oskar Singer: Zwei Autoren des Lodzer Gettos Studien zur Holocaustliteratur.* Berlin: Peter Lang.

Fishman, Joshua. ed. 1974. *Studies on Polish Jewry, 1919–1939.* New York: YIVO.

Flam, Gila. 1992. *Singing for Survival: Songs of the Łódź Ghetto.* Urbana: University of Illinois Press.

———. 1999. "The Role of Singing in the Ghettos: Between Entertainment and Witnessing." In *Holocaust Chronicles,* ed. Robert M. Shapiro, 141–53. Hoboken, N.J.: KTAV.

Fode, P. 1969. "Hirhurim al yihuda shel ha-mahteret be-geto lodzh," *Yalkut Moreshet* 11. November..

Fodor, Rene 1953. "Agresye fun kinder in a toyt-sakone." *Yivo-bleter* 37.

———. 1956. "Di virkung fun der natsisher okupatsye fun poyln af di batsiungen tsvishn muter un kind bay yidn." *Yivo-bleter* 40.

Fogel, G. 1947. "Tsum yortsayt fun stolyar-shtrayk in Lodzher geto." *Dos Naye Lebn,* no. 10 (November).

———. 1958. "Di geto fun litsmanshtat." *Tsukunft,* no. 4. April.

Frank, Shlomo. 1958. *Togbukh fun Łódźher geto.* Buenos Aires and Tel Aviv.

Friedman, Philip (Yeruham Fishel). 5714 [1954]. "Goalei sheker ba-gitaot polin" [False Messiahs in Poland's Ghettos]. *Metsuda* 7. London.

———. 1980. *Roads to Extinction: Essays on the Holocaust.* Ed. Ada June Friedman. Philadelphia: Jewish Publication Society.

Fuks, Tanye. 1947. *A vanderung iber okupirte gebitn.* Buenos Aires.

Gilbert, Martin. 1985. *The Holocaust.* New York: Henry Holt.

Girsht, Y. L. 1947. "Lererkursn far yidish in Łódźher geto." *Yivo-bleter* 30, no.1.

———. 5709 [1949]. *Min ha-meitsar .* Jerusalem.

Goering, Hermann. 1940. Decree of 17 September 1940 (*RGBl* N-170), "Über Behandlung von Vermögen der Angehörigen des ehemaligen polnischen Staates."

Grossman, Chaika. 1950. *Anshei mahteret.* Merhavya.

———. 1987. *The Underground Army: Fighters of the Bialystok Ghetto.* Trans. Shmuel Beeri. Ed. Sol Lewis. New York: Holocaust Library.

Gutman, Israel. 1982. *The Jews of Warsaw 1939–1943: Ghetto, Underground, Revolt.* Bloomington: Indiana University Press.

Hersh, L. 1939. "Yidishe demografye." *Algemeyne Entsiklopedye, Yidn,* vol. 1.

Hershkovitsh, B. 1950. "The Ghetto in Litzmannstadt (Łódź)." *YIVO Annual of Jewish Social Science* 5.

Hershkovitsh, Bendet. 1947. "Litsmanshtat-geto." *Yivo-bleter* 30, no. 1 (Fall).

Hielscher, Friedrich. 1954. *Fünfzig Jahre unter Deutschen.* Hamburg.

Hilberg, Raul. 1961. *The Destruction of the European Jews.* Chicago: Quadrangle Books.

Hupert, Sh.. 5745 [1985]. "Melekh ha-geto: Mordechai Chaim Rumkowski." *Mehkarei Yad Vashem* 15.

Itonut 'gordonia' u-mahteret geto varsha. 1966. Hulda.

Jasny. See Yasni.

"Die Judenausrottung in deutschen Lagern. Augenzeugenberichte" (mimeograph). 1945. Geneva.

Kaczerginski, Szmerke. 1948. *Lider fun di getos un lagern.* New York.

Kaufmann, Max. 1947. *Die Vernichtung der Juden Lettlands: Churbn Lettland.* Munich.

Kermisz, J., ed. 1946. *Dokumenty i materialy do dziejów okupacji niemieckiej w Polsce,* vol. 2: *"Akcje" i "Wysiedlenia."* Łódź.

Klinger, Chaika. 1959. *Mi-yoman ha-geto.* Merhavia.

Kronika shel geto lodzh. 1986–1989. Trans. and annotated by Arye Ben-Menachem and Joseph Rab. 4 vols. Jerusalem: Yad Vashem.

"Di letste minutn fun Dr. Wajskop." 1950. *Undzer lodzh,* no. 1.

Loewy, Hanno, and Andrzej Bodek, eds. 1997. *"Les Vrais Riches," Notizen am Rand: ein Tagebuch aus dem Ghetto Łódź (Mai bis August 1944).* Leipzig.

Loewy, Hanno, and Gerhard Schoenberner, eds. 1990. *Unser einziger Weg ist Arbeit . . . : das Getto in Łódź, 1940–1944: eine Ausstellung des Jüdischen Museums Frankfurt am Main.* Vienna: Löcker,.

Melezin, A. 1946. *Przyczynek do znajomości stosunków demograficznych wśród ludności żydowskiej w Łodzi, Krakowie i Lublinie podczas okupacji niemieckiej.* Łódź: Central Jewish Historical Commission.

Michael, Robert, and Karin Doerr, eds. 2002. *Nazi Deutsch/Nazi German.* Westport, Conn.

Mostowicz, Arnold. 1988. *Żółta gwiazda i czerwony krzyż.* Warsaw: Państwowy Instytut Wydawniczy.

Nayshtat, Melekh. 1948. *Khurbn un oyfshtand fun di yidn in varshe,* vol. 1. Tel Aviv.

News of the YIVO / Yedies fun YIVO, no. 156 (Spring 1981).

Nirenberg, Yankl. 1948. "Di geshikhte fun Lodzher geto." *In di yorn fun yidishn khurbn.* New York.

———. 1996. *Zikhroynes fun Lodzher geto.* Buenos Aires.

Noakes, J., and G. Pridham, eds. *Nazism 1919-1945: A History in Documents and Eyewitness Accounts.* 3 vols. New York: Schocken Books, 1990.

Oshry, R. Ephraim. 1996. *The Annihilation of Lithuanian Jewry.* Brooklyn: Judaica Press.

The Persecution of Jews in German-Occupied Poland. 1940. Free Poland Pamphlet no. 2 (May). London.

Pinkas ha-kehilot, Polin. 5736 [1976]. Vol. 1, *Lodzh ve-ha-galil.* Jerusalem: Yad Vashem.

Polonsky, Antony, ed. 1993. *From Shtetl to Socialism.* London: Littman.

Poznański, Jakub. 1960. *Pamiętnik z getta łódzkiego.* Łódź.

———. 2002. *Dziennik z lódzkiego getta.* Warsaw.

Proces Artura Greisera przed Najwyższym Trybunałem Narodowym (stenogram). 1947. N.p.

Puś, W., and S. Liszewski, eds. 1991. *Dzieje żydów w Łódzi 1820–1944.* Łódź.

Ringelblum, Emanuel. 1952. *Notitsn fun varshever geto.* Warsaw.

———. 1961. *Ksovim fun geto.* Vol, 1, *Togbukh fun varshever geto (1939–1943).* Warsaw.

Robinson, J. 5727 [1967]. *Nituk o retsifut be-vaadei ha-kehilot be-tekufa ha-natsit.* Jerusalem.

Rosenfarb, Chava. 1972. *Der Boym fun Lebn.* Tel Aviv: Ha-Menora.

———. 5738–40 [1978–80]. *Ets Ha-haim.* Tel Aviv.

———. 1985. *The Tree of Life.* Melbourne: Scribe.

Rosenfeld, Oskar. 1994. *Wozu noch Welt: Aufzeichenungen aus dem Getto Lodz.* Ed. Hanno Loewy. Frankfurt am Main.

———. 2002. *In the Beginning Was the Ghetto.* Ed. Hanno Loewy. Trans. Brigitte M. Goldstein. Evanston, Ill.: Northwestern University Press.

Roskies, David, ed. 1989. *The Literature of Destruction.* Philadelphia: Jewish Publication Society.

Rubin, Icchak (Henryk). 1988. *Żydzi w Łodzi pod niemiecką okupacją 1939–1945.* London: Kontra.

Rudnicki, Adolf. 1963. *Kupiec Łódzki.* Warsaw.

Scharf, Rafael F. 1991. "Rola Ch. Rumkowskiego w Łódzkim Getcie." In *Dzieje Żydów w Łódzi 1820–1944,* ed. W. Puś and S. Liszewski, 301–310. Łódź.

Sefer ha-zevaot 5705 [1945]. Jerusalem,

Shaar, Pinchas. 1999, "Mendel Grossman: Photographic Bard of the Łódź Ghetto." In *Holocaust Chronicles,* ed. Robert M. Shapiro, 125–140. Hoboken, N.J.: KTAV.

Shapiro, Robert Moses. 1987. "Jewish Self-government in Poland: Łódź, 1914–1939." Ph.D. diss., Columbia University.

———. 1993. "Aspects of Jewish Self-Government in Łódź, 1914–1939." In *From Shtetl to Socialism*, ed. A. Polonsky, 296–317. London.

———. 1994. "The Polish *Kehillah* Elections of 1936: A Revolution Re-examined." POLIN, vol. 8. London.

———. 1999. "Diaries and Memoirs from the Łódź Ghetto in Yiddish and Hebrew." In *Holocaust Chronicles*, ed. Robert M. Shapiro, 95–116. Hoboken, N.J.: KTAV.

———, ed. 1999. *Holocaust Chronicles: Individualizing the Holocaust through Diaries and Other Contemporaneous Personal Accounts*. Hoboken, N.J.: KTAV.

Shner, Tsvi. 1951. "Le-toldot ha-haim ha-tarbutiim ba-geto lodzh." *Dapim le-heker ha-shoa ve-ha-mered*. Vol. 1.

Shulman, Y. 1958. "Rumkowski—der elteste der yuden." *Yediot bet lohamei ha-getaot al shem Yitshak Katzenelson*, no. 20 (April).

Sierakowiak, Dawid. 1958. "Dziennik z getta łódzkiego." *BZIH*, no. 28.

[Sierakowiak, Dawid]. 1996. *The Diary of Dawid Sierakowiak: Five Notebooks from the Łódź Ghetto*. Trans. Kamil Turowski. Ed. Alan Adelson. New York: Oxford.

Shvartsbard, M. 1955. "Notitsn fun geto." *Bleter far geshikhte* 8, no. 3–4. Warsaw.

Singer, Oskar. 2001. *Herren der Welt: Zeitstück in drei Akten*. Ed. Sascha Feuchert. Hamburg: Walter-A.-Berendsohn-Forschungsstelle für deutsche Exilliteratur.

———. 2002. *"Im Eilschritt durch den Gettotag . . . ": Reportagen und Essays aus dem Getto Lodz*. Ed. Sascha Feuchert et al. Berlin: Philon.

———. 2002. *Przemierzając szybkim krokiem getto—: reportaże i eseje z getta łódzkiego*. Trans. Krystyna Radziszewska. Łódź.

Tabaksblat, Yisroel. 1946. *Khurbn Lodzh, 6 yor natsi-gehenem*. Buenos Aires.

Tarłowska, Irena. 1947. *Łódź w walce o wolność*. Warsaw.

Trials of War Criminals before the Nuremberg Military Tribunals. 1949–1953. Vols. 5, 14. Washington, D.C.: U.S. Government Printing Office.

Trunk, Isaiah. 1948. "Yidishe arbet-lagern in varteland." *Bleter far Geshikhte* 1, nos. 1–2.

———. 1949. "Shtudye tsu der geshikhte fun yidn in varteland in der tekufe fun umkum." *Bleter far Geshikhte* 2.

———. 1950. *Shtudye tsu der geshikhte fun yidn in varteland in der tekufe fun umkum (1939–1944)*. Warsaw.

———. 1953. "Mayrev-eyropeyishe yidn in mizrekh-eyropeyishe getos," *Goldene keyt* (April).

———. 1953. "Milkhome kegn yidn durkh farshpreytn krankaytn." *Yivo-bleter* 37. New York.

———. 1962. *Geshtaltn un gesheenishn—historishe eseyen*. Buenos Aires.

———. 1962. *Lodzher geto*. New York: YIVO. Jerusalem: Yad Vashem.

———. 1963. *Shtudyes in yidisher geshikhte in poyln*. Buenos Aires.

———. 5728 [1968]. "The Organizational Structure of the Jewish Councils in Eastern Europe." *Kovets mekhkarim Yad Vashem* 7, 137–153.

———. 5730 [1970]. "The Relationship of the Jewish Councils to the Problems of Armed Revolt against the Nazis." *Ha-Amida ha-yehudit be-tekufat ha-shoa—diyunim be-kinus hokrei ha-shoa, Yerushalaim, 9–13 be-nisan 5722—7–11 April 1968*, 160–80. Jerusalem.

———. 1972. *Judenrat: The Jewish Councils in Eastern Europe under Nazi Occupation*. New York: Macmillan.

———. 5733 [1973]. "Ha-yudnratim ve-yahasam le-baayot ha-meri ha-mezuyan neged ha-natsim." In *Shoat yehudei eyropa: reka-korot-mashmaut*, ed. I. Gutman and Livia Rothkirchen. Jerusalem.

———. 1973. "National Polyarchy in the Situation of the Jews in the Occupied Territories." *Dapim le-heker ha-shoa ve-ha-mered*, second series, vol. 2, 7–22.

———. 5740 [1980]. "Typology of the Jewish Councils in Eastern Europe." *Defusei ha-hanhaga ha-yehudit be-artsot ha-shlita ha-natsit 1939–1945: Hartsaot ve-diyunim*, 11–22. Jerusalem.

———. 5739 [1979]. *Judenrat: The Jewish Councils in Eastern Europe during the German Occupation* (Hebrew). Jerusalem.

———. 1979. *Jewish Responses to Nazi Persecution.* New York: Stein and Day.

———. 1982. "The Historian of the Holocaust at YIVO." *Creators and Disturbers: Reminiscences by Jewish Intellectuals of New York.* Ed. and compiled by Bernard Rosenberg and Ernest Goldstein. New York: Columbia University Press.

———. 1983. *Geshtaltn un gesheyenishn—tsveyte serye.* Tel Aviv.

Turkow, Jonas. 1948. *Azoy iz es geven:* khurbn Varshe. Buenos Aires.

Turski, Marian. 1999. "Individual Experience in Diaries from the Łódź Ghetto." In *Holocaust Chronicles,* ed. Robert M. Shapiro, 117–124. Hoboken, N.J.: KTAV.

Unger, Michal, ed. 1995. *The Last Ghetto: Life in the Łódź Ghetto, 1940—1944,* Jerusalem: Yad Vashem.

———. 2005. *Lodzh: aharon ha-getaot be-folin.* Jerusalem: Yad Vashem.

Wasiak, Stanisław. "Bilans Walki narodowościowej rządów Greisera." *Przegląd Zachodni,* no. 6.

Yasni, A. Volf. 1950. *Di oysrotung fun Lodzher yidn.* Tel Aviv.

———. 1960. *Di geshikhte fun yidn in lodzh in di yorn fun der daytsher yidn-oysrotung,* vol. 1. Tel Aviv.

Yediot beit lohamei ha-getaot. 1950–1958. Nos. 7, 11–15, 20.

Yivo-bleter, vol. 30, no. 2 (1947), 37 (1953).

Zelkowicz, Joseph. 2002. *In Those Terrible Days: Notes from the Lodz Ghetto.* Trans. Naftali Greenwood. Ed. Michal Unger. Jerusalem.

References to illustrations appear in italics

References to illustrations appear in italics

Subjects Index

90, 224, 244, 270, 304, 312, 379; mortality among, 200, 219

electricians' workshops, xlii, 56, 264, 367. *See also* Small Appliance Department

electricity and gas, 52, 68, 103, 160, 185, 428n87, 449n224; Departments of, 51, 52

Electrizitätwerk, Łódź A.G., 51

Electrotechnical Department, 150, 193–194

elites, ghetto, xl, 110, 230, 323–324, 343, 371–372

embezzlement. *See* corruption

Emissions Bank, 80, 81. See also currency; money

employment, xii, xxxii, xxxix, xli–xlv, xlviii, lii, liv–lv, 6, 11, 19, 20–21, 45, 46, 51, 56, 57, 63, 83, 89, 90, 93, 95, 96–97, 111, 120–121, 144, 153, 159, 162, 163, 165, 169, 171, 177, 187, 189, 192, 200–201, 235, 242, 261, 268, 287, 315, 321, 324, 325, 333, 367, 453n67; structure of, 156–158. *See also* administration, ghetto, employment in; forced labor; workshops and factories, employment in

encyclopedia of Litzmannstadt Ghetto, 47, 339, 340

epidemics, 5, 16, 20, 21, 57, 58, 72, 176, 177, 196, 198–201, 202–207, 209, 212, 213, 215, 217, 218, 219, 223, 297, 306, 326, 364, 388. *See also* diarrhea; diseases; dysentery; typhoid fever; typhus

equipment. *See* machinery

evacuation, xxx, xlv, xlviii, lii, 11–12, 14, 19, 260, 263, 290. *See also* deportations; liquidation, ghetto; outsettlements

executions. *See* murders and executions

extermination, Jewish, xlvii, xlviii, 3, 9, 10, 32–33, 107, 165, 175, 182–183, 229–230, 239, 389. *See also* "actions"; death camps; deportations; "Final Solution"; liquidation, ghetto

extortion, 224–225, 270, 355

family life, 298–300

fascism, xxxv

favoritism, 48, 53, 59, 111–112, 119, 121, 131, 136–137, 225, 242, 255, 256, 312, 323, 325, 343, 371

felt and straw slippers workshops, 68, 156, 168, 171, 270, 331, 380

"Final Solution," xliii, lii, liii, lvi, lvii, 10, 33

Finance Department (Office), 19, 48, 49, 68, 77, 78, 92

Finance Ministry, 150, 423n12

Firefighters and Chimneysweeps Brigade, 44, 68, 79, 80, 81, 93, 111, 129, 228, 242, 245, 266, 271, 275, 288, 316, 323, 467n4

first aid stations, 36, 57, 192, 236, 252, 271, 288, 321, 327, 374

folksongs, xxvi, 337, 381, 382. *See also* Herszkowicz, Yankele [People Index]

food. *See* food supply; Provisioning Department

food supply, 23, 43, 60, 104–105, 108–110, 112–113, 117–122, 125, 131, 134–135, 139, 142, 165, 170, 174, 214, 226. *See also* Food Supply and Management Office—Ghetto; kitchens; Provisioning Department; provisioning pyramid; ration cards; rations, food; stores and shops, food

Food Supply and Management Office—Ghetto (*Ernährung und Wirtschaftsstelle—Getto*), 45

forced labor, 36–37, 45, 46, 60, 64, 65–67, 84, 119, 148–197, 221, 225, 226–227, 309, 314, 329, 331, 334, 391. *See also* labor camps; women's camps

fraud, 44, 73, 352, 353, 357

free market. *See* black market

Fritz Hilgenstock (firm), 178

fuel, 129, 151. *See also* coal; heating; wood

funerals, 222, 223, 346, 349; Department of, 387. *See also* cemetery

furriers' workshops, xlii, 68, 101, 150, 154, 166, 258

garbage miners, 11, 125

garments. *See* underwear and clothing workshops

Gehsperre, 242, 243, 244, 275, 460n206. *See also* Shpere; deportations

gender, 18, 46, 95, 96–97, 219, 220, 252, 258, 298. *See also* men; women

General Secretariat, 39, 53, 68

General Zionist Party, xxxiii, 330

Gestapo, xl, xlii, xlix, l, 14, 34, 67, 107, 109, 162, 164, 178, 179, 228, 245, 246, 251, 252, 253, 254, 258–259, 261, 262, 263, 265, 291, 292, 306, 310, 311, 315, 320, 324, 329, 333, 353, 354, 356, 363, 395, 396, 398, 402–403, 443n50

Geto-tsaytung [Getto-tsaytung], xv, 316, 347, 351, 352

Gettoverwaltung (German ghetto administration), xv, xix, xxiii, xlii, xlv, 2, 4, 38, 39, *43*, 52, 62, 107–108, 111, 118, 119, 130–131, 149, 150, 151, 155, 165–168, 173, 175, 177–178, 191, 196, 211, 245, 247, 253, 259, 264, 268, 287, 306, 308, 311, 319, 333, 348, 349, 418n7, 419n33, 433n66, 436n53, 446n135, 467n4

Ghetto Fighters' House (Lohamei Ha-getaot), xiii, xiv, xxiii

ghetto guard, xxxi, 17, 20, 27, 30, 117, 200–201, 227, 260, 296, 325, 363, 428n83, 442n15, 442n17

ghetto scrip. *See* currency; scrip, ghetto

gloves and hosiery workshops, 68, 101, 155

Goods Exploitation Department, 191

Gordonia, l, lv, 330

Green Market, 227, 261

ISAIAH TRUNK (1905-1981) participated in the work of the Central Jewish Historical Commission in Warsaw following World War II. After immigrating to the United States in 1954, he became a senior research associate and chief archivist at YIVO . His book *Judenrat* (Macmillan, 1972) won a National Book Award. It was reprinted by the University of Nebraska Press in 1996.

ROBERT MOSES SHAPIRO is Assistant Professor of Judaic Studies, Brooklyn College, City University of New York. He is editor of *Holocaust Chronicles: Individualizing the Holocaust through Diaries and Other Contemporaneous Personal Accounts*; and of *Why Didn't the Press Shout: American and International Journalism During the Holocaust.*